The Armchair Mystic
Adventures Within!

Fifteen Years of Meditation, Visualisation, Pathworking and Astral Travel, revealing The Inner World, its Geography, Inhabitants and Nature.

By

Richard Abbot

Natural Living Books & Passerine Publishing
Northamptonshire, UK

Copyright (c) 2015 by Richard Abbot

All rights reserved. No part of this book, in part or in whole, may be reproduced, transmitted, or utilised in a form or by a means, electronic or mechanical, including photocopying, recording, or by any information storage or retrieval system without permission in writing from the publisher, except for brief quotations in critical articles, books and reviews.

A small section of this work was previously published as Steps Toward The Light, by Natural Living Books, 2005.

International Standard Book Number: 978-0-9554758-7-0

First edition: 2014

Typeset, printed and bound in the UK by Natural Living Books

This is a Natural Living Books Illumination Device ID34

Cover by Aaron Munday
www.12orchards.com

Illustrations "An Entrance to a Cave" and "The Temple of Opportunities"
by Colin Clark
Richard Abbot's extensive catalogue of work
including books, online lessons, audio and video can be viewed at
www.thehermitage.org.uk

THE ARMCHAIR MYSTIC
By
RICHARD ABBOT

After thousands of years, are we really any nearer to discovering **who we are** *or* **what we are for**?

"In occult stories of Initiation, a mystical experience is usually treated in an allegorical or symbolic manner. The candidate is made to pass through the most fantastic experiences and the most harrowing and gruesome trials of his courage, faith and obedience. Such stories are purposely intended to stimulate the desire for Initiation, yet are blinds which do not reveal to the profane any of the real secrets.

The candidate may pass such fantastical experiences in the Inner World, but if he is truly an initiate he must meet in real life that which they symbolise, for true initiation gives real balance, real power and real spiritual growth, which will clearly manifest in the daily life."

With thanks to Harriette Augusta Curtiss and Muriel Graves.

An Entrance to a Cave by Colin Clark

CONTENTS

Introduction
CHAPTER I　　　MAIDEN SOLO VOYAGE
CHAPTER II　　　KALIA
CHAPTER III　　GEOFFRI de BOUGAINVILLE
CHAPTER IV　　SARIA d'ESTRAING
CHAPTER V　　　ANDREI
CHAPTER VI　　　NG
CHAPTER VII　　DERRICK
CHAPTER VIII　　SOPHIE
CHAPTER IX　　　AMOS
Invocation of The Nine Lights
Family Connections
CHAPTER X　　　SERAPHIA
CHAPTER XI　　　HERMES
CHAPTER XII　　EDUKI
CHAPTER XIII　　HELENE
CHAPTER XIV　　MITHRAS
CHAPTER XV　　　ELI
CHAPTER XVI　　HERMES RETURNS
CHAPTER XVII　　SOCRATES
CHAPTER XVIII　MERLIN
CHAPTER XIX　　LAO TZU
CHAPTER XX　　　THE LORDS OF CHANGE
CHAPTER XXI　　THOTH
CHAPTER XXII　　THE VOICE OF VOICES
The Worlds I Now Inhabit
Afterword - Notes on the Method

INTRODUCTION

The feeling that there must be more to life than 'this' is a common one, present throughout history and across cultures. It is the driving force behind those who attempt to build a better future, as well as those who would rather retreat to the past. It is the fuel behind all forms of faith and human exploration and is as much the cause of inspiration as it is of despair, of practical action as it is of daydreams. It may then be said that the idea of 'more to life than this' rests at the very heart of the human condition.

So is this an idle fantasy? A troublesome distraction from the now? Or is this feeling based on reality? Are we compelled to try to connect with something more because we actually, deep down, know that it exists?

I see everybody as part way through their mission to reconnect to this 'something more', which I call The Inner World. Some are well advanced in this, others have barely begun. This book is the story of my quest towards a fuller, deeper and richer life experience. And it began by closing my eyes.

By closing my eyes I came to see that Life never really ends. Rest punctuates the activity and busyness of Life, as sleep punctuates regular consciousness. Death, sooner or later, punctuates our current *form*, only for our Life to continue first in an invisible fashion, and then again a differently visible one. But it's all one Life, on going, ever present. More of that later, though. For me it is all about how to experience some of the Life that is otherwise obscured?

The first step is to consider, more deeply, the Life that we currently have. But care is required here, for deeper consideration may mean changing our view of things we hold dear. For example, does it really matter if you are late for work? Or if you don't reply to that text immediately? On one hand of course it does matter, if you want to keep your job, but in the scheme of things it is absolutely meaningless. These small fry issues are in fact very important and comprise the first steps toward a different experience of Life.

From very early on in my quest I was fortunate enough to work with a teacher, someone who had been there before me. He was human and flawed, but he knew stuff that I did not know and could not discover elsewhere, so I remained as his Student of Life for twenty years. It was he that introduced me to the spiritual concepts of Guides, Guardians, Angels and the Inner World, concepts that made no logical sense for a very long time, but which I constantly sought to verify in the only way I could - through experience.

And so began, sometime around 1995 in Lincolnshire, England, my introduction to a world I did not know existed but which would increasingly come to dominate my Life. We used a process of discovery laid down in 1960's California by Edwin Steinbrecher called The Inner Guide Meditation. Chances are that if you have ever listened to a meditation track, or performed a guided visualisation, it was based on this. My teacher, Arthur, worked with this, refined it within his own practice and passed it on to me.

My first attempt was under Arthur's watchful gaze, and as a stimulant-addled twenty something, five minutes of this and I thought my brain was going to explode. My second attempt a year later, again with Arthur, was a little more successful. In the specific meditative state I could just about make out some unexpected imagery and sensations. The experience was vague, hazy and unclear but it was enough to convince me that there was indeed 'something more to life'. Even so, I simply took the audio CD from Arthur and put it on my shelves. It was another three years before I listened to it again.

What follows next is my real time diary, recording my attempts to explore into and beyond this meditation. It is a true and accurate record of my successes, failures, techniques, realisations and frustrations. It will demonstrate, very clearly, all that can be gained – and lost – when we commit our lives to the quest for more.

CHAPTER I
MAIDEN SOLO VOYAGE

Undated, sometime in 1999. I was surrounded by an array of obstacles – I did not understand the process, I was too busy, I couldn't get any peace, I was too tired, too fidgety. You name it, it presented as a problem, even to the extent of actual happenings to distract my attention. If I had believed for one second in 'signs' I would never have closed my eyes, let alone attempted to navigate my sea of emotions or penetrate my mind.

I undertook my first excursion, eyes closed, against quiet background music of seawater lapping on a shore. In my mind, I invented a cave around me, and allowed the cave to form itself as it would. Unexpectedly I found the air was salty, with a slight chill breeze. I found the floor was damp with sand and seaweed, and the walls were rough and rocky. It was dark, but quiet and peaceful. I reached out with my mind to sense as much as I could. I could feel the damp sand on my bare feet and I could feel the weight of my body on my feet. I was there, in this cave, as fully as I could possibly be. At times I felt as though I was watching an image of myself, but when this happened I got straight back into my body and regained the view I had from my own eyes. I used as many senses as I could to re-affirm my presence in the cave. Some detail was still vague and hazy, and when this was so I simply allowed it to become clear or not, as it wished. I was at pains not to create the experience, rather to let the experience form by itself.

On the left hand wall there was a door, tiny and low to the ground, too low for any human to crawl through. It was old, but substantial. I felt I could and should try to get through it. As I decided to do this I simply found myself travelling through the doorway. It did not open, but my form shrank and I just moved through it.

I emerged into a lush and vibrant landscape. The dark and cold of the cave had been replaced by a glowing light and penetrating warmth. The lifeless nature of the cave had been replaced by thick undergrowth, expansive bushes and trees. Thick green grass and small animals were all around. The air was still, and the temperature was just right. The scene was not overgrown or neglected, but the forces of nature were strong here and life grew very extensively, very quickly.

I bent down to pick a flower and to raise it to my nose. It was pink with many petals. As I plucked it from its stem it gave off a high-pitched squeak, "Ouch!" I had hurt it! What? If plants had feelings and could express themselves, then so must animals. I called out for an animal to take me to my Guide.

A Zebra immediately galloped up from the right. It was a strong and proud animal, not at all shy or easily scared. I followed behind as the Zebra led me further into this new world.

The undergrowth became thicker and more difficult to penetrate and at times the Zebra slowed right down. When this happened I reiterated my desire to be taken to my Guide and the Zebra would pick up the pace. The animal was leading, but was I directing?

The Zebra meandered some more and came to a halt in front of an angel, a winged man, dressed all in white. He exuded an aura of huge power. His eyes were piercing cold blue, and they looked right through me.

I was pleased to meet my Guide and very happy that he was a being of such stature and authority. I moved forward to greet him, just in time remembering the procedure that it was vital to check who he was.

"Are you my True Guide?" I asked.

"You have travelled far, come nearer," came the reply. I had spent many years in the regular world failing to receive straight answers to straight questions and this answer disturbed me. I repeated my question.

"Are you my True Guide?" The angel disappeared, with a hiss and a curse. I felt that I had done the right thing and his reaction had proved he was not my Guide at all.

I turned back toward the Zebra and the animal nodded over to the right of where the angel had been. I moved in this direction and the feet of an unknown figure came into view. After a little while I could just about discern his dress, similar to that of an ancient Assyrian. His skin was bronzed and worn, he carried a short dagger, and his clothing was all flowing purple robes. He wore sandals, was tall and broad of stature and although I could not see all his face, his eyes were warm and full of depth.

"Are you my True Guide?" I asked.

"Yes," he replied without hesitation. I was very pleased, and felt great warmth toward him. I could see behind my Guide there were one or two other characters lingering around. I did not approach them and felt they were also False Guides, waiting to distract me.

My Guide reached out his hands to take mine. I allowed him to do this and I immediately felt an outpouring of trust, warmth and kindness from him. It was akin to a brotherly love, or the love one has for a close member of one's family.

He took my left hand in his right and we both turned to face the distance. High in the sky was the Sun, warm and bright. With his other hand, my Guide pointed up toward it. He asked me, and I gave him my permission for the Sun to come down. I felt no apprehension at any time throughout this. A swirling mass of heat and colour came down from high in the sky and became part of me. Reds and oranges of all shades coursed through me and I was rejuvenated, feeling healthy and full of life. This Sun did not stay long, but long enough for me to never feel quite the same again.

My Guide suggested it was time to go and I wished him goodbye. He said I would see him again soon. The Zebra arrived to take me back to my doorway. I returned the same way I had arrived and found myself back in the cave. I dissolved the cave around me and I returned to the physical.

It would take me a further four years to integrate this experience. These were the worst four years of my life, having again glimpsed 'something more' I failed, for a million reasons and none, to reconnect to it. But it never went away, it was always available. It's just that I was not available to it.

The years that followed ushered in a slow realisation of the significance of the Inner Guide Meditation (IGM) process. I tried many other guided and unguided meditations, visualisations and pathworking exercises, but none of them hit the spot in the same way that this process had. I found an increasing number of exercises and courses on the market which extracted and expanded one or two parts of the process. There were courses that tackled the first part only, the stillness of the cave. I found that expanding and deepening that aspect brought great relaxation. But nothing else. I found a series of books, cards and audios dealing with Power Animals, building upon the part of the IGM where I had encountered the Zebra. This too was beneficial and comforting, but within very tight bounds. Over the years I became increasingly of the opinion that the IGM was a very special kind of practice, but also that it could be taken so much further. I just did not know how.

Shortly after the Millennium, Arthur passed me a book by the Irish mystic and author, J H Brennan. This book, Astral Doorways, was exactly what I had been looking for. Brennan explained – in words simple and clear – that there exists an invisible reality beyond our usual visual sight, and that it can be reached through dream, vision, meditation and through projection of the mind through a symbol, such as a Tarot card, a hexagram of the I Ching or a Tattva symbol. Arthur had said as much but my relationship with him was often so confrontational (on my part) that he could say 'here's a chair, sit down' and I would sit on the table. I was not always well disposed to hearing what my teacher had to say so he often presented me with books written by others, which he knew contained the same message in different form. I devoured Brennan's book, combining his insights with the original IGM exercises, Arthur's words and my own ideas. I thus began to explore using the seventy-eight cards of the Tarot as doorways to that elusive, yet ever-present, 'something more'.

CHAPTER II

KALIA

[AUGUST 2003]

Monday 18th. Evening. The Wheel of Fortune. As I arrived in the Inner World I was immediately confronted by a small, dark skinned woman. She greeted me on my right hand side and I immediately asked where my Guide was.

"I am your new Guide," she replied. I could see the Assyrian from before in the background. He called over.

"I must go now. You will be in safe hands," gesturing over to the small woman. "Your first Guide is often a man," he said, "and as you progress you meet others. We never leave you, but your new Guide will take care of you now. The man's voice was kind but full of strength and authority. I felt calm and comfortable with this unexpected turn of events and turned to the small woman in front of me.

"Are you my True Guide and do you have the power to protect me here in the Inner World?" I remembered my maiden voyage and had to be sure with whom I was dealing.

"Yes," came the unfaltering reply. She smiled broadly and we embraced. There was no explanation, discussion or debate.

We approached a tall Ferris wheel, heavy of metal. It was painted brightly with many flashing coloured lights adorning its spokes. In its shadow however, there was a smaller circus Wheel, enclosed within a wire-fenced compound. Although this wheel was dwarfed by the iron one behind it, and it showed signs of wear and tear, there was more happening by this smaller wheel. I could hear cheers of joy and screams of despair. Happy people going up and sad people coming down. The wheel travelled around, steadily but inevitably, never stopping to let anyone on or off. Its passengers could not see, they could not connect up to down, or action to consequence. They did not realise that the lowest point was at the same time the point of improvement, The Wheel turning inevitably upwards from there. The scene was meaningful, directly relevant to my Outer World situation. When life is problem free, I thought, you must take full advantage of it, for it cannot last, and The Wheel must turn downwards from its highest point. There could be no escaping these changes, these cycles. They were the only constant in life.

There was a ticket booth at the entrance to the smaller compound, occupied by a being whose shape I could not define. I asked the being if there was anything he could do for me?

"You are getting too clever for your own good," came the reply, as it passed me a wrapped object in the shape of a key. "You will need this later," came another voice. I took the gift in my right hand, and pondered on what it was for as I swapped it to my left. I took my new Guide's hand and entered the compound. The key obviously fitted some kind of lock, and I scanned the scene for its location. I could see no lock, no door. Nonetheless, I knew the key was valuable and that I couldn't lose it. I asked, but my Guide would not look after it for me.

There were many questions to which I had no satisfactory answers, in this place and in my usual Outer World. Just as that thought flashed across my mind I found that we were stood at the foot of four steps leading up to a large doorway. The wooden door was heavy and old, and the steps worn away in the centre. I was immediately conscious of being on hallowed ground. My Guide waited at the foot of the steps as I approached the door. I could now see the keyhole, for which I unwrapped and inserted the key.

I knew immediately that this was The Library. Not just a library, but The Library, the place where there is a book for everything and everything is known. I could feel myself rising up and out of my physical body, becoming lighter and lighter. I did not dare release myself totally, but did rise for some time and some distance. There were shelves upon shelves of books, stretching up and along, as far as the eye could see. I was aware that there was no need to remove any from their shelves to discover what lay within. Asking a question would simply elicit the answer. I asked what I thought were the big questions of Life.

"World War One? What was its cause and its lesson?"

"Incompetence, bigotry, intolerance of other cultures. All caused by the male." Came the clear reply. Not a voice, nor a presence, just a knowing. Unexpectedly clear and strong, the answer was straightforward and simple. No complex theories or ifs and buts. I pressed on. I would consider the value of the answers later.

"And World War Two?" I continued.

"Illness, madness. All that killing caused by the male again." There was a pause. "Hitler was a very ill man from early on. He lacked balance within himself, and never saw the need for it in others." I pressed further and asked about President Kennedy. "What about him?," said the voice, "your question is vague, so will be the answer." Another pause. "The FBI were involved in his death, but the whole affair was bungled. The significance of the event is found in the fact that Kennedy was unsuitable to be President. His demise was for others to learn the fallibility of the male and to destroy the cult of personality."

I felt I could continue here all night, asking as many questions as I liked, so long as I was prepared for the answers. The simplicity of the answers was difficult to bear though, there was certainly no room for my favourite pastimes of debate and discussion, so I left it there. I was instructed to leave the key on a table at the side as I departed. As I did so, the image of the Librarian, who had been in attendance all that time, began to come into view. He was immensely old, possessed of great wisdom and authority, but was no mere stuffy academic. As I closed the door behind me the Library vanished from sight.

I returned to my physical body, absolutely exhausted. As I proceeded to write this record, I could scarcely hold my pen or focus on the paper in front of me.

I lay on the sofa in my living room for the rest of the evening, head spinning, body wretched.

Afterwards. In these early days I would often discuss my experiences with Arthur. It was my way of trying to make sense of them. In this, Arthur never contradicted me, and only intervened to add a word or phrase here and there. On this occasion he said only one thing, correcting my use of the word Librarian. "The bad tempered Keeper," he said.

Wednesday 20th. 6.40pm. The Empress. After meditating gently upon the image of this Tarot card for some minutes I closed my eyes and allowed whatever wanted to form before me to do so. Fighting the urge to 'try' or to 'invent' anything in my imagination I was confronted with a feeling of silliness, that I was somehow doing this wrong, or wasting my time by doing it at all. It was at that moment, the moment closest to opening my eyes and giving up, that I saw a doorway, jet black in colour, which turned into a landscape as I passed through. My Guide was waiting on the right.

"You must trust both your intuition and your judgement more," came the voice from the Guide. I connected this directly to the contractual arrangements I had with my current employer, in the regular world, whom I was in the process of leaving. "He is an opportunist and must be handled carefully. But you can play him at his own game. Do not be too rigid. Just sort the car out. Anything else can be as vague as he requires it. Commitment is not necessary. Avoid that and simply see how things go." The advice was unsolicited yet relevant in every respect. I could not have consciously summarised my situation better. I asked if there was anything else I needed to know. My Guide referred to a colleague of mine, a fellow explorer of the mysteries. "He is in here." I asked if we should go to see him. "No, he is not ready, and you should not have encouraged him to come in before he was." I had over zealously explained to him my thoughts and experiments in this Inner World, in spite of my knowing that he was even less receptive to learning about such things than I was.

In the distance I could just make out another figure, surrounded by life and activity. I suggested that we head to see what was going on. The figure was strong, sexual, warm and loving, yet could be forceful when necessary. She sat on a raised chair, akin to a throne, but not as grand as any throne I had seen before. Her influence was clear to see. She radiated life outwards to all that surrounded her – plants, grass, birds, trees. There were no children in attendance as far I could see, which I found to be out of keeping with the rest of the image, but I did not raise this concern.

"Go!," she said, "you have physical matters to attend to. Be strong, fit and clear when you come here. Attend to the physical. Always be rested and not at all hungry when you come here." I tried to argue but the words just would not come out. "Go," she insisted firmly. My Guide urged me to listen to her. I took heed, wished her farewell and left immediately.

I gave it two hours, back in the Outer World, where I had a light dinner and a shower before returning through the same doorway as before. Again my Guide greeted me on my right.

"Welcome back. You are fresh now. It is very important to address the Outer World first. It is just as important as the Inner World you know, not more or less, but equally so." I asked if we could carry on where we had left off. "Yes," replied my Guide. Before us appeared a gravel pathway, full of twists and turns. At its end, the woman sat as before, surrounded by the vibrancy of life. She was its giver, and holder of the ultimate responsibility. At her feet was a young crone, dressed in dark rags. Her hair was greying and her skin was lifeless. She was hunch backed and miserable. "I do all the work while she gets all the credit," the crone pointed up to the woman as she scurried off to her small shack not far away. My Guide and I followed. Although the shack was not far away the landscape now changed significantly. It was muddy and dirty and there was no life, joy or noise. The crone entered through a small door at the front and left it ajar behind her. I knocked and entered slowly. The crone was huddled in the corner, crying. She stopped crying when she saw me. I repeated her words back to her – that she does the work and others get the credit – and asked her to explain herself. Her reply was unintelligible and I felt the image start to break up in my vision. I left her shack and seemed to be able to pull things together again. I asked my Guide who the crone was and what she meant?

My Guide insisted she was nothing for me to worry about and took both my hands in hers. She was small and so were her hands, but her grip was firm. She repeated that it was nothing to worry about. I asked if it was my attitude toward my mother that had brought the crone to life. I had answered my own question. It must be that. I turned toward where the shack was and it vanished in a flash of bright light.

"Well done," my Guide was pleased with my insight. Returning to the woman on the throne I asked if she were the mother, not knowing where these questions or insights were coming from.

"I am," she replied. Her image became clearer now. I did not recognise her face, but she was dressed brightly, with jewellery and long, flowing hair. She was mature – though not old – and experienced. I asked it there was anything I could do for her?

"Call your mother. It won't kill you. You have no idea what it's like being a mother." Her voice was firm. I could see many small children around the feet of this lady. I asked her where the Father was? "You'll meet him soon enough!" came the reply. A small girl came running up to me.

"Will you be a Father one day?" she asked. She knew that I wasn't. I leaned down and replied that I did not know. I turned to my Guide and the Empress, who were next to each other, asking for some clarification. They both smiled benevolently and it seemed that they nodded their heads.

Now my Guide suggested that it was time to leave. I asked why I could not stay longer? She relented, but insisted that it didn't get too heavy.

I looked my Guide up and down. She was short, maximum five feet tall. She was dark skinned, and wore a sackcloth type tunic with sandals. It was very primitive and basic dress, maybe even that of a slave. But then there was also a vague sense of some kind of wrist jewellery. I felt that I could see through her clothing, and she mildly scolded me for this. I turned then to look around at the nearby environment. There was a large green tree in the background and as I looked further it became clear that all around and behind the Empress was lush greenery, thriving plants and flowers of all types. This was in contrast to the area where I had entered. Around the doorway the grass was now worn away and everything was somewhat barren. As well as it being a well-worn pathway, I got the sense that trouble and destruction were encroaching from the Outer World.

"This is true," said my Guide, before I could even speak. "But I thought we said not too heavy?" I nodded in agreement. "Now it's time to go," she insisted. I prepared to leave, but at the last moment turned to ask her name. "K, Kalia," came the answer. I doubted this information at first, unsure if I had heard correctly. "Kalia," she repeated, "but what is in name?" I replied that back in the Outer World, names possessed tremendous significance. "That is right," she said, "in the Outer World!" There were faint signs of exasperation at my ignorance.

We embraced and she ushered me toward the doorway, waving goodbye as I returned to the Outer World. When I arrived back and opened my eyes I looked first at the clock. Expecting around five minutes to have elapsed, I was amazed when I saw that I had been gone almost thirty!

Saturday 30th. 7.05pm. The Moon. I arrived through the doorway, greeting my Guide, Kalia, on my right. She didn't waste any time in addressing my Outer World anxieties. She said that the house where I lived in Cheltenham would be sufficient for a few years yet, and my ownership of it provided security which would actually serve to improve the quality of my journeys into the Inner World.

I surveyed the landscape around me. There was a wide puddle of dark coloured water on the floor, directly ahead, filled with rushes and wild plant growth. There were small insects and frog-like creatures around it. Out the other side of that puddle a pathway extended into the distance as far as I could see. It twisted and turned and there were large, wild animals on either side. A tall building was on the right, about half way along the path. In a flash it was struck by lightning. Someone's world had come crashing down, I thought. As this happened, a bat flew out of a derelict building on the other side of the pathway.

It was a foreboding sight and I asked Kalia to come with me as I headed down the path. She said that I needed to go alone, but that she could follow behind if I insisted. I edged forward along the path. A wild dog was barking on the right. It was close but yet I felt no danger from it. It continued to bark as we passed by.

As we proceeded further, the sky darkened, the grass edges surrounding the path were wet and the animals all around us were noisy. Straight overhead was the Moon, full and bright. We travelled along this path for some time before the landscape became much brighter. I immediately sensed we were near the Library again. But this time I have been given no key. I turned to Kalia.

"Where is the key?" I asked.

"The dog has it," she said. Of course, the dog had been barking for a reason! I ran back down the pathway toward where we had seen him. He was still there and I asked him where the key was. He dug furiously into the ground and there it was. I pulled it from the ground and patted the dog, thanking him for his help. He was happy, and eager to help some more, but I had to leave him to return to the Library. I was suddenly conscious that I had no questions prepared. Kalia suggested that I simply enter and see what happened.

As I rose up the steps and went in through the door, I could see the hall much more clearly than before. It was huge in all dimensions, the walls were long and stretched back as far as the eye could see and rose so high that I could not see the roof. The floor was made of white stone, and the whole room pulsated in an electric blue. The Keeper was waiting and as I looked around I found myself transform into a mass of energy, a soft and calm, light blue energy, as opposed to the vibrancy of the room. I was very conscious of my own energy and being and nothing else seemed to matter, to the extent that my physical body felt like it no longer existed. Eventually something resembling normal consciousness returned and I was confronted by the stern gaze of The Keeper. He said that it was time to leave. I foolishly asked him if he was the Hermit and he refused to answer, ordering me to leave. He was not happy and as I left, the door slammed shut behind me. I returned the key to the dog and the animal quickly buried it again. The whole thing was very confusing and I asked Kalia for some clarification. She smiled and said the unknown had to be confronted and ultimately mastered,

"A silver lining hides behind every cloud," she said, "and this pathway is the path of life where the more you learn the better it gets." Her face was clearer now. She had dark skin and bright white teeth. She was of African or Middle Eastern tribal descent. She wore a simple sackcloth dress with sandals and silver jewellery. I waved goodbye.

[SEPTEMBER 2003]

Wednesday 10th. 7.30pm. The World. I had some free time, at last. After reflecting upon the image of the card for many minutes I closed my eyes to enter the Inner World. Unexpectedly I was confronted with the image of a hill, with its peak chopped off, flat and square. On top of the hill was a large black doorway. Having entered the Inner World via a mind doorway I could now see another doorway leading elsewhere.

Kalia greeted me, and a stream of consciousness about matters in the Outer World burst forth. My recent house move was complete, but it was important that I did not take for granted those who had helped me with it.

We moved further into the Inner World, the hill and its black doorway still in the distance. There was a celebration on top of the hill, in front of the darkened entrance. There was a dancer and three creatures sitting around, watching and enjoying the spectacle. The dancer was more than just an entertainer though, she was on the same level, even of the same kind, as her audience of three creatures. I could only make out one of these as a Bull. I asked the creature next to the Bull if she were a Sphinx.

"No!" was the empathic reply. I felt somewhat inferior to these creatures and sensed that I should defer slightly to them. I did so and Kalia followed suit. The dancer had much to say.

"There are reasons to be cheerful now, and cause for celebration. There will be travel and a feeling of satisfaction. Enjoy, but then prepare for your next cycle." I interrupted the dancer.

"Does the black doorway lead to another level?" I could not hear her answer and felt pretty inadequate in the presence of these beings. Trying to correct that I asked if I could do anything for the dancer. She extended her arm toward me. She was holding a white baton with decorative ends which she used to draw a thick line diagonally through the middle of my palm.

"Follow your path, and become all that you can. That is all."

Kalia and I bowed and moved back down the hill. I wondered what to do next. Although the sky was dark the Moon above us was very bright. Suddenly, over from the right of the scene came lightning. Very localised, it did not seem to affect the weather above us in any way and only touched one building, striking it directly. I asked Kalia if we should go over. No sooner had I said those words than we were there, with a man emerging from the wrecked building, coughing and spluttering.

"Can I help?" I asked.

"What happened?" he was confused.

"Complacency." I returned, "you took it all for granted." A sense of realisation came over his face, as if this was a revelation. He shouted to his friend.

"Luke, we've cracked it!" They both rejoiced and cheered at what they had realised and ran off into the distance, planning for the future, safe in the knowledge that they had learned from this mistake. I commented to Kalia that I did not know where my presence of mind had come from and in any event that my words did not seem very helpful.

"But it is everything to them," she replied. "You should remember the price you have paid for your knowledge and experience, the long road you have travelled to get even here." She was of course correct. One person's obvious is someone else's revelation.

We walked back to the doorway through which I had arrived. The way back was not as clear or immediate as in other visits, but after some confusion we arrived there safely. I asked Kalia who she was and where she came from. She replied that she had been a member of an ancient Middle Eastern tribe. She told me the tribe's name, but it was so alien that I could not hold onto it. I asked her to repeat the name, but to no avail. I was tiring now and asked her if I could find the name in history books back in the Outer World. She laughed and said that they would not have recorded it.

"They don't record many things!" she said, smiling. She urged me to return soon. I kissed her and held her arm tightly before wishing her goodbye and returning to the physical.

Wednesday 17th. Death. Entry through the doorway was at first very difficult. I could neither see nor sense anything at all, but then from nowhere came Kalia's voice. I felt a temptation to fill the black void surrounding it with inventions from my own imagination, but I resisted and slowly an awareness formed itself.

It was dark and raining, then the rain slowly dispersed and was replaced by a thick white fog. I could sense Kalia's presence on my right, but still could not see her. I also sensed a figure directly in front of me. Now I had vision, but only of his eyes. They were piercing though neither threatening nor menacing. The figure gave off a feeling of weighty inevitability and as he became a little clearer I could sense that he was very routine and matter of fact about his work. He was covered head to foot in a black cape and walked with a large bladed scythe, but rarely used it. He had a single white rose pinned to his cloak. He was powerful, but did not always demonstrate that power. As he travelled, wherever he had been there was light.

"I represent change, of a higher form," he said, his voice was not at all threatening. "I am not, as you think, evil. I just - am."

"Is there anything I can do for you?" I asked.

He laughed aloud. "It is more a case of what I can do for you!" he continued. "Do you not know who I am?" he asked, not giving me a chance to reply, "I am Death. The bringer of change." I did not dare push the conversation any further, and looked to Kalia for some confirmation about his nature.

"You can only see what you are ready for," she said. Thinking that I might not be ready for this I suggested that we move on.

A horse drawn Chariot sped up, stopping straight in front of us. Its horses impatient for action, it wasn't going to hang around. Kalia and I jumped aboard. The Chariot was pulled by one white horse, one black, both very strong and fast moving, covering a large distance in no time at all. After a while we came to rest at the foot of an overgrown hill. We got out of the Chariot as quickly as we had got in, and I looked up the steep incline. Kalia was on my left, and I felt uncomfortable. I asked her to move to my right.

"If it makes you feel better," she said, and switched sides. We climbed up, some way through the thick undergrowth and eventually emerged into a large clearing. We stood and surveyed the new landscape. Suddenly lightning struck close to my left foot. I looked down, the earth was singed and smouldering. I looked across to the left, there was a Tower under attack from above. Two men emerged from the wreckage, shaken and disorientated. They asked what had happened.

"Your pride was mistaken," I said and pointed to the smouldering foundations, which were steadily sinking into the ground. "You sacrificed your freedom yet you work best when you are free." These insights effortlessly floated out of me. The two men seemed to understand my analysis and ran off, rejoicing, into the distance.

"Where now?" I said to Kalia. "The Library?"

Instantly we were there, at the foot of those well-worn steps. The door now had no lock and no key was required. The Keeper welcomed my return. This journey was unlike others so far. My sight of the Inner World had been reduced and replaced by a sense, a feeling, but one that was no less informative. I had heard – back in the Outer World - that this could be rectified by mental exercises and stimulation of the Third Eye.

"Do I need to do this?" I asked The Keeper.

"Yes," came the straightforward reply. And it was done. I could suddenly see everything again, in vivid colour.

"No exercises?" I asked.

"No exercises. Your vision will be reinforced by regular visits here, to the Inner World," said The Keeper. Our time was again limited and nothing more was said, the Library dissolving around me as I fell to the sandy earth. I was very confused. The impressions and senses were unfamiliar, but maybe that was the whole point? Maybe I had been trying too hard to order this Inner World in the same way as my Outer World? "Accept whatever comes," was the message from Kalia, "try neither to order it, or to predict it," she continued. "To behave as all those men do, back in the Outer World, will not work here. This is effectively an alien landscape for which none of your laws apply."

Death had been the precursor to this discussion, this realisation. I had remembered the many early Saturday mornings of long train journeys just to try and soak up a bit of Arthur's knowledge. On those occasions my Tarot Card of the Day had frequently been Death. Death of old ways of thinking, old methods. These were tough lessons and took some accepting. I had resisted change for years, I often did not see the need for it, and more often resented it. But today's challenging encounter with Death had left me little option but to accept it.

[OCTOBER 2003]

Wednesday 1st. The Chariot. This time the mind doorway was purple. As it faded, I saw Kalia, waiting. Together we walked down a steep precipice to a large circular, barren racetrack. The landscape was rocky and sandy. There were no spectators. The Chariot sat in front of us for a short time while I took in my surroundings, but quickly sped off, the Charioteer seemed somewhat impatient. After completing a lap or two he returned again. I did not hang around this time and, with Kalia, jumped in.

The Chariot now travelled fast and I had to hold on tight. The ground was bumpy and the two horses that pulled us, again one white, one black, were arguing with each other. But their argument seemed not to distract, and if anything to propel us faster and further forward. The axle groaned under the strain but held firm.

The speed at which we travelled seemed amazingly fast and was exactly the rate at which, I felt, life should be lived. "An ideal shortcut method," I thought. I asked to take over the reins but the Charioteer insisted that I was not ready.

"That," he said, "is real magick." I kept silent. He had other things to say. "Money is a false desire. The desire simply for money is an empty one. Money only flows from achievements and accomplishments. When you accomplish something worthwhile the rewards will be great, but not before that." The advice had been unsolicited, but very relevant to my Outer World concerns.

We then arrived in front of a ruined building – a Tower – and the Charioteer said to look at the people around it.

"They built it falsely," he remarked, "on meaningless desires. And look at it now." I thanked him for illustrating his point. Kalia and I now disembarked and the Chariot roared off. I again shouted my thanks to the, now distant, Charioteer. He said it was fine, I could help him another time.

"Woe is me!" wailed one of the poor unfortunates in the wreckage of the Tower. I offered to help, trying to pass on the point given to me by the Charioteer, that false hope, not rooted in truth, had led them here. "No, it was because our belief wasn't strong enough," moaned one of them. I urged him to discard his beliefs and deal only with what he knew. He looked cross eyed at me, literally, but then his face changed as the truth dawned on him. He jumped to his feet and he and his friend departed jubilantly. I questioned Kalia on the sense and reality of all this.

"It makes perfect sense, and is as real as anything else you had ever experienced in the Outer World," she replied, seemingly content where I was not. It was time to go. "Come back again soon," she said, smiling a beaming white toothy smile, a soothing sight after a most intense and fast moving visit.

Wednesday 15th. The Wheel of Fortune. The purple doorway loomed large above and in front of me. I rose up in a diagonal fashion toward it and passed through. As I did I realised it was the same size as my physical body. Kalia was waiting to greet me and we went down a hill into a fenced off area containing many different fairground attractions. The scene was however, as far as I could see, missing a Ferris Wheel. We arrived at the fence that surrounded the compound, and an Eagle swooped down very close to me. He settled on the fence and stared closely at me. He was intimidating, but indicated we were safe to proceed toward the ticket booth. A Bull was behind the counter and did not seem very happy about it. A Lion was close by, roaring threateningly. I thought that if I could tame this Lion I would prove myself as very strong indeed. The Lion read my mind and indicated that I was not ready to do this, but promptly rolled over, tempting me to give it a try anyway. I backed off.

I shunned the more extravagant rides that surrounded us and approached the ticket booth. As I did the Ferris Wheel, exactly as before, came into view. I asked the Bull for permission to enter and he agreed. Kalia and I climbed in one of the cars, having to jump a little, as the Wheel did not stop. As I travelled up, I could see different people and events, through various snapshots of time. This Ferris Wheel took on a new dimension and became the Wheel of Life, a measure of time's quality, as distinct from its quantity in hours, minutes or seconds. Each movement of the wheel was a snapshot in time, important in its own right, dependant on the others to form the whole. The Wheel was as such a clock, by any other name, forever turning and moving on, sometimes fast, sometimes slow. But never stopping. Some of the scenes I witnessed were of action and movement, others of silence and rest. But none of them endured.

I had seen enough and it was time to move on. The Wheel continued to turn as our car reached the highest point. At once we jumped out, flying high into the sky, then gently floating for a while before drifting back to earth, coming to rest next to the ticket booth, at the feet of the Bull, the Lion and Eagle. The Bull went to hand me something and I questioned him on this.

"That is how it works," he said begrudgingly. I have no awareness of taking anything from him at this point, or any memory of what it was he gave me. The other creatures wished us well, as we turned back up the hill. It was mere seconds before I remembered giving Kalia a hug and returning to the physical. Immediately before snapping back home I could sense a fourth creature around, but in my tiredness I couldn't quite define it.

Friday 24th. 6.30pm. Justice. Entry through this doorway was difficult. It was hard to concentrate and doubly hard, today, to resist the temptation to invent. Finally, as I emerged into the landscape I cut my bare feet on the sharp white rocks, drawing blood. Kalia confirmed this was indeed blood, but not as I knew it. The scene was unclear and some time passed before I became comfortable and familiar with the scene. I then asked Kalia to take me further into this part of the Inner World.

The Eagle from before had been circling and suddenly swooped down and landed in front of me.

"Who are you?" I asked with some trepidation.

"I – we – are Justice," replied the Eagle gesturing toward my left where a woman, a Bull and a Lion were waiting.

"We are Justice," spoke all four in unison. The woman now took over.

"We exert Justice upon the Universe, maintaining balance through constant re-adjustment. The balance of the four elements is key to all life." They continued in unison. "When the four elements are in balance, there exists peace, prosperity and happiness. When the four elements are moved out of balance we move to correct them, but we cannot do everything. We cannot go back, we can only move to change other things in order to re-balance the whole. Understand, we cannot go back. We can only look to new actions to provide the re-balance and re-dress the situation requires."

The woman who stood with the three creatures seemed kind and compassionate. The Lion roared, and the Bull encouraged the woman to continue the explanation. The Eagle, however, interrupted and stopped the proceedings. Kalia was at my right. I bowed slightly toward the creatures and asked them if I could do anything for them.

"Write about these experiences. And look after those close to you," came the unambiguous answer. The Eagle again called a halt and the creatures dispersed.

These creatures seemed, after this encounter, very advanced indeed. Kalia confirmed this, but said to not worry about it and to hurry back again.

As I left I cut my left foot on the same white rocks as I had when I arrived. I felt no pain once I had returned to the physical, and in the space just before opening my eyes I felt further insights wash over me. The four creatures maybe ruled the Inner World, but did they rule the Outer World too? The Inner and Outer formed a whole, but if the Outer World was out of balance (which daily evidence seemed to suggest it was) then would the Inner World be under threat too?

[NOVEMBER 2003]

Wednesday 12th. 6pm. The Devil. The doorway was a rich purple and as I emerged on the other side, Kalia was on the right, waiting for me. Previous trips through other doorways had always begun with relative serenity and calm. But not this time. Deafening noise, whistling wind, thunder and lightning were all around. It was oppressive and frightening. We had to fight through this terrible weather to reach the beginning of a rocky pathway. Although all around was devastation, Kalia indicated that it was as it should be.

As we walked along the pathway, Kalia and I spotted a woman lying on the ground. She was naked, but for bright red body paint, interspersed with yellows and whites. I could not have imagined anything more attractive and my gaze was fixed on her. She wasn't beautiful, or welcoming, but I lusted after her and she knew it. She became very expressive and graphic doing everything possible to tempt me toward her. I asked her who she was.

"I am the Dark Side," she said, "where you cannot control your emotions." She flung me to the ground, demanding immediate sexual gratification. I was very tempted, but resisted, taking flight with Kalia high up into the sky. From this distant vantage point I could still see the naked woman, but my lust had vanished and my emotional attachment had gone. To have stayed in her presence and fed my desire would also have meant feeding the Dark Side. Going against myself in that moment, by denying the light, would have increased the influence of the Dark Side and allowed it to co-opt powerful human emotions along the way. But from this higher place, in the sky with Kalia, I could see that any manifestation of the Dark Side – in this case through sex – may act as a release, but may just as quickly destroy our dreams and enslave us in the false belief that *it* is the only solution to our insecurities.

Thinking that these realisations would remove the problem I came back down to earth. But the Devil, the red painted woman, would not go away. As Kalia and I travelled along the pathway, the woman followed us, always lurking behind a bush or a tree. Further along the path she tried again to tempt me, and almost successfully, but I managed to resist. She was angry at this and disappeared. Kalia congratulated me and I felt relieved. I noted that the Dark Side appeared more of a burden in this case, than an enjoyment. I certainly would have enjoyed myself with her, but would I ever again be free? The voice of the painted woman wafted through the air. She would be back.

My awareness then shifted to a completely unconnected sight; that of a golden chair, far off in the background. The image did not remain long, and it was time to go.

As I left Kalia, she said that we should meet again soon and that my experiences on this journey would have to be tested. She also gave me a warning.

"The Dark Side will be more sophisticated in future."

Wednesday 26th. 6.30pm. Temperance. Eyes firmly closed I saw a slim and beautiful young woman by a pond, fed on one side by a stream where water gently flowed in. It mixed around in the pool and gently flowed away on the other side. On one side plants grew and thrived, on the other they withered and died. It was a cycle, as one passed, so another bloomed. The woman seemed to exert influence here.

"Balance is needed at all times," she said. "If you cannot introduce it into your own life then it will be introduced for you," her voice remained calm. "As you grow as a person, so does your Dark Side. There can be no way around this. For both, in balance, represent growth." As the woman shared this with me, the Eagle, Bull and Lion were circling around the scene. These three creatures discussed amongst themselves "whether I could handle it" yet. I did not know to what the 'it' referred. There was then some mention of the need to publish these experiences. That would be a long-term goal, it was said. The Dark Side was also mentioned.

"You need to keep it under control, and then very occasionally give it tightly controlled licence." Arthur had said as much before. But then came a bombshell.

"It is your job to re-balance the Inner and Outer Worlds," said the woman. I was lost for words. "Your job, and that of others. You will receive assistance in this task." My experiences in this place were becoming ever stranger, the possibilities ever bigger, my potential ever expanding. The words spoken seemed to be dripping with urgency and I felt that, in this place, I had abilities that were almost magickal. An insight came from one of the creatures. "You certainly do." The other creatures moved to prevent any more being revealed.

The woman by the stream urged me to turn and help Kalia as she was emotionally hurt. I turned and gave her a hug and we both seemed to grow, not in size, but stature. It was a tremendously natural feeling of love, affection, warmth and trust. In this comforting state we walked a little while in the Inner World before I returned to the physical.

[DECEMBER 2003]

Monday 22nd. 5.30pm. The Hermit. A purple coloured doorway formed in front of me and began to increase in size. Engulfing me, I stepped through to be greeted immediately on my right by Kalia. It was good to see her. We spoke briefly about my life in the Outer World. She assured me that all would be fine, but that I had further pain and thus learning to encounter. We turned to a light shining in the distance. I asked if we should approach and investigate. No sooner had I posed the question than there we were. An old man was sat on a log, dressed simply. His hair and beard were white, his face was not entirely clear, but his smile was gleaming white, natural and sincere, his eyes bright and clear, piercing yet calming. He was the Hermit.

THE HERMIT

"What do you wish to know my child?" he said. I asked about a client in the Outer World. The Hermit said things had gone well and that my client's Guide was very pleased. I asked about my partner and he said that in time I could show her these things too. I asked what I was to do next. The Eagle had appeared, and wasted no time speaking up.

"He's not ready," he said to the Hermit. But the Hermit spoke regardless.

"Teach and guide others," he said. Suddenly, a golden disk, divided into four sections, was pushed into my heart. I instantly knew what the four sections represented - independence, communication, versatility and psychic ability. This knowing was as clear as daylight and was accompanied by a shocking force. The immersion of the disk into me almost knocked me over as I felt a power welling up inside me. The Hermit spoke, his tone now more serious.

"Changing the world in accordance with desires is something that must be performed with great care." He pointed to a nearby tree. "I could destroy that, if I wished. But if I did, it would upset the balance and I would have to pay a price. Change through magick and manifestation easily becomes a slippery slope where all your time is consumed firstly initiating, then forever re-acting, correcting, re-acting again, and correcting again, ad infinitum. All this time you are not moving forward or learning anything, just lost in a sea of endless consequences." He said that I may have a slight awareness of what it was like, to live through crisis after crisis, never recovering before the next one befalls you. I certainly did and I didn't want to go there again. The Hermit continued. "Most things are as they are for a reason – good or bad. Lasting change can only occur once the lesson contained within each thing, and connecting to other things, has been learned." The Hermit asked if I wished to know more. I was still soaking it all in and could not reply.

The Library appeared. I wanted to go in but felt that I had nothing of value to ask. The offer was repeated but I resisted. The last thing I saw, before the building vanished, was The Keeper waving and smiling through the window before hurrying along to his business. Kalia interrupted and called a halt to proceedings. The Hermit wished me good luck and reminding me once again to "teach others." Then he was gone. A flash of understanding came – time out in the Inner World delivered real peace of mind, while time out in the Outer World often amounted to no more than distraction.

Suddenly I became aware that I could fly. So I did, all over the place, up and down and round again. Anything was possible, the old restrictions and rules gone. I could distil myself down to an essence of swirling colours, and when I did so it felt wonderfully liberating. Unfortunately these freedoms did not last long as I quickly felt absolutely exhausted. Kalia insisted on ending the session there and I departed. I returned to the physical, aching, tired and drained.

[JANUARY 2004]

Saturday 3rd. 12.30pm. The Moon. The scene was black and it was very difficult to discern anything at all at first. I then realised that was because it was night-time in the Inner World! The night held little fear for me back in the familiar life, but here in the Inner World, I was filled with a sense of foreboding.

Kalia was at my right and said that if I could release my fear of the unknown then I would be able to see clearly. Easier said than done I thought. I tried to feel and locate my fear and then to release it, remembering Arthur's old saying 'the more you learn, the better it gets'. It worked. New realisations washed over me. Both light and dark were an integral part of the whole of Life, and neither could be lived without. I could now clearly see a road snaking into the distance, with two stone pillars, one on either side. In between the pillars, up in the sky, was the Moon, full and bright. We started to travel along. A Serpent hissed from the left roadside and darted out, grabbing my left arm. I felt that if I did not panic, and was instead calm and focused then I could dismiss the creature, but if I over-reacted in any way then it would only grow stronger. I just knew that was what I should do, so I focused as best I could. I could see the creature hanging on to my arm, looking particularly dangerous, but again I felt that the Serpent was a necessary part of Life. With focus I felt no pain and slowly the fear diminished. The Serpent relaxed its grip, dropped to the floor, and went on its way.

Further along the road, various other beings appeared. Firstly, an old man, with a long white beard, appeared on the right. Then further along, a ruined building with people evacuating and running for cover appeared on the left. I offered them some advice, as best I could. There were quite a few refugees from this ruined structure. Many of them ran back down the path, from where we had come. One seemed interested and asked whether the disaster of the falling Tower had been brought about by him and his friends. Wondering why they singled me out for guidance I simply answered that in my view complacency was the fastest way to kiss something goodbye. He signalled his understanding and gratitude and ran ahead into the distance.

Another scene of devastation appeared next on the left. Five people wandered aimlessly amongst the ruins of another building. They had lost all their money and possessions and were without a clue what to do next.

"Who are we?" wailed one.

"What are we for?" moaned another. They had few inner resources and now they were bereft of outer ones too. Accepting the faith they placed in me I answered.

"Each one of you is unique. You each have an identity and a purpose, different from each other. Each of you has a particular job to do in a particular way, one that no-one else can do." They looked at me intently, like they had never heard this before. "Stop trying to be part of a club, and start tuning in to who you are. Start doing things your way," I said.

"But what if we get it wrong?" said one of them, suddenly nervous. "We couldn't handle it if it went wrong again!" They all nodded in agreement at this.

"Fear is a measure of the amount you have learned," I said. "The greater your fear, the less you have learned." The truth seemed to dawn on them and they turned to each other, slowly realising that they were not the masters they imagined themselves to be.

Further down the path there now appeared an enormous white palace, high up in the mountains. It was beautiful, intricate and ornate. White and shimmering. It must have been a huge task to construct. I felt that it had been built through dedication and devotion, rather than through greed or coercion. I looked back down the path and saw that all this time we had been on an upward track into these mountains and toward the palace. At that moment of realisation though, at that point of awareness of how far we had come, I instantly snapped back to our starting point, as if tied with an elastic band that had stretched as far as it could.

The Library was now on my right and The Keeper beckoned me in. I was wary and unsure as yet again I did not have any questions prepared and I certainly did not want to waste his time again. I pressed on with the first thing that came into my mind.

"Is there a map of this Inner World?" I asked.

"Yes," came the straight answer. I continued, lamely.

"And can I trust my intuition, to find this map?"

"Yes, you and your Guide are a powerful combination," said The Keeper.

"And will I see all that I need to?" was my final, even lamer question.

"Yes."

I could not think of any more questions and The Keeper vanished. It had been a poor attempt on my part.

I now became aware of the three familiar creatures. The Bull and the Lion were silent, while the Eagle did most of the talking. Kalia, my second Guide, was soon to depart, and a new Guide introduced. This would not happen just yet, said the Eagle, but it would be soon. I protested at this, neither ready to leave Kalia, nor meet someone new, but there was no reply.

I returned to the physical and opened my eyes, exhausted. I felt really old, though I seemed to look no different in the mirror. Yet again, the intensity of these journeys was increasing. I kept being confronted with the unknown, and with the dawning realisation that I was not as informed as I thought I was.

Saturday 10th. 11.55am. The Empress. Entry through the doorway was not at all smooth. I seemed to be floating, somehow lacking control. Eventually, though, I passed through, unscathed.

The Empress was seated on her throne surrounded by small children. She was feminine and mature, experienced and wise. All her energy was devoted to her simply being a mother. She told me that children, especially boys, looked up to their mothers, listened to them and respected them.

"Mothers can introduce significant change in hearts and minds," she said. "Mothers are held in high regard, and are often given the benefit of the doubt. The future can be changed by our mothers." A small boy pointed up to me, asking who I was. I could not remember my own name, so I just picked him up. "One day," said the Empress, "you will have that responsibility. Not yet though!" This was not something I was ready for. Kalia suggested that it was time to leave them.

"Time for home?" I said.

"Not quite yet," she replied.

The Library appeared on the right of the scene. Again I was apprehensive, but knocked and entered nonetheless. The aged Keeper was straight to the point.

"What do you want?" I wanted to know about my partner and I. "Which one, you or your partner?" I hesitated.

"Me," I said. He told me I had witnessed some terrible things in a previous life, but that I had done as much as I could to put it right. I had made a number of mistakes, but had not accrued a Karmic Debt as I had done what I could to rectify the problems I had been involved with. The Keeper continued, this time about my partner.

"She was a carer in a previous life, which is why she wants to be taken care of now."

I thought it was best not to outstay my welcome and thanked The Keeper. I hugged and kissed Kalia but before I left I sensed some steps in the distance, leading up into the sky. Did these steps lead up to another level? I was excited and started to climb them, but Kalia pulled me back. The Bull and the Eagle circled around but said nothing. There was at least one other creature nearby but could not be certain where the Lion was. It was now time to go and I returned to my physical body with a sharp jolt.

Monday 19th. 5.35pm. The Wheel of Fortune. Kalia was the first thing I saw as I moved through the doorway. There was also a sheer rock face which we climbed straight down and headed toward a gated area containing the Ferris Wheel. The wooden ticket booth was again occupied by the Bull, taking money from the many visitors. The Eagle was perched on a railing watching the Lion rolling around on his back in front of a crowd of visitors, daring them to come and play with him.

The Eagle turned his attention to me and was critical of my ignorance, that I had not been expanding my knowledge as much as I should. The Bull encouraged me to count the pennies and the Lion described how I needed to be bold and brave, even if my bark was worse than my bite.

The Eagle pointed to a key which lay on the ground. As I located the key the doorway to the Library appeared. I hesitated, but the Lion reminded me of the need for bravery, the Eagle spoke of the need to think things through and the Bull spoke of the need to pay attention to the small things. I picked up the key and ascended the steps. Opening the door, I was immediately confronted by The Keeper.

"What can I do for you?" he asked, his tone direct and to the point.

"I want to know about me, and my history." His reaction was calm, and I began to recall images from my past. There I was, a young woman in late 1920's Europe. There were flashes of violence and anger, much noise and many uniformed men. I looked at a newspaper headline with a friend and was dismayed at its angry tone. The sun was shining and I tried to enjoy it with my friends, for we were safe, somehow protected and part of a tight knit circle. My friends just looked away from the problems and I often did the same. I then saw a final scene where, suitcase in hand, my conscience finally overcame my fears and I fled into the night. The Keeper told me that Hitler was a "misguided mystic with ignorance in his mind and hate in his heart," then continued. "With love - or at the very least tolerance - in your heart and a desire to always learn, you will be able to access and handle power." I was satisfied and we wished each other well. The Library dissolved away.

Back at the ticket booth, the Eagle swooped down and rested on my right shoulder.

"Tell me what you have just learned," he demanded. The message had seared into my mind so I had little difficulty repeating it. The three animals concurred that I was ready now to advance further and handle more responsibility. The Lion and Eagle departed into the distance. The Bull followed but was some way behind. It was time to go now and I said farewell to Kalia.

[FEBRUARY 2004]

Saturday 14th. The Emperor. Kalia was instantly recognisable as I emerged through the doorway and into the landscape. She was already dancing and happy to see me. In the distance I could see a man, sitting on a throne, dispensing instructions to those around him. We approached this man of authority and I asked him who he was.

"I am the Emperor," his voice was stern and firm. "The Father. And how little you know about that," he said. "It is a love in spite of everything and against everything. A strength and a sureness. No sweeping fluidity like the Mother, but a rigidity." He was very definite that I should not interrupt. "My traits are needed throughout the universe in equal measure to the yielding and flexible nature of the female, the Mother. One cannot exist without the other."

I looked away from the Emperor and saw another man on his knees, crying in agony. He was beset with problems; he had broken his leg, then he had been robbed, and finally he had lost his job. He expected even worse to befall him and saw no end to his miseries. The Emperor suggested that I try to be a father figure to this poor man, but this was hard. The man was under attack, maybe unfairly, but he had followed his own worse instincts to this place. I assured him that his pain would pass, and suggested that he not allow himself to be led by others to this place again. My efforts seemed inadequate. I asked Kalia what else I might say to help him. She said it was simply a matter of offering him my love. I did this as best I could and he hugged me tightly. His relief might not last long and his suffering would surely return the moment I left, but at least now he might just live to fight another day.

Kalia commented on the length of time since my last visit and hoped that I could come back again more regularly in future. She said that performing defined actions and routine tasks immediately after visits to the Inner World would help to ground me sufficiently to be able to continue my normal, necessary life.

The Keeper was also at hand. I entered the Library and asked about a new client. A book became available to me detailing her exterior strength, but also her sensitivity. Despite her confident appearance she suffered chronic indecision and hesitation. I was warned that there was little I could do about this and that to her, and other sensitives, more information simply means more confusion. Indecision and low self-esteem are a testing combination, especially when the person presents themselves as stronger than they really are.

I exited the Library and the Eagle and Bull were waiting, although nothing was said. I asked Kalia to tell me more about this place, this Inner World.

"Is it a different planet?" I asked.

"Your perception is irrelevant," she replied, inscrutably. We ran into the distance together and then took off into the air. We could fly and proceeded to loop-the-loop, soaring and diving. The limitations of the Outer World did not apply here, our scientific laws unnecessary. In the Outer World, we travel around, arriving back where we started and therefore accept the world as round. Our limited minds can conceive nothing else. But just because we cannot conceive another answer it does not mean that there is not one. Kalia urged me not to bring Outer World rules in here, and suggested that I assimilate all this and return in a few days.

Saturday 21st. Strength. This doorway proved difficult to enter at first. I could hear Kalia calling me but I could not see her or seem to make it through. My senses were on overdrive trying to focus on the slightest of things. This lasted some time and was quite frustrating. Suddenly though, vision arrived. The Lion appeared straight ahead of me, to the left. Kalia was behind me on my right. The Lion roared, quite aggressively. Other people in attendance had it under tight control, on a kind of energetic leash, then in an instant that control was passed to me. I was then atop the Lion, riding it like a horse. It took both physical and mental strength to remain in control, but the Lion did as it was told so long as I concentrated. We sped toward a high precipice. The Lion roared and reared up, trying to unseat me, but to no avail. We then both jumped from the top of that cliff, landing back exactly where we started. I still had the animal under control. Success, I thought. I then made the mistake of relaxing my concentration and moved to stroke the Lion. It was lucky that it did not bite my hand off. A silly mistake, I thought, something that strong is going to want to use its strength. The Lion did not possess the intelligence to discriminate between the friendly and the threatening hand.

"That is what I'm for," said the Eagle as it swooped down and landed on top of the Lions head. The Lion tried to swat it away with its huge paw, but the Eagle was far too quick. The strength of the Lion was rooted in its size, its mass, its solidity. I had not understood muscle and strength before, but I certainly did now. Speed did not sit well with strength, and strength could, without motive, destroy or create.

Lightning struck in the background and I could see a sad man, lost in poverty and desolation. But rather than financial suffering it seemed to be an emptiness, an inner poverty. Kalia and another figure, a female lion-tamer, confirmed that it was safe for me to take a closer look. The man was a strong communicator with a versatility and a need to be on the go. I directed him towards a brighter future where his individuality, communication skills and thirst for travel would feature much more. I urged him to free himself from restrictions and rules. He welcomed my words and did not fight them. He departed the scene feeling much better about himself. Kalia congratulated me, mentioning only that there were a couple of things I had omitted to tell the man. I foolishly neglected to ask her what those were! My mind, instead, turned elsewhere. I asked Kalia who she was.

"I am you," she said.

"But where do you come from?" I probed further.

"The lands you know as Mesopotamia, over ten thousand years ago. But do not rely too much on your documented histories," she smiled.

"So what did you do there?" I pressed further.

"I was compassionate, I spoke up for those who could not speak for themselves. And I had a good time!" she smiled again. I looked around and could see the Inner World much more clearly, in much greater colour and detail. Everywhere was a hive of activity. Previously I had assumed that the scene was made up only of me and Kalia, plus maybe the three creatures and whoever we were visiting. But not so. There was a marketplace of people, events and happenings distributed everywhere around me. "It's always been like this, but you could not see it before," said Kalia.

All the doorways we had entered seemed to open into different parts of the same place. I was now on the verge of completely detaching from my physical body. I felt a strong lump in my throat, but did not dare go any further than that. Slowly the feeling subsided. Further insights came thick and fast. As sickness and hatred prospered in the Outer World so it did in the Inner World. Kalia gave me a golden coin to make some demonstration of this, but it did not register with me how this would work. The Lion roared loudly. I asked Kalia what I could do for her. After all she was helping me out quite a lot here. She reminded me to "not be a stranger and return soon." The Lion tamer said that I already had what I needed and that now I should go and use it.

[MARCH 2004]

Wednesday 3rd. Strength. I returned, some two weeks later, taking time to review my previous experiences. Re-reading my journal raised more questions than it answered, as if I were opening doors and peering through, rather than exploring them fully. Yet, at the same time, I was doing as much as I could, or dared. The most recent loose end played on my mind the most, when Kalia had given me a golden coin and I had neither asked nor known what to do with it. As if to highlight this point the Lion roared loudly as I arrived carrying this anxiety.

Kalia told me that the Pentacle she had gifted me represented the power to achieve anything I wished on the physical plane – money, objects, fixing the body, health and healing – anything material. The power was accompanied by a secret, that it must not be used until genuinely needed, as opposed to wanted. Use of this power for any form of 'want' will be an action of my Dark Side. The power was not time-limited and will always be available to me. I asked to leave the Pentacle in the custody of Kalia, for I did not trust myself with something so enormous. The Lion was now silent. I took this as a confirmation that my decision was right. Who knows what I might do if I had, like the Lion, strength without judgement?

Wednesday 10th. The Lovers. I entered the Inner World with ease and clarity. Immediately visible were a couple, making love. It was not just sex, but an act of inspired creation and the raising of power. All around them flowers blossomed, grass grew and birds sang. It was a beautiful scene, punctuated only with an awareness that joy could not always be relied upon, for when sex is matched with hate or resentment then that hatred just grows. If darkness is the seed, sex will multiply it.

Turning aside from the couple I saw the Eagle, waiting patiently. I approached it and we flew off high into the sky together. When the Eagle disappeared from my side I slowly glided back to the ground. I asked Kalia about the last time she was alive in the Outer World. I was testing her really, trying to catch her out on what she had told me before. She simply said that it was a long time ago, way before I was born.

The Chariot pulled up. We jumped aboard and sped off toward another loving couple. All was well between them, until lightning struck. I went over to help, consoling the man as his partner walked off into the distance. I presumed to give the man advice, telling him to never take things for granted, as that was the fastest way to lose them. He nodded before the scene faded. I was now stood next to Kalia and could condense and distil myself down to my smallest essence, a swirl of coloured energy. In this form I span around intensely and at great speed. This was very tiring and I returned to the physical shortly after.

Tuesday 16th. The Magician. The Magician was dressed in a bright orange cloak with a hood pulled over his head which fell forward to cover much of his face. All that I could discern were clear and bright piercing eyes. He explained that he had full control over the four elements of life - Earth, Air, Fire and Water - and that I did not. As a result, he continued, "there is no need to draw upon any higher power to achieve your aims and goals, it is simply a case of getting your dominoes in a line." I did not quite understand, so he continued with some Outer World examples of the four elements. "You can attain some control of Air by actively thinking in a specific direction. You can attain some control of Water by allowing yourself to feel. I should reach out for some control of Fire by bold and original actions and you can master the Earth by simply getting on with things and finishing what you start." This was a most interesting instruction! He continued. "You can employ these four approaches in your daily life, or for even greater effect you can begin writing. This is the arena where you will see the four elements working together in maximum harmony."

Monday 22nd. The Hierophant. Kalia, greeted me on my right. The Pope, dressed in much ceremonial splendour, had a crowd of people gathered around him. He commanded this audience with calm, measured and rational tones. A Lion sat nearby and roared at the Pope, decrying the conventionality and conformity of the sermon. The roar of the Lion scared the audience away and they fled to the left of the picture. The Pope was now bereft, his traditional garments faded in colour before my eyes, he removed his triple crown and morphed back into an ordinary man. He shuffled off into the distance, without the robes of office he was nothing, empty. There was no inner power and his appearance had been everything.

The Lion, together with the Eagle and Bull came closer to me. In the far distance I could just make out the shimmering white palace, atop a mountain. Kalia reminded me that she still had the Pentacle in safe keeping, ready for me when I needed it. She asked if I required it now. I said that I did not and she promised to keep it until I did.

The Lion was annoyed that I had not visited here more regularly.

"Convention is boxing you in," he said. "You were to use this time to expand your internal horizons, not to replace uncertainty with stifling normality. Your learning has not even begun!" Harsh words, with which the Bull and Eagle agreed.

"Do you think he is ready?" asked the Eagle, swirling around my head, faster and faster. I felt myself rising up into a kind of vortex created by the bird, up to a different level of awareness. But I also felt a resistance and a pain. It was clear that I was not ready and I did not push it.

"Think outside the box!" said one of the creatures.

"Destroy the box!" said another. I could not determine which creatures had spoken.

"That is enough." came the message from the three creatures in unison, and Kalia urged me to return the next day.

Monday 29th. The Emperor. The Emperor sat upon a throne, which in turn stood upon a raised mound. He was all powerful yet at the same time not complete. He acknowledged this.

"I am only half," he said. Of course! It was the Empress who offered completion and balance. "I build and assist others with their building. I sit at the top of the hierarchy, alongside one other." The Emperor was respected by all around him, for when he spoke everyone recognised his truth and authority. His comments were always knowledgeable, thoughtful and wise. He had a reputation and sought to uphold it.

My awareness moved away from the scene as four insights overcame me. I failed to see how they were connected to my life right now, but nonetheless had a strong sense of their future significance. There seemed to exist four very powerful forces. Men, and to a lesser extent women, constantly fought against them, with varying degrees of success. These forces could bite you hard if you accidentally or deliberately misused their power.

Death was the first force. Words came from nowhere. "Change occurs in order that you may learn. Therefore all changes bring lessons. Side stepping these lessons of life, or worse still, selecting those lessons that you wish to learn and discarding the ones you do not, only ever stores up even more painful changes and lessons for later on. There are no short cuts. Everything that happens is a chance to learn."

The voice continued. "The Dark Side. You all have free will, the ability to turn away from Truth. When you knowingly do this however, it is the action of your Dark Side." There was a still pause. "The Lightning Struck Tower shows you that taking your relationships for granted is the fastest way to lose them." I was concentrating as hard as I could to hold these insights clearly in my mind. The pace continued. "The Sun. Your most prized possession is your health, and good health always leads to personal power. But the abuse of your power, and waste of your health, will always land you in hot water. It is universally true, especially so with the male, that power is always misused until control is learned." The voice spoke no more.

The Emperor came back into view. He was solid and certain, able to take control of the crowd because he first had control of the fundamentals of his own life. He asked my desire.

"Power." I replied, honestly. He demonstrated his own power as a flash of light shot out from his hand and ripped through the air. The display was impressive but he simply said that wielding this power gave him no sense of accomplishment whatsoever. The image faded and I returned to Kalia, who urged me to leave now but return again soon.

Tuesday 30th. The Devil. Kalia greeted me immediately, on my right. She waited while I became aware of another figure, straight in front of me, a small woman, pale skinned, brazen and provocative, with bright red curly hair. Her eyes were piercing and her body was firm and toned. But for all this there was also an intensity and a frustration about her, as if she were her own prisoner. This seemed to reflect the attractive, enticing, but limiting nature of the Dark Side itself. Like a drug bringing very high highs, but lower – and longer lasting - lows each time. Ever more restriction, increasing limitation and narrowing of options. This was not a good path. All these reflections caused me to withdraw from her even though her hands now started to move all over me.

The Library was now over towards the right of the scene. Kalia asked if I needed to visit. The Keeper was ready, but I had no questions prepared, and the image quickly faded.

The Eagle, Bull and Lion appeared, harmlessly fighting with each other. All of a sudden, the three creatures and me were at the starting line of a race. The countdown began, I was up on my blocks, waiting, waiting. And we were off. The Eagle shot straight ahead into first place, way ahead of the Lion in second. The Bull was a poor third, while I limped along in last place caught somewhat unawares by the whole thing, by far the slowest of all. After we had all passed the finishing line they turned to me and explained that this race illustrated the degree of control I had over each of the four elements, which each of the contestants represented. The speed to which the creature advanced indicated the amount of control I had. My limping in a poor fourth showed that I had little control over Water, which represented my emotions and feelings. This was undoubtedly true, a real vulnerability and a recurring weakness which needed to be addressed.

I then received some unexpected insight about my car, in the Outer World. I was told to get rid of it and thus be free from the aggravation and pressure of paying for it, opting, instead, for a less expensive model. It was now time to go, but I had some difficulty in actually leaving. Probably because I did not want to go. But I did.

[APRIL 2004]

Thursday 8th. Temperance. Prior to setting off I was tired and weary, unenthusiastic and demotivated. But I persevered toward Kalia who, recognising my depleted energy, somehow provided gentle healing rays. She said that in due course I could do this for other people, through her.

There was a woman stood by a stream, lightly dressed, watering the plants and the undergrowth. It was as if – through her – that all available water could be re-distributed, spread more evenly, taken from some and given to others. Her constant attention to balance encouraged growth and development all around her, and she explained how overbalance – too much or too little of the necessary requirements - always resulted in disease and illness. The plants were all thankful for this, and told her so. I too needed a re-balance, currently experiencing great emotional drain as others increasingly looked to me for answers, fed off my experiences and left me depleted. This visit was strange in that the scene was so clear within my mind that it almost filled my head. This was exhausting and I could not hang around any longer.

When I returned to the physical I did not feel, for some hours, as though I had fully returned at all.

Tuesday 20th. 5.30pm. The Hanged Man. The first thing, upon greeting Kalia was to ask her about her name. I had read in the Outer World about the ancient goddess Kali. I asked if that was her. She smiled, said that it indeed was, but that the writers of the books had got it all wrong!

The Hanged Man hung upside down, one foot tied to the branch of a tree. He was cheerful, happy and relaxed. As I approached, he athletically flipped himself up to sit on top of the branch, his foot somehow still tied to the tree. He explained.

"I am seeking a new direction, a new sense of being and a new perspective." He continued, "I do this of my own free will and can leave this place any time I like. All knowledge, you see, must be paid for. But it's worth the price for the more you learn the better it all becomes." The rope that secured him had worn a groove in the branch of the tree. He must have been here some time. "Patience, patience. Not your strong point." He said, shaking his head and tutting. So true though. I had never had any patience and this often got me into difficulties. He reached out toward me and in his open hand was a talisman packed to bursting with 'patience'.

"It is something you cannot avoid and must learn," he said. The talisman seemed imbued with his state of mind. Waiting for others might not be that bad, I thought, closing my right hand around it. Now able to see through his eyes everything had much more depth and detail, and was eminently more understandable. The patience he spoke about was simply a resting of desire and a quietening of the mind. Only then could come awareness and acceptance of what is, as well as what is not. Kalia took the talisman from me, and threw it far into the distance. Like a boomerang, it rebounded immediately and struck me hard on the forehead, knocking me to the ground.

"And there is no escaping this lesson!" she laughed.

The Hanged Man dropped back into to his upside down position.

"Make sure you give me that back before you go," he shouted over to us.

Kalia pointed to a group of people over toward the left of the scene. We approached so that Kalia could get in amongst them. She ushered some of them into a wooden pen. These people were miserable, deep in suffering, having lost their possessions and their money. Kalia spoke to me.

"Take note. These poor people's suffering is self-inflicted." I thought that was a bit harsh, but before I could open my mouth Kalia continued. "They cannot hear me, for they do not want to. But you should! They did not think or take any time to approach old problems from new perspectives." I heard her, but still wondered how that mistake would lead them to this place. "Escapes and short cuts have never and will never work. Remember that well!" By now she had finished herding these people into the pen and walked back over to me. My concentration was waning now, and the scene became fuzzy and unclear. I was not sure whether I had even drifted off into sleep, but either way I was jolted back to consciousness violently, yet still within the Inner World. I remembered what the Hanged Man had said earlier and thanked him as I handed back his talisman.

Kalia urged me to leave and get myself in better shape. The journeys continued to become more demanding and draining. I was entering the Inner World in reasonable shape, but was returning as a wreck. My recording of events by hand was almost impossible to re-read, due to my illegible handwriting. The Hanged Man seemed to offer a clue. Looking at regular things in new ways – for example by entering the Inner World – required considerable effort, and patience. It could not be rushed. I suspected, though without sufficient evidence as yet, that these experiences were using a previously neglected part of my brain, and that was why it was so tiring.

Saturday 24th. 7.30pm. The Star. Access through the doorway was easy on this occasion, but en route I did feel noise, confusion and unknown chattering voices. I had spent time immediately prior to this journey reading a variety of occult literature, much of it of dubious value. I felt this was the cause of the interference in my mind.

Once within, the sky was dark, the only light coming from the brilliant stars in the sky. They sparkled, shimmered and shone. A woman was beside a pool, hardly dressed and beautiful, though not sexual. She effortlessly carried tall jugs of water and poured one of them all over me. The woman said that it was fun and it helped. "Optimism is the key now," she said. "You are beginning an up phase and should take a positive view of new opportunities. Fluidity and simplicity will work well for you now." She mentioned an acquaintance of mine, and said that he was so wrapped up in complexity he could not see the wood for the trees. "Truth is always simple, obvious and feels right," she said. "Recognise the flow and go with it." We spoke of the other beings I had encountered in here so far and I asked how such things might appear to others who might follow in my footsteps. "The basics are the same for everyone," she said, "but I would appear to be different to someone else than I do to you. Or more accurately, that individual would perceive me differently." She smiled and urged me to relax, stay flexible and adaptable, optimistic with an eye to new opportunities. Hers was a powerful yet softer presence than others. Her messages at an end now she wished me well before disappearing into the sky, becoming one of the millions of stars that hung there. I called after her, asking what I could do for her in return. The answer resounded through the sky,

"Relax," she cried, "One day you can join me in the stars." He voice trailed off. Why can't I do this now, I thought, trying to rise up and follow her. Kalia accompanied me with a heavy sigh. We travelled up and up, high into the sky, until I felt a sense of great foreboding. Maybe I'd gone too far? Suddenly, the woman of the Star transformed herself into a hideous monster with dozens of eyes and blackened skin. I had been warned off and I was not about to argue. I hurriedly retraced my steps and landed back on the ground, on my feet, with

Kalia squarely in front of me. I looked up and could see nothing but the Star twinkling, happily and gently above us.

"You can only learn what you are ready for," said Kalia. It seemed that I only knew this by finding out what I wasn't ready for! Keen to know more about my limits I asked her about the works of Aleister Crowley.

"His findings are no longer relevant," she said. This was surprising to me. "His work was simply a stepping stone. Human understanding has moved on since then." This was not what I had been told back in the Outer World. "The Internet," she continued, "a huge step forward in the Outer World, one step closer to telepathy you might say." I did not understand her point and hammered on with mine.

"But did Aleister Crowley journey to this place, the Inner World?"

"Oh yes, but he had not progressed this far," came the reply. Silence was my only response. That simply could not be true and I questioned it again. The answer came back emphatic, a slight boredom in Kalia's voice now. "He did not get as far as you." At that she called a halt to the conversation and jumped on my shoulders, tickling and playing with me, then jumping back off and immediately running round and round me, faster and faster.

"What shall we do now?" she said, and then before I had a chance to answer, "do you want to see The Keeper?" the Library appearing next to her. I felt a twitch in my physical body and, although I hesitated, Kalia urged me onwards. I entered the Library and The Keeper was impatient.

"What do you want?" he said.

"What am I alive for? What is my job?" These were the only things that sprang to mind.

"You are here to show the Light!" he cried, exasperated at my question.

"Show the Light?! Who to?" I said.

"Everyone!"

"Everyone?" I was amazed. No further answer came back. Both time and The Keeper's patience were running out and my physical body was twitching even more.

"But how do I do this?" I said.

"You will be shown how!" he cried. The exasperation had now mixed with humour in the tone of his voice. He was not angry, but wearily annoyed. "If you are on track and in balance then your financial situation will be taken care of." The Keeper finished. I thanked him and left the building. Kalia urged me to leave quickly and wished me well until next time.

Tuesday 27th. Temperance. I lingered on the outskirts of the Inner World, in a sort of limbo-place-between, for some time. When I finally entered I performed joyous acrobatics with Kalia. She lifted me high above her head and span me around faster and faster. I returned the favour and it was all great fun.

The sparsely dressed woman was busy by the river. She drew the perfect amount of power from the Sun and delivered the perfect measure of water to the land. The trees grew and the landscape blossomed. I said to her that I thought she was very beautiful.

"Thank you," she smiled, "you must understand the similarities between me and the Star," she said, "but also our differences. The Star is about the present, whereas I deal with the longer term." Remembering what The Keeper had previously said, I asked if I had attained balance in my life yet. "Yes," she said. This was better than I was expecting, so I tested her again, unsure and disbelieving as I was. "Yes, you have balance now," she said, "but you must be constantly vigilant in maintaining it."

My attention turned to Kalia. She reached up and caused thousands of pounds of money, in note form, to fall from the sky. There was so much that I was drowning in it.

"Does that make you happy?" she asked. The notes were grimy and smelly. They kept falling and falling, the pile so heavy now that I could not move and would soon suffocate me. I did not know how much had fallen, nor where. Some of it had certainly blown away into the distance. I felt very dizzy. Kalia repeated the question. "Does all this money make you happy?" I replied that it did not, but still wondered whether this amount need be such a burden in the Outer World. "You better believe it is," she said. "Though of course, never forget that all must eat." Instantly the money was gone, replaced by a three small piles of notes at my feet. "Anything beyond what you need is just a safety net," she said. The piles vanished. "Your attitude to money needs to be looked at," she said, "and it will be. Lesson over." We both turned to the woman by the stream again, and the three familiar creatures appeared.

"Your task for the future," came the voice of the woman, "is to improve the standing that the Bull, who represents physical action, and the Lion, representing boldness and bravery, play in your life." She continued. "The Eagle, representing thought, and you, representing emotions, have the upper hand and thus you are in balance now. But you must remain so." I did not understand how I could remain in balance by changing. "By doing what I have just said," replied the woman. "As you grow and become more, so you will need to re-balance this new you, with all four elements." She vanished in a puff of smoke, somewhat annoyed by my doubts. I dwelt on what she had said though. I definitely had a see-saw of mental vs. emotional, and it did cause problems. If, as she suggested, I could overcome this by taking bold actions or, less grandly, just starting something and seeing it through to the end, then that would be worthwhile. I was aware that inaction often resulted from too much emotion, but that too much mind could itself be quite paralysing. The woman's words struck a chord and I stored them away for future use. I was tired now and wished Kalia goodbye, returning, back to the physical.

[MAY 2004]

Wednesday 5th. 6.00pm. The Sun. I shot straight through into the Inner World and was happy to see Kalia on my right. She was just as pleased and did cartwheels along the ground in celebration. The Sun rose quickly in the sky, settling high up on the right hand side of the landscape. As I reached up toward it I found myself moving upwards. I pushed my hand into the Sun and grasped a chunk of its energy, breaking it away from the main mass. The Sun reformed to repair the gap and I felt no pain. I returned to the ground and launched that energy far and wide into the air. It exploded loudly and colourfully. Where it landed on the ground some plants immediately flourished, others shrivelled up and died. Back in the Outer World, I had been suffering with a small but irritating issue with my left foot and I applied some of this Sun to the affected area. I was suddenly aware that I had a new array of skills. I could change my shape and also lose my shape. As I did this my body and face dissolved away leaving only my life essence, my inner energy. I shrank this down even further, smaller than a blade of grass, then immediately expanded bigger than a giant. Kalia was beside me throughout all this. I took from this that the Sun was an energy and a power which could be directed, but only with a focus, or perhaps, a reason behind it. Kalia urged me to go over all my recorded experiences within the Inner World to ensure I had completed this cycle. There were a few Tarot doorways I had not yet travelled through, and I was to make sure I got the maximum benefit from them.

Some small children now appeared on the horizon, travelling from left to right. The first one ran, the second one rolled head over heels behind him. There was maybe a third, younger child. I could see no more and I returned to the physical, emotionally refreshed, but physically drained.

Saturday 15th. 11.30am. The Hierophant. Entry was slow and the scene was not immediately clear. I greeted Kalia on my left. She reprimanded me for leaving so quickly before. I said that I had not meant to upset her, but the whole experience was still somewhat alien to me.

The Pope was preaching to a crowd over toward the right. Suddenly, lightning struck and blew off his crown. The audience laughed and ridiculed him. They mocked and left him in droves. Maybe his conventional beliefs had little substance or value? They certainly could not withstand any sustained attack. I spoke with Kalia and asked if I could travel to other planets.

"Not quite yet, but it can be done," she said, very matter-of-fact. I asked if there was anything special on the planets to see. "There is nothing on any of the planets to see," she said. I asked where this place – the Inner World – was. "A different dimension," came the answer. I asked if it was a different planet. "No," she replied.

The Library appeared, and at once I was inside and before The Keeper. I asked about a recurring client of mine.

"She needs your support." He said. I replied that was exactly what I was providing, but The Keeper seemed intent on telling me that I could do more. I felt annoyed about this and very soon the Library disappeared, leaving me back in front of the Pope again. I did not like the things he had been saying to the crowd and The Keeper's comments had annoyed me. I turned on the Pope with the full force I could summon. I willed that he would be propelled from his platform, into the distance. His whole body lifted up and smashed against a tree in the distance. The Bull, Eagle and Lion looked on aghast. The Pope picked himself up and returned to his podium. He instantly grew one hundred feet tall, towering directly over me. His power and anger grew along with his size. I had made a bad mistake by over-reaching myself in this way. The air was silent and tense as the Pope stared down at me, ready and undoubtedly able, to inflict retribution. An eternity seemed to pass before he relented and shrank back to his normal size.

"I will not punish you, this time," he said. "But you must realise that the negative cannot exist without positive. You may despise rules and regulations, but other people love them, and need them." I did not agree but was not about to show it. "Order and tradition are one part of the story of life. People cannot live without these things. It is just a question of balance," said the Pope as he departed. It had been a lucky escape. I offered my apologies to him but he was already gone. I apologised to Kalia and the three creatures instead. Immediately I was transported to a road next to a crying woman. She had been left by her husband and felt stupid and broken. I asked why he had left her but she could not answer. What was clear though was that she had relied on the traditional and conventional wisdom of marriage. This had broken down and caused her real upset and emotional disturbance. I knew many women who had suffered this way, brought up to believe in the institution of marriage and then forced to watch and wonder while that world collapsed around them. These people felt let down and this greatly contributed to their sense of unease and disengagement from the world. The creatures and Kalia tapped into my concerns and seemed satisfied with what I had learned. I wished them all farewell and left.

Sunday 16th. 12 noon. The Hermit. Kalia greeted me and urged me not to repeat the mistakes of my last visit. I said that I would not, but she took some convincing. We walked along as she spoke.

"These forces that you encounter, the Hierophant, the Emperor and so on, they are not to be messed with you know." I asked her why not? "Because they are the Forces of Life," she said. Her words hung in the air, but I moved the subject on rapidly, asking her how old she was. "13,384 years old," she replied, with total clarity and without any hesitation. "Unfortunately, I cannot tell you everything you want to know about that period," she said "but suffice to say, back then the Inner World existed in balance and harmony with the Outer World."

We arrived at some thick bushes and I led the way through them, travelling some distance before reaching a clearing where the Hermit sat. He was bright eyed, wore simple clothing and sat with his legs crossed on the ground. Around him were only a very few possessions.

"I've been expecting you," he said, taking my hand and looking in my left palm. "Your progress in this world will be swift," he said. "Once you understand and master the four elements." I nodded my understanding. He continued. "The guidance I can offer will apply mainly in the Inner World, and we will begin with your future." Suddenly Kalia, the Bull, the Eagle and the Lion all became part of me, and I became part of them. The moment was powerful for I finally felt complete and whole, like I never had before. I could see everything around me clearly, as it really was, uninfluenced by how I wished it to be. I again became conscious of the Hermit's voice. "The key lies in the Four Elements of Being and the Twenty Two Principles of Life. The four elements combine to make up every individual and the twenty-two principles combine to present to each individual the lessons they must learn." My brain was on full stretch to try to come to terms with this, and the Hermit could see I was having difficulty. "Remember, truth is always simple. But often it is so simple that you cannot see it!" He laughed, immediately clearing the tension in my brain. "Let us move on," he said. Immediately I felt myself floating in the sky, levitating, not for a reason, but because I knew I could. The Hermit interrupted. "How can you do this?" I replied that I didn't know how but just knew that I could. "But where's your evidence, how do you know you can?" he probed, testing me. I started to doubt myself, wondering if I was imagining it all. I instantly fell to the ground. The Hermit laughed and bent down to help me up. "So, do you think you need evidence?" he said. I said that just because I couldn't fully explain something it didn't mean it wasn't true. "That is right. Try to remember that!" he said. We both sat down on a nearby log. "It is nearly time to go. But please understand that everything you are working for is built upon the foundation of your health, and if you lose that you will lose any chance of progress. It is not just physical health, though. Your emotions can deplete you, so please eat as wide a variety of foods as possible." I took it all in. "Fresh foods." he added. "If you cook it, you kill it!"

It was time to go now. The Hermit wished me well as he packed his few belongings into a bag. He stood up straight and concentrated, shrinking himself down to the size of a fly and buzzing off into the distance. Kalia and I left the clearing. I wished her goodbye and casually remarked how attractive she was.

"Thank you. I am indeed attractive, but you do not yet know why." I asked her to expand on this remark, but she cut me off in my tracks and said goodbye.

[JUNE 2004]

Tuesday 15th. 6.30pm. The Fool. Entry through this doorway was initially slow, difficult and uncertain. I struggled to keep hold of any focus or clarity. I had deliberately eaten a full dinner some ninety minutes previously, in the hope this would give me the necessary fuel, but if anything it seemed to be hindering my work.

After a while, through the blackness of confusion, I could make out a vaguely rectangular doorway and within it the first glimpses of a landscape. Although I could see this I struggled to move smoothly toward it, in the end simply lurching, physically and mentally, through the doorway and into the Inner World. Kalia faced me head on, grabbing my right arm, with her left, elbow to elbow.

"What have you learned?" she asked. I was struggling to establish myself in this landscape and could feel myself slipping back. I lurched forward again as Kalia and I grabbed arms. She now urged me to "stop and locate your true self." I had no clue what she meant, but I tried to follow her instruction by surveying the landscape, which formed itself as I looked. It was fresh and bright, with mountains in the distance and lush greenery in the foreground. A white bird flew high in the sky and descended rapidly. It was the Eagle and it came to rest on my left shoulder.

The Bull now approached me at great speed, and just at the last minute came to a halt directly in front of me. The Lion was last to come into view, approaching me from the right, in no hurry at all. Kalia stood with the three creatures. No one said a word. In the end it was me that broke the silence, asking Kalia if this Inner World was a place where I could travel in time? She answered straight back.

"The Astral Planes are the places for that sort of thing." Pushing on, I asked if I could eat in the Inner World? "You gain energy differently in the Inner World than you do back in the Outer World," she said, "but give it a try, see what happens." I reached down to a bush that bore some strange shaped fruits, but as a grasped hold of one what seemed to be a serpent's head appeared from around the Bull and hissed at me, showing its fangs. It did not seem too happy at my attempts to take the fruit. I drew back and looked over to the Lion who was motionless and unresponsive.

Kalia pointed me away from the three creatures and toward a faint voice in the distance. It was the faint sound of a tuneful pipe that grew louder as we got nearer. I could then distinguish a voice.

"Disaster falls, disaster reigns, but I have no cares, for I am unchained!" The words were sung with joy and feeling, the singer happy and optimistic in the face of his troubles. They were spoken by a giant figure, colourfully dressed, carefree and skipping along the road. He seemed quite effeminate, which did not match his size or demeanour. Perhaps it was simply that he was innocent and untainted? A small white dog yapped persistently at his feet, but it followed his master diligently. I approached the man, a little apprehensively, asking if I could do anything for him. He mused and laughed.

"You can do nothing for me. The question is," he paused "what can I do for you?" I had no answer. I knew that his appearance was not what I was expecting. He seemed innocent not at all world weary, but at the same time he projected a strength and a wisdom, which I did not associate with innocence. "Understand," he said, "that I am immeasurably wise." His voice deepening. "And because I know so much, I know that I know absolutely nothing!" His voice boomed into a theatrical laugh. This man was The Fool, but he was no fool!

At his invitation I climbed onto his shoulders, then on top of his head. I sat there comfortably as we travelled down the road. I asked him where we were going.

"Towards the future!" He was full of confidence, but I now felt tired. "That is far enough," his voice more calming now as he set me down and wished me luck for the future. I saw him wander into the distance, and climb up to a cliff face. He danced and tip toed along the edge, caring not for the danger. He was singing, and happy, then suddenly fell. It was a long way down, and he hit the floor hard, but without delay or fuss rose up again to continue his journey toward the future.

Kalia now suggested that I leave and return tomorrow. The creatures signalled their agreement. The Lion roared, the Bull blew air from his nose and the Eagle shrieked. I returned to the physical, tired and disorientated.

Wednesday 16th. 6.30pm. The High Priestess. This was one of the rare occasions where I glimpsed the subject of the doorway – The High Priestess – before I saw my Guide. I stood by the sea, the landscape was rocky, and the tide lapped up on the shore. The Eagle soared high in the sky and then straight down in front of me. In the middle of the otherwise deserted scene was a tall, serene woman, covered in a long blue dress. She carried a white scroll in her right hand.

"What do you want to know?" she said. I had no idea what to ask.

A serpent appeared to her left. Rearing up toward me it opened its mouth wide, bared its fangs and hissed. It was powerful, but the woman did not flinch. I decided to follow her lead and calmly asked the serpent to leave. As I focussed my desire that it leave, the serpent faded away into the distance, hissing as it went.

Kalia suddenly appeared on my right. She grasped my arm in the usual way, elbow to elbow. I experienced an unfamiliar sensation as I became aware that I was, in fact, in two places at once. I was very conscious of sitting in my green armchair, and similarly conscious of being off in another world, at the same time.

Conscious of this Inner World, I knelt down before the High Priestess. As I did so she 'knighted' me with her scroll. I felt a faint electric shock, but was shortly to feel a great deal more as the High Priestess pointed with that scroll toward a magnificent white, glistening palace, high in the mountain, over toward the right.

"That is where you are going," she said. I took her at her word and asked if there were anything I could do for her in return. "Just get there as soon as you can, so you can tell me if I am right about it," came the wholly unexpected answer. This did not seem correct at all, and I said to her that she must have been there herself. I was confused. "No, I've never been there," she said.

The sky, the air, all around us started to turn the lightest shade of blue, and I began to feel a twitching in my physical body, pulling me to return. I did not hang around, wished Kalia farewell and returned, drained and exhausted. It would be another week before I returned.

Wednesday 23rd. The High Priestess. Movement toward the doorway was swift, in spite of yet again feeling somewhat tired. I could see Kalia doing somersaults and handstands from right to left as I arrived. She was pleased with my progress and greeted me warmly.

The landscape was cold and the shore was over toward my left. The serpent again reared up as I approached. I felt less threatened this time and it must have sensed this for it embraced me, circling my whole being and running up my body and around my spine. This seemed a perfectly natural thing, and not at all frightening. I could see the serpent's old skin discarded on the floor. I felt immediately renewed and rejuvenated. Maybe there was no need for food or rest here, just renewal? I checked my experiences with both the High Priestess and Kalia. It all seemed to stack up.

"The difficulty," said Kalia, "is that many of the things that you have read about in the Outer World, particularly with reference to the serpent, are false. These falsehoods directly contradict your own Inner World experiences and cause tremendous conflict." I could accept this, and for once I felt full of energy. The High Priestess spoke.

"You will be going on from here and on completion of this cycle moving to a new level of awareness. But, knowledge is power and power is always abused until control is learned." She said I was to be wary of flexing my new muscles. She then stood aside to reveal the Library hovering in the middle distance. I wasted no time and leapt forward, up the stone steps and through the heavy front door. The room contained a swirling mass of pulsating shades of blue, from soft to electric and The Keeper appeared from nowhere. He resembled the Hermit that I had met recently and asked him if he was one and the same.

"No – I'm The Keeper!" came a bad tempered response. I felt that I ought to get to the point, and asked him where I went from here. He took both my hands in one of his and with his staff pointed to my head line on each palm. This line, on each of my hands, forked at the ends. "Writing and expression," he said, "it is all yours now, no limits remain on what you can achieve, but you must move forward and reach out for it." But I wanted specifics. "You will have dealings with an artist. He is a positive man, but you must be wary of those around him." I opened my mouth to probe further. "That is enough," said The Keeper and drew the visit to a close.

I was tired now, the energised feeling I had experienced not long before had quickly drained away. I thanked the High Priestess and wished her goodbye. She bent down and kissed me on the cheek. She was so much taller than me. I turned to wish Kalia goodbye and she kissed me on the cheek too.

"Let's play a game!" said Kalia. I protested that I should go, but she insisted. She led the way and shrank her whole body to the size of a blade of grass. I followed suit. I was tiny but my consciousness remained intact. I could see everything as before, just from a different perspective. An average sized fly buzzed above our heads. We both grew back to our usual size and I departed.

Saturday 26th. The Tower. The card image made me a little apprehensive. This fear, along with other thoughts and feelings from the Outer World, drew all my attention and I strained to be rid of these distractions, trying instead to focus on the black doorway in front of me.

Kalia was immediately present on my right and all around was a scene of devastation. A wooden shack with a corrugated tin roof lay directly in front of us, and suddenly the dark sky was illuminated by a lightning bolt, striking the building, accompanied by a deep, booming thunderclap. The building was now a wreck and a family were hurrying to escape. The father cried that his child was still inside, and I rushed in to help. I felt no sense of danger at all as I entered the remains of the building. It was as if I were immune, and that any threat was not directed against me. I rescued the child, yet strangely, at the same time, I was unsure if I had actually gone in at all. I seemed to watch myself emerge from the building, which was something that I had always guarded against allowing to happen. Nonetheless, the escapees spoke of their complacency and that they had taken their home and status – such that it was - for granted. The lightning had been a 'harsh illumination' of where they had gone wrong.

Looking around I could now see the surrounding area contained buildings of differing shapes and sizes that at one time or another had all been struck by lightning. All their experiences had been harsh, but what replaced the old was better and stronger, and as the physical structures were changed, so were their inhabitants. I felt that the lightning only struck when the inhabitants strayed from their paths. I confirmed this with Kalia and she agreed.

"You are doing well," she said, "but this means that you will soon be leaving me as another cycle draws to a close." I was upset by this news, but before I could react too much the creatures had gathered around again. The Eagle sat on top of my head, although I could not feel his claws. The Bull arrived hurriedly. The Lion was slower and ambled up on my left. Kalia stood at my right. The Serpent entwined my spine and I felt, for just a fraction of a second, that the creatures and I became one. In that micro-moment I possessed increased understanding and power, and felt whole and complete. This feeling was intense, but did not last long before the animals dispersed and Kalia again spoke. "Be sure to write down these experiences immediately on your return, and then come back soon." Time was up and I waved goodbye to her as I departed. Looking at the clock as I opened my eyes I saw I had been gone a little less than ten minutes, although it seemed considerably longer.

Wednesday 30th. 2.45pm. Judgement. The first thing I could see was a tall and impressive building to my left. It was solidly built and looked well able to resist the lightning which was striking it. It resisted the first huge blows and stood still in the face of the onslaught. The second wave struck again very quickly, in the same place as before and the bricks and mortar came crashing down to earth. People ran from the remains of the building into the distance and I called after them, but to no avail. They either could not hear me or were not listening.

The Sun shone brightly, directly overhead. Over to the right of the scene was the white palace up in the hills. I also saw a large tree directly in front of me. Its trunk was twisted and knarled, but it leaves were luscious and healthy. It lent slightly to one side and its uppermost branches were flat so that the whole tree resembled a 'T' shape. Kalia appeared on my right with a serious look on her face.

"It is time for us to pass judgement upon you. And you upon us," she said. "In other words, it is time to judge yourself."

A trumpet fanfare sounded, from the direction of what I assumed was a now ruined building. But to my amazement it had been rebuilt, stronger and more secure than before. The fanfare signalled the arrival of the now familiar creatures. The Lion and the Bull encircled me. The Eagle sat calmly and coldly watching me while Kalia was beside me, outside the circle created by the Lion and Bull. The Serpent had again knitted itself around and into my spine.

I listened closely but heard no comment or pronouncement from any of these assembled creatures. I just felt a one-ness with them, including Kalia. My human form seemed to disappear and together we all merged into a swirling mass of dark reds and oranges. Typically this did not last very long and I soon returned to my human form, within the Inner World, and the creatures dispersed. The Lion bounded off up the hillside in the direction of the palace. The Eagle flew off towards the horizon, and the Bull charged headlong into the new building, trying to bring it down. Kalia remained and pointed up toward the palace.

"That is where you are going next," she said. "Always remember, the further you travel in the Inner World, the more vigilant you must be in the Outer World." The words seemed ominous. Putting these nuggets of wisdom into practice was always the hardest part. She continued, "you may find that before you journey on, you need to verify one or two of your previous journeys, perhaps undertaking some of them again, until you are satisfied of their value." The advice seemed sensible and I nodded along. I could now make out a new figure to the right of Kalia. He was tall, heavily built and shrouded in a dark cloak. I asked his name.

"Geoffri," he said.

"Are you my next Guide?" I asked. The answer was unclear. I was unsure whether Geoffri was a genuine Guide and I drew back from him, asking him no more questions, and he disappeared. Kalia had said I would be moving on, and as this was the last Tarot doorway it seemed like an appropriate time. But I felt comfortable with Kalia and was very unsure about a future without her. I felt tired now and back in the Outer World my next door neighbour returned from work and slammed her front door, snapping me back to the physical.

[JULY 2004]

Thursday 8th. 6.30pm. The Fool. My thoughts flitted around all over the place as I recalled the events of the day, their conclusions and implications. As one matter was closed, so another seemed to spring to life. The day had been difficult and fast moving and although I was itching to get on with my life in the Inner World I felt in limbo, in between the thoughts of the Outer World and the feelings of the Inner World. For a long time I seemed unable to control this and only after great persistence and stubborn refusal to quit did I enter through the doorway. This time though there was no landscape.

The Fool was dressed impossibly colourfully, in the style of the Joker from a pack of playing cards or even the Pied Piper of Hamlyn. Every colour was hyper-real and accentuated. This young and strangely androgynous figure beamed a brilliant white smile. His small white dog yapped incessantly at another figure over towards my right. This shape was tall and dark and stood just behind Kalia, dwarfing her and wearing a dark cape which seemed to cover the whole length of his body. The harder I looked the less I could see his face. He was still, watching, not moving. I asked him his name. He disappeared, but returned moments later. I was confused and asked him if he was my Guide. He did not answer.

I turned back to Kalia. She said that I would find out who he was shortly, but first she gestured toward to the colourful Fool, who was now tottering along the edge of a cliff face, almost inviting danger. He was granted his wish when he overbalanced and fell off. He did not cry out or seem at all perturbed about his fall. He slammed to the ground and speared himself on the jagged rocks. This would be the end for any normal man in the Outer World. The Fool simply got up and started again. I looked over toward Kalia, still conscious of the tall and shadowy figure behind her. The Fool turned around with an elaborate swirl, and in a theatrical tone of voice said,

"I thought you were here to see me?" This was the first line of a tune, to which I could not make out the words, other than something about the need to 'begin again'. I quickly dismissed this, turning back to Kalia and the dark figure. I felt compelled to look at him and I asked Kalia what was going on. The figure disturbed me, with its presence shrouded in mystery. Everything that I had learned in the Outer World led me to doubt the presence of dark shadowy figures in unknown situations.

I urged Kalia to do something about him. She turned to the figure and she grew in size until it was she that dwarfed him. She reaching out to grasp the figure, screwing him up in a ball as he turned into paper. With an enormous lunge she propelled the paper ball far into the distance and returned to her original size and shape. I leaned across to hug her, but was again confronted by the same shadowy figure, in the same place right behind her. He was evidently going nowhere. I was confused and wary and felt a pull back to the Outer World, returning to the physical with a start.

The whole trip had been jarring and disjointed, as had been my attitude at the outset. I was in a hurry, and being in a hurry in the Inner World seemed not to deliver results. I had also forgotten the golden rule spoken of by many mystics of the past, that Inner World beings are 'bound to tell the truth.' When I had visited Kalia on previous occasions she had never failed to answer all questions truthfully. This new being, the dark cloaked figure, had caused me considerable confusion, but I had overlooked the value of Kalia's considerable local knowledge.

Monday 12th. 6.00pm. Judgement. This time I made sure of rest and relaxation before any journeying. I took a nap, and had eaten light dinner an hour ago. It seemed to do the trick as entry through the card doorway was swift and certain, free of any mental flapping about. I immediately recognised Kalia and Geoffri.

Kalia greeted me warmly and we embraced. She had always been expressive and fun loving and this time was no exception. We went for a short walk with her sitting on my shoulders. After a little while we came back and there was Geoffri, waiting. It was at this point that she introduced him as my next Guide. The difference between them was great. She was small, warm, fun loving, female and dark skinned. He was tall and slender, covered head to toe in a black cape that completely obscured his face. I did not feel the same degree of apprehension as I had earlier, but neither did I feel an outpouring of affection. Kalia explained why. She said that I had not instantly warmed to him because he was the next thing I had to learn. She continued in more detail.

"If you know everything that is going to happen, and if everything that happens does so according to your expectations, then nothing is ever gained. The purpose of your life is to learn, and if you always know the answer then you are not learning anything. If you are not pushing yourself and not moving forward then what is the point?" This was fair enough. I, like many others, spent a good deal of time and effort, back in the Outer World, trying to foresee and forestall attempting to avoid nasty surprises and always trying to stay one step ahead of the game. This had benefited me materially, but was a threat to inner progress. Perhaps I should be more willing to confront the future, more eager to face the unknown? Maybe through facing the future, and making the inevitable mistakes, I would ultimately do better? Being inactive, and then wise after the event, seemed a poor second prize. "Geoffri will guide you to your next level of awareness and understanding," she concluded.

The long cloak that Geoffri wore was jet black and covered his body completely. Suddenly, and with flourish, he flung it off to reveal himself in his full glory. He was indeed tall, but now also muscular and dressed colourfully in reds, greens and browns. His face was pale, his hair ginger, almost red. He had a full beard and glowing green eyes. His appearance screamed action and adventure. Where Kalia had been passive, he was active. Where she had been sensitive, he was forceful.

He put his left arm around my shoulder, so that he stood on my right and pointed toward the distance, toward the future. He was keen to get going. I felt comfortable with him now, and my previous sense of foreboding had evaporated. Nonetheless I thought it wise to go through the correct procedure.

"Are you my Guide?" I quizzed him.

"Yes," came the reply, without hesitation. Up to that point he had seemed jocular and very informal. Now he snapped to attention, demonstrating that he understood the seriousness of my questions.

"Why did you wear a black cloak?" I asked.

"I was the unknown, surrounded by darkness and foreboding. You have made the unknown, known, and I have removed my cape!" He looked earnest for about half a second and then let out a raucous laugh. He put his arm round my shoulder again and grasped tightly. He had the air of Robin Hood about him, very male, but lacking the ability to really hurt anyone or anything. I was conscious that Geoffri seemed to come from a completely different time period than Kalia and I asked why.

"We are attached to you through duty," he said.

"And love!" said Kalia, from the background.

"Yes, and love," replied Geoffri. "We all appear in the clothing from our last time on Earth." I asked him what era he came from. "Around 1200AD, as you would call it," he said. I asked him if it was significant that he looked like Robin Hood. "I represent Robin Hood!" He cried. "I am who the legend was written about!" He seemed pleased to share this with me, but also eager to press on with the future. But this was all going too fast for me and I asked him to slow down. He stopped immediately and indicated that as I commanded, so he must obey. I called back to Kalia. I felt sad at the thought of leaving her. My apprehension for Geoffri had disappeared, but I felt nostalgic for the warmth of Kalia.

"It is too soon," I said. "I'm not ready for you to go yet."

"It is Geoffri's turn now," she said, comforting me. "Your passive time is coming to an end, and it will soon be time for action."

I welcomed that news, but I still didn't want her to go. "I have others to see now," she said, "but I will always be around, if you need me." I hugged her tight. I had just got to know her and now she was leaving. I pleaded again for her not to go just yet. Geoffri took a deliberate step back and Kalia drew closer. "If that is what you want," she said.

But it was now time to go and as I felt myself moving back to the physical I waved to them both. Kalia was at the front and Geoffri stood tall behind her. I knew deep down that a new future beckoned and it would be Geoffri who would take me there.

Realisations: It was around this time that I started to question these experiences much more rigorously. I had been tripping along with detached amusement, but had been increasingly surprised at the clarity of the scenes, and the wisdom of the advice. But the greatest shock was how tiring they were. I used my brain all day long, and yet half an hour sitting in chair was proving exhausting. How could this be? What was going on? It took me a long while to identify that I was deeply enmeshed in a series of conflicts, which all came together in this work. The mental and emotional energy invested in these conflicts must have been immense.

First, the experiences were not what I expected, and this was hard to accept and overcome. Seeking to validate my encounters proved fruitless, for no one seemed capable or interested in either verifying - or disproving – what was happening to me. Indeed whenever I discussed this work with supposed experts I encountered only resistance and vagueness. I found this deeply disappointing and troubling, and I did, in hindsight, allow this to undermine my confidence in the work. I could not accept that the experts were not expert.

Secondly, the mismatch between the help and support I received in the Inner World and the almost constant struggle I faced in the Outer World was sharp. The acceptance that I received, and the constructive progress I could make in the Inner World seemed, in comparison to the Outer World, almost literally unbelievable. The programming of my psyche, from its Outer World dealings, seemed so deeply set to failure and disappointment as to reject the genuinely good things that were happening in my Inner World. Arthur was really my only

Outer World support, and even that was often a fractious and confrontational relationship.

Add all this into the mix with a society which I concluded was travelling in exactly the wrong direction and I had a toxic mix of elation and disappointment – both generated as a result of these excursions. This was going to be a hard journey.

Tuesday 27th. 6.30pm. Justice. At first I heard voices, and then shapes came into view. There was Geoffri's voice, then his form, and then Kalia's in the distance. She remained, just to make sure, but Geoffri was in charge now, at first covered by his cape again. With my permission he boldly removed it and started dancing around. I said Jeffri, with a J, was a silly name. He replied that it should be Geoffrey or better still Geoffri from the old French it originated from. He looked into my heart with his piercing green eyes and said that he could see everything about me.

The creatures were again around us. The Bull was raging and snorting through his nose. The Eagle was on top of the Bull's head, too clever and too quick to be batted away. The Lion roared. Kalia remained, but was faint and growing fainter by the second. The serpent moved slowly on the ground.

In the distance, with a clear pathway up to it, was the shining palace. The animals pointed up there and Geoffri led us up the pathway, toward the front door. This huge door needed a key, which I did not have. I wondered where I might find it, and immediately the Eagle dropped one from the sky, which I caught in my hands.

Joyfully I went to put it in the lock when a huge lightning bolt smashed into the pathway that all of us were all on, shattering it all to smithereens. We crashed to the ground. Geoffri looked at me and said that I was not ready for this step.

"Think before acting. You are in charge here and must direct me." I was not sure that I fully understood his words, but had certainly learned by now that they were not meant to be cryptic or complex. If he said I was not ready then I simply had more to experience in order to make myself ready. I also sensed that time acted strangely here, which meant the necessary experience, the missing piece of knowledge, would be presented imminently.

As all this was running through my mind the serpent coiled itself loosely around my leg, then moved up to my whole body, opened its jaws and swallowed me whole! It was mere seconds before I was ejected out the other end of the serpent's body. I felt completely different. It was all getting weird, and too real. Surely these creatures were merely representations of what was going on my mind and my life, constructs of my imagination? Immediately as that thought passed across my mind I felt a sharp dig in my ribs. I would even say that I felt it in my physical body. It was Geoffri.

'I am as real as you are,' he remarked, half indignant, half joking.

The animals were all still there, sitting, resting, looking on. I felt a pull back to the physical but also a sense that the creatures were not ready to let me go. After a short while, one by one, they granted permission for me to leave, wandering off in their own directions. Geoffri wished me good health and said to return as soon as I could.

The transmission home was instant and I had to check myself that I had fully returned. I became conscious how very fine the line was between these two realities and how very fine would be the line between a real experience and a fantasy. How would I possibly tell the difference?

CHAPTER III
GEOFFRI
[AUGUST 2004]

*M*onday 2nd. 7.15pm. The Magician. Kalia was calling me and appeared to my right. She kissed and hugged me. I was glad to see her although she confirmed that I would not be doing so again. She had others to see now, and Geoffri, who was lingering close by off to the left, would take good care of me.

"It is time for action now," she said. "I will be around if you ever really need me."

I asked her if my sequence of Guides related to the passing of time – oldest first, most recent last. She did not answer, and confronted with the silence I asked again. She replied that I was not ready for the answer and that she could not tell me.

The Magician from the Tarot appeared straight in front of us. Huge, like a giant, he performed various tricks to us. In his colourful dress and 'trickster' appearance he seemed more like the Fool, but he summoned the four creatures and said that he had control of the Four Worlds. I queried this. He confirmed that his statement was accurate. I climbed onto his hands and he made me disappear and re-appear on the other side of the landscape.

Geoffri was anxious to get moving. I could see that Kalia had climbed high toward the palace on the mountain and said that I was heading there with Geoffri. It had to be him, she could not take me there. Waving goodbye she faded from the scene, flashing her bottom cheekily at me as she left, smiling! Geoffri said to me that he was not replacing Kalia, simply adding to her. I was fine with this explanation, but I still felt that it was the end of a beautiful relationship.

A walkway appeared before us, similar to before. It snaked directly up toward the doorway of the palace. Geoffri accompanied me almost to its very end, but suddenly the Magician appeared, pointed at the last section and made the final four feet or so of the path disappear. The drop to earth was huge, and although four feet seemed not insurmountable the gap was just big enough to be dangerous, and to give pause for thought.

"You are not ready," came a voice. "There remains one piece of the puzzle before you can enter here."

"So what is it?" I asked.

"When you know that then it will be time to enter," came the reply. The voice was not Geoffri's, nor I think the Magician's, and seemed to emanate from behind the closed door. But there was no time to argue or debate for the entire walkway collapsed beneath us sending Geoffri and I falling to the floor. I was struggling to maintain concentration at this point and could pursue it no more. Geoffri waved with both hands and a broad smile as I disconnected.

"I am not like other men," Geoffri said. "Come back soon." The Magician was still in attendance and calmly confirmed this.

Tuesday 10th. 7.15pm. The Hanged Man. Geoffri was calling me, laughing loudly and joking around. Kalia was absent, but Geoffri smiled and reassured me that everything was fine.

The palace shimmered high in the mountains and Geoffri said we were to again travel to it. Over toward the left a man hung, upside down, suspended by one leg only, from the branch of a tree. I suggested to Geoffri that he may be able to help us with directions. Geoffri was pleased with this and we went over to investigate. It was strange talking to an upside down face. He explained that everything I had been taught in my youth or thought that I knew was, in fact, wrong.

"You have it all the wrong way round," he said. "Everything has to be turned on its head for truth to be realised - men-women, science-spirituality, good-evil, everything, all of it. Only now can you begin to see and start to accept this." I asked if I could help the man and show my appreciation. He pointed up to the palace.

"Hurry!" he said. I felt the presence of the three creatures and many of the other powerful figures from the Tarot gather around us as Geoffri and I stepped onto the path. Again we travelled successfully up until the end, and again as before, there was a gap – not huge, but too big to jump over. There was nothing for it but to trust and step into thin air and walk over the gap. I had seen Indiana Jones and it had worked for him! I did not see any other way so I stepped out, and did not fall. I was not amazed by this, as perhaps I should have been, it just seemed totally appropriate. I banged the white door knocker on the large and heavy door. No answer. I looked at Geoffri for some suggestion, but after an uncertain response I decided to push the door open anyway.

I stepped through to a marbled hall. The room was vast in all dimensions – tall, long and wide – and was bathed in bright white light, a very different kind to the landscape below. Geoffri was with me and around our heads flew energies, colours and voices, all too alien to define. Many realisations came to me. Everything was seeded and began here, in this place. I could feel myself rise up and up and out of my physical body, and as I did so a tremendous sense of enlightenment overcame me. I felt that everything could be seen from here and momentarily felt myself looking down on the entire world. This all took a mere matter of seconds before I felt a sneeze growing inside me. Unsure of the effects of a raucous sneeze in this place I departed from the Hall and returned back down the pathway to the ground of the Inner World.

The creatures and assembled figures were all very happy, cheering and clapping. Then one by one, they all disappeared, followed by the palace, and then the entire landscape until it was just Geoffri and I in the midst of a barren desert. I still had not sneezed, and returned to the Outer World disorientated.

Saturday 21st. The Lovers. I was in poor physical condition. I had drunk too much wine the night before, slept badly, and both my body and head ached. Nevertheless, faintly, Geoffri came into view. I could not see the landscape, save for two lovers in the nearby undergrowth, engaged fully with each other. Theirs was a give and take relationship, a thing they worked at, actively. Their relationship provided balance and was not an escape from reality for either of them. Together they were ever evolving, moving forward, mutually supportive. I turned to Geoffri. He was on my right.

"How do I know this is all not just my imagination?" He immediately switched position to my left hand side.

"Because then I would be over here," before flashing back to my right side, "but I am here so it's not!" I could not even begin to comprehend this, except to say that my throbbing head and immobilised brain seemed incapable of any imaginative trickery today. He playfully said that any kind of relationship, so long as it was positive for both parties could work just fine – homosexual, heterosexual, whatever, it did not matter. "Just bear in mind," he said, "that the female is devoted to the emotional and spiritual, the male to the physical and mental."

I was tiring. Smiling, he wished me well and said to come back soon. I returned to the physical, but felt strange and wondered if I had returned fully, or even been anywhere at all!

Although I did not know it at the time, this was to be my last journey for over a year. I had not planned it that way, but in hindsight it seemed that reaching the Hall of the Palace had released, or created, a great force within me. Maybe not all of it was positive, certainly not all of it was easy to handle. The coming period without Inner World contact would see me involved in all manner of earthly pursuits, largely to do with money. I would also take my first faltering steps at organising Mind Body Spirit events across the UK. Additionally I would foolishly spend a good deal of time trying to gain election to public office, and having failed would then move house one hundred miles across the country. Although I did not visit here my thoughts were never far away from these Inner experiences, and I spent probably too much time questioning what had happened so far. It just seemed too fantastic to be true.

As these doubts deepened so my life would take a turn for the worse. A malaise was about to sweep over me. I would push on with what I considered progress in my spiritual and psychic development work, but I was really only ticking over, struggling to assimilate what had happened. It would only be many years later, when formally writing up and reviewing my handwritten journal, that I could see this period clearly. It provoked three major insights, any of which might take a lifetime to resolve.

Firstly, we can only learn what we are ready for. There is no point trying to divine or calculate the entire mysteries of the Universe in one sitting. Not because the information is unavailable – on the contrary in fact, it seems to be all there waiting. The real question is can we handle it? Can we assimilate it? Will it drive us mad? Because it just might. When presented with information that is contrary to existing beliefs the most sensible thing would be to adapt our beliefs.

Unfortunately, more often than not, the result is actually a visceral rejection of the new information. Combined with this there is always a temptation to do the wrong thing and to know it. On one level I could not handle the information I had so far received, but on another level I absolutely could. On one level I resisted the experiences, but on another level I welcomed them. It was a matter of where my awareness and attention was on any given day. If our Outer World is filled with trivia, and our time devoted to things that simply do not matter (although we might swear blind that they do) then how much energy can be left over for the Inner World? The modern pressures of information overload and instant download might bring us results in the Outer World, but they do not support an Inner quest. I had to learn to be ruthless about saying no to anything and everything that deflected me from this work. The worse distraction of all was, and still is, me. I got bored really easily, but slowly came to realise that not everything that I put my energies into was really worth the effort.

Lastly the cult of instant gratification did not help me. Progress can only ever be followed by consolidation, which can only then be followed by progress and then more consolidation. The myth of perpetual growth and straight line upward development is impossible in reality. Sooner or later there must be a pause for assimilation, a rest while we address the foundations and secure them for future development. This seems to underline my first realisation – we can only learn what we are ready for. If the foundations – spiritual, mental, emotional or material – are as sand, then the structure of our life will sooner or later collapse. It is perfectly appropriate to visit the Inner World and contact our Guide regularly, but there really ought to be a reason for the visit, and if guidance is given it must be acted upon. Further revelations, experiences and insights cannot be achieved until previous work has been fully understood. Put another way, intoxication by new information, experience or insight must be followed by a sobering up, into that new information. What happens in the minutes, hours and days after an Inner World experience are maybe more important than the Inner World experience itself.

[SEPTEMBER 2005]

Thursday 1st. 8pm. The Cave. Over twelve months had passed. Bypassing any Tarot doorways, I entered the cave from the seashore and floated around for a while, struggling to gain a footing. After a while I entered the Inner World proper and called for Geoffri. He greeted me warmly, his voice booming with laughter just as I remembered it. He pointed up into the distance – the Mountain of Wisdom he called it – suggesting that we should try to scale it. We began to climb physically up the mountain, and we got so far before Geoffri suggested that we fly instead. So we did, swooping up and down in the sky of the Inner World. Immediately I sighted, on the ground, the Library, shimmering and buzzing in electric blue. I approached and stood before The Keeper. He indicated that I could speak and request whatever I wished to know.

"What is the Spirit Council?" I asked, questioning something that I had heard talked about in the Outer World.

"Ah, at last a decent question," replied The Keeper, instantly causing a large book to open in front of me. I placed both hands on its pages and the required knowledge flowed into me. There was no formal organisation called the Spirit Council, but there was a collection of "overseeing intelligences, very high in the pecking order of Life." Although I had, in that moment, an awareness of these beings, they defied all attempts at description or illustration, other than being "very light." The book closed and I thanked The Keeper.

"Should I sell my printing business?" I asked.

"That is a matter for your Guide," he replied. I turned to Geoffri who instead suggested the name of someone from the business world that I should try to meet. Other Outer World information rushed over me and we seemed to be deviating from the original purpose of visiting the Library. The Keeper had no tolerance of my vacillating state and kicked me out as the building vanished. I rolled to the ground, unharmed.

Geoffri and I resumed our flight up to the mountain top. I could see Kalia in the distance, unmistakable and smiling at me. Touching down part way up the mountain a golden flying Chariot, drawn by one single leopard appeared swiftly. I questioned why such an animal would be in charge of a Chariot but received no answer. Geoffri and I climbed into the Chariot, and I took the reins. I found that while in the driving position I could alter my size and shape at will, first very small, then very large, as we drove off the cliff face at ever increasing speed. Faster and faster, the ride grew bumpier and bumpier, until it was all too much and lost control. I fell out of the vehicle and watched it disappear from view.

As I tumbled down and down the landscape started to turn black and red. The further I fell the blacker and redder it became. Images of murder, horror and violence flashed before my eyes, more awful as each second passed. It took some time but I felt Geoffri grab hold of me and we returned to the stability of the ground in the usual Inner World landscape. I was grateful for this, but was losing concentration. I tried for one last question to him.

"How will my financial and business life develop?" He replied straightforwardly.

"Money will be available in abundance, when required." I returned with some difficulty to the Outer World, tired and disorientated.

Wednesday 21st. 9.50pm. The Cave. A series of brief and confusing images came into my mind, but I burned through them with all the concentration I could muster. I could perceive a portal in my mind's eye of transparent black. Beyond it was a windswept and rain drenched Geoffri. I could not make out what he was saying. The scene was foreboding and although I could glimpse the palace the overall landscape was not welcoming and I resisted further entry.

Almost as soon as I went to step away I immediately found myself exactly where I wanted to be. It was a sunnier scene altogether. Waves lapped up on the beachy shoreline, which was bordered by grass and the usual hilly terrain. And there was Geoffri. He greeted me warmly in a masculine lower arm to lower arm clench and asked me to state my question. I was not ready for such directness and could not concentrate either on the question, Geoffri or the landscape. Maybe my meditative accompanying music was too loud?

Forcing myself to focus I asked Geoffri about my proposed business sale back in the Outer World. He said the timing would be much better in a numerological nine year. I asked about Pleiades and about Angelic Light work (two things I had encountered on my Outer World travels). Geoffri laughed and said that I knew the answer already.

"All this is hollow, End Times stuff for those who fear the future. People who follow these religions," he said, "are to be pitied. The small grains of truth contained within these teachings are the only positives for folk who are utterly lost."

I asked about the ethics and practice of magick and ritual for monetary gain. He handed me a golden coin with a five-pointed star, the pentagram, inscribed on its face. I felt it gently singe my hand, the heat travelling right through me, charging me up with something.

Behind us appeared the Library. Excited, I entered the building, but again without a prepared question. When would I learn to be prepared? The Keeper was friendly enough but was in no mood to waste time. Question-less I was bundled down the steps after a few seconds and the Library disappeared.

I asked Geoffri about the palace up in the distance. He said that we could visit briefly. It comprised a huge marble hall, bathed in white light with a purplish mystical tinge. Was this to be my very own Inner Temple?

All throughout this time a shadowy figure had been lurking. Small and unclear in a black hooded robe, it was not at all threatening but lingered nonetheless, somewhere in the middle distance.

I looked around and saw that three creatures had arrived. The Bull and Lion were not totally clear to me, but they seemed quite downbeat. The Eagle was much more noticeable, sharp eyed, cold and potentially cruel if the need arose. Suddenly it was time to go. I went to leave, but then paused. I asked Geoffri if I was to return the golden coin to him. Being told that I must I duly passed it back to him, but my right hand in which I had carried it was branded with the marks of the pentagram.

"The Midas touch?" I asked, half jokingly.

"If you like," he replied, now busy attending to some plants behind him. I regained awareness in my chair in the corner of my room in the Outer World. I noted that this time there was a very definite downward sensation, a sinking feeling, as I rejoined my physical body.

[OCTOBER 2005]

Monday 10th. The Cave. Life in the Outer World was stressful and challenging. I had a great deal to do and little understanding of how to do it. My state of mind was unquestionably affecting my Inner World experiences. Access was slow and vague, without the clarity and certainty that had occurred in the past. Nonetheless I managed to penetrate as far as Geoffri, who was sitting with the

Lion. I greeted them both and the Lion started to wrestle me. It knocked me to the ground and mauled me incessantly. It did not hurt in the sense of claws, teeth and blood, but was more like being forcibly woken up in the morning, not painful but disturbing. I felt that this message was given so that I could understand a little more of the Lion's fiery nature, its boldness and its power. Maybe it was an indicator that I needed to harness such traits in my own life. I had to admit that they were often lacking. The experience did not last long with Geoffri intervening to despatch the Lion. Geoffri urged me on and we wasted no time in taking off in flight toward the palace. I ascended as a blue energy, devoid of my physical body or any awareness of it.

Once inside there were many colours, sounds and sensations, all exuding a power of their own, although I could not decipher what − or indeed who - they were. One of these forces, positioned centrally in front of me, spoke directly.

"It is down to you," it said.

"Who are you?" I replied.

"God. Or as near to God as you will understand." I questioned this, disbelieving, seeking confirmation. "You know the answer," came the reply. I retreated back down to the ground of the Inner World. Suddenly a flurry of answers and realisations came over me. I saw insights into my personal future and that of those around me. I glimpsed opportunities that I had not previously considered and obstacles I had not been aware of. (Confidentiality prevents me from mentioning these in detail, but suffice to say I was pleased when every single insight was subsequently fulfilled and verified, even if some of them did take years.)

Again now there was a lengthy pause in my explorations. I was having conversations with God, without having read the book or attending the workshop. Given that I did not really believe such things this most recent experience was going to take some time to assimilate.

[JANUARY 2006]

Saturday 14th. 12 noon. The Cave. On my first visit for three months Geoffri tried to greet me while I swayed between both worlds. I seemed not to be able to be fully present in either the Inner or Outer space. The pipes on the radiator in my little meditation room were rattling and my skin was itching. I had read of the 'veil' that seems to exist between the Inner and Outer Worlds, and this seemed to be an experience of just that. A veil that was penetrable, but that also blocked the observation of one World from the other. I persisted but without success. I returned to the Outer World, groggy and disheartened. I turned the radiator off and put on an extra jumper so I would not be disturbed a second time.

Thirty minutes later I returned. The wait had proved worthwhile. There was now no veil, just purple and green kaleidoscopic flashes which filled my view as I seemed to rise up – rather than move forward - into the Inner World. Geoffri greeted me in his trademark lower arm clench and I slowly assimilated his world.

It proved hard, and I struggled to keep concentration. It had been a long time since my last successful visit. The sky was clear blue, full of light with wispy clouds. The ground was soft and warm, not at all alien, but very supportive and welcoming. I had to check myself a couple of times as Geoffri had started to behave differently than the last time I had seen him. He simply remarked that he was being his usual playful self, only messing around, but it unnerved me.

The palace on the mountain caught my eye again. I tried to catch all the details of its appearance. It was bright and shiny white from a distance, but as I got nearer it became crystalline and translucent. Its internal floor was black and white checkerboard and I felt – but could not see – currents of colour and energy all around me. I felt overwhelmed. All manner of 'God', 'Jesus' and 'Cosmic' related metaphors filled my mind but proper clarity remained difficult to grasp so I returned to the ground with Geoffri. It was question time.

I asked him about the possibility of time travel – could it be done, and if so, how? I was immediately transported to Bosworth Field in 1485. This was the battleground where Henry VII defeated Richard III, and was pronounced King of England. All around were Knights in dull (why not shining, I thought?) armour. Viciousness, brutality, murder and sexual debauchery were all around me. The ordinary soldiers were starving to death and the scene was brutality in the extreme. The scene was as real as walking down the street. There was my answer. It was possible alright, but was it desirable?

I changed tack and asked Geoffri about Angels, that modern day fascination of so many well-meaning folk that I encountered.

"These people only see what they can handle," he said. I took this to mean that when confronted with new information and experience, we process it within the parameters of our previous knowledge and experience. As I saw only briefly the horrors of 1485, as much as I could bear and no more. Others could only comprehend the softer side of life. "If the only way to experience and understand the Inner World is through seeing Angels then that is better than nothing," he said. I asked whether this was not a bit dangerous, a bit delusional. He remarked that it was all under control. "The advance of the Inner World," he said, "is now unstoppable and Angels are just a step along the way, an evolution of thought, if you like. But the real problem," he continued, "is the unrecognised fear that folk have for the Inner World. Ignorance of its existence and a general unawareness of the uniqueness of life have combined to form a powerfully negative force where people in the Outer World know that there must be more to life, but are morbidly fearful of doing anything to try to find it. This is where Angels and other such passing fancies serve a great purpose – they are all preferable to doing nothing at all." I returned, confused, disorientated and exhausted.

I recognised later that I was as guilty of asking questions and doubting the answers as anyone else. Indeed I had recently read 'In Search of the Miraculous' an account of Pieter Ouspensky's travels with the Russian mystic Gurdjieff. I found it fascinating except for the irritating self-doubt and internal debate that Ouspensky engages in after every encounter. I heard myself saying 'Just let it be, man!' until I realised that Ouspensky sometimes sounded more than a little like me.

[FEBRUARY 2006]

Saturday 4th. 12.45pm. The Cave. My recent difficulties within the Inner World had led to me going on a healthy living regime in the Outer World, shunning alcohol, eating better and resting more. The results were clear and positive. I was first greeted with a profusion of colours, pulsating blue, yellow and purple. I greeted what I first thought was Kalia, in a dark cloak this time. The figure said that it was usual for someone to regress back to an earlier Guide as a way of integrating the progress made so far. This seemed sensible, but I felt it would cause no harm to check.

"Are you my True Guide?"

"Of course not." She scowled and disappeared in a flash, revealing Geoffri. He had been there all along, obscured by this other being, who I now suspected not to be Kalia at all. Confused much I ruminated with him on matters of the Outer World. We concluded that it was down to me to lead and create the progress required. "Down to me" I thought, where have I heard that phrase before? The progress would be gentle, in a way that others could handle.

"Getting into a debate about matters of truth or fact," he said, "is unhelpful. You know what must be done. You should now get on and lead." This direct language pierced to the heart of the matter and was helpful.

Geoffri now pointed up to the palace and instantly I seemed to rise higher and higher toward it. I felt a tightness in my throat and a buffeting noise in my ears, so I descended again. I could discern the checkerboard floor of the hall, but that was all.

I remained with Geoffri but focused on the pulsating colours in my mind's eyes - still blue, yellow and purple in a kaleidoscope pattern. This continued, even intensified, for some time. I was then drawn back to the Outer World by the noises of one of our cats and this restored my regular consciousness. I shook hands with Geoffri before I departed.

It was around this time that the period directly after each journey started to take on greater significance. In the quiet time afterwards I stopped having to go for a lie down, and instead started to regularly note down the realisations, points and insights that settled within me as I returned. They were intended to apply directly to me and, on occasion, more widely to others.

Realisations: My physical body may only be a transport device containing the real life energy, but this does not mean I can overlook its condition. Physical aches, pains and illnesses definitely reduce my ability to access the Inner World. It may be that a disability might not cause the same problem, but the trauma of a disability might. Looked at from this point of view, the Inner World is not a place of refuge, comfort or escape from sickness.

Alcohol and drugs are out. A heightened, temporary, experience can certainly be achieved by the judicious use of certain alcoholic, herbal or chemical stimulants. I had some past experience of this, but had not developed the ability to use these things in moderation, and I wondered if anyone else really had. It is all a matter of control, and the substance too easily takes control of you, fuelling the illusion that you are in control of it. I have seen nothing whatsoever to make me believe that a sustained and fulfilling Inner World experience is possible when using alcohol, drugs, sedatives, anti-depressants, or medication of any kind.

The avoidance of artificiality might apply to foodstuffs as well. A diet of processed foods full of man-made ingredients leaves me feeling sluggish at best and exhausted at worst. Top up with some alcohol and my body is a mess. Successfully accessing the Inner World is akin to Olympic training, requiring courage, discipline and a proper diet. My inability to do all these things has contributed to - and maybe even been a reflection of – the difficulties I have had accepting my experiences. Imagine the torture the energetic body must be going through. Used to the confines of the physical body, it then begins to catch regular glimpses of freedom, only to be slammed back down into the toxin ridden, decaying and degenerating physical body.

[MARCH 2006]

Monday 6th. 7pm. The Cave. I preceded this journey with care. I sat resting with some gentle music for sometime beforehand, and I made sure that my dinner had digested before I began. Entry was then swift, smooth and untroubled. Geoffri greeted me immediately, but he seemed that bit further away than usual and I had to reach out for him. Kalia also seemed to be in attendance, or was it a new figure dressed in a hooded cloak? I quizzed this unknown being about its true intentions, but there was no answer and it disappeared.

"The Dark Side surrounds you," said Geoffri, "it surrounds us all, but you have turned away from the Light." I could recognise this and was sorry that I had allowed the Outer World to obscure my contact with Geoffri. It had been a month since my last visit.

We ascended to the palace and arrived in the Hall with the familiar black and white flooring. Our point of entry was different to before. It felt like we had swam in, underwater. My breathing changed and although I could not see clearly I could just discern unknown shapes and voices around me.

"You will not return here," came a loud voice, "unless you prove you can cope. Control your feelings. Do not allow your frustration to boil over." That was all and I returned to the ground of the Inner World with a bump. Now there were noises and distractions in the Outer World and Geoffri urged me to return there, address them and come back another day.

"You should formally write out this journal," he suggested as colours of violet and yellow filled my view and I returned to the Outer World somewhat dazed.

Realisations: Being told off in the Hall specifically related to one Outer World matter. For seventeen years I had been a student, learning from Arthur. I say learning but there were many times when I had argued and many times, and increasingly so now, where he seemed to stop teaching. He maintained throughout that I was the cause of the trouble, and undoubtedly I was, but the difficulty remained. Part of the problem was that the esteem I held him in was not justified. At times I felt him to be almost God-like, but of course he was not. He was very human. Wise, learned, experienced, strong, powerful, charismatic and compassionate, but with moods and problems of his own. He had probably grown weary of the repetitious arguments, and was now ageing fast. He had started to contradict himself, and I had no patience with this. Now through a simple misunderstanding we had exchanged harsh words and the relationship had become strained to breaking point. I accepted my part of the blame, but he did not. This annoyed me, but it still was not really the issue. He was only a human being and it was high time I came to terms with that.

Saturday 18th. 11am. The Cave. Entry into the Inner World was preceded by much ritual preparation and at once I saw what seemed like my life flashing before my eyes. My breathing quickened and my heart started to pound. This lasted for some worrying minutes, but as it receded I could see the colours come into view, predominately purple and yellow, followed by Geoffri's clear and welcoming voice.

While trying to pierce through this mass of sensory input I realised that something was profoundly different. I could actually sense Geoffri's presence in the room with me. I had not ascended up to meet him; he had descended down to me. Or that's at least how it seemed. I greeted him, but he was overtly sexual and encouraged all manner of undesirable behaviour. This did not seem right at all, and I could glimpse another figure in the background, which I instantly recognised as the real Geoffri. I turned to the first figure – the one who appeared in the room with me – and asked him directly if he was my True Guide.

"Of course not, would your Guide do this?" he mocked and I cast him away in a flash. Who or what had I invoked? I refocused on the real Geoffri and quickly ascended with him. He was much calmer and more centred than the first figure. Once fully in the Inner World, I sensed yet another figure, small and cloaked over to my left. I wondered whether it would be my old friend Kalia, but the pull back to the Outer World was strong today and I did not probe further, simply holding the scene as was, as best I could.

Geoffri pointed over in the distance, to the scene from the Wheel of Fortune card, the Ferris Wheel bound by a wire fence, the Bull attending the toll booth. Suddenly I was a passenger in one of the carriages, travelling all the way down, then back up again, then down again. But of course it was not just a simple fairground attraction. In the moment I was reminded of the natural order of life – up and down, profit and loss, progress for one followed by progress for another. The Eagle and Lion appeared and the Bull came closer.

"You are too harsh, too judgemental," remarked the Eagle, flapping its wings. The Bull charged fast, flattening me and then spoke.

"You must stand up for yourself, and not be swayed by others so greatly." The Lion playfully batted me around the head with his paw, demonstrating only a fraction of his full power. I could not discern his words, if indeed there were any. The intervention of the three creatures was powerful although at no time did I feel threatened or fearful.

At once I was conscious of Geoffri at my side and of the pull back to the Outer World, but it was not time to go yet. The Library appeared, vibrating blue as usual, but the pull on me was now impossible to resist and it faded from view. I felt myself slipping back to the Outer World, but not before Geoffri threw me a golden pentacle. I felt its power in my hand and absorbed it into my stomach. Geoffri said to return it next time.

Realisations: Mundane Outer World matters preoccupied my attention and seemed to spoil my Inner World experiences, either making entry more difficult, or bringing premature exit. Just as I felt I was reaching some small acceptance of my inner experiences they were now being interfered with and I felt uncomfortable with this. If, as Arthur had often indicated, my future role was that of an Illuminator, rather than a Transformer, then why was I not fully utilising my chance to explore the Inner World properly? Was the Outer World the Dark Side? While these and other thoughts whirled around my head I reminded myself of the progress that had been made so far. Balance and patience were important, and a constant straining for progress might obscure these experiences altogether.

[APRIL 2006]

Thursday 6th. 8.30pm. The Cave. After some gentle relaxation and a soft perception of Geoffri from the Outer World I entered without trouble. I could feel a tingling in my third eye region and definitely felt as though I were in two places at once.

The landscape contained many figures scattered around, but as I confirmed Geoffri's identity all but one disappeared from view. This seemed to be Kalia, but I could not be certain. We had a brief loving and intimate encounter. It felt right, but I never confirmed who she was. I turned back to Geoffri and asked him if this place could be described as a different dimension? He answered.

"One half of the human brain is directed toward the Outer World and one half is directed toward the Inner World. You can therefore be in two places at once. Bi-polar people, of course, have this ability strong and prominent, but due to a total lack of understanding these poor souls are encouraged to fight against it, not realising the strength and possibilities that could be derived from embracing and exploring it."

I now asked Geoffri about the pentacle he gave me on my last trip. He replied, "you should keep it, for you have earned it." It became infused deeper into my stomach and became an integral part of me. I felt the energy very strongly and surmised that it may have symbolised a partial mastery of the Earth element. I then asked where we should explore next. Quick as a flash the Library appeared, with The Keeper behind a counter and the walls high with books as far as the eye could see. I asked this Keeper about time travel. He replied.

"It is possible. By ascension to a different plane within the Inner World."

"But how?" I asked, impatient for more. He pointed out of the window of the Library toward the palace on the mountain top.

"By visiting there, and making a lot more mistakes than you have so far!" As usual he was in a hurry, and I rolled backwards down the steps as the Library disappeared.

I asked Geoffri if we might ascend toward the palace, and as we did so I felt my energy shift and my body vibrate. I rose through the floor and into the main Hall with its checkerboard floor, but could go no further, nor hold this position. I was exhausted by the experience and sank back to the earth of the Inner World.

Geoffri, and the other vague figure from earlier, wished me goodbye telling me to return soon to "simply explore, maybe via the Tarot doorways, just in order to gain knowledge." I opened my eyes in the Outer World and still felt spaced out.

Realisations: I had been in two places at once, experiencing two dimensions of space in one dimension of time. This might have further ramifications. To be in *one* place at *one* time was the standard state of affairs on Earth, in the Outer World only. To be in *two* places in the *same* time required simultaneous Inner and Outer World consciousness. To connect with *one* place at *different* times is possible while practising any form of divination, while *two* places at *different* times would be theoretically possible during travels in time and space.

Easter Monday 2006. 7.45pm. The Fool. Between visits I had reviewed my notes and reflected on my experiences with Geoffri. The presence of the second figure beside him seemed to herald the imminent introduction of a new Guide. I felt unprepared, so I revised the basic questions that I should always ask. Are you my True Guide? Do you have the power to protect me in the Inner World? What is your name? What should I do next? There would be many others of course, but these four would establish a firm connection with any new being.

I now closed my eyes and immediately a purple doorway appeared before me. Its edges were well defined and I floated between it and me for some time. I could hear Geoffri's voice, but could not enter. I took breath, shuddered and passed through.

There were two figures. On my left was the Fool himself. Brightly coloured, fleet of foot, dancing like a jester. The figure on the right said nothing and did not react either to the Fool or to my urgings.

"Are you Geoffri?" seemed to bring no response. After some time Geoffri appeared in full colour, moving wildly and energetically from the hills in the distance. It was good to see him. We discussed the situation in my Outer World as the Fool played around to the left. The things I was pursuing in the Outer World were simply distractions, escapes from the reality of my current situation.

"They should be brought to a close," he said, "there is no point trying to enlighten people against their will. If their learning has taken them off in a different direction then so be it, it is not your job to bring them back. Everyone must learn in his or her own way and in his or her own time. You cannot force the learning on anyone, but must simply be the catalyst whereby they might do the work for themselves, when they are ready. Do not to worry about letting these things go," he said, 'there is always more to do with your time – there always will be!"

We both turned toward the Fool and immediately flew up into the sky with him. My whole body pulsed and vibrated as we returned to the Earth of the Inner World. I stood before the Fool and asked him what I could do for him.

"Always keep learning and moving to the New Day. That is the secret," he said. As I moved away from him, ready to return home he stuck his foot out and tripped me up. He smiled playfully, "trips and falls, mistakes, are all part of the plan, and all to learn from."

As I prepared to return to the Outer World I felt a growing itchy right ear. It was distracting, and Geoffri urged me to return soon.

Realisations: I was increasingly being asked about Arthur, in my Outer World, and specifically how he had come to gain all his knowledge. This was a hard one to answer, but it boiled to down to his willingness, even eagerness to make mistakes. This hunger seemed beyond even the acceptance of accidental mistakes. He actually seemed to go looking for them! Like the Fool he seemed to love them, and so did an acquaintance of mine, who when confronted with difficulties would remark without rancour or irony, "that'll be another opportunity for growth then."

Monday 24th. 7.30pm. The Fool. For some time I floated in a void between the two worlds. It was blissful to be neither an inhabitant of one nor the other. Scenes from my life came to mind, that feeling of life flashing before your eyes. Was this akin to the process of death? The purple doorway cleared before me and there was the Fool, alternately shrinking and expanding his form, tiny one minute, then one hundred feet tall the next. In his enlarged state he lifted up his foot as if to stamp on me, and then as he brought his full weight down on top of me I penetrated right through him, untouched and unscathed.

Another fun loving being on the left of the scene beckoned me to join him in his games and laughter. I felt wary and called for Geoffri. He came running immediately and it was comforting to see him. I was drifting and struggling to hold my concentration, and it was Geoffri who brought me sharply back into the Inner World with his encouragements to focus. The Library noisily ratcheted itself down before us and along its front steps rolled a wooden box secured with a padlock and chains. I seemed to be able to open it without any trouble and inside was an electric blue sphere of energy, pulsating and vibrating. First hovering, then moving fast, it implanted itself into my brain. It was like being plugged into mains electricity, but this was energy of 'knowing'. It told me that I had now received "the burden of knowledge" and all of this in one go seemed too much to cope with. I felt that this sphere was somehow not of this world and as it merged into, around, and with my brain I was almost knocked backwards. Its force was astonishing and I felt truly changed by it. I had knowledge. And it hurt.

The scene faded from view as Geoffri urged me to go home, relax and return soon. I opened my eyes, shell-shocked and disorientated.

Afterwards: I did not believe that I had suddenly received all the knowledge in the Universe, that would have been silly. But I did come to think that somehow I had been granted, or earned, a degree of knowledge. Knowledge behaves differently to belief, hypothesis, suspicion, idea or opinion. Knowledge is accompanied by weight and certainty, and it does not ever go away. During the coming months, as a result of my interactions in the Outer World I would often feel as if I were going mad.

[MAY 2006]

Monday 8th. 7.30pm. Nine of Wands. My usual review of the day's events took place before I could pass effectively through the doorway of the card. Once inside I perceived Geoffri and beside him an unfamiliar blond, male figure, slightly effeminate, although also with strength of character. He signalled his intention to help me. I was suspicious of him and yet also felt drawn by him. It was confusing and unclear, until Geoffri called over whereon the man instantly departed, scowling into the distance. Another False Guide? A True Guide should not elicit such confusion, I thought.

I next noticed a wooden hut, made of branches and canes. Inside was a new man and beside him was the Lion, alert and on guard, watching me. The man inside had worked hard to build what he had and was ready for any occurrence. He was secure, his position stable and accomplished. But therein rested the problem because he was also stubborn and determined to keep what he had at all costs. He embodied security, resilience, stubbornness and inflexibility all in one. I did not speak to him.

As I left the hut the palace on the mountain came into view and I rose up to the now familiar checkerboard floor, but could not journey any higher. I felt tightness in my head and sensed powerful forces and moving shapes within the hall, but left when instructed to do so. It was a lot to take in. I begged my leave from Geoffri, and after some soothing words from him I returned home.

Realisations: I had been performing these journeys from an eight foot square box room that I had decorated with a more occult-type feel. But preparation of the outer space was also preparation of the inner space, and around this time I settled on a best practice: A full stomach was essential for me. Neither stuffed and bloated, nor rumbling with of indigestion or hunger. Phones must be switched off or on silent, cats put out or asleep, and computers powered down. Washing, showering or bathing with a cleansing focus was very helpful. Arthur had taught me to see – actually, visibly - black shards of negativity running down the plug hole during washing. I had sometimes introduced an incense, to subtly switch the mind into a different state, but I did not always do this. Is it only me that finds some incense addictive? I found music helpful, and reserved certain instrumental tracks only for this purpose.

Especially in winter I found it vital to pre-set the correct room temperature. Knocking pipes and clattering central heating systems must be addressed. Cold toes and fingers might be a distraction, and colds are easily caught during the exhaustion state of the journey.

A comfortable, yet alert, seating position is essential. I settled on the traditional God form pose, seated upright, legs uncrossed, arms resting on my legs, the two halves of the body separated. Lying down, for me, was too likely to lead to sleep. I would vary in my use of occult practises. I increasingly began the sittings with the Lesser Banishing Ritual of the Pentagram, although I by no means used it consistently. It was through the repetition of these pre-practices that I was to deepen my experience over the coming years.

[NOVEMBER 2006]

Saturday 25th. 10.30am. Ten of Cups. I took some time to review all aspects of the pictorial representation of the card before entering. The black doorway expanded in my mind's eye and I immediately came across the Lion, who opened his jaws so wide that he swallowed me whole, spitting me out again seconds later. A painless though interesting experience.

I could hear the voice of a small ginger haired, tartan kilt wearing figure flashing before me. This could not be Geoffri and I tested his intentions. His smile turned to a scowl and he departed, allowing the real Geoffri to appear in his usual tall, powerful and kind guise. I queried the presence of the other man with Geoffri.

"Merely a False Guide," he replied. Apparently he had been hanging around for a while but had now been despatched for good. As if to reassure, Geoffri now turned to show me a collection of familiar faces lined up to my left. First was my old friend and previous Guide Kalia, and then came the large Bull, then the larger still Lion. The Eagle circled above them all.

Then the steps of the Library honed into viewed, descending downwards and slotting perfectly into position on the ground, just as if they had always been there. I looked to Geoffri for a lead and he urged me to enter. I climbed the steps and inside the building were the usual electric blue lighting and a sea of books on shelves. At a central table stood The Keeper, his face invisible.

"What do I do now?" I asked. The Keeper simply rose his hands and waved to all the books around him.

"You must learn all this," he replied. I looked around. The books contained a collection of everything that had happened and will yet happen. They were not arranged by event or by time, but by the most important reference of all – the individual life.

I reached up to a book marked 'Teddy Kennedy' – there was no need for formality here it seemed. As I reached out and touched it I seemed to assimilate all the knowledge contained within it – an alcoholic, even now, and an adulterer. I reached for another marked 'Lebanon' and immediately understood the tensions that existed in that region of the Outer World. It was like being given a secret briefing, and then being challenged to accept what you learn as fact rather than opinion.

"That will do for today" said The Keeper and I rolled out of the Library down the steps and back to the feet of the animals, Kalia and Geoffri. The building disappeared from view.

"Come," said Geoffri and suddenly we were in the presence, high up in the hills, of a beautiful woman, naked with long hair. She was happy and had everything, yet inside her was sadness as if she had nothing. All she wanted was love. Nothing else mattered to her. We made love – not sex – but love. She was yielding yet not weak, needing but not needy, wanting but not demanding. She needed love like others needed oxygen. It lay at the very core of her being. We made love again, and although she did not want me to leave she accepted the inevitable, now content. Were her needs particular to her or descriptive of the true nature of woman?

I felt myself ascend to the palace. The Hall had the usual black and white floor tiling, now with large pillars on either side. I could see no further but felt my body convulse with tremendous force. I was in the presence of something extraordinary and I felt like I would explode if I did not descend out of there.

Back on the ground of the Inner World Geoffri, Kalia, and the three creatures all bade me farewell and said that I should return soon. These were often the last words spoken, "return soon," almost as if I might not. This was curious but would have to keep for another day. I opened my eyes, disorientated and light headed.

Realisations: The Tarot seems to be a much misunderstood technology. It has seventy-eight different apps, each of which does something unique, takes you somewhere new and teaches you something worthwhile. Entry to the Inner World, via the cave, is the most direct route, but different parts within that space can be reached by suspending disbelief and allowing the figures depicted in the cards to come to life. It matters not whether these pictures are actually alive or not, because they behave as if they are. By working with the cards in this way I have yet to encounter a problem that cannot be resolved, understood, approached or explained.

The Library can be viewed as a central collection of objective truth, presenting itself differently to each visitor. To me, a lover of books and a lifelong printer and publisher, it presents as bound tomes on shelves. To a software programmer it might present as a giant touch screen containing countless files for download. To a comic enthusiast it might present as a collection of graphic novels, to the farmer it might even appear as an infinite collection of talking animals and plants, to the photographer a collection of slides, to the cook an array of bottled ingredients. The information seems to presents itself here in the way the enquirer is best able to handle.

Monday 27th. 7.15pm. Queen of Swords. Geoffri pulled me through into the Inner World. Although I was wavering I thought this was an unusual move and tested him on it. He disappeared, then reappeared as miniature, rising up again as a giant, then returning to his regular height. This was Geoffri alright.

He gestured over to a clearing with some rocks, some children and an older lady. Geoffri told me that she would not speak to me but that I could observe and read her. She was a masculine female, using the tools of the man to make her way. She was not materialistic, but full of disappointment and keen to protect herself from further hurt. She was quick to judge and to find fault, harsh and demanding, though not outright nasty or wholly negative. She was just cynical and maybe a little bitter.

The Library appeared by my side and I climbed the steps inside. The shelves hurtled past me at great speed and suddenly I had in my hands the book marked 'Adolf Hitler.' I paused. Did I really want to know this? Too late, the answers flooded in. The last great evil man. There was no limit to what he would have done given the chance. He was a powerful black magician and a fool with no common sense or fundamentals to build upon. Much progress has been made since then, with every mass murderer after his time being a little less evil than him, and none of them able to act on anywhere near his scale. This was not the summary that my conscious mind would have given.

The shelves hurtled past again, the book now gone from my hands, replaced by 'Bill Clinton.' The book spoke - a kind man, but weak. A serial adulterer, many affairs, not just the once or twice where he had been caught. Hillary has become like the Queen of Swords. Again, wholly different to the conclusions I would consciously have drawn.

That was it now, the lesson over as quickly as it had begun. The book disappeared, followed by the Library itself. Geoffri wished me farewell. The disconnection was so swift that when I opened my eyes I was dazed and could not focus properly for at least a minute or two, as if I was on an unfamiliar planet.

[JANUARY 2007]

Thursday 4th. 8.00pm Ace of Pentacles. I varied my pre-journey routine slightly this time, discarding some music that had accidentally become attached to negative Outer World associations. Whether this helped or not, entry was swift. I greeted Geoffri more warmly than before. He smiled broadly and his features seemed clearer than ever.

I floated around the scene and transported myself immediately across the landscape toward where a castle was being constructed. The builders' progress was slow but sure and the work was still in the early stages. The workers were tiny and attending to small details such that the structure could become golden and magnificent later. A graphic example of 'big oaks from small acorns grow' and a perfect representation of the Ace of Pentacles. The Library appeared again and once inside I spoke directly to The Keeper.

"Is everything knowable?" I asked.

"Yes," he replied, without hesitation or emotion.

"For everyone?"

"Yes."

"Past, present and future?"

"Yes."

What further questions were needed? The Library would elicit all answers when asked directly and genuinely. There would be no trivia and all was possible - when I was ready. The Keepers answers were delivered strictly and swiftly. He was unforgiving of fools but generous with true seekers. That was enough. I was bowled out of the Library. One day, I thought, it was be nice to leave in a more dignified fashion.

I looked up at the palace and began my ascension. Again I felt pressure upon me and an intensification of colour as I rose. I could go no further so I retreated to Geoffri and quizzed him about aspects of reincarnation instead. The answers were revealing.

"I am you, and you are me," said Geoffri, "as was Kalia before that." These were my past lives and my Guides possessed the best qualifications of all, they knew me and knew how to help me because they were me! We seemed to be coming forward in time as Geoffri had originally appeared to me in the dress of the Middle Ages and Kalia had presented herself in simple cloths from the Stone Age. I was now struggling to maintain focus, so after a lot of floating around I returned home.

Realisations: Both my Guides so far had been my previous incarnations. They were me and I was them. A shocking revelation, but I should be getting used to those by now. It was also becoming apparent that Geoffri was always available, always present, not just in the Inner World – although that was where he was most accessible – but everywhere, at all times. It was just a matter of stilling the mind, allowing him to communicate and not prejudging the answers.

Subsequent practise of these techniques with pupils in the Outer World revealed that the Inner Guides were always either our previous incarnations or someone who we had been strongly associated with and connected to in a previous incarnation. There was never any getting away from yourself!

Saturday 6th. 12noon. Judgement. The conscious mind was active, and this presented some obstacles as I struggled to understand the full divinatory meaning of the card I had chosen. In frustration I abandoned this mental dialogue and instantly a purple doorway opened up before me. I felt light headed, but could not enter through this opening. Instead I felt myself to be in the middle of an impenetrable forest. Thickly wooded, my movements restricted on all sides, unable to see the wood for the trees, so to speak. I opted instead to become one of those trees and suddenly everything became clear. I was now in the Hall of the palace. A voice came from one corner.

"Do not invoke us unless you mean to, for we will surely harm you."

"Not all of us will,'" came another voice, softer this time. I swirled around the room, unable to stay still in this heady brew of energy and power. My next awareness was being with Geoffri, outside of the palace.

"What is the problem?" I asked.

"Whose problem? Your problem?" he replied.

"Yes, mine." It was difficult to focus on the right question and to hear the reply clearly. I was impatient. I asked about the book I was currently writing (the manuscript that would become *A New Day*). New information had come to light recently and I feared having to revise large chunks of the work.

"Does the book need a re-write?" I asked.

"Yes." I was not happy with his answer.

"Whole or partial?" I said.

"Partial, mainly at the end, section two." This made sense. I knew instantly what had to be done.

"How long will it take me?"

"It is significant work, many hours, but quicker if you apply yourself in a focused manner. The deadlines you have set are still largely achievable if you focus and apply yourself." His words were helpful, though not entirely welcome. I gave him my best wishes and goodbyes. As usual he urged me to visit again soon. Upon returning home I had to sit for several minutes assimilating the information before I could write up my account.

[MARCH 2007]

Monday 12th. 8.00pm. The Hierophant. Prior to this journey I had always used the Cosmic Tarot deck for these journeys. I now swapped to using the Morgan Greer deck, its more basic and primal imagery seemed more appropriate.

After entering through a purple doorway I sensed Kalia to my left, but also many other figures to my right – one in the foreground, the rest smaller and cast in shadow behind. I floated around for a while, struggling to hold my position and eventually asked the male figure in the foreground if he was Geoffri. He indeed was. His face was unclear and he was smaller than I had previously remembered. He explained that he was Geoffri de ...... (words unclear), a French noble man of the 12th Century AD. I asked him if he was my True Guide, as I felt wary about him. I moved to hold his hand and felt the right connection of warmth, love and acceptance.

An unknown woman now appeared on the scene, beautiful and naked, with red hair and womanly curves. I touched her gently and was aware of the difference in feelings I had for her to those I had for Geoffri. This might have been expected, for the woman was unfamiliar and new, whereas Geoffri - being me - was extremely familiar. Geoffri and I were so connected that anything I did not like about him I also did not like about me. Any wariness I felt for him must therefore also be wariness of myself.

I floated around for a while longer, surveying the landscape. I felt a buzz and release throughout my body, as if I had momentarily disconnected from the physical. I returned all too soon and wished Geoffri a warm farewell.

Realisations: I seemed to be skirting around the edges of a long documented mystical phenomenon – the recurring (I wanted to say crystal) palace on the mountain. Geoffri referred to this as the Mountain of Wisdom. Arthur Norris had called it the Temple of Opportunities. Various old documents I had accumulated spoke of the need for 'Mastery of the Temple.' Some thought that the Temple might be constructed physically, but it was now clear that the Temple existed first in the Inner World and the task was to achieve Mastery of that. This would be no small task.

Tuesday 13th. 8.00pm. Nine of Wands. I divined the Nine of Wands as the card of entry and immediately became aware that the Inner World contained levels. What were they? Did the Outer World gravitate toward the Physical and Mental, while the Inner World associate with the Emotional and Spiritual? This seemed the best conclusion from Arthur's teachings.

I floated around and entered, and my gaze turned to the mountains in the background. Geoffri was to my right and a dark cloaked figure to the right of him. A wooden shack appeared on my left. I greeted Geoffri, but also made sure to check his identity.

"'Are you Geoffri? Are you my Guide?"

"'Yes!" he cried, performing a cartwheel, revealing himself as he had on previous occasions as happy and smiling. I asked who the cloaked figure was. I was apprehensive of him and pointed as if to despatch him. He (or she?) fell to the floor. I pulled the hood down and there was no-one inside, the garment had collapsed to nothing. I got the impression that I should not have done this. Geoffri agreed, but we did not linger over it. My actions had been born from fear of the unknown, but with my Guide at hand what was there really to fear?

The Library appeared, emanating electric blue. I forward rolled into the main hall – for in the Inner World I was agile and athletic! The Keeper, hooded, was in attendance and asked that I speak a question.

"Arthur Norris?" I kept it simple, needing to know more about my teacher. A book from the highest shelf came down to me.

"You have pushed him too far. He is only human. He will always be there for you, but leave him alone currently. He has other issues to deal with. Ask another."

"Adolf Hitler?" This book was lower down on the shelves.

"But you know all this?" said The Keeper. I wondered for a moment how I knew this. I failed completely to remember asking for the same book on a previous visit! The Keeper continued, "It was a sign of how far Germany had sunk that it would embrace someone so low. Smelly, uncouth, unkempt and lazy. A totally unremarkable man."

After a moment the indication came that time was up, and the building folded away, sending me rolling back down to the ground.

"What is your name?" I turned to Geoffri.

"Geoffri de Bougainville. I lived in a castle in Southern France on the Spanish Border in the late 1100's. I was a nobleman, but lost everything, foolishly. The trouble was related to women. I will try to make sure that we do not do the same again."

"But who are you?" I probed further.

"I am you," he replied. I remembered these words from before and they produced a warmth in my heart, like when you arrive home after a long journey. It confirmed my previous insights that these Guides were previous incarnations of me, and we were all part of some kind of soul family.

"How many come after you?" I asked.

"Female, male, then female, then others," he replied. It was not really an answer but I accepted it as normal and correct. I felt at home in the Inner World in Geoffri's company for the first time.

We advanced to the wooden hut. A man was inside, busily engaged in planing some wood. He was building his own house, busy and unwilling to engage in conversation.

"What is your name?" I asked.

"Dave," came one voice.

"Christian," came another. Both these seemed unlikely, but I did not argue. I looked around and could see for the first time that the man had a family – a wife and children playing outside. He carried the responsibility of providing for them.

"Anything I can do?" I asked faux-helpfully.

"Yes, bugger off and leave me in peace." He was not abusive, but spoke firmly. I complied. Feeling as though my head was filling up with information that I would struggle to remember I bade Geoffri a warm and heartfelt farewell and returned home.

This was all remarkable information, yet unlike some previous expeditions it all seemed perfectly acceptable and normal. In fact, upon my return in seemed as though it was the Outer World that was uncomfortable and alien.

Realisations: The response from The Keeper when I had asked about Adolf Hitler had provided all the proof I needed for the independent and verifiable existence of an Inner World. I had asked for the book on Hitler before, but had forgotten that I had done so. When I asked again the answer was consistent with my notes, even if I had failed to remember them. The same applied to my quizzing of Geoffri's true identity. I had been down both these lines of enquiry before, and the consistency of answers, coupled with my inability to remember my experiences proved very revealing. This was real.

Wednesday 21st. 8.00pm. Ten of Wands. Entry was uncertain, unclear and difficult. There were two or three men, each carrying large bundles of wood, each staff freshly cut and still carrying its shoots and buds, but I could not see Geoffri. I called out for him and a large figure approached who transformed himself to the size of a giant. Was this him? I asked, but received no clear answer. I asked again and proceeded through a series of none too certain encounters before I finally fully recognised Geoffri, and even then it was only a vague sense. There were many alternate beings around to confuse me and I decided on the one I felt most comfortable with, though I was less than sure.

We both glided toward the men with the batons. They seemed to be in almost willing slavery, restricted by their heavy burdens. I asked if I could help and one of the men threw me a bundle of five sticks to carry on my shoulder. I buckled under the enormity of the load. It weighed heavy in all dimensions – mentally, emotionally and spiritually as well as materially. I collapsed on my back.

The Library appeared and although I could see no Keeper I entered and asked my question.

"Philip K Dick?" I had been reading his work in the Outer World. The book appeared in my hands and I flicked through its pages like lightning.

"A fool, a crazy fool, yet one who was not fearful of what might happen." This was interesting, someone else who just did his stuff without fear of the consequences.

The Chariot came speeding up and I quickly embarked. I stood to the left of the Charioteer but could not discern Geoffri. We travelled fast along a sandy beach and high up into the air toward the right of hills and mountains until we emerged in a barren landscape with a deserted race track. No spectators or competitors, just the three creatures in the centre of a circular track, watching and waiting. We had sped twice around the track before I noticed the Chariot was being pulled not by horses, but by two fast cars, one black, one white. We continued faster and faster until we took off from the ground, soared high up into the sky and I was thrown out by a sudden movement. I was now right back where I started, at the feet of the men carrying the burdensome sticks. Geoffri was now also there and we advanced toward the Temple high in the mountains off to the left.

I rose through the floor of the main hall with less difficulty than before. This felt significant as my whole body seemed to disconnect and I felt so powerful and knowledgeable. There were voices within the hall who questioned my presence between themselves. One voice was clear.

"You are not yet ready," at which I landed back on the ground, outside the Temple (as I felt I should now call it) with a thud. This time the ground was damp, green and fertile. The men who had been carrying the sticks had been constructing a house and their efforts were bearing significant fruit.

I asked Geoffri if I would see Kalia again. She seemed to approach from the right and I felt warm toward her. We embraced and I asked about my other Guide, the first before Kalia. Another shape in a cloak appeared. We all stood together before I kissed Kalia and waved goodbye, eager to record all this lest I forget the details. I felt very disconnected and disorientated on my return.

Afterwards: Doubt and confusion ruled my mind at this time. Arthur had taught me this process, but left scant notes or supporting materials and I could find very few texts covering the subject, and those that did exist seemed overly complex and ritualistic. I paused and meditated on the number eleven. This was one of my four key personal energies. Broken down into 1 and 1 might this suggest that I must achieve a sense of individuality, independence and purpose in both worlds? Once I had managed this then maybe the doubt could be dispelled?

Thursday 22nd. 7.30pm. Strength. I arrived in the middle of a grassy, shrubbed area and greeted Geoffri to my right. I recognised him instantly and felt warmly toward him, in contrast to previous occasions where I had been somewhat unsure. This time I felt confident that it was indeed Geoffri. I asked him his name and history again and he repeated exactly as he did before – Geoffri de Bougainville, the Franco-Spanish nobleman of the 12th century.

The Library – in electric blue – appeared in front of us both. I asked Geoffri whether I should enter?

"When the Library appears you must always enter," he replied. I forward rolled into the building and was greeted more warmly than usual by The Keeper, an old man in dark blue robes, hunched over a staff. I looked around the hall, it was small in width and length, but rose high up, further than the eye could see and beyond. The floors were wood panelled, and in front of me were shelves of old handmade books. This was the area of the Library reserved for everyone who had ever lived and ever will live. Behind me, I turned around, was an area of subjects – green bound books for nature, orange for world affairs, gold books high up on the shelves for spiritual knowledge. I could now appreciate more of this Library than I ever did before. Who should I enquire about? David Cameron came to mind, and so suddenly did the awareness, which poured into me as the book opened up before my eyes. A secret in his past, a dark secret, the media have it and it will be exposed. The information came to me as a knowing, rather than as spoken or written words. I moved on in my subject matter, Tony Blair.

"A dark secret in the future, yet to occur. Sometimes the pendulum swings one way, then another, and then sometimes not at all, such is the nature of things. It is all to learn from." I did not probe further. My time was up and I backward rolled out of the Library to the feet of Geoffri.

Suddenly a very attractive girl came into view, naked, red haired, dancing provocatively, shapely, sexual and strong willed. I asked whether it was a good idea to make love to her, but before any answer presented itself we were doing just that. It was fast, powerful and intense. She departed, almost taking a piece of me with her. I felt as though I would meet her again.

The Lion approached, being ridden bare-back by what seemed like the same girl. She was powerful and strong, wore no garments, signs of office or power. Her strength flowed from within.

I climbed aboard the Lion, behind the girl. She had the immense creature under tight control and we paraded about, seemingly effortlessly. She dismounted, and I continued alone with the Lion. The creature did not stay calm for long, at first argumentative and restive, and then fully independent and beyond my control. It flipped me high in the air and just as I was about to land in its mouth, the girl, named Evie or Eve, kicked the Lion to one side and I landed on the floor, on my back, unharmed. The Lion roared at me but did no harm. Eve wished me farewell and departed. I said goodbye to Geoffri and departed also.

Realisations: I liked the red haired girl, on top of the Lion. She appeared more akin to the Scarlet Woman in Aleister Crowley's interpretation of the card, which he renamed as Lust. It was cross references like this, which only become apparent after the event, which led me to think that instead of being a predictive or divinatory tool, the Tarot is, at its heart, a map of the Inner World. In this way, every spread, every layout of cards, as well as being a conscious attempt to trace the dynamics of the Outer World, is a subconscious, maybe even primal attempt to connect with and understand the Inner World. Every Tarot artist endeavours, on some level, to draw the Inner World which they sense but may not see. Every Tarot reader is peering through the veil in an attempt to co-relate the invisible to the visible. I do not treat this as mere psychological mapping, but a substantive attempt at grouping, visualising, displaying and interpreting an objective reality, which is governed by laws, inhabited by life, experiencing growth and undergoing constant change. The Tarot is our map to this reality.

[APRIL 2007]

Tuesday 10th. 8.15pm. Eight of Swords. Geoffri greeted me, but there were also many other unknown figures hanging around. I was confused, but then remembered the importance of experiencing this Inner World from the perspective of one's own body, looking out through one's own eyes. This action provided the clarity required, and with the shadowy figures all gone I now felt more comfortable in my surroundings.

I could feel sharp white stones under my bare feet, then realising that I was in a quarry, with Geoffri directly in front of me. I could discern two other beings, one small unknown directly to the right and one dark hooded figure in the background. All doubts about Geoffri were resolved as soon as I re-confirmed my point of view. I now turned to the figure in the foreground and enquired on its identity. At this the being disappeared in a flash, leaving only Geoffri and the dark hooded figure, black cape, face and body invisible, standing impassive. The next thing I remember I was flying high into the air with Geoffri and could see the shimmering Temple in the mountains to the left, but we did not travel there today and returned to the ground.

There was something happening over to my left and with Geoffri I forward rolled through the air toward it. The landscape was green and lush. There was a crumbling old house with broken drains and gutters. A woman outside was injured, with a crutch lying on the floor. She was bedraggled and greasy haired with mess, filth, and dirty small urchin type children all around. The woman looked broken and ugly. However I felt that my viewpoint had shifted out of sync and I had the tiniest sense of watching myself. I re-orientated immediately, to occupy my body within the Inner World. As soon as I did this I could see all around me that the scene was the chaos and destruction, but now the woman herself was beautiful, with brilliant sparkling eyes. I asked if I could help her and we kissed. She said that all she needed was support and then she would be fine. I lifted her up and she leaned on me because of her broken leg. Immediately she was able to cope with everything, to be able to sort out her own situation for herself. All she needed was support. Not what I was expecting at all.

Geoffri and I rose high up in the air. I looked down to the woman who was waving her thanks. We rose and rose, high into the sky of the Inner World, up toward the Temple and through its floor. I could feel the same presence I had felt many times before, and I felt light and free with a lump in my throat. But I also felt that this experience was maybe not for today so I allowed myself to drift back down to Earth. I glimpsed the Library hovering in the distance. I saw the woman one more time and we kissed goodbye. I felt her name to be Mary, or maybe Maria?

It was time to go and Geoffri wished me well. The dark hooded figure was still lingering behind him. He (or she) came forward slightly and shook my hand.

"Are you next?" I said.

"Yes."

"But I haven't been with Geoffri for five minutes," I protested.

"That's OK," said Geoffri himself, indicating that all would be revealed once I returned home to the Outer World.

Realisations: I was committed to establishing a best practice for these journeys, and I felt that through trial and error I was getting there. Total relaxation, on a foundation of personal progress in the Outer World, went hand in hand with this work. Learning and accepting the realities of Life, including the making of important mistakes, was also an essential partner to development in the Inner World.

The experience must always take place whilst in the body and looking through the eyes. Kisses must be on the body, handshakes must be with the hands, and while walking barefoot we must feel the surface underneath. 'Through my eyes, with my hands, on my feet.' I did not know where this motto had originated, but it was an essential part of the instruction, making all the difference in the quality of the encounter. Anything else was illusion and fantasy.

The Dark Path tempted me to overcomplicate the procedure, pre-empt the encounters, overly systematise the results and obsess over precise conclusions. The Light Path in contrast, would simply involve turning up, being present, engaging, recording, accepting, and – later on - concluding, once the heart and mind could find agreement.

Exploring the Inner World through the scenes of the Tarot was turning into a multi level initiation, each card bringing something new to learn, a new scene, new beings, new thoughts and feelings. A serious Life Qualification might even be bestowed if I could one day pass all seventy-eight stages. Maybe?

Thursday 12th. 8.00pm. Temperance. I could sense a dog barking by my left foot. Looking down I resisted the urge to kick it away and instead asked it what the matter was. The animal gestured toward my right, behind Geoffri, to the cloaked figure of the previous encounter. I enquired if she was my next Guide?

"Yes." Her eyes were piercing but I could see nothing else of her.

"Isn't this a bit quick?" I asked. Surprisingly she agreed with me. I looked to Geoffri but I was again unsure – what was it that continually made me wary of him?

Over to my left was a naked and beautiful girl, with long dark hair. She was standing by a stream measuring water into cups. She stood in front of a simple wooden machine that appeared to be doing the same. Adjustment – Re-adjustment. Balance – Re-balance. Give – Take. Give – Receive. She continued with these basic messages while I looked at here. She was soft and not at all grasping, as ready and willing to pick up the cups as to put them down again. My eyes were drawn to a pathway behind her, which snaked off to the left. It rose high up into the hills, spiralling round and round, and I set off in that direction. As I rose I was urging Geoffri to stay close, but he was struggling to keep up. I finally found myself in a hallway, the sensation of arrival was similar to that in the palace, yet things seemed different here. This was a corridor as much as a hall – long with one doorway at the end and two pillars on either side of the door. I seemed to be looking down on it. Each wall was painted different colours but the shades seemed unusual and not of the colour spectrum I was familiar with, yet at the same time perfectly correct and appropriate. A voice came from the distance.

"He does not know what is going on!" it cried.

"He soon will," said another. I was wary, and descended out the way I came and back down to the Earth, again to be greeted by Geoffri and the new hooded figure. She was unhappy that I had gone on without her and I again expressed my wariness and unreadiness to leave Geoffri, even after all the struggles I had been through in order to accept him. Amidst this inner turmoil I returned to Geoffri and sat down on the floor, cross legged in front of him. He assumed the same position, such that we were eye to eye.

"Who are you?" I asked, experiencing a case of extreme self-doubt.

"Geoffri, your Guide," he replied.

"How do I know that?" I asked.

"Because I am you. Because I love you," he reached forward to touch my arm. It felt genuine and warm.

"So why do I resist?" I asked. As soon as I had verbalised the question the awareness came flooding in. I needed to resolve the nature of my relationship with Arthur and then let it be. I was to journey back to see Geoffri regularly. I was to ask Arthur if he required anything from me, and to understand what an effect he had had on me for such a long time. His effect upon me ought not to be underestimated and some loneliness at his inevitable death must be expected. I ought to take as many opportunities as are available for illumination, grab them all, because although tiring, his current state is better than the alternative. If I could place my relationship with Arthur in its rightful position, in perspective, good and bad, then further progress awaits. At this, Geoffri gestured toward the new being, and indicated that much awaited me, when I was ready. I felt like it might not be too long.

I hovered around for a while. Here had been a practical illustration of the value of conversing directly with your Guide. It was just a question of putting that advice into practice. But impatience was my enemy and I wanted instant enlightenment, indeed this had been the problem all along with Arthur, though I was starting to realise that where I could allow things to develop over time then they often did so more fully and wholeheartedly.

Tuesday 17th. 8.15pm. The Tower. In the semi-relaxed state prior to entry it seemed as if I could already see the landscape, but with my eyes open, overlaid and in between the table, chair and bookcase of the Outer World. The room around me turned visibly misty and milky and I could feel Geoffri's presence at my shoulder. I was in the Inner World, but not. In the Outer World, but not. I could imagine how this might become dangerous, but I persisted until I was completely transported through.

To my left was a collapsing wooden building, raised on broken stilts, the scene having been recently struck by lightning. There were two men, one with his head in his hands mourning the disaster, one busily combing the wreckage, already suspecting the causes of the problem and urgently trying to rebuild.

I saw Geoffri to my right and greeted him, forcing myself to check his identity. He confirmed, and immediately I was aware of many other figures around him, who, in the next breath vanished in a puff of light and smoke. Except for the now increasingly familiar, small, hooded figure.

The Library appeared, hovering slightly in the air. I jumped up the steps and burst in through the door, immediately looking up and around. The building itself was always draped in an electric blue light, which emanated from the billions of individual electric blue lights, one for each book. I reached up above The Keepers table to the book marked with the name of a close friend. The contents presented themselves in their usual direct manner, "...some sadness, a life incompatible with expectations." I reached a little further along the shelf to my own book. The Keeper appeared, suddenly active, pointing forcibly at me with his staff.

"Take care," he said, 'be sure that you truly wish to know." How could I not? I peeked inside my book, "..sadness and pain, caused by impatience and one's own actions." There was more, but the words tailed off to nothing as I concluded that this was enough. I assumed that the contents of the book were my potential future, although I did not confirm this. Or maybe it was my past, or maybe an inevitable future? Whichever way it was I found myself ejected from the Library, landing on my back on the ground. I looked up at Geoffri, and saw the new figure in the dark cloak sitting beside him. I could see a little more of her now, but she was still very unclear. She held out her hand. It was tiny and thin, fragile and gentle. Geoffri once more indicated that all was well and that this character was the future. As I moved toward the Tower on the left she seemed to advance with us both, just a few paces to the side and behind.

I approached the remorseful man, and looked directly at him, asking if he required any help. This seemed to comfort him a little, but he really wanted to know what his disaster had been about, what it had been for?

"To learn from," I said, thinking I could guide him that far at least. "Mistakes always lead to learning, and then always lead to progress." The clarity of my own answer surprised me.

His friend was still climbing up the damaged building, hoping he could save it. He had a checklist with him.

"This was wrong," he spoke, ticking things off. "Yes, this joist was poor. I can fix this." And then to another, "and this. This can be mended." He progressed through his work quickly and enthusiastically, wanting to get to the core of it. The forlorn man was uplifted when I pointed toward his friend and indicated that at least those who learn the lessons can escape repeating them. He now joined in and set about the task of repairs, but with more deliberation than his eager friend.

I now felt a tickle in my throat, and a need to cough. It became uncontrollable, and I snapped back to the Outer World. Geoffri shook my hand, elbow to elbow as I departed, repeating his frequently used parting words.

"Come back soon."

Monday 30th. 8.00pm. Eight of Swords. I entered with the specific purpose of visiting the Library for information that might help one of my Outer World clients. As I moved toward the Inner World I felt Geoffri's arm come out to greet me. At that point I felt myself to be in two worlds at once.

The Library was straight in front of me, hovering just off the ground, and Geoffri urged me not to delay. I entered but could not find the required book on the shelves, until I realised that it was already open on a lectern straight in front of me! The Keeper was again present, as was a smaller, younger, friendlier figure. As the old man instilled an element of apprehension and urgency, the younger assistant made me feel that I could relax and take my time.

The information I required came flooding through. My role was to help her distinguish her essence from her appearance. The precise words that I needed to say to her became clear. She believed that she was cursed, and suddenly I had the perfect form of words to counter her superstition. That was all, but it was enough. Clear, direct and unambiguous. I wished The Keepers assistant goodbye and found myself once again with Geoffri, and the unknown hooded figure. Still not fully clear, she seemed less threatening and lighter than before. I turned to Geoffri and asked him what life was like when he was still alive in the Outer World.

"Do you want to see?" he said. Of course I did. He walked through the air and disappeared through some kind of portal. I followed and suddenly we were both elsewhere, flying high above a castle. At first I felt myself watching myself, and knowing this to be wrong I pulled myself back into my body.

There was now a large dining room, with plenty of food arranged over a large table. I could see a man – Geoffri, me – wearing a golden crown and next to him was a woman, very attractive, with a pink headdress. It was a classic medieval scene, yet real and multi-dimensional. Suddenly I was back through the portal back to the Inner World.

I looked over toward Geoffri's right and was greeted by a woman crawling around on her hands and knees, not quite destitute or in poverty, but restricted and boxed in by eight swords stuck fast in the ground in an irregular pattern, close enough together to block any escape. She tried to reach though the swords toward me, but cut herself. I reached through to her without difficulty, my hand passing straight through a sword without pain or injury. To try to give the woman a little respite I forced one of the sword deeper in the ground, right up to its hilt, enabling her to step out momentarily. The sword rose back up slowly however, and she willingly climbed back in before it returned to its original position. She was grateful, having at least seen some light at the end of her tunnel. I wished her goodbye, and returned to the centre of the scene. I sensed that it would not be long now before I would properly meet with my new Guide. The mountains in the background caught my eye, but I returned home to the Outer World.

[MAY 2007]

Saturday 5th. 10.30am. Three of Swords. Having divined the card I entered to be greeted by Geoffri, and the unknown figure, again behind him and to the left. The Library appeared directly ahead, and Geoffri urged me to attend.

I asked once more of my close friend, and the book appeared on the lectern "...sadness, but with a desire to be happy. Leave her in this world in a better condition than when you found her." I had no real desire to interpret this, but many thoughts flashed through my mind.

"You know the answer," came the voice of The Keeper. Suddenly I was out of the Library and next to a warring couple, attacking each other with words. Words full of expectation, belief and disappointment. Words full of hurt. Then my concentration was lost and I felt myself drifting, suddenly aware that I was outside of everything, looking down. I could see – actually see – the outline of the entire galaxy, beautiful and complete in its own right, full of billions of individual stars, single and different points of light. Although I now felt a pull back to my physical body I could not get hold of myself at first. Eventually I returned home, disorientated. It took a little time to get myself straight.

Monday 14th. Ten of Pentacles. Geoffri was present, but this time I approached the Inner World through a door preceded by a walled pathway. New awareness came flooding in. I asked for insight on earthly, mundane matters and answers regarding another one of my pupils came easily – frustration, unfulfilled ambitions, and unfulfilled potential. But why?

"Emotions are the essence of humanity," I was told. "The human body is composed of 75% water and the fourth creature in the World card is human, showing water and emotions. The urge of humanity is to feel, yet like all things imbalance is fatal." So many need emotional expression, I thought, but this is both dangerous and limiting if it fails to recognise the other elements of life. My pupil was totally governed by how she felt, but how could she separate her mood from accurate inner guidance? And how might she, and others, free themselves from being prisoners of emotions? After all, negative emotions are so readily held onto, for they are often viewed as better than no emotions at all. The voice then continued, "to open up the full world, you must open up to your emotions – let all the hurt inside out and then be free of it, free to understand it and ready to transcend it. You must unburden yourselves of your negative feelings and emotional hurt before you can strike any balance and then progress in life."

My attention now turned toward a castle on the left, populated by the scene from the card. There was a happy man, proud of his mastery of the physical, and a miserable woman for whom this meant nothing. I was reminded of one of Arthur's old sayings, "A man's greatest disappointment is often his status. A woman's greatest disappointment is often her man."

[JUNE 2007]

Wednesday 6th. 8.00am. The Lovers. This journey simply involved a partial disconnection from the Outer World and heightened awareness of the meaning of this card. I did not journey, but in the half-way state insights flooded into my mind.

I looked at the two figures together. Partnership, relationship, co-operation – these things cannot be discounted or ignored. There is always the negative, but the human connection offers the chance to overcome it. The ultimate partnership is with your Guide. But being unable or unwilling to meet ones Guide indicates the influence of the Dark Side. Once the Dark Side grips you it is very difficult to see it or to do anything about it. This is heart breaking to watch, but it need not be that way. The balance brought by a Human-Guide connection makes it possible to help others to overcome their Dark Sides, for everyone must learn in the end.

[JULY 2007]

Tuesday 10th. 8pm. Five of Swords. A troubling time in the Outer World had preceded this journey, hence the gap in my explorations. Geoffri immediately greeted me on my right. He was more colourful and vivid than I remembered. He wore a multi-coloured long tunic, had bright eyes and a ginger beard and hair. He beckoned behind him to my old friend Kalia, to a vague shape behind her and then yet another who wore a black gown.

"Behold the future!" He exclaimed and the unknown figure removed her gown. She was beautiful and I felt an instantly strong connection with her. Although I could not precisely discern her features she glowed with a pink, green and blue aura showing sex, warmth and compassion all at once. I embraced her and became part of her energy. It was unlike anything I had seen or experienced before. Her name – I think – was Saria – although I could not determine this or anything else for certain.

We both travelled off to the left, toward the Temple where I seemed to enter the hall. I felt energy and shapes around me but my mind began to drift, and I felt myself back on the ground of the Inner World, but in a new scene. There were now two men, one hurt and angry, cloaked, on his hands and knees scurrying to pick up his belongings. Another, further along the road, was dead. Saria was immediately communicative when I asked her what had happened.

"We must press on," she replied, "always forward, even when disaster strikes we must learn the lesson, change and go forward. It hurts but it must always be forward." The man on his hands and knees confirmed her words, begrudgingly.

I remained in Saria's company for a while, simply enjoying being there. I asked her for healing on my shoulder and I felt a surge of energy throughout my body, so much so that I had to breathe deeply in order to take it in. I felt renewed, as if injected with a new breath of life.

"Will I see Geoffri again?" I asked.

"Not for a while," she replied. I moved to return home and she remained large in the scene until I opened my eyes. She was magnificent and I loved her.

Realisation: These beings - from the first unclear one to Kalia, Geoffri and now Saria - wanted to help. It seemed to be their prime motivation.

CHAPTER IV

SARIA

[JULY 2007]

Thursday 26th. 8.00pm. The Magician. I was immediately greeted by a very dark lady, dressed in colourful Indian robes. She looked regal, like a powerful Indian goddess. Something was amiss though, her features were too clear and her energy too aggressive, so I looked beyond and to the right. Now I could see a plainer figure, dressed in a simple robe with a hood obscuring her face. As she came nearer I could feel the last remnants of Geoffri's presence gently dissolve.

She came up closer and it was Saria. She removed her robes and underneath she was naked and beautiful. We embraced and kissed, she was magnificent and sensual. We made love; she was active, but feminine. She was a woman who needed a man, yet she was comfortable in her womanhood.

We uncoupled and I approached the Library to be greeted warmly by The Keeper – and for once he had some time to spare. I asked about matters of the Outer World, particularly a close friend, and I was transported to a different part of the Library with a new text in my hands.

"She is not fulfilling her life's purpose. She is creating a nest and amusing herself but is not fulfilled. Another academic course of study will help to rebalance her."

I pondered on this information, and how I might make use of it, but The Keeper grew impatient. I left the Library and fell back into Saria's arms. We made love again. Saria was a wonderful being of love and affection, warmth and knowledge. She accepted me as I accepted her. We remained in this embrace for sometime but then I remembered that the Magician was nearby so we approached him. He was tall, strong, muscular and bearded and worked physically at something that was more a bench than an altar. He was powerful indeed and admitted that he could make anything happen that he wished.

"But *should* I? That is the real question," he remarked. I asked of matters in the Outer World, of a goal I had been striving for. "Oh yes, it is perfectly possible. But is it desirable?" I did know how to answer this, so after a short while he explained himself. "If you set out to make something happen then you are unavoidably saying that you can justify and explain why that thing should be present or absent. You must know that all is written already and if you force the hand of the Universe then you are saying that you know better than the Universe. And maybe you do, but you had better be certain. For if you don't know better and you still force the hand of the Universe then your essential learning will have been averted, except that the learning cannot ever be averted. So the lesson, whatever it might be, will come round again – harder and faster than before." Complex but helpful stuff, I thought. Could I do anything for the Magician I asked?

"Think about these words first," he said. I promised to try.

I embraced Saria again and kissed her affectionately. She was real, yet not composed of earthly stuff. Electric, magnetic, ephemeral, full of light, with a kind of a form but also malleable. This had indeed been an insightful journey, full of experiences and information.

Monday 30th. 8.00pm. Queen of Wands. I saw the image of the card through half closed eyes and entered easily. Saria was on my right, dancing, dressed in very little, attractive and light, positive and open. We embraced and I become a part of her, though without her becoming a part of me. We held this state for some time, indeed if I'd had the chance I might have held onto it forever. But no, for the Queen of Wands seemed to call out. We approached her, hand in hand, very close. Saria was not totally distinguishable, but her presence was real.

The Queen sat on her throne, in command of all she surveyed. I knelt at her feet. She wanted me to do this but yet, at the same time it also displeased her. She told me what she required.

"I want someone who will do as I say, yet never do as I say. I want to dominate and be dominated. I will never allow myself to look up to someone, to worship or fear them, or to look down in pity or anger. I must be with one who is perceived as my equal. For in that lies safety and full enjoyment. Fear or worship creates distance between us which makes entering fully into a relationship almost impossible." At that she disappeared from view.

I turned back to Saria. What could she teach me? She proceeded to shrink to the size of a grain of sand and I did the same, so small as to be almost invisible. Then I felt what it was like to be the size of a grain of sand – utterly dependent on others for meaning and existence. What is a single grain of sand? It was such a limited existence, yet to be part of something much bigger – a beach, for example – provided meaning and purpose.

We returned to full size and made love again. It was so real, almost as if she was really there in the physical. I could feel her and sense her. We embraced and kissed, I slowly departed, uncoupling our hands as I departed. This was a fantastic new relationship.

[AUGUST 2007]

Thursday 9th. 6.30pm. The Devil. Entry was difficult. My body was tired and I had not eaten since the morning. My mind was in overdrive and I could not help but replay the events of past few days, over and over. Eventually, my tension eased a little and I saw immediately to my left a dark coloured horse, worn and ugly, from which guttural and bestial sounds emanated. I then greeted a woman on my right with long flowing dark hair and lustrous white skin. I could not see her face and was a little unsure of who she was. I called for Saria and this figure gave way, but kept coming back. She was beautiful, but I could not be certain who she was. I wrestled with this for a little while, but came to the conclusion that it must indeed be Saria, although I did not actually ask her!

Together we approached a nearby house. She asked whether I really wanted to see inside. Now hesitating I did not enter but observed through a window. There was a male figure roughly penetrating a woman over a table. This was animalistic control, not love, but compulsion. The difference between this scene and my relationship with Saria was stark. I embraced Saria and we kissed for what seemed like a magickal eternity.

I reflected upon the scene. The man was undoubtedly exerting his control over the woman, and to an extent they both fed on this, but it also seemed as if the man himself was controlled, as if something else was feeding upon him, and by extension, her. I felt myself floating high above the scene now, Saria trying to call me back down. I did as she asked, but not without some difficulty. I now felt totally disconnected from my physical body and in a new and unfamiliar state of awareness. It took some time to reconnect. Feeling totally spaced out on my return I was certain that something significant had been revealed. If only I could put my finger on it.

Monday 20th. 8.00pm. The Cave. I visualised the beach that led into the cave, and then, once inside I passed through a hole near to the ground, shrinking to the size required in order to pour myself through. Appearing on the other side I was greeted warmly by a small, pale skinned and naked female. She wore shoulder length, straight black hair and blue and gold jewellery about her neck and wrists, and no clothes. Ever cautious, I addressed her directly.

"Are you my Guide?"

"Yes, of course," she smiled warmly. I smiled back and knew that it was Saria, although she seemed different to our last meeting. We embraced and kissed but before long a wave of information and ideas overwhelmed me as I followed her down a stream of never-ending steps. Where did she come from? Was it China, or France? The answers came. She was a servant girl, a slave, in the 1200's in France. But I had saved her, she said. These words made no sense. I did not know how I had saved her and she would not tell me. Hang on a minute, is this my Guide? I was satisfied that it was, but I could offer no explanation as to what she meant.

Gradually the scene faded and we were back in the place where we met. We made love. She was unashamed, and at the end we were both transformed. She wanted love, needed it, she grew from it and changed because of it. She looked different now, stronger, taller, and grander. She had been fed with love. As I was depleted so she grew, and as the woman was deprived so the man grew. I felt very strongly that this ever shifting balance was universally true, and harmony could be found by the simple art of give and take in order that both might grow. I embraced her and returned home to the Outer World, though not as dazed as usual. Today's communication had been directly with my Guide and not all of it had been verbal. I left with a new sense of knowing – and some new ideas.

Monday 27th. 8.00pm. The Cave. I could feel Saria's presence before I even arrived in the landscape, but today my concentration was scattered and broken and so was my journey.

Her appearance was as last time. Small, with straight black hair. Pale skin, curvy and not skinny. We embraced and I felt her sexual energy emanate strongly.

I glimpsed the Library on my left and approached, not knowing what to ask. I greeted The Keeper with a handshake, but then realised that it was not him at all. The real Keeper was dressed in blue robes over toward the right. I approached and asked for information about the state of affairs of my Outer World. The insights came clearly and directly and I remained in front of The Keeper for some time longer, but my mind was drifting. I was not ready to explore any further in his presence. I sensed that his nature might be described by some as virtually God-like, and that he maybe resided up in the Temple or visited there from time to time. I did not know any of this for sure though.

I rolled out of the room and toward the floor. I saw Saria again, but my head was full of disconnected ideas and visions and I had to leave in order to record them. We embraced and I returned home.

"Take care of the small things," she said, "before they become big things."

Realisations: It seemed that everything in the Inner World, every sense, intimation, clue or inference springs forth exactly at the required moment. What is given there always seems to be significant, absent of trivia, debate or commentary. In the Outer World we are constantly practising – maybe quite rightly – assessment, discernment and judgement, sifting the wheat from the chaff. But in the Inner World everything seems loaded with meaning, and a stressful, complicated Outer World only seems to block our connection to and understanding of this. I was starting to conclude that a simplification of my Outer World was called for, in order that these Inner Realms may expand. I was unsure how I might go about this, but from looking around at others I was absolutely certain that a complex Outer World did not support a burgeoning Inner one.

[SEPTEMBER 2007]

Wednesday 12th. 9.00pm. The Cave. I perceived Saria immediately and we embraced warmly. Again, she was smaller than me with straight black hair. We turned together to face the Inner World. Its colours were luminous and vivid. People and creatures seemed to be all around us and I could access the Library seemingly at will.

"What can you tell me?" I asked her.

"Anything you need to know," she replied, very matter-of-fact. I asked where I should look to purchase a property in Cheltenham.

"Suffolk Square or Suffolk Row," she replied, "That is where you need to be. It will suit you." I returned, half dazed. It was a very short but very clear and intense experience. On my return it seemed as though the very essence of the natural world, its colours and vibration, had changed.

Realisation: My bond with Saria was very real and this seemed to help to improve the overall experience. I concluded that it was important to take the trouble to get close to the Guide. I wish I had done more of that with Geoffri.

In Hindsight: After many months I finally bought a flat some half a mile away from the location Saria described. It was a different vibe entirely and although the flat had been acceptable at first, I went on to experience severe noisy neighbour problems, which ultimately cost time, money and energy. The property failed to live up to expectations and in the end I landed up renting it out. It had been a bad move, one that so easily could have been avoided. The lesson? The wise and mature person acts upon whatever is said by their Guide, however unwelcome, illogical or unlikely it may seem.

Monday 17th. 9pm. The Cave. I embraced Saria and we flew up in the air of the Inner World, her on my back. Ascending up through the floor and into the Hall of the Temple I felt a lump in my throat and my consciousness halted at that point. My breath quickened, but as I tried to moderate it I felt my whole being move in time with my breathing. I suddenly felt very light and my awareness was moving around all over the place – present in totally different Outer World places within split seconds of each other. First I was in Berlin, then London, Cheltenham, remote and rural Cotswolds, then Northamptonshire. Distance seemed to be no barrier, and although I what I could 'see' of these places was very limited I had a powerful sense of being present in each of them. Although this whole experience did not last long it was draining, and I soon felt tired and disorientated. The experience was "borderline astral projection," said Saria. She understood my exhaustion and wished me to "rest, then return soon, where all will be revealed". Upon arrival back in the Outer World I felt spacey and disconnected.

[OCTOBER 2007]

Saturday 6th. 4.00pm. The Cave. I was happy to greet Saria almost immediately. She looked the same as before, wearing just as few clothes. We embraced. I looked into her eyes. They were big and blue, open and welcoming. The Outer World had been exceptionally demanding, and looking into Saria's eyes was the last thing I remember before I must have dozed off. Was it possible to fall asleep in the Inner World? If it was then I had managed it. I had a vague sense of receiving information during this time, but I cannot recall what.

Realisations: Although my sleep was more restorative than it used to be, I was never truly totally asleep. As a teenager and young adult I remember undergoing what I referred to as a complete shutdown during sleep time, a thick black line of total demarcation between one day and the next. But now I was acutely aware that such a thing was no longer happening at all and that life was *always on going*. It might be punctuated occasionally by rest in the form of sleep, and then sooner or later by a longer and deeper rest in the form of a death, but the process of Life marched on and we were never completely free of it. As such our story would never really end, and the consequences of our actions would forever stay with us. During sleep time our awareness of all may be dialled down, but never, it seemed to me, totally extinguished. Even in sleep there seemed to be no escape. Even in sleep I was still wide awake.

Monday 29th. 7.30pm. The Cave. I needed to know how, specifically, I might help one of my clients. I asked this of Saria and we were instantly faced with the Library. I rolled forward inside and greeted The Keeper, who enquired as to my purpose. As I answered the book of her life appeared before me. I placed my hands on it and absorbed all the information. There was a great deal said, and although not all of it was pleasant, it was helpful providing an explanation of what was wrong, followed by an understanding of what to do about it. I thanked The Keeper and dissolved away from the Library. Saria appeared in front of me again and I thanked her, moving to depart. I raised my hands to hers in a kind of 'High Five' fashion. In the moment of contact she imbued me with power that coursed down my hands and arms until I could feel it in my whole body.

Emerging back into the Outer World I visualised my client imbued with this power that I had received from Saria. I imagined her cleansed and strengthened, at least for the meantime. It took some time for this charge to dissipate and for me to start to feel normal again.

Postscript: Throughout this time I continued to develop my own private practice, giving readings, tuition, healing and assistance. My efforts were always concentrated on a small number of ever changing clients for whom I solved problems and unpicked dilemmas, a handful of irregular students who dropped in and out for tuition of one kind or another, and a larger group of people for whom thirty minutes of insight and guidance would be enough for a lifetime. I could see that the Outer World was a deeply challenging place for many people - simply getting out of bed was too much some and even when folk tried to move forward they seemed beset on all sides. In order to stay clear of a deluge I avoided offering unsolicited help and intervened directly in people's affairs only in rare cases, when specifically requested to do so. These instances really were the exception, after all, who could imagine that such things were possible, least of all by me? But in those unusual instances I responded and appealed to the Inner Realms for knowledge and assistance to guide them. For without this, it seemed to me, they would be utterly lost.

[NOVEMBER 2007]

Monday 12th. 7.30pm. Nine of Wands. I approached this journey in a more ritualistic fashion, preparing myself and the space with great care. The small act of lighting a candle seemed to help me focus and I did this deliberately and slowly. I felt I had been neglecting my work here and needed to reconnect with it respectfully and reverentially. These words grated with the Outer World me, but I felt them to be very necessary here.

I recognised Saria and embraced her warmly. I also saw many people from the Outer World and gained insight into their situations in relation to mine. Holding myself at this halfway-point enabled me to unbundle some complex Outer World issues and to say things to people's faces in here, that I could not (or would not) say to them out there. Too much had been happening in the Outer World, not all of it good, and although I had not intended for the visit to pan out like this it was, in fact, just what I needed.

I asked about one particular individual, one of a pair of twins, the significance and truth of this phenomenon. The answer was direct and unexpected.

I now spotted some steps and railings, leading up to a doorway. The door was old, heavy and unfamiliar. I knocked. It opened. I entered.

"Is this the Library?" I asked.

"No," came the clear answer. I ventured further. It was dark, but I felt that in here I could gain knowledge of things yet to come. "This is the doorway to Outer Space," came the same voice. All this seemed surprising and unfamiliar, in a way that my Inner World contact had not been for some time. I asked further questions related to my Outer World and received clear and unambiguous replies. Amidst the all enveloping darkness there was life, voices and points of light. I could make out a passageway which led down a corridor. I moved along and felt myself going deeper and deeper, seemingly for a very long time. The further and deeper I went the more disconnected from the Outer World I became. There was a light at the end of the tunnel, behind a curtain. I reached out to pull it back and I was immediately engulfed with a powerful white light which filled my very being from within. I soaked up all that I could get until the light was exhausted, returning back up the passageway, almost floating now, out of the darkness, out of the door and back to Saria. I felt bigger, more alive, more knowing, more accepting than I felt before, but also more disconnected and fuzzy headed when I finally opened my eyes.

The Outer World I now returned to seemed alien and strange, even unnatural, needlessly problematic and difficult. I thought that this was a strange assessment for me to make and it took some time to return fully, the disconnection so great that I wondered whether I would ever return fully. What was that place? How could I go there again? I thanked all concerned, from the distance of the Outer World and sat quietly for a few minutes. Everything around me looked and felt different now. I was accustomed to transformative experiences, in the parlance of some I had 'died' during these trips many times already, and perhaps I had become too glib about this? But this experience was the most intense so far. Did it signal the end of a dark period of my life, or was this just another signpost along its road? I looked at the clock. It was 8.40pm, almost an hour since I had entered the Inner World.

Tuesday 13th. 7.30pm. Two of Cups. I was troubled by some indigestion, but I persisted nonetheless. Travelling through the doorway of the card I was not at all clear where I had landed. Trying to relax into the unfamiliar, I used this time to review and dispense with outstanding matters of the day. This helped, temporarily, allowing new thoughts to flood into a clearer space. These thoughts were less heavy and afforded me a better outlook.

I felt myself to be in a court room, facing a severe judge, but this scene faded as quickly as it came and I greeted Saria, embraced her, and then walked hand in hand toward the same steps as before. At the top of them I could see a doorway opening up and although I asked Saria to enter with me she would not. Alone, I ascended the steps and the door opened immediately. I could feel the intense white light once more and ran toward it, down the corridor, deeper and, deeper, until I was completely engulfed by it. It was full of love and healing energy, filling me up from within. I took my fill until there was no more left and I returned to Saria who was waiting by the doorway as I emerged. We made love right there. I wished her well and returned home.

Realisations: My indigestion had definitely affected the experience. I likened it to the old days of watching television through the interference. You could follow the story and even see the picture in parts, but it gave you a headache and earache. Delicate preparation of the physical body was so important.

Saturday 17th. 10am. The Sun. Saria's name became clearer to me now, spelt or pronounced more like 'Sa-ria'. She was much shorter than me with a big smile and straight black hair. We embraced and she told me that my travels in the Inner World were to be written in depth as "Adventures Within". She continued.

"The Inner World contains common themes, applicable to all people, yet as in the Outer World there are personal differences. Use your Eleven vibration to explore and master this. Document it all. Skills and methods to string the experiences together meaningfully will follow."

I saw the Sun, high in the sky, and asked it to come down in human form. A male shape of flaming red detached itself from the Sun in the sky, appeared before us and touched my heart. I was energised and repaired, but I did not dare take too much.

I watched the Sun-Man and Saria talking, although I did not understand their language. It was part telepathy, part speech and part unintelligible sound. I enquired what they were doing.

"Silence!" came the sharp reply from the Sun, who was clearly the authority here. I apologised profusely and they continued their in-depth exchange. When they were finished the Sun asked me if I wanted anything. After some agonising I asked him to direct his rays toward an ex-colleague who had lost her way in the Outer World.

"A good request," said the Sun-Man, "but I cannot do that. You, however, can help her, by showing and reminding her of her path. She must appeal to me directly, which of course she is currently unable to do." I thanked the Sun-Man, who at that moment morphed back into the rest of the Sun in the sky. I turned to Saria.

"Where next?" I asked.

"The Temple," she suggested.

A vagueness of Outer World issues crept in again, but after a while the image of the Temple, high in the mountains, was clear once more. Suddenly I was within, swirling around its colours and energies.

"What is this Temple dedicated to?" I asked.

"You," came the answer. "You and everyone else, your potential, all that you can be." I again felt energised and stood, arms outstretched, receiving and sensing its aura and power. Within this Temple I was elevated, but perhaps I did not fully realise how much, for good and ill. It occurred to me that I had spent a good deal of time in the Outer World over the years, looking for a dodge, a shortcut, and a fast track to exactly this kind of experience. I realised what a waste of time that was and saw that I had consistently been nudged exactly where I needed to be at each stage. All I now had to do was to review, understand and assimilate it all. But my full acceptance of what I had received was still absent.

I returned to Saria, thanked her again, kissed, embraced and returned to the Outer World.

Realisation: Could I really expect to assimilate, understand and accept my Inner World experiences during one thirty minute session, once a week? Obviously the answer was no, but right now that was all I could handle.

Tuesday 20th. 8.00pm. Two of Wands. I was concerned, and in great doubt. Was this Saria or not? The harder I looked at the person in front of me the less sure I became. And the more I looked past the False Guides the more they kept appearing. In the end I abandoned any attempt at a connection with Saria and looked elsewhere in the scene.

Managing to scramble aboard the Chariot as it sped off, we flew high into the sky at great speed. I accepted the reins, but instantly regretted it, for I did not have the required skill or control to stop us careering though the air with increasing speed and danger. Finally, in a state of virtual exhaustion I managed to wrestle the vehicle under some control and brought her to a halt on the ground. It was a demanding experience. I thanked the Charioteer, and the suddenly present Saria. How could I learn to drive this Chariot? Or perhaps the question should be how could I become a better Charioteer? It seemed to be as much about my attitude as my knowledge. What did the Chariot represent? My mind turned to my practice of readings and tuition. Regardless of the superficial reasons given, people contacted me because on some level they recognised a chance to experience some Light. But they might only recognise that for one moment, so it was important to try to build on their enthusiasm swiftly, before the Dark Side in them re-established control. Client appointments for dates way off in the future were rarely kept to, so the opportunity, like in the Chariot, arrives in the moment. I was thankful for this realisation as I had frequently witnessed clients self-sabotage, vacillate and generally fight themselves when trying to keep future appointments. I would now deal with this differently.

Postscript: Preparing my handwritten diary for publication, the first part of today's entry appears barely legible, a spider's web of scratchy letters and half-spelt words. This was a classic indicator – as highlighted by Arthur years before - of the lingering presence of a False Guide. These dark characters might be figments of imagination, embodiments of internal fears, unresolved issues, functions of the dead hands of myth and fantasy or expressions of religion. These were no less real for being false. They might be just the right kind of attractive, but their web of deceit, carefully spun by ourselves upon ourselves, must be penetrated in order to reach for the Light, the Light that is frightening, affording no hiding place nor offering any shades of grey. My experience of False Guides is that they never deal straightforwardly, so I have concluded that there is no point trying to engage, argue, or fight with them, for in fact this only strengthens them. Instead, I simply look beyond.

I try to practice the same in the Outer World where I urge people to look beyond whatever is in front of them. They might then discover, for themselves, their True Guides. This will enrich both their Inner and Outer Worlds whereas the lies and distortions of False Guides degrade both. A true Inner World experience may not be easy or blissful, but over time the rewards will be obvious. The challenging nature of Life cannot be done away with, but I have learned to beware of those who profess a rich Inner World yet cannot tie their own shoe laces. There are exceptions to every rule, but it is unlikely that such people are visiting any world other than a totally imaginary one, populated by seemingly powerful and significant, yet False Guides. I have watched those whose lives career from one dramatic disaster to another, yet claim higher guidance in all that they do. They may well be guided, but falsely, and if truly then they can only be refusing that guidance.

Saturday 24th. 11.00am. Three of Cups. For what seemed like a long time there was only blackness, but when I finally called for Saria she came and embraced me immediately. We both looked around. The Sun was in the sky, but so was the Moon. I thought that we could have called down a visitor from the Moon, but we did not. The Temple was high in the mountains. It seemed different now and I could actually see my surroundings with my own eyes, rather than just in my mind's eye. Even though the image was a little unclear I looked around the Hall of the Temple and was greeted by a Sphinx. It spoke.

"I am an amalgam of the four living creatures, and I am available to do your bidding. But," warned the creature, "I will act when called, regardless of the merits or correctness of your request." So I must take responsibility and be the decider now. I dismissed the creature and said I would call on it only when required. The Temple now disappeared and I rolled back down to the ground, landing next to Saria. We saw a white doorway and enquired within, asking the reason for the inhabitants' clear and obvious unhappiness.

"Communication and honesty," they replied, "these should have been used to solve our issues as they arose, rather than allowing them to fester." We moved on.

I turned to Saria, and indicated that I needed to know more about her. She said to make a list of questions and visit through the Hermit next time. I returned home disorientated and markedly more tired than when I entered. My experience of seeing through closed eyes seemed a real breakthrough in the quality and realism of the experience. Maybe this was the pay-off for all the practise and persistence? I emerged into the candlelight of an unfamiliar Outer World. Everything looked and felt ever so slightly, imperceptibly changed.

Realisations: Way back when I first started these experiences I had been passive and receptive, the goal simply to be as sensory as possible in order that I notice as much as possible. This now seemed to be changing as the situations demanded my increasing involvement. It became increasingly empowering, but with a matching weight of responsibility. Maybe this responsibility could be handled better if we get the two worlds in balance? If the Inner World represents 50% of the Universe then shouldn't we spend 50% of our time and direct 50% of our energy there? The chains that fix us to the Outer World are strong and they seem to work hard to prevent this from happening.

Sunday 25th. 2.00pm. The Hermit. For once I had remembered to act on an Inner World suggestion. I found Saria and the Hermit sitting alone in the clearing of a forest, preparing a meal, surrounded by very few possessions. The presence of the Hermit seemed to be key to unlocking further detailed information about my Guide.

Her full name was Saria d'Estraing. She was a seventeen year old servant girl to the King of Aquitaine, in France, 1286AD. She was raped by the King and died that year. At that time she was beautiful with straight dark hair. In her short life she witnessed much, including great abuses of power. More importantly though, she said, in the Outer World all I needed to do was call and she would be there. I thanked her and the Hermit, who pointed out the pentacle imprints in my palms, but warned against their unwise use. I thanked him for this, kissed Saria goodbye and said I would return the following day.

On my return to the Outer World I immediately began to doubt my experience and question the facts as they had been communicated to me. I was fearful and fragile that something like that should have happened to Saria – to me. A voice spoke.

"Impatience is a sign of the inability to take the rough with the smooth."

Realisations: The King of Aquitaine in 1286 was the King of England, Edward I. Although lauded in history as a great king, I had no difficulty seeing him exactly as Saria had described.

Monday 26th. 7.30pm. Five of Cups. I could see Saria more clearly now, and she seemed more familiar, this being the third successive day of visiting. She addressed this, suggesting that I had seen a lot recently and maybe ought to take a day or two off to rebalance myself in the Outer World.

"There is much that needs to be done in that sphere to continue your overall progress, none of which should be taken for granted," she said.

I sat on a rock with my back to the usual entrance and surveyed the landscape before me. Directly in front was lush green grass, but then in the middle distance a couple of unidentified beings as the greenery changed into scrubland. Straight ahead in the far distance the Sun burned through a misty sky. To my left I could see the shore, a rocky one, and the sea beyond it. To the right of the shore in the distance were the mountains that contained the Temple. Back to my point of view, and to my right there was much less clarity – large areas of darkness. Saria remarked that these dark areas would be visited soon enough.

The Library appeared some distance in front of me and I dived through the door way, greeting the blue clad Keeper with deference. He was pleased with this but still abrupt, asking me to come to the point. I asked about a client in the Outer World and The Keeper banged his staff on the solid floor with a loud crash.

"You already have that information!" I asked instead of another and new awareness washed over me, "...sadness, disappointment, illness, defeat and resignation. Disconnection from reality. Look beyond her to her husband, whose ambition and ideas she has followed, to her own detriment." There was no book however and the Library quickly faded away. I thanked The Keeper and departed, surveying the scene once more before returning to the Outer World. The scope of the scene was deeper, longer, richer, more colourful and longer lasting than ever.

Realisations: As instructed by Saria I took a good look back through my diary. My Guardian came first, to provide basic protection, only appearing when needed, and only then if I recognise him. His purpose is not to teach, but to protect. A series of teaching Guides then followed, whose purpose was education and development, and these only appeared in turn once I had learned enough. Arthur had suggested that the first teaching Guides might appear from the age of ten onwards and that very young children have neither a Guardian nor Guide permanently in situ, though occasionally some would have visitations from their Guardian, manifesting as their special friend.

[DECEMBER 2007]

Saturday 1st. 9.00pm. The Empress. Saria greeted me and we embraced warmly. The Library presented itself and I greeted The Keeper respectfully. I asked about another client, the appropriate book appeared and I soaked up the insight through my hands. Content, I did not want to detain The Keeper, but as I went to leave I was offered, though did not request, the book of Adolf Hitler. I accepted and received the information unquestioningly, "...a cold, hard man, masculine, not at all feminine. Irredeemable." I wondered about the relevance of all this but The Keeper indicated that I would soon understand before removing me from the Library. I next encountered the Empress, who was in the process of giving birth, yet spoke to me.

"Regardless of what you might read in the Outer World, the majority of females need to give birth in order to feel anywhere near satisfied and complete. There are exceptions to every rule of course…" Again this was unsolicited advice, but relevant and helpful. I embraced Saria and returned home.

Tuesday 4th. 9.00pm. Page of Swords. I asked Saria which essential oils could ease my painful lower back. She surprised me with her answer.

"Barks would be better – liquorice root, camphor and comfrey to ease and warm, and then lavender to penetrate afterwards." My question was part of a wider issue. I was adjusting my diet, but much more had to be done. I saw the Page of Swords, but the physical discomfort I felt interfered with the image. The Page was playing at life, immature and the cause of trouble to others. He was not yet mature enough to be let out into the world alone. He thrashed around with his sword and although it was apparent that he could be some small help and protection, but he was just as likely to cause damage and difficulty too. This was an interesting insight into his nature. After a while I embraced Saria and returned home.

Sunday 9th. 8.00pm. Seven of Swords. Before entry I lit a red candle, and placed it on the table before me. After a while I greeted Saria and could see a bright white light in the top left corner of the scene, toward where the mountains and Temple usually were. The Library was in the middle of the scene and we travelled there. The inside seemed bigger than before, as if an extension had been built. The Keeper explained that it was my perception that had grown, not the room.

"As perceptions grow so do the scope of possibilities," he said. The Hall was its usual electric blue and contained row after row of information. I asked about Arthur.

"A pain in the heart," came the only reply. I had nothing else to ask so I rolled out and back to the ground. I looked around and saw a man burying seven swords in the earth. I asked him why.

"The truth hurts, so I am hiding it from those who cannot handle it." He was fully occupied with this so I asked if he needed anything. His reply was to drag one of the swords across one of my palms. It did not hurt, but it did leave a scar. "Scars are signs of learning," he said and hurried to finish the burial of his swords before his friend called him over. He did not want him to see the truth, for it would hurt him.

The Temple beckoned now, and Saria said that I must go alone. I entered and stood in the Hall, surrounded by the pillars. The power and light flowed through me, but there were blockages in my own energy system. I felt that alcohol must be completely abandoned and my foods must become more varied and pure to enable this energy to flow more freely through me. I saw a red spinning chakra wheel within me, picking up speed. I soaked up the light and could hear mutterings and voices, but could sense nothing beyond that. I asked as many questions as I could muster.

"Why is this Temple on a hill?" There was an answer, but it was unintelligible.

"What interest does my conscious mind have in this imagery?" I said.

"None," said an unknown voice.

"OK, what esteem do I hold these images in?"

"None," said the same voice.

"So why do they appear to me?" I could not understand the reply, so I tried one more question.

"Is this objective truth and reality?"

"Oh yes."

I thanked whatever had appeared in the Temple and bowed, before instantly returning to be next to Saria. I hugged and kissed her goodbye.

Friday 14th. 6.30am. The Fool. I felt alert and awake for this early session and the images seemed clear and strong. I greeted Saria on my right. The sky was a warm pink, and the Library manifested immediately. Entering, the hooded Keeper was carrying a staff.

"What can I do for you?" he asked. I enquired about another client. Immediately I was stood before a lectern with her opened book in front of me. I placed my hands on its pages and knew what I needed to, "...sorrow, pain, abuse, family difficulties, disappointments. She is seeking shortcuts to avoid further difficulties, and is only semi-detached to reality." This realisation was no more than I had suspected, but I had only to think this thought to illicit a curt response from The Keeper.

"But worth the confirmation!" He was right. I thanked him and departed. I had not intended my thought to be heard by him, but in the Inner World what difference is there between a thought and a word?

Saria and I greeted the Fool. He was young, slender and colourfully dressed. Running round in a circle, faster and faster around the edge of a large cavern, the scene seemed dangerous but the Fool did not care. Even after he tripped and fell, he simply got back up again and carried on, undeterred. I observed the Fool for some time but my awareness drifted off and I arrived back home with my eyes open before I knew it.

Sunday 23rd. 12noon. The Planet Jupiter. I had been preparing for this day, and had selected it for a time when all mundane responsibilities had been attended to or were on hold for Christmas. I wanted to test the limits of this procedure. I printed a photograph of the planet Jupiter, the sharpest and most detailed I could find, and mounted it on some board. Looking upon the image I allowed my eyelids to droop, and then to go cross-eyed, as the scene changed before my very eyes.

Jupiter (c) NASA

I was instantly hurtling toward the planet. It was surprisingly very cold. Obviously, basic science tells us that space it is cold, but I had expected the planet Jupiter to be associated with warmth. Anyway, I hurtled through the atmosphere. Like Earth's it was a protective layer, usually impenetrable, but somehow I got through and came to rest, landing on the ground. I say ground, but I still felt like I was hovering. The scene was utterly indescribable, totally alien and unfamiliar in every way. The human concept of language seemed so feeble in this setting. Yellow seemed an appropriate colour to attribute, but in truth it was as if the whole place was beyond the level of my senses to comprehend, see, feel or process. I asked if anyone was there, looking for a sign to check that I was not simply imagining this.

A loud roar boomed out. Louder and fuller than any thunderclap, different in tone from anything on Earth, natural or man-made, the sound knocked me backwards. There was life here alright, intelligence and consciousness, entities of some description, though I could not see them. I asked if I could do anything for them. A voice came loud and clear.

"There is nothing you can do for us – go now!" I hesitated, part frozen with amazement and fear.

"GO <u>NOW</u>!" roared the voice. I was away like a shot, back up to the atmosphere and home.

Realisations: This was almost unbelievable, yet it had happened. Just as I would normally go to the shops or pop round a friends house, today I visited the planet Jupiter. This journey of the mind, of my consciousness, was instant, taking no time at all. There was no long trek across millions of miles, taking years in suspended animation. I was there, and then I was back. But the experience had a price. Walking down the street would never be the same again, and getting on the train or bus took on a whole different dimension. I was now somehow disconnected from everyone else, and while I do recognise how fortunate I have been, it did not make life any easier. Re-reading this years later I see that at the time it was a step too far, way beyond my capacity to deal with. During the coming days I would sleep for upwards of fifteen hours at a time and still feel tired. So what did I learn from it? I recorded these insights in the minutes straight after my return.

1. We are absolutely not alone in the cosmos.
2. Life is not just physical, but also energetic. First contact with other intelligences has already been made, not by me, but by others. But it could all too easily be overlooked, ignored or, worse still, dismissed as a figment of imagination. How many humans have been medicated or institutionalised for sensing the invisible intelligences out there?
3. Life is colour. Wherever there is colour there is also life. Jupiter was vivid.
4. We need to grow up fast as a species and treat our home and fellows with care and concern.
5. Humanity is at a low level of understanding in comparison to some of the intelligences out there. Human arrogance is a major threat to all life, maybe not just on this planet.

The weeks following this experiment were challenging. I was physically exhausted and succumbed to a bad cold in the first week of January. Discussing the matter with Arthur he remarked, "although you may be on a high level of development and understanding on Earth, it is not the case on other planets."

Life could be spiritual or material, visible or invisible, gas or solid, colour, fire, water, human, non-human, plant, animal or anything else beyond our comprehension, and these different forms of life were not necessarily lower forms of life. Quite the contrary, in certain cases the level of development of an alien life form might be higher than that of humans. Yet we think we are so clever.

My experience of life on another planet was literally earth shattering. I no longer felt bound by the form of planet Earth, seeing it now simply as a temporary teaching school. Other worlds offered different lessons and different experiences, in different states and modes of being. But it was still a lot to take in, and without the grounding I had received from Arthur, aside from the fact that I probably would never have got there in the first place, the journey would probably have sent me completely insane. As it was the combination of amazement and disbelief was difficult enough.

Wednesday 26th. 7.30pm. The Cave. I greeted Saria warmly and affectionately. It felt more than good to link up with her again. It was now an essential part of my life to come here and spend time with her. Together we lay on the ground and looked up at the sky for a few short moment until both the Temple and Library appeared. Entering the Library I found my hands on an opened book, all about me.

"You must finish what you start, only then can you continue further down the path toward learning and reach completion of this phase." Without a chance for the information to sink in I was out of the Library, without seeing The Keeper. Kissing Saria goodbye, I told her how valuable she was to me. She smiled and I emerged back into the Outer World.

[JANUARY 2008]

Friday 4th. 9.30pm. The Hierophant. I embraced Saria passionately. It was good to be back. We sat and surveyed the landscape of the Inner World. The sky was a pinky red and the temperature was warm. The Temple was high in the mountains to the left and other mountains, which I thought were part of a different land, stretched into the distance. As soon as I saw the Library I rushed straight in, asking The Keeper if he was the Egyptian God Thoth.

"Yes – as you would understand the name." It was so interesting, because for many months I had known that information, I knew who he was, but I did not know how I knew. I asked him for the book on a client. It revealed that he was in pain, having stepped completely into the unknown. He said that this would be ultimately beneficial for him, but in the short term very difficult.

"It is down to you to offer to help," he said. I argued a little with this information, but not for long. I enquired as to his boss, a man whose bad behaviour had preceded his stepping into the unknown. "Nothing good can come from him," was the clear reply. "He must be side lined for any positive work to be possible." I thanked the Keeper and left.

The scene was calm and tranquil as I approached the Hierophant over to my left. Further insights from my questions in the Library flooded in. My client has lost his job, his status, and his position. Although he was not about to starve, he had in fact, been reduced to nothing because he lacked any fundamental knowledge of himself and his purpose. His title of 'Manager', like the robes of the Hierophant, once gone, left him bereft.

The Chariot drew up quickly. I climbed aboard, was given the reins and in no time I had crashed the vehicle. I still lacked control. I concentrated and tried again, now a little more successfully. The Chariot lurched up in the air, looped the loop and I just about got it back down again in one piece. I disembarked and wished Saria farewell. As I left I caught a glimpse of an oriental face with straight black hair. I did not know who this was. I was simply happy that, although I had been tired when I entered, I emerged refreshed.

[FEBRUARY 2008]

Friday 1st. 9.00pm. Queen of Pentacles. I felt at ease as I re-connected with Saria. Balanced, energised, whole and complete again. We embraced warmly and I saw now that she was significantly smaller than me.

The Queen of Pentacles was to my left, tidying her house and beautifying her surroundings. She had achieved material security and from that stemmed her emotional fulfilment. Nothing was said.

I pointed up toward the Sun and a fragment of it came down, further re-energising and re-charging me, clearing the fuzzy headedness and fatigue I had been suffering. I resolved to return here more often. The Chariot then approached. Wasting no time I jumped aboard and it took me up to the Temple where it ejected me. In the Hall, voices spoke.

"Who are you?" I asked.

"Masters," said the barely audible voices.

"You," said another. "This place is your place, where the disparate aspects of yourself can converge and reunite. It is safe and secure here, and is the only place where such things can happen. Mastery, understanding, knowledge and power can all be reached here. This Temple is your Temple, your foundation and your stepping stone to higher things." Trying to remember it all I departed and wished Saria well.

"You should return more often," she said. She was correct, but as I hand wrote this account immediately afterwards it seemed as though my consciousness was separate from my physical body. This must be why I struggle so much, I thought.

Saturday 9th. 5.00pm. Four of Wands. I greeted Saria. We embraced and sat talking for a short while, and as our connection strengthened so I could see and understand more. She was small, with short black straight hair. Surprisingly she was of Polynesian descent with a slightly oriental look, and had been trafficked across the world to France. She spent her short life looking for love and affection, but instead was only ever abused and taken advantage of. Although she had seen plenty of evidence of the evil that men do, she never fully understood it and was pleased that her future self had seen greater glimpses of the truth.

The Chariot was somehow present again, but the image was unclear and I could not seem to correctly discern where it was. Instead we ascended to the Temple, where I received great power into my hands, a charge flowing into them freely until they buzzed and tingled. I could also catch sight of some vague future versions of me, as yet only partially formed. This suggested that my future was considerably more mapped out than I had anticipated.

There was a higher intelligence in the Temple, external to me. In response to my request a chair appeared over to my left. "Here," I was told, "you can sit, projecting yourself into the past or the future, or into space."

I projected back into a street in Berlin in 1933. It was awash with colours, with much noisy cheering and rejoicing. All was vibrant and healthy. I then moved forward to the same place twelve years later in 1945 and the happy scene was replaced by death, decay and collapsing rubble all around.

I now felt myself project as a being of light and energy out of my body and into space. I travelled for some distance but then suddenly felt that I could go no further. I returned quickly and bowed to the unknown surrounding entities as I departed the Temple and returned to Saria.

The scene from the Four of Wands was now before us, a glade containing growth, warmth and protection. It was a happy place, whose protection came from its inward looking nature. Its lack of expansion and growth, a problem in so many other areas, was its strength. Limited yet contented, children and adults played harmoniously, and resting after their hard work. I did not join in but thought afterwards that I should have done.

I turned back to Saria. Since the very beginning, most of my Inner World experiences have taken place to the left of my vision, but now I could discern something to my right side. It was unknown, and consisted only of vague colour and light. I turned toward it, and Saria guided me forward. It was as if I was a baby again, born into a world too bright to see, my eyes not yet accustomed to the vibration I found myself in. I stumbled along, toward a vista on my right that I had never seen before, where lay new discoveries. After a while of this I returned to the centre and bid farewell to Saria, returning home.

Callisto (c) NASA

Sunday 10th. 2.00pm. Callisto, moon of Jupiter. Since my previous visit to Jupiter I had obtained some photographs of other celestial bodies within the Solar System and mounted them on a metal backed board. After lengthy relaxation I placed in front of me the card containing an image of the second largest Jovian moon, taken by Voyager 2 in 1979.

I was instantly conscious of a place buzzing with growth, life and development. As I entered the field of the moon I could recognise gas and energy, multi-coloured, swirling, changing and moving. No faces, no voices, no noise as we would know it, just an overwhelming knowledge and awareness that filled me up. The inhabitants were invisible, with no physical form whatsoever. The population was composed of many levels of evolution, understanding, awareness and knowledge, as it was on Earth. On Callisto the energies were finer, less visible and not as heavy. There was no physical or material solidity to life, but all life here still underwent a programme of learning, interaction and development. It seemed a freer and more blissful place, although I felt there were darker forces here too.

The population was grouped around the core of the moon which provided them with everything they needed to sustain their existence. They occasionally observed and visited Earth and while they did not regard themselves as on a higher level than us I sensed that they observed our antics with amusement and sometimes bewilderment. I was enjoying mingling with them. I had bowed in deference when I arrived, even though they had suggested there was no need to do so. Suddenly though another energy, more forceful and with greater authority became apparent. Its form was again indiscernible but it commanded me to leave. I did so without hesitation.

This was further proof to me of the existence, within close proximity, of independent alien intelligences, some of whom were friendly and communicative. How much we could benefit by our conversation together and knowledge of each other. But then again, given the state of our World, and how we treat the aliens already among us – the Animal Kingdom - it is little wonder that they have yet to make themselves fully known to us.

I returned home a little shaken. What a poor level of understanding we have here on Earth.

Monday 11th. 8.00pm. The High Priestess. I greeted Saria and saw the High Priestess immediately to my left. She was tall and dressed elegantly in light blue. She had blonde hair and much power.

"You think you know, but you do not!" she screamed, pointing a wand directly at me. "Listen, you think you know about woman kind, but hear this. You the male, must initiate and then support so that the woman can follow and create further development and growth. Most males are weak and simply look to control women, to subdue and extinguish the female fire. To be truly a man, to truly lead, is to be strong enough to stoke the fires of woman and to handle the results. If the fires are stoked but then the woman undermined she will not feel right about herself or about you. Illness and a lack of confidence will then ensue. The male must take charge and lead, but then step back in order to support and not control. Begin, initiate, then stand back, ready to support when needed." She paused, as if awaiting a signal from me. I had nothing to say. "Then know this," she continued, "this is vital - a strong man is required now, by all women, as their springboard." Revealing stuff, I thought. Man must not step back; he must step up, secure in his power and comfortable in hers. Once a man gets a woman moving then there will be no stopping her, but she will soon turn to the negative if she cannot find the fulfilment she seeks. I thanked the High Priestess for this information, bowed to her and turned to the right of the scene which was, as before, a vague mass of coloured lights, very unlike the left side of my vision. Through this I could just make out a forest. Densely wooded but not foreboding or dark. I sensed that this was where some of the Major Arcana, specifically the Hermit, resided, forming a fuller picture of the Inner World.

I embraced and kissed Saria before leaving. I returned home a little disorientated. I thought that The Hermit would be appropriate for the next visit.

Saturday 23rd. 12noon. The Hermit. Saria was on my right though halfway between worlds. It seemed as though she was visiting me as much as I was visiting her. As we embraced I became aware of much colourful activity on my right side. My vision of Saria was now very clear. She was again small with oriental eyes and short, straight black hair. I could make out individual details of her appearance as she led me to the forest on my right and then into a clearing, climbing over logs and fallen trees along the way. This was a rarely trodden path that eventually opened up to a clearing where sat the Hermit.

He was alone, old and wise, though not frail or weak. The clearing itself was his home and I could only enter it with his permission. I felt Saria take a step backwards as I greeted the Hermit. He spoke.

"Magickal acts always bring the results that are needed, though not necessarily in the way that you want or expect them. Even then the magick takes time to work. In fact, it all takes time and one must have the patience." I asked the Hermit his age.

"862 years," came the reply. I doubted this and asked for confirmation. "My age is 862 years and I am as old as Time," came the, even less user friendly, reply. He pointed to the Temple. "All is possible, for you, within that sacred space. You must energise it, protect it and discover more within it. I will tell you everything you need to know, when you are ready to know it."

I wished him farewell and returned to Saria, warmly embracing her goodbye. On arriving home I noticed I was breathing heavily, very disorientated and unable, at first, to hold a pen in order to write all this down.

[APRIL 2008]

Sunday 6th. 4.00pm. Queen of Cups. I saw Geoffri. Then Kalia. This was unexpected and confusing until I looked around and saw Saria, waiting patiently. Together we all approached the left of the scene where there was a blonde, voluptuous woman, the Queen of Cups herself. She was expressive and strong, though not controlling.

"Seek number compatibility information in the Outer World," said a voice. I did not understand her words but the scene became clearer and there were green fields, trees and fences, stretching into the distance. I sensed that this was vision of a place in the Outer World, not in the UK, and that I would recognise it when I saw it.

Saria and Kalia were smiling at me, their faces beautiful and very clear. I departed the scene, wishing them well.

Afterwards: I had never before interpreted an Inner World experience as a direct vision of the future, but I could not shake the sense that the rural scene was an Outer World place that I would someday visit. If the Inner World is the place of creation - the reality that precedes the form of the Outer World - then is part of my future already arranged, without my conscious involvement? I has been so busy looking at the Temple, the place of deliberate and intended creation, that I had not taken into account forces and currents over which I had no control, which were perhaps already shaping my future.

Monday 28th. An evening of reflection. It often seemed as though the actors in the story of my Outer World Life conspired to pull me away from the Inner. Even if this were true, it was always me that allowed them to do it. This quiet evening – without any kind of journeying - reminded me that The Inner World is always available, waiting, an enduring part of Life. And there is always an excuse not to connect with it.

Wednesday 30th. 7.30pm. Three of Swords. As soon as I settled down to concentrate I felt the pull and instant connection of the Inner World. I had been much less stressed out in the Outer World during the past couple of days and the benefits were clear. Stress, and 'mind-busyness', were definitely obstacles to full Inner World appreciation.

I entered wholly and saw Saria to my right, the same, small, dark straight haired semi-oriental girl as before. We embraced warmly. There were other dark figures behind her and to the right, but they were unknown to me and we waved them away. Saria accompanied me as I ascended to the Temple. I felt that I was in the Hall fully, as if the location was with me as much as I was with it, that I had travelled to it and it to me. I had glimpses of this merging before, but now I could hold onto it for a much clearer experience. The Hall was huge with white stone, marble pillars and an altar. Colours and unknown entities swirled around above the checkerboard floor. I felt it to be a place of power, but also of knowledge and of safety. I felt at home there. But suddenly felt that it was time to go and in the moment of realisation I felt the floor open up beneath me and I went crashing down to the ground. How interesting that a thought here produces instant results. It takes much longer in the Outer World.

I landed at the feet of Saria. We embraced again and wished her farewell. It had been good to see her.

[MAY 2008]

Sunday 18th. 5.30pm. The Hermit. My first sightings were vague. It seemed frequent practise was essential to maintain complete clarity and unambiguity. The parts of the brain used for this process were like the muscles of the Olympian - in need of exercise.

Saria was on hand and we made love briefly. It was deeply comforting to be with her. We approached a wooded and overgrown area, with the Hermit hidden beyond in the clearing. His attitude was directed simply toward living, and did not concern himself with arguments or disagreements. He said everything exactly as he saw it. Debate or discussion, was to him, a waste of energy and he was perfectly focused on minimising all outside distractions, his attention directed inward toward the accumulation of knowledge.

"The more factors in your Outer life, the more time and effort is required to disengage from them. And disengage you must, if you desire a fulfilling Inner life," he said. So true. We discussed what I needed to know, but the scene was beginning to fade and I struggled to concentrate. The only message I was clear on was that in the Outer World, in the company of the Hermit, I was junior, and although I did not like that I must accept it. Perhaps, in fact, that was the only message.

Saria and I now approached the Temple. I stood in the Hall, arms outstretched, legs apart, and imbibed the atmosphere, the knowledge and the power. The room was blue, with wisps of green swirling around. These colours and energies seemed to enter my stomach and promote some kind of healing. I could feel myself in the centre of the Hall but a noise came from the Outer World and suddenly I was back on the ground outside the Temple with Saria. I took my breath and I wished her farewell, returning home a little foggy.

Realisations: A traveller must, I suppose, always be junior in the company of the locals, in this case the Tarot Archetypes of the Inner World, and their Living Counterparts of the Outer World. Arthur identified himself as the Living Hermit, so I would have to deal with being junior to that.

It seemed increasingly clear now that regular practise of these journeys was the essential component of success. Repetition was needed to reinforce the new brain connections that were being made each time, so that each subsequent trip might build upon the last, and not be wasted revising the past. This re-wiring was transformational, adding new mind possibilities and creating fresh dimensions in Life. But the change would only hold if it were repeated.

Tuesday 27th. 8.00pm. The Cave. I entered and greeted Saria, but also a gentleman dressed in silver and white. I knew instantly that this was to be my next Guide. I could immediately see how he – for this was definitely a male energy – was different to those that came before. He was tall, upright and solid, not unpredictable and adventurous like Geoffri.

Saria herself seemed to be dressed differently this time. I approached the Temple of Opportunities and entered it. I sensed an elderly man, bearded, cloaked, kneeling down before the plain stone altar at the end of the room. He vanished instantly as I approached behind him. I did not know nor enquire about him. I could see many colours and formless entities swirling around as I looked up and down and around my Temple.

"Where do you wish to go?" said a voice. I asked to visit a friend, and instantly I was there, witnessing her actions at that precise time. I returned and asked to witness another. In both cases the details and insights I could see and hear were the most private and confidential. I expanded my scope and asked to visit the Prime Minister Gordon Brown. Immediately I was there. He was a painfully pale man, wore a blue tie and was hunched over a table in informal discussion with close confidantes. I could not hear what was being said, but they looked worried. Although this is completely unverifiable, I felt satisfied of its truth.

In the Temple I traced a flaming golden pentagram in front of me, six feet high and across. I stepped into it, arms outstretched, allowing it to energise me and protect me. But it also burned me.

I said thank you and left, somewhat eager to return to the ordinary world, a little frazzled and singed. I kissed Saria on the cheek and wished both her and my new unknown friend goodbye.

Having returned to the Outer World I felt my business was unfinished and that Saria had somewhere else to be. I returned quickly and kissed and hugged her. She said that we could have done more together, but that our time was up and our progress acceptable. She turned and introduced Andrei, a tall blond, military figure. I recognised his appearance and dress immediately as Imperial Russian.

I tested him and held his hands in mind. He was tall and strong, but also calm and kindly. He presented me with a staff that would be mine for the duration of my time in the Inner World. I said that I wanted to take this slowly and he accepted that. I went to bury the staff inside the Temple but was instead instructed to conceal it elsewhere in the Inner World. I bid Andrei farewell and returned to the Outer World, much more at ease with myself. Upon my return home I cast the I Ching and drew Hexagram 3 – Ch'un – Difficult Beginnings.

CHAPTER V
ANDREI
[JUNE 2008]

Tuesday 10th. 8.00pm. The Cave. Moving through the cave I found the staff exactly where I had hidden it. I greeted Andrei immediately. He wore a blue military tunic with a gold braided and buttoned front, and black riding boots. He was well dressed, no regular foot soldier. I knew – although I did not know how I knew - that his was the uniform of a Russian Hussar. He had blond hair and sharp eyes. I confirmed his identity but questioned why I had the staff. I could not hear the answer so I discarded it. Andrei looked downcast at this, so I apologised and retrieved it. It was large but I found that I could shrink it, almost telescopically, integrating it into myself.

Andrei pointed up to the Temple and without him I arose to its Hall. I counted four pillars on either side of me, one plinth at the end of the Hall and one throne at the place I had entered. This made ten stations. I imbued my staff with power from all of them and asked what could be done in here.

"Anything. Everything," came the reply, "but only when all else fails, when the objective is needed not merely wanted and when it conforms to the individual pattern of Destiny and their essential learning." Not quite sure of those words I asked whether affecting others, in here, wasn't just bending someone's will? "It is always the bending of will. So long as you know what you are doing! In this place, your intentions, once they are clear and a true part of your life path, become real."

I asked about a particular matter in the Outer World and received a direct answer. I agreed wholeheartedly to follow this guidance and suddenly there were cheers and celebratory exclamations all around me. The intelligences were happy indeed.

I departed the Temple, after having my whole being infused with a golden energy, and returned to Andrei. He pointed straight into the distance, toward the start of a long and twisted path. This was what I needed the staff for. I tried to advance toward the start but there was a force field in the way.

"It will happen in good time," said Andrei. I asked him some direct questions about his life. He said he had died in 1905 fighting in the Russian Civil War.

"But there wasn't a civil war in Russia in 1905!" I exclaimed, feeling very clever at having caught him out. I knew my history and now I was onto something, perhaps I could start to deconstruct this whole world, and finally discard all this as an illusion?

"Yes there was," he replied, calmly. I was not buying that and left. I said goodbye but as I arrived home I realised I had forgotten the staff. What had I done with it? I returned immediately to find Andrei waiting with it. I took it and buried it in the same place as before.

"Don't forget the staff! The Living Staff!" echoed a voice.

Realisations: I thought I had a pretty good grasp of history, but I was wrong. There was a civil war in Russia in 1905, the first Russian Revolution, predating the more commonly known one in 1917. It seemed relevant that all these Guides were from periods of history to which I had an affinity. I had always been interested in the history of old Imperial Russia, and now I knew why. I even knew what Andrei was thinking and what he had been through (ultimately he had been killed in an uprising, leaving his wife and children behind.) I knew this because he was me. I was Andrei. The images seemed very clear. Was this because they were not so long ago? In some ways I felt the same then as now, just with different experiences, different clothes and a different body. In others I felt different, certainly less thoughtful back then, probably more obedient.

Reconnecting these threads of myself through time made me feel anciently old. But the upside was a greater perspective. The more I settled with these ideas the more content I became as the limitations of my earthbound existence melted away. What did house and car matter other than as a means to an end, for shelter and transport? What did it matter which party was in government, or whatever was the latest fashion? These things all came and went in cycles. The issue of Life was awareness. To lead a closed and unconnected life, such as I once had, seemed empty and pointless. How did I cope before I had this understanding? How do others cope now? No wonder the state of the Outer World was so bad, torn as it was from its partner, the Inner Realm. I now accepted what Arthur said many years before, that the object of life was simply to pursue your destiny, learn its lessons, develop self and love others. In that order.

[JULY 2008]

Saturday 5th. The Cave. I paused on the beach, outside the entrance to the cave, while I steadied myself. Once inside I looked around for the staff. I had to shrink it down to pocket size before I could successfully move into the Inner landscape. I greeted Andrei and was now free to allow the staff to expand to its true form. Then it was Andrei who changed. First he was smaller, and then taller than me. I tried to do the same, but lacking any control I just flailed about all over the place. After a while I managed to normalise to my right size, trying to find a centre or base point from which to shrink and expand in future.

I properly greeted Andrei now, embracing warmly as, shall we say, soul-brothers?

"There is a lot to do," he said, turning to point toward the Library and Temple high up in the mountains.

I entered the Library and as usual The Keeper was abrupt. He wanted me to act on information I received, not just take it passively and for its own sake. I enquired about two clients and was given direct and focused insight, and in one case a suggestion. I departed and rolled down back to Andrei. I had forgotten to say thank you to The Keeper, and as I returned to do so I got the distinct impression that he was none too happy about it.

The Temple of Opportunities
by Colin Clark

I rose up into the Hall of the Temple, while Andrei waited back on the ground. Again there were four pillars to my left and four to my right, a plinth at my front at the very end of the room. Further, two collections of energy were in front and a little above me in the form of colourful swirling clouds, one to my left, one to my right. They were sensing me, assessing me.

I looked above and saw that the roof of the Temple was open. Above it were pink, blue and silvery clouds, stars and galaxies. This was the Universe. I rose to the level of the roof line, seemingly on an elastic band, feeling myself at the edge of everything. I looked into this abyss and could see it all. This was the threshold to travel anywhere in space and time – anywhere at all. I rose higher and higher in my body and could feel myself disconnecting from the physical and becoming more aware of everything else. But the elastic started to pull me back and I returned to the Temple, falling to my knees in front of the pillars and the intelligences. I rose back to my feet and imbued myself and my staff with the golden healing energy that hung in the air. After maybe ten seconds of this I prepared to return home. The assembled intelligences seemed pleased with my progress and wished me farewell.

I returned to the ground of the Inner World at the feet of Andrei. I was exhausted and collapsed onto him for support. When I had recovered I asked if he would answer me when I was in the Outer World, and he in the Inner World? If I called his name and listened carefully would I hear him?

"Whether you can hear is different to whether I will answer," he replied. "Try it."

Walking back to the point where I had entered, I waved goodbye and shrank back again to get through the hole, casting a pentagram to protect the entrance. The staff seemed to be there as a prop for me, a support and maybe even protection if needed.

I returned to the outside of the cave, cast another pentagram at that entrance, and then after a few moments willed myself back home to the Outer World. And it did take some will. I could have easily not returned. I was disorientated, tired and fuzzy with a powerful urge to go and do something bad. It had been a long journey, maybe forty five minutes or more. I went to the kitchen to prepare a large cheese, Marmite and crisp sandwich, which with dairy and wheat intolerances was a very bad thing to do.

Tuesday 8th. 8.30pm. The Cave. I stood on the beach for a while. The sky was multi-coloured yet the atmosphere was relaxing and peaceful. Just this, as a meditation, would be enough for some. But not me. Inside the cave I collected the buried staff. Transferring through the opening low to the ground with the staff in my right hand I greeted Andrei warmly. He was dressed in his familiar blue military tunic, again a little smaller than me, blond hair, bright eyes, and this time I noticed he wore a well groomed moustache.

I looked over to the right of the scene and started to explore, but it was dark with a brick wall preventing our progress so we returned to the centre. I approached the Library and asked about a client. The answer was swift and abrupt. Other images flashed into my mind but I went no further.

The Keeper grew impatient and ejected me from his premises. I managed to regain entry and apologised profusely to him. He said that he would always be available for queries but that others needed him too. I sensed from this that he was an independent figure separate from me, accessible to all. I chose not to go any further and wished him and Andrei goodbye. He said he was always with me and smiled.

Monday 14th. 8.00pm. The Cave. I had managed to organise my Outer World into some kind of order and security. I was free of heavy burdens and energy drains. I was rested from a holiday and, for the moment at least, financially secure. This was a good strong basis for development, I thought and I wondered how far one could really develop as a human being without some sense of material security. I accepted that people had different material *desires*, but did they really have different material *needs*? Did not everyone need enough for essentials – food, clothing, shelter – enough for some creature comforts and a little superficial enjoyment, and then enough to help others when necessary. Although we may *want* more than this, and our circumstances might allow us to *take* more than this, does any of us *need* any more than this? And how does the amount we take influence our Inner progress? Taking more in one Realm might translate as taking less in the other?

Reflecting upon all this I entered from the sea shore through the cave. I immediately felt myself larger than normal and held the Living Staff outstretched in my right hand. I greeted Andrei but found myself rising up, higher and higher until I seemed to no longer be in the Inner World. I was travelling very fast across the sea, with no sight of land. Suddenly I came back down with a bump and properly said hello to Andrei. I asked him about Nikola Tesla. He said to enquire at the Library, which presented itself at my left. The Keeper was as usual in attendance and I greeted him correctly and with deference. I then held the Tesla book in my hand.

"...a fool, a buffoon, wrong on many counts, financially suspect. Do not believe the hype that has grown up around him." There was a pause. "However, he did discover the answer – an equation in electromagnetism that held the proof of the existence of all things psychic. He had not realised the implications of this, but the secret had been there all along." I drifted off into other thoughts but became aware of The Keeper again. I apologised and departed. This time he did not seem so angry.

I approached the Temple and entered the Hall. Again there were four pillars on either side and one in front. Andrei stood outside. I knelt before the room, heard voices and sensed communication.

"What next for him?" said a voice.

"We must make sure he is ready," said another. I asked that the intelligences show themselves. I can recall only fragments of what happened next.

The pillars were alive. They had either given way to plinths, with beings seated on them, or themselves had morphed into beings. In the first position to my immediate right (Pillar One) stood an alien being, small, brownish grey, unclothed, cold, even lifeless. Very similar to those Roswell stories that I did not believe. The three adjacent pillars on my right each contained something but I knew not what. Crossing to the left side, the pillar furthest from me (I will call that Pillar Five) contained a swirling cloud of colourful energy. Another one of the pillars on my left contained the traditionally recognisable image of the Egyptian God Thoth. He was very real and alive, old and with great wisdom. I got the sense that these intelligences had presented themselves in ways that I would best recognise, which may not be their truest form. Maybe they would look different to others? I did not ask.

I looked dead ahead between the two rows, at the central far altar on which sat a triangle containing an all-seeing eye. This cosmic eye pierced my third eye with such a powerful light that I felt that I must be in the presence of a significantly higher intelligence. This was unexpected, the ray of energy so powerful that it knocked me to the floor. Recovering after a little time I uttered a vague thank you (although I did not know to who or what) and departed. I greeted Andrei again and fell at his knees. He urged me to record the whole experience while it was fresh and to return soon.

Upon arriving home I had a buzzing and burning sensation in the position of my third eye, where the energy had struck me. It felt real enough to cause me not to discard the rest of the experience as fantasy. The feeling lingered that entire evening.

Tuesday 22nd. Reflections on Basic Meditation Practice. These experiences were teaching me that practice through repetition, even when results are not immediate apparent, brings a rich experience and in the end always yields results. It just takes time!

"...we are training ourselves to hold open a space that something may enter. This is an outcome of a discipline, an established practice, a way of living. Partly, what we do; more, who we are, even more, our commitment to live that life, regardless."

These are the words of the guitarist Robert Fripp and although he was speaking about music his rules apply just as well here. Nothing can be achieved or realised in life - and especially in the mystic/spiritual/psychical/occult - without persistence and determination. I'm not talking about bull headed, selfish, blind ambition, rather the ability to train the mind and the will to persevere, regardless of the internal and external distractions and the million and one reasons not to. This means that the inconsistent and the flaky will never master any aspect of themselves or of life until they cease being inconsistent and flaky. 'Open Up and Feel the Vibrations' might get us started, but that is all it will do. This awareness came to me today, and I hoped I could hold it close by.

I had recently played around with holding two large clear quartz crystal points, one in each hand, during my practice, to help me to disconnect from the Outer World. I reckoned that the items themselves held little intrinsic power, other than what I might invest in them, so in a sense it was fruitless. But the repetition of the procedure became significant. I was creating a ritual, for example using these crystals, sitting in the same chair, at a same time and day of the week, and it helped to create and *hold the space so that something may enter.*

Standard meditations and visualisations have long been known to ease physical discomforts, but my journeying practice grew difficult whenever I had any physical ailment. Coughs, colds, aches, pains all got in the way of the work. Personally I cannot work in cold temperatures. I learned, while attempting to perform Tarot readings at an outdoor Christmas market one freezing December evening, that my hands and mind freezed up in unison. Lately I could not do this work if I was hungry or thirsty either. There were so many things to take into account. It was not merely a case a crossing your legs and going "Om!"

[AUGUST 2008]

Saturday 2nd. 4.00pm. The Cave. After collecting my Living Staff from the usual place I greeted Andrei. It was good to see him.

I started off down a path to the right of the Inner World landscape. It was dark both actually and symbolically. There was an indeterminate goal in the distance, high up in the mountains, beyond the wind and the rain, the thunderclap and the scene of a Tower being destroyed, but it was too foreboding and I came back. The Library had appeared during this time but I declined the offer. The Keeper seemed pleased with this and departed the scene.

I ascended to the Temple and felt increasingly disconnected from my body. In front of the two rows of four pillars I asked that they identify themselves. To my right the first pillar was an alien form, the second a collections of atoms, electrons and protons. The third was a thin, blue-ish energy cloud, barely visible to me. The fourth was empty – or was it invisible? On the left, running back toward me, the fifth, sixth and seventh positions were beyond description, empty, yet not. The eight position, next to me on the left, contained the very clear image of Thoth.

I really wanted to see a lot more but pulled back from straining too hard to view these beings. Trying to stay focussed and centred I approached Pillar One, the alien. He did not move or speak. He was around four feet tall, smooth skinned, dark eyed, four toes on each foot, two fingers plus a thumb on each hand. He showed me his palm, it was completely smooth with no lines or marks. I did not feel scared but doubted what I was now experiencing. What was the alien doing here? I held back from asking this directly as I felt myself rising higher and higher, losing connection with my body. My breathing lessened until I was barely snatching oxygen. I did not fight this for I could see the whole Universe and flew around within it. After I while must somehow have returned to centre. I found myself outside the Temple, back with Andrei. I crawled back into the cave and returned home utterly exhausted.

Afterwards: I sought specific guidance on this from Arthur, three days later.

"...there are four types of life form," he said, "within you and around you in the Universe. The first three are Physical, Emotional and Mental and all these ultimately wither and die. Only the Spiritual lives on, never dying, only transforming." I suggested that an example of an emotional life was the weather. He did not answer this, but continued, "the next step is to get your Guide with you in the Temple, sit in the throne and ask what is to be done. Seek and offer help and enlightenment. Await transformation. Total disconnection from the body must not happen until greater control is achieved. Extreme care and caution are needed now. A total disconnection from the physical body, even for a short period of time, can take a long while to reconnect, maybe never." This would be classed as insanity, I thought. "This is a serious, real and present danger in this work," Arthur concluded, with emphasis.

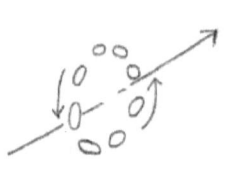

"'Your purpose – identified by your Four Roads of One, Three, Five and Eleven – is to travel out of the Outer World and then return back again, communicating your findings in grounded and practical ways. All the great mystics of the past lost their grip on reality in one way or another. That must not happen to you."

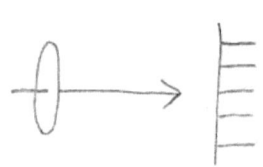

Tuesday 5th. 8.30pm. The Cave. I greeted Andrei warmly, it was good to see him again. He explained that I needed my staff if I were to take charge and exert some control in this world. I asked that he accompany me to the Temple. He said he was happy to do so. We ascended into the Hall where I sat down on the throne facing the other beings.

The Alien on Pillar One felt I was being presumptuous and rude. I rose and kneeled to him, so our heads were at the same height. I could immediately see something different as he filled my head with all sorts of information. His third eye looked into mine and after a while Andrei stepped in and cut the connection.

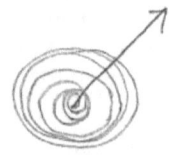

Diagram of Alien Propulsion System

His name was Yi-Chun (that was the closest Earth English approximation). He was from Proxima Centauri, the planet Niberia 5. He gave me a script that they used, full of unrecognisable symbols and letters.

He detailed his method of propulsion. I recorded it as best as my limited brain could manage. There were eight clear crystals, all facing the same way. They were charged and revolving anti-clockwise which somehow produced or resulted in forward directional movement toward a plate or flat surface. The charged crystals created a vortex which forced motion outward in a given direction. If you are at the centre point then you are propelled forwards. So long as the charge is great enough the propulsion force would be powerful enough to.... (next part unclear). Afterwards I thought that the charging of the crystals might take place via electricity, heat or magnetism, but without charging they were inert. These ideas came but I did not understand any of them.

I passed onto Pillar Two, the image of an atom, with the neutron at its core, orbited by electrons and protons. Yet this was an intelligence by itself. I greeted this intelligence, trying to show some respect, and then moved on.

Pillar Three showed itself as blue and orange gas, fast moving, ever changing, but again with consciousness.

Next, Pillar Four now showed itself as a pink cloud full of love and caring. This energy derided the alien for his harshness. I turned to the other row. I could not comprehend, recognise or see anything in positions five, six and seven. I knew there was something there, but it was beyond by vision, senses or understanding.

Lastly to Pillar Eight, nearest to my left, the figure of Thoth, anciently wise with great knowledge beyond my comprehension. Sharp and pointed in his demeanour, he was razor accurate and insisted on accuracy and quality. I returned to my throne, bowed again and spoke to them all.

"Listen. I want to know what I can do for you, and what you can do for me." I expected to feel foolish, but instead felt quite apprehensive. The Alien was amazed by these words, and repeated the information from earlier, with such intensity that although I could not understand it, it seared into me. But it was too much. I had to make my apologies and retreat. I was exhausted and disorientated. Andrei helped me to return to the ground of the Inner World. He suggested I ask something a bit more basic next time, because I would be unable to deal with this information for some time to come. I buried the staff and returned home. I had overdone it.

Thursday 7th. 9pm. The Cave. Holding clear quartz in each hand, points inwards, I reached the beach, with its clear blue/pink sky. I entered the cave. The scene was clear and well defined. I located the staff and entered, immediately meeting Andrei.

"Why do I have this staff?" I asked.

"To lean on, and to command," he replied.

"Will the beings of the Temple tell me what I need to do next?" I continued.

"Yes."

"Will you tell me, Andrei?"

"No, only they can" he replied, "but take care, some of them are good, some are evil. All of them are powerful and operate at a level that you cannot comprehend. They will seek to tempt you but you must be strong." We flew up into the Hall. This time there was a caped solitary figure of great power, straight ahead beyond the two rows of pillars. I bowed to him and all the other, empty, positions as I had done before, assuming my place on the throne. As I did so the eight entities manifested and the pillars filled up. Thoth and the Yi-Chun were arguing over something minute, not serious, just jockeying with each other. I took control and spoke.

"What am I here for?" The answer came, but I knew not from which Pillar.

"To learn. And then to lift up the human race beyond its petty factions."

"So what are you here for?" I asked them.

"To learn from you," came the reply, and after a pause, "there will of course be a price."

"What should I do next?" I asked.

"'We will tell you," said one voice. "No, we will show you," said another. "It will be obvious if you remember all you have learned. You will just have to say yes." The atom then chipped in,

"And that will be the hardest part."

"Where am I?" I asked.

"Inner Space. Inside your mind. And out of this world."

The conversation continued, into long details that I could not recall. Eventually the entities formed a circle, generated an energy, and I stood in the centre. The energy started to be transferred, but Andrei intervened. I used my staff to reach over to him and he pulled me out. I was safe, but the entities remained unmoved. All this information was tiring and difficult to comprehend, but the beings had come here to see me. I asked the Alien if he could time travel.

"I am here aren't I?" he replied. I said no more, bowed my head and thanked them. Retreating, I fell to the floor of the Inner World at the feet of Andrei. I used my staff to get up.

"You must be careful with these beings," he said. "Discarnate and incarnate beings from across space and time, and they have not come for nothing. They want something and you must decide how far you will go." He smiled and urged me to return soon when rested. I buried my staff, threw the protective pentacle at the two entrances and stood for a while on the beach before returning to the Outer World. It took some time to re-assimilate myself. This was all totally ridiculous yet very serious stuff.

Saturday 9th. 9.00pm. The Cave. As I entered Andrei warned me against using the Temple just for the sake of it.

"The beings do not like having their time wasted on trivia." Point taken, he continued. "You must attend with a purpose and then spend the appropriate amount of time re-establishing your balance, by acting on the information and insights revealed. Balance!"

I did not like the sound of this and offered some half-hearted resistance, but I knew it was fruitless. In the very next breath I found myself in the Temple, on the throne without Andrei. I had not controlled my travel and found myself here without realising it. A dangerous move, I thought. All the beings from before were in attendance, silent. I commanded them to speak, and they were not happy with me. I commanded Andrei to my side. He urged caution and respect. I apologised to the beings, and bowed low as a mark of respect. These were higher beings, higher forms of life than me. Not merely different, these were better, more perfected. I ought to show respect and maybe a little fear. As soon as I realised this they were immediately satisfied. The position directly opposite me at the end of the pillars contained a figure, cloaked all in black, its features and body completely obscured. I asked that all the beings show themselves. Suddenly the Hall filled with brilliant bright white light, so bright that even some of the beings had to turn away. The light penetrated everything and gave it life.

"Who are you?" I enquired to the figure at the end.

"God. The Source." Then a pause. "I am too much for you, too much for all living things, all at once. So I cloak myself in darkness, revealing myself only when appropriate."

I disliked the word God but recognised that this situation was no joke. I bowed low to God and to the other beings, thanked them all and retreated, back with Andrei to the Inner World landscape outside, and then through the cave to home.

Realisations: I felt the positioning of the Pillars in the Hall was significant. There was I – Human – at the opposite end of the Hall to God. It was as if we together brought everything into balance. The light of God filters down to man and man attempts to journey toward God. The concept was ages old. The eight beings facilitated the balance, provided the link and enabled the journey. An existence without God would mean an existence without Man. God needs Man to complete the great purpose and man finds his purpose through God. It sounded a bit religious, but there was no escaping the experience and besides, God might be interpreted in many ways. Was Man the Ninth Pillar of Completion, and God the Tenth of Rebirth?

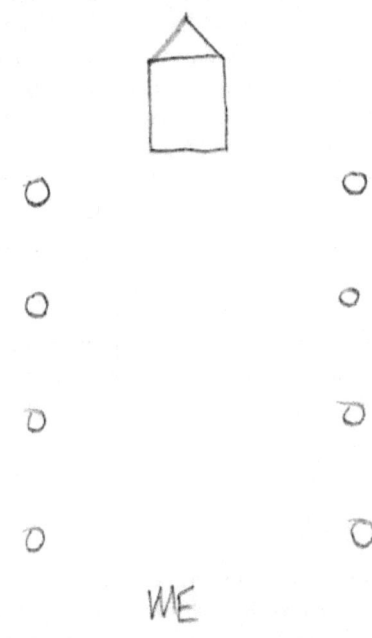

Layout of The Temple

Saturday 23rd. 10.00am. The Cave. I stood on the beach and surveyed the landscape. This was the Dream World, where all matters of the Outer World might be understood, rebalanced and healed. Connection to it is essential for health and wellbeing. Along the shore there seemed to be other cave entrances, and they all seemed protected in some way.

I entered my cave and collected the Living Staff. This time it seemed to contain a very large gemstone, set into its tip. I do not know how it got there, and could not ask Andrei as he wasn't anywhere to be seen. I called for him, but only a small man approached me from the right. This was not Andrei, and I could not see clearly due to the crystal atop the staff. I seemed to black out everything. I cast it back into the cave, where it fell onto the sandy floor. Andrei appeared immediately, unmistakeable.

"You cannot bring anything from the Outer World into your Inner World," he said.

"But what about the staff?" I asked.

"I gave that to you," he replied. "Without the crystal." We walked and I pointed into the distance directly ahead. "The Forest of Souls," said Andrei, "many people to meet there…" But he was cut off by the arrival of what I knew from before as the Kundalini Serpent. I checked with Andrei and he confirmed that it was safe to reach down and let it bite me. I did so and it engulfed my entire body, starting at my spine. I became the serpent, it became me. It was energising and burning and just about manageable, unlike when this happened a few years ago. I felt stronger and more capable now.

The beings had begun to congregate in the Temple, but the encounter with the Serpent had drained me and I called off the meeting. I saw the Library and ran to get a chance to ask particular questions about two students, receiving direct replies that required further research in the Outer World. I thanked The Keeper, who was in an amenable mood. I warmly thanked Andrei whereon I departed, disorientated on my return.

[SEPTEMBER 2008]

Monday 1st. 8.00pm. The Cave. I lingered on the shore line and the sea came and went, along with many images from the day. It was difficult to shake the Outer World, but just being by the shore and the cave at the mouth of the Inner World itself brought much insight and balance. I felt very light and could sense an approaching separation and disconnection from my body. My energy rose up to my throat and halted. I felt strongly that there were earthly matters to attend to before I could proceed any further in the Temple. The physical plane was my foundation, so those material things had to come first. Andrei's voice penetrated my thoughts.

"If you are in need then call. I will be there." It also seemed as though the Temple of Opportunities was at the centre of some debate and I was not allowed in today. I secured the cave, closed myself down and returned home.

Wednesday 24th. 8.00pm. The Cave. I was tired, and my access through the cave was vague, but I found my way in and greeted Andrei warmly.

"They want to speak to you," he said. I ascended to the Hall, seeing Yi-Chun, the alien, closest on my right. I sensed that on my right were the visible beings, the alien most physical, and becoming less physical as the sequence ran away from me. On the left maybe were the invisible frequencies, higher as they came nearer to me. This was conjecture on my part. The alien reached forward to connect with my mind, but something - I think Andrei - moved to stop him.

"To fully understand the propulsion information you were previously given you must fuse with the alien mind," he said. I resisted. It would be too much of a strain. Andrei nudged me to take charge of this situation. I could sense all the beings, at least most of them, but they were impassive, unresponsive. I enquired what the alien was.

"An example of what the human race may become. Natural evolution combined with genetic engineering will create a being capable of living this way, highly evolved mentally, but deficient in other areas." The voice was neither that of Yi-Chun nor Andrei. I asked if the Roswell Incident was a reality. "Yes, it is a glimpse into your future." I took the words without any understanding of them. At that split second the roof came off and I connected with the whole Universe. I could sense and see everything and had real trouble breathing. I sneezed and immediately returned, feeling very otherworldly. In this half-state I remembered that I had not taken my staff with me into the Temple. Perhaps that was why they would not heed me?

CHAPTER VI
NG
[OCTOBER 2008]

Friday 24th. 8.00pm. The Cave. Access was instant and Andrei wasted no time in introducing me to my next Guide. Her name was Ng, short for Ngebula or Ngebura, I could not be sure of the spelling. She was a black African tribeswoman, living just before the time of Haile Selassie in the 1920's, in the Horn of Africa (Somalia or Ethiopia). She was only a teenager and she did not live long. She was slim, even skinny, but friendly and warm with a big innocent smile. I was reluctant at first but Andrei reassured me everything was as it should be before saying goodbye. Ng and I made love. She had a bald head and big white teeth, around eighteen years old, or maybe even a little younger. After a while of just being with each other we set off across the landscape, eventually passing by the Forest of Souls.

"For another time," she said and rose up to the Hall in the Temple of Opportunities. At first she stayed outside until I requested that she accompany me. I took my position on the throne and banged my staff on the floor to summon the beings. I bowed before them and before God. The alien tried to link with my mind again, but I resisted.

"What is the Grand Purpose?" I asked, to whoever would appear.

"First, the circle of life: learning, growth and development. Each day better and fuller and wiser than the preceding one. Second, learning lessons: as you learn them so do I, as I learn so do you. Third, experience: to experience the full joy and liberation that is life and growth for the marvel that it really is. The beings are here to teach you and you to teach them. They know things that you cannot possibly imagine, and you know things they cannot be aware of. As you all enrich yourselves and each other so the whole is enriched and the whole is expanded for everyone. As one grows so do all. There is painful growth and learning as well as happy growth and learning. Growth and lessons that make you cry as well as ones that make you sing. But no matter for it is all growth and life and preferable to the nothing that came before. The joy of life is living in all of its forms. It is the preconceptions and inability to learn that creates the problems. If you feel pain it is in order to adapt and grow in that area, maybe even to change your mind, for even pain is preferable to nothing, so long as there is learning at the end of it. The recognition of your path and its pursuit is your harmonisation with the Grand Purpose, which is designed to be understood by all, but can only be realised by breaking it into smaller pieces." This was the voice of God, of that I had no doubt. I thanked all concerned, bowed and released the room. Heading back to earth with Ng I decided to go quietly and quickly while I remembered all this. I thanked her for her time and wished her well.

[NOVEMBER 2008]

Tuesday 4th. 9.00pm. The Cave. I saw Ng very quickly. I felt as though I were travelling through my third eye, down a corridor, toward a beach. We made love. It was passionate and raw. I became her and she became me. I could see from her perspective and her from mine. We connected through our crown chakras at orgasm. I knew so much about her and about her life at that moment... beatings and ill-treatment because of her colour by men in gangs. I cast back to today and could see how, from this perspective, the election of Barack Obama would be such progress.

There was another figure in attendance, tall and wearing a red mask. I waved him away with my staff, which I noticed now had that previously forbidden large crystal set at the top. I entered the Library for the book on Barack Obama. The Keeper, dressed in electric blue, obliged, "...pain in youth, weakness and indecision, kindness, goodness and generosity." The last few pages of the book were blank. Was this because his life would be cut short or because the future was not yet written?

It was the Temple next, and I summoned the various beings, trying once again to identify them. Some were still invisible. Pillars seven and eight were coloured gases, five and six were clouds, three and four were scientific, and both one and two were physical beings. The alien on Pillar One would again attempt a mind swap. If I could achieve this safely then it would be of huge value, but it would not happen today for my staff and Ng blocked the way. I turned to the front and asked the position at the end to again identify itself.

"Jesus," was the reply. "Ascended Master. Archangel." I scoffed loudly and turned to Ng saying that this was all rubbish. Instantly his being filled the room. Huge and angry he looked down on me. I realised my mistake instantly, and bowed low to him, as it seemed did the other eight beings.

The pull back to the physical now became very strong indeed, with itching and pains within my physical body. I apologised and headed back sharply, managing to wish Ng goodbye before I went.

Thursday 13th. 8.30pm. The Cave. I greeted Ng immediately and warmly.

"I have to go now. Our time is up," she said. I was very sad at this, but she was only young and her message and lessons were simple – love, kindness and tolerance. She had partially taught me those things and the figure to her right would now follow her. We kissed and hugged and I waved to her as she departed.

In front of me stood a figure clothed in red from head to toe, all features covered and obscured. Maybe this was because I was not ready to see him fully. I asked if he was my True Guide for I detected no love or emotion of any kind. I could hear no answer. I got the feeling that this person had moved to the negative in some way last time round, but had now learned the lesson and had something to pass on – when I was ready to hear it. But maybe that time was not yet, for he just stood still, unmoving, in front of me. I produced a sword to protect myself (where did I get that from I wondered later?) and carved the figure down. But there was nothing there, nobody. I looked beneath the fallen robes and from nowhere appeared a leprechaun, which then morphed into a giant, and then a leprechaun again. This was not correct.

Ng appeared again, she had come back to help. My physical body sneezed, a sure sign that I was not seeing the whole picture. She assured me that the figure in red was safe and he appeared once more. I said I needed to depart and she replied,

"We will both be here on your return." We went through the goodbyes, I bowed to the figure and him to me, gesturing, but not speaking.

Afterwards: This would be my seventh Guide. I decided to apply numerological principles, engaging with this energy by approaching the whole matter with the prime energy of seven - scepticism.

Monday 24th. 7.30pm. The Cave. As promised Ng was there, with the red clad character who immediately threw back his hood. Ng calmed me. He spoke as Derrick, an American gangster from the 1920's. He now wore the clothes that he last wore on Earth, a sharp pinstripe suit with a traditional fedora hat and a gun. Ng stood aside and waited while I got used to Derrick. I tested him and he seemed friendly and warm, if a bit of a rogue. He had learned some important lessons but died prematurely. His gun and clothing now dissolved away as I saw him as being of pure energy and me as the same. My staff melded into me. He presented me with an amulet, some kind of badge of accomplishment, which again energetically merged into my chest. I felt calm and looked around, able to see the Inner World with a broader perspective now – the Library, the Temple, the Forest of Souls, The Eastern Sea over to the left which led to another world *as yet unexplored* plus a mountain where the Hermit lived. We both approached this place of the Hermit and he greeted us warmly. I sought no particular advice and the trip was unhurried, my breathing calm and regulated. I felt fine and could see the landscape clearly throughout.

Ng was waving goodbye, saying that it was all well now. I let her go and myself returned slowly to the Outer World, wishing Derrick farewell.

CHAPTER VII
DERRICK
[DECEMBER 2008]

Monday 8th. 7.30pm. The Cave. Standing by the shore the cave door seemed a long way away, but I climbed up the beach entered the Inner World with my staff to see Derrick. He was dressed as before, in the 1920's American gangster look, and he behaved as such. There was an antelope to his left, wanting to lead me off into the Forest of Souls.

I instead entered the Library. The Keeper appeared, and we bowed at each other. I asked for information on a client. The book appeared, placing two hands on the open pages I received the information but I felt it wasn't enough, it was nothing I did not already know. I enquired further. Impatience – that was what I needed to know about her. It was never enough for her either. I thanked The Keeper and returned to Derrick who was practising shooting his gun. I felt this was inappropriate and directed energy at him from my staff. His Outer World shell disappeared and just his energy remained. Freed from the associations of his past Outer World life we embraced warmly.

I approached the Temple of Opportunities and felt myself rising up. In front of the stone throne I greeted the eight beings. Again the alien immediately tried to create a mind fusion. I resisted with the energy from the staff and from Derrick. I requested that the ninth being also attend. He identified himself as the Lord of the Earth. Master, but not Jesus. I could not see him but could sense his enormous presence. I was thinking what my next move might be. The alien again tried to mind link and again I resisted. One day I would fully embrace this, but not yet, it would be too draining and exhausting.

The Lord of the Earth, was authoritative, but I questioned him on why he had identified himself as Jesus last time and God before that. He said he did not call himself Jesus. "That was the name you attributed to me. Although I had not disagreed." It didn't wash. I felt this there was something amiss and demanded that he demonstrate and prove to me his power and status so that I would know for sure. The alien tried to interrupt, but I stopped him, maybe with too much power for he fell off his plinth. I quickly apologised for that. My actions had shocked the other beings. The Lord intervened and prevented the alien from interfering further.

"We will meet again soon to do what is required," he said calmly. This had turned into place where I took instruction, not where I made things happen. Who was meant to be in charge here? Derrick said that I had not yet asserted my authority in this place but that I would, in time.

"Go to rest," he said. I felt the call of the material to be very strong and I left.

Realisations: In retrospect it seems unbelievable that I demanded the Lord of the Earth to demonstrate and prove his power to me. What was going on in my mind that day? Clearly I didn't quite believe that there was such a being. I had moved onto a Guide I felt little connection with, certainly in his outer form. But whoever said that all Guides have to be love and light? Is it not sufficient that they appear simply as what they were when last on the planet, and are involved in our development, for our progress is also theirs? Who said they have to smile about it? Amongst this confusion I had forgotten that I had been given the Living Staff specifically for support, as a living embodiment of my knowledge, hard fought and hard earned. I was allowing the Outer World to distract me and undermine that. If that could stop then I would have less reason to be so needlessly and shamefully arrogant with the Lord of the Earth. I think probably I got off lightly.

Saturday 13th. 11.00am. The Cave. Rather worryingly I could not locate the cave on the sea shore. It was not in its usual place, or I had not entered the scene at the usual place. There were some tense moments, but eventually I spotted my cave some way off in the distance. I entered, collected my staff and this time walked straight through the wall, rather than through any opening. Seeing Derrick in his energetic humanoid form I quickly greeted him. There was a small creature to the right, saying he was my Guide. I left Derrick on a boulder for a second while I tested this. I lifted up the small creature in my hand and asked him directly,

"Are you my True Guide, and do you have the power to protect me in the Inner Realm?" The answer was 'no', followed by the creature changing into a butterfly and flying away. I returned to Derrick and asked him to identify himself. He did.

"I am your True Guide, and I have the power to protect you in these Inner Realms." I said that we should talk before going any further.

"How should I behave in the Temple?" I asked.

"With respect for oneself and for the others there. With strength and humility. There is no need to 'cow-tow', but arrogance is not appropriate either," he said.

"What about protection?" I asked.

"I will protect you from harm," he replied.

"Is it really the Lord of the Earth?" I quizzed.

"Only he can answer that."

"Who is he?"

"Only he can answer that." I don't know why I tried to catch these Guides out. It never worked. We moved toward the Temple and rose up into the Hall. I stood in front of my throne and there were no other beings there. I requested that they arrive and the eight beings appeared in the usual two rows of four. Derrick cast a protective circle around me and I greeted all the Kings (the urge to call them this came from an unknown source) in turn with a respectful nod of the head. It was difficult again to be certain in which positions these Kings were rested. The alien was on Pillar One, and although he was his usual active and communicative self, it seemed as though he was a different being this time.

Pillar Two was now a Venus Fly Trap not the atom from before, three and four were unrecognisable. Five was now the atom, six some coloured gas, seven was a pink energy and eight was a black energy.

The end of the rows, directly opposite me, was empty. I commanded the Lord to appear. The roof in the Outer World shook. Yes, the Outer World. I commanded again that the Lord appear. The roof of the Outer World shook even louder. I actually felt the chair in the room in the house physically shake, as if there were an earthquake. I bowed my head slightly and the other beings turned toward the ninth position and offered respect and deference. A white light appeared, but no figure or being that I could discern.

The white light identified itself as in charge of the development of Planet Earth. Its power was limitless, but so was its responsibility and one tempered the other. It only acted in extreme cases and then only within defined boundaries. If the continued existence of the species was under threat then he would intervene as he did with the Hitler regime ensuring that came to an end, even though the aftermath and price was huge, the price for doing nothing would have been greater. All the beings present were tasked with assisting him in his work and I was a very junior member. I began to ask what I should be doing next. The Lord intervened with a warning.

"If you were to ask such a question and receive the answer you would be compelled to act. There would be no excuse for inaction." He urged me to wait and I fell in line with this. The Lord called an end to the session and the beings bowed.

I returned to the surface with Derrick. He suggested that I go back to the Outer World to recover, but return again before Christmas.

Postscript: This is now totally beyond my comprehension. Who are the Eight Kings? Are they individuals or representations? Where do I figure in this? What must I do to act on this lesson/information? This is beyond my current knowledge. What do they do? Where do they live? How did they get (t)here? Where is (t)here? Who is the 9th? Lord? Name? Job? Appearance? Why am I there? What is across the sea? What is the Forest of Souls? What is my specific life purpose? It seems that the more I explore the less I know.

Tuesday 16th. 8.30pm. The Cave. I was greeted by two figures. I asked that my one True Guide identify himself. The more defined humanoid of the two, on the right, dissolved away leaving a roughly human shaped energy on the left with no face.

"Who are the entities in the Temple?" I asked. The answer came clearly.

"Examples, representations of each mode of life. They form, with you, the whole of the possibilities of life." Many of these forces, their behaviour and relationships were incomprehensible to me. I could work out that the alien seemed to represent a different, yet complementary, form of physical life to that of humans, but anything else was still way beyond me. At that thought he attempted the mind fusion again. I was tempted, more out of frustration than anything, but Derrick intervened to stop me. The Lord of the Earth now appeared. I asked him where he came from.

"Earth. Millions of years ago, in its early days," was the reply. For a moment it was as if he *was* Earth. Either way he was certainly wrapped up in the progress of the race and of the planet, although the two might not necessarily be linked. But I was tiring now, struggling to concentrate, and disappointed at myself for this. The Lord left, as did the eight others.

I looked around at the empty Temple and walked out of the Hall toward the surface of the Inner World. I walked for a while with Derrick but then left him and returned, leaving my staff in the usual place. I thought that next time I must ask more detailed questions, but not be so impatient for the answers.

Wednesday 17th. 4.30pm. The Cave. The scene was clear and bright as I entered with good awareness and focus. Again there were two individuals waiting for me, and again I requested that my one True Guide identify himself. He did so and we merged together then separated as I rose up to the Hall. I met the usual scene and became aware of two of the many messages the beings had been trying to give me. They arrived in my brain as fully formed concepts, and did not unravel in the ways that speech or trains of thought do.

First, direction. Life without direction is subject to randomness and chaos. Everything has a direction and a goal, with everything either moving toward it or not. Even the lost have a direction, they just cannot find it. This applies to all things, from cellular level upwards.

Second, part of the whole. Everything is connected, and is part of something else, even invisibly. Everything is a meld of differing factors and components. One's life energies are interconnected with others. Thus we are all connected.

Another concept began to present itself when the alien attached himself to my third eye. At once I felt a blockage clear from my mind and information flood out. After some time we swapped and I attached to his head and gained an understanding of his life form. It had no need for clothing, as his nourishment and dietary intake sustained the body at a high enough temperature to avoid the external skin and extremities freezing up. We humans had lost that ability. The being had large eyes that protruded a little from its head, in order that it could see more and have greater peripheral vision, extending almost behind it. The eyes looked black but they could in fact perceive both auras and brainwaves so in their species there was no such thing as lies because you could never get away with it. It also revealed details of their Propulsion Cube. Everything elemental and atomic is contained within the cube, producing spinning energy, controlled and harnessed. This was based on an understanding of the stages of life. Physical life (cellular) > water/vapour based life (sea creatures) > air dependent life (birds, insects, humans) > spirit based life (the inhabitants of the invisible world) > and round it goes again.

I commanded the Lord to enter and he appeared in a brilliant white light.

"What is the purpose of my life?" I asked.

"You were born at a particular moment, when things visible and invisible were, have and had been occurring. Events leave invisible traces and your birth at that point makes you the amalgam of those things. The purpose of your life is to play out those things in order that the lessons of the time are learned. Your birth is the healing and progression of the events of that time. New life comes to cast out the old ways. The Universe – all of life – is a mixture of interconnected parts. Your life is one manifestation of one point of that Universe. This happened, so you came here to make sure that the direction of life is maintained and built upon. It is because of others that you are here. Everyone needs to hear your message, even if it is wrong, so that they can assimilate it into their own development. Your life is snapshot of the Universe at that time."

I returned, after bowing respectfully to the other beings. I knew this answer to be right and true, yet I was still uncertain. Why do I doubt this so? Where is the proof that life on all levels is interconnected? If the Lord were right then at any point one can touch the stars, because one is already a star, and as such connected to everything else at every time. This is truly the concept of No Limits.

Thursday 18th. 3.00pm. The Outer World. Entering the Post Office on the High Street I felt the energetic vibration of everything around me. I could see and feel spots of light, stars, gases, purple, blue and black. Nothing seemed solid, it felt like matter were breaking up into its constituent parts. This gave me a grave sense of foreboding, almost apocalyptic, but on reflection maybe this was the unending nature of the physical world, constant decay followed by constant rebirth? Entropy – the increasing disorder and randomness of things – is one side of the equation of Life. The greater the uniformity the greater the entropy, and thus the greater the decay – the Post Office in the High Street was uniformity-central!

Here was the cast iron proof of Arthur's teachings and the words of the Lord. Every individual is fundamentally unique, yet all individuals are interconnected. The greater the expression of this uniqueness, the greater the positive effect, change and adaptation that springs forth. In this positive circle entropy decreases, whereby less things fall apart, less frequent. On the other hand, uniformity of thought, feeling and action means the denial of uniqueness, entropy increases as does decay. Uniqueness is life. Conformity is death.

Thursday 18th. 9.00pm. The Cave. The very act of entering this reserved space in the Inner World was, today, enough to change my entire attitude and outlook. I was greeted by lots of small people at my feet, all very pleased to see me, before the scene moved onto Derrick. I asked that the Sun come down and it did, healing me with its rays. Derrick also placed his hands on my eyes and sinuses to soothe them. We went along to the Library and The Keeper presented me with a closed book about a colleague. It spoke of intimacy problems, beatings and abuse which she has not gotten over. I was not sure whether she was witness to or recipient of these experiences but in either case she had been profoundly affected. That was all I needed to know.

We moved onto the Temple and I greeted the eight beings. I turned to the ninth position occupied by the Lord in the hope that he might offer some proof that I wasn't going insane.

"This is about acceptance, not knowledge, or faith. Acceptance of truth and your place in it. If you really need evidence then you ought to go to the top of a hill, outdoors, observe, connect and wait." I agreed that I needed this. I would return once I had done it.

Afterwards: This Lord discarded both faith – the keystone of all organised religions, and knowledge – the root of scientific materialism. I could readily accept this. Faith could so easily be a symptom of naivety and illusion, and what is knowledge without understanding? He was advocating independent and personal experience as a key to understanding Life.

[JANUARY 2009]

Wednesday 14th. 8.00pm. The Cave. My extended absence of nearly one month, might not have been a good idea. I could see my cave entrance and was distracted by a bright pink light and happy sounds coming from another cave of which I was unfamiliar. I looked inside and it seemed not quite real though attractive and enjoyable. Were these the inner workings of someone else's life? Could they be visited? Could I, therefore, live their life? I turned away from all that, allowing my cave to come into view.

I entered and caught a snapshot of Derrick. At first I had trouble controlling my size within the Inner World but then also had trouble holding focus on Derrick. There was another figure, a tall bearded male, stereotypically Jesus like. I looked past him to the right and saw the energy that was Derrick. We embraced. He was warm and quietly correct, hardly an earth shattering energy but just right.

Derrick shared his knowledge with me. It came not in the form of words, but of simple understanding, as if I were now plugged into his experiences. It was only much later that I understood the importance of this. His download ran like this: The ability to accept truth depends both on your state of mind and on your ability to control your Dark Side. The Dark Side is always waiting to disguise the road of delusion, whose destination is misery, as the joyous shortcut to bliss. This Dark Side is always present and it must first be identified and then controlled. At all times we must know the status of our Dark Side, be it active, restive or quietened, on the move or off the leash. If something in our life is out of place that is a sure sign of the uncontrolled march of the Dark Side. Derrick's advice flowed from his personal experience. He knew this quest could only be completed in the fullness of time, and that may be more than one lifetime. He was firm that everyone must do something to placate their Dark Side, now, before it gets a grip.

Monday 26th. 9.00pm. The Cave. I remained by the sea shore for some time while I reviewed recent events in my mind. I entered with the staff in my right hand and saw immediately a small and happy dancing girl to my right, followed by the familiar reddish energy of Derrick on my left.

"She is your new Guide," he said. I protested that I had only been with him for a short time. "But you have learned all that I can teach you," he replied. I understood that as a Guide is activated in the Inner World so corresponding experiences are revealed and developed for learning in the Outer World. This had been the case here.

We went toward the Temple, Derrick on my right as I ascended up to the Hall I felt myself rising up out of my body. I greeted the assembled, who arrived at the same time in their usual positions. I banged my staff on the ground and bowed to greet them all. The alien wanted to connect and I allowed this. He extracted information from me and I from him. I felt I need not fully accept the reality or otherwise of alien life in order to have this experience. Maybe the experience would reveal its own truth?

He projected his species writing script into my mind. They wrote with symbols and pictograms, in a way more akin to hieroglyphics than our language of letters and numbers. Their script enabled mental concepts to be more fully explained.

  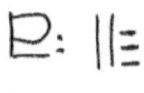

Alien Script

I had no idea what they meant but he told me that it could not be deciphered character by character. Suddenly our method of communication, our typewritten letters and numbers seemed so primitive. I disconnected from him and turned toward the light in the ninth position, straight ahead. A voice spoke.

"It is recognised that you have attained a degree of acceptance, especially of your Dark Side, but you have yet to face the full power of it. When you do you will understand and only then will you control it. Until that time illusion and self-deception are likely." The light continued, "you will be sent the necessary people and circumstances with which to explore this further. Expand your Outer World for these opportunities." The assembled beings agreed. I thanked them all and departed.

Returning to the scene outside the Temple I approached the Forest of Souls with Derrick. These were souls waiting for their next incarnation, whilst recovering from and assimilating the last. There were some 'Souls of Knowledge' who were ready to go, and there were others in denial refusing to accept what had happened and their role in it. One soul was ready to re-incarnate and shot down to Earth like an invisible shooting star. It was born into the physical and immediately started to cry and scream. The transition process had been painful and traumatic but had opened the door to further learning for that soul.

We returned to where my new Guide was waiting. I found I could communicate much earlier in the process now, and no longer felt the tiresome urge to question, deny and finally accept. Her name was Sophie and lived in the 1930's or 1940's. She was French, short haired, attractive and fun loving. We made love and I felt totally at home with her. Her energy was electric blue and she enjoyed life.

I felt that I ought to be with one Guide or another, not both, so I bade farewell to Derrick with a manly handshake and embrace. He seemed to disappear off into the Forest of Souls. I stayed with Sophie for a while and then wished her goodbye too. She urged me to return soon to get to know her better. She was my eighth Guide.

"You must detail all these findings in a book. This is part of your upcoming completion phase. Start now." I did not recognise this voice, which presented itself in the half way space between the Worlds.

Postscript: Back home I researched the alien script. The closest similarities were to two *ideomorphs*, supposedly dated to 14000BC, found in Seine, France, and Athlane in Ireland. Henry Agrippa's Celestial, Malachim and Transitus Fluvii alphabets seemed similar, though not identical, and parts of the symbols were similar to the astrological notation of the planets Jupiter, Saturn and Uranus. Or maybe there was no direct link to our history and that the script I had received was new and original. Perhaps I should meditate on the symbols? Were they representative of the planets – keys or glyphs for them? Was there a link between planet, Guide and station in the Temple? I had more questions than answers.

Our Solar System of Sun, Mercury, Venus, Earth, Mars, Jupiter, Saturn, Uranus, Neptune and Pluto makes ten bodies. If the Earth corresponds with my position in the Temple, and the Sun takes the ninth position of the Light then we have the Solar System *within*. The stations have been populated by external energies, but maybe could (or should?) be populated by my Guides? Maybe I was dealing with the Kabbalistic Tree of Life, yet the positions seemed not to match with what I had read. Again, so many unknowns. I seemed to uncover one answer, only to reveal fifty more questions.

CHAPTER VIII

SOPHIE

[JANUARY 2009]

Saturday 31st. 12noon. The Cave. I tried to enter the Inner World via a different cave further along the shore, but it was protected by an invisible barrier. I did not force the issue and entered the correct way through my cave. I saw a central area in the cave, a kind of fountain, but without water. It must have always been there, I had just never noticed it before. I felt it was designed to contain a being, maybe my first Guardian, who sits and waits until called, resting in this space between the two worlds.

I passed fully into the Inner World and saw Sophie straight away. Small and with short dark hair, full of life and fun, and a blue tinge to her aura. She jumped on top of my shoulders and did various other acrobatics. She had been a circus performer. We went over to a fallen tree and asked her more about her last life on Earth.

"It was 1940. Hitler came and took me under his wing. He selected me, as he did many young girls, all of us impressionable. He was a visionary, a dreamer, but also very weak and did not have knowledge or control of the very dubious people around him. Sadly everything about him is viewed through the lens of the Holocaust. That wiped out any chance of working out what and who he was. He was not interested in sex, although sometimes he would stroke my cheek. I was lost and impressionable and took it all in and looked up to him really. He liked that. He liked people to listen to him. A kind and gentle man really, but then sometimes with such a terrible temper. My time with him did not last long before my background - which he knew about and liked - was used against me by others. I was in the circus, friends with gypsies, you see. I was removed and never saw him again." She looked sad for a moment, but then picked herself up and started to dance. Her words had been on one hand shocking, but on the other, well, old news. I knew it already.

[FEBRUARY 2009]

Sunday 1st. 12.30pm. The Cave. I was aware, in addition to the beach and shore, of land and grass above the cave. This was yet another feature of what might comprise a starter meditation for those in need of a gentler introduction to the Inner World.

Moving inside I greeted a strange, dark being. He explained that I would soon understand his purpose. Nothing else was said. Moving through to the Inner World I saw Sophie, again dancing and acrobatically jumping around. We embraced and kissed, enjoying each other. After a short while we walked in the direction of the Forest of Souls, and she told me all about it.

"This is where souls wait between lives, adjusting to their past or future Karma. Some are angry at past or future difficulties, some are unable to accept their Karma, but this is the place where we rest after experiencing one level, before we experience another. It is just another stage in the process." She seemed cheerful about it. "Some souls rest peacefully," she said, as we negotiated our way through toward a crypt. "This is not the end but a period of peace, rest and tranquillity, activity suspended between lives. Some of us cope with it better than others."

We moved out of the Forest and across toward what Sophie referred to as the Eastern Sea, which was in fact to the left of my view.

"What lies across this sea?" I asked, staring out at a vast ocean.

"Nothing," she replied. I noticed a sailor returning from a voyage. We approached him and helped him ashore. He was tired and near to collapse. He had searched for a long time but to no avail.

"What you seek is always right under your nose," he said, looking up to the Library and Temple behind us. "I have searched for meaning and answers across the sea, but my Guides, the Library, the Forest and the Temple were here all along. I am finished now." It was a sad sight and Sophie gestured to some helpers, who were immediately on the scene, to clear away his body. I understood the message, there was nothing beyond the sea, the answers were right here and now in the Inner World. I wished Sophie farewell. I could not remember if she was my seventh or eighth Guide. I asked, and she seemed to say that she was the eighth.

"Look at your notes for the answer!" she said, "but come again soon, we will not have long together."

Realisations: I spoke to Arthur in an attempt to clarify some of my recent experiences. "Progress in the Inner World can only be achieved if there is progress in the Outer World." He said in a serious tone. "Force produced by efforts in one World always brings movement – or the need for it – in the other." He continued. "There are nine Guides, then nine more, and then nine more. There is a turning point at each stage, a decision to be made on where to go next. This is a crunch point before re-birth." I asked him if this happened in the Temple of Opportunities?

"The cycle of nine applies in both Worlds. The first cycle relates to getting yourself right, through learning about self and the necessary acceptance. The second cycle relates to identifying your nine Guides. The third cycle is your interaction with them, balancing of their energies with yours." I recorded Arthur's guidance word for word, in the hope that I would understand it later, because I sure as hell did not understand it now.

Tuesday 3rd. 8.30pm. The Cave. I entered and encountered a red haired, green eyed monster to my right. It had sharp teeth and was ready to bite. It definitely seemed female and I warned it off.

"Are you my True Guide?" I asked. The answer was no and she instantly disappeared. Sophie embraced me and we went to the Library. I asked about the controversial US Vice Presidential candidate, Sarah Palin. The Keeper was not amused.

"Do not come here asking questions that you already know the answer to!" and booted me out of his building.

We moved on and up to the Temple of Opportunities where the beings were gathered. The alien again was impatient to plug into my mind, but this time I refused. I looked around and still could not quite discern all the beings, although I felt perhaps that this did not matter. I saw the ninth position straight ahead contained an empty stone chair.

The alien requested access to my mind again and this time I agreed. He implanted into my mind and I into his. I could see a very clear star map.

Star Map of Yi Chun's Home

There was a large area of black nothingness in one part of the map. Bordering that was a star system from where the alien originated. I tried to focus in closer but could not. My mind felt numb. I retracted and broke the link. The being from the ninth position now spoke.

"That is enough. Soon you will choose the next step." I replied that it was in fact no choice, for the hand of Fate was always at work. "There is always a choice, because there is always a price." He indicated that one option lay elsewhere, gesturing up to the skies, black and stars everywhere. "Soon..." his voice tailed off.

I signalled that the beings should leave, thanking them all respectfully. I returned to the ground in the Inner World. Sophie smacked my behind playfully and said she would see me soon.

"There is still so much to do. It never ends, the amount to learn and master," she said. I glanced to the right hand side of the scene before I left. I thought that we must visit there next time. The quality of the experience had changed again. I returned with dry lips and dry mouth, and a fuzzy head.

Thoughts: As the Outer World is common to all, but our experience of it is individual, so it must be in the Inner World. There are many examples of people, unconnected in the Outer World, having the same idea at the same time, brought to them by their similar connections to the Inner World. As there is an electronic web of knowledge that we can all access via a computer in the Outer World, so might there be a psychic web, an invisible collection and interconnection of human vibration, accessed by the greatest computer of all – the human brain when switched into the correct receptive state?

Saturday 7th. 12noon. Nine of Cups. The card expanded, allowing me to move inside it to greet Sophie. I saw a woman with a market stall, lining up nine large golden cups for display,

"There is one for each type of human life. You must drink from all nine cups, fully and in balance, moving on, not desiring more or less, nor preferring one cup to another," said the stallholder. I thanked her and wanted to know if I could do anything for her?

"'Do as I ask," she said.

I turned to Sophie and asked about her history in the Outer World. She replied that she had told me enough already and there was no more of relevance to say. I then asked about how else I might access this Inner World?

"Correct and appropriate symbols or images always lead somewhere." She continued, "as you know, entry can be made via the hexagrams of the I-Ching, but this is more difficult." She signalled the end of questions and answers by jumping on my shoulders. I felt very comfortable with her, like I really knew her, so there was no chance of misunderstanding or offence.

The right of the scene was in total darkness, with the faintest shadows of animals and Guides, seemingly waiting for action. I moved through the darkness and spotted a point of light in the distance. Sophie urged caution. I pressed on further ahead toward the light, but she remained behind me. I thought twice and decided to follow her lead and returned back to the centre of the scene.

"That is for another time," she said. I agreed, waved goodbye to her and the stall keeper and returned to the Outer World, reversing back out through the card. Feeling sick and disorientated upon my return, I had to hold my head to check it was real. It took some time to feel normal again. I held onto the wooden legs of the chair, but my breathing remained irregular and my motion uncertain for a few hours afterwards.

Questions: Did the Tarot provide us with a map of this journey and this terrain? The concept of nine ran right through the cards. The physical nine are shown in the Pentacles, Ace through Nine, revealing nine cycles of human life and nine planets in the solar system. (The ten is all cases is a higher level of the Ace, $1+0=1$). An emotional nine show themselves in the cups – maybe nine Guides, nine previous versions of you. Then there is the mental nine, swords, showing nine lessons? Then nine spiritual stations in the wands, nine spiritual lessons, nine Masters, nine points in the Temple? Maybe this arrangement needed work but it felt as if someone had been here before and left us a map.

Wednesday 25th. 8.15pm. The Cave. There was strife and conflict on the shore, and in the cave next to mine. Moving through into my space silenced these noises. I greeted Sophie and we warmly embraced. It was good to see her. She climbed atop my shoulders and performed her familiar circus acrobatic routine. I asked her where next?

"Look over to the ninth one," she said, "and soon be ready." The ninth Guide was just a shadowy figure but the process was familiar. Sophie offered me some words of wisdom. "You cannot pretend like you are living an ordinary life, when you are not. The darkness seems like it is closing in because it always seems like it is closing in – it is just a balance that is being struck. The middle of the night is always black and the night might last a long time, but it will never last too long." This was helpful. She continued. "You can only make your contribution and be you – be The Illuminator. If you work magick you will actually succeed in changing yourself." I felt myself rise up higher and higher, as if on the top of a totem pole, getting lighter and lighter in the process. Sophie urged me to talk more deeply with a client of mine. "This may open doors to your uniqueness and your value."

I felt myself instantly explode and was, in that moment, conscious of the whole of the universe. Stars, gases, clouds. Birth. Death. The vision hit me like a thunderbolt and was a physical, emotional, mental and spiritual sensation. I had experienced nothing like it before. I returned to Sophie shocked and dazed, but not scared. The awareness was real. I embraced her and returned with my staff through the cave, leaving protection behind me as usual.

Afterwards: The Outer World was stressful and troublesome in many ways; the Inner World – although difficult – seemed to offer some peace of mind. My brain seemed balanced and painless - in harmony - during these visits. It was a strain at first, but now it was natural, even essential. I felt that this was the secret of life – the healer of many things - getting the balance between the two worlds.

[MARCH 2009]

Thursday 5th. 7.00pm. The Cave. I greeted Sophie. A figure dressed in an orangey brown cape was close by to my right, but I wanted to be with Sophie a little more.

"You've been here a long time," she said. I disagreed, it had not been very long at all. "Long enough" she said, "and you'll move on in the next one or two visits. Try that experiment we discussed. You will learn a lot and it will get the demons out."

We sat for a while, observing the landscape while I reached a new understanding of her. I would miss her, she had been my favourite so far. I drew great strength from our time together. But I must be certain to continue these experiences factually and not romanticise them. Best to do as the woman with Nine Cups had suggested – drink fully and then move on.

Afterwards: In the following days I would, again, argue with Arthur. The room I used for this work was becoming damp and the clock in the corner had stopped. I had developed a bad back and bruised muscles, from no activity whatsoever. How much of this was due to a fear of progress and unwillingness to adapt to my changing, internal, situation? I had certainly become attached to Sophie. It would be a while until I asked this question again.

Tuesday 24th. 8.00pm. The Cave. Greeting Sophie warmly, resigned to what was coming, I allowed her to jump on my shoulders. After enjoying each other's company for a little while she turned to present a figure in a brown Hermit-like smock and hood. His face was not visible, but I could detect a kindly glimmer in his eyes.

"Are you my True Guide?" I asked.

"Yes," came the unflinching reply. I sensed him as direct, kind, strong and warm. He maintained solidly in my vision and I repeated the question.

"Yes," was again the answer. At this Sophie kissed me and I waved goodbye to her. I would miss her. The year 1950 seemed relevant now. "That will keep for later," he said. Catching sight of the Library I moved inside in the usual way and greeted The Keeper. I asked about a client.

"Perform a Tarot reading about her proposed project, but communicate disappointment gently. She must do more now in other areas of life." Her Book of Life was thick. I asked of another. This time the Book of Life was thin.

"She has learned little. You must teach her whatever she will take. Do this and fulfil your purpose." The Keeper now gestured for me to leave and closed the large door behind me.

I rose up to the Temple. My new Guide stood aside, waiting outside this time, insisting that I had the power and the knowledge to cope with this alone.

The same Eight Kings formed in two rows, with one bright light at the end. The alien in his usual station, connected with my mind and I with his. He was a simple and direct, yet incisive being. He honed in on what mattered and did not allow his mind to experience anything other than his goal. This was very much of the One energy. I released the connection after a while. I then tried to feel out for some relevant knowledge and guidance. The answer came that I was not doing enough with my skills, knowledge and power. "To progress you must do more," said a voice. I dismissed the group. It felt as if I were really there in my body.

I returned to the ground and saw the new Guide. His gave his name as Amos. In keeping with other contacts I had not yet seen his face and that seemed quite natural. I wished him well and returned home. I cast protective circled pentagrams in bright neon pink.

The music track that accompanied this visit had run out. I had been in there over forty minutes, but I felt better and rejuvenated for it, no longer tired or exhausted. I must visit more often if I am to progress, but then again I am obligated to take the time to act on what I learn. I turned to look at the clock beside me. It had started to tick again!

CHAPTER IX
AMOS
[MARCH 2009]

Tuesday 31st. 8.30pm. The Cave. I entered the cave instantly. Amos was straight ahead in his brown cloak. There were other beings around so I tested, and confirmed, that it was him. After a while I gave permission for Amos to merge fully with me. It was a more incredible experience than I could imagine. I felt bigger, taller, wiser, more powerful, could see everything more clearly. Yet I knew that this was not really me. I felt tearful at the love I was feeling, as though he really loved me, properly, without any demands being placed on me. I asked if he would return with me to the Outer World, now he was part of me.

"Of course. I already have, but if it makes you feel better we can wait," he replied. Suddenly I felt under pressure to handle this new situation. I could see how easily insanity or a split personality might develop. I changed my mind and said for Amos to wait until I returned again. He sat down on a log, looked a little downcast and I wished him goodbye until next time.

Realisations: As well as being bigger, more whole and more real, this integration gave our relationship a continuity - Outer World and Inner World together. Meeting my Guides had been rewarding enough, but fusing together like this took the experience to another level. I felt a breakthrough. Completion of this section of work in the Inner World was now in sight.

[APRIL 2009]

Monday 6th. 8.00pm. The Cave. Various thoughts and emotions from the day swirled around my mind, barring my progress into the Inner World. Eventually I managed to clear my head and focus enough to move into the cave and beyond. I saw various figures, all similarly dressed including one dark red force to my left. I managed to ignore all these peripheral images and caught a glimpse of Amos. I hung on and I focussed straight on him. He welcomed me as we merged together.

I rose up to the Temple but did not summon any of the beings. Instead I opened up the roof to reveal the vast scope of the entire Universe. Trying to let go of my physical body, I wanted to rise up and merge with this amazingness. My breathing turned into gasps for air and my heart beat quickened. It was as if I had a lump in my throat and could not reach past that. I willed myself to travel to Jupiter but it was as though there were a shield up, preventing me from doing so.

"No," said a voice. I persevered, but to no avail. I could feel the breath of life enter me in the form of a wind, but I could not free myself into it. I returned to the ground of my Inner World and became again conscious of the presence of Amos. I collected my staff and returned through the cave, performing the usual protection. I felt invigorated and more aware. Was Amos still with me?

Afterwards: I felt an unknown presence close to me in the immediate aftermath of returning to the Outer World. Events the following day included tiredness and dreaminess. I wanted to be left alone, but unexpectedly took three phone calls for readings in quick succession. Everything seemed raw and hyper-real.

Tuesday 7th. 8.15pm. The Cave. This time I made sure that all Outer World jobs and tasks were attended to. I observed my, sometime neglected, rituals of cleansing the space and holding crystals. Sure enough the images were clearer than before. As I entered the cave I queried the dark cradle in its centre, just before the entrance to the Inner World. The answer came, source unknown.

"This is a place of refuge. A womb."

I passed into the Inner World and Amos leapt out of my body. I felt immediately lighter. He said it was a draining experience living in my body, and he needed to rejuvenate.

After a while he came back into sight and merged back with me. With the help of Amos I had a greater awareness. But who was in charge – me or Amos? I supposed that it must be me, and it never for a moment seemed the other way around.

I looked around and asked the identity of the many other beings who were gathered. There had been extra beings hanging around as long as I could remember, but their number seemed to have increased over the years. It had always been a lingering concern and I thought that they were False Guides trying to tempt me from my path. I did not sense any answer to my question from Amos. I asked them all to remove their hoods and they simply vanished. Only one remained – a small baby, crawling on all fours by my right foot.

I looked around the landscape and saw many features in greater clarity. I rose up to the Temple and accidentally commanded attendance of the beings. They appeared but I wobbled, not having a reason for summoning them. I apologised and they departed. Then the roof open and I was at one with the Universe. I basked in this heightened state and, maybe a little intoxicated with it, requested to visit the Dawn of Time on Planet Earth.

Instantly I was four billion years in the past. There were mountain ranges, and red, angry clouds in the sky. Small critters scurried around at the edge of some grey water which was teeming with particles. It was not a barren scene, there was plenty going on. I would describe it as more of a raw scene, but most interesting of all was that the sky was dark with no stars whatsoever. The red clouds gathered and moved violently, not gracefully. There were crashes and howls, but not thunder as such. I could see no Sun and there was no rain. It was all violence and anger, though not death. I was there in spirit, among the critters and with many gases and colours all together forming life. I could see no plant life, just a soup of lakes and ponds, dark but not dead, and violent eruptions from the mountains. It was shockingly real and totally alien, but I could maintain the vision no longer. I returned back through a kind of Kaleidoscope, and found myself back in the Temple. I bowed to the Light at the far end of the Hall.

"What am I to do?" I asked.

"Learn, develop and grow, 24/7. It will get harder, but that is your task." I fell back down to the earth of the Inner World with a bump and returned through the cave. Amos came with me as my consciousness returned to the Outer World.

I opened my eyes perfectly well but my body would not respond. For many seconds I could not move my physical body even though I felt I had fully occupied it. It was not like a standard Out of Body Experience where the body feels present but disjointed. I was most definitely in my body but could exert no control over it, as if my muscles did not work. I was worried. After what seemed like ages, but was probably only ten seconds, my control returned and everything switched back on. The quality of the Inner World experience had improved greatly. When I had been in the Temple I really had been there, fully and completely. The difficulty in coming back to The Outer World perhaps proved the experience.

Wednesday 22nd. 8.00pm. The Cave. Entry was again marred by thoughts and distractions in the Outer World. Tired and hungry I eventually entered my cave. I proceeded through to the Inner World and Amos leapt out of me immediately and stood on the rocks high above. He needed a break from being in my body. It seemed hard for him, so I expected the time apart would be lengthy, but in the event he slid back into the top of my head quite soon afterwards. I surveyed the scene and saw it clearly. The Temple was fed by a staircase of shimmering stars which I ascended. I greeted the eight intelligences and the one Light at the end of the Hall. This was a grand and mighty place indeed, but I was not fully in control and floated about for a while before taking myself under control.

"You have done well," came a voice, "you will be granted more time to complete your work." This was unexpected. I then realised I did not have my staff. I had forgotten to collect it on the way in. I thanked the assembled and returned to the floor of the Inner World. I felt faint and tired and returned to the cave with Amos. The staff was untouched. I left.

Realisations: I could imagine that entering the cave might prove so emotional for those of a sensitive nature that they might not be willing to move toward the further unknown experiences beyond it. Who of an uncertain and emotional nature could possibly be ready for these kind of adventures? Similarly, those of a predominantly mental nature (and I include myself in that category) may be able to undergo the experience, but find themselves unable or unwilling to invest it with enough commitment or emotional energy in order to make it seem real. It would be easy for the mental person to theorise and conceptualise the experience, and never quite bring themselves to believe it. It's all very well saying that we should approach this work with an open heart, but some people are more naturally biased emotionally or mentally, without a switch between. I only hoped that the missing links in the chain would eventually become clear.

Monday 27th. 7.30pm. The Cave. I gained entry easily although once inside I could still sense noises from the Outer World. I persevered and Amos leapt out of me so I could feel his presence separate and distinct from mine. I could see many shapes over to his right. They were much clearer than before.

"False Guides," said Amos.

"Why?" I asked. "Why do such things exist?"

"There must be False Guides to lead you to the darkness, just as there are True Guides to lead you to the light." There were many of them. An attachment to a False Guide might prove difficult to untangle.

Amos merged back into my head and I felt the boost of energy he gave me. So long as I ate well, then with this body of light I could be very resistance to illness. Amos suggested that I return home to attend to an outstanding matter in the Outer World and return tomorrow. I replaced the staff and exited the cave, securing the protection as usual.

Tuesday 28th. 8.00pm. The Cave. Immediately that I sat down in my Outer World chair I felt myself disconnect and begin to rise up out of my physical body, but as soon as I could perceive this I started to anticipate it. And at that precise moment I snapped back into full consciousness again. Recovering some control while on the sea shore I was attracted by another cave entrance to the left (South?) of mine. There seemed to be much activity inside. I approached closer, but then felt the need to retreat. It was not appropriate, I thought, maybe even forbidden to trespass on others privacy.

I entered with the staff and Amos emerged out of me. Perhaps in due course we would achieve full and permanent integration? Right now though there are many True and False Guides present. Amos climbed up the rocks and mountains toward the Temple and the Chariot approached. We climbed aboard it quickly and travelled the short distance to the foot of the mountain of the Temple. There was a ladder present and I climbed it. As I did it felt like I was rising inside of myself until I entered the Temple through the floor. Amos was again part of me. I had the staff and used it to request intelligences and the Light to appear. The Light was a white sphere. It spoke.

"Approach." I walked down the centre of the Hall and stood in front of it. I communicated that I was genuine and respected the Light. It seemed to like that. I stood and looked into its eyes – for it did have eyes, eyes that contained a bright and penetrating force. Nothing was said. I tried to form and project thoughts and words but nothing happened. I eased back and then the words came.

"Who are you?" I said.

"Your next Guide." It replied. This was so strange an answer that my mind must have drifted off. Coming back to awareness I looked around and there was nothing. The roof to the Temple opened at my request and feeling that everything was possible, I requested a visit to a different time.

"21st December 2012." I asked. No answer or awareness came. Nothing. I waited. Suddenly I could see small children running around in the hallway of my house. That was it, nothing else. I did not like the look and sound of that, some three and a half years in the future.

Returning to the Temple, I thanked the assembled beings and cleared them. Slowly returning to the floor of the Inner World I laid face down on my front while I regained awareness of Amos' presence within me. Other beings were trying to merge with me as well, but my staff allowed me to repel them. In fact this object seemed to have a life all of its own, the crystal at the top directing protective blasts of energy where needed. Well, I suppose it had to be called the Living Staff for a reason? I slowly left the same way I had entered. Amos was with me all the way, now fully a part of me. The journey lasted around thirty minutes. I had not used any crystals or external paraphernalia. I felt like I no longer needed them.

Afterwards: Many questions were raised here. Immediately afterwards I concentrated and sought the answers.

Q: Is that my next Guide, the Light? A: Yes.

Q: Will Amos be leaving? A: Soon.

Q: Will the new Guide merge with me? A: Yes.

Q: Is this dangerous? A: Yes.

Q: Should I mix it with alcohol? A: No.

Q: What about food? A: Extreme care is needed.

Q: What is the Light? A: A higher vibration, a different density.

Q: What about the other beings in the Temple? A: You must join them and become an Ambassador.

Q: What happens after the ninth Guide? A: Nothing, no answer came.

Discussion with Arthur: He spoke. "Acceptance is the lesson. Impatience is the enemy. Open up, let go of all opinions, beliefs, ideas and knowledge. Everything you think you know is wrong. Totally wash and kill the old self. Surrender and accept whatever comes. Identify what matters and what is relevant at any given time." He continued. "Total harmony with your Guide is required at all times. You must not simply believe or be gullible, the experience must feel right. You, in turn, will become a Guide, but not yet. Your Outer World will transform and grow richer as a result."

"How much value can I be to others? Will they be better or worse off with my influence?"

"Look at the energy of Eleven, the number you are now operating with. Care with its negative is needed – obsessive, delusional, fanatical, frustrated, lack of confidence, lack of self esteem and a fear of failure."

This was interesting. My on going question had been based on the perceived difficulty of teaching this knowledge. "Why does no one want to know?" I would often say. But given Arthur's words maybe I should also consider that I had some lack of confidence in my ability to teach it. Maybe it wasn't that they rejected the teachings, but that I felt unable to pass them on, or passed them on unsuitably. This was difficult, but it was a subtle and significant shift in my perception.

"Create your own Universe," he said. "Everyone can do this. The implications of the statement 'you are the only one there is' are massive. Spell them out."

Reflection upon The Hermit, Card IX of the Tarot: The similarity between it and the Fool struck me for the first time. They are both alone, travelling light, searching for something or someone, exposed to nature and accompanied by a living creature for support, a dog for the Fool and a Living Staff for the Hermit. The Fool for the most part looks up and toward the journey ahead while the Hermit for the most part looks down and back to others. The Fool is present with all the Light around him. The Hermit has harnessed that Light and uses it to create his own Universe.

[MAY 2009]

Tuesday 5th. 8.30pm. The Cave. I entered the usual way, collecting my Staff. The crystal tip popped off but then re-attached itself. Amos leapt out of me and stood nearby.

"Would you like these False Guides?" he said, pointing to some red shapes to my right. I resisted using the power of the Staff and crystal. Amos leapt up in the air, and flew up to the top of the mountain. I followed via a ladder. At first my ascent seemed slow and uncertain, but I felt myself getting lighter and detaching from my physical body. The lump in my throat stopping me from fully releasing but I continued nonetheless. Then I was in the Temple. All the beings were assembled in their usual places. I saw the being of Light at the end and approached.

"Who are you?" I asked, as if it were the first time I had been here.

"Your next Guide," came the reply, exactly as before. Now there were two beings. One was an ethereal feminine being of white light seated on a stone throne. One was a tall physical man standing to the right. I was confused about which one to choose and remained so for some time. Eventually I asked the standing figure to approach me. "You were right to choose me – the power behind the throne." He was tall and red haired. A King. Booming with laughter, his features became clear almost immediately. I hesitated further. I had expected the next Guide to be female or even amorphous, but this was a tall male King. This seemed not to be correct. I turned back to the being of light. She gave her name as Seraphia.

After much indecision and questioning I retracted my words and made a new choice - her. She was not forceful or persuasive in any way and I allowed her to merge with me. The experience was beyond orgasmic. I was suddenly aware of an explosion of energy and light throughout my entire being. I was invigorated and knowledge came flooding in. The roof of the Temple opened and I became instantly aware of all possibilities. I was now connected to all knowledge and understanding. Where could I go next? What knowledge, place and time did I wish to understand? All was possible now if I could accept and let go. This awareness was acute and profound. I returned to the floor of the Temple. My physical body could not cope with such journeys and would have to be left behind. I sat on the throne previously occupied by the being of Light, Seraphia, while the King now retreated downcast.

I walked back to my position and departed the Temple by flying down to the floor of the Inner World. There were many other people there now, waiting for me. I departed in the usual manner. Seraphia came back with me to the Outer World. I felt dazed and confused but invigorated and enlivened at the same time. I had spent a great deal of effort, in many journeys over many years, wondering, justifying and trying to evidence my experiences in the Inner World. The concrete nature of the Outer World held little interest now. Having dipped my toe in the dreamlike state of the Inner World while rooted in the physicality of Outer World reality, I had transformed into someone who felt that the Inner World was more real and meaningful than the fake plasticity of the Outer. How could any satisfaction be gained from a purely Outer World existence? Our moods there may be up or down, lasting seconds, hours or years, but if they were not underpinned by a rich, expanding and developing Inner World then little of worth would be achieved. To those who would ultimately read this account and conclude that the Inner World is a fictional construct and a figment of imagination I say that the counterfeit world is more likely to be the Outer World, the place where man digs his own grave every minute of the day.

INVOCATION OF THE NINE LIGHTS

It seemed like a good time to have a break, to take stock, to look back at where I had been and what I had learned. It seemed like a significant moment and although I could not rest in any way – there was a nagging sense that a great deal had been left undone – I felt it necessary to mark, review and reflect. In this space an invocation - an appreciation, a realisation of all that had occurred - arrived fully formed inside me.

"I stand before the Universe

One bright star among many bright stars

I recognise my nature. It is four, shining

I confront my twin. He is four, darkly

I recall my past. It was nine, and now is one

I speak from beyond, guided from within

I am unbound, alive

I am the Universe"

FAMILY CONNECTIONS

My *Core* Soul Family is formed of ten living individuals. Nine of them are alive and well in the invisible dimensions, one of them is living visibly and presently in the material dimension. All ten of us overlap on the emotional and mental planes – the places of change and adaptation. The physical plane is finite and fixed, at least until the emotional or mental planes act upon it. The spiritual lies above all these and is more profound and enduring than anything else.

All members of my family seek unity and integration with the others. Although they exist independently in their own right, they are each only one part of the whole, invisibly and eternally interconnected. If one hurts then we all hurt.

The family are me and I am them. Each of the nine are previous physical plane manifestations of the spiritual life force that exists now within me. My nature is different from the nature of each member of my soul family, but the thread remains in place.

These nine individuals identify themselves as Guides, and as previous incarnations, who are better placed than them to advise me? As my previous family members hailed from France in 1940, America in the Roaring Twenties, Imperial Russia, Medieval France and Ancient Mesopotamia so I can recognise a long standing affinity with those places and times.

My *Extended* Soul Family includes all the individuals that I have connected meaningfully with in past lives. All these memories are contained within the threads of DNA. It is probably inevitable then that we seek out those connections in this lifetime, whether it be for the purposes of completion or continuation.

The *Global* Soul Family is formed of the entire human race. Our threads and connections like a spider's web that spreads out and touches everyone, directly or indirectly. Everyone is a minute thread away from everyone else.

CHAPTER X

SERAPHIA

[MAY 2009]

Wednesday 6th. 7.30pm. The Cave. I entered the cave as usual and felt Seraphia disconnect. The Library was available and I entered without her. The Keeper allowed me to stay while I just looked around and soaked up the enormity of it all. Could there really be a book for every soul that ever existed? As this thought passed through me I sensed The Keeper growing impatient.

I left and decided not to ascend to the Temple, but instead to get to know Seraphia who now stood in front of me.

"Who are you?" I asked.

"Your Guide."

"But what is your purpose?"

"To Guide you." She was calm.

"Why?" I probed.

"To learn."

"But why?" I was not satisfied.

"So I can learn."

"Why?"

"The more you learn, the more I learn. The further you ascend, the more I ascend. My success is yours, yours is mine." She was patient in the face of my persistence.

"Where did you come from?"

"Around 40,000 BC, as you would say, from a land you know as Iran. Some mistakenly refer to our civilisation as Atlantis, but this is all wrong. We had an advanced society – wheels, astrolabes, machinery, though not so advanced as yours – but the seeds of our doom had been sown and our civilisation collapsed backwards, all due to the same issues you face now."

I looked upon her differently. I saw a serene and beautiful, fair haired and fair skinned woman of that time, nearby a pool of water, with columns surrounding it. I felt her merge with me, again very powerfully and we left in the usual way.

Realisations: Questioning Seraphia as I had been seemed to deliver insights that took me beyond the mere answers, giving me pieces in a jigsaw that enabled me to see more of the whole picture.

One of these was that The Temple of Opportunities could be accessed via the astral plane directly from the physical body, when I was ready. Travelling out from the roof of the Temple would bring much original knowledge and inventive insight, if I could handle it. Regular conversations and links to Seraphia would strengthen the clarity and volume of the voice and the depth of the information, but I must accept her words and not add to my trauma by resisting them.

Thursday 7th. 9.00pm. The Cave. I entered as usual and Seraphia detached from me, running up to the top of the mountain toward the Temple. I followed and felt myself ascend from my body. The scene moved rapidly. I felt an energy enter me but it was not Seraphia. It was a smaller and altogether unfamiliar sensation that exited as quickly as it came. I reconnected with Seraphia. She stood aside as we communicated. She gave me two specific pieces of information that needed my attention in the Outer World. I then asked where my next inner progress would lie.

"Dowsing, with your hands," she said. "Not using a pendulum, although that would be practise, but to move your hands over areas and over bodies, sensing the energies and discrepancies, feeling the results, over maps and places and feeling the energies. Healing and dowsing using my hands." Her words had hardly registered when she returned to my body very forcibly. Feeling her presence within me I left the Temple tired and dazed. I sensed an aspect of myself run off back to the Outer World ahead of the rest of me. I tried my best to gather and locate myself in the Inner World, as composed as possible, before returning home.

Saturday 16th. 4.00pm. The Cave. As I arrived two energies leapt out from me. One ran off to the right, and Seraphia exited to my left. Had I accidentally allowed an unidentified energy to remain inside me? That couldn't be good. I rose up to the Temple and greeted the usual eight pillars and assembled energies. The ninth position was of very pure white light, much clearer than before.

"Call me Seraphia," said the Light. I allowed her whole being to merge with mine and it was supremely powerful. I outstretched my arms and commanded that the ties that bound my client be freed in accordance with her Karma. I left it to intelligences higher than mine to decide what degree of freedom she should be granted. I clearly saw an image of her Outer World life being reordered. I did not try to force the issue any further as I sensed another energy being over to the left. As I became aware of this force, so I felt connected to all sorts of other energies and information. I felt I would have to up my game in order to maintain this level of connection, this higher vibration. This meant more regular visits to the Inner World. Feeling the strain I thanked and disbanded the energies. They leapt up and transported themselves out of the Temple and back to the ground of the Inner World before disappearing.

Monday 18th. 8.00pm. The Cave. I stood in the Inner World. It surrounded me, in front, to the sides and behind. A being of light exited from me and presented itself as a Sun-like figure. I felt neither overwhelmed nor concerned. The atmosphere and process seemed still and calm. I followed this Sun character to the Temple, rising up in the process. The two rows of four pillars were all around me and again I had to intervene with my Living Staff – my Kundalini serpent energy – to prevent a mind meld with the alien.

In front of me there were two or maybe three figures. One directly in front had piercing eyes of white light. Not evil or foreboding, but certainly powerful and not to be messed around with. There was maybe another being to the left and then another, a small red skinned being in a black hooded cloak. I thought that he might be a representative of the Fire element, but I sensed not heat but movement and freedom. Quick, dangerous and instant. Everything then nothing. I became a little part of the fire and burned away happily, feeling old issues burn away too. It was not as intense as I expected.

I looked at the assembled beings and wondered aloud who was my Guide. I called for Seraphia. She appeared to my right, just behind me. I tested her and she answered.

"I will always come if asked, but only if asked. I will answer if questioned, but only if addressed truly – as Seraphia. I am always awake, but sometimes resting. I must be called by my name and truly needed. Then you must listen for the answer." She paused before continuing. "Your internal brain chatter will interfere with the signal. Anything that suggests a short cut will be the interference in the signal. This is the Dark Side. Information."

Her voice seemed to come from the back right of my head, exactly where she was standing. The questions, in contrast, seemed to come from the left front of my head.

Realisations: The internal dialogue of Guide vs. Mind might easily cause a man to go insane, and this was one of my biggest fears. It was right back to acceptance again for I still struggled with what I was experiencing, even though I now had a lengthy collection of evidence. There were a couple of grey areas and seeming inconsistencies here and there, but they were as nothing when compared to the volume of correct, accurate and helpful insights. Courtesy of Arthur I had the knowledge and foundation to be able to distinguish reality from illusion. I knew what my life was for. I knew what I needed to do next. I knew that the Guides could be tested and were 'bound to tell the truth', smoking out any False Guides in the process. I knew that the true voice of the Guide feels right, truth is simple and that the unexpected was not imagination. But I must take control, initiate and ask for the answers. I also knew that throughout this journey of discovery thus far my life had only improved. This evidence could not be overlooked. Note to self-try to remember this!

Tuesday 26th. 7.30pm. The Cave. Pausing before entry it occurred to me that the pink sky and the shoreline might be comparable to the moment before birth, a threshold, no longer of one world, waiting to pass into the next. As if the womb was a gateway between.

The cave contained the newly identified central area, which itself seemed almost womb-like, and the Living Staff now seemed to resemble a DNA-helix. The suggestion were of death, rebirth and of crossing over. And with Seraphia being my tenth Guide it would all be perfect timing to 'take the zero out of ten and start again.'

As I entered I could see Seraphia standing on a rock facing me. A small dark entity escaped away, to my right. I then entered the Temple with Seraphia and greeted the assembled intelligences. I turned to the alien for a deeper greeting, but felt a strong presence in the ninth position, straight ahead. I approached two shapes there. One human form on the left identified himself as my next Guide. The other one, nearer to me, was more powerful, but did not make himself know. I asked his name.

"Are you Michael?" I asked. There was no answer.

"Melchedizak?" Again, no answer.

"Are you an Ascended Master or an Angel?" I probed further.

"Incorrect language," came the reply. The light from the being was white and powerful, and while not threatening, it was not warm and comforting either. It was just power, a neutral force. I allowed the entity to energise me. Instantly my whole body rocked and I felt my heart rate quicken. The power was too much to bear. My breathing quickened to cope but I could not tolerate this any longer and released the power. If I could not integrate this then I feared the consequences for my regular life, so left it alone and allowed the entity to go free. I felt lighter again and turned my attention back to the alien, accepting a mind touch with him.

"Are you Pleadian?" I enquired.

"I am from Niberia 5, Andromeda," he said as he gave me a star map. This had all happened before, so why was I asking questions that had already been answered?

"Are you Arcturian?" I continued.

"No." Throughout this period his attention was focussed on the structure and formulation of my eyes. I released the alien without resistance or argument and allowed Seraphia to re-enter me. After the previous two experiences this was light relief.

"Maybe I should try to take some energy back with me to the Outer World?" I said, half jokingly.

"No. That is the physical. These dimensions are different," replied Seraphia.

Discussion with Arthur: He listened solemnly as I recounted some of my recent confused experiences. "Decrease the frequency of your visits," he said. "Take time to understand what happens on each journey before embarking on the next." He suggested three weeks in between each. "You must guard against impatience. You cannot use your Guides for short cuts, but you can prove and verify your experiences by staying alert to new learning in the Outer World. And be careful to guard against suspect characters in the Inner World."

He said nothing more, but I remembered one of his maxims 'if the answers to your questions cause disbelief then you asked too soon!'

[JULY 2009]

Thursday 9th. 7.00pm. The Cave. The inside of the cave seemed more womb-like every time I visited, a place for rest, recovery and growth between worlds. Through to the landscape there were now many beings, more than in the past. Two of them were prominent. One straight in front was motionless, waiting. She indicated, when asked, that she was Seraphia, but I felt nothing. My attention had been distracted by something more colourful flying in the sky toward me. Although attractive I did not think this could be my Guide. My attention switched again. Now the Library presented itself and I approached swiftly. I knocked and was allowed to enter. I enquired on a client and the book appeared. '...selfish, silly, sorrow and sadness. Some self-inflicted, some accidental.' That was enough. Thanking The Keeper I left and went to sit down on a fallen tree, next to Seraphia. A serpent was moving across the ground. I threw my Living Staff down nearby and they fused together, changing their shape. The serpent's energy now flooded into me, I felt as though the serpents head was even fusing into mine. All this happened in an instant.

Nothing was said before I wished Seraphia goodbye, but she was now unwilling to let me go, saying she wanted to save me, protect me and help me. This seemed strange and I departed the way I came. Whenever it was time to return home I always sensed a pull from my physical body, in this case in my legs.

Tuesday 21st. 8.00pm. The Cave. The imagery was at first dim and muted in colour, but also clear and defined in appearance. I called for Seraphia and many entities were apparent, but I protected myself with a wall of energy until I could be certain who was who. Once established we spoke of the chakras, "effectively," she said, "the seven batteries of the energetic body. Correct diet and a little exercise is all they need for power. But they indicate levels of development and take time to activate fully. When diet is good then all is possible."

The Library appeared. I entered and bowed to The Keeper, although I had no question for him. Instead I asked if I could help or do anything for him?

"Add to the Library,'" he said, "write in yours and others' Books of Life and enrich the race." I thanked him and left, ascending to the Temple where I summoned the Eight Kings. I greeted them all and without hesitation approached the ninth, bright white light, straight ahead, welcoming it and allowing it to fill me with its energy, increasing my knowledge, understanding and awareness. The roof to the Temple was removed and I connected with the stars. I could see what certain people were doing at that time, what was really happening in the world, what was possible and what was not. I was plugged into the Universe, could see, sense and feel it all. This did not last long though, and when it was time I did not resist the disconnection, thanking all those around me, including Seraphia. I returned home, feeling refreshed and revived. There was indeed something much greater and it was a good feeling to connect with it.

[AUGUST 2009]

Tuesday 18th. 7.30pm. The Cave. I entered, collecting the Living Staff along the way. Again there were many beings around and I could not see Seraphia at all. I called for her to appear and an unfamiliar being came before me. It was black all over with blue electric specks and flecks of light and energy. This was a new Guide. Seraphia showed herself to the right and but only momentarily before fading into the distance, smiling and biding me farewell. I turned to this new figure.

"Are you my True Guide?" I repeated the familiar mantra.

"Yes." The words felt right, so why was I apprehensive? "Because this is a step into the unknown," he answered before I had even asked the question. I knew that he would soon reveal himself fully. We merged and I felt powerful and alive. This time it felt very different though he assured me that all was well.

I held the Living Staff out in front of me and allowed this to merge with us, as the staff itself transformed into a serpent. The sense in my body was no longer one of heaviness or stillness, but of a vibration in a million different directions. We looked around the scene. I could see the Forest of Souls, and the sea with the boat on the left. The boat interested me, but I declined to visit.

With this new Guide, and the serpent, part of me I felt that I must look up to the sky above. It occurred to me that I had never done this in the Inner World before. Save for in the Temple I cannot remember ever looking up. As I did so I could see the same scene as from the Temple – stars and points of light, every event in the life of the Universe, past and present, shining before me. At will I transported my consciousness to the Battle of Naseby in 1645 and witnessed the battle scene on the hill I had physically been standing on just days before. The sensations felt real enough, but in a way it was just another battle, like so many in history. I asked to go further and to witness an event that would mark this experience. Instantly there were two boys on the battlefield, seven and fourteen years old respectively. They were doing the menial tasks of fetching, carrying and messaging, but had been caught up in the fighting. I then witnessed their death. It was horrific.

"Be careful what you desire to see and to know," said a voice. I returned home through the cave, this time bringing my new Guide with me.

Realisations: The passage from one Guide to another always seems to bring a shift in consciousness and awareness, and a change in the conditions of the Outer World. At the time I had suspected that Seraphia was a False Guide, but in hindsight It was clear that I was wrong about this. Reviewing my notes reminded me that Guides came in all shapes and sizes, assisting in a variety of ways, some of which were not always apparent at the time. Sometimes we have great feelings for them, sometimes they stay with us for lengthy periods. Sometimes not. But the connection was always real and significant. It would seem that each Guide would allot us at least one lesson, challenge or task.

Seraphia was the first Guide of the new cycle, and the tenth overall. This next being would be number eleven. Perhaps I had expected something more earth shattering from Seraphia, but perhaps I had received exactly that but just did not notice or appreciate it.

I had been trying hard to hone my technique, for I sometimes still struggled to achieve a smooth or lasting entry. I noted four lessons, all of which required active involvement in the experience:

If a being or entity is unclear or unidentified, seek their identity before getting involved.

If the scene is unclear, request or demand clarity.

If the body is not fully connected, request or demand that it is.

If we cannot smell, see or hear, request or demand that we do so.

CHAPTER XI

HERMES

[SEPTEMBER 2009]

Monday 7th. 7.00pm. The Cave. I was greeted by a rush of beings, all trying to approach and enter me. With my Living Staff now an integral part of me I used it to erect a barrier to this assault. Now the energies simply bounced off. In amongst the crowd I recognised one, coloured in black, blue and white. I greeted him face to face and allowed him to enter and merge with me. His energy was dark, not negative, but cosmically black, rather than bright white. I tried to transform this energy into pure whiteness and asked the being his name.

"Hermes," came the instant answer.

"But aren't you a God?" I asked, stunned to have received such an answer.

"Not as such. Ask me a question if you don't believe," he replied. I asked the secret of time travel. "Focus, intensity and association," he said. "Associate yourself as much as possible with the period in question. Focus upon it and direct your energy toward the goal. The greater the focus and intensity and the clearer and more accurate the association, then the better the results."

I asked further about earthly matters. His answers were unexpected, clear and unambiguous, though not all palatable. I could feel my energy body slightly disjoint as I rose up. I approached the Temple of Opportunities, I rose higher and higher still. Greeting the assembled beings in the Hall I approached the light source ahead. I saw the shape of a Bull, then the six pointed star - the Seal of Solomon - which I was to use to protect myself before proceeding any further. This was so completely unexpected that I departed and felt myself on the floor of the Inner World.

I requested immediate clarity and I received it. I could see houses and buildings in detail the like of which I had not witnessed before. As I directed my consciousness so it expanded and became clearer. I approached a house with nine large swords by the doorway. What did these folks have to teach me?

"...accidents, pain, suffering. Slow down on your journeys." Message received loud and clear.

I returned to centre but felt a pull back to the Outer World now as Hermes left me.

Realisations: Again, acceptance! I now had a Guide who identified himself as Hermes – Thoth, the messenger of the Gods. What was I to do with this?

[OCTOBER 2009]

Tuesday 13th. 8.00pm. The Cave. I manifested the cave before me and could feel strong winds buffeting as I approached. I did not enter through the traditional cave door instead felt my being merge with the Inner World quite naturally. I looked to my left, then right, and called for my Guide. The black shadowy figure appeared from before. He had many electric blue points of light, buzzing and full of energy.

"Who are you?" I said. I had to test, I simply could not trust.

"Hermes. Thoth," he replied, crystal clear. We merged together. I felt at one with him, a comfort that I had not experienced for some time. I asked to review my Outer World progress. "You have the ability to draw in and direct power toward ends such as healing," he said.

"I need some words of power in order to do this, to act as a trigger," I said. Instantly they were given to me. He continued, "matters in your Outer World need attention. You will be busy with them for sometime." He said. "Any time travel book that you write will adapt in its form and take much longer than you anticipate. Your other projects should also be developed but there was also a need to attract and save money. There should be no unnecessary spending."

I queried about journeying across the Eastern Sea of the Inner World. We instantly climbed aboard a boat that was located on the shore on the left but it would not go anywhere. It was tied firmly to the shore and I could not free it. It seemed correct for it to remain there and for me to leave it like that. The sea journey was a long one that might be pursued another time. I returned again via the cave and had to be sure I had fully returned, trying to avoid any confusion.

[NOVEMBER 2009]

Wednesday 18th. 7.00pm. The Cave. One month since my last visit. I was weary. Could I even do this? After a degree of acclimatising I entered the cave and drew a hexagram within my being and a pentagram at my feet within a circle. I located the Living Staff within me and passed through the energy barrier. I was immediately greeted by Hermes/Thoth. He appeared as before. After greeting him warmly I asked,

"What is the deeper secret of Time Travel?"

"The secret is that time does not exist. Cycles exist, certainly, but time in terms of years and dates is a construction of man to spread order and control. Cycles are such things as the day – a new day is a new life, a new cycle. A twenty-eight day month is a cycle of the Moon and thirteen cycles of those make up the cycle of the Sun. You can count the years if you wish but to travel in time is not to bridge the vast gulf of space and time – it is simply to reach out with your hand. The past and future are right there – now. They never went away for they, and everything, form part of the Universe – everything that ever was, is, or will be. The key as always is to accept the way it is, was, or will be. Seeing truth, not wasting time fighting it. The project will take some time to complete in full, maybe a year and don't be surprised if no-one publishes it.' He laughed.

"Why?" I was disappointed.

"Because it is way ahead of its time. People still seek complexity and detail whereas in reality it is all really, really simple, if you allow it to be. But press on, just do not neglect other matters." The words spoken by Hermes/Thoth did not seem revelatory, though I noted that they were straightforward, contained no mumbo jumbo, symbols, sigils or magickal arts. Just reach out because other times are there – just there. And if other times are just there then so must be other planets, places and dimensions.

I was in a hurry to return and record this information so I wished Hermes farewell. He seemed friendly. I retraced my steps, this time leaving the staff buried in the cave and glimpsing two doors on the way out.

Tuesday 24th. Discussion with Arthur. I filled him in. Again he was unmoved, and spoke directly. "Visit the Inner World only when necessary. You have failed to assimilate your experiences thus far." I told him about meeting Hermes. I was sure that would put a different light on things. "Hermes represents quality, correctness, accuracy, precision and speed. Take to time to understand this. Slow down, all is well."

[DECEMBER 2009]

Monday 14th. 6.30pm. The Cave. Having taken time to mentally prepare myself I entered without difficulty. I was energised and protected with a flaming hexagram which surged through my body. I was approached by numerous figures, but ignored them and greeted Hermes instead. We were beginning to talk when I sneezed. This snapped the link, but I felt I could reconnect without going through the cave again. I double checked his identity and another being approached eager to identify himself as my Guide but I dismissed him and I greeted Hermes properly.

I asked for specific guidance and help to which he replied in detail. On matters of business and money he provided a clear direction. I was due to go on holiday. Desperately needing a break I requested that we might have a disturbance free time. He said he would oblige. I sensed there would be a cost, but that I should pay it nonetheless. Outer World matters satisfied I then asked of the nature of the Qlipothic Tree.

"This is a shadow world, the Dark Side," he said. "Each Tarot card depicts an energy, experience or person trying to find its full expression. Reversed cards can be seen as the Qliphoth - the blocked, distorted or failed expression of those energies. Not evil as such but whenever there are blocks to the true expression of energy then there are always lessons not being learned." I soaked this up, making connections in my mind with specific cards. "Your progress is good, just continue in the same vein," he concluded. I did not detain him longer, wished him farewell and departed. There was a strong link between us which I felt might not require active entry into the Inner World in order to communicate. I would need to test this to be sure though.

Following some of the answers recently received from Hermes I embarked, around this time, on various journeys to other places and times in history. This research appears separately in The Key to Time, which will be released, one day.

[FEBRUARY 2010]

Saturday 20th. 10.30am. The Cave. In a recent excursion I had noticed two doors in the cave. This was new information so once inside I set about looking for another entrance. There were two possible contenders. One was in the centre of the cave, part of the womb-like area I had witnessed before, almost like a well or a cradle. The other was a small aperture to the right of the old door. At first I tried the central cradle-like doorway, but I could not move forward from the entrance to the cave. When I switched my attention to the one to the right the same thing happened. After shrinking myself down in size I found that I could enter this small entrance. As I moved along it became a dark corridor with no end in sight. I pursued this for a while but felt the strongest urge that I should come back.

I re-grouped myself and again approached the central area, which now seemed much more like some kind of well. I hesitated, but then just went for it, throwing myself like a diver headlong into it. I was instantly falling and falling with a noise akin to that of an aeroplane taking off. There was great noise and the rush of air. I felt totally disconnected from my body, no longer sitting in my chair in the room. I felt as though the music, which I had used since I began, was no longer appropriate. It had become associated with the Inner World, and this experience was something very different.

I applied my tests to this new situation. Did it feel correct? Yes. Was it unexpected? Yes. The only possible conclusion was that I had managed my first steps at true Astral Projection.

Monday 22nd. 7.00pm. The Cave. I entered in the usual way. The central well was immediately apparent this time and I jumped in feet first. There was the same rushing and noise as last time, but less dramatic. I was swimming in a sea of blackness, down and down. I could see nothing but felt that I was dislocated from my body wobbling from left to right and behind by about a foot, moving back and forth through the chair back. My consciousness was fully focussed on myself. I could see nothing else and did not try to. I was just floating, mildly disconnected and mildly disorientated. It was like being lightly stoned, and although I felt a little sick that soon passed. Perhaps I needed to release my self control and properly let go?

Whilst in the state I could not see the room of the Outer World, but could acutely sense the movement of my neighbour's car and the air bubble in the radiator. I, the disconnected me, felt a little different to the bodily me. I was seeing the world with a different perspective than before. After some time of this I connected straight back to the Outer World, without returning the way I entered.

[MARCH 2010]

My long time teacher Arthur died on 10th March. I had spoken with him only days before.

Thursday 11th. 7.30pm. The Cave. I entered the cave and at first did not attempt to go anywhere or do anything. I simply familiarised myself with the scene, observing and sensing. It was as usual, as it had always been, but now with a new feature, an opening in the floor and the ceiling of the cave, off to the left. I raised the Living Staff from the ground and absorbed it into me. I wanted to jump down into the well, where I had been before. I willed myself to do this, head first, then feet first, then as a forward roll, but each time I could see that it was not me doing it, but me watching myself. As soon as I returned to my point of view each time I could see that nothing was actually happening.

I had almost given up trying and certainly stopped focusing when I could feel myself before a different scene, one I had never seen before. It was a mountain range, at either dawn or dusk, with a series of hi-rise buildings. The air was hazy and the vision vague. I did not know where it was but I would recognise it if I ever saw it again. Then it was over just as quickly as it had arrived. My mind then flashed to my nephew Joseph in his bedroom. He was pretending to go to sleep. He saw me, or at least sensed me.

I could not feel my body, but then became aware of it as soon as I thought 'I can't feel my body'. I tried to return to the physical but nothing happened. I brought my consciousness back into my body, but for some long seconds I could not move at all. Some seconds passed before I regained the link, but writing these words took some concentration and I still felt rather weird hours later, disjointed and disorientated, as if my legs did not belong to me. The journey had been uncontrolled and unclear.

Postscript: Three years later I would enter a hotel room in San Jose, California and witness through the floor to ceiling windows the exact same scene glimpsed during this journey. It was unmistakable, hitting me instantly with great reassurance.

Monday 15th. 7.00pm. The Cave. Inside the cave was the floor to ceiling Vortex Elevator, off to the left. I could see it more clearly now. Standing inside it caused me to dislocate from my body, by about five inches to my left and my back, a diagonal shift from my seated position.

The experience built slowly and I started to feel drunk, disoriented, yet with a real sense of moving higher in my body, maybe just below

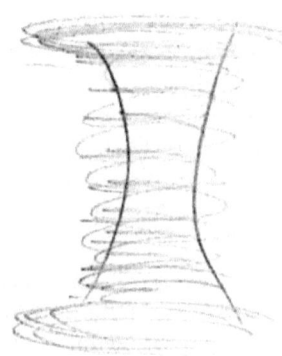

Vortex Elevator

the throat level. My being seemed to be oscillating, swaying from left to right and I felt like I was going to burst. I felt bigger than my body. The pressure grew, getting bigger and bigger, before I let it subside. I slumped energetically back into my body and slowly returned to normal. The physical body is so very heavy. I hadn't been anywhere this time but after the snap back to the physical, I was disorientated and my movements very slow afterwards. My eyes took a few blinks to adjust to the Outer World again.

Tuesday 16th. 8.00pm. The Cave. I proceeded straight into the cave, straight into the Vortex Elevator and to direct communication with Arthur. Although I knew that this could be done theoretically, when I actually managed it I was elated. His image was very clear to me. He spoke.

"It was all about the learning, that was all that mattered. In the end, the learning is what counts and lasts. Pain is only temporary." He continued, "you can see me over the next two weeks, then intermittently in case of urgent need, but I will then be resting for five years, after which I will return to work with animals. You did well, but you are the one to continue this work. Life will be intense from now on. 'No commitments, no promises' is the key to spreading the light across the world." I tried to remember every single word. "You were always the one, there are others of course, but only you can do this now. Return again tomorrow with Outer World questions. Continue to write, practise and go forward and it will all happen in the end." It was Arthur alright, there was no doubt. His words were so typically him.

Wednesday 17th. 7.30pm. The Cave. After immediate entry I was straight into the Vortex. Greeted by Arthur he held my hands smiling like he used to, warm and friendly as he was in times past. I had no questions for him now. It did not seem appropriate any more.

"Remember, there is never enough time," he said. "I have to go now. You have everything you need - if you can remember it. It is time to go." He started to fade into the distance. I waved to him and said thank you. He smiled and waved back as he faded away, the link now severed except for disaster or real need. Arthur was gone.

Monday 22nd. 7.00pm. The Cave. My doorway into the cave was bright and golden, with no other doorways visible. I entered and passed by the Vortex Elevator on the left, going through the usual doorway into the Inner World landscape itself.

I immediately became very tall, with the staff in my right hand. I glimpsed Hermes who was the same. We settled down to our usual size and he then merged with me to became one. It was very powerful but not overwhelming. I could see more now and we discussed Outer World matters and various pupils.

Hermes, within me, wanted to go off toward the Temple. We rose up, him slightly ahead of me, but still integrated, just. We arrived and stood in the usual position. The eight energies lined up in two rows of four, this time in a different order. The alien in the first position to my right, then the Saturn glyph, followed by a coloured gas and then the fourth position unclear. On the left the furthest position was unclear, then a pink cloud, then the swirl of the electrons and neutrons in the atom, then the closest on the left was also empty. The difference between the arrangement now and before disconcerted me, but I found certainty at the head of the rows where shone the brightest light. We approached, I knelt before it and requested guidance.

"USA, particularly San Francisco is the way forward now," said the voice. I requested protection and help in all my endeavours there, the flight, the trip, all of it. "Of course, but do not pester me with such requests again."

I was urged to look at my palms. They were now permanently imprinted with a golden pentagram on each, which I could use, among other things, to heal headaches. I was told, by a voice unknown, that I was now moving to another level, overcoming the annoyance of some people I had met and starting to apply myself for good and benefit. It would be hard work but as long as I was aligned then there would be no problem. I appealed for balance in my other work.

The roof of the Temple opened and I rose up to the heavens and stars, becoming part of them, almost totally disconnecting from the physical. Book learning was important, I thought, but practice and experience more so.

I returned to the Inner World's ground and thanked the assembled assorted entities. Hermes was happy to stay with me and so we left to the Outer World, and protected the doorways on the way. I buried the staff in the usual place. I was now the possessor of an enormous amount of knowledge, insight and information which I had yet to put into practice. Doing so would in turn aid my understanding and help me to assimilate it.

Tuesday 23rd. 8.00pm. The Cave. I entered through the usual doorway into the cave but paused with the Vortex to my left and the well or cradle in the centre. I climbed in this cradle and allowed it to act as a resting place as I curled up inside. Suddenly and without warning I felt my ears buzz and my eyes vibrate, as if I was shaking very rapidly. I felt myself getting taller and taller, higher and higher. I tried unsuccessfully to hold this state and project myself to a few places. Locations for which I had an affinity came easily, though I kept pulling myself back and experimenting with the phrase 'control now'. One of these trips gave me the vista of being above my own house, wafting over the garden and the roof. To call my vision 'sight' would be inaccurate, it was more like an ability to sense people walking along my street. From my new point of view they were neither to my left or right, but definitely below me. I could also see my back garden and the slope of its terrace seemed a lot steeper from above. I flew around the hedgerow and neighbouring field. Sometimes I felt I was getting ahead of myself, losing the perspective of my own eyes and watching myself, but this was only occasionally. For the most part I was pretty certain I was seeing the existing land in a new way. After this short but eventful period I felt a slight pull and returned back, intact, recovering my composure in the womb-like cradle for a while before I left the cave. I came round in the Outer World a little disorientated.

Postscript: It now seemed important to draw a distinction between the possibilities *within* the cave and those of the landscape *beyond* it. I could not perfectly scribe the conceptual dividing line but it increasingly appeared as if they offered two very different types of experience, which may require different skills and approaches.

[MAY 2010]

Tuesday 11th. 8.00pm. The Cave. It felt too long since my previous visit, and I was annoyed that Life always seemed to get in the way of this work. At first I was not even certain of the right entrance as there were numerous cave doorways available to me. I finally entered through the regular one – a pink background with a purple pentagram hovering as protection. The cave was just as fuzzy as the shore, but once through to the Inner World everything became clear. I greeted at first a black figure, a monster who sought to devour me. I was alert and despatched him quickly using my Staff, spotting Hermes to my right. He merged into me with a shudder. Many questions and answers on daily Outer World matters were exchanged, truthfully, but not entirely happily. I asked about my book on time travel. Hermes laughed.

"No-one will publish it," he said.

"Why?" I asked, downcast.

"Because it is ahead of its time." He continued. "To be The Hermit, even wanting to be so, takes skill and practice. Focus on what is relevant, abandon arguments and wait for people to find you. The Hermit light has gone out from the world for the moment. It is up to you to fill it." When and how I would do this were unclear. I thanked Hermes, felt him depart and returned to the Outer World feeling just as dazed and confused as I used to.

Tuesday 18th. 8.00pm. The Cave. I saw the pink energy doorway with its purple pentagram and entered through it and into the cave. I paused before climbing into the cradle and I caught myself trying to anticipate events. It had been a very material, heavy and distracting day. After some relaxation the buzzing started of its own accord and I seemed to partially detach from my body. I was flipping between the viewpoint of my physical body and my dislocated body. I flipped and slowly somersaulted around. I felt a little sick as I did this but slowly and gently got my bearings. But I still kept pre-empting the next move and I was not wholly out of my body or my mind.

Suddenly I could see a different view. It was as if I were twenty feet tall. I could see my neighbour's garden, from above. I surveyed the scene, noting the details and looking further afield around the foot of the garden and over the bottom toward the fields, all from that same height. I now wanted to visit a building some twenty miles away. As I thought this I was immediately there, no time having elapsed. I could see the building from the view of the park opposite and soaked up this new, clear and sharp viewpoint.

When I felt it was time to go I snapped immediately back into my physical body with a start, shocked and a bit disorientated. Some more practice was required!

[JUNE 2010]

Wednesday 23rd. 8.00pm. The Cave. I entered the Inner World, past the Vortex which I could see led into the wider Universe, and was greeted by many various shadowy beings, all dancing around me, though none too closely. I requested the presence of Hermes and after a few uncertain moments his form appeared on my right and then merged into me with a shudder. I enquired as to my recent progress.

"You have been absent, developing and indulging in material and earthly matters. That was important, but now it is time for other things. Let us go to the Temple, the next level," he said.

I rose up to the checkerboard floor, with the two rows of four plinths, the throne behind me and a bright light ahead. This scene always seemed the same, and this helped me to accept it. The alien being was in his familiar position, nearest to me. The plinths seemed to have colour, or even chakra, significances, but I could not be certain. I approached the bright light and asked many questions.

"We are happy with your progress so far," came a new set of voices, in unison. "Your impatience has caused problems, it is easy to hurt others with it. You must take care of this – the people of the future are all sensitive and emotional." Images of tasks I was required to do in the Outer World came to me and I noted them down. The light grew stronger. As I approached I felt it rush into my body, filling me completely. "Provide this energy to others when healing," said the voices.

I enquired about Arthur. I sensed he was up above me. I looked up and the roof was gone and a billion stars shone in the sky. I could not see him, he had gone elsewhere. I then enquired whether I should speak to the assembled eight energies? "That is for another time," came the reply. I gave my thanks and departed, Hermes accompanying me back to the Outer World.

[JULY 2010]

Tuesday 20th. 8.00pm. The Cave. The shoreline was stormy and windy but the doorway to the Inner World was clear. I passed swiftly into the cave and beyond, collecting my Staff. I was greeted by two or three entities, which was far less than usual. Among them I asked Hermes to identify himself and then verified this. Once I was satisfied Hermes merged with me in a flash.

He expressed disappointment that I had not done more writing. He said it had been a mistake to pass it to a friend for her appraisal. She had been lovingly harsh with her critique.

I asked about an Outer World predicament, related to property. He said I needed more information before the situation would reveal itself fully. He said that learning the correct lessons here was essential and instant knowledge would only be a shortcut.

I rose up with Hermes to the Temple and greeted all the beings. Unsurprisingly the alien tried to suck information from me but I resisted. I did not want him attached to me today. I could feel him in my brain and did not like it, but at the same time I felt this was for the betterment of all life – not just humans.

I approached the brightest light at the end of the Hall and it spoke.

"Naturally you have struggled without Arthur, but you do have everything you need with which to grow. Any more is mere greed. The town in which you live is not the best option but you should treat it as a base from which to explore the world. Remember, you have in place all that you need from which to expand."

I left the Temple and talked on the ground with Hermes for a while. I asked him to separate from me so that I could be clear who was saying what. He suggested that it would be wise to learn more about the nature of The Hermit. I assumed he meant for me to do this when I got home, to read some books or something. But suddenly I was in a clearing in the middle of a forest, being greeted by The Hermit himself. He seemed a little cantankerous, not unlike Arthur, which was quite comforting! We spoke extensively about the matters of my ordinary life, and he came up with insights and connections I would never have made by myself. At the end of the session I thanked the Hermit and returned to the cave with Hermes. As I wrote this account down I noticed, for the first time, the similarity of the two words Hermes and Hermit. How had I not noticed this before?

Hermes merged with me and we returned to the Outer World together. Much time had elapsed and I could not recall everything that happened. The background music track completely ran out. I had been gone over forty five minutes.

Postscript: Reviewing this account in preparation for publication I can see that I was not really taking these experiences seriously at all. I continued to visit, ask questions, fail to act on them and then return to ask them again. I failed to recognise the lessons and experiences placed in front of me in this life and instead devoted great energy to wishing I were somewhere (and occasionally someone) else. These avoidance tactics needed to cease, but it was almost as if one part of me wouldn't allow the rest to quite believe what had taken place. It was as if there was a great insecurity, negativity and lack of confidence within me that prevented me from standing up to be counted, to believe that all these amazing and fantastic things could happen to me. I had encountered many individuals of dubious character and intent on my travels in the Mind Body Spirit arena of the Outer World. I always said that 'not everyone in the spiritual field is all that spiritual themselves.' But I still found it hard to stand firm in my own knowledge in the face of this. This was all down to my Dark Side, which really wanted someone else to carry the burden, but I was trying to understand the way that this Dark Side played itself out. I was carrying so much mental and emotional baggage. For a man who spoke of having no beliefs I sure was carrying a lot of them around with me – they were just different ones than other people carried. My central belief being that I cannot be The Hermit, I should not be The Hermit, and I do not really want to be The Hermit. Yet I knew this was a load of rubbish. I suspected that The Living Staff may be able to help me and I set about researching it that.

Monday 26th. 7.30pm. The Cave. In the Outer World I prepared by protecting the four walls of my room with connected golden flaming pentagrams. I then rang the bell in each corner to invoke my four energies. Moving into concentration I immediately felt disconnected from my surroundings. The experience was intense, in contrast to some trips where the imagery was vague and my feelings ambivalent. It seemed that the Outer World needed somehow to be restrained, circumscribed, to stop it from crowding out the Inner.

I entered the cave and I sat in the central cradle. Straight away I felt myself rising and rushing. My head was dizzy and although I could not see anything I could at the very same time see whatever I wished, whatever I brought focus and concentration to. My mind flitted from person to person and place to place in the Outer World. I gained much insight into whatever I looked at.

My awareness returned back to the cradle and I climbed out, entering the Inner landscape as usual. I was floaty and disconnected, feeling weak and tired when a dark figure shot out of me. Was this Hermes? I called for him and I was greeted face to face with a rich black energy. I could discern the eyes, or at least their energy, but nothing else of form. It was not scary although it perhaps should have been and certainly would have been under different circumstances. I could see the wisdom of ages in this formless shape.

"It is time to meet your next..." he said. I do not remember exactly whether he said the word Guide or not. I imagined that he must have done, but I registered that the word was absent. From the right appeared a white figure of energy. His name was Eduki.

"It is time for you to move on. I will always be available," said what must have been Hermes as this new being approached. I welcomed him and he merged with me. Immediately my entire body began to shake and I was gasping for air. It was as if something bigger than me was in my body and I could not contain it. I had to let it out. Now he stood next to me. He was a tiny being.

"I am only small," he said. "What is the problem?" only half jokingly. I could not answer this but said I would return soon. He urged me to do just that. I was out of breath and disconnected on my return to Earth. The music track ran out.

CHAPTER XII

EDUKI

[AUGUST 2010]

Sunday 8th. 10.00am. The Astral. From the cradle in the cave I felt a tremendous thundering and juddering sensation. Even thought I had felt this before it was still such an alien thing to me. I did not expect success in my efforts, but just as that thought passed by so the goal was achieved. I arrived in the cotton wool whiteness of the Astral Plane and immediately stated my intentions – to visit Arthur.

Two figures greeted me. Firstly on my right was a disembodied and vague energy, then on my left was Arthur, recognisable in his form of around ten years ago, when our relationship was at its best. He wore his trademark light blue jumper.

"Why present yourself in two ways?" I asked. At this the dis-embodied energy immediately surged into the recognisable Arthur. Much was then said which I had some difficulty recalling. I gained insight into human Outer World characters and then I asked some developmental questions.

"Why can I not distinguish the voice of my Dark Side from the voice of my Higher Self?" He seemed surprised that I could not do this.

"It is to be practised," he said. I recalled the strong resistance I had to attending a recent Outer World meeting. I had overrode my feeling because I thought that it stemmed from my Dark Side whereas in reality it was a prescient warning. I had been annoyed at myself for not listening. Arthur addressed this. "Experiences must be entered into fully and then detached from. The Dark Side resists new experiences and writes them off before they start, failing to recognise that even in a situation destined to fail something can be extracted from it. So it is vital for you to explore this and then vital to realise the truth. One cannot happen without the other. The Dark Side nags, the higher voice does not, but it may be followed by a sense of foolishness if you do not listen to it." I asked about a fellow student of Arthur's, one who had got into great trouble recently. "Why have the teachings had such a harmful effect on him?" I asked. "Because he never really listened and could not understand. At least you listened, sometimes, even if you did argue."

"How often can I come and see you?" I asked.

"Only if genuinely needed, or if indicated by the Hermit card," he said.

"At any time of day or night?"

"Oh yes, there is no sleep. I am resting from activity but far from dead!" What a thing to say, I thought. He continued. "The key to progress lies in simplicity. All the books you have contain elements of truth, small facts and knowledge, but so much has to be waded through in order to get to the core. I have direct access to the core, without the need for all the nonsense." I then asked about a new client who had requested healing. "Proceed with the healing method as I taught you, but do not place energy directly on her heart. Work around it to strengthen the supportive tissue and being. Be aware though of the profound effect you are going to have on her." I started to form a follow up question, but too late. "That's it now," he concluded, "enough." I asked if it were possible for Arthur's life essence to merge into mine?

"That's enough for the moment," he replied. I returned from what was undoubtedly the Astral Plane and sat motionless in my chair for sometime, unable to move, while consciousness slowly returned to my body.

Thursday 26th. 7.00pm. The Cave. I entered with my Staff, allowing it to fuse as part of my spine. Looking around for Eduki I saw that, to my right on the ground, was a tiny being of whiteness in an indiscernible bodily form. It was minute but potent. Suddenly it disappeared and then re-appeared on my right shoulder, still small. After checking his identity I allowed him to merge with me. It felt like I was on fire from within. I queried the spelling and pronunciation of his name, was it Adooki, Eduki, Edooki?

He originated from Sumer, around 35,000 years ago (or was that BC?). I tested his gender and he was male. His true name was Eduki. He seemed to be very old and very wise.

"Your times are much more advanced than mine," he said. I felt his energy strong and clear, but I could not hold it steady. It was too powerful.

"What do you want with me?" I asked.

"You have much to do. Many to help," he said. I asked if this is what my planned event at the weekend was for? "Yes, very much so," came the reply as Eduki shot off into the distance. I thanked him but felt totally shattered and exhausted. My arms ached and I was disorientated. I was left with the nagging feeling that I was not doing nearly enough with my knowledge. This would have to be addressed. I left the staff and returned.

Eduki was his name, but I still did not know who he really was. From nowhere I was gripped with the fear that I was running out of time.

[SEPTEMBER 2010]

Tuesday 7th. 8.00pm. The Cave. I entered as usual and spotted Eduki on my immediate right. He fused into and with me. I asked him where he was from?

"Sumeria, as you would know it," he said, "35,000 years ago. Check the history books if you like but they won't tell you even half the story. We were knowledgeable, but not advanced like you are today."

"What can you tell me that is new, that I do not know?" I asked, waiting for a revelation. After a pause came the reply.

"There is no 'I', only 'We'. Levels of 'We'. Me and you. You and your other parts. You and other beings. Them and the world. One affects all and the structure of life is four fold," he said. Well I did ask for something different, outside my own views. He continued. "Thoth is father to many by the way his energy divides into four and then recombines as part of a new four within his offspring and descendants. This continues to others and then others." Fascinating!

We now appeared together in the Temple before the usual two rows of four energies and the Light at the end. I bowed before this Light and then before the rest. Here, before me, I felt, was the nature and structure of the entire Universe. I gently approached the Light.

"Write, write, until your fingers burn," said the voice. I bowed and bid my farewells.

Eduki and I jumped down to the ground again. I noticed then that he had separated from me and was now moving off to the left. I departed but after opening my eyes found I could not move. It seemed some time before I could manage to even pick up a pen, and then my writing was all but illegible. The Outer World seemed surreal and at fault where the Inner World seemed correct and natural.

Realisations: If, as Eduki claimed, the interconnectedness of human beings runs far deeper than I had previously supposed then the ramifications are enormous. It would mean that any understanding attained by anyone at any time in any part of the chain of Life has the possibility to affect all other parts of the chain. As one grows so the rest of us are able to grow, and as one hates so others pick up on it, and maybe feed on it. It might even give succour to those who toil away, isolated and seemingly unrecognised, that they are in fact invisibly influencing the chain of life.

Tuesday 14th. 7.45pm. The Cave. My mind had been engaged in Outer World matters all day, and with this mental acuity still present I made a smooth arrival in the Inner World, where two strangers were hanging out. Looking past them I called for Eduki. He quickly appeared as a mass of white energy formed in the shape of a pentagram, merging into me at my full size.

A huge awareness of Outer World issues flowed through me, chiefly that the Outer World was just as important as the Inner and although I should increasingly prioritise Inner matters this cannot be at the expense of the Outer. As long as I maintained this balance then all would be well. I asked Eduki if he was coming back to the Outer World with me. He said no. I released him, thanked him and departed. A swift, short but valuable experience.

[OCTOBER 2010]

Friday 1st. 10.30am. The Cave. Straight away Eduki merged into me from the left. This caused my whole body to shake and shiver. He said that we should enter the Temple but before we could move anywhere the Library appeared. I briefly entered and asked The Keeper about Arthur. The answers were surprising.

"A life of error, but deliberately so! When the opportunity for error or mistake presented itself he always took it. This was a vital and deliberate part of his development which shows the importance of error, the importance of getting it wrong. He embraced all these things and they were the key to his success." I could not process this in anyway and simply tried to remember it. Thanking The Keeper I departed and went to ascend to the Temple, but Eduki would not come with me.

"I cannot," he said.

"So who can?" I asked. Suddenly Geoffri appeared. It had been a long time, but I recognised him immediately and felt warm and protected by his presence.

"He can go with you." Eduki remarked. I entered and was greeted with the usual scene but in greater clarity than before. The eight positions and energies related to numbers. From my nearest right ran one to four, with five straight ahead, then six, seven, eight and nine on the left running back toward me. There seemed to be a relationship between me and the energy in position number five. Only positions one and nine were fully visible, one being the alien and nine a collection of atoms. Wild possibilities and half-connections flooded into my mind, while I tried to remember the scene as best as I could. On leaving I gave thanks, and re-connected with Eduki. Geoffri and I embraced and he somersaulted off into the distance.

"So who are you, Eduki? A Guide?" I said.

"No," he replied, 'I am, as you would term, an Ascended Master or Form of God, not here to guide or protect but to teach." Strange words to accept, but there they were. He issued forth insights into Outer World matters, but I was tired now. I asked a couple of Outer World questions to which he replied directly and clearly, but he said he could not return to the Outer World with me. "This is my domain, and you should return here soon." I departed and felt suddenly very weak, almost ready to sleep, or even collapse and die. It was an odd sensation, only fleeting, that I was spent and could do nothing more. I arrived back in the Outer World with a jolt of my physical body. My legs had paralysed completely and I could feel nothing of them. Sensation and life returned within minutes, rather than seconds or hours.

Monday 4th. 6.00pm. The Cave. I entered and greeted Eduki but following on from last time I did not seek to confirm his identity as my Guide. The moment I acknowledged him but accepted his true role I could clearly see all my previous Guides arranged to my right. Kalia and Geoffri were the most prominent, but they were all available to me now. Eduki stood separately and watched while Geoffri entered into me and I became again aware of his knowledge and being. In total silence I felt the vital importance of accepting my task as an earthly Guide. In this space I carried no doubt around that idea. In order to accomplish this I was infused with the significance of the changing of the seasons, and how, as an integral part of nature, I was approaching my hibernation time, my annual consolidation and my movement inward.

I was comfortable with all this and a voice urged me to "take on no additional responsibilities or commitments. Time is needed now to assimilate and reinforce your knowledge." The visit seemed to flow much better than before. I was not fighting the information and had not yet had my dinner so maybe that helped? There was, literally, less to digest!

I returned out and back to the Outer World, accompanied by Geoffri. There was much to do now of an Inner Nature. The nine Guides had differing skills and abilities. Maybe I could access whichever was appropriate to my circumstances and challenges at a given time?

Thursday 7th. 6.30pm. The Cave. Access was swift, entering with the Staff in my right hand. Immediately I experienced a rush of beings toward my right. I stood firm with my Staff while I assessed the situation. Everything and everyone became still, then Eduki greeted me on my left and advised me on my troublesome Outer World matters.

"Material progress and aggravation go together like hand in glove. If you want material progress you must engage in aggravation, and be firm in your resolve from the outset. If you do not want the aggravation then you must step back from the material world of money and business. So long as you remain then the secret is to be firm and direct, yet subtle and co-operative from day one of all your dealings. Trying to recover your position late in the day by force is unlikely to ever yield results. Get involved." It took me a while to grasp it, but perhaps by being involved you can create, shape and direct what you are involved with, whereas standing back, disconnected and only ever reactive actually causes you to be overwhelmed? "These beings want to become one with you," he said, now gesturing to the nine Guides. I resisted this, it seemed like a lot to take in. Eduki urged me to apply myself to this task and to complete my assessment of where I had been and what I had experienced thus far. "Only then can you take the important next steps of completion." I felt that all this should have been done before now, so it was time to catch up. I wished them all well and this time after many years of being nudged, pushed, directed and guided, returning home resolving to begin the work in earnest.

Thursday 28th. 8.00pm. The Cave. I was greeted by my family of nine Guides. I could not, at first, make each of them out although I felt a sense of togetherness with them all. Turning to my left toward Eduki, I appealed directly for help with my current Outer World situation.

"I will help to avert the worst aspects of it, but I cannot interfere with the learning," he said, "you have striven for and gained too much. That always brings problems. The idea of abundance is to have enough, not excess. Until you face up to the consequences of your decisions you will have to pay the price."

"But," I pleaded with him, "I need more money in order to be secure and safe."

"Yes, but there is too much. You could live much more frugally, spend less, and be nearer to your goal. All this is unnecessary and self inflicted and until you can accept that the lesson continues. No one has ever advised you to have no money, but your assets are not the point. Security has been compromised. You will reach your mythical financial goal, but not in the way that you think."

The message was annoyingly direct. I had expected something a little softer or vaguer. As I returned, buzzing with this very real experience, my family of Guides seemed to speak as one, "Do not forget the work." Their voice was at the front of my mind as I opened my eyes.

[NOVEMBER 2010]

Thursday 4th. 7.00pm. The Cave. All manner of thoughts and insights of the Outer World assaulted me. Eventually I found myself in the cave and then the Inner World, greeted warmly by my family of nine to my right. I identified Eduki and one or two others – Kalia and Geoffri, certainly – although I sensed they were all present.

I received information about Outer World matters, specifically about property, and the need to be active and attentive to problems. This raised a difficult issue, for the guidance now given contradicted what I had received from Arthur some years previous. It must be that Arthur's guidance had been wrong. But "no" came a voice, "it just means that the correct advice changes as times change." This was hard to handle and I felt a loosening of my connection to the Inner World. I could see that my family looked downcast and some of them turned away in sorrow. I was tired and weary of the whole game.

"Why does no one want to know the truth?" I said.

"No answer can be given until you complete your review of all your Inner World experiences." I did not know whose voice this was, but I knew that I needed to do this as well as to rest. I felt so tired sometimes, physically, spiritually, emotionally and mentally. I wished Eduki and my family goodbye and returned home. It seemed like a sad state of affairs but I must pursue the work with much greater vigour. Early starts were needed if I were to complete my review of the diary, for posterity if nothing else.

Tuesday 16th. 8.00pm The Cave. I entered with the Living Staff as it transformed into a serpent and fused into my spine. On my right were the nine versions of me. They rushed toward me and I asked them to line up so I may count them - tall and short, male and female, light and dark, positive and negative, warm and distant, successful and unsuccessful incarnations of me. Overall they seemed pleased with how I, and in turn they, had worked out.

"Never been this advanced before," said one, though I could not discern who. Geoffri came to mind and I queried that as a French nobleman surely he was more successful then I now?

"But I lost it all," he said, without elaboration. I did not ask further though maybe I should have done, maybe I should know how I undid myself in previous lives? I asked instead how to differentiate the voices of guidance, the nagging and persistent from the quiet and gentle. Some awareness came to me, although I knew not from which direction. "The nagging one is the mind, the Outer World or maybe the Dark Side. The other is small, fleeting, will speak once, or maybe twice if asked. This is the sound of the Inner Voice. It will be tiny at first but must be tuned into and listened out for. The true Inner Voice will not nag or worry. It will say its piece and then move on to the next situation. The trick is to be receptive and available to it. The Inner Voice never goes away, it is always available, but you are not always available to it." I asked the nine why no-one understood or accepted what I was trying to say and teach. "But you are ahead of your time! By more than twenty years!" Put like that the problem was straightforward. I thanked them. Nine was the number of completion. Nine beings in the Temple signified Universal energies, for example one represented the individuated physical form whether it be human or alien. Nine steps in the Tarot plus four components of structure in the world. I turned to Eduki for clarification of my thoughts. "I can add nothing to this,'" he said.

I went to leave and Eduki called me back to implant two pentacles, branding me in each hand, first left, then right. They represented and bestowed money, financial skill and healing energy. I thanked him and departed.

Thursday 18th. 6.30pm. The Cave. I greeted the nine to my right. They moved to surround me, linking hands to form a circle with me at the centre. They lifted me up above them and as I rose so did they. From this invisible world where they lived their goal was to advance my development and understanding, which in turn advanced theirs.

Back down on the ground we disbanded the circle and I greeted Eduki. The clarity of the image was so intense that it almost seemed that he stood right next to me in this room, and that this room had become part of the Inner World. He was tall and slim, wore white robes and shone brightly. I asked him who he was.

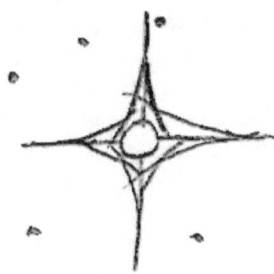

More Alien Script

Closer View of Yi'Chun's Home

"Your link to God," he replied, matter-of-factly. I felt safe enough to at least explore this and together we ascended to the Temple. I stood in front of the usual nine energies – the Eight Kings plus The Light. I turned to One, the alien on my nearest right. It was a small grey/brown being with eyes that closed into a slant and then opened as big and dark. He was not malevolent, but he was cold and distant, inquisitive and observant. One was his expression of Life, he was Alien as I was Human. We joined arms and hands. He could see the contents of my mind, and I his. He had not fully understood what it meant to live an individual life. In his species everyone had a specific task which was unique, but expressions of colour or personal energy were seen as wasteful and did not take place. In this sense we were very alien to him. I then asked for information and insight in exchange. Unusual images appeared in my mind, together with some characters or script than he used.

I again saw a star map showing his positioning. I would recognise the formation if I saw it again.

I turned to the position straight ahead at the end of the room - an extremely bright light. I approached it humbly, bowing my head and it entered me forcefully and powerfully. I was to use this to heal a client and thus to prove to myself that it could be done.

"Demonstrate the healing technique clearly. This is just one fraction of the power available – for all ends." I accepted it, thanking all present and returned to the ground outside the Temple. I was in no rush to return home in case I might forget something. I thanked Eduki, who urged me to return soon, and wished my family goodbye. They were smiling and happy. I returned and could still feel my hands tingling from the white light.

Monday 29th. 7.30pm. The Hermit. I entered directly through the Tarot card, with no cave this time. Eduki appeared as a white shining light on my left, with my nine friends on my right. We huddled around in a circle. They were nine and I was one, together we made ten, a new level and a new chance. I explained that I was here to visit the Hermit and turned to Eduki to guide me toward him. I asked what I should do with my nine friends?

"They will follow," was the reply as Eduki led me over to the left of the scene. At the foot of the mountain was some thick undergrowth that I had to climb through. I tried instead to dissolve it away with my mind and for one second thought I had succeeded, until a strong branch rebounded and smacked me on the forehead. I resigned myself to moving through more slowly and deliberately. Finally, a clearing was reached I asked if I could approach the Hermit.

"You may come closer," he replied. He was of late middle age, male, alone, roughly dressed and shaven. He was not intimidating or aggressive, but carried an aura that you did not mess with him. He sat on a log and I explained my situation with the nine as I approached him.

"We are already aware," came many voices around me. There was now a circle of Hermits all around. "We have many faces," they cried, "the Hermit has many faces." I did not know how to interpret this statement. Is the Hermit all things to all people? Or approached differently by different people? Or both? I asked what I should do to gain understanding of the Hermit nature. The lead Hermit replied. "You should review every single text you have, including those you have written yourself, for these answers. You will find it all there, already in your possession. The clues are Hermit, the number nine and the colour brown. Do not delay in this." I thanked him and moved to let him go, but he asked me to come closer. He took my wrists in his hands and would not let them go. I asked him what he carried his lantern for? "It is the Hermit's Guide – my inner light – the only thing that can be relied upon to guide me."

"Where may I find my lantern?" I asked.

"You already have it. It is your uniqueness and your knowledge of it. This is the great secret." Suddenly, all the many Hermits approached me, not attacking but overwhelming me. I was not scared, but a voice called out.

"He is not ready," it said, and the Hermits retreated, with one final cry.

"Go now. Integrate your nine selves. Then you will be strong enough." I rose up effortlessly and somersaulted out of the clearing. I wished Eduki and my family goodbye and promised to return soon.

[DECEMBER 2010]

Tuesday 14th. 7.00pm. The Astral. I could not see Arthur but I could immediately sense and hear him.

"We must look only to the future now," he said. "You need to focus on completing the integration of your nine selves. Do this by fully transcribing your diary experiences. Everything else is on hold until you can do that." I still could not see him. He had no form now and no longer presented himself in the old familiar way. He was beyond that now. "I will be back to work with animals. So many species have been lost," he said regretfully.

I asked him about the Tarot and the value of using separate suits for separate areas of life. He replied simply, "Try it. You still do not know what you have access to, what is at your fingertips, but you will." It was definitely him, free of the pain of the physical body. "But, remember, there is so much to do."

This place, the Astral, seemed to be one of waiting and rest. Nothing seemed to go on there, a world of potential one might say. As usual there were more questions than answers, but at least there were some answers. A series of images flashed into my mind, a kind of schema for this Astral World in relation to the others.

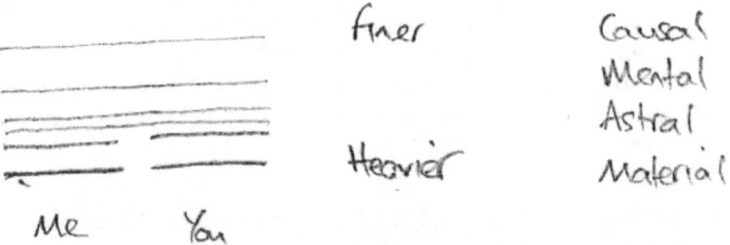

The Relationship of The Worlds

Upon returning home I felt light headed and disconnected with a lump in my throat.

Friday 31st. 11.30am. The Cave. I had some initial trouble holding a fixed focus but kept trying. As I passed through the cave I retrieved the Staff, allowing it to become part of me. I felt a buzzing electricity run through me. Moving into the landscape Eduki was there, and now, to my right, was an unknown a male figure. Eduki gestured toward my family of nine and they surrounded me in celebration. I asked to identify each one in turn and as I spoke their names they formed into their distinct identities. Amos gave me a wise nod, and Sophie a quiet smile. Derrick acknowledged me but sat on a rock some distance from the others. Ng was there, smiling and waving. Andrei, uniformed in bright blue tunic, stood to attention and saluted. Saria cartwheeled and smiled while Geoffri boomed with laughter. Kalia was much smaller than the rest, and smiled softly and warmly and the Assyrian guard, now identified himself. His name was Jordain and he was dressed in gold and purple, impassive but present. We all formed into a circle. Joining hands I was in between Amos and Jordain. We danced around. It seemed like a scene from card XXI The World. I stopped.

"What happens next?" I asked.

"We are always with you now," said Saria. "And you ask us matters related to our station. Geoffri holds position three for matters of society and communication. Derrick holds seven for privacy and study. Andrei holds five for movement and adventure. Sophie is eight for money and power. And so we get to know each other all over again. You see?" They all seemed happy and content, as was I. It was now time to take the next step and become one. One by one they each merged into me. It was a powerful experience, very intense. Flashing lights and sounds appeared inside me and all around. I took a deep breath and turned to Eduki.

"And what about you?" I asked. "As these are Guides, are you a Master?"

"Yes,'" he replied. "And Seraphia. And Hermes." He was dressed all in a white and now had a semi oriental appearance. A dog barked at my heels and Eduki gestured down to it. The animal started to move and I allowed to lead me off wherever it might. It led me to the Temple of Opportunities.

I positioned myself in the usual place. The dog barked as if to summon attendance of the beings. The two rows of four pillars filled up, but this time the energy of the operation was different. I was no longer fractious or uncertain. Everything was now calm and measured, as if the energies were taking stock of me. I felt bigger, as if I had greater presence and the alien was noticeable in his restraint, no longer trying to mind touch with me. The position directly ahead from which the Light had previously shone was empty. I pushed no further and decided to leave. I suggested to Eduki that as a Master he might be more at home up in the Temple.

"That's a different level." He said, patting me on the back. "Return soon!" The nine stayed within me and we all went home together.

Afterwards: Throughout all these years I had deliberately resisted looking back at my diary because I did not want to just 'pick up from last time' or force previous trips to define the parameters of new ones. I felt it was important to be absolutely clean each time and allow the incidents to take on a life of their own. I also have an extremely bad short term memory. I can tell you what someone was wearing twenty years ago but I could not tell you what happened this morning or yesterday. I can hold information in the moment if I concentrate hard, but I have to write most things down immediately or I forget them. I don't misremember, I forget. I intended to use this handicap as a proof-mechanism. If the trips and the information gelled together over time, bearing in mind that I would had forgotten what was said in between visits, then this would tell me that something real was actually going on. Finally now, upon reviewing my lengthy diary I discovered exactly this. I found that questions repeated on subsequent visits provided identical answers, and my attempts to catch the Guides and Masters out by twisting the questions never succeeded. By reading my diary I found the evidence I needed to dispel my lingering disbelief. The journeys had now finally proven their own validity. Eduki suggested that now I had cracked this egg I could move on.

[JANUARY 2011]

Saturday 8th. 8.00pm. The Cave. I entered and merged the Living Staff into my spine. Eduki was on my left now, a slight oriental man with a long beard dressed in white. The nine beings leapt out of my body and arranged themselves around me. I slowly identified them all in turn and the results was exactly in keeping with my records from last time. I asked whether the Guides took up stations in the Temple? They all shook their heads

"No, no, no," they all said in agreement. "We are within you, forming a whole. Without you and without each other we are incomplete. We enter the Temple together as one." So I turned to Eduki and asked if he took a station there?

"I see you there," he said, but gave no further information.

"Is my numbering sequence of the stations within the Temple correct?" I asked.

"Yes." Eduki then said that the best use of my time would be to return to the Outer World study of my notes where even more would soon be revealed. "The nine will come with you," he said. They merged back into me and I felt enormous, the tenth, the rebirth of the nine at a new level. There was an enormous surge of power within me. Eduki spoke forcefully. "Do not abuse this power." I returned. It had been a short journey.

Sunday 23rd. 4.30pm. The Cave. I visualised that all my external distractions and temptations were moved as one block onto my left hand side. Repeating this with intense concentration enabled the cave to come into view. But I knew that this could only be a temporary solution, and these matters would have to be resolved soon.

I entered, collected my Staff and greeted Eduki, dressed in his familiar oriental clothing, on my left. The nine emerged from me and lined up on my right. I identified them all present and correct. I asked that we join in a circle and I spoke of my Outer World financial problems. They shook their heads.

"We cannot answer this." I noticed that Derrick was absent from the circle. When I asked him to join he did not delay, and unexpectedly spoke.

"There is a great deal of crookery here," he said. "Do not lose out or have your efforts disadvantaged. Come to negotiated resolution. Hold firm and do not be the one taking the loss." He clearly understood my predicament, maybe having experienced something similar himself. I asked if I should correct the matter magickally in the Temple? They were not keen.

"This is not necessary," they said together, looking down, shaking their heads. I was most insistent that I should do this as I was not confident I could negotiate myself out from substantial losses. They looked downcast at this. "It is your choice, but we do not agree," they said. I took a deep breath and allowed them to merge back into me. Derrick was the last to do so after which I felt complete again. I turned to Eduki and presented him with the same problem, asking to force the issue in the Temple.

"It is not necessary. You have all you need to solve this without such action. Bring your full Outer World intelligence, sensitivity and power to bear upon the matter and you will resolve it." I maintained that I was very concerned about the financial implications and wanted external forces to help me. "It is not advisable," he said, 'you have all you need. It would be overkill."

"But what if I cannot sort it, and then I need magick, won't it be too late?"

"No," he said, "using magick in this way is an act of desperation, only when all else has failed." I did not like this, but I dared not go against my nine Guides and Eduki.

"Does this matter have a wider significance in my life?" I asked, trying to see the bigger picture.

"Of course," he replied.

"Am I facing the Abyss?" I asked.

"'Oh yes," he said.

"He has already passed it!" said Hermes, appearing from nowhere on the left.

"Yes he has, if he but knew it!" said Seraphia, now on the right. I looked to Eduki confused,

"But there is always more to learn," he said energetically. "Return home and continue with this matter, but do not neglect the work." The three of them wished me well. I let out the most enormous sneeze and returned home.

Thursday 27th. The Astral. I entered through the cave door and approached the central cradle. I entered it and ascended with a loud buffeting in my ears. I could sense Arthur to my near left. I had commanded myself to reach him and I gained the sense of moving forward. I greeted him warmly and it was a fast paced exchange. I didn't think I could hold my concentration very long.

"Where is this?" I asked.

"The Astral," he replied.

"Which is what?"

"The formation. And the beginning. Let's say the early stage of things."

"Thank you for everything," I said, "over the years."

"What are you doing now?" he said.

"'You don't know?" I asked.

"I don't know everything!" He replied as if his new state and location distanced him somehow.

"I am trying to follow in your footsteps," I replied.

"Hard, isn't it!" he said. 'It'll take some more time yet. Carry on as you are, making money but getting the balance." I asked about a fellow student of his, who I had done some study with but had fallen off the path. "Ha! Serves you right!" he replied, alluding to the frequent phone calls I was receiving from him, as Arthur had done from me. "There's not much that you can do, except maybe be less harsh with him. There is no need to generate resentment." I repeated that I was grateful for all he had done.

"What are you doing?" I asked him, enquiring if he was ready to return to work with animals yet.

"Not yet. It'll be a while yet." There may have been further words but I could not recall them. He suggested I return to rest and that having now made a good basic contact subsequent journeys would be easier. I thanked him again and said goodbye. I commanded myself to return, but it took a while to reconnect. It all felt correct and appropriate. I was pleased to have spoken with him. My card for the day had been The Hermit.

[FEBRUARY 2011]

Monday 7th. 7.00pm. The Astral. I entered the cave and before me was the Astral Cradle, as I might call it. I paused to notice what was going on around me, and review my recent experiences. I was deluged by a variety of sensory information. During this time I did not achieve full disconnection or projection, but did manage to arrive at some further understanding of the process.

The temptation, for me, once fully projected would be to not return or not want to return. I recognised this within me as a very real danger that I could not allow to happen, for it would of course totally defeat my life purpose.

My process of projection was a movement out as much as up. It was accompanied by enormous and shocking buffeting sounds as I felt myself separate to the left and then to the right of my body. I tipped forward and back, in and out of my body, then to the sides. The movements were subtle but definite. I could also discern colours and vibrations stronger than usual. A sense of rising was accompanied by that of emerging, or breaking out. I did not find the process to be about vertical movement.

It was certainly true that the more heavily involved I was with the material world the harder the process became. But conversely the easier the process the harder it was to engage back with the material world. Maybe the amount of progress I had made was correct after all.

[MARCH 2011]

Monday 7th. The Cave. My entry to and location of the cave was not at all instant and took considerable concentration. Finally within the Inner World nine beings jumped out of me. I could just about remember all their names. They responded and I was satisfied they were all present. Derrick stood slightly back, outside the group, tipping his hat forward to obscure his face. I coaxed him in and we all linked hands, dancing around and around, faster and faster, rising up at every circuit. I moved into the centre and all nine shot into me. Colours exploded all around my vision.

Composing myself I saw Eduki, Seraphia and Hermes in front of me. Eduki stood a little more in the foreground, Hermes slightly to the back. I asked a series of questions. Hermes took the lead in answering.

"Who is my Holy Guardian Angel?" I said.

"I am."

"Hermes? You?"

"Yes," he replied.

I found this difficult to accept. There must be a condition to this answer. Eduki and Seraphia noted my resistance, and were uneasy at my unease. I bowed my head slightly and said that I accepted the answer from Hermes.

"Who is Lam?" I continued. I had been reading speculations about Aleister Crowley's alien contacts.

"A fiction," said Hermes.

"What about the alien in the Temple," I asked.

"Something entirely different," he replied. I had many more questions but Hermes gestured me toward Eduki.

"What happens next?" I asked.

"You continue in the same vein. You must complete writing up these notes and answer all questions that arise. Then you will be ready for the next cycle." He continued. "Once this work is completed there will be a new phase. That is when you will start to put all this into practice, gain more pupils and become of more help. The future is dark for many. Outer World events threaten many people. It will soon be your turn to help guide them. So many need it." I returned. I scrawled notes in what I noticed afterwards was appalling handwriting. My music ran out.

Monday 28th. The Cave. Almost as soon as I closed my eyes I could feel the pull of the Inner World. It was then a swift journey to the cave and through to the Inner World. The Staff morphed into a serpent before fusing into me. This rush of energy was accompanied by the appearance of the nine to my right, with Hermes, Seraphia and Eduki to my left.

Again among the nine Derrick was distant. As I approached him wanting to know why, the others parted. As I spoke to him he momentarily appeared as a criminal, raging loudly at me. This subsided when I showed no fear and tried to find out why. He insisted on standing slightly distant while he explained his time in the Outer World. He had been a gangster. Using his power to procure sex he had abused his status and his position. His had been a dark incarnation and he carried this with him still. I understood this but commanded him to join the group circle. He offered no argument and immediately fell in line. Interesting, I thought, as I commanded so they must comply? This theory was soon put to the test when Derrick retreated again. I commanded him to return, louder and louder but it wasn't working now. A different approach was needed.

"I forgive you," I said to him. "We are all trying to make amends." He turned to me, surprised, and pleased. Then I understood. Derrick was a dark individual, sullen, isolated and contrary. Therefore, inevitably, at least one part of me was the same. I could see that this was true, and by forgiving Derrick I was also to an extent, forgiving myself, allowing both myself and him to no longer be like that. It felt good to have soothed, if not completely healed, the breach. Derrick now joined fully in the circle and we started to dance around, faster and faster, until we took off and the nine flew into me again. The next thing I knew I was in the Temple of Opportunities. Hermes did something, producing some kind of protection.

The stations this time were planetary.

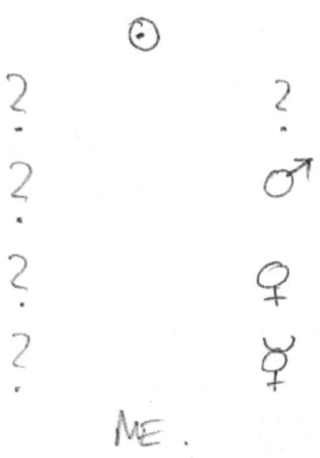

Planetary Arrangement of the Temple

As I had now completed my inner nine, so I would now complete my outer nine. This would involve new connections to new forces and a great deal of study and learning. I was urged to come back on subsequent nights. There was much to do. I felt exhausted but things were starting to make sense.

Tuesday 29th. The Cave. Entering the cave I fused the Staff into me and passed through. Hermes, Seraphia and Eduki were all present. My nine were not there, but, said Hermes, "they will be if commanded." I did so and they emerged out from me. I asked Hermes if he was Mercury, and if Eduki was Mars and so on. "This is not the place for these questions," he said, urging a visit to the Temple.

"I would rather do it here," I replied, although I did not know where my sudden dominance had come from. Eduki looked at Hermes, a little shocked. There was no reply. I relented and the nine flooded back into me. Feeling a rush and vibration I was in the Temple. Hermes, Seraphia, Eduki in their positions as before and a bright light at the end. Hermes spoke. He seemed to be the most senior.

"There is much study and practise to do now," he said, 'Much assimilation and integration." Many Outer World issues and images flooded my mind. I asked what should be my priority? "Practise, study, read, and then approach the daily issues of life with that knowledge. This will teach you all you need." I approached the Sun-like Light at the end of the Hall and outstretched my arms in readiness to receive the light. It flooded and enlivened me. I knelt and thanked the assembled intelligences. I was now both able and willing to walk freely up and down the central aisle between the two pillars. I asked where the alien had gone.

?"That is something else," came the voice of Hermes. "Oh and don't believe all that you read," said Hermes, tapping me on the shoulder. I laughed. I returned to the floor of the Inner World. I checked the nine were outside of me in order. All correct and appropriate, including Derrick who seemed now fully engaged and a connected part of the group.

Postscript: Before this journey I had been reading a lot of mystical and occult books. In every book that drew me I found something, even if it was only one line of sense. But there were many books to read and practices to master. Life from now on would be busy. I had these unusual teachings and all I had to do now was follow where they led.

[APRIL 2011]

Saturday 2nd. 9.30am. The Planet Mercury. I performed a deliberate protection exercise, known as the Lesser Banishing Ritual of the Pentagram and positioned a NASA photograph of the planet Mercury about twelve inches in front of me. It took some time to focus on the image and I kept thinking that is not what the planet looks like, although I did not know where I got that idea from.

Closing my eyes I felt my awareness of the image shift subtly. The planet was scarred and cracked, burned and singed. It was, to all intents and purposes, scorched and ruined. I called for Hermes and his guidance, and it took a while to fully isolate his voice.

"Mercury is a dead planet," he said, "it has achieved its state. Others, like Earth, are worlds in progress." He continued. "Earth is like a hive and its inhabitants like bees, with many of them just going through the motions." He reminded me that, "you must remain in the world, removed from it on one hand, but still active within it. Withdrawal and isolation is not the way."

I could see that colour and life went hand in hand. The NASA image of Mercury was colourful, but in reality the planet was a grey rock, devoid of colour and of life. This was its final state. Its energy had gone elsewhere.

My vision was now of Earth, not Mercury. I could see the planet from space. North Africa and Japan stood out, seeming to glow. I wondered what future space travellers would see. Hermes said that such events were coming soon and would be transformational for many peoples consciousness.

I returned home, but could not move my legs. I tried not to panic, but they just looked lifeless. It took a while for sensation to return, after which I performed the same protection ritual to close.

Monday 18th. The Astral. Arthur. I found the shoreline and cave without too much trouble. I passed through into the cave and could perceive the cradle beside me. I merged into it, and it into me and instantly I felt a rush of air and buffeting in my ears. Then within seconds the noise had gone but I had not moved. I thought for a moment that I had failed, but then I realised that the Astral was not 'up', but 'in.' And there I was.

I called for Arthur and off to my left there was a shapeless and formless energy mass. It spoke harshly and critically. This was not right, this was not Arthur. I called over to my right. Slightly behind me and to the right was Arthur. He wore the dress he was so familiar in – blue jumper, very bulky, more in his prime than toward the end of his early life. This felt much more correct. I approached him, he was welcoming. I said I was trying to do the work.

"So now you know how hard it is!" he said. "But, to be fair, you are doing it." He continued by saying that the key to the work is to create ripples in the pond. "By themselves individual actions mean little and have little effect, but cumulatively they have greater impact. See, consult, read for as many as possible." Looked at this way the task was not insurmountable or daunting. This was the kind of advice he always used to give – unexpected, straightforward, a new look at an old problem. I asked about two clients who would visit as a couple in the coming days. "There is a little attention seeking here I think, one of them likes to show you off," he said, "but it won't hurt. Look at the practice it will give you." He suggested great results could be gained by exactly replicating his Arpedio method of healing. I resisted this and he gave me a familiar facial response, as if to say 'really?'

I asked about finances, because being a Hermit seemed not to pay too well. He was reassuring and said something about "having enough," continuing "you have plenty of knowledge, put it into practice." I had no come back to this.

"Is that all?" he asked, exactly as he used to. I felt a giant sneeze coming on. Arthur picked himself up and waved goodbye. He seemed content enough. I sneezed and snapped back violently.

[MAY 2011]

Sunday 8th. 12noon. The Cave. I entered swiftly intent on speaking with Saria, Andrei, and Sophie regarding property matters. On arrival I could feel all nine escape from me and line up. It seemed good for them to come here, which was after all a home for them.

The three I selected split into a separate group. I wanted insight around my Outer World idea of buying garages to rent out. Sophie said, "a high quality location is critical." Andrei said, "somewhere people travelled into, a town centre maybe?" Saria said, "somewhere solid in a good condition." I asked what else did I needed to know, where could this plan go wrong?

"Impatience to do a deal, any deal," said Jordain, suddenly present.

"And paying too much," said Geoffri, also suddenly involved. This was worthwhile information, which in a sense told me what I already knew.

"Think about it, plan it, calculate it," urged Derrick from the sidelines. They all seemed involved now and in agreement that given all these things it was a good idea. I thanked them and turned toward Hermes, Seraphia and Eduki. I bowed my head slightly and held aloft the Staff. Hermes pointed up to the Temple. I checked that this was him and that his advice was correct. Once I was satisfied the nine fled back into me. Suddenly we were there and the Hermes, Seraphia and Eduki took up their positions.

I bowed low and banged my Staff on the ground. The light from directly ahead - The Lord of the Earth - was blinding and the three turned away shielding their eyes. I approached, firmly and confidently but with a degree of deference and respect that I had not managed to master before.

The Lord confirmed that the broad sweep of my progress was good. Hermes remarked that my book – *The Key to Time* – would not be published. "We have made it so," he said. "Your challenge now is to keep on keeping on. Individual obstacles will present themselves for specific knowledge and learning, but the overall direction is correct so far. Keep learning, reading, writing, progressing, helping." His voice continued, "The essence of eleven, your current dominant energy, is two ones, the need to achieve independence in both worlds."

I thanked the assembled and returned back to the ground of the Inner World. I could see the Forest of Souls ahead and approached it. It was dark, the resting place between lives, resting to come to terms with whatever happened. Resting to recover energy. Resting while the world catches up. I returned to centre, aware of the Eastern Sea to my left, while to the right of the scene was an unknown and unexplained area.

"You have lots to do. Determination and discipline are needed now," I was told. I returned and the music had again run out.

Realisations: The nine Guides can be invoked to answer different questions, but I must make sure I don't compound my blind spots, by ignoring the Guides who might help the most. It took Jordain, Geoffri and Derrick, who I had not chosen, to provide the most useful information.

Thursday 12th. 6.30pm. King of Pentacles. It had been a while since I entered directly through a card, but it was clear and instant. Many Kings of Pentacles from the Outer World flashed through my mind, most of them negative stereotypes of bankers, stick-in-the-mud bosses and unimaginative chairmen. This King however was seated at his large and expensive mahogany desk amidst a vineyard. He was the very picture of wealth and control.

"How can I become like you?" I asked.

"Are you sure you want to?" he replied.

"I would like to have the choice, at least to investigate the idea," I said. He passed me two golden coins, one for each hand. They burned into me as I took them from him.

"Now rub them together," he said. As I did so many smaller golden coins and dust sprang into the air. "Money does not like to stand still. It needs to meet other money and opportunities in order to grow. There is no point just putting it in your pocket."

I asked about a particular lock-up garage investment I had been pursuing.

"Yes, but not that one," he said. "It should be one of quality, in a quality location."

"What about the stock market?" I asked.

"It is a market under the control of the market-makers. Their goal is to relieve you of your money, so it is just a game and they are your opponents. Mistakes have and will be made in this field." I wanted more specific investment knowledge.

"Is the commodity boom over?" I asked.

"Yes, look now to major international drug companies." He replied. This was at variance to my Outer World conclusions so I queried it again, but he did not defer, reminding me that my impatience was a killer. "You must be as the rain," he pointed over his shoulder, "sometimes you bang your head against a brick wall, but market makers and others that want to take money from you are all relying on your lack of determination and persistence. Prove them wrong." He paused. "If you are going to do this you must drive your efforts from your desk. Comfortable and quality surroundings are needed in order to inspire you. You will not be successful in a huddled mess. But as you do more in this world of Pentacles you must ensure that you do not lose sight of the other factors or the purpose of your life." I thanked the King and asked if I could do anything for him. He gestured that I should simply act on his words.

I now turned to the right and greeted Seraphia, Eduki and Hermes in that order. Eduki was most dominant and spoke straight away.

"There is much to do. You may have integrated the nine into you but now you must live them, daily. This is no longer a pastime, it is serious and committed daily life." There was a renewed urgency in his tone, like we were readying for something. He said much had been learned but that I should go now to eat and "return soon." I snapped back to my body, shaken and disorientated.

Friday 13th. 4.00pm. The Cave. My nine Guides flew out of me and assembled to the right. Seraphia, Eduki, and Hermes appeared to my left. I greeted them all, and again Eduki was active.

"Shall I address you as Master Eduki?" I asked. The answer was unclear, but it seemed an appropriate thing to do. I asked of his provenance, but again the answers were unclear. All that I could discern was that he was oriental with a long white beard. He asked if I were ready. I said I was and followed him up some stone stairs.

"This is sometimes called Jacob's Ladder. The Stairs of Life, the DNA Helix," he said. "The purpose of Life is to ascend this and activate the DNA, adding new possibilities. DNA is not fixed, it changes as the person changes. It changes significantly, not trivially." I imagined arguing that in a court of law and he advised me not to bother. "As experiences and learning takes place so the individual DNA changes, just as the lines on the hand change." We found a doorway. "Enter," he told me.

It was the Temple. I stood in the usual position, all as normal, but now the spaces were filled by the entities from before, although I could only clearly discern the alien in the first position to my right. I banged my Staff on the floor, calling them to attention and protecting myself. The alien wanted to mind touch, but I resisted, instead approaching the Light at the end.

"What do you want?" it spoke.

"To know what I am here for, exactly, precisely," I said.

"Continue exactly as you are, but now make it bigger, do more of the same. It seems not much, but in fact it is everything. And it will keep you occupied all of this lifetime."

"And the next," came another voice. I returned to the alien to mind fuse. He allowed me to go first and I placed my hand on his head. I instantly felt cold all over, but could see the stars of Niberia 5 together with him and his species transporting themselves around their planet. They used a vehicle which could hover just above the surface, over land or water, and there seemed to be a lot of water around. The vehicle had a spiked, downwards nose and this seemed important, but I could not make out the type of propulsion. The being seemed to be the only one in the vehicle. We switched and he mind melded to me. I heard a chatter, a vibration and a tone. It was not voice, but a sound, communicating with others.

"I did not know that. We did not know that," was all that I could make out. I broke off contact and thanked all those around me, returning to the ground with Eduki. He said to return soon and the nine came back into me. Before leaving I asked Eduki how to energise the Tarot cards, to make them more suitable and receptive. He referred me to Hermes,

"By association, and through the hands. Charge them with the intention and goal. Wrap them appropriately, bring stones, money, materials, solomonic seals, wrapping, silks, and incenses of correspondence. Imbibe them with the task at hand." Totally exhausted now I returned home.

Wednesday 25th. 4.00pm. The Cave. Around this time I had started to pull together what I had learned into some kind of overview. My working title was Principia Specialisimus – the fundamentals of being a special human being. But I was missing something. What was it? I arrived in the cave, allowed my nine out of my body and called for Hermes.

"Tolerance," was the answer beamed into my third eye. This was of course blindingly obvious and a step beyond the mere celebration of differences.

"So why do we lack tolerance?" I asked.

"Because of your inability to follow your uniqueness and others perceived responsibility for that," Hermes replied.

"So what am I missing that will making Principia Specialisimus the explanation of everything and of all the teachings?" Eyebrows were raised at this.

"Are you sure?" came the answer. I insisted that I was.

"Very well, you will be sent the information, and guided toward the experience in the next few days." I was impatient for something now, but the same answer was repeated to me again. I would have to accept that so I welcomed my nine back into me, thanked and departed.

Afterwards: The following days panned out exactly as Hermes had indicated, the 26th and 27th May 2011 had seen me receive, during prolonged meditations, a detailed explanation of the nature and purpose of human life today. It was called *You Are The Only One There Is*. It is presented and expanded upon in *Emergence*.

Saturday 28th. 2.30pm. The Cave. I approached with the intention of filling in the final missing pieces of Principia Specialismus. I sensed Hermes immediately, before I had fully entered.

"Now apply the given principles to your own life." Much like the rest of the information, that was a comment I had not expected. I completed the entry procedure and my nine departed from me. I greeted Eduki, Seraphia and Hermes to my left. I faced them squarely and asked if those words had come from them. Hermes confirmed they did.

"This is the creed and code of Hermes. Now apply it to your life and make the appropriate changes." I wondered whether this meant to my connections with others?

"Not necessarily," I was told. "Only by applying it will you see its truth." I thanked them and the nine peeled back into me. "No-one else has these teachings," continued Hermes. "They appear in fragments, scattered throughout parts of life. Nowhere else do they appear whole." I returned home, overwhelmed.

[JUNE 2011]

Monday 6th. The Cave. I fused the Living Staff along the length of my spine before I entered the Inner World itself, passing straight through the cave wall. I greeted in order from left to right Eduki, Seraphia and Hermes. Then my nine.

"Who should I address my questions to?" I asked.

"Whoever is appropriate for the question. The nine know about you, the three know about everything else." Eduki appeared front and centre, so I spoke to him. First I asked about how to assist a friend, with her neighbours dispute.

"It is not appropriate to coerce, just to protect," he said.

"On that topic, do I need protection when I attend my MBS events?"

"Oh, yes, very much needed. Protect everything that matters."

"But computers do not react well to the power and energy raised by such efforts," I protested.

"Computers are getting better, their power flows are cleaner, and they are more able to withstand it. Brand new computers are better still, but each new device might take some adjustment and harmonisation with your energies." This was valuable to avoid frying every new piece of technology I bought.

"Should I exhibit my services in Holland?" I asked.

"Yes, but not in the small towns. Visit them if you wish but to achieve what? Go where the open minded population is, Amsterdam, The Hague, Utrecht, Groningen. Recognisable places with sizeable populations like Rotterdam. There is no hurry on this, it is a long term plan."

I asked that Eduki now enter and return with me to the Outer World. He obliged and his merging was hugely powerful and effective leaving me feeling somehow not me.

Tuesday 7th. 7.30pm. The Cave. I performed the protection ritual known as the Lesser Banishing Ritual of the Pentagram and I entered intending to speak to Hermes about Outer World obstacles and reversals. Instead I greeted Eduki as he emerged from me. No-one else was around. I quizzed him about my concerns on the direction of society.

"Are you sure you want to know." He said. I did. "Very well. It is time to live up to and to put into practise all that you have learned. Theory without action brings – has brought – frustration," he continued, "the World needs you." I questioned this, surprised at his words. He did not flinch, simply saying "there is so much to do."

"But I cannot do it all," I said.

"You don't need to. You just need to do some of it," he replied.

Wednesday 8th. 4.00pm. The Cave. I had some difficulty identifying Eduki and spoke to a vague and uncertain shape.

"Are you my Guide?" I asked.

"I will guide you for the meantime," came the reply. This seemed unsatisfactory. I pushed further, he replied more directly and clearly, but still I was in doubt. In truth I was still a little in doubt about the whole thing.

"What is the problem?" I asked. "Why do I still doubt and resist?"

"That is a funny question, because it is you that has all the answers!"

"Is it you that I can hear and sense, in the Outer World during the day?"

"Yes, of course." he replied.

"Will you come back with me now?"

"No. And this will help you to tell the difference." The Living Staff fused with me and the nine entered me. "Persistence," he continued, "is essential. Binging on knowledge or information is not beneficial. It must be practised and developed regularly, with discipline."

Sunday 12th. 5.30pm. The Cave. I entered intending to astrally project to Arthur or some Outer World location. I scanned the possibilities. Manhattan Island, Moscow, Brisbane. I did not go any further.

I entered the floor to ceiling Vortex Elevator in the cave. After a little resistance I partially disconnected. Then something surprising happened. I saw myself. One second I was in my body looking at my astral form, the next I was in my astral looking at my physical form. My earthly body was tired and worn, ugly in comparison to my astral light body. I was in need of a thorough energetic wash. I could see dozens, maybe hundreds of hooks and dirt from others, which all needed to be cast off. My cleansing needed to be multi-dimensional, physical, emotional and mental. I had picked up a great deal of rubbish which must now be discarded if I am to handle and direct the energies that are trying to flow through me. I returned home to begin this work immediately.

Monday 13th. 7.30pm. The Hermit. I entered through the card and greeted the Hermit in a forest clearing. He was not overly welcoming. I asked if he were, in fact, Arthur?

"No," was the abrupt answer. I asked about the Living Staff and Serpent. He threw his staff in the middle of the clearing before us. It transformed into two separate serpents. They both approached and swallowed me whole, one from my head, one from my feet. I could feel it in those areas, not yet elsewhere in my body.

"The preparation for initiation, but not the initiation itself," said The Hermit. "Dark and Light. Strength comes from recognition, control and balance of both. Not being victim to the Dark Side but recognising its reality. Not being fooled into thinking that all is Love. The goal is the recognition and use of both in balance." That was all he had to say and he referred me to Hermes who was stood nearby.

"Who are you then, Hermit?" I asked the man.

"A practitioner of the Teachings of Hermes. As you will be too."

I turned to Hermes and asked if he would assist me in my Outer World money making ventures?

"No," he replied firmly.

"But can I command you to do so?" I continued.

"Yes, but it is not advisable." he replied. I recognised that I did not have the power to do this. I asked next of the Staff. "You have your own Staff now and this in turn will be as powerful as the one belonging to The Hermit."

"What is the Book of Thoth?" I asked.

"An instruction manual for life." he replied. Throughout this exchange his answers were instant, without any form of delay or pause. I thanked him and went home.

Sunday 19th. 10am. The Cave. Hermes spoke the moment I arrived.

'The nine are inside you now and will answer if addressed directly. They have no need to manifest here and it will only cause confusion if they do so, although they will obey if you command this. Address each to their own number and association and he or she will answer. These nine combine with you and make ten, the new level achieved as shown in The Wheel of Fortune. Every day is an initiation now, a trial, but with some time off as the occasional reward."

I had the growing sense that much of what I had built up in the Outer World would not survive this transition so I asked about this impending destruction.

"Might it be the destruction of my old behaviours and attitudes rather than all that I have achieved?"

"Oh yes, it can be," he said. "But that is up to you." Indeed it was, as always. "That is enough for now," he concluded. I departed humbly.

Thursday 23rd. 7.00pm. The Cave. I immediately saw Seraphia, Eduki, and Hermes. They seemed clearer than before. I was still concerned about my future. Every January I performed a Year Ahead Tarot reading for myself. The cards for August, now only a month away, were doom laden – Ten of Swords and Sun reversed.

"The death of belief," said Hermes. "The death of an old belief. You will survive, look at the cards which follow, but you cannot move forward without things like this." His tone suggested that I should really know this already. Of course I did, conceptually, theoretically. But now it had to bite. I thanked him and departed.

[JULY 2011]

Monday 4th. 8.00pm. The Cave. I reached Arthur in his usual position and demeanour. It had been an extremely challenging time in the Outer World, with all sorts of disasters and difficulties finding their way to my door. I asked him what was to be done.

"This work – being The Hermit - is a different level of challenge than you have undertaken before. It requires daily practise and constant mindfulness on the task at hand and the energies around you." He offered to merge into me, and to return to the Outer World with me to assist through the next little while. I accepted this and felt a surge of energy. I opened my eyes and felt different – older. I better not forget to let him out again!

Wednesday 20th. 5.30pm. The Astral. Arthur left my body. As I felt him go I became lighter and more in control. This was serious stuff. For the past week I had been struggling through the days, really very tired.

"You should have let me out sooner," he said, then continued, "I will return again if necessary. Slim down your life. Money is important, but more than enough is a waste, it takes too long to attend to. Focus on what is important and re-orientate your life around it. Finish your writing so you can move on with further studies." I said goodbye and departed, still tired but relieved.

Saturday 30th. 10.00am. The Cave. I tried to identify all the nine Guides lined up before me but I could not remember all their names. This was very poor of me. I asked Derrick a little about his remaining distance from the others. He spoke again of his – not totally healed - sense of isolation, disappointment, frustration, and how these things were therefore also within me. I tried to welcome him back into my body but Hermes intervened and cautioned against having only one of the nine within me.

"You are the Law," said Hermes. "Things can only proceed at your pace. This is the same for anyone." He stood silent, waiting. It was up to me to present myself, willing and able, for the next tasks. Eduki spoke. "You must complete all that you have on your plate."

"Or drop it," interjected Saria. Hermes advised me to certainly not take on anything new, though "in due course you must teach these method to others and make an extensive development of it. Rituals and practices for money and success along these lines are acceptable." Again Hermes fell silent and stood waiting.

The nine merged back into me, followed in turn by Eduki, Seraphia and then lastly and most powerfully, Hermes.

[AUGUST 2011]

Tuesday 9th. The Cave. Straight into the cave, the nine within me and the three emerging from me. The Outer World was on fire, it was the midst of a series of riots across England. I asked Hermes what could be done to protect the world.

"You should volunteer whole heartedly for such a task, without reservation." I replied that I was not certain about that. "You must be all in," he said. I agreed that the situation was serious and he smiled and merged with me powerfully. "Regarding these current riots you have to treat each person as an individual. To calm the flames visualise a burdensome cloud, weighing heavily upon the troublemakers, making them feel sleepy, stoned and drunk. Ask to see the key ringleaders and visualise yourself knocking them over." I did this and saw them in Manchester, Bristol, Glasgow, East, North and South London and in Brighton. I focused hard on this, but did have a slight concern. Should I really be doing this? "This is the correct course of action - today. But you must always check directly with me before any future interference - for that is what it is." He also encouraged me to share this with others. I thanked him and departed. So it was possible after all, to intervene and influence events.

Tuesday 16th. 8.30pm. The Wheel of Fortune. Using the old procedure I enlarged the card and stepped through it to witness a fairground behind meshed steel fences. The Bull was on the entrance booth.

"There is always a price to pay," he said. I paid it with the golden coin I had implanted in my hands. I looked up toward the large Ferris wheel and asked of its significance.

"It is The Wheel of Life," came the voice of Eduki, who had accompanied me. "The Wheel must turn, up and down, good and bad, dark and light, progress and consolidation, reflection and action." He continued, "the horizontal points on the wheel, see 3pm, 9pm, signify the 'to' and 'from' states of change. This is the nature of things. You have been down and now you are on the up."

The creatures, who I had not seen for some time, were at the top of a large slide. From left to right they were the Lion, then Eduki, the Bull and then the Eagle. Propelling themselves down the slide The Lion was by far the fastest, followed by Eduki and the Eagle very close together. The Bull came in last. This seemed like a different result to their last race, some years ago.

Suddenly a new figure appeared. It was Thoth, in his form of a man with a bird's head. He was clear and distinct in outline, without colour. The four urged me to attend him. He was outside the fence so I left the park.

"My bird's head is not literal," he said, "it is the only way I can be understood by those who view me. It represents my advanced mental and intuitive state." I assessed him some more. He wished to merge with me and I allowed this. It lasted many seconds – seemingly far longer than usual energetic mergings. I shook, maybe even physically. He left something, some part of him within me.

"What will happen next?" I asked.

"Let us see what the next few days brings," he replied. The creatures and Eduki were very pleased, celebrating. The Bull and the Lion were particularly vocal. The image of Thoth seemed to be burned in my mind. I thanked all concerned and departed.

Thoth

Wednesday 17th. 8.00pm. Three of Cups. I saw three sisters. Blonde, ginger and dark haired, curly, short and long haired, taller, shorter, rounder. Three distinct types.

"We do everything together," they said in unison, dancing around a wooden tree stump with flowers and plants all around, in sumptuous robes with rugs and ornate decoration everywhere. Their faces were pretty and smiling.

My attention was caught by Thoth, and my mind was flushed with his name. After a little floating around on my part I managed to hold my focus upon him. He passed me a scroll, but I looked and could see nothing on it. He insisted I look again. I could still see nothing. I was feeling frustrated and racking my brains as to why I could not see anything.

"It is blank for you to write your truth on," said Thoth, ushering me back toward the three sisters. All around was pleasure, enjoyment, the fine things, carefree celebrations and indulgences. They offered themselves to me and I made love with each of them in different ways. They wished this, it was their goal, to attain my essence. After this complete immersion in joy I asked them to show me their distorted expressions. Now they did not share anything. They took each for themselves, were overindulgent, greedy and wasteful. For all they had they were still not satisfied, constantly searching for gratification and never finding it.

"It is insights such as this that you must write in your scroll, to create your truth of the Tarot," said Thoth, concluding "all your packs of cards are to be consecrated and charged for this purpose." I gave thanks and departed.

Thursday 18th. Ten of Wands. A man was struggling with ten large sticks. He could not see where he was going because of them. All his energy was focused on maintaining his grip of them and he was unable to move forward. Not being able to see ahead was bad for me, I knew that much. Too many projects and burdens at once was not a good situation to be in.

"We struggle on because we have done for so long," he said. "We accumulate these sticks over such a long time that we forget there might be another way. It becomes almost automatic," he said. How true.

"So what happens when you realise this?" I asked. The man paused, threw down his sticks and walked off into the distance. It seemed such a waste, all that effort just to throw it all away. Surely a better way would be to transform the ten sticks into one and begin the journey again at a higher level, carrying only one burden and thus able to see forward? The man now wore a harness that prepared him for his struggle.

"It is simple," said the man. "Tens are achievements yet also burdens. They are not yet at the new level, but are worn out from the old level."

Tuesday 23rd. 7.30pm. Death.

'You will always be alive, even when you are dead.'

I immediately greeted the cloaked figure of the Grim Reaper. There was no sense of evil about him whatsoever, if anything he just projected a plodding, matter-of-fact, inevitability. There nothing in the slightest bit scary going on. Hermes appeared to my right to prepare me for "the next procedure, induction," he explained. "Death is another kind of Fool. A wash, a purification," he said. Outer World matters filled my mind. I could not release them. "They need to be let go of now," Hermes insisted. I turned back to the Grim Reaper at Hermes' request and allowed him to perform his work. His black cloak engulfed me completely. I felt extremely light headed, dizzy, vibrating and shuddering harder and harder. This lasted for quite sometime and I took it as a sign of the much needed purification and renewal. Once the operation was over I thanked Death, but he had already moved on to continue his business elsewhere. I requested information from Hermes on a name from the Outer World. Hermes gestured me toward the Library. It was on my right hand side and I struggled to see it clearly or to get the correct point of view. I re-orientated the scene and saw the book I required. It was a disappointingly slim volume. The book spoke to me, "not much of a life, a lack of responsibility."

This was a friend of a friend who had sought me out for healing. I had tried to encourage a reality check in her but she seemed convinced that I was some kind of miracle worker. I asked The Keeper how I could move beyond this and try to help the woman. The Keeper seemed pleased and provided all the information I needed, and more. Hermes also seemed to be present at this point. The information was detailed and specific, a list of measures, that if I could persuade the woman to cooperate with would surely provide relief.

"This is a large undertaking," said Hermes, "but one that will reveal much to you." He went on to remind me "Inner World experiences are merely the catalyst for the real Outer World initiations. It begins in the Inner World and is practised in the Outer World until fully understood in the Inner World. This is how knowledge is gained, the congruence of the two worlds." I thanked Hermes and went to leave.

"No, thank *you*," he replied.

Thursday 25th. 5.45pm. Four of Wands. I stepped immediately onto a pathway, divided into four lanes, each paved distinctly. I was surrounded by garlands, hung from four large staves. I touched one of them, it was hot and alive. As I walked through them and along the pathway I could see a castle on top of a mountain in the near distance, but there was no one around. It was a restful, peaceful, but also silent and sterile environment. A good place to rest, but not so good a place to live. I asked about the possible negative expression of this place. Eduki answered, "boredom, stagnation, consolidation, rest not utilised or welcomed or embraced fully."

I moved further along the path and then inside the castle which was plush and luxurious, but empty and stale. I asked for further guidance on the woman who thought I could miraculously heal her. Hermes appeared and spoke.

"Diabetes is a disease related to overstimulation, and its symptoms are a reaction to that stimulation, be it physical, dietary, emotional or mental. There is little you can do with this woman in terms of guidance as she is caught up in the world of competition and thus lost for now. But you can still make some attempt at healing."

Eduki also chipped in an urged me to make this effort even if I had already discounted the results. I thanked them and said I would return.

"Wait, something else," said Hermes. "You should visit Aleister Crowley, at the very end of his life." (I did in fact do this on 25th and again on 28th August and this is recorded in *The Key to Time).*

Realisations: The cards I was using were stage one of an initiation. Visiting a card in the Inner World activates stage two of the experience in the Outer World. Thus, as the Inner World becomes weirder, more amazing and more challenging, so must the Outer World.

[OCTOBER 2011]

Monday 10th. 7.00pm. The Cave. Directly into the Inner World. There were so many figures present, including Hermes/Thoth, flying high in the sky. I followed him and felt the rush and noise as we merged together. His voice was clear and true.

"The Complete Works of Arthur Norris Volumes One and Two. Volume One is straightforward, a collection of all you have. Volume Two should contain all things magickal and the details of the Dark Side. Remember your eleven, it is two ones - you and others, your work and your work for others. A Magician can do both." I saw the image of a Magician pointing up with one hand and down with the other. I let this sink in for a while.

"Are you coming back with me?" I asked.

"Oh yes," he said. And I returned at least knowing what to do next.

Wednesday 19th. 8.00pm. The Rosy Cross Back of the Thoth Tarot.

The Rosy Cross

Through and beyond the heart of the rose was nothing, a total void. I felt myself disconnect, falling forward then back, to one side then the other. I could see nothing but in this void I sensed that I could in fact move anywhere.

Within the void I thought of the year 1942. Instantly I was surrounded by and aware of gunfire and tanks, death and metal. I could smell the burning and hear the incredible noise.

Still with the void all around me I thought of the year 2162. I saw this place, this house its street, garden and beyond to the main road a mile away, levelled. The ground, currently a valley was totally flat and empty, with a wind whipping across from the East. It was as if the levelling had been deliberate, the purposeful creation of a new landscape? The image was real and shockingly clear.

I asked to visit God. The buzzing in my ears grew louder and the sense of disconnection grew stronger as I felt a presence above me.

"What do you want?" came a voice.

"What do you want of me?" I asked. I was nudged toward Hermes.

"You have contact with Hermes." And the presence disappeared. Hermes spoke.

"My teachings shall come again, through you." And that was it. I returned. Maybe Arthur's teachings were the foundation, the road toward the greater teachings of Hermes and Thoth? I felt the presence of Hermes all around me as I opened my eyes.

Sunday 30th. 12noon. The Cave. I collected the Living Staff and allowed it to transform and fuse into me. The Staff itself lodged into my spine and the crystal that was inset at its top merged into my brain. This seemed entirely natural and normal. I now saw Eduki and Seraphia to my left and Hermes up above the ground, in the centre. The nine were outside of me, to the right. I asked that the Guide or Guides I should work with right now step forward. Eduki and Hermes came closer.

Eduki identified himself as my Guide and then said that Hermes was a Master. At the very same time I heard the word 'servant' in my head. The image of Thoth took a step back. I checked all this again with Eduki and held out my hands for evidence of his commitment. He dispelled all my doubts and his image came more closely into view. He was dressed in purple oriental robes, decorated with symbols and patterns. He wore a long beard, pointed at the end. I asked where he came from?

"I once worked with Confucius. But of course he got most of the credit!"

We talked about Outer World difficulties. They troubled me immensely, more than perhaps they should. I had incurred great financial loss in one of my businesses during late August and many of my Outer World plans had been wrecked. "We can re-build you!" said Eduki, pointing to the Sun. "But you must take regular visits here to rebuild your connection, to set right any wrong turnings." The Sun came down in male form, with it arms outstretched. It approached me and it fused with me. I burned and tingled, but did not tense up or fight it. I allowed healing and restoration for some seconds before I released it, thanking Eduki and retracing my steps. The nine seemed happier now, smiling, laughing and waving. That must be a positive sign, I thought.

Monday 31st. 7.00pm. The Cave. The Staff with its large inset crystal fused into me once more, the crystal within my brain as some sort of receiver? That's what it felt like. I could see Hermes straight in front of me and my nine had arranged themselves around some kind of campfire. Seraphia was off to the left, impassive with Eduki. I called for "whoever was of maximum benefit." Hermes stepped forward. I had been consulting with a writing coach as I prepared my book The Key To Time. At my request Hermes spoke about this.

"She has some good input, it will make your writing better, but you should not expect the book to be published." I resisted these words, but Hermes seemed disinterested in arguing about it, wishing me farewell and gesturing toward Eduki. I wanted to know how my recent Outer World disasters had come about? "Within Arthur's method of the Four Roads," he said, "you went to the negative of each, all at the same time. Think about at. One – impatient. Three – spendthrift. Five - misuse of freedom. Eleven – obsessive. You know your numerology, see yourself!" I disliked this intensely. He continued, "When all four roads run to the negative a Black Hole forms, which sucks in and destroys everything of worth. One or two of the roads operating negatively could be managed, but all four spells disaster."

"But how to turn this around?" I asked.

"From the ground up. One - slow down. Three - be optimistic and control spending. Five - use freedom and do not fear it. Use it better and more wisely. Do this and prospects are bright. We can talk about Eleven later."

[NOVEMBER 2011]

Tuesday 1st. 8.00pm. The Cave. I heard a voice, "there is no need to visit, come back next week" but I did not trust it. I entered and greeted Eduki warmly. He repeated his words, saying I was to rest and focus on the work at hand.

"We may even give you a helping hand," came another voice.

"But is he worthy?" said another.

I replied that I did not know whether I was worthy, but that I was taking matters seriously. I also sensed there was something available for me to take but I did not reach out for it. I said I would return on Monday. Eduki said to rest until then.

Monday 7th. 7.00pm. The Cave. I strained my concentration and commanded that the cave come nearer to me so that I could enter. Collecting and fusing my staff and crystal I entered the Inner World landscape. The nine looked downcast, Hermes was present but flew away from me. Seraphia said and did nothing. It was only Eduki that approached me, speaking immediately.

"The people you meet for readings and healing present themselves for a reason in that moment. These people are in a constant battle between conscious and subconscious, ego and higher self if you like. Catching them in their moment of openness is all important. It rarely works to wait because matters conspire and their Dark Side has a chance to intervene. It is so vital to catch them in the precise moment that they present themselves, and not even five minutes later." This was an important lesson. I saw what was really meant by the Power of Now, the time of maximum weakness of the Dark Side and maximum availability of the higher/conscious self. Otherwise they say yes and they mean no, or mean yes when they say no. They intend to attend and then they don't, they don't mean to attend and then they do. At MBS shows I had seen it all.

"So if they present themselves to me it is because, on some level, they know that I can help them? And even if they present themselves with attitude or resistance or begrudgingly they are nonetheless presenting themselves and I can give them what they need, as opposed to what they want? But the window is in that moment only?"

"Yes!" came the answer loud and clear. I asked Eduki for healing of my bad cold and he directed me toward the Sun where I received all the rays possible. They penetrated into my bones and it felt good. Eduki called time and I went home.

Monday 14th. 4.00pm The Cave. I greeted Hermes and after some deliberation on my part about whether or not I had made the right connection to the right being he spoke directly to me.

"All magickal effects to you are cleared." I felt something move straight out of my back. I then asked about my book project, *The Key To Time*, and the potential of working with a publisher/agent I had recently met. His reply was clear. "This is the first book you will write for me. The woman is beneficial for you, but it is doubtful she will be able to get it published." My vision turned into this woman at the end of a long corridor. "But you will only see this for yourself, for sure, by working with her." His tone was one of resignation and I remarked back, "this whole process is rather hard."

"You are free to go at any time," he said. I was surprised. "No one works here unwillingly. You are free to return to normality whenever you like." I remembered my mundane life, before all this, and did not fancy it back. But this was really difficult and not at all what I thought it would be. Hermes gestured me toward Eduki and promptly vanished.

"He is not happy," said Eduki. I replied that I was indeed committed to the work. "But you don't always act like it," he said. I asked now about a magazine business plan I had. Eduki replied, "networking is the key. Progress can be made here after 10th January." I asked about the chance of taking a holiday. He seemed keen for me to do this, but less pricey than before.

I asked then about some praise and appreciation I had recently received. "Oh yes, they all love you when you are Richard Abbot. Just not at other times."

Finally I asked about uploading some images of my Outer World library and Inner Sanctum to social media. "They will all think you are crazy!" came the laughed reply. At that Eduki merged into me and we both departed back to The Outer World.

Tuesday 15th. 8.00pm. The Cave. I called out for Eduki, rather than looking for him. Straight away he appeared to my left. I could not anywhere discern or identify Seraphia. Hermes was vaguely around, but distant, and the nine seemed a little happier than they had recently over to my right. I asked Eduki if I might see my Dark Side?

"Are you quite sure?" he replied. I said I was. Fool! Instantly I could see myself at my office desk, hunched over, biting my nails, thinking. I looked old and worn and closed off from society and contact. My greatest strength, my mind, was my greatest weakness. Thinking had paralysed and frozen me. Highly advanced thinking it might be – I would say – but really little more than a cul-de-sac for life. Eduki called a halt to the image "that is enough for today." I asked if I might recapture access to the Temple, the nine, the communion with Extra Terrestrials and all the other things. "Yes, but it will be a long hard journey." I left deflated and returned home.

Afterwards, notes and ideas of what to do with my readings and courses sprang into my mind. A bright blue table cloth, copies of *The Key to Time*, Arthur's Book One and a Hermitage banner all appeared before me.

Wednesday 16th. 7.30pm. The Cave. It seemed like Hermes. But it couldn't be, given my previous encounters with him, how unhappy he was with my progress. I called for confirmation and a second figure appeared. Instantly the first one vanished in a puff of smoke. But it was the same figure. It was Hermes. I was relieved that the contact had not been severed. I asked if he would please channel his teachings to me?

"All in good time. First you must assemble the teachings already given to the previous Hermit." Visions of a book cover with Arthur's face came to me, as did the need to complete this as soon as possible. I felt frustrated. I asked about my real passion, my book of *The Key To Time*. What were its lessons?

"Consequences," he said. "Time travel leads one to believe that consequences do not follow actions, as if you have somehow escaped the linear train of cause and effect. But this is not so!" Hermes continued. "Accountability is real and all are accountable to time." This immediately seemed like a profound insight. "Certain times are allocated for certain potentials and actions, other times are not appropriate for them. Flitting back and forth in time leads you to conclude that you can do what you like, when you like. But you cannot. You can only take demonstrable actions when the time is right, and no one can escape the patterns of time, as shown through numerology. You can only learn, develop and grow when the time is ready." Hermes continued, I listened intently to this fascinating insight. "Discipline. This is a sub-lesson. Time travel suggests that you have almost unlimited power over yourselves and your environment. Not so however, for you must still pay great attention to the now, and to your life today. Life will not simply roll forward correctly unless you make it."

That was all. I thanked Hermes and departed. On leaving he injected an essence of an energy into my brain behind my eyes "to enable you to see." But see what? I did not know, but was aware that this new type of vision would be required somewhere. Eduki was also present and I thanked him as I left. "Visit tomorrow" he said. I queried this, but he confirmed that tomorrow was necessary.

Thursday 17th. 8pm. The Cave. I greeted Hermes immediately after calling for him. I was intent on completing my *Key To Time* experiments and analyses, regardless. I been pursuing them for months now but on each trip there had been an intervention, something or someone not from that time or place. They seemed to be wanting me to stop. The presence was unaffected by whatever I said or did.

"Who is intervening in my time experiments?" I asked.

"It is me!" he replied. My heart dropped like a stone. "You should not be doing these experiments. The work is totally out of time, ahead of its time, and this is not a good thing. It is too much, too true, too real, not appropriate for now, maybe a hundred years will pass before people are ready. Complete and finish it if you must but it can only be despatched to a very small and select group of people. And you should still expect nothing. You have been walking into certain bodies in those travels. The spiritual body and the material body are always attracted to each other, and thus you cannot help but do this. In the olden times people were more susceptible and aware of subtle energy shifts." I felt it was therefore also the peoples Guides that were telling me to leave. Hermes continued, "the whole thing is too powerful and too true an account. Being ahead of your time, the arrogance and pride of being first, is dangerous and delusional. This time is not for these things. Give it up and focus on what matters."

So this was the cause of all the trouble. One hundred years ahead of its time! Not only pointless but actually destructive for it takes me away from what I should be doing and what people need me to do. Dammit! This would take some assimilation.

[DECEMBER 2011]

Monday 5th. 6.00pm. The Cave. As I passed through the cave I collected the Staff, which fused with my spine and caused my brain to become one enormous crystal, multi faceted and multi-coloured. I was greeted by Hermes, but doubted him and called instead for "The Real Hermes." Instantly a winged horse ridden by a man appeared from my left. I asked that he identify himself and he confirmed he was indeed Hermes, although I doubted this also.

"What do you want?" he asked. I wanted to know what else I needed to complete Arthur's book. "You pretty much have it all," came the reply, "now comes the human part, the layout, design and printing. I thanked him and he flew off to the right. "And soon there will be more," he said, laughing.

I turned and called for Eduki, who appeared from my left and merged into me. I asked to visit The Keeper and Eduki pointed over to my right, where the Library appeared. I approached. I could feel my crystal brain increase its vibration and power. I entered and asked for The Keeper, bowing as I did so, making sure to show some humility. "What do you wish?" he asked. I spoke the name of a new client. A huge volume crashed down from the shelves above, on top of me. I moved out from underneath and started to thumb through it. It was full of blank pages – missed chances and spoiled opportunities. I asked for the essence of her. Suddenly I could see the Outer World through her eyes, from her point of view. The experience was so strange that it has stayed with me ever since. Her vision, from her eyes, was so restricted. She concentrated so intensely on things that she could not see what was taking place around her. It was as if she were surrounded by a dense fog that narrowed her vision and removed her horizon.

"Gently lift up her eyes to the world," came a voice. That was enough.

I asked about one other person, someone very ill, yet who had been in remission many times. "Her time is up," came the reply. I thanked The Keeper. He was in a friendly mood. "Come again," he replied. I bowed and retreated toward Eduki. The staff and the crystal moved out from me and I returned them to the Earth, checking that all was in order. Eduki confirmed all was well and would remain so.

"Is there anything else, anything you have for me?" I asked him. He seared a burning golden coin into my hand and told me to use it. I felt it physically as I returned home.

Tuesday 13th. 7.30pm. The Cave. I took up the Staff and crystal and greeted Eduki. Or tried to, for he was as small as a blade of grass. I shrank down to what I thought was his size, yet I was still too large. "It is the small things, seemingly insignificant, that matter," he said, "they are too easily overlooked". I accepted this at face value, yet maybe in hindsight I should have probed more. Instead I asked about my next steps. "In here. In the Temple," pointing ahead and a little to the left. "The Library," gesturing to the far right. "The Forest," straight ahead and right. "The cards, the Sea," pointing to the far left. "And over there," he said finally, indicating an unknown area to the far, far right. "You choose where next." I asked instead about the Outer World.

"The book – Arthur's – is key," he said. I felt further work had to be done on this, and Eduki reminded me how important it was. He said to return again tomorrow, were we might access the Temple provided enough had been learned in the interim. I moved to leave yet felt as though I was almost disconnected from my body, without even trying.

Wednesday 14th. 7.00pm. The Cave. As I entered the cave I felt light headed and as I passed into the landscape beyond I felt myself floating upwards. Eduki accompanied me as I floated up to the Temple. I sat on a stone throne and brought the session to order with my Staff. Eduki was at my right. A few of the pillars were populated. There was a bright light at the end, dead ahead. Eduki urged me to move toward it. I approached steadily.

"What do you want?" came an unfamiliar voice.

"To fulfil my Destiny." I replied, this being the very first thing of worth that I could think of.

"But do you?"

"Do I have a choice?" I shot back, only afterward thinking this might have been unwise.

"That is no answer. Fulfilling your Destiny requires changes." I immediately felt apprehensive. "Changes that you will become ready for," continued the voice.

"This what I want," I confirmed.

"Then we will make the arrangements." The light dimmed and then disappeared.

I turned next to the alien being. I looked closely into his eyes, which were deep and black, with no reflection. They simply absorbed light and information. The alien placed his hand on my head and absorbed from me. I asked for a return. He pointed to my heart, first drawing a clockwise, then anti-clockwise circle. It was all to do with the direction in which the heart pumped blood, a crucial factor in human health and wellbeing. Pumping the wrong way, or not pumping with sufficient force, making an incomplete circuit, would not cleanse the body properly. I saw then the form of an atom, with particles flowing around the outside, and then saw the Moon move around the Earth, both anti-clockwise. I was not entirely clear on this, but felt it would be useful in a healing environment.

But then the experience was over. We both came down from the Temple to the ground of the Inner World, next approaching the Library. I asked The Keeper for the book of my father. "That is the right request," he said.

This book was large, but the final pages were empty. The end of the story was not yet written. I took this an indication that he had learned something during his time. It did not receive any specific facts, but being with the book enabled me to clear my thoughts around him. It would be hard to talk with him about these matters in the Outer World, but it would be a test of my ability to look beyond mere words, and deal primarily with the higher self. The Keeper seemed in no hurry, but after while I left anyway. Eduki suggested that I visit again before the weekend.

Friday 16th. 5.00pm. The Cave. I entered this time through a white tunnel of light, which simply formed itself in my vision. There was Eduki, with the nine sat in a circle next to a tepee. But then there was two Edukies. I was confused, but managed to settle on the one to my right. He was the taller, younger, less oriental of the two, but I felt comfortable with him.

"We should try to integrate these nine one more time, to try to complete this once and for all," he said. Jordain then presented himself, the first Guide I had met all that time ago. I faced him and asked, "What lesson must I learn from you?" he replied clearly and directly.

"Individuality, leadership, focus, independence." I then felt an all over red-ness of energy and action envelope me. I allowed Jordain to merge into me. It was so much more intense than I could have imagined and I was eager to proceed to the next one, Kalia. But then I paused. Maybe I should proceed with this one at a time, maybe one per day, or even one per week? Eduki was pleased with my realisation, "a sign of some control of your impatience," he remarked. "Take one at a time, and watch for the sign indicating the next step. It may be days, or weeks." I accepted this and moved back into the Outer World, with Jordain, to assimilate his red-ness, one-ness, energy and vigour. Truthfully I did feel that this was some kind of backward step, some kind of demotion, having to go back and do this all over again. I felt some frustration as a result, but I was prepared to suck it up and do it. That would not always have been the case. Thanking Eduki, I returned home.

The Days After. The presence, or perhaps I should call it over-shadowing or in-dwelling, of Jordain brought several experiences and insights in rapid succession. I felt the urge for immediate learning and development, the thirst for independence and individuality – to make my mark as only I could - and the need for action, to make things happen, now. I was eager for a shift. I was energetic and active. I became aware also of much selfishness within me. I developed a keen eye for openings, fresh starts and new beginnings and experienced much bold, forward momentum in all areas of my life. I did not see how this could be sustained indefinitely though, unless one was to career through life, constantly breaking through and breaking free again.

There was the on going sense of burning, as if I were on fire. I was eager that this fire should be a cleansing one, but much of this energy was wasted.

Tuesday 20th. 8.00pm. The Cave. Eduki told me there was further learning to play out with Jordain. I asked about the relationship of this first Guide to the characteristics of the number one. Did this apply universally to everyone? "No" came the quite unexpected answer, "this is for you. Not everything applies to everyone. Numbers are the path you have chosen." He continued. "New acquaintances in the Outer World will bring home to you the negatives of this number one. You need to know this for full integration to take place."

Jordain did not emerge from me. He remained within, only at the end of this visit did he face me, eye to eye. This was in no way threatening, merely a steady looking at oneself, before merging back into me peaceably. I tried to remember that the Inner World experience stimulates the matching Outer World experience, through which only together can there be completion. But Jordain was more a part of me now than ever. The process felt more meaningful than before, more substantial than all those years ago. Eduki signalled that all was proceeded according to plan. "Return in a few days," he said, not specifying exactly when, "but be careful. Power corrupts."

Monday 26th. 7.45pm. The Cave. Upon arrival Jordain immediately jumped out of me. Eduki was to my left, and Hermes also appeared. I asked about the pressing matters at hand in my Outer World and was referred immediately the Library. The matter related to some new contacts I had made, who had evidently been drawn toward the energy of Jordain, as well as, or maybe instead of, me.

"They want you to write the book of their lives for them. And you can do this. But do you really want to?" I struggled to fully focus but heard The Keeper say that I would need to put into practice all that I knew in order to deal correctly with these people. He then ejected me.

Eduki was more supportive. Hermes then said, "you still do not see the effect you have on people. But you will. Take this break to revise all of Arthur's work and then put it into practice. The time for theorising is over." I asked if I had a powerful Dark Side? "Yes," said Eduki, "it is highly destructive to self and others. Now take Jordain with you, he had been attempting to help but you have tried your hardest not to listen." I turned to Jordain, and asked if he would protect me. He confirmed that he would. I was still somewhat resistant but Eduki confirmed my suspicions.

"Others find Jordain highly magnetic and are drawn toward him, and thus to you. But you must exert your control for you also need his protection." Jordain faced me head on and merged back into me. I could physically feel this.

The Days After. I wondered whether Jordain's appearance had occurred not only as part of a process of learning, but also as a protective force in my life. Around this time I felt genuinely in danger and under threat from Outer World events and happenings. Could Jordain, the number One and the colour Red provide the impetus I needed to make it through?

An escalating series of Outer World events had been brought about following my most recent contacts in the Temple. I had indeed met the people predicted by Eduki, and I had handled my meetings with them badly. I had not valued their initial good feelings toward me and I had failed to guide them appropriately. I had generated much ill will as a result of my words and actions. My influence had proved quite destructive to them and the blame for this was entirely mine. I hoped that I could learn from it, that it might ultimately help me to embody these teachings, scars and all. Theorising about life was just not enough. It had to be lived.

[JANUARY 2012]

Monday 23rd. 7.00pm. The Cave. It had been almost one month since my last visit. On one hand, this gap was certainly a momentous waste of time, but on the other maybe not so much. The lessons of life take as long as they take. I was greeted by Eduki on my left, next to Seraphia and Hermes in the middle, with the nine to their right. Hermes stepped forward as the others deferred.

"Ebooks, ipads, e-readers. The work must be distributed in these ways," he said, "that is all I can say." He disappeared and Eduki gestured for me to sit down with him and Jordain at a nearby rock.

"You are trying to bring the wisdom of Hermes back again. This is no small feat. You will be provided with all you need in order to do this. But it will be your needs that will be met, not your wants." I enquired about someone I had met for the first time a few days before. Eduki shook his head. "Impatience. Many seek the theoretical knowledge, but as you know yourself, practising it is a different matter." Eduki gave me a name of someone who I was aware of but barely knew, indicating that they would become significant in the future. I queried the fleeting nature of my Outer World human connections, as it did not seem too satisfying. "But that is how you best help people, connect when they need you and then move on either when you have helped them, or when it is obvious that you cannot."

I asked about a client with a particularly challenging family situation and was directed toward the Library. The Keeper was friendly and the book of the client descended but was empty. Try as a I might I could see nothing within its pages. I reported this back to Eduki, who seemed doubtful that this could be the case. Nonetheless he said that the Outer World library I had amassed contained all the answers I needed in order to help her. He encouraged me to manufacture a talisman, in brown, grey or silver, on the waxing Moon, leaning toward her protection. "Investigate this," he urged. I asked if we needed to talk about anything else, but he replied that all was going well. I begged to differ, but did not say so. Home.

Wednesday 25th. 7.00pm. The Cave. I called for Hermes and as I saw him descend I also felt Eduki and the nine gather around me. They initiated this as a formal meeting. Hermes asked what I wanted.

"Are Hermes and Thoth the same?" I asked.

"The same energy, with different interpretation. Same as The Hermit. Same as Nine, Hermetic Wisdom, The Teachings of Hermes, and down from there." I asked him to confirm this. "Yes, this is so. Is there anything else?" I hesitated. He asked again. I said no and he departed. I saw a downwards pointing triangle before me. Hermes on the left, Thoth on the right, connecting down to Hermetics, the Hermit, the colour brown, the number nine, and then me. Somewhere on this spectrum must be a point that is close enough to be recognisable to others, friendly and welcoming enough to be The Hermitage, yet still directly connected to the source Hermes/Thoth energy and still strong in its force. But how to find that point, for the image of Thoth directly is too big and scary for the average person. I reflected on this for a while.

I went to leave but Eduki said we needed to talk about a long standing pupil of mine. He confirmed that she was in contact, via the Inner World, with one of his kind. "So it is now time for you to step back from your work with her. She must prove her own worth now in this task. She has leaned on you enough." I departed, thanking both Eduki and the assembled nine.

[FEBRUARY 2012]

Saturday 4th. 10am. A Practice in Astral Projection. In the Outer World I located my centre of attention, exactly as Arthur's method, in between the bottom of my stomach and my genitals. I concentrated and caused it to move up through my body. As it reached my heart space I gained an awareness of blood rushing through my body, but not only blood, information, knowledge, awareness. I felt some tightness now in my chest. As I moved it up to my throat I felt a sense of excitement and anticipation. I tried then to direct it out from the very top of my head. I could gain only fleeting sensations – a forward/back rocking motion, followed by the same but side to side. I felt myself increase in size, to get bigger, longer, taller. It felt like I was too big to fit into my body, as if I my life force had to be condensed and compressed to even fit into a body shape.

I continued to experience this variety of sensations, none of which could be called 'true' astral projection. Maybe I had the wrong idea about what astral projection actually was? Maybe I was really only searching for a greater scope of awareness? I had certainly accomplished that. My senses were being assailed by all sorts of unusual input. I could see now that it is the invisible which drives the visible, the inner energies propelling the physical body.

Suddenly I felt a buzzing and buffeting sound in my ears. It continued with some intensity for quite a few seconds, then stopped. All I could see was a kaleidoscope of flashing lights. And then nothing, complete stillness, whiteness all around, but not even whiteness, more like nothingness. A fog, a cotton wool, but without colour, form, smell or shape. Unvaried and unchanging.

I instinctively called for Arthur, and he replied. "The book is ready to be published, but only to a limited few. You should expect criticism and problems to come from it, but continue exactly as you are. Nothing of worth ever comes easily." This was characteristic Arthur, never addressing the thing at the front of my mind, always the issues underlying it. I was in no doubt that I had made contact, although I could not 'see' him in any way. And then I lost the connection and came back to regular consciousness in my green chair, somewhat disorientated as I opened my eyes.

All this reinforced the idea that these experiences could never be accomplished with a busy and distracted mind. The more Outer World sensory input, the less room for this type of work. Perhaps more dangerously the greater the Outer World input the greater the chance of seeing, within the astral, exactly what you want to see, what you are already familiar with, some kind of mash-up of Outer World imagery with an astral ghost thrown in for good measure. This would be imagination, not real experience. I had first practised today's astral method under Arthur's watchful eye some fifteen years previously. At the time he had remarked, "you are not ready yet." Little did I know how long I would have to wait.

Sunday 5th. 11.00am The Cave. I entered the Cave in the usual way, but before proceeding through and into the landscape beyond via the established route I looked around for another exit. The Vortex Elevator became clear and as I stepped inside I felt a swirling within me, like a pendulum moving in a circular motion. It became stronger and stronger as I entered it. I felt the familiar buffeting and vibration, the preamble to full release from the body, but today I was tired and I could not manage it. I sneezed violently and snapped straight back to my body.

This short experience allowed me to recognise that awareness and vision were two different things. In these fleeting experiences I could gain heightened awareness of whatever or whoever I turned my attention to, but not a full vision. During and straight after these trips concerns of the 'Muggle' World seemed very far away indeed, and much of the things that pressed upon me during the working day seemed to become almost insignificant, smaller and much less noisy.

But how to explore this and remain practical at the same time? My curiosity wanted to visit Area 51, the Vatican Secret Archive, Downing Street, the Oval Office, North Korea, other planets and galaxies, but would any of this be allowed? Was any of it really worthwhile?

Monday 6th. 5.25pm. The Cave. This time I moved through the cave, past the Vortex and into the landscape, greeting Eduki on my left. There were other voices around at first, but after some time I became comfortable with him and allowed him to enter into me. I asked about a particular challenging client in the Outer World. Eduki shook his head.

"She is trying to find her place, her purpose, just like everyone else. But you can only stand firm on the basics with her – that is, her uniqueness and the need for others to follow theirs." I had felt her to be an extreme case, extraordinarily challenging and difficult, though constantly coming back for more, but Eduki did not seem phased or think her in any way extreme, "you must not lose your temper with her," he said.

I asked next of the Vortex. "It enables you to go out from the crown of your head." As he said these words I instantly felt myself rise to this point. "From there" he continued, "anywhere. Inner or Outer World, through force of will and with control. Past, present or future, inside or outside. Straight to. You may visit the Temple via this route, the Vortex, or in the standard way through the landscape without it. It is less a question of going up, as it is going higher, to a higher awareness and vision."

My awareness then turned to Outer World matters, specifically money and a recent large bad debt incurred in one of my businesses. "No one is immune from the Karma of others. Where involved with others you are involved in their Karma. There is no escape from this, not personally, locally or globally." Annoyingly truthful words, which resolved the situation not, but at least enabled me to learn something from it. I asked next of the Library, what is its purpose? We both suddenly appeared in the Library, before The Keeper. I asked the same question of him.

"You know all this," he said impatiently.

"I need clarification," I replied. He gave me the words of a specific question which I repeated back to him. "What is this place and what is it for?" He then replied clearly.

"It records everything. Every individual. By person, not by event. Past and future. Things learned and not learned. Done and not done. All is recorded. Take yours for example." My book appeared before me. It was bigger than I had remembered and had sections I had not seen before, now with dividers. It detailed this life and previous lives. "But use them wisely!" he said.

I got the impression that the level of answer I was now likely to receive, in this place, was at a higher level that before, maybe more comprehensive, more meaningful, more profound, and probably more difficult to accept. I placed the book back on its shelf and asked the The Keeper if he always needed to be here when I accessed the records. "Yes" he replied, "until I can…"

We departed freely, without being ejected. Eduki said he would come back home with me. "You need to revise these experiences. Then you will get your full and comprehensive understanding."

Tuesday 7th. 7.30pm. The Cave. I had spent the day doing exactly as Eduki had suggested, re-reading my previous diary entries. As I arrived Jordain – or at least some kind of shape – leapt out of me and ran off to the right. I went with Eduki to sit on a rock and he waited some time for me to speak first.

"So Jordain," I said, "has been with me all these weeks? To teach me about the nature of the number one?"

"Yes," Eduki replied.

"About individuality, independence, the importance of going ones own way and not being subsumed by others?" I continued, "but I knew this already."

"Theoretically, yes you did. But now you also know about it in practice," Eduki was calm. This was not logical, but it was completely sensible.

"So now it is time for Kalia?" I was eager to get on.

"Not yet. There are a couple more things to do first, some final lessons. It is only a matter of days. Come back here again when you can, tomorrow preferably, but when you can." The One energy had been, with hindsight, apparent throughout the previous couple of months. It had manifested strongly in my Outer World as new experiences, people, places and events. It had even manifested itself in my redder than usual skin tone! But as we were not done yet, when Jordain approached I allowed him to enter me and we returned home.

Wednesday 8th. The Sun. As I arrived in the landscape Jordain shot out and off to my right, while Eduki appeared on my left. He was dressed all in red but with black collars and cuffs. These were long and traditional oriental robes, and the detail was clearer than before. Hermes was up above us, Seraphia to my left and the nine to my right.

Eduki led me up a rough stone stairway, a series of ledges, to the top of a mountain. The Sun was high in the sky directly above, and I asked it to come down to me. It appeared in exactly the same shape and size as me, an almost perfect double, yet alive with burning orange and red flame. I allowed his rays to flow right through me, feeling the energy, the heat, the movement, the life touching right down to my toes, my insides, my fingertips, my bones. Powerful, and burning. I remembered my first direct encounter with the Sun through Arthur, some twenty years before, when I had completely overdone it, took too much, more than I could handle and felt literally burned and singed for quite a few days afterwards. That memory was carved into me and while this time I took as much as I could, I did not push myself to take more. It may even have been possible to take the Sun-man directly into me, but I did not do this. I felt a powerful awareness of the healing and transformational properties of this energy. If such a thing could be harnessed on Earth then we might be free of war, pain, illness. The Sun would burn it all away, and would always be available for replenishment, when needed. Anyway, when I felt that enough was enough I thanked the Sun and it departed back up to the sky. I returned my awareness to Eduki and the rest of the Inner World. The realisation dawned. The Sun, card nineteen, was the ultimate expression of the One that I had been working with all this time (19: 1+9 = 10. 1+0 = 1). It was the shining individual of power, charisma and force. The power of the Sun 19, flowed through The Wheel of Fortune 10, introducing change, and was focused down by The Magician 1 with focus and intent.

"Next time will be Kalia, but not today," said Eduki. "Would you like to see Arthur?" he asked. This was most surprising. He immediately appeared in his recognisable form.

"You see how difficult this is?" he said. I sure did. "And how power is always misused until control is learned?" I saw this too. And then he was gone. I thanked Eduki and departed for home.

Monday 13th. 6.00pm. The Cave. Eduki, Kalia and Seraphia were all to my left. Seraphia was flying in the sky with her wings. Kalia was exactly as I had remembered her, black skin, white teeth, young and lively. She jumped straight into me. I could feel her and me and Eduki, all holding hands and circling round in a dance, getting higher and higher, lighter and lighter all the time. Suddenly we were so high that I could see the whole of the Planet Earth from space. Eduki and Kalia held onto me, on either side. Now I could understand why people were so lost, sensitive, shy, scared and lonely. I could understand where the Light came from. It reflected from nature and from wherever the population was. The greater the population the more Light there was. I asked them both what should be done about the situation (some might say emergency) on Planet Earth?

"Keep on exactly as you are," came the reply, "things will develop of their own accord. Simply respond to people as they step forward. Help guide them to a bigger picture. As insights visit your consciousness so they do to others. Ready for one, ready for all. One getting ready, all getting ready."

I asked Kalia about the number Eleven, specifically as it related to me. She was very helpful.

"Extremist, angry, violent, not being able to see the bigger picture, not being able to see the whole picture. In Eleven, the two ones might easily obscure each other, or one might be invisible or out of sight because of the distortion and enormity of the other. For you it is also about being grounded, practical and getting on with the daily business of individual help, as well as the big picture stuff."

I returned to the ground of the Inner World, actually feeling the descent. I saw Jordain and moved toward him, but he would not accompany me. It was Kalia's time now, and she merged back into me again, "we will complete the whole later," she said. Eduki waved goodbye and I returned home.

Thursday 23rd. 7.00pm. The Cave. Kalia jumped straight out of me and ran off to the right. Eduki was sat shaking his head. Matters in my Outer World had not gone smoothly and I had failed to deal effectively with certain situations. Eduki cautioned me of the trouble that would surely follow next.

"But how do I address this? I asked. He summoned Kalia over and I asked the same of her. She spoke.

"Emotions – the number two – are a weakness more than a strength, sometimes." I checked that I had heard this correctly, surely it was a matter of fifty-fifty, equally a weakness and strength? Kalia repeated herself, with emphasis. "Definitely more weakness than strength. They cause you to hide from yourself, to not stand up for yourself and to run away from difficult situations." I asked how this could be addressed. "By giving a little to each pole. By being even handed and calm, sharing and taking. Giving a little. Compromise. Any other path of the two tends towards difficulties. When the time comes you will have to give up something to resolve this. You will know what and when." Balance and calm-headedness. That was good advice.

I turned to Eduki and asked about Arthur's book, and the idea of a limited print run. He urged me to keep it closed to certain people. He did not specify who exactly, and I did not ask, hoping I would know when the time came.

I thanked them both. In spite of everything they seemed relatively content with my general progress. I asked Kalia if she were coming back me. "Oh yes!" she said enthusiastically, merging in wholly, clearly and powerfully.

Friday 24th. 10.00am. The Cave. I wasted no time in asking Eduki where, on the planet, I should be?

"California" came the direct answer, "but lots has to occur before this can happen." He explained about the need for physical fitness, an attractive physical appearance, white teeth and clear skin, "drink lemon and lime instead of alcohol," he said, "feeling better about your appearance will help you engage with others more, and thus progress faster."

I turned to Kalia who cautioned me that some people I knew were feeling left out of things. It would be a good idea to involve them more in the work and to make some display of commitment. "All this will result in progress," she said. I was keen for a move of house, town, even country, but no answer came about when this was likely, only a veiled warning that "things must improve and change here first," and that "physical collapse or degradation might result in your withdrawal from the world, which is not really what we want." I did not really understand these words, but one of Arthur's many predictions about my life came to mind, that I would progressively experience much greater involvement with people, with much reduced interest in them. Or did he say that the other way round? Kalia merged back into me and I returned home.

Monday 27th. 6.00pm. The Cave. I greeted Eduki on my right and Kalia (who emerged from me) on my left. We sat as they gave me specific Outer World pointers and a mundane action agenda. Specifically they spoke of a healing procedure to be given to a very sick friend of a friend. I had some resistance to even offering this, but in the end I had done and was awaiting her decision on whether to attend. The healing practice involved a full immersion and commitment, as well as specific techniques. After this discussion we sat together for a while before returning with Kalia.

[MARCH 2012]

Monday 12th. 8.00pm. The Cave. Kalia was in playful mood. She grabbed hold of me very tight and we flew into the air. We swirled around the Temple and entered. She stood beside me to my right while I received unexpected instructions.

"Here are the entities that you command," said an unknown voice, as I looked around at eight beings and energies ranged on the plinths around me. "Here is where to travel in space and time," the voice continued, as I looked upwards to a roof open to the stars. "Here then is where you place your intentions," the voice went on, as my focus moved straight ahead to the centre of the Temple. "And here is where you energise it," the position directly opposite me at the end of the Temple became apparent. "Anything at all is possible here, given the rules you already have." The voice grew silent.

I asked about a long standing client. Hermes appeared and told me that I had been wrong about her. I could not accept this and left the Temple. With Eduki to my right and Kalia to my left, back on the ground of the Inner World I asked the same question. Eduki spoke.

"She is a strong character, whereas you are plagued with doubts and uncertainties. She constantly takes liberties with you, but you have allowed her, and others, to do this. Work of this nature must always be charged and paid for. It does not register when given for free. You must strengthen your resolve, for the number four – which is strong within her - always causes trouble." I asked if I might perform some working to this end within the Temple. They both seemed pleased with the suggestion and then we were back there. All stations seemed still occupied. I spoke.

"I desire to become stronger in resolve and of backbone. To say no when I mean no. To be willing to say what I need, to say what works for me, and to discard what I no longer need. I desire this as well as opportunities to learn about this." The Light in the opposite position to me asked if this is what I really wanted. I confirmed that it was. Suddenly I felt that my backbone was made of steel and I sat bolt upright in my chair. I felt myself joining together with the eight beings and the Light to energise the desire that I had placed before us in the middle of the Temple. Then came an enormous explosion, the debris and energy of which shot high up into space. I thought that I should expect challenges, but that I must do this anyway and thus become more. I thanked all and returned home.

Wednesday 14th. 6.00pm. The Cave. An on going, long standing problem in the Outer World was the effect that I allowed others to have on me. Their attitudes, their refusal to see, their failure to try, their criticisms, even their demeanour and general day to day behaviour demoralised me and fed my own self doubt and distrust of the Inner contacts and voices. I consulted on this with Eduki who immediately offered to merge into me. The quality of my being, as he did this, became very different. I could see how embodying an approach like that of Eduki might change the whole dynamic of life. A better pair of scales would enable me to adjust the balance between what I must pay attention to against what I am merely distracted by. The quality of my Outer World interactions might improve if I sought a stronger Inner World relationship. In other words, if the deepening of Inner World contact seems to create annoyance with the Outer World, then the answer is to go deeper, not shy away.

The answer was summarised by Eduki. "More frequent visits here. Once a fortnight is not nearly good enough. The goal is to reunite the nine strands of you, and then go forward with me, but this process is incomplete. The energies must be lived. Floating around it and pretending will not do it." The suggestion was that my work rate and attitude might improve if I were really to pursue this. Eduki continued. "To fully integrate is to fully feel the Karmic weight and wisdom of all your previous lives. This is enlightenment as much as any one person can experience – the reunion of the strands of yourself." I felt much weight upon me with this task. It was serious and the more I delayed the bigger the problems would be. The truth was that I was continuing to struggle in the wake of Arthur's death.

Saturday 17th. 11.00am. The Cave. Kalia left me and departed to the right. I struggled to concentrate but managed to ask Eduki about the integration of the nine strands. He confirmed that Harriette Curtiss' ideas were correct.

"Natural inner phenomena stimulate the desire and are the precursor only to allowing these things into the Outer Life. It is a bit like going over everything again," he said, then continuing, "the nine strands represent things known to you from past experiences, whereas Seraphia and I represent future selves. We guide you toward new learning experiences that the nine will be unfamiliar with. You will be guided to meet the right kinds of people to enable you to broaden your understanding of this in the coming times, to see how others interact with it." Kalia merged into me and Eduki suggested that I leave now to take a rest.

Monday 19th. 6.00pm. The Cave. Kalia again ran off to the right. I now suspected that this was for her to report back to the rest of the nine. How effective it would be to get all nine to line up inside of me, and act from that position of knowledge. At that point Eduki came forward and merged into me. Together we approached the Library, but my concentration was flagging and The Keeper was not impressed. I pulled down the book of a close friend, who had been struggling.

It was large, thick and old, with blank pages throughout. She had missed lessons out and these must now be learned.

We left and entered the Temple. I stood in my usual position, face to face with the Light. The assembled entities seemed uninvolved and uninterested. I commanded them to engage and they did. I placed my close friends issue centrally and all the entities gathered around and we linked together, energising the goal, "to provide my friend with the money she needs, no more, no less." Together we launched the charged goal up into the cosmos above. It was done. I thanked all those assembled. Eduki spoke.

"Multiple visits to the Temple to revivify this working might be necessary." I asked about the wisdom of such a direct intervention in another life, even though it had been requested. He provided the only possible answer. "You are The Hermit now."

Tuesday 20th. 8.00pm. Ten of Pentacles. I had enquired with the cards on behalf of the same friend, as to her difficult financial situation. The Ten of Pentacles had figured prominently in the answer. I entered the card and greeted Eduki. "Ten is One, but reborn, from the result of the Nine," he said, "but there is no escaping bad decisions." There was a figure close by, in a garden near a house. He spoke.

"Ten Pentacles are the rewards of patience. It takes time and is the result of money making money. It does not come about only from individual and personal works. Money itself must work hard if there is to be more money."

"But how can matters be set straight? I asked.

"Only by forcing the issue and intervening," he replied. I then found myself in the Temple, alongside Eduki. The scene was very clear. I commanded the assembled intelligences to gather. I was told that my friend had "stored up good Karma in the bank" and the intelligences seemed willing to oblige. As before we gathered, together with the Light, with the matter centrally and repeated the energised words, to provide my friend "with the money she needs, no more, no less." We shot it into the heavens above where it shattered into a million pieces, each propelling themselves to exactly where they needed to be, where they might have greatest effect.

I asked the assembled intelligences who they were? "Another time," said one voice. Fair enough. I thanked Eduki and departed. I was exhausted and could barely write the record of the experience down. Yet he urged me to return soon, "There is still so much to do," he said.

Saturday 24th. 4.00pm. The Cave. Eduki, Kalia and myself together stood facing a large triangle, point uppermost. This then inverted itself, pointing downwards.

"Is there a Hall of Learning?" I asked them.

"The Hall of Records. The Library," said Eduki.

"But that's for people, what about things?" I asked

The faintest of replies came, "people are things, things are people." I concentrated harder and Eduki continued. "The Temple of Opportunities is effectively what you might call The Hall of Learning." I asked next about the existence of Watchtowers, whereupon he pointed up in the distance to a tower I have never before noticed, on the extreme right of the scene. "This can be explored another time," he said, "for the meantime you should return and protect your new working space." He was right. I had recently relocated my Outer World working space from a small six foot square box room into one of the main rooms of the house. I departed, attempting to take the Staff and Crystal back with me, but they would not move through the threshold into the Cave, although Kalia happily returned with me.

[APRIL 2012]

Tuesday 10th. 7.30pm. The Cave. Entry was swift and smooth. Once I had battled a False Eduki away the real one came closer and clearer. Kalia went off to consult with the other eight. I asked Eduki why I had such difficulty in dealing with others in the Mind Body Spirit community. I found the 'love and light' mentality empty and lacking. This had been a running sore for years and his reply was faultless.

"You do not realise how much you know. You know things that others only seek. You are maybe fifty years ahead of the rest, possibly less if progress is made in the world. You are basically a social man who has been deprived of society and isolated by what you know. But complain not," the voice grew clearer and deeper, maybe it was not even Eduki at all now, "for you have that which many seek, yet cannot find. Identity. You were taught directly by a Master, but you asked for that knowledge and this is the price you must now pay. Understand that The Hermitage now takes priority." I asked that these words be confirmed, three times. They were without variation, equivocation or qualification on each occasion. My very poor short term memory could not have reproduced these words. The voice continued. "The Hermitage takes priority. Build it and they will come." This was being suggested as a solution or at least easement to my woes. "You find it hard to believe and to accept that you know more than others and seek social interchange and contact, but always fail because of what you know. Do not complain. It is a heavy price, but one worth paying for you have that which others seek but cannot find." There was more from this powerful voice. "Use Facebook and the like for comments and postings. Do not use it to interact, or to look at others, or to wish you or they were nearer or further away." I asked about the healing methods I had been practising. "Counter-clockwise motions on the feet stimulate the blood flow in the correct direction, or at the very least they harmonise with it and work alongside it." I tried hard to remember all this as yet more words came, "All this is not about you any more," addressing my perception of a lack of success and achievement in this field, "build it and they will come. Much will be found about the Hermit nature and the associated nine energy in the books by Harriette Curtiss. Your transition from three to nine has proved difficult, but acceptance is now taking place. All is well." By the end it had not been Eduki's voice.

Friday 13th. 4.30pm. The Cave. Eduki wore white this time, and merged with me. It was an electric sensation. I could still see through my eyes, but now his too. I enquired about a long standing client, asking whether we should consult The Keeper on this matter. Eduki suggested the Temple, but we found ourselves in the Library anyway, with The Keeper immediately demanding to know my business there. I spoke the name of a friend, who had accidentally and carelessly fallen foul of the law. A tablet computer, not a book, appeared in my hand. The report was positive, she had learned some things and had in fact progressed. I asked if it was acceptable to try to help her.

Immediately I was in the Temple. The only difference to the standard arrangement was that all the eight pillar positions were filled with my previous Guides. This did not compute, there were nine of them and only eight positions. I pressed on regardless and addressed the room. "We need to help her."

The voices replied in unison, "no, you need to help her. We can only mitigate, not remove the punishment all together." We gathered in the same manner as we had previously done, and spoke the demand. "Clemency and leniency for (name spoken but removed from this record for privacy) on 23rd April at 10am." The efforts were then released into the ether.

Suddenly I felt completely exhausted and drained of all life. This has been a real release of energy, much more powerful than before. I thanked the assembled and descended from the Temple.

Eduki and I passed through the threshold, this time also bringing the Staff and Crystal back with us. It was also around this time that I started, with increasing frequency, casting pentagrams over the doorway to my Inner World as I left.

Tuesday 17th. 7.30pm. The Cave. Eduki emerged from my right and we stood looking at each other for a while. I asked about the Staff, which I had collected on the way in.

"It is now yours to take with you, back to the Outer World. It provides the required strength, the crystal giving the receptivity and sensitivity needed." I was very appreciative, so I enquired as to my next steps forward. "We will need Hermes for this," said Eduki. Instantly Hermes flew down from the skies on horseback. This vision was so real, so life like that I was stunned into silence. "Take time to study in here," he said. "Your next initiation is to make The Hermitage real in the Outer World. Then I will merge into you," he said, before swiftly departing.

Many ideas flooded into my mind – a new website, cloths, banners. Choose the best people for the jobs regardless of their views of the work itself, and don't delay. If these are people not used to the subject matter then so be it. That in itself would be their initiation.

"Come tomorrow and visit with more of your Guides," Eduki said. "In the meantime I will come back with you."

Wednesday 18th. 4.30pm. The Cave. Eduki departed from me and Kalia approached. I felt the strong urge to re-check, verify and if necessary to go over old ground.

"Who are you?" I asked her.

"You," she replied.

"So I am a direct re-incarnation of you?"

"No – I am a part of your family connection."

"One of my four segments?"

"Yes," she said, "which explains why some of your incarnations were as you suspected, and others who you might have expected did not appear." I did not totally understand, but another voice then intervened, "there is more information and research to be done here, but you did ask!" Indeed I did.

My head was then filled with visions of Hermitages in Canada and the South of France. But I could not believe this and concluded with my mind full of doubt. With a million questions I returned home.

Thursday 19th. 7.00pm. The Cave. I asked Eduki about the notion of initiation. All I could hear was the word "Ipsissimus." He suggested we visit the Temple for some insight on the matter.

I asked the nine assembled Guides about this, but again ran into the problem that there were only eight pillars.

"Do not get hung up on the numbers," came a voice. But I was. I could not contemplate nine into eight. I must be missing something simple and obvious, I thought. I could at the same time sense an in-rushing of energy into the eight positions, yet as my doubts grew it turned into a subsequent out-rushing. I then thought that the previous inhabitants of the eight positions, the alien entities, had perhaps been unwanted guests? Maybe I ought to protect this space more strongly next time? Questions everywhere, no answers. I returned, disappointed. The nine were disappointed too. It seemed we were so close to a breakthrough, but how could nine go into eight??!

Eduki returned with me, but even this could not allay my discontent. Maybe Jordain was not really one of the 9, and was a separate being, a protector, the archetypal Guardian? Maybe the nine were in fact the other eight plus me?

Afterwards: Ipsissimus is an arcane word relating to the highest degree of initiation within the Hermetic Order of the Golden Dawn. Much dispute and confusion surrounds this grade, with some claiming it is as astral connection, with others saying that it cannot exist within a living human. This was not new information, but how did it pertain to me? I had concluded that it could not, but then I stumbled upon two Latin root words, Ipsissima Vox (the very voice), and Ipsissima Verba (the very words). So the word Ipsissimus might refer to a human relating the precise words and meaning of an Astral Master – without filter or interpretation. This must be the goal.

Tuesday 24th. 8.00pm. Astral Projection Practice. Limited success. I experienced the forward/backward, then side to side rocking motion, partial disconnection and sense of being taller and higher than my body. But I was constantly having to check, correct and stop myself from imagining results rather than actually experiencing them. Finally I seemed to established some contact with Arthur and I asked him about producing a Volume Two of his works?

"Yes," he said, "but it's over now. It's time to go." He said smiling. I took this that further contact was not appropriate. I returned very unsure of things.

Wednesday 25th. 6.30pm. The Cave. This visit took on a most unexpected twist. After Eduki exited from my right side I clearly saw Hermes coming down to greet me.

"You have done well," he said.

"I find that hard to accept," I replied. He reached out and touched my head. I could feel nothing at first and he disappeared, but then when he was gone, he was somehow not gone. Eduki, who had been standing close by, spoke, "We are ready to go beyond." We stood together outside the Temple and then ascended into it. Once again I was struggling with the notion of nine into eight, then I had a flash of inspiration (or madness?) and dissolved all eight pillars. There were now none, and thus there was room for everyone.

The Temple then filled up with all nine Guides, each entering on my right. Eduki stood there the whole time with Hermes straight ahead. One by one I allowed all nine Guides to merge into me, beginning with Jordain. This process took maybe twenty minutes as I chatted briefly with each and then felt them move into, around and through my body. It was a shattering exercise. I then allowed Eduki to do the same, while Hermes looked on. I had protected the four walls of the Temple with flaming pentagrams, and the floor with a flaming hexagram. Then a voice spoke. "Where do you want to go?" I could not answer. I had seen and done enough, maybe more than enough, for one day. It had been a major achievement I felt, certainly a first. I had consciously created an initiation that made sense and felt right. The Tarot card of the Day, that morning, had been the Ten of Swords which made the experience all the more powerful and surprising.

It was a watershed. I was certainly not free of problems but I had reunited the old strands of myself throughout history. This experience created a knowing, which was now sealed within me, and consciously available at all times. I felt it. But I could also see that this was an enormous responsibility, one that I had been searching for since meeting Arthur in November 1989. All that I knew must now be practised. Limited no longer, except by the laws of Life. Ipsissimus? Unlikely. But if so, I was forbidden to say.

Sunday 29th. 9.30am. The Cave. There were many noises drawing me back to the Outer World, making my entrance through the cave unclear and uncertain. There were two figures representing Eduki. After some testing and deliberation I chose one of them, as best I could. Hermes was right there and not at all happy about some recent Outer World behaviours and choices I had made. I was moving around all over the place, but finally managed to find some still space and I felt myself settle around in and around my chest area. I asked Eduki about my book, *The Key to Time*. "Only Hermes can answer this," he said. So I turned to Hermes himself.

"We have spoken about this. You cannot release it. It is too much, because it is too true." Could there be danger associated with it? "Complete it for your own personal satisfaction and produce one copy, but none for other people."

I turned to Eduki and asked about the Temple. He confirmed that it was indeed "your world." The question now was what did I want to bring into my world? I though The Hermitage would be a good place to start. Eduki confirmed this was a good idea. I still thought that given how the possibilities were endless whether I should not be thinking a little bigger? Maybe I should begin by protecting it further, setting a foundation and invoking the necessary forces into it? These were vague thoughts without end or answer. Eduki merged into me and we returned home.

[MAY 2012]

Wednesday 2nd. 6.30pm. The Cave. I entered and could feel Eduki to my right, emerging from me. I asked for an audience with Hermes. He obliged and appeared down from the sky.

"The Key To Time…" I began.

"You have discovered it!" he was angry. "I showed you where to look and you found it. There is nothing more to say. You have it all." At that he dismissed me, suddenly gone and not at all happy. I knew that I kept asking the same questions hoping for a different answer, and I knew that I found this infuriating when my pupils did it to me. I turned to Eduki and he explained the problem. "It is the publishing that is wrong, not the exploration as such though that is fraught with disaster. It is up to you what you do with the material now, your choice entirely. Visit again once you have resolved the matter." I felt so strongly that the material should be published, in spite of everything that was said. Eduki merged back into me and we returned.

Afterwards: In the end I finalised the manuscript and professionally printed four copies only. I have shown the cover design a couple of times, but the content and books themselves remain on my shelves. Even years later it still rankles, but I dared not go so flagrantly against the guidance.

Thursday 10th. 6.00pm. The Cave. I could feel Eduki, almost physically in the chair beside me, to my right. In the Outer World I had recently come across an opportunity to become a trustee of a college. Discussing this with him he confirmed that it was "theoretically a good idea," but that the other trustees were "primarily interested in preserving their lifestyle." We both agreed that, from this perspective, it might not be entirely suited to my personality. I thought it revealing that whilst I was connected fully to the Outer World the idea had merit and attraction, yet when discussing it at this Inner (higher?) level, the obvious, yet somehow previously hidden flaws could be seen. It sometimes seemed that I needed these inner connections to get any decisions right at all!

Eduki suggested that today I should return without him. "It is tiring," he said. I took this to mean for him, although it was undoubtedly so for me too. I insisted that I needed his presence with me in order to do my work. He agreed to merge back into me, speaking the words, "The path toward the Nine is through the

Five. The Hermit via The Hierophant. If you cannot be the Hermit, be the Hierophant."

Thursday 17th. 6.30pm. The Cave. I saw Eduki immediately to my right, his image was clear and sharp. My previous days had been constructive. I had moved my mental focus toward the establishment and building up of The Hermitage Development Centre, and attending MBS events. I had relegated my printing business to secondary importance and I was busy tidying up loose ends as my emotional and mental shift bedded in.

Eduki said that it was now time to introduce a new Guide. I was resistant, but knew from previous experience that resistance was futile. My Tarot Card of The Day that morning had been The Wheel of Fortune. I simply said that I wanted to spend a little more time with him, to clear up a few points and thank him for everything. He agreed, and we sat down. Discussing a current client he spoke clearly, "help her as best you can, show her what you can, but she is conflicted and seeking the easy way. Go as far as you can." I asked about previous Guides. The nine were in me now and this was clearly a new cycle. "It all begins again," he said, "never ending learning is the name of the game." I asked about a colleague's ideas around using astrology to precisely map Karma. "Interesting, but of limited use without the fundamentals of life," he said. I asked about happiness. Vague I know! He said "It is a right, but the more time you spend – especially now – looking out, the more unhappy you will be. The imperative is to look inside for answers, solace and comfort." He now seemed eager for me to move on. I looked around and there was a figure standing right in front of me, with an aura of blue and white, somewhat reminiscent of the Star card, yet not. Her eyes were blue, but I could see nothing else. Her name was Helen, maybe spelt Helene. We embraced, and I confirmed her identity a second time.

"I am here to teach you love," she said. I asked about a vision I had seen some days before of an endless mountain. I took it to be the future of my life. "I will help you climb it," she said. I could then see the Temple of Opportunities in relation to the mountain, but without clarity as to how, or if, they fitted together. We spent a little time together and she answered many of my Outer World questions. This time I did not fight the transition. This seemed to help and the process was comforting and comfortable.

"Just continue exactly as you have been doing recently," she said, "being more aware of how you spend your days." We made love, and afterwards she merged into me and we came back together. Eduki was all but forgotten.

CHAPTER XIII

HELENE

[MAY 2012]

*M*onday 21st. 6.00pm. The Cave. Helene emerged from my right side and I turned to face her. Her eyes were completely white, with no pupils, and a bright energy shone from them, a soft, yet highly powerful blue emanation. I had some uncertainties about her name, and varyingly contradictory impressions came upon me. I tried to let them all go however and asked solely about my next steps.

"Study, but do not take on any new projects. Read a book, experience a method, or undergo a happening, and then check back with me. This will be the form of your learning. There is much to know. There will be crises to knock you off your path but you must persist. It may take some time, maybe one year, or more." She entered me again and I returned home. From my chair in the Outer World I felt calm, collected and centred, not overawed or confused as I had done on other occasions. I walked to my desk to note all this down in a state of acceptance, rather than the resistance and exhaustion and had so often been the case over the years. I hoped this new feeling would last.

Wednesday 30th. 6.00pm. The Cave. I entered the cave, via the sea shore, although I noticed that the cave was not in its usual position. Once inside and through to the Inner World I could see no beings whatsoever. There were none of the Nine and no Eduki. This was of course correct, for the nine lived within me now, and Eduki had departed. Still, it seemed different. Helene merged out from my right and stood beside me. She carried the same blue-ness about her as before, and again her eyes were pure white. We embraced for a while and I asked her about a recent discovery I had made. For maybe two years now I had on my shelves a CD, which I had only just got around to listening to. It was a Book of Shadows of an old Master called Frater Sisto. She spoke, "ah, an old man, whose time has passed. He did much work and had some good points, though he was not correct in everything." I asked what to make of his teachings, which were primarily related to the elements. "You should begin with the daily breathing practice that he suggests and fully write up his notes in order to understand them. You might then listen to the recordings by Dolores Ashcroft, although these will be less useful to you." I asked about an idea I had for a book about the numerology of US Presidents. "You can do this later, it does not have to be done now," she said. From out of nowhere a rabbit appeared at her feet. I stroked it and it hopped off to the left. This caused me to look around, and although the components of the scene were all in place – The Library, the Mountain, The Temple – it seemed like a new vista had opened up. Should I heed the rabbit and look at smaller things, rather than bigger things? "Start a new daily routine," said Helene, "to include the breathing practices as given by Frater Sisto." I thanked her and asked her to confirm her name. "H. Helene," she said. I asked, for it had been in my mind since we met, if she were Helen of

Troy. "If you like," came the enigmatic reply. I couldn't really believe that she was. Was she? She had decided to come back home with me and said that I should return "very, very soon."

Thursday 31st. 5.00pm. The Cave. I greeted Helene immediately. I was in a doubting mood and had to go over old ground. "Is this the Astral Plane?" I asked.

"No," she said softly.

"Then where is?" Hearing me out she pointed up to the Temple, to which we immediately rose. I was greeted by a voice.

"What do you want?"

"The Astral – where is it?" I asked.

"Ah..." replied the voice, "the Astral. Place of illusion and phantasy." My awareness turned to the open roof of the Temple and the stardust of the Universe. "So where do you wish to go?" came the voice.

"Mars." I said.

"Really? Very well."

Although I was sat perfectly still I could now feel myself rocking forward and back in my chair but could still get no more than a vague image of the planet. After a while I returned to Earth. Helene explained that the Astral was accessible from either the Outer World or The Inner World. She urged greater practice of the Sisto methods and the writing up of these Inner World notes for greater understanding, plus a return daily. She underlined the need for daily development, and pointed out that there was more to learn than there was time available. I came home.

[JUNE 2012]

Friday 1st. 5.30pm. The Cave. Helene was on my right. She enveloped me in a loving and supportive fashion. I knew not whether it was wings or a cloak, but it was pleasant and comforting. I asked her about some recent attempts at deeper self analysis. "Some of your characteristics and behaviour are part of your nature, the negatives of which must be controlled. To do this operate from the positive perspective of your numbers. Some of the other traits, well, you have picked up along the way," continuing, "you need a regular daily routine now. Time in here, time in your chair, your room, the Inner World, in order to grow and move forward." She was direct and forceful in underlining, again, the word daily. "A daily discipline and practice, in spite of all the inevitable reasons not to. Daily. But this is enough for today," she concluded, wishing me well. She would stay here today. I returned home.

Saturday 2nd. 3.00pm. The Television. I thought I would try the principle of a moving meditation into a solid object, rather than a headspace. I choose the TV set. It was an old style cathode ray tube TV with the bulge out at the back and the curved front screen. I began with the picture on, but sound off.

As I entered, electrical impulses seemed to fire off all around me. And there was dust, mountains of dust and fluff, all somehow impeding the signal. Some of the electronics were not working. I initially thought that maybe this was the case in all TVs, some of the elements working depending on the functions being used, but then it dawned on me that it was more to do with the age of the television set, approaching the end of its life. I returned back home. On one hand I was quite impressed by possibilities raised by this little excursion, but on the other hand I did not feel I had learned anything new.

Later that day. The Cave. Helene was stood to my right, radiating an enormous amount of energy. She was bigger than me, fuller than me, though physically she was slim and slight. She remarked that everything was as it ought to be, but "to stay with me a little longer so you can consolidate all that you have learned so far. Go through your diaries from the very beginning, including from the time of writing *Steps Toward The Light*. Can you achieve this by Christmas?" I replied that I should be able to have it done much sooner.

"No." She was insistent. "You will not be able to do it sooner. Is Christmas possible?" I said I would aim for this deadline. I tried to clarify what she meant by consolidation, what things I could cross off and what things must I attend to. "Musts are the daily breathing practice, which you should already be finding benefit in. The daily visits to me are vital. You must go through your notes, books and all courses. Discard the Presidential project and finish, for your own benefit, *The Key To Time*." I asked about the many unread books on my shelves. "This should all be part of the revision/consolidation/learning. They will fill in the details around what you already basically know, but since these many books have already appeared in your field of life they should be finished." I got the additional impression, though I did not seek confirmation of it, that as a result of this something would be presented to me. On that note she merged out of me, "visit tomorrow," she said, kissing me goodbye. I returned home. Who was Helene? Was she connected to Hermes?

Sunday 3rd. 4.00pm. The Cave. Helene was apparent on my immediate right. Again with piercing eyes her blue cloak enveloped me. Caring and supportive she wiped my face, saying, "You need a purifying wash, a cleansing from within." I asked her about the lack of recognition I had received for my work. "Reactionary comment will always put backs up, and some people will always take offence, but rather than being a showy and attention seeking version of Three, be an authoritative Three. Three and The Hermit are incompatible unless you use the number, rather than allowing it to use you. Be original, considered, thoughtful and slow down. Deliver your words clearly and with authority. Do not discount the responses before you begin. Do not expect resistance – you might get it anyway – but do not take the power out of your words beforehand. And above all, do not apologise for having something to say." I thanked her, those were helpful and relevant words. "Next?" She wanted more questions from me. I asked why I had not always visited the Inner World when instructed to do so. Why did I have such resistance? "Because you did not really want to know. Which is why your visits must now be daily, to catch up. Come again tomorrow," she said. I was tired and questioned the need for tomorrow. "Yes, tomorrow. That is all for now."

Monday 4th. 4.00pm. The Cave. Helene greeted me to my right. I asked if she was in fact Hermes, in a kind of disguise, but then retracted my question. She gave no answer and merged into me, deeply and intensively. She was well and truly aligned inside me, my eyes were her eyes and vice versa.

"Increase the intensity of the breathing exercises, up to thirty-five breaths now, with eleven more for the Akasha." The comments were very specific and related directly to the Sisto methods I had spoken to her about. I checked that it wasn't me asking these questions of myself? "Yes, increase the intensity," she said. "What else?" I asked about working on a project with a friend in the Outer World. She did not waste any time answering. "Yes, of course, if you wish, but nothing is without consequences." I pressed it no further. She then said that I would soon again have access to my flat in Cheltenham.

"Ha, that will be years away," I scoffed, but she held firm, "maybe sooner." Another tenant in the building had undergone a psychotic incident which had nearly caused the building to be razed to the ground. "This happened," said Helene, "because the building was unprotected." Obviously she meant energetically so. She continued. "I am inside you now and will come back with you tonight. Repeat the breathing in the morning and notice the difference. Report back in here tomorrow." My logical mind was unclear about how she could be within me in the Inner World and at the same time as being so in the Outer World? If this were so then it should just be a matter of being able to hear her voice in the Outer World as I could in the Inner World? There was the faintest murmur of a "yes" to be heard as we/I returned home, although with the lingering question of what was my voice and what was hers? I looked around at the room in my house. It seemed to sparkle.

Realisations: The difference between Helene's voice and mine is immediately apparent, and varies in tone, volume and pitch. Whenever I start to say no to her words then confusion immediately wells up inside me, whereon getting the correct voice back becomes even harder. On the other hand if I say no to myself it seems much more cut and dried. It certainly seems to be the case that the voice of Helene does not argue. It simply states, informs, guides and then waits for the monkey mind to find its way back to it again.

But what about free will? To be fully guided from within might somehow imply surrender to something greater, in this case Helene being a manifestation, an aspect of God itself, certainly higher in the order of knowledge and life than little old me. This possibility seems to remove any illusion that we are somehow in charge of our lives. The only real decision it seems that we can make is whether to ignore or accept the guidance presented to us. But how do we know the guidance is reliable?

False Guides are a real problem, both in this terrain and in the Outer Life. Liars – let's call them that - are never fully wrong and completely deceitful, otherwise they would be easy to spot. Instead they give us just enough to believe them, and then fill in the rest with blinds and complexities. False Guides offer short cuts, encourage you to off load blame elsewhere, breed bad behaviours and generally judge you in some way or another.

But this is difficult territory, because we all sometimes need a good kick up the backside. A True Guide will be able to provide this, but not in the same way that a living human being would. A False Guide on the other hand might well encourage you to turn your ire on 'them pesky others' who bar your progress.

It is hard to work out the True Guide from the False one. But it's worth the effort, for the more I have worked with these energies, the more obvious it has become how utterly useless I am without them and how, without their guidance I have no chance whatsoever of making it. And if that is true for me then it is true for others. I have frequently got it wrong, but my Guide never has. And together we can learn what is required. Together with my Guide I/we have grown enormously powerful. But without my Guide what really am I?

The proof of a good Inner World Guide contact is that your Life gets demonstrably better, richer, more interesting, and with more possibilities. Ever decreasing limitation is the law of failure, which is the result of bad guidance along ever narrowing passage ways.

Tuesday 5th. 5.00pm. The Cave. Entering the Inner World, Helene emerged from me and came face to face, eye to eye.

"How was it for you?" she asked, cheekily.

"Confusing." I said. "I did not know your voice from mine. Is there some kind of sign you could give?"

"Its easy," she replied. "My voice tells you unexpected things, out of the blue. Address your Dark Side, the negatives of each of your numbers is you, everything else is my guidance." Upon asking she repeated these significant words without hesitation or variation. I now stood back and looked at her more intently. Today she was wearing a red cloak. I asked her, who in fact, was in charge in this relationship? Her mouth opened wide like a monster and she devoured me whole. It did not hurt and it was not scary, perhaps just a signal of who was really boss. I felt different, I suddenly felt some pressure to get on. "You are now driven. Because there is so much to do," she said.

I asked about the Monarchy. "It is in a transition which will accelerate soon enough, but it may hang on in a diminishing format for another hundred years. You are transitioning to a Presidency of Europe and will soon have very important decisions to make, but that is for another day. Have tomorrow night off," she said, "try to help your young nephew and come back on Thursday." She merged back into me and I was somewhat disorientated.

Thursday 7th. 6.00pm. The Cave. I asked immediately about a possible trip to the USA next Spring.

"Oh yes, you must pursue this. You will need much preparation and you should expect travel and format changes, but it is very positive. Embrace new technology to promote it. Now you see why we wanted you to have gone through everything by Christmas! It will be a matter of promoting yourself toward what people want, but in fact giving them what they need."

"I drank some alcohol last night." I said.

"And how did you feel this morning?" was the reply. The answer was, of course, bad. "Yes, you overindulged. You simply cannot handle it any more. Moderation only from now on please." I asked then of a working opportunity with a friend and was cautioned against it, "care needed, a large price to pay, you could lose everything." After some back and forth on this I resigned myself to the advice. "Come again tomorrow, or at the very least on Saturday" she said, returning with me.

Saturday 9th. 6.00pm. The Cave.

'The New Age is the perfect home for the delicate Ego'

Helene spoke immediately. "Well, where are we today?" I had attended a usually busy MBS fair in Lincoln with the intention of doing readings for people. The day had been very quiet and those that did visit seemed more interested in sticking plasters than solutions. I found this depressing and it raised two big questions. First, the effectiveness of Arthur's teachings on people's everyday lives.

"He was only one man, and he did not have enough time with them to really make a difference. The more time you can get with them the more difference you will make. You need time in front of people to get the message across as well as assistants working for you, delivering your message and singing your praises. It is actually better not to get close to any of these people, your distance keeps their desire for more burning strong and strengthens their adherence and connection to the work."

The second question related to the popularity of these events in general. "Well you can see for yourself. Some might call a smaller show a consolidation where as in fact it is simply collapsing from within. The darkness has taken root." Can it all be consolidated and managed I asked? "Possibly, but more likely will be a complete collapse. 2012 is shaping up to be an awakening of consciousness but not in the ways that they imagined. This is harsh but true. Many of these folk have been living in a dream, and now it is time to wake up." I cannot remember everything else that was said, including the conclusion about whether to continue attending them, or what their immediate future was but the fragment "it is collapsing due to the negativity involved" stayed with me. I do not recall whether the guidance was specific to this event, or this organiser, although I felt it was more generalised. After some reflection I questioned the insights I had been given. "It is harsh, but it is the way it is," she said. "It is collapsing under the weight of its own contradictions." She insisted that even though I would be travelling tomorrow that I still find time to visit.

Sunday 10th. 3.30pm. The Cave. I performed this entry during a break at the Lincoln MBS. I felt it was important to try to perfect the method any time, anywhere. I was immediately given a warning about one specific individual at the event. This was very helpful.

"So what do you think of these events now?" asked Helene.

"As you said, collapsing under the weight of their own contradictions." I replied.

"Yes, but what would they do without you, where would they be then? You are holding this up!" That was a big call and a big task to continue to do so, but I felt in my heart that it was correct. What a realisation, given all that is happening in the scene, what would these folk do without me? Maybe they would be better off. "Come tomorrow. That is all for today," as she merged back into me, with Arthur's words ringing in my ears, "this is why you are so needed."

Monday 11th. 7.00pm. The Cave. Helene emerged at my right and turned to face me head on. I asked the question that had been bugging me ever since I first met her.

"Are you Hermes?"

"Yes," came an unambiguous reply. I was stunned. I had expected to be scolded for such a ridiculous question.

"But why appear like this, why not identify yourself?"

"So as not to disturb you." There was not much I could say to this, beyond a grudging acceptance. I moved on instead to practical matters, and asked whether the breathing practice that she/he had urged me to pursue was not just an exercise in glamouring, building up a bubble to avoid life. "It could be, but you will only be permitted to glamour yourself in so far as it contributes and enables your illumination of others. You will not be allowed to go further than that." I continued,

"How can I stand firm in the face of attack?"

"Allow the attack to hit your outer energy field and then fizzle and drip down to the floor, lifeless. You have the Staff and crystal, the crystal like your brain is for use as the greatest receptor ever devised and staff is for the inner strength that you need." I should feel the staff in my spine when needed I thought.

"What is the future of MBS shows?"

"You must continue them until you have an alternative – video pieces to camera is a good place to start. Get started!" That was all. Hermes merged back into me, instructing me to return tomorrow night. This was already a punishing regime.

Tuesday 12th. 7.30pm. The Cave. Hermes merged out and faced me again. I detected a smile upon his face, but I could not hold the vision with any certainty. He ushered me to sit down and ask questions. First of all I was concerned that my daily pore breathing exercises were in fact just a constant taking from the Universe, and thus imbalanced.

"What you are doing is reuniting, reconnecting, to the Universe, to this world. Finding your place in it. You are entitled to as much of this natural condition as you can get, so long as it is used to produce or deliver something for the benefit of others, to fulfil your purpose of illumination. One must serve the other. Rest now, you are tired. Have a night off and a day off. Return to it all on Thursday." I sensed that an important part of the process was to notice the difference between doing the practices and not. Hermes did not merge with me on this occasion and I returned directly home.

Thursday 14th. 7.00pm. The Cave. Hermes urged me to update him. I asked about the Outer World choices now facing me, particularly the business opportunities.

"You have either disconnection from me and immersion in the material world – this will lead to wealth, but tremendous ups and downs, followed by a sudden and abrupt end to your life, while probably still quite young. Or you have the path of guidance, which is far harder, but much bigger and more fulfilling. This will result in a long life."

"Do I have a choice?" I asked.

"Oh yes, very much so. There is always a choice. We want you to work with our guidance but it is up to you."

"Why me?" I asked.

"Because you stepped forward."

"But which is the right path?" I was vacillating.

"You know which is the right path," he replied. I switched tack, and asked more about the Temple of Opportunities. "This presents itself for making things happen on path, broadly speaking. To effect changes related solely to your purpose."

"And if I chose to use that power on another path, say a material one?" I asked.

"We would not allow that." There was no menace in the words, it's just how it was. Hermes said he would not come back with me today, but that I was to visit again tomorrow.

Maybe the two paths were not mutually exclusive? I tried to convince myself of this but with little success. The guided path was clearly the bigger of the two and as such the material path would bring misery and sorrow. I suppose it comes down to whether I wanted to live or not?

When I used to ask Arthur about his experience with the magickal possibilities of manifestation, he always replied the same way, that he had everything that he needed. When he first introduced these possibilities to me, in my mid twenties (which in hindsight I think was way too young) he dangled the deceptive carrot that "you can materialise a Bentley, if you wish." He was right, but I saw now that it wasn't that simple. Law of Attraction People beware what you wish for!

Friday 15th. 5.00pm. The Cave. It had been an exceptionally busy and profitable few days in the Outer World, and I was tense and tired. I saw Hermes sitting by a log, waiting. He, or maybe she, looked like a young girl and it took me some time to accept that it was Hermes. He or she merged into me and asked me to report. I shared my suspicions on Outer World developments and meetings.

"My life could be this profitable, this busy, this stressful, every day, every week – if I wanted," I said.

"Oh yes, it could. In the meantime look upon it as a windfall with which to do something constructive, to pay some things off maybe?" I lamented about the time and energy input required to make such money. I felt it to be nearly all consuming. Hermes urged that I use these thoughts and recent experiences to reflect more upon the choice I needed to make. "When the time comes you will have to swear an oath in the Temple of Opportunities." This was an unexpected development. I had better give this a bit more thought! Or was not the answer staring me in the face?

"Return tomorrow morning" she said. I thanked her and she appreciated it, but did not come back with me this time.

Saturday 16th. 10.00am. The Cave. Hermes appeared very differently today. Now she stood taller and seemed larger, dressed in a blue cloak. It was very much a female energy now.

"You have gone wrong," she said.

"With what?"

"There should be more love and more trust." In what? I was confused. This conversation was headed in an unforeseen direction. "You cannot control the direction that people move in. You must let them be themselves." I argued all around the statement, all the while knowing that it was pointless to do so. She continued. "Let them be them, imperfect and messy, confused and confusing, go along with their decisions even if you don't agree. You are not them, but they each have a contribution to make." I confessed that I had no clue how to actually do this. "Then you are not ready for the oath," she said. "Come back on Monday. Continue with your breathing practice, taking the opportunities to act as they arise." She did not come back with me, An unexpected turn of events, and therefore probably a valuable one.

What is this oath Hermes speaks of? What does it require? What is the sacrifice, what is the reward? Who and what is the oath to? Is it really sensible to hand over this much control of my life to another, non-terrestrial entity? The words of Arthur from twenty years prior chimed in, loudly. "In order to get anywhere with spiritual development you have to surrender to God."

Monday 18th. 4.00pm. The Cave. Hermes was friendly, warm and smiling, beckoning me to sit down on an old log. This time he was male. He smiled knowingly. Yesterday's Outer World teaching experiences were enjoyable but difficult. He seemed to know this already, even though he had not been present. Or had he?

"That was you!" he smiled, referring to one particularly challenging course attendee, "you were just like that with Arthur." I knew this to be exactly and terribly true, always waiting for someone to say the right words that would make life better without ever really making any effort to look hard at myself. "You are not ready for the oath," she said. She? Hermes was female again. "There is much else to do. Go through Dolores Ashcroft's work and your own notes of the Inner World. Pull a Tarot card daily and enter the Inner World with that. Make it your morning card and do this daily. Contact me when you enter each time." I asked if this process had been referred to by others as the Knowledge and Conversation of the Holy Guardian Angel? "This is what this, us, is now," she said, "Arthur was very good at simplifying these things you know." I felt the weight of it all, and I obviously wasn't ready. Would it be possible to not come everyday and instead have a break? I found it so tiring. "That is up to you," she said. "But certainly come here directly before giving this healing session on Thursday. Otherwise its over to you." We embraced and I departed.

Tuesday 19th. 4.00pm. King of Wands. I had not entered the Inner World via a card for some time. Eventually, after just reflecting and contemplating it I received the vaguest impression of a tall man directly over to my left, with Hermes on my right. Hermes indicated for me to step toward the man. I shouted to him. That may not have been what Hermes had in mind!

The man explained that he directed everybody and every event using his wand to enforce his will. He was above the minutiae of things and got others to do that. Women did his bidding via his wand also. "But do not think me manipulative," he said, "for in fact I operate as close to an honest connection with Spirit as you are likely to get." The grounds and the house that he lived in were "rather like yours" he said.

The Library appeared and I entered, bowing to The Keeper. I asked of a friend of mine. There was no book. Instead a feather wafted down from the ceiling. "She has never done anything positive – off her own back – in her life." I asked of another. "She needs rest, time to reflect. She has not really come to terms with her illness. The diagnosis and the language used fills people with dread and negativity as much as the illness itself." I thanked The Keeper for his directness and did not detain him. Hermes bade me farewell.

Wednesday 20th. 5.00pm. The Devil. "You will need me with you today," said Hermes, closely accompanying me as we moved toward the dark and foreboding Forest of Souls.

"This is where the souls wait until their time to return. At the correct time they must leave," she said. "Your mother was your carrier, but she chose her own path. Your father was not helpful to her, but she had opportunities to grow and change and she did not take them. It will be some time until she returns." The occupants of the Forest did not look universally happy. I got the impression that it would soon be time for Arthur to return, but how and where?

I saw The Devil, in the depiction from the card, in the sky, flying toward me in attack, but Hermes deflected it. This Devil seemed connected to hunger. The Dark Side was hungry, but the Light knew when there was enough. Hunger might show itself in many ways – sexual, financial, food, drink, company, knowledge. Yes, the Dark Side could definitely be hungry for knowledge, and be not prepared to wait for the understanding that must always accompany that knowledge. A thirst for anything if not matched up with patience, was a manifestation of, and takeover by, the Dark Side – the urge for more, for its own sake.

In the card the Light was indeed present but the Devil obscured it, turning it toward his own ends, debasing it, rather than moving up toward it. This is the condition of our modern world, but also, unavoidably, the condition of me. Hermes seemed happy with these insights and merged into me. We returned.

Thursday 21st. 5.00pm. Page of Pentacles. Hermes was very close by as I entered, and a child was off ahead in the distance. Hermes urged me to visit and to understand this figure before any questions were asked.

The child was an apprentice, a student, definitely not a Master. He or she was learning how to control the most basic of material things – the body and the immediate physical environment. The child did not yet know the purpose for which the powers of the material world could be used. He or she – for I could not discern which - was only getting to grips with Life, simply playing. This was a youngster gaining experience, but only of the physical dimension.

I turned back to Hermes to ask about Arthur's healing practice. Here, I was that child. I did not have a solid handle on what might be achieved with the technique or how, really, to bring the power into full flow.

"But you will, you will. In the meantime, good work has been done." I was surprised but happy to hear this. I asked about the video clips I had been preparing.

"This is also good work, but you must keep it accessible and practical." She gave me two topics. "Make a list of more, and plan ahead." She emerged properly from me and said to return tomorrow.

Friday 22nd. 5.00pm. Judgement. Hermes was to my right, and a scene of people were running round and round in circles, heads bowed down, neither looking up to the Light, forward to the future or into themselves. They were solely concerned with short term, external matters. I asked about some friends, one of them long standing, and their resistance to the Light.

"These people know where you are, if they want you. All you have to do is to shine your Light and people will find you. Focus on those that do." I wondered whether I might be able to help an old school friend, who had no interest whatsoever in this subject matter.

"You can try," came the words, tinged with an aroma which suggested that was all I could do.

"How might I avoid landing up like these people?" I asked.

"To do that you had better not ignore the guidance," she said.

Turning to the scene of people, there were folk running from all around to hear a pending announcement. Somehow I felt that this represented a failure to move with the times. If you yourself cannot move with the times then you will be called to judgement, under which all people are moved on or sentenced accordingly. The energy of Judgement always shows where there has been a failure on the part of man to act according to the Inner Guidance, which is always available. The Judgement is external, delivered by factors and forces in the wider world that cannot be argued with.

Hermes suggested I move to a smaller number of breaths in my daily practice, but to make them deeper and try to fully accumulate the energies within my body. After that I could build up the number again. She did not merge with me, simply saying, "come tomorrow." Arthur always did say that Judgement was a big card.

Saturday 23rd. 4.00pm. Eight of Wands. I could see eight enormous staves flying through the sky, like rockets minus the destructive power. Hermes pointed up at them. They changed course and came swooping down, I ducked.

"Large projects, tasks that all demand energy. They are all in formation, you must try to catch as many as possible. This is a card where many demands of your external time and energy are made and you should rise to the challenge. Results only ever come from energy and effort." I thanked Hermes for this, and then turned to ask him about my mother.

"There is of course a long connection, as she carried you, but the Karma of this was played out long ago. It was demanded and has been paid." Thought turned to my father and sister. "In a way it is worse with your sister." I was not quite sure what was worse, and how.

"But am I compelled to go and see them?" My relationship with them was fractured and my visits now very rare.

"It is your choice." I thought on this for a while but my mind turned to my relationship with Hermes, which to me was much more important. She agreed that this was so.

"Is this process the Knowledge and Conversation of the Holy Guardian Angel?" (I was not consciously aware that I had asked this at least twice already. Whatever answers I had received were obviously not penetrating).

"Are you sure you want to know?" she said. I confirmed that I did. Suddenly, Hermes, who had started today's session as a meek and mild little girl was transformed into a huge and towering figure. Her cloak enveloped me and I was now the tiny one. She emanated force and power and confirmed who she was, before merging into me powerfully. I felt myself almost tear in two. "Step up the breath practice to seven repeats and hold them," she said, "and tomorrow we will heal your friend. I will return with you, but tonight there must be no alcohol."

We returned. I did not freak out as I had done during similar transitions. But were those transitions anything like this?

Sunday 24th. 5.00pm. Four of Cups. Hermes moved out and away from me, off to my right, far away. I caught sight of some vivid green ivy and shrubs in a rich and well kept garden. A man was resting in it, superficially satisfied and content, but his mind seemed anxious, restless and concerned for the future.

"What troubles you?" I asked.

"I have a good situation here, but I know that I must change, grow, do more. I have attained certainty and equilibrium, you can see it all around you, but I feel the presence of new influences. These concern me. I know they will be beneficial, yet they will also upset my space. So I embrace them, but reluctantly. It is truly a fearful situation, for although the new has not even arrived I can feel the stagnation of the existing, which only five minutes ago was abundant and joyful." Very much a Sunday night/Monday morning feeling that I recognised well, where we know what we must do, and we know that it will be fine, but we still don't want to do it. The Four comes in to disturb the Three. I wished the man well and thanked him.

I looked around and could see Hermes away to the distance on the right. A serpent was at my feet and it hissed for me to follow it to Hermes. I could not seem to manage this movement to my right, so I edged directly forward instead. The serpent was ahead of me. The further ahead I walked the more barren was the ground beneath me, the brighter over head was the Sun and the whiter its light. I could just about perceive a horizon but nothing else other than an increasingly intense white light. The serpent was now gone but I remained where I was.

The figure of Hermes, in the traditional form of Thoth, floated in front of me like an hallucination. I asked for the real Hermes to present himself. This figure before me said he was Hermes. I again called for the original Hermes and a female form appeared on my right hand side. I now could move off in this direction, toward a greener and more lush land, rather than the nothingness of before.

"You did not follow the serpent," she said.

"I could not do it," I replied.

"Practice, and you will. This is a very dangerous time for you. The barren field you just visited is full of illusions and phantasms." I asked how she had managed to heal my friend today so miraculously. "I did not. You did." I could not believe this. "Yes, you did. You allowed and managed the energy to flow through you. It was the result of all these years of practice and could not have happened before now, but this is also dangerous because you are starting to see the full extent of your powers and you will be tested as such." I asked about the appearance of dark forces that supposedly follows the Knowledge and Conversation of the Holy Guardian Angel. "This is happening and will continue to do so. You must be careful of who you interact with. You must let out your Dark Side, but under control. The consequences are severe if you lose this control. Some people will cling to you like limpets and you will never be free of them." I asked if Hermes would come back with me for tomorrow's teaching session. "You do not need me. So long as you prepare you will have it all there. Just call if needed."

"And how shall I call you?"

"By my name." Obvious I suppose.

Afterwards: Shape shifting by Hermes was very confusing. Why was he doing it, why be male then female? It took me a while to work out the fundamental answers to this. First, the mythology of Hermes proved very revealing. He was a trickster, a natural shape shifter, manifesting in the ancient stories as whatever he needed to be as the circumstances dictated. In some myths he was even hermaphrodite. Secondly, the differing nature of the Inner and Outer World had to be considered. The Outer World is the realm of Form. Everything that exists here has a structure, a framework, a physical dimension around which the invisible collects and penetrates. The Inner World however is the realm of Force, or maybe we might prefer to say Energy. The two realms overlap to some degree, where things of seeming form – pillars, mountains, towers – appear in the Inner World landscape, and where the invisible forces – vibration – exert an effect in the Outer World. But primarily each stays and is rooted in its own domain. Therefore it is quite ridiculous to expect Hermes, or any other *force*, to adopt a specific, fixed and consistent *form* in either world.

Monday 25th. The Chariot. A low slung American style sedan car appeared before me. I got into the passenger seat instinctively, but then realised that no-one was driving. I climbed over to the drivers side and we took off. I only just managed to keep control of the vehicle until I bailed out over the Temple.

Hermes was waiting. I surveyed the Hall, and no other beings were present. The roof was off and anything was really possible now, but Hermes and I left. I told him about my Outer World day. It had been too busy, and I did not function well with this manic activity, or even enjoy it much any more. I used to thrive during that kind of day but now it just seemed too frantic, too panicked, too reactionary and without direction. Hermes confirmed that this indeed was the problem – no direction. I needed a much clearer goal and purpose, and then to employ the necessary discrimination to all forms of activity outside of that goal. It was not enough, any longer, to simply be busy, as under the Chariot I was bound to be, without a meaningful focus and reason for that busyness. Hermes suggested I return when I was in a better frame of mind. I was annoyed that the day had impinged so much on my Inner World efforts. I had been up to my eyes in work, without a break from 9am with many changes of direction and constant juggling of projects and schedules. It was a good job that I had heeded the advice of the Eight of Wands a few days prior and worked to clear my desk in advance of this or I would have been in absolute chaos. Hermes indicated that my work would be like this for sometime. I replied that this was not what I wanted. "It is your choice" she replied. I returned, she did not.

Afterwards: The accuracy of my Tarot Card for the Day had never let me down, in twenty plus years, but it had now taken on a life of its own, sometimes talking about what was coming down the track in the following days. This was even more helpful.

Also, the symbolism of these Inner visits was outstanding. Automatically getting into a car on the passenger side, assuming that someone else was would be driving it? Symbolic of wider life issues, me thinks!

Tuesday 26th. 4.00pm. Seven of Pentacles. There was a man, sat at a table, counting his money. He had a large pile of coins at the left end of the table, with some smaller pieces on his right. In between counts he would write things down. I asked him what he was doing.

"Planning. Counting. It all takes time," he said, without looking up from his work. It didn't seem like he had much fun or any time for enjoying his gains, but maybe that comes later, I thought. What could I learn from this patient man? "Time. Details and thoughts take time. Quite rightly too," he said.

I turned to Hermes at my right and we sat down. I had noticed that there were not the abundance of figures and beings in this world now that there used to be. I asked about Karma, and my failure to be recognised for my works. Was it all Karma, as a result of fighting Arthur so hard? I expected that this was so.

"It is nothing to do with Karma. That has been played out in one area already, with one of your clients. The problem is that you have not yet found the language with which to communicate."

"Why have I not?"

"Because you are intolerant of them." Hard, but true. I was. But how to fix this?

"By remembering that you were once as they are now. Do not forget this. It is not Karma. Meeting Arthur and being The Hermit mean regular encounters with unvarnished truths and a constant call back to seeing the way it is. Other people do not want to do this. You did not always want to do this."

I switched gears, always feeling against the clock in this process. "This place, is it the Astral?" another question repeated, previous answer unheard!

"No, this is the higher mental plane. But your terminology is wrong and incompatible. Look around you, does it fit any description of the Astral that you have ever read?" Of course it did not, and the terminology did not always bring clarity. "Visit next time via the other doorway in the Cave," Hermes said. "Practice nine breaths and hold," she said, calling after me as I went home. I felt very tired.

Later that day I visited the cave again and located the Vortex Elevator. I entered it and requested "The Astral." Instantly I felt the familiar rushing, buffeting, rising sensations. These ceased after a while and I emerged into a fog. All I could see was white, which meant that I could not see anything at all. I turned my head to scan around and I saw Arthur, walking toward me in the familiar motion that he had, head to one side, dressed in blue. He greeted me warmly and said he had been waiting a long time for me to make it through.

"I was trying to get you to see, to pass it on," he said. I understood, now, if not then. I asked him about the Inner World. "That is more of a mental place," he said, "this is more emotional." I could feel my forehead, the third eye position, throbbing like crazy, almost to the point of pain. "Come again tomorrow," said Arthur, "it takes a little getting used to." Various other matters of specific relevance passed between us, so many in fact that I struggled to remember them all. But it was definitely Arthur. He spoke directly in a manner and with a voice that was unmistakably different to Hermes or any other.

One of the topics was his method of The Four Roads, together with the notion of the Four Worlds. He said that you could not directly equate one with the other, but that they were different uses of the number energy Four. "You can make whatever you like here, you know," he said. "But be careful." My mind instantly turned to money, but before I could say anything Arthur chimed in on this. "You have enough. There will be problems, but you will have enough." I could see that care was needed in this 'make anything you like' game.

I returned to the Vortex Elevator and allowed myself to descend, with a definite sinking feeling. I had performed this trip in total silence with no accompanying music, and this seemed to help. The throbbing in my forehead instantly disappeared and I returned home.

Wednesday 27th. 2.00pm. The Astral. I repeated the procedure exactly as yesterday, entry via the Vortex, from the Cave, requesting 'Astral' as I entered it. It was the same again, all white fluffiness, but through the fog Arthur appeared. He was sat in the same place as before, as if he were waiting. He beckoned me to sit down and I asked him various questions,

"Which numbers are connected to the Earth?" I asked. He gestured me toward an image, hanging in the air, of an arrangement of numbers:

3   6   9

2   5   8

1   4   7   <<< "These are the Earth numbers," said Arthur.

Arthur

This did not seem right, but he insisted that I research the question from that starting point, including the works of Austin Coates to discover the answer. I asked about the current, general Outer world situation.

"You are right in your concerns. There is a very real danger of Tarot being outlawed along with other things too. You can only do what you can in the face of this. There are other factors at work though, good signs, the rise of women for example. We shall see whether this brings with it a positive use of emotions or the domination of fear. This is the decider of which way things will go. Come again tomorrow?" he said. I replied that I was unable to visit tomorrow. "Well, when you can then" he said. I thanked him very much and he said that he thanked me. I waved goodbye.

During the first part of this experience I felt the same pressure on my forehead and third eye region. It lessened as time passed but again I felt very tired on my return.

Later that day. Two of Pentacles. Immediately I connected with Hermes, but from a distance for all the activity was taking place above me now, rather than straight ahead. "Rise up to meet it," he said.

As I did I could see graphs, lines rising with other lines falling. Profit and loss. Progress and consolidation. Matters were not established enough to have a productive life of their own, things within this Two where too dependent on external ups and downs. This forward and back, this lack of balance, all brought dissatisfaction. I asked Hermes about one of my share holdings in the Outer World. The answers at first were confusing and I doubted them, but then there was clarity, "They will find oil, but not as much as expected." I scoffed and said that this was old news and had already happened. "With more to come!" she said, continuing, "and don't ask me again!" This was an interesting response, for at the time I felt it was a justifiable question designed to prevent losses, rather than gain profits. But how skilled we are at justifying ourselves. Hermes had spoken and she did not lie. I thanked her. "That is all, come again tomorrow, in fact, now daily." I picked up the Staff and crystal and fused it into me as I left.

Thursday 28th. 5.30pm. Knight of Swords. My first impression was of a very flashy looking Knight on horse back with much noise and fury, but little light. He was determined to demonstrate how clever and skilled he was, and demonstrated this by leaping into the skies. I tried to keep up but could not, in spite of his demands. He wasted too much energy on appearance and possessed little wisdom, limited knowledge and only shallow technique. His superficiality limited him in a number of ways, but it worked well as a protection and disguise.

Hermes said that was enough for today and to have a night off and a small drink if I needed to, "but to be back to it again tomorrow."

Afterwards: If you wish to live by the Air, then be a King, not a Knight.

Friday 29th. 3.00pm. The Astral. I entered the cave and then the Vortex Elevator. I requested 'Astral' as before and felt the usual rushing and buzzing, exiting to the white fog to see Arthur. I asked him about the books, Volumes One and Two of his teachings.

"I would rather not," he said "do not make it about me. It's over now. Make it about you." Other things flashed through my mind, but suddenly I felt so tired. "Alcohol, this needs to go. There is not enough time. You will be fifty years old before you know it, then sixty. Use the precious time you have been given." I was even more tired now and he replied that I should come again very soon to answer any unfinished questions. I thanked him and returned home, exhausted.

Later that Day. Knight of Cups. I could see a figure to my extreme left. The sense became so strong that the left side of my head started to itch. Hermes was on my right and gestured me to investigate. I could see a hooded figure, curled up, scared, frightened, moody, emotionally unstable, inconsistent and vain. I approached him, or maybe her, and she ran off toward the Forest of Souls so fast that I had no chance to catch her. "Scared," said Hermes.

Cups related to Water, and contained as much negative as positive – flaky, dreamy, passing in the night and inconsistent. Without maturity they always brought an overwhelming of emotions and flights of fancy.

Hermes called time on the day and merged into me in preparation for tomorrow.

Saturday 30th. 6.30pm. Five of Wands. It had been a busy MBS fair, and challenging. The card had indicated the day well – clashes of interests, competition for attention, readers fighting to be noticed, noise, kerfuffle. Shyness was never going to win the day. There was much noise, disturbance and interruption. I asked Hermes, how in the face of this, I had coped.

"Not good. You let your mouth run away with you. Single Aspect Tarot readings, as taught to you by Arthur, do not track one issue through the year, they track the most important issue each month. You led her to believe things would develop incorrectly." In truth I knew this had happened the moment a particular reading had ended. "You must be sharper tomorrow." She gave me specific hints on some of the individuals I had been dealing with. I was tired yet Hermes insisted I visit again tomorrow.

[JULY 2012]

Sunday 1st. 6.30pm. Knight of Cups. I heard news that my mother had died.

I saw the Knight. He was angry, frustrated, downcast, emotionally unstable and immature, his development arrested and his life stagnant. I turned to Hermes.

"How do I move on from this point, indicated by this Knight?"

"How indeed!" she replied. "It is time to take the high road, to be the bigger man, to show compassion with your father and sister. They are more open now, well at least your Dad is." I could not in all honesty face this.

"So what if I do not do this?"

"That is fine, but there will be repercussions. Rise above the level of the Knight and show leadership." This was very difficult and I said that I might have to come back to the subject. Some things, regardless of the guidance, just cannot be done and the consequences, whatever they might be, have to be swallowed.

Monday 2nd. 6.00pm. The Astral. I entered via the usual procedure in the Elevator Vortex. White fog all around, and Arthur to my left, with my mother off to my extreme right. She was alone and crying. Then she saw me, "What are you doing here?" She seemed very surprised, as indeed she might.

"This is what I have been doing all these years," I said. I told her that I wanted to say things and asked her to listen. I said that I thanked her for all she had tried to do for me and I forgave her failings. I had not told her about this aspect of my life because she did not want to know.

"Yes I did," she protested.

"No you did not. But let's not argue." I said.

"It was your father," she said. I said that I understood but that she had made her choice a long time ago and it didn't have to turn out like it did. I told her that I loved her and that I would come to see her again. She asked me to stay a while. I agreed but said that I did not want an argument. From this perspective we could both see what my Dad and sister were currently doing and she realised, at least in part, the trouble she had caused and contributed to. I said that as she had now left her body to leave the anger there with it. I could help her move forward, maybe. "It starts with the only evil is the male," I said to her. "I know that!" she replied, continuing, "I will do it differently next time. I would have been proud of you had I known that you could do this." I replied that we can only deal with what we have now. She was very sad and I said that I would come again sometime. I returned in the usual way. This was as much of the high road that I was able to take.

Later That Day. Temperance. I entered via the card and immediately saw a pyramid straight ahead of me. I turned to Hermes who was on my right. I remarked that I had never seen a pyramid here before.

"Well, you can see one now," he said. At that, it became two pyramids, on top of each other, one inverted, point to point. "This is the Key To Time," said Hermes. "All matters are related to timing and speed. Things and people arrive only when they are ready to. It can never be sooner without negative effects." I could see how the energy of One became Four, and then how Four became One. This movement generated much positivity, tolerance, patience, acceptance, contentment with what is, stability and an embracing of the statement 'you can only learn what you are ready for'. This powerful energy had another polarity though, impatience, urgency, and thus delays, instability and hunger for knowledge and food. The inverse pyramid always brought problem and difficulties – I remembered that the banking system was an inverse pyramid – which in the end had to be made right again.

Afterthought: The relative wealth of recent times has been produced by the inverse pyramid of fractional reserve banking, where the system is designed so that there is never enough money available if everyone wants theirs out at the same time. This upturned pyramid has now fallen over and when it is righted we might find ourselves less well off, but sustainably more so.

"This card will always mean these things for you." Hermes said.

"So the pyramid is an astral connecting place, a place to rise on the planes? Maybe this is what they were once used for?" I thought aloud. Hermes confirmed this was so.

"It will be an intensive day tomorrow, rest now, return then," he said. I thanked him and remembered that my Tarot Card of the Day that very morning, had been Temperance – reversed!

Tuesday 3rd. 4.00pm. The Cave. I entered and immediately saw Hermes to my right. I had been reading extensively about the nature of The Hermit. Harriette Curtiss in *The Key to The Universe* had identified The Hermit in three ways – with his Staff, his Lamp and his Robe. This was new information, what was this robe? I asked Hermes and she instantly enveloped me in her cloak and merged into me from behind. At first this was a jerky, jolted motion, but then it smoothed out. Hermes spoke more about the steps required in the healing practice, "counter-clockwise motions on the feet, caps off the fingertips, accumulating Akasha in the hands." In this merged state we returned home for the imminent healing appointment.

Later That Day. Nine of Pentacles. I could see the scene depicted upon the card, but I was distracted and took some time to get into it. I asked the woman in the scene about the plus and minus of her situation. She replied, "the fruits of life may come naturally and abundantly (+) or through lies and deceit (-)."

Hermes emerged from me and I asked various questions about colleagues and friends. A theme was developing whenever I asked about others. "Maintain your distance, let people know you are around, but do not get too involved." I asked of the purpose of the Nine who now resided inside me. "To reunite your various aspects through time and across incarnations. There are many more than those nine, but they are the key ones. An old soul will have many previous lives and inevitably some difficult Karma along the way which is why they so easily default to negativity in this lifetime." She merged back into me and we returned. Had she been referring to me?

Wednesday 4th. Four of Wands. Four staves had been erected by effort and work. I heard "Joy through Work." Here was great satisfaction and contentment achieved by a concerted effort of developing the four roads and working with the four elements. I asked for the reversed expression and saw laziness, lack of application, and unwillingness to exert any effort. Here was an expectation that the rewards of life would present easily and without stress.

There were some people about and I asked if they had anything for me. Two girls inserted four wands into me vertically. They merged into my body separately and then fused together as one in my spine causing an electric charge to run right through me. The girls ran off and I turned to Hermes, and involuntarily called him Merlin. I went to correct myself but he spoke first.

"Same idea." Parking that for the moment I asked about the grades of initiation, as people in the Golden Dawn and other mystic societies had written about, titles like Magister, Magus and Ipsissimus. "Must we do this?" he said, "this obsession with status and measurement." I replied that it was handy to know as an external reference and marker of ones own experiences. "Very well, you are, to all intents and purposes, Magus of your own Life. You are yet to master the Temple but this is do-able. You are not yet Ipsissimus – Beyond – but this will come."

"Beyond? Beyond what?" I asked.

"Beyond everything, all encumbrances." He paused. "Do you want to master the Temple now?" he said.

"If I am ready?" His answer was "yes" and we appeared instantly in the Temple of Opportunities. I asked Hermes what to do. "Summon the beings," he said. The eight pillars filled up with energy. The alien was in his old familiar place in position one.

```
         Light
    5       4
    6       3
    7       2
    8       1
         Me    Hermes
```

The alien kept interrupting and wanting to connect to me. It would not cease and I asked Hermes what to do. "Allow it, so that you may also connect with him." We linked, head to head. He fed into my brain and all the way down my spine, and was invasive and persistent. I asked that he stop but he would not. I repeated this a few times, but eventually I forced my right hand outwards toward him – I actually physically did this – and he recoiled back. I felt strongly that this was the correct course of action and an essential step to exert my authority in the Temple. I was then told that I had been declared Master of the Temple and my desires and requests, in this place, would now come to pass. As simple words on the page it sounds too easy, but I knew the effort required to get here and the emotional and mental rubicons that I had to cross in order to exert my will in any way at all. I felt the process might enable me to flex my muscles a little more in the Outer World, but was also mindful of the dire consequences of wrong action. I thanked Hermes and returned back to the ground of the Inner World. He said he would let me be now and to return tomorrow.

Afterwards: Hermes had previously said, "In the Temple you can go anywhere and do anything, but you must be in complete control of that environment, including those beings." During this reflection I flipped back to the Temple, to exactly where I had been earlier. The alien was still there, where I had left him.

"Thank you for attending. I now release you and wish you well." I said to the alien with the intent of banishment. Hermes spoke. "That is better. You respect them, they will respect you. But respect with firmness." We returned again to the Earth of the Inner World. Hermes smiled and was pleased. He put a cloak around me. "Back tomorrow."

Thursday 5th. 3.00pm. Four of Pentacles. There was a white haired man to my extreme left, and I was a little wary. He was sat in a chair amid his gardens, next to his large house. I asked him what was going on.

"Safety, security, no risks, no speculations, no chances. Steady and incremental movement through life. Some say boring. I see investments building up, step by step." I asked him to show me the negative of this.

"Ohhh, stagnation, boredom, investments locked away that you cannot access," he replied nonchalantly. And did the man have anything for me? As if his words were not enough! He gave me a cloak, in deep and rich purple with bright golden pentacles embroidered into it. He draped it around my shoulders. I thanked him and turned to my far right where Hermes was smiling. I drew the cloak into me, allowing it to soak into my skin penetrating my shoulders and back. I could actually feel this physically. Hermes explained.

"Now, the situation of The Hermit – your situation – is that all consciously directed thoughts and goals appear rapidly into form. A confused and unfocused mind will encounter delay, but when concentrating upon the goal at hand it realises itself swiftly."

"So I need to be really careful what I think about?" I replied.

"Very true," replied Hermes, gesturing me to the Temple. I queried how exactly I might behave within it, and how particularly to deal with the alien. Hermes seemed pleasantly surprised at my question. "Behave with reverence and respect, but also be in control. You are in charge. If you cannot handle the alien then freeze him in stone until you can." We were in the Temple and the place filled up with the assembled energy beings. The alien was indeed very active so I froze him into a rock with a blue tinge. I turned to position number two, and could just make out a small figure, human or human like with very short straight hair. I asked what it did.

"I am here to help you in the further realms," she said, unexpectedly. I had no idea what this meant, and further questioning produced only silence. Hermes was close by and nudged me onto the next position, number three.

"I am here for the nearer realms," said this one. I could not discern her form or see her face. Onto position four, then five, and so on. As we advanced I could hear, discern and understand less and less. Four had many particles, five was a cloud, six an even thinner cloud. Seven and eight were just imperceptible noises and vibrations, slight senses of movement. I said to Hermes that I did not understand this. "But you will, you will," he said. "Visit again tomorrow, both days of the weekend." I commanded those assembled to depart. After releasing the alien from his stone I returned home.

Afterwards: I would have to be very open in order to make sense of all this. I needed new information, but it was also clear that power was being made available to me - power to protect myself and my work, but not the power to run riot! I briefly reconnected to Hermes who simply said that my progress was fine and that I should read Franz Bardon, *Initiation in Hermetics* to discover more. "I must go now," he said. I was not his only concern.

Saturday 7th. Four of Cups. A young boy was playing around on horseback. There was much fun, jollity and lack of seriousness, all underpinned by a sense of safety and rest. Asking for the negative I received boredom and a pointless void.

"What have you learned today?" asked Hermes. I had been giving Tarot readings all day to a wide variety of people.

"That different people have different needs, and wants," I said.

"Yes, you must strive to give them what they need, while being mindful - and not simply dismissive - of what they want. You should offer the balance of both, for this is not generally what others do." After a pause for me to reflect upon this he called time on the session, but not before dropping in the seemingly unconnected comment, "give them the keywords to use, as they see fit," and flashing images of the South West of France into my mind. He merged into me and we returned.

Sunday 8th. Two of Swords. The atmosphere was one of guardedness, defensiveness and the need for protection from shifting currents. The swords seemed to be working to keep out an invisible enemy, but still tension and apprehension dripped from the air. Asking for a reversed interpretation the scene morphed into one with the same characteristics, but a different overhanging atmosphere, this time one of dishonesty and bad faith.

Hermes took one look at me and declared, "Too tired. Nothing can be achieved today. Return tomorrow." I said that I was present and willing, but there was no argument with Hermes. Tomorrow it would have to be. We are not always masters and deciders of our own time, I thought.

Monday 9th. The High Priestess. Here was the very attractive form of the High Priestess. She kindly showed me her realm, that of water, its flowing energy and great power. "It transmits and receives both power and information, appearing naturally in woman," she said, "but it needs the firmness of man as anchor, base and platform. Without this the energy flows everywhere and anywhere, without direction or purpose, sometimes destructively, and always all consuming. There must be balance wherever this force is introduced. When balance is present there will be many positive results, but when absent much negativity."

She offered herself to me and we made love, I could understand what she meant now. I turned to Hermes, ever present, and asked various questions of him, related to Outer World events, clients and acquaintances. Particularly I asked, again, of my writing project, *The Key To Time*.

"We have already discussed this," he said firmly. There was no going back here and no appeal to the decision. He shifted gears. "You have a lot of reading to do" he said. "Return daily here for Tarot card practice and get your reading done." I returned home without him. He knew I was still tired but his language and instructions were insistent.

Tuesday 10th. 5.00pm. Knight of Pentacles. I had to physically turn my head in order to get a clear view of the scene over to my far left. It was of two young men, one hard working, busying himself with manual tasks, skilled though not yet a master. He might be classed as a 'doer', getting on with life. The second called me over. "Look," he said, "it is easy." I took a seat next to him and watched the world go by. This man had plenty to say, though much of it was critical and negative. He was watching but he certainly was not doing. Of course this was his choice, but I decided to call him out on it and ask why. His response was nothing but a hiss as he turned away from me. I moved back toward the other young man, enterprising and active. He offered me a golden coin, larger than my whole hand. He pushed it into my heart. He said it was a "sign of work and of effort, application now for results later." I felt a throbbing in my chest and suddenly the scene was gone. I could now only see Hermes. He said that I could handle tonight's upcoming readings and tuition on my own, "just draw on all that you know," he said. I returned home alone.

Wednesday 11th. Two of Wands. I was instantly aware of a large tower, right next to my point of entry. There was a man on top of this castle, as I felt I ought to call it. I found the door, entered and willed myself to rise up to the top.

On the ramparts a man was gazing out across the landscape, scanning it, looking for something. He held a globe in his hands. Not just *a* globe, but *the* globe - the whole world that rotated as he moved his eyes across the horizon. He turned to faced me and tossed the globe in my direction. "Here, I don't need it," he said, turning back to the landscape as I just about managed to get myself behind the incoming throw, which I caught, but not with my hands. As it merged into my stomach I realised it was much larger than it had looked and I could feel it welling up inside me, like an expanding balloon. It was large, but not satisfying and if anything it now made me feel sick and just I wanted it out of me, so I regurgitated it out of my mouth.

"You are right," I said to the man, "it isn't enough."

"No," he replied, "it is not, there has to be more," his eyes still fixed on the horizon. I asked the man if this might be called a Watchtower. "Yes," he said. "There are four of them and we each search for the new. You rose upon the planes in order to experience this one." I asked if he might show me the negative manifestation of the same, "Ah, that's when the new comes looking for you," he said. Great insight! I thanked him, descended and returned home. Hermes remained present and reminded me again to "return tomorrow."

Thursday 12th. 5.00pm. Knight of Cups. My vision was patchy but I could make out an eager and energetic young man. His youth was obvious and he was not as experienced or knowledgeable as he might one day be. Helpful, but not yet strong, a leader of sorts, but not yet the boss. Young in age, experience and depth. Did this matter? It would depends on the circumstances, I thought. Mounting his horse the young man drew nearer to me. At his invitation I jumped on the back of the horse with him. Immediately we are up in the air, flying, swooping and diving, but within seconds we had fallen to earth. The man admitted that he could not yet totally handle having a passenger. I admitted that I had some difficulty being one!

Hermes appeared and instructed me. "Visit your Mother, via the Astral. Withdraw from here." I said goodbye to the young man.

I found the Cave and the Vortex Elevator and went through the usual procedure of gaining access to the Astral. All was fluffy and white, amidst which I could see my Mother, sad and crying. I went over to here and again she seemed surprised to see me. She wanted me to stay for a while, but the only conversation was about me forgiving her.

"I am sorry," she said. This experience must have been especially testing for her to say that.

"I forgive you," I replied, "but you must try to see what you did wrong as well as what you failed to do." No answer came, but I remained seated with her. There was an interruption from the Outer World - the phone was ringing, very unusual at this time of day, but I ignored it and remained with her. Suddenly there seemed to be an enormous distance between us. I could feel it expanding and we moved further and further away. I came back down the elevator, with the definite sinking feeling and flashing colours as my vision adjusted. Before I returned home Hermes simply said, "that is good."

Friday 13th. 9.00pm. Death. I was staying away from home, overnight at a residential retreat where I was running an introductory course on the mystic arts. This was therefore a patchy and unclear attempt at connecting with the Inner World. I had no accompanying music, could not reach Hermes and did not actually feel very comfortable in my spartan Outer World surroundings. But I could witness the Grim Reaper, cutting me down to size, reducing me in some way using his scythe. This pruning was painless and perhaps much needed. I remembered the title of the weekend course that I was running – 'Tools for Transformation'. What could be more transformative than Death? And whose transformation, the students? Or the teacher? It seemed to be all about letting go, particularly of my Mother, following yesterday's encounter. Maybe it was time for her to be reincarnated? I did not have the answers, nor, without Hermes, access to them. I could concentrate no more and returned.

Monday 16th. 6.00pm. The Cave. Back home in the usual armchair. As I connected with Hermes I expected a poor mark from the weekends performance. I did not rate it as having gone very well. Yet, despite my thoughts he seemed pleased.

"A little too much information, and not quite enough basic practice, but it was good. You may have an apprentice, but it is early days. There is much to sit on and reflect about. The weekend has caused you to rise to new heights – use it, work at that level or inevitably slip down again, which will bring even more frustration." Unexpected comments all of them, but welcomed nonetheless.

Tuesday 17th. 4.00pm. The Cave. Entering the cave I found the Vortex Elevator and arose. Flashing lights, buffeting, then still whiteness. Arthur was present on the left and he beckoned me over. "Time is up now… Don't forget to keep on learning and growing… It never stops… You have done well." Just fragments of maybe longer sentences that I could not recall, as he faded into the distance "Goodbye!" And that was it. He was gone.

I turned to the right, where my Mother was waiting. She was upset and angry. I told her about the inevitable continuation of life, but she did not want to know this. I said that I could return another time. She remained angry, and I felt that she would be so for some time to come. I felt no sadness about this, like many things in our relationship, it was just a matter of fact.

I descended the Vortex Elevator and entered the Inner World to a firework display. Hermes was smiling and immediately merged into me. His words were hard to remember, something along the lines of it just being me as The Hermit now. I asked about the Thoth Tarot and its suitability for use.

"For self? Yes, to learn about it. But for others? No." I asked about a colleague and was straight away directed to the Library and the once again bad tempered Keeper. Was he bad tempered because of me, or by anyone who disturbed him? Did memories like to be turned over and recalled like this? Is the past best left in the past? He produced the book of the life of my colleague. "There is potential here," it said, "but she is in need of much healing energy." I hovered and lingered with this information for sometime before returning with Hermes.

I reflected that all these developments and changes were likely to make me busier than ever, and that changes in the nature of the Inner World must presage something new in the Outer World.

"Books," said Hermes, "are there for you to sift through, developing the good and discarding the bad."

Wednesday 18th. 4.00pm. Four of Cups. Using the Thoth deck entry through this unfamiliar image was difficult at first, but with patience I saw that the four cups had lined up on a mantelpiece. They all overflowed with molten gold, and that gold seeped into all corners of the house, creating and maintaining a brilliant luminescence all around me.

I asked for the reversed vision (which also happened to be my personal card for the day). I now saw an overwhelming lack. Lack of commitment, scarcity of supplies, tight budgets, people at arms length to their work and friends. I turned to Hermes who indicated that this was correct. "Entry to the vision may have proved a lot harder with this deck, but they did add a new scope to the reading," he said.

Thursday 19th. 6.00pm. The Tower. A falling Tower, rubble, smoke and noise everywhere, with some individuals to one side. Then suddenly the Tower was whole again, we had gone back to its pre-state, moments before the ruinous event. I entered its doorway and ascended up its centre, emerging at the top. I was told very clearly that this was the Tower of Reason, Logic and Mind. Emotion, the unpredictable and unmeasured, came to smash it. As the lightning struck I, together with the building, crumbled to the floor.

I lay on the ground with the rubble all around me, but found that I was unharmed and Hermes merged right into me. His was an enormous energy to hold and his voice came from within me.

"You will be financially taken care of - if you stay on path. And not if you don't." But what about the last few days, I wondered. I had suffered heavy financial penalties and much reduced profit expectations. "What are you complaining about? You were not concentrating, but with everything in recession you still have work don't you?" No sympathy there I thought, but he was correct, even at reduced profit margin the work was still worth having, and was much better than nothing.

I asked about a colleague who might be able to assist me in future and I was assured that "the wheels are in motion, let us see what happens." Hermes confirmed he would be returning with me to the Outer World. "It is time to redouble your efforts," he said. I just felt tired and dizzy.

Afterwards: The Tower reminds us that things which make no sense logically can still register emotionally. But in the reversed state the event does not come from nowhere, instead we go looking for it, by deliberately turning away from logic and reason and consciously embracing chaos and unpredictability.

Friday 20th. Four of Swords. Four people were camped out around a fire. The crackling of the flames induced peace and serenity into the resting group. But inverted there was no rest, matters outstanding were unsettled and there was very little peace of mind. And how much can one really rest among unfinished business?

Hermes was present. He cautioned me that I had been a little harsh with an old friend. I expressed my frustrations at him to Hermes, whose advice was clear. "Yes, and it's not over yet. Avoid the call if you do not wish to get dragged in." Turning to another colleague, who I had queried on already a number of times in recent days I was urged to attend the Library for further information.

"Potential, great potential. Someone here to pass the work onto. Maybe," came the voice.

Back to the four men and the fire. I had evidently disturbed their repose for one by one they impaled me with the full length of their swords, slashing down through me each time. It was a curiously pleasant and relieving sensation as I felt all manner of negativity, prejudice and belief wash right through and out of me, as if to empty me of forty years of nonsense. This continued for quite some time and with each cut I could feel the rush of fresh air into my being. Hermes was close by and nodded along that this experience was a wholly good thing.

Saturday 21st. 10.30am. The Cave.

'Knowing Self is better than Knowing Stuff'

I allowed Hermes to merge into me. "How may I purify all my foolish and nonsensical beliefs, habits, thoughts and actions that I have picked up in the Outer World these forty years?" I asked. "How can I be a better vessel for you and this work?"

"This merging and these visits will, over time, achieve this. Accompany this with the breathing exercises. These things done regularly, with no alcohol, form the path forward. Negativity and habit are all about the hooks that you place into things, and the hooks they place into you." I said that I really wanted to achieve this task now. "Very well, it shall be done. Rejecting alcohol is the number one method of purification you will ever find and it will improve everything as a result. I will leave that with you." And then he departed. I did not, at that moment, want another drop of beer or wine ever again.

Later That Day. Seven of Wands. A solitary man was fighting off attack from all comers. "So many things to do, so many responsibilities," he said, "but all can be overcome by knowing self, understanding self and controlling self – the Inner Self that is," he said, deflecting an incoming spear. "Else there is embarrassment, and matters reflect badly on you as a result."

As the onslaught ceased he passed me his wands. They were each different and he forced them into my spine. It was a harsh motion and caused me to sit upright in my chair. "Know yourself," he said cryptically. Hermes indicated that this was enough and I departed.

Sunday 22nd. 4.00pm. The Lovers.

'The more you put things together the more they keep falling apart. But they fall apart differently to how they were put together, such that they can never, quite, be exactly re-assembled.'

"We have nothing to hide from ourselves or each other," came the voices of two figures, in unison. "We know ourselves so that we may know each other." They looked at each other devotedly. "Love is the sacrifice of one part of yourself, so that you may come to know one part of another." The male, with my permission, penetrated me, and afterwards I did understand a tiny something about what it was like to be a woman.

"We feel," she said, "that we are somehow lacking. The feeling is deep, and the man - literally but also in other ways - fills that gap."

"And we feel" said the man, "that we are somehow lacking, something, but we are not sure what. The envelopment and disappearance of ourself during sex resolves this."

I thanked them both, they operated and had spoken as a true partnership and the experience had been highly instructive. I turned to Hermes to ask what

Karma I had accumulated during past lifetimes. I had to concentrate very hard in order to hear any kind of answer.

"You had the Karma of wilful ignorance. Which accounts for where you are right now."

"And what about Present Life Karma?" I asked.

"None at all," he replied. "You nearly had some but that has been taken care of. And you may collect some more very soon, if you are not careful."

"So far so good then?" I said.

"Yes, but care should be taken," he replied. He merged into me and we returned home.

Monday 23rd. 6.00pm. The Lovers. "Men must make love to women - or lose them," Hermes said. "And then where will you be? Woman, women, must feel loved. Then, and only then, might men get what they need. It goes in that order."

I asked Hermes of the Middle Pillar Exercise.

"It is a worthwhile practice. The philosophy involves much old fashioned Christianised ritual, but you can update this, indeed others have tried. But as a practice, it is solid and reliable. I returned, dazed.

Tuesday 24th. 4.00pm. Two of Cups. At some unknown half way point between the worlds I was struck by what I can only describe as 'cosmic simplicity'. In this momentary state of bliss I could see how everything in life worked together, how one movement affected another, and how seemingly unconnected aspects of life were invisibility threaded in, out and back round again. I saw a full pack of Tarot cards, laid out in a specific way, which seemed to depict this, though I could not hold this image nor my overall awareness for more than a few seconds. As my attention shifted elsewhere the image already seemed like a distant memory of something I had once glimpsed in a dream. Hermes intervened.

"When are you entering the Temple?"

"When you say that I am ready," I replied.

"No. YOU must say when you are ready"

"I am not ready for the oath." I said. "I do not understand what would be required of me." Hermes explained. "Imagine reproducing the Middle Pillar Exercise in the Temple. You can see how many results that would bring. Those beings are all involved in your development, but the key is to explore those connections in a controlled manner. When the alien takes you off to his home world you must re-focus immediately on your return, and not allow the experience to spin you out into despair, amazement and bewilderment, or to send you off at a tangent as it did with *The Key To Time.*" It was a lot to take in. I thanked Hermes and said I would return later.

"Tonight," he said, "there is so much to do."

Later That Day. The Cave. Hermes merged into me and we rose up the Temple. I produced the Staff from my spine and called the beings to attention with it. The scene and atmosphere was different to before, I could even see the Temple now superimposed upon my Outer World. I banged the stone floor with my staff and thanked them all for attending.

"I now know that you are all invested in my growth and development and I appreciate that." There were faint murmurings of approval. I drew in power from the roofless sky above and protected the inside of the Temple with a complete round of four connected and circled pentagrams.

"I select the alien, Yi'Chun, from Niberia 5," I said. He approached and we connected. Though much smaller than me we adjusted ourselves to be head to head, straight on. I could feel a penetration into my brain and I gave some resistance to this until he informed me that this was an equal arrangement, and I simply had to say what I required. I told him that I wished to travel to his planet. He agreed.

I was now vibrating fast and furiously, a definite sensation of rising up and out of myself, but still could not quite escape the confines of the Temple. He gave me some more script, this time unintelligible.

"More practice needed," said a voice. That was enough for today. I thanked all those assembled and returned home alone.

Afterwards. That evening I had a splitting headache in exactly the position that the alien had penetrated me. I never get headaches, but this one was enormous and I was struggling to assimilate the whole experience. I had to talk myself into not freaking out; "you can handle this," I repeated very slowly.

A Little Later Still. I made another attempt at visiting the alien's planet. Applying a heady oil to the region of my third eye I entered through the cave and into the Vortex. I kept hearing the voice. "The Astral doesn't go that far," but I persevered.

To my surprise I emerged into a green landscape, and then further afield a vast array of buildings, all very low rise, as far as my eyes could see. It was sunny and warm, and rather familiar, in that respect at least.

Now there were more alien beings moving around the scene on hover board-type devices, which travelled not far off the ground, powered by some kind of battery. I asked one, "what can you possibly want from me?" They seem extremely advanced and I could not see them lacking anything.

"We need to know about love," came the voice. "Everything we have here is ordered and purposeful, with reason and utility. We lack what your species has." I replied that I could show him this and then asked, "what may I discover from here?" There were a multitude of voices in reply, some cautionary, none quite discernible, fragmented. I asked about their use of energy, how did they heat their homes and cities?

"There is no need for external heating. The body can self regulate. By agitation it can generate and sustain its own heat. Our food does not need to be heated. This is all possible for you too." Incredible. I could instantly see how we might begin this task but was then overwhelmed with the thought that it might take hundreds of generations to master this. But how obvious a solution – to address the inner maintenance of life, not the outer protection of it.

"What is this planet called?" I continued.

"Sh-Loch, is the nearest human word," came the answer, pronounced with a whispered, short, upwards *sh* followed by longer downwards *loch*. I looked around as he spoke and cast my eyes on a tall, dark metal-like tower emerging from the ground nearby. It was bigger in scale than anything I had ever seen or read about on Earth. I was warned to not enquire any further about this.

"But how do I know it is even real?" I asked.

"We do not play tricks. Reflect upon this and visit again." A series of sonic booms radiated out from the middle distance. I thanked the voices, and returned home.

My mind was a mess. This was all complete and utter madness in the eyes of 99.9% of the human population, but it happened to me and was as real as making a sandwich or having a shave. I clutched my head tight with both hands, in disbelief and amazement. If I could have reached inside and pulled this experience out with my fingers I would have done.

Wednesday 25th. 4.00pm. The Devil. Hermes spoke without any delay. "Under the Dark Side you can never be free. You will always need to fulfil its demands and satisfy its urges. So the question must be *which route is better*? To willingly, and in full knowledge, indulge the Dark Side, in the hope that it will then give you some respite? Or to take the path of refusal, resisting all evidence of the Dark Side's existence and domain?" He paused before providing his own answer. "The path of ignorance can never be the path of bliss, for until it is acknowledged the Dark Side will chase you around and harass you every minute of the day." A miserable analysis, I thought to myself. "Not at all. A love of life may grow, but only once its desire has been satisfied. Love is not a product of desire or indeed anything to do with it."

I asked for a reversed interpretation. "Release from an on going burden and a new sense of freedom. It is temporary though, for the Dark Side will, must, come again."

I recognised, at least in theory, that the energy of the Devil might be liberating and freeing, if it were brought under conscious awareness and control. I asked for another piece of the puzzle. An attractive female dancer with bright red hair appeared before me. I desired her very much but before anything could happen Hermes called a halt to proceedings, saying to return tomorrow before I left for my weekend course.

Thursday 26th. 12noon. Eight of Cups. I could pick up only floating insights, like information was being poured into my mind and then bobbed around, part submerged. I could see, hear and smell nothing.

The card spoke of dislike, dissatisfaction and disillusion, but reversed there was a galvanised action, an attempt to fill the void. Maybe not success, but certainly an attempt.

"That is fine, that is it," said Hermes, "come tomorrow."

Friday 27th. The Sun. The Sun came down to me in the form of a burning man. Flames licking upwards from every millimetre of his shape, he merged into me. Hot and intense, but manageable now that I had done this a few times and could regulate what I took. It spoke. "I am the ultimate power in the Solar System." I asked if he were comprised of the four elements – Fire, Air, Water, Earth. "No! Just fire." D'oh! That was obvious and I felt very foolish. Another, unknown, voice intervened. "Akasha, universal energy, is more powerful still."

In the positive the Sun made itself available – as the Fire element – for constructive harnessing toward positive ends. But as a negative it was simply raw, misused, unrecognised energy.

Hermes appeared. "An interesting experience for you," he said, "very good. But with consequences." I did not probe further as to what he was talking about. Instead I asked for my book of life from the Library. As I entered the building The Keeper said, "but you have already seen it." I said that I would like to do so again and a large, bound tome, old and worn, appeared before me. It was no more than 75% full, with many blank pages, scattered throughout. "The ending remains unwritten," said The Keeper, "everything that happens to you, everything that you do, say, think, feel contributes to the overall learning of life. Whether this is positive and enjoyable, or negative and painful, the learning creates the entries in your book. There are no mistakes, simply lessons yet to be mastered. So long as the narrative of a particular experience, encounter or happening is running in your head then the lesson remains unlearned. Nothing can be deleted or erased. Nothing is ever truly forgotten and everything forms part of the story of your life. But you do not need to visit me in order to know this…" As The Keeper's words tailed off I thanked him and departed.

I asked Hermes if visiting the alien was appropriate today. After some backward and forward between us I accepted his advice. "Another day," he said.

Afterwards. Later that day I had experienced another to and fro with Hermes about something I had particularly wanted to do, yet also felt apprehensive and unsure of. His remarks where informative. "When will you stop fighting yourself? If you are unsure then you are unready."

Saturday 28th. Seven of Swords. I was in attendance at a weekend conference which was going, in my view, extremely poorly. I was concerned how to make sure my presentation the following morning would go down better.

"You do not have to give the farm away," said Hermes. "Tomorrow will be another day. They, as you, think badly of what has happened so far. It will be better tomorrow."

Sunday 29th. Five of Swords. My reflections on the day took up most of my visit. It was the end of a pattern of behaviour, the end of an old way of relating to becoming the Hermit and move toward a more professional stance. My visit through the doorway of the card seemed to confirm this, with a vision of people packing up and moving on, all of them stepping into a different relationship with The Hermit.

"Sit, and spend time with him," said Hermes, referring to The Hermit.

Monday 30th. 6.00pm. Queen of Cups. I could see a long haired feminine woman. The length of her hair seemed important. She used it as antenna to pick up on her surroundings. It was all about a feminine power than flowed, instead of being static. I could see how inability to embrace this side of her nature would cause her and others many problems. I moved toward Hermes and addressed him about the weekend's conference. He was not happy.

"When will you learn that you can only meet people where they are? There is no point or benefit in trying to do otherwise. All groups of people must be first met with a blank canvas and only when they present themselves individually into your awareness can you assess where they are and what they need. Disappointment pours forth from expectations. Have a blank canvas and no expectations! Come again tomorrow before your healing client," he said.

I returned home doubting the contact I had just made and guidance I had received. I questioned the presence of malign influences, but the truth was nothing so grand. I had simply been told that which I did not want to hear.

Tuesday 31st. 1.00pm. Death. The Grim Reaper, the figure of Death, was still, unmoving and waiting patiently. I wanted to connect with him.

"Then you must step forward," said Hermes.

I did so and gave permission for the figure to merge into me. But after multiple attempts nothing happened. "It is not yet your time," said Death. Hermes nodded.

Instead I held out my hands and Death touched them. The connection was strange. It was not an energetic charge, or even a magnetic draining. It was an instant emptiness. Momentarily there was nothing in me and I was nothing. I thanked the figure and without response he just turned away and shuffled off slowly.

Hermes now merged into me in an altogether different experience, both different from Death and different from usual. It was like being charged with a new current, a new fuel. I moved to the Temple and Hermes with me. The energies assembled and I protected the four walls with the flaming, connected, encircled golden pentagrams.

The alien wanted an answer to his previous question of love. I said that, having thought about it maybe I wasn't the best person to do this task for them. He did not seem bothered by my reservations. I allowed him to connect and again I felt a sharp pain in my third eye region. He downloaded what he needed and then consulted with a colleague who also appeared to be present in his realm, but not fully in mine. They seemed content and busied themselves with the results. The alien explained that they were "unable to gather this information outside of the Temple." I then asked for my return exchange. "What will it be?" he replied, immediately attentive to my request.

"What do you understand by intuitive and divinatory arts?" I asked. He explained.

"All things are connected. Some things are connected to similar things on the same level, some to similar things on different levels, yet everything regardless of similarity or level, is connected in some way. Intuition is simply the connection of dis-similar things on different levels. They seem unconnected but intuition bridges the gaps which, to your eyes, are invisible.

I thanked him and disbanded the assembled crowd. Hermes returned home with me. I was very tired.

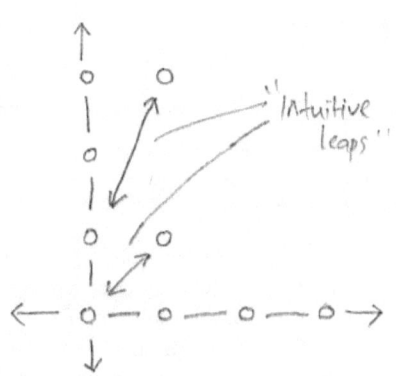

How Intuition Works

[AUGUST 2012]

Wednesday 1st. Knight of Swords. Hermes gave me some insights regarding illnesses and numbers. He said, "one shows itself as skin complaints, two as self esteem issues and depression. Three may have cosmetic surgery, which may be prone to go wrong." He said something about four but I could not remember it. He continued, "five is prone to disability or immobilisation." The next words I could recall were, "eleven suffers greatly from degenerative and nervous disorders while twenty-two may be hit by cancer." He did not wait for me to catch up and moved onto a new topic. "The Tarot court cards are behaviours to adopt and/or avoid, within self and/or within others. These behaviours can be taken or left at will."

The Knight from the card image now arrived as a young man on a black steed. A valiant fighter, but young and inexperienced. His arrival signified a new project that required clarity, precision, eagerness and rigour. The Knight was not yet the King. This was me I thought, not yet the King. Hermes intervened and said that my visit with nephew Joseph tonight was important. I returned home.

Thursday 2nd. 7.00pm. Hanged Man. The scene was similar to a crucifixion, but with the man happy to be in this predicament, seeing things differently from other eyes and perspectives and giving his own vision a radical shake up. At my request the scene inverted to demonstrate how the afflicted meaning might appear. Now there was an unwillingness to do what was necessary. This was not born of safety but selfishness, and no desire to change. I could feel myself experiencing some of this. I turned to Hermes for reassurance.

"Am I doing OK?"

"We can only go as fast as you let us," he replied.

"But is the speed we are travelling OK?" He repeated his answer, without modification or new emphasis, "we can only go as fast as you let us." A feeling of dissatisfaction and defeat slid over me. I returned home.

Friday 3rd. King of Swords. A man sat at his table, directing and dissecting matters with his sword. He was the master of the mind, of discipline, precision, accuracy and definition. In a second, as I willed it, he became over-critical, harsh, rigid and cruel. There were the two sides of the same coin, a crossing of the line of harshness within the same field.

The King indicated that I might be able to take the sword. Hermes agreed, and as I lifted it I could feel the qualities of the King merge into my hand, move up my arms and migrate throughout my body.

"There is much learning and studying to do," said Hermes, pointing to the many books on the table in front of the King. I returned home.

Saturday 4th. 3.00pm. The Fool.

'With effort the void may be filled with joy, but not so by default. The common order is formed from the misapplied energies of self and others.'

I asked Hermes about a new Outer World teacher I had become interested in working with. Hermes was cautious.

"The tendency, temptation even, is for happy thoughts to crowd out constructive ones. The attraction of the easier path is ever present, it never goes away, but if anything is to be built it requires much effort and work. Not all her work may be categorised like this, but much of it can." He urged me again to return tomorrow. I questioned what these very short trips were really achieving? "All will become clear, when the time is right," he said.

Sunday 5th. 7.00pm. Hierophant.

'The road to the Nine of the Hermit runs through the Five of the Hierophant.'

"I teach about Life," said the Hierophant, "and through Life extends the Mysteries. Most everybody wants to know about Life, but not everyone wants to know about the Mysteries. But through Life we can demonstrate the Mysteries. That is all." With that sentence he leaned over, with his patriarchal cross and branded my outstretched right hand. "The sign of the teacher," he said, and dismissed me. Hermes seemed very pleased with this beneficence. Symbology running in my mind I asked him about the Unicursal Hexagram symbol, the six pointed star that could be formed in one motion. "Re-enter this place via that symbol, then ask me again."

I did exactly that, setting the additional card from the Thoth deck up in front of me and entering to be greeted by Hermes. I took a deep breath in an honest attempt to hear the fullest possible understanding of whatever he might say.

"Aleister Crowley was a man of extraordinary vigour, and equally extraordinary ego. It takes some ego to think that you alone are responsible for, and the conduit of, a New Age. This hexagram is a perversion of the natural and beautiful hexagram of two perfect intersected triangles."

"So what is this for?" I asked.

"It was for his selfish purposes, his warped view of love and sex." I questioned further about whether to work with the image more deeply.

"It is not advisable. It represents illusion made real," he replied. I persisted with the sense that the symbol relates to space and time, but Hermes did not confirm this and I did not press it. "Return tomorrow," he said as I faded back home.

Monday 6th. 8.00pm. Six of Wands. The Chariot pulled up. There was a trailer attached containing many rocks, and well hidden among them were lumps of gold, well concealed from impatient and superficial glances. This represented good news that was not always immediately apparent, I thought. In the difficult presentation there would be no gold, or even no Chariot at all. Or maybe a Chariot that you might not even see.

Hermes said to try to keep up with this pace of daily practice and to return tomorrow. He gestured toward this journal as being a priority upon my return home.

Tuesday 7th. 7.00pm. Justice. A powerful figure sat perfectly still on a throne. She presented scales and a sword and spoke slowly, her words dripping with power.

"These scales weigh and assess the Inner and the Outer, cause and effect, positive and negative, creation and destruction, action and thought. Then by this sword – informed by these scales – I act, dispensing Justice. With these scales Justice may seem harsh, but it is always fair, informed as it is by universal principles, not human prejudices. Without these scales attempts at Justice can only ever be an unfair reaction to, and provocation of, human events, without reflection or judgement. The only thing that may heal the absence of a sword, or a sword uninformed by scales, is the passage of time."

I knelt before her to receive Justice. There was a pause during which I heard a loud voice cry out. "No!" as Hermes intervened to pull me away.

"You are right, you do not want Justice to be passed on you, just yet." She knighted me gently, seemed pleased, and disappeared. I turned to Hermes and he spoke. "You are in consolidation and preparation from now until the end of the year. Consolidation and study. There will be no further developments until this is completed." I came home.

Wednesday 8th. 6.00pm. King of Pentacles. I struggled today to see anything at all, neither image behind the card, nor Hermes. Then he spoke, "I am in you now. Visits here in this way are no longer necessary in order to meet with me." An interesting development. Hermes continued, "the King represents your will – or lack of it, built on weak physical foundations as it is. You are tired, an improved diet is much needed, more vitamins and nutrients." This was absolutely true, I was deeply tired. "But you are now ready for the oath," Hermes said, "so come back tomorrow if you wish to take it." I felt very uncertain about this but nonetheless could still feel Hermes inside me. The Inner World would continue to be relevant but no longer in the same way. Home.

Thursday 9th. 11.45am. The Astral. I took the Vortex Elevator into the usual white fog of nothingness. Arthur was there, on my right, dressed in the attire so familiar to me. "Any questions?" he asked. I was instantly flummoxed. "Brain death!" he said, laughing. That had been one of his sayings, back in the day.

I stepped back and thought what I would like to ask him. I had remembered back at the first signs of the economic collapse in 2008 that Arthur had felt the recession and difficulties would be short lived. I had disagreed with him at the time, but had deferred to his judgement. I quizzed him on this.

"I was wrong about that," he said "but Cameron and Osborne have made matters worse than they needed to be. The sooner they are gone the better. Even a Labour government would be preferable." I asked about UKIP's prospects. "Stranger things have happened," he laughed, and then made his excuses to leave. He had passed me an additional warning about the attitude of a particular client which I must take heed of. He waved goodbye.

An awareness seeped into me as I descended from the Astral state. It is the descent of the Life Essence into heavy physical matter that causes the inner spark to be forgotten, obscured and distracted from it purpose. The physical and the spiritual are a long way apart, and become ever more distant as the child grows up. The best hope must be to instil the spiritual within the child at a young age. At that thought I was home.

Later That Day, 2.00pm. After some delay I saw the High Priestess. She rose from her throne and approached me, pointing to the left.

"The Pillar of Mercy, compassion, love and forgiveness." And then pointed to her right, "and the Pillar of Severity, the facts, the way it is." She paused. "All life is an interplay of the two. Would you like to see this?" she said. I very much did.

She pulled back the veil that hung from the two pillars behind her and I passed through it. Everything was alive, vital and moving, energetic and buzzing. "The connections of life," she said. I returned back through the veil. "So what is the reversal?" I asked. She explained. "When you see the vitality of life and cannot handle it, or resist it, maybe cannot see it at all, or only partially. Whatever way, it is poorly handled." I stepped back a little.

"Do you want to taste me?" she said. I was stunned and hesitated but I could not say no. She drew back her robes. Her lips were full and fragrant. She spoke. "Through this comes knowledge, you come to know me and I you. It is the knowing of others in this way that brings life, connection and love. This is the knowledge that men seek."

I said to Hermes that I would return soon. This time it was I who was enthusiastic.

Later Still, 3.30pm. At first I was confused by the presence of two Hermes-like figures. The first, with shining eyes, but no form said, "to take the oath we must go to the Temple." I could not shake the sense that I was not yet ready. The second figure was more playful as he descended from the sky. His energy seemed much lighter.

I chose the first shape and he merged into me powerfully, like an electric shock, intense and long lasting. We ascended to the Temple and once in place, I called the beings and said that I was here to take the oath. Hermes pointed to the Light source positioned directly ahead. I protected the four walls of the Temple with the pentagrams and turned toward the Light.

"I wish to take the oath." I said.

"What oath?" came the reply.

"The oath to become The Hermit."

"You mean the oath to go beyond The Hermit?" came the reply, half question, half statement, serious in tone and gravity. "This is an undertaking in excess of anything you have thus far tackled. It requires a commitment, a binding of you to me in order to receive guidance at a level you are unaccustomed to. It will involve an effort of time and energy you are unfamiliar with. And it is not a commitment that can be broken without the severest of consequences." I remarked that this all sounded rather dark. "Not at all. We compel no one to do this," was the impassive reply, without any attempt to convince or dissuade.

"What are the rewards?" I asked.

"They are beyond comprehension."

"Reveal yourself." I asked. The assembled beings seemed shocked by my words. I saw a swirling mass of colours and shapes, all beating together like a heart, but not like a heart. I was suddenly so tired.

"We have provided you with the necessary avenues for developing and managing yourself, but the rule must be maintained - you must hurt no-one in the process." The whole thing was heavy with consequences and penalties for misdeeds. I was deeply uncertain, or perhaps more truthfully I was completely sure, completely sure that I did not want such a life. Yet at the same time I did, and always had done.

"Return again later," said the voice.

I disbanded the room, but with the lingering impression that I must make up my mind very soon, and absolutely not summon or invoke such things again until I was ready to cross the bridge. Hermes said to return later.

Back at home, I experienced a virtual physical collapse, but then a stiffening of my resolve. I rested for a while, motionless.

Even Later Still. 4.30pm. I returned one more time with the firm intention of crossing the line once and for all to take the oath. Hermes stood face to face with me and we merged. Once the Temple was protected and the beings summoned I again spoke the words, toward the Light.

"I wish to take the oath to go to the Hermit and beyond."

"Do you understand what this entails?" came the patient voice.

"No, not fully." I was only being truthful.

"You must understand!" came the loud, suddenly not so patient, reply.

"I understand the weight of it, but not its specifics. I will not complain." The Light, and maybe the whole room, emitted enormous, almost mocking laughter. "Not to you anyway." I said. There was a pause.

"Very well. It is done." And then a further pause.

"That is it?" I asked, confused.

"What did you expect?" laughed the Light. "The ramifications of this have now spread throughout the entire Universe. Nothing will be the same again. Changes start now. You do not need to do anything, and yet you must do everything. Begin by daily practice and writing."

I disbanded the assembled being and the room. Ever so faintly, out the corner of my eye, I caught glimpse of an old man shuffling off into the background. How strange and how unexpected.

Hermes spoke now, "Return here twice daily."

"Twice?" I queried.

"Once in the morning with the card, once in the evening to the Temple."

"I am concerned that I do not know enough," I said

"You have everything you need," he replied. I returned home, shell shocked.

Friday 10th. 6.00am. The Hierophant. A series of images flew toward and around me as if I were a particle in a kaleidoscope. The one that hung in the air, stronger than all others, was a flaming golden pentagram. I then penetrated through to the same Hierophant as before, although he now sat to the right facing me.

"The Nine reaches through the Five," he said, "therefore it is essential to know lots of different subjects and many kinds of people in order to keep your flow of knowledge moving. When you stop then everything stagnates. There are many, many people who want a piece of you. Some will even demand it, but you cannot specialise on just one person, you must keep moving. As a teacher it is so vital to keep learning in order to stay ahead of your pupils." He again blessed me with his Cross, this time on my forehead, before fading out.

Later That Day, 5pm. Hermes seemed in a celebratory mood. "You should aim for one book a day," he said, gesturing to the many unread tomes stacked up in my Outer World. "Daily practice, every single day. The Temple of Opportunities awaits in order to make important things happen, but does not exist for trivia, nor for enabling or correcting hurts. No one must be hurt in any of your work."

I wanted to visit the Library to enquire about the Book of Life of a colleague, but Hermes suggested that this particular use was not appropriate. Exactly at that moment, back in the Outer World, the door bell rang!

After dealing with the disruption I returned and apologised to Hermes. I tried to also do so to The Keeper, but found that the Library was firmly closed.

"How are we to avoid the temptation to use these forces and powers for darker ends?" I said. I had no intention of doing so, but I could see how the temptation might be hard to resist.

"You must resist it!" came the straightforward reply. Home. Feeling disjointed.

Saturday 11th. 6.00am. Nine of Cups. I could not remember seeing the imagery of this card in a long time, and I could gather only flickering images and fragmented insights, which at first related to the negativity of the card – disconnection, removal, failure to meet each other fully and openly. Moving beyond these difficult concepts I could see the ripeness and fullness of the nine's emotions expressed in a flowing manner, openly and joyously one minute, but partially, reservedly and clumsily the next. It could be circumstances that prevented a full connection between people, or it might be resistance on the part of one or other. It was a confusing mismatch of imagery, negative intertwined with positive.

"Do not consult your notes on the card meanings before you visit here." Said Hermes. Ah! That was my mistake.

Afterwards. I reflected on the nine, which had been very prominent recently. 3 x 3 = 9. Nine was the maximum power possible, three lots of the trinity. But the power of nine that overflows from the cups is poorly handled, refused or unrecognised in the reversed position. Simple really.

Later, 5pm. I asked Hermes about the correct sequence of elemental breathing, as taught by Franz Bardon, but before I could get the words out, or even have the thought fully formed, the reply came. "It is in his book."

I wanted to apologise to The Keeper for my last visit. "I will only approach you in the future for serious purposes." I said. He seemed pleasantly surprised by my approach, but I did not linger.

I turned to Hermes. "How do I know what I should or should not bring into form in the Temple?" I had being wrestling with this for some time, if anything was possible, where do you start?

"Your Four Roads will tell you," he replied.

"But wouldn't opportunities for growth open up along those roads, naturally, without forcing the issue in the Temple?" I said.

"Not necessarily," he replied, "past choices may impede new doorways when travelling any of your roads. Only then can the Temple set this right."

"But how do I distinguish between wants and needs?"

"It should not be about wants or self gratification. It should be about learning and expanding, constructively following the four roads. In the Temple you must be as specific as possible" I took this as a clue to the answer, but not the answer itself. Hermes concluded, "that is enough for now. Return tomorrow." I had been increasingly trying to set the agenda during these visits, but it was still clear who was in charge of them. And it was not me.

Sunday 12th. 6.00am. Knight of Wands. I began the session with a pattern of breathing I was finding very effective. It was Israel Regardie's circular breathing exercise – in for four, hold for four, out for four and empty for four.

A man on horseback was moving across my vision. I called over to him and he dismounted, striding over to greet me. He had much energy and vigour.

"You have to be 'in it' to make things happen you know," he said. Completely glossing over his remark I asked if he had anything for me and what I might do with it?

"Here," he said, producing a small wand, "use it to stir the pot. It doesn't look like much but you will be surprised. I moved the wand into me and it lodged in my lower stomach. "Stir the pot, shake it up a bit," he said, mounting his horse and riding off. Hermes was nearby and confirmed that everything about this experience was acceptable. "But before you go," said the Knight, "The Keeper has something for you." So I entered the Library and bowed in deference to The Keeper.

"Your behaviour last time was poor, but your apology heartfelt. You may choose one book – a free choice – to learn from," he said in a conciliatory manner. I thought for a while and chose that of a contemporary. The book appeared and the information poured out of it, "mental issues, a life of study, ripped off by others, devious – he cannot help himself – and unaware of the dark side." I turned to the back pages of the book and was clearly told that I should be part of his circle. I protested. All my interactions with him so far had been problematic.

"When it comes to money – yes – but there is much to learn here." That was unlikely and unwelcome news. I thanked The Keeper and returned to Hermes. "Why do I keep wanting to call you she?" I asked. "Because I am, at least partially," he said. I questioned the history that I was aware of, of the god Hermes. "Well there you go," he said, "another falsehood." I came back home.

Later, 6pm. I returned for a deeper conversation with Hermes.

"Should I have asked for the book of my own life?"

"Yes, of course."

"Can we do that now?"

"No, you missed your opportunity. Another time."

"What happened to Seraphia?"

"You did not make use of here while you could. She is now gone. You must use opportunities or lose them."

"Will I get another chance?"

"No, although we will try to make up for the learning in other ways." Hermes was eager now for us to attend the Temple. "One more thing," I asked, "what about me running a Shadow Work course?" Hermes was positive but brief, "It could be the first Hermitage course."

We entered the Temple. I summoned the beings and prepared the walls protectively.

"I welcome all those invested in my growth and development," I said, with as much authority as I could muster. "I desire that my appearances at forthcoming MBS fairs be profitable and constructive." I gathered all the beings around me and with my staff I proclaimed the words again. Raising the Staff high we sent two bolts into the starry sky, one for each location. They split off in the two separate directions. I felt a rush of energy through me, but held no expectation about the results.

A voice spoke. "It is done." I thanked and disbanded the group. Turning to Hermes for a final word about my upcoming and expected busy schedule. "Yes, you will be kept busy. But be careful, the people will be unpredictable." I thanked him. He seemed pleased, although I am not sure I any longer knew what my behaviour ought to be in this realm. Home. "Tomorrow," he called after me.

Monday 13th. 6.00am. Six of Swords. A man jumped out from nowhere, darting around on tip toes with six unsheathed swords. He turned to me, "disruption and imbalance in all things, domestic and mental. Deceit, lies, let downs, rocking the boat. You have attained balance, yet all these things come to disrupt that." I asked if he had anything for me? "See this Caduceus," he said. "Take it," at which point he threw it directly at my head, it penetrated by skull and merged downwards directly into my spine. "It is the only thing you can rely on." Before disappearing he uttered his final words, "in matters like this sometimes the best thing you can do is to get the hell out of it." A Chariot pulled up, the man climbed in and they were gone. All this to do with lies and deceit in the home and family, the need to not rely too heavily on others, and the need to find equilibrium and balance in the only true place – within.

I could see that with the six dignified swords we could move away from this, while in the reversed we were stuck, forced to experience it.

Later. I was emotionally overwrought. It had been a busy day. Hermes spoke.

"You are in danger of creating a self fulfilling prophecy with your attitude of doom. Those around you are not well and need your healing attentions. You have found many pupils and even some potential teachers, but you must find a way to meet your clients on their level. Arthur told you this many years ago. You must be present in all ways, be there to smile and greet them, get into this zone beforehand. Clear your thoughts first, you have too many distractions. Even if you cannot relieve yourself of all of them, you should do whatever you can."

I said that sometimes I felt his presence to be harsh and unloving. He immediately enveloped me in his cloak (or was it wings?) This was a real and genuine connection and I could find no reason for it to be otherwise. I did not want to disconnect but returned home anyway disjointed and confused. Had I overdone it? No. I had simply taken the oath and this is what should be expected.

Tuesday 14th. Eight of Cups. I could immediately see a figure rushing away from me, escaping into the distance. I hurried after him, shouting out that I would like to speak to him.

"Where are you going? Why leave when you have so much?" I said.

"Because something is missing, and I can't bear it any longer. If this were the reversed situation I would be scooping up the bounty of the all the cups for maximum enjoyment, but I am not, because something is missing. Nothing is wrong with the enjoyments that are available, but they are not enough, and thus I am incomplete."

I asked if he had anything for me. He produced a cup from his heart. "Here, seek not in others what you should be able to find within yourself. Seeking from others produces only disappointment." I fused the cup into my own heart and thanked him. Hermes was around and seemed pleased with developments. "See you later," he said.

Later, 4pm. I tried to engage Hermes in a conversation about the Dark Side. He agreed and we retreated to a nearby fallen log to discuss matters in detail.

"Money," he said. "The key lies in spending less. You will be sent the right people in your Hermitage work. You cannot complain too much as your business career has been lucrative for many years, so things have just gone back to how they used to be, acceptable, though with smaller profits. Reset your expectations lower, spend less and all will be fine. No drastic action is necessary." This was sensible and reasonable, and it felt like a level headed judgement from a voice of experience. "But in other matters," he said, "you are in danger of making promises you cannot keep. You must be careful not to let your intentions run ahead of your ability to deliver. The small matters and the quiet people of life are so easily overlooked, but that is where your attention should now be. Work through your outstanding tasks in these areas steadily and gently. And come again tomorrow."

Wednesday 15th. 6.00am. Page of Wands. A young boy, no more than ten years old, was shouting into the mountains, cupping his hands to make the sound travel faster. I asked him what he was looking for?

"Me. I am looking for me!" he shouted enthusiastically.

"But you are here?" I said.

"No. People like me. I don't want people that are different, for then I have to make adjustments. I want people like me so I can focus on me and nothing else. But then sometimes for the longest time I cannot find those people." What a strange situation. I thanked him for his time, although forgot to ask if he had anything for me. Hermes indicated time was up and I returned home.

Later, 6pm. I felt I might be able to speak to Hermes without entering the cave, but I dared not risk miscommunication or a wrong connection. I saw a crack across my field of vision, like my perception being altered or distorted in some way.

"There is a great deal to play out yet with some of the people you know," he said. "For the moment say the least amount possible, words are always a form of contract." I asked about my on going practice with the Middle Pillar Exercise "Am I not just creating a bubble for myself?"

"Yes, but the bubble is real! It is not illusory. Others will feel the effects and so will you. See you tomorrow."

Thursday 16th. 6.00am. Queen of Pentacles. A woman greeted me warmly, she was solidly built, with large hips. "Hello, I am involved heavily in the physical world. It weighs me down, for there is so much to do and it absorbs all my energy. I therefore have no time for daydreams, thoughts or fantasies, and I have no energy to give to them. I do not really mind though, I like it this way. If I were not so burdened I might seek the things that you seek but then again I might not. I am happy." If this were the case dignified, then reversed could only be an unhappiness with the situation, and the presence of too many burdens. "Here, see what it is like," she said, offering me a burden. I did not take it, I was distracted, or perhaps I allowed myself to be distracted. Hermes appeared and spoke again of the same Outer World characters he had done yesterday.

"It is early days, too early, there is no certainty with new people or situations." Home, exhausted and overwhelmed.

Later, 5.30pm. I encountered a horseman, riding vigorously toward me. He and the horse were large and fast. I raised my hand into a stop signal and they obeyed. I turned to Hermes we walked to the fallen log nearby.

"Is it safe to speak with you without coming into the cave?"

"Not yet. The difference between my voice and voice of your own sub-conscious is, well, all the difference in the world. When you get into the correct state, into the chair and into the cave the words you hear will be reliable."

"So is everything that happens now a result of the oath," I asked.

"Yes."

"So what next?"

"Follow up each and every opportunity as it arrives. There will be many, and you will be inundated. There is not enough time really, certainly no time for laziness, many books still to read."

"But…"

"So get on with it, please. Until tomorrow."

Friday 17th. 6.00am. The Devil. Many figures were assailing me as I broke through. There was one particular woman with red hair. She urged me to do anything I liked to her, anything and everything that I desired. I did. It was satisfying, but enjoyable would not be quite the right word.

"It was satisfying for you," she said, "but now is when I begin. You will never be free of me. I manifest through everyone that you meet. There is no spell, no binding, no magick that you can do to stop me. The only thing you may do is to feed me, to calm me temporarily. But once you feed me you will have to keep on feeding me. There will be no end to it." Hermes words intervened, "be very careful."

Later, 5pm. I asked a series of questions to Hermes about Outer World contacts, clients and acquaintances. "You can only help these people to a limited degree," he said, "there is much darkness in these people and you must not allow them to mistake your intentions. And unless you make yourself clear they might do just that." I asked if one of them in particular was one of the Four Evil Princes spoken of in the Abramelin Operation. "No, they do not exist, but you will be tested on each of your four roads, and this is one of those tests. Too much has been said now, leave the matter at arms length."

We attended the Temple, protected its walls and summoned its beings. I asked that a client and her family be protected from bullying influences. The beings talked among themselves for a while. "We can do this," they replied. I produced the Staff, banged it hard on the floor as we energised the idea. It was then catapulted into the skies as I focussed additionally on the perpetrator of the bullying. We disbanded and Hermes again reminded me to "return tomorrow."

Saturday 18th. 6.00am. Seven of Swords. I did not recognise the man before me, and I tried to engage him in conversation. He was carrying some swords. I assumed there to be seven, though I did not count them.

"What's with the deviousness?" I said.

"People cannot handle the truth, so I give them half the story. For this may in time lead them the whole way, when they are ready."

"But why do you just not blow people away with the brightest white of truth?"

"You think that works?" he laughed.

"No," I said with deep resignation. "I know it doesn't. But even so, are you sure that you aren't just being devious for your own ends?"

"Sometimes, when I have to be. Few can handle the unvarnished whole. You will see this soon enough. When you finally plan what you are going to do then you must not delay, but intense planning and thought of this kind," he pointed one of the swords at his head, "takes much time and patience. The mind is a powerful thing, and once you have arranged something in your own mind, you can arrange it in the material world." He continued, "you are not very devious are you?"

"I would prefer to be honest, it is less to think about."

"Yes, I see. Well here is something for you" he said, implanting one of his swords straight into the centre of my heart. "This will help you. Go well!"

Hermes, present all the way through, nodded in confirmation. "There are a great number of hidden factors to take into account right now, you must look beyond wants toward needs."

Later, 7pm. I entered through the Vortex Elevator. Hermes was waiting on a log for me. I asked him what I might learn from today's excursion to a fair, delivering readings to very different kinds of people.

"One of your lessons is laziness, you often cannot be bothered. That is why we are doing the daily practice and discipline, for if we do it enough then it might become automatic." Now he tells me! He continued "You must meet people where they are, and you must be present and available when they are ready to meet you. Having said that you are not responsible here for the visitor numbers. Rest now, and sleep."

Sunday 19th. 6.00am. Two of Wands. There were two men. One was peering through a telescope, standing next to a globe. But this globe was in fact the whole world. He surveyed the horizon, while the other man stood to one side taking notes. This was the one I spoke to.

"He is searching intently. Dissatisfied, but if he searches long and hard enough, taking his time, he will find what he needs. But if disturbed, distracted - or disturbing and distracting to others - then he will be confused and it will take much, much longer." At that the man turned away. Seeking and finding where only part of the story, our reactions when we seek and find are just as important. Hermes nodded his approval.

Later, 7pm. I asked Hermes if it were correct to say that Inner Guides were not Gods.

"Yes. Although you are now working with me – a God-Form." He paused. "So what have you learned today?" he asked. I mentioned some personal insights "It is the women," he said, "that you must focus on, to try to lift up. They are the future, if there is to be a future."

Monday 20th. 6.00pm. Ace of Swords. A very large sword had been stabbed into the ground. I tried to get to grips with it, but it was too big for one man to remove and I kept cutting myself on its sharp blade. I looked around for something to help me, and then saw a much smaller sword to the left. I could pick that one up, but still could not integrate it into me fully. It was sharp, solid metal but at the same time kept changing its shape and form. I had to summon all my skills and concentration in order to avoid being viciously cut. Hermes indicated that all was well with this scene and its difficulties.

"What do you think about astrology?" Hermes asked, connecting me back into an interesting recent experience. I replied swiftly, saying that after years of investigation I now thought "it was rubbish." Hermes laughed and unexpectedly answered. "Correct!" he said. And then I was home.

During a break at a quiet fair I had asked an astrologer to look at someone's chart. I had given the birth details as 5th January. She input them into the laptop, printed off the chart and spent thirty minutes giving me a very accurate reading on the persons character as I knew it, insights in harmony with those I had myself gained from knowledge, experience and numerology. But at the end of the reading a look of horror appeared across the astrologer's face, "I'm really sorry, I have input the wrong details." The software was American, inputting 5/1 produced May 1st, not 5th January. Before I could say much she had input the fresh details, printed off the new chart and started a fresh interpretation. Nothing she now said made any sense, every insight contradicted what I knew about the person, important things were no longer emphasised and minor points became big. "I always said that I wasn't an intuitive astrologer," she said. So it was that experience, plus a few others like it that had caused me to abandon astrology as a serious practice.

Later, 8pm. It was a noisy and disjointed entry. I made contact with Hermes and he spoke.

"You are busy, but it hasn't even started yet. This is nothing. Get back to your breathing practices, you must not let these slip. You cannot invoke me for any purposes other than those of your path. Well, you can, but you should not! The people who arrive in front of you are the correct ones at that time. Do you want another one?"

"No," I replied. "I barely have the time and energy to deal with what I have."

"Good answer." Came his reply. "Just remember, many people seem willing to help, but when it comes down to it…" We returned to the earlier conversation on astrology. "It is the complexity that is the problem," he said. "You had the evidence yourself. A circular arrangement of planets and stars does not influence you to the degree claimed. It simply does not work. Now press on as you were, there is a great deal more to do."

Tuesday 21st. 6.00am. Seven of Swords. "Sometimes you have to let people fill in the blanks for themselves," said Hermes. That was all I could get.

Later, 8pm. I entered the Temple with the intention of giving some distant healing. The Temple seemed so much more crystalline and shiny than before, much brighter and bigger. But Outer World matters overtook me and I could not complete my task.

Wednesday 22nd. 6.00am. Justice. A line was drawn in the sand, with a very large sword. At the end of the sword was an imposing figure who I could not make out fully. I asked the figure to explain herself.

"I demarcate. I draw boundaries," was her reply.

"Why, what for?"

"The nature of my Eleven is expansive, but one cannot have expansion without some form of counter measure. The nature of expansion is unlimited, so I have to limit it. I do this with the economy, business, finance, life, love, learning, family, food, drink, everything. You can only learn what you are ready for and if you are not ready then you cannot learn. Expansion from insecure foundations will always invoke some action from me." She passed me two smaller swords. I merged them into my arms and something strange happened with my eyes, a buzzing, tingling, sensation. "Discernment," she said. I could see the connection now between 20 – 11 – 2, Judgement - Justice - High Priestess.

Thursday 23rd. 6.00am. Queen of Swords. I approached carefully. "Excuse me, what do you do with the sword and why do you have it?"

"For protection," she replied, "I would much rather be free and expansive, but having been hurt somewhat in the past I use the swords of tongue and eye to ensure it does not happen again. I look out for danger in order to head it off, and use my words to avoid and control its impact."

"What can overcome this?" I asked.

"A King, but not of Swords, for there we are equal. Of Pentacles by whom I am grounded and channelled, of Cups if I can handle it, and of Wands if I can defeat it."

"Do you have anything for me?"

"Yes," she said, happily pinning something to my chest. "You will spend one day seeing how others see you. It will be most revealing. Just one day."

I thanked her and turned to Hermes. She was laughing. "A good idea!" she said, "Return later." An image was received in my mind of the USA. "Next year," she said.

Friday 24th. 6.00am. Two of Swords. I saw two cross swords directly in front of my vision, they were connected at the centre by a circle. As I approached the connecting ring fell apart and the swords uncrossed, making way for me.

A Protective Mark

"Emotion tempering reason," said a figure seated on the log to one side. All around us there were sword fights and battles.

"What may you teach me?" I asked.

"Balance, compassion, judgement, detail," he said. Suddenly Hermes appeared, "Numbers are the key to the Tarot." I asked if the figure had anything for me. "No, not today."

Later, 5pm. I approached the Vortex Elevator in the cave and rose to the Astral to see my mother.

"Is that you?" she said as I emerged.

"Yes."

"I don't like it here, what is it?"

"This is a place of rest, and preparation for next time." She signalled her understanding, or at least hearing, of the words. "When you come back again it will be to learn more lessons. It's all about the learning, development, change, growth. It doesn't matter whether it is hard or easy, so long as there is some progress. That is the only real key." I don't know how those words came from inside of me.

"But my progress was hard, I was a Capricorn." She complained. Back in the Outer World she had read her Sun-sign astrology in the newspapers pretty much every day.

"Yes, but things are there to be overcome," I replied. "You will return as whatever is most suitable for your learning."

"OK," she said.

"I must go now. Love you, Mum."

"Love you too," she said.

Back via the Vortex, into the cave and out to the landscape. Hermes was waiting.

"You need a visit to the Temple," he said. I could see it, large and shining in the distance to the left of the building, very similar to the Ancient Greek Temple of Artemis, but somehow brighter.

"But surely I need a specific purpose?"

"Don't you have one?" he asked. I did not. "What about today's events?"

We ascended to the Temple, I summoned the beings respectfully but firmly, although this time I did not protect the four walls. "I request. No, I command that all the people who need me at this fair seek and find me."

"Do you want to be busy?" came a voice.

"I need to be!" I replied.

"Correct," came the answer. I repeated it again - for people who need me to seek me out, and for those that do not to not bother. I energised the request with the beings help and a spark flew out of the Temple roof in the direction of the fairs location. I thanked them and departed. Hermes said to leave and enjoy the evening. Home.

Saturday 25th. 7.00am. The Hanged Man. A man was hanging upside down from a branch, whistling.

"Why are you so happy? Contorted in this way?" I said.

"Ah, well, you see, there are things I had not considered. Whether it was my old life or my new one I had got certain things wrong. And now I want to know how and why. That's what it boils down to in the end you see, learning as much as possible about as many things as possible."

"And in the reversed situation?" Suddenly he flipped, and was no longer suspended from the tree, but sitting on the branch.

"Well, now you can see, there is no learning. I am superficially happy, but there is no development or change. I cannot be bothered. I am selfish, lazy, not willing to put the effort in."

"What else?" There was a pause.

"And I am not committed, in time or in presence. To really learn from a situation or a happening one must fully commit to it, to be fully present in its time and space. Otherwise we are not really showing up." I asked if he had anything for me. He produced a sharpened wooden arrow head from his pocket and handed it to me, "This helps to keep me on my toes. As your friend says, it's about sitting on pointed sticks. These keep you learning and moving forward."

Later, 5.30pm. A slightly disjointed entry. This often seemed to happen in the evening sessions when I was tired. Hermes sensed this and said "you need rest and recovery before tomorrow." Rain was lashing down hard on the window, disturbing my concentration. "You must be available, yet stay detached from all that find you."

Monday 27th. 12noon. Ten of Cups. The scene generated feelings of serenity and peace. There was a waterfall, children laughing and playing, a family gathering. "Step in," called a voice. It was the picture of joy, laughter and delight.

"So what happens in the reversal?" I asked.

"The apple cart is kicked over," said the woman. "You kicked it over. Others may have wanted to, but you did it."

"How do we right it?" I said.

"You don't. The cart once kicked over cannot be righted. All that can happen is for you to begin again, to rebuild from scratch."

"How do I do that?" I asked.

"Here," she said. "A seed," and passed me an apple. It entered my stomach directly. I thanked the woman and turned to Hermes. "Come," he said, "there is much to discuss. You must have some questions?" We walked over to the fallen log and I began by asking for some background and additional information on the Middle Pillar Exercise.

"This is a powerful discipline which balances and aligns the energy centres of the body, but you must be perfectly flat on the ground in order to do it. Otherwise there is a danger of misalignment. This is what was picked up by a therapist recently, your misalignment."

"But is this whole chakra re-alignment thing not just a fantasy?" I asked.

"No, not with the peripheral knowledge you have. It is very real, but you must be protected with the pentagram before each session. Vibrating the words does bring an additional effect, but is not strictly necessary. You have the core of the practice, now you must build your own method." That was very helpful, I moved on to ask about elemental breathing.

"This is different. This is an accumulation of power, it builds you up and strengthens you but the power – if not controlled – will always be misused. Franz Bardon's book does not make clear that the exercises are a thing in their own right, not just a precursor to developing something else. The something else being 'how do you use and direct your own power'. This is known through your Four Roads." Excellent insight again! But what about Nine, the Hermit number? "We are moving toward full integration of the Nine into you. This will be complete by the Spring and then you will transcend your Four Roads. These will still of course be within you but you will become the Nine. This is the goal." Finally I turned to a repeating client and her on going difficulties. "She is clearly having unfamiliar learning experiences. You can tell her this, she is undergoing an enormous transformation, an awakening. She is experiencing conflicting emotions, joy and sadness, regret and hope, love and anger. It is churning her up inside but this is something that she must go through alone. Be there, listen, guide, support as you would with everybody, but do not judge. She must face it alone. Tell her this and come back tonight."

Later, 6pm. Entering the Vortex I travelled directly to the Astral and could see Arthur. Although he was moving away from me I asked that he stop and speak with me. He reluctantly agreed. I asked him about Multiple Sclerosis. "Healing, particularly directly on the affected area, alleviates some of the symptoms, but it will not cure it. MS is a wasting disease, a shuttering off from one area of life. It can only be cured if that issue is addressed." I thanked him and left, returning to Hermes in the landscape of the Inner World.

"Arthur is correct, but if you are to attempt to heal such an illness then the question is whether you can bring enough power through to have the required effect? You can see that in relation to her Four Roads, your friend is well, hardly pursuing them, is she? All in all, theoretically it is possible, but we will have to see if you can actually do it. Visit again later for more if you wish." I did not much wish and eagerly returned home.

Tuesday 28th. 6.00am. Three of Swords. A large, blood red talking heart appeared before me. Enflamed, engorged, throbbing, yet sensitive, the slightest thing tipping it into pain, almost like a trigger ready to unleash the swords. It was overloaded with emotion, too much, too conflicted, too torn. In the reversed state there would be no escape from this misery. I asked for a gift, and received three swords "with which to build a cage for your heart, to stop you from getting hurt," it said. I turned to Hermes.

"Why did you not visit last night?" he said.

"I am sorry, I was so tired."

"Then it must be twice today." I was resigned to agree with him.

"Is she ill?" I asked, about someone close to me in the Outer World.

"Oh yes."

"Profoundly? Mortally?"

"No, but it is not minor either. The doctors might be sensible though."

"I don't like doctors." I said.

"Even if they help her?" Enough said. Home.

Later, 4pm. I entered and allowed Hermes to merge into me. I requested a visit to the Temple to create some results for an upcoming event I was due to attend. Hermes refused. "It is for needs, on path, only. Not wants. You have already called upon the magick for this matter, you cannot do so all the time. There is no substitute for actions in the material world."

"So if I make those material efforts, and I am still in need can I return in a week or so?"

"Maybe." Hermes replied. "I will give you a night off from visiting here, so long as you use it for rest and reading," he said. I thanked him and he returned with me.

Wednesday 29th. 6.00am. Six of Wands. A man had lined up six stakes in the ground. "These are my accomplishments," he said proudly. "Effort brings accomplishments, and acts of will bring victory! Here, have one!" He pressed one of the stakes into me. I hesitated for a moment but then stopped resisting. "And reversed?" I asked.

"That apple cart again, the malign influence of others, disturbing the efforts and diluting the will."

I was already tired and the day had barely begun. "More later," said Hermes, "go and get yourself ready for the day."

Later, 6pm. Various Outer World matters had to be discussed with Hermes. "All women," he said "and some men, want to be held firmly. As water they need containers, they lack the solidity that men provide. But that is not the issue here. You need to be ready for the next phase of our work where we will step up the practice. In the meantime you must continue to walk a fine and balanced line between the work of the Inner World and the enjoyments of the Outer World."

Thursday 30th. 6.00am. Strength. A woman dressed in fine clothes was lying on the ground, trampled by a Lion.

"My desires, my will, my power – I cannot control it," she wailed, "and it walks all over me and my life."

"And if you could control it?" I asked. Suddenly she snapped upright and took the Lion back under her control. She mounted it and was in total charge of the animal, directing it exactly where it needed to go.

"This takes experience," she said.

"How do you keep control?"

"Your weaknesses are its strengths. Know yourself above anything else, because this animal lies within you." Suddenly the animal was gone, and only the woman remained, or did she? She was shape shifting, one minute woman, next Lion, next both. She seemed to be able to do this at will.

"Do you have anything for me?" I asked.

"Yes, here is a stronger heart," she said. At those words I could actually physically feel my heart beat faster as she leaned in to merge something into me. I thanked her and departed.

Later, 8pm. "Are you ready to shift gears?" said Hermes.

"Do I have a choice?" I asked.

"Always. Are you ready to go to another level or not?"

"I do feel better, stronger, than I ever have, so yes." I replied.

"Do you want an assistant?" he said.

"I can cope with more work, I cannot cope with an assistant," I replied. Hermes did not reply. The scene faded and I could not get it back. Home.

Friday 31st. 6.00am. Three of Cups. A table with fine food and drink was laid out. A bearded man led a group of party goers.

"What are you celebrating?" I asked.

"Achievements. It is here that we celebrate the achievements of the other three – the Pentacles, Wands and Swords." And reversed I wondered? But before my wondering was even half formed the table of delights had been turned over. "There's that apple cart again, empty celebrations, unearned and for no reason, or overindulgence," said the bearded man.

"Can you tell me anything about this?" I asked.

"Surely not!" laughed the man, "you know all about overindulgence!" Indeed I did, how astute of him to know. I turned to Hermes and asked him about a business opportunity in the Outer World. "Yes, the pictures could be produced in print form and sold at these shows you attend, if you get the printing exactly right. The owner of the copyright is greedy though." I asked then about a new client, one with many issues. "That is a job for the Library," he said, pointing to the now apparent but previously invisible building which seemed to have the ability to appear any time anywhere. I approached and knocked the door,

"Yes," came the old voice.

"May I enter?"

"Yes, what can I do for you?"

I spoke the clients name and a book appeared, its pages flung open to reveal words, which were then spoken into my ear, rather than read by my eyes, "bitter, resentful, fearful, does not really want to learn." A big sigh from me.

"What do you do with people who do not want to learn?" I asked. The Keeper was not impressed. "You should know the answer to that!" he scolded and shooed me out of the Library. I repeated the question to Hermes, but answer there came none. My own mind said that nothing could be done.

Later, 6.30pm. After drifting for some time in my attempts to connect I managed to see Hermes. He spoke "Ask others to assist you in your plans for America. This is what you have been waiting for, everything has been practice up until now. Back tomorrow, ready to pick up the pace."

[SEPTEMBER 2012]

Saturday 1st. 6.00am. Three of Cups. "Here's to a celebration of achievements!" cried one, "and a celebration of being alive," cried another. "Nothing more!" cried a third member of the group gathered around a table full of food and drink.

I turned to Hermes and spoke of Outer World matters, then moved onto the work proper.

"An adjustment of your daily routine to give more time for focused practices such as breathing will be beneficial," he said. "Franz Bardon is a very old school academic but the merit of his words can be discovered in intentional practice and the subsequent realisations that flow. For example, visualise strongly the sphere above the head in the Middle Pillar Exercise, above the head, not in the head." I found this most helpful. "Do you want an assistant?" he continued. I had changed my feelings since the other day and said that I did. "So be it." I looked up at the Temple in the distance, it was massive and dominated the skyline. "It was always there, that big you know, you just couldn't see it. It waits for you when you are ready."

Sunday 2nd. 6.00am. The High Priestess. The High Priestess was unmistakable, to my left. I looked at her straight on and she started to talk.

"Feelings, love, psychic senses – all are like water. Exactly like water they flow, going wherever they can, into the smallest nooks and crannies. This is the power of water, to get everywhere, to find the one piece of information or insight or word to make it all better again, to find the weakness, or the crack in the façade that will bring the whole house down. Just like water." I asked of her reversed expression. "Same, but poorly handled. Either you cannot deal with the consequences of wherever the water has flowed and penetrated, or you try to impinge upon it or impede it in some way. Either way the resulting blockage and distortion creates problems." I asked for something more tangible. "I have something for your heart, to handle its flow better. Come into my world," she said and I willingly approached her. She enveloped me with her veil and I felt an all pervading emotional power pour through my body. After a while of soaking this up I thanked her and departed.

Later, 5.30pm. "What am I missing?" I asked Hermes.

"Time *is* the key," he said, smiling and laughing. "An investment of time is always required. It is only a step change in your level of commitment that will do now. Theory and practice are both important, time is needed to absorb the knowledge and then more time is needed to practice it – this is the investment of time and it will be all consuming. Only then will it and you be ready. Return again tomorrow."

Later, Talking With Dice. I selected an ordinary die, six sided. I projected my consciousness into the deepest point of the object, its absolute centre, and took on the viewpoint as if the die was all about me, above me, around me and below me. It was quite a different sensation to normal life.

"What is this and what is it for?" I asked.

"Its function is to give choices," said an unknown voice.

"How does it feel about that?" I probed.

"It might like a break, a rest sometimes. Its own options are somewhat limited so it might like a companion, or it might like to escape, to be a rogue die, to make a bid for freedom." I thought on this, indeed when a die gains a partner it become dice, changing its name and thus its behaviour. It was interesting that the answers were not received in the first person, from the die itself, in a sense it was me answering my own questions, the voice my projection. But isn't that the purpose of a die, to be the carrier of the throwers desires, to be imbued and charged with the dreams of everyone that picks it up? Given all that, does it really remain an inanimate object? And what about different sided dice, how would they behave?

Monday 3rd. 7.30am. Four of Wands. The door to the Inner World, and then the Temple itself were decked out in garlands.

"Did you not see that before?" said Hermes, "It has always been like this," he continued. "The Temple is there for whatever purpose you want, on path. On path you can have whatever you want, in terms of rich experiences. Would you like another experience?" I said yes.

"Then it is done. Now to serious matters, you too easily make promises to others than you simply cannot keep. Therefore you are now in a holding pattern, a time for you to work out what you want, and then to make it happen in the Temple. Come back later and we will explore this further." I had no idea what I wanted in the Temple, but I agreed and thanked him. I had over-committed myself and this had to be resolved.

Later, 8pm. Hermes seemed pleased with the events of the day, "A great learning experience" he said. "It is now all about what you want. In transcending the four roads, moving beyond them, what do you want?"

"Success at my forthcoming event?" I couldn't say this was an all consuming desire but it would be nice to get a result there.

"You have left that a bit late," he said. It was three weeks away.

"I don't know then," I replied. Hermes laid it out for me. "Well, this is where we are now – decide what you want, in accordance with your path, and make it happen. Simple and easy things will be do-able with the click of your fingers in the Outer World, but more difficult things will need you to resort to the Temple." I did not know what I wanted though. I was too practised in reacting to whatever was available, rather than setting a specific course toward something. What did I want?

"Explore that question next," he said, "and then return."

Back at home. That was a great question for the Tarot - 'What do I want?' Keywords and book meanings would have to be the starting point of interpretation, otherwise how do you know you aren't intuiting illusion?

Tuesday 4th. 7.30am. Page of Wands. A boy to my left was busy building something.

"What are you doing?" I asked.

"Building my house," he said. He carried a small staff and was tracing lines on the floor with it. He pointed up the Temple. "It's going to be like that," he said.

"How are you going to do it?" I asked, after all he was only a Page, unskilled and immature.

"I'm just getting on with it," he said, walking quickly and eagerly, his mistakes glossed over, untouched by doubt or error. He wore a necklace, the face of a Sun on a chain.

"What is that?" I asked.

"Here, you have it," he said. With that it merged into my chest.

"Enthusiasm," said Hermes, appearing from nowhere. "In the Temple this is what is needed. You cannot wipe away what you know, or what happens, but a new sense of possibilities and opportunities will serve you as you move forward in the Temple and decide what you want. Optimism, confidence, energy, vigour." I turned to the boy and asked if there were anything else? "No, that's it, bye," he said.

"Reflect," said Hermes, "and return later." Home.

Later, 7pm. I gained entry and approached the log where I normally sat with Hermes. Throughout my encounters with him I could only, very rarely, glimpse him in any sort of form. Most usually I could see nothing at all, but could sense a strong presence and could hear his speech. This time however I could actually see a silvery grey shadowy vagueness, as a light cloud, but not even as defined as that.

"This is as much of me as you can perceive," he said. We turned to the vexed question of what to do, and what did I want?

"All the books written about Nine, and the Hermit, talk about helping others." I said.

"Go on."

"And freeing yourself from responsibilities, ceasing to wish anything for oneself."

"Continue."

"So it seems that I should be making things better for others?"

"Yes. So…?" he replied.

"Let's start with my friend who is ill." I said, uncertain and far from convinced myself.

"Her learning cannot be interfered with," he said, "ask her for permission next time you see her. You must do this with all other individuals who you might desire to help – ask their permission."

"Hmmm, what about a bigger canvas then, say globally?" I replied.

"Now you are talking," he said.

"Or nationally, by helping people in this recession?"

"Well, again, everyone must learn."

"So the best I can do globally is to shine my light the strongest it can possibly be and assist all those who fall into my path?"

"Yes. You will need protection as well as you light up. Do you want to know how to make all this happen?" Hermes asked. I confirmed that I was in. We ascended to the Temple and I protected its walls with purple flamed pentagrams. I summoned the eight stations and they appeared from left to right in colours red, orange, yellow, green, blue, indigo, violet and opal. Dead ahead was a bright shining light. Hermes nudged me forward to enter it.

To describe it as powerful would be to insult it. The appropriate word simply does not exist, certainly not in English, to describe the force that penetrated every granule of my being, the vastness and the compactness of the energy, its ability to be everywhere and nowhere and all points in between all at the same time. But for all this I knew I was only glimpsing a fragment of the whole. Suddenly I was very scared. This was a new feeling for me in this environment, and I could suddenly feel hands around my throat, choking me.

"He is not ready," came the voice. I regrouped, composed myself and breathed deeply, still in the Light Space. I reaffirmed my identity, "I am Richard Abbot, I am The Hermit," but unable to move forward any more I pulled back. Looking at the Light from the outside now it was a vigorous bright void which I could see into and beyond. I turned to Hermes and said that I could not do it.

"Tomorrow," he said. "Again tomorrow." I returned home, head spinning at the information, the sensory input, the energy flow and the leap I could not yet make.

Wednesday 5th. 7.30am. Queen of Swords. A woman, unhappy, though more cold and harsh than sad and remorseful. She had switched herself off due to her continual failure to be supported. She was trying to be a man and failing.

"What do you have for me?" I asked.

"Here," she pierced a sword through my heart. "Now see what I see," she said. I could see it alright - anger, coldness, intolerance, distance, lack of connection. It all seemed very real and very close.

"How do I deal with this?" I asked Hermes, who had now appeared.

"Avoid. And if you cannot avoid those of this nature then be the King of Wands. Firm and still is the only way. The King of Swords will fight, the King of Cups will be defeated, the King of Pentacles would just walk away. This Queen has experienced much disappointment with men, and now over thinks and over plans everything. Notice her counterparts in the Outer World."

Later, 7pm. A good conversation with Hermes.

"Dignified Tarot cards bring positive learning experiences. Even the negative cards, dignified, with their negative learning can be ultimately beneficial and in the end positive. Reversed cards are not the Dark Side but a distortion caused by human free will and a resistance to meeting the positive learning experiences."

"The Temple?" I asked, "What actually is it?"

"You will be reborn," he said. "Die and be reborn. It is a matter of surrender. You have issues with that." And with that we were there. I protected the walls so the eight coloured energies could manifest exactly as before. Hermes urged me to step forward toward the Light. As I did do I could see a vivid purple disk in my minds eye, vast and flashing. Then I was totally engulfed and swallowed up by the brilliance of the Light. My whole body convulsed with this overwashing and penetration of energy. I started to cry. This continued for what might have been ten seconds or ten years – in that moment there was no way to know. There was no ebb and flow or change in the level of energy. It was just on me and in me. And then it wasn't. I was gasping for air, but I stepped forward for a second dose.

"No," came the voice.

"You are The Hermit now. Use the power wisely." I bowed to the Light in response. I turned to the eight assembled energies and integrated them each into me, in turn. So I was the ninth? I then turned to Hermes, who explained.

"When you return I will no longer be here. You now possess instant knowing of all that is needed, when it is needed."

"But who will I see?" Hermes gestured to another figure waiting to one side.

"You no longer need me, although I will be here if you do. You must now work the protective rituals that you have on yourself and your property, this is very important. It is your time now. You have everything you need, everything, but remaining on your path will be the challenge." He wished me farewell.

I am The Hermit. Maybe.

The words spoken by Hermes confirmed exactly and precisely the method of working operated by Arthur. In our many long and winding conversations he would practice what is now know as 'being present' but which to him consisted simply of answering exactly that which I asked him, without thought or reference to anything else. He would sometimes contradict himself and then when I called him on the contradiction he would act as if no such thing had ever happened. At the time this was greatly annoying, but the truth was that he neither remembered nor cared what had been discussed before. As explained by Hermes, Arthur possessed instant knowing of what was needed, when it was needed. Not before or after. He often spoke with dismissive tones about the past, almost as if it did not exist, which within this new paradigm delivered by Hermes I suppose it did not.

Thursday 6th. 7.30am. Page of Swords. A young boy was trying hard to wield a sword. But it was too heavy for him and he could only slash wildly and uncontrollably. He was a student, a learner, but I asked him a question.

"What do you have for me?"

"Nothing. Just look how others fail to cope for insights on how you fail to cope," he said. "Psychic, mystical, spiritual endeavours should not withdraw you from life. If done right they, in fact, swirl you more fully into the maelstrom of life. But they also give you the tools with which to grow and prosper within that maelstrom." I turned around and I could see Hermes.

"You said you were going," I was confused.

"It caused some discomfort," he said.

"Yes, it did!" I was pleased to see him.

"But my time is up. You must now look to the new," he pointed and I saw a dark figure to my left with red eyes. He was powerful, but not supportive, more threatening. No. "I reject you," I said and cast a cross with a circular central link at him. He vanished. I turned back to Hermes, who seemed to approve. Suddenly a doorway appeared above his head and a new shape emerged from it, coming down to greet me.

"Hello child," he said. The shape was shimmering white. An old man? Bearded? It was hard to say. He had powerful eyes, large and sun filled. I asked his name.

"Me…Mi…Meth." I could make out no more and it was my hearing that stuttered, not the spoken word. He said nothing more, but I said that I needed to reflect a little and would come back later.

"But not too much later," he said.

"Contact established," smiled Hermes, wishing me well with the final words, "an assistant is needed to take your place at shows."

Later, 7pm. The white haired, bearded man was right there where I had left him. He was tall and upright, very straight. The scene was clearer and I more settled.

"How shall I address you?" I asked.

"Mithras," he said. Repeating himself slowly. "Me-thras. Research my history and pronunciation."

"It's a bit stereotyped isn't it?" I asked, sceptically. There was no answer.

"Not Metatron then?" I asked.

"No." He laughed. "I will come with you to your next fair if you meet me here tomorrow night," he said "Now go and talk with your pupils, they are your responsibility now."

CHAPTER XIV

MITHRAS

[SEPTEMBER 2012]

Friday 7th. 7.30am. Ten of Cups. It was a rosy day in a beautiful garden, with many figures enjoying the fruits of their labours. Suddenly, as before, the wooden cart full of juicy apples is kicked over. The perpetrator was immediately identified by the others and expelled from the garden, forbidden to return, at least for a long time.

"Hey, here is something for you," said a voice as one of the apples was pushed into my heart. I offered no resistance and turned to Mithras. "This is fine," he said "you have a busy day, visit again later and we shall merge. Now go well, child." I felt his language was a bit stereotypical and it caused me to doubt its truth. "Not really" he said, "when the stereotypes were all based on me!" Ha! Who can argue with that! Home.

Afterwards I checked back through my notes and recognised that I had been divining (not selecting) the same cards repeatedly – a classic sign of unlearned lessons. The reappearance of the apple cart on numerous occasions reflected a danger of me kicking over an apple cart in the Outer World.

Later, 6.30pm. I saw Mithras immediately and he was visible in some detail. But I just felt that his appearance was too much of a standard wise old man.

"I meet you where you are," he said. "This is not my form, but a form that you can deal with me in."

"But how do I know that this is true and good?" I asked.

"Do I need to demonstrate?" he said. At which his eyes sparked up like two light bulbs - no pupils, just one mass of light in each eye.

"No, no, it's OK" I said, convinced enough by this, for now. I had been researching the Cult of Mithras and asked him about it.

"It was a pivotal time in history," he said, "any number of practices could have taken and held. It just happened to be Christianity which did."

"But the Cult of Mithras excluded women," I said.

"Think again. The Cult did, but the teachings did not," he replied.

"But what about the trials and initiations of the Cult?"

"Time enough for that another day," he said. "We must merge. I will enter you to protect and assist for tomorrow and Sunday, but you must expel me on Sunday night. It is dangerous to both of us to leave it longer than that." He stood directly in front and merged into me. It lasted longer and ran deeply and powerfully. At the end of it I felt him shrink down to a tiny molecular grain and reside in my heart. He spoke. "The schedule continues unchanged. Up early in the morning, and practice in the evening. Remember to expel me on Sunday night. This is very important."

Home. Some hours later I could still feel him resting inside me.

Saturday 8th. 7.00am. Ten of Pentacles. "Steadiness," said an old man, seated at a table with piles of coins stacked up high. "Steadiness, accumulation and charity," intervened Mithras. "Charity is very important." The old man at the table – who was not Mithras – flipped one of the coins up in the air and it fell into my right hand. As I caught it I felt it dissolve into and through me. Both the old man and Mithras signalled that all was correct.

Later, 7pm. "What have you learned today?" said Mithras.

"If you are present inside me, then people find me," I replied.

"Yes," he said. "They will."

Sunday 9th. 7.30am. The Lovers. A man and a woman were making love. The man was on top of the woman yet explained to me all that he was doing.

"I am giving, not taking," he said "Try it and see." I merged into him and experienced exactly what he experienced. We were giving love to the woman, not taking her for our own satisfaction. Every movement was given in order to enliven and empower the woman to stand and to be stronger, as opposed to nailing her into submission. I said to the man how interesting this was. "Isn't it!" he said.

I asked for the reversed scene. It was all just hard sex now, taking from each other as opposed to a giving to each other. "Love and sex are not the same thing. And love may well become more unavailable the more we search for sex," said the man. Mithras was present and confirmed all was well, but hurried me on my way.

Later, 7pm. Intending to expel Mithras as he had instructed, I was surprised to see him waiting as I entered the landscape.

"But you are already out of me?" I asked, a little confused.

"This is what you see," he said, "but it is not the full story. I am still energetically within." At that his visible shape merged inside me, then moved out again. I felt a pull, a sucking out of me as he left, and it must be said, a sense of emptiness.

"No more today," he said. I thanked him for his help and returned home.

Monday 10th. 7.00am. Four of Cups. A stream. A young man, lying by the side of the water, basking in the sun. The stream was part of a garden, well kept and luscious, though almost silent. I sensed within him some despondency, some tension, not full relaxation. This was his pause between frenzied activities. It was his rest time.

Reversed? "A failure to take the time even to breathe," he said, "continuing the party after every one else has gone home. Enjoyment, yes. But on borrowed time. Neither one thing nor the other."

"Do I need anything from you?" I asked.

"No. You know all this," he said. Indeed I was familiar with such behaviour. I thanked him. Mithras signalled me to end. "Return later and we will talk," he said.

Later, 6.30pm. Mithras wasted no time, speaking as soon as I arrived.

"You long ago ceased to be an ordinary member of the human race. You are not marked out for earthly things," he said as he pointed up to the stars above. "Try to keep your material life on course as best you can, for when it shifts and changes it will be painful. There is nothing you can do with certain people, they will not be helped even though that is what they ask for. Avoid too many distractions. Plain speaking is required."

I asked for some assistance with the events I was running. He confirmed that the Temple was the place for this. We ascended there and I performed the protective procedure as usual and summoned the eight beings. I saw once again the Light at the end of the room, opposite me.

"I summon all those interested and invested in my development. I require success, profits and abundance, good works at our forthcoming events." I was asked to confirm this and I did.

"So be it," said a voice. Three streams of light shot out of the roof of the Temple and landed in the respective towns, detonating like mini-bombs.

"Tomorrow please," Mithras said. "Though sooner if you can would be helpful." But I was much too tired for that.

Tuesday 11th. 7.00am. Seven of Cups. A man was stood in front of seven golden goblets, which all hung in the air. He was utterly confused and self contradictory – full of fantasies intermingled with nightmares, ifs, buts and maybes, possibilities unfulfilled. His mind was whirling. Suddenly, reversed, all the vessels dropped from the air. They were replaced by one large cup, one goal, one direction. Focus and clarity had been attained. The man wanted me to experience the scene from his point of view. I moved toward him but the large cup just moved further away, with each step I took it receded into the distance even more.

"The only way to achieve the clarity you desire," he said, "is to know yourself inside out, what you are like, what you need, what you don't need. Your future potential is a long way off. Make no promises to anybody, do not speak of the future or the past. You see things clearly now, the fantasy is over." I thanked the man. "Thank you," he replied, quite unexpectedly, "we are all interested in your progress."

I turned around and could see Hermes.

"Why are you here?" I asked.

"Because you need help to remain on your path," he said.

"How do I reach you?"

"Just listen," he said. Mithras nodded in confirmation and they both urged me to return that evening.

Later, 6.30pm. There was just one sentence, spoken by Hermes or by Mithras, I knew not which.

"Taking time to reconnect with the Inner Reality is important, especially when rushing around."

Wednesday 12th. 7.00am. Five of Swords. "You have been skewered by your own efforts and meddling," said a voice. Mithras then intervened. "Your intention to help others is admirable, but in many cases you have hit a dead end. There is very little that some want to learn. And if the basics are not addressed, they stay at Level One."

"So what do I do?" I asked. There did not seem much point to it all if my efforts were in vain.

"You have a responsibility to those who find you, and you can loosen those ties somewhat by changing the way you think and approach them. That will make it much better for you."

Looking around there was a man fending off the attack of five swords coming at him through the air. He maintained his freedom of movement in spite of the attack and passed me a golden coin and it fused into my chest, "to change my heart."

Later, 7pm. Mithras enveloped me in a vortex of blue/white light and faced me square on.

"Listen carefully," he said. "You are not of this planet. You cannot connect with people the way that others do. So do not try. If you train others up to their potential then you will gain all you need - that is all that your life is about. We need you on track with this. Now rest tonight" I thanked him.

Home. These past weeks I had experienced one of my periodic 'doubts about the work.' The gap between what I saw, heard and learned in the Inner World and what I then had to deal with in the Outer World seemed just too big. Yet at the same time I could not, in all conscience, abandon the Inner. Far from living in both worlds, I was actually living in neither. At least I now finally realised that.

Thursday 13th. 7.00am. Two of Swords. "The volume of trouble has been turned down, but the trouble is still there," said a woman, negotiating the many swords laying on the ground. To the left was the sea and it was angry.

"Reversed?" I asked.

"In the dignified you have turned down the volume successfully, but in the reversed others are turning it up again. Your input verses others."

"Is it always like that, for reversals?" I asked.

"No, but it is sometimes." I thanked the woman and turned to Mithras.

"Move onto the next section of Franz Bardon's work today please." I wondered afterwards that perhaps there had been no please. Why should there be? Home.

Later, 8pm. I greeted Mithras and he explained the concept of 'Healing With Numbers.' I could see his form quite clearly. He was dressed in Greek style toga with a Plato-like curled beard. I questioned his form and its clarity but he would not entertain or engage with those doubts and we sat down for the lesson.

"We must practice the energy," he said and merged into me. After a little time he shrank himself down to a dot within me. "You can direct me around your body as required. Into the feet to enable walking with purpose and to help with feeling the right way forward. Into the brain to assist thoughts and decisions, into the heart for a different kind of feeling, the throat to assist communication and the hands for writing or typing. When you want the action to be directed or informed by me then move me to the appropriate area of the body. For readings the area will be the throat. At first you will have to concentrate hard in order to hold me for long periods of time, but it is worth the effort to achieve the goal. Set aside times when you may hold me there and the people will present themselves. You will have to enter this place to achieve the connection at first but after practice you will be able to do it anywhere. Now return, read, practice and come back tomorrow." Mind totally blown, I returned home.

Friday 14th. 7.30am. Judgement. An announcement of great importance was imminent and many different people could be seen running to hear it, through stricken lands of earthquake, fire and destruction.

"It is announced," came the voice, "that Richard Abbot has passed the necessary stage of initiation and is now The Hermit, with all that that entails."

"Do I need anything else though?" I thought, concerned at the finality of the statement.

"These words are enough," came the reply. Mithras now spoke.

"This is a reason to be happy!" He said. "You are going to be fine, unlike some others. Make very sure to return later."

Later, 6pm. "How will I find the time to do everything?" I asked Mithras.

"You must be judicious in what you take on, what you engage with, what you say yes to. Be more willing to say no. Try that today and visit again for an extended period tomorrow. There is so much to do and you will fall behind if you are not alert."

Saturday 15th. 7.00am. King of Swords. A man is leant over a table with a large map. He is dividing up the terrain into regions and zones. I approached him.

"Sometimes it is better in life to segment, divide and separate. You will find it very useful when there is much to do." Very helpful, I thought, in all areas of life. He threw me a sword. "Here, this will help," he said. I caught it with my right hand and it merged into and became part of my right arm. "That is all," said the man, turning back to his map.

"Come back in a while," said Mithras. "And I will take you on a journey."

Later, 10am. I had been diligent in preceding these visits with a series of my own breathing exercises, adapted from the work of Franz Bardon and Israel Regardie. The time I had available each day tended to dictate the frequency, duration and intensity of this, but today was a clear day so I really got into it, to such an extent it left me absolutely buzzing. Maybe today I was in the Inner World before I had even journeyed there! When I finally closed my eyes my vision was made up entirely of bright white horizontal lines.

I could feel Mithras' presence even before I entered the landscape, and I offered no resistance when he entered me powerfully. This was always a strange experience, especially given that he was much bigger than me, but then would shrink down to the size of a grain of sand. He spoke.

"Be in your heart, you can know things there." I felt my heart beat increase. "Be in your fingers, you can know things there." My finger tips tingled. "Be in your sex, you can know things there." My groin throbbed. "Be in your ears, you can know things here." My hearing became acute and seemed to expand its range. "Be in your throat you may speak the truth, and in your brain you may understand it all."

He expanded to full size again and was then present throughout and inside every part of my body. It was almost suffocating, for it did not seem that I could contain him, that I might burst at any moment. The only thing that seemed possible was for me to reduce the size of my own being to make some room for him. I did this and the over-shadowing was complete. I was secondary now, though carrying both him and me. I did not know how long this state could be sustained. It felt certain that over time, if I could not fully cope, there would be all sorts of problems.

"Open your eyes," he said. I did as instructed and could see the Outer World from both his and my own perspective. Everything that I turned my eyes or head toward looked completely different than I had ever seen before. Everything was penetrated and permeated by light, the colours of everything were a shade lighter than I had seen before and the form, solidity and mass of objects seemed a degree less than the last time I looked at them. Looking at my desk lamp there seemed to be no obstacle to it floating up into the air.

My brain was now processing two experiences, what I was seeing and what Mithras was seeing. If I went about my day like this I might experience all manner of wonders, I thought. My appearance and situation would no longer be of the slightest importance, save as it might enable me to experience even greater wonders. I justified all this by saying that it would also enable me to be a greater help to others, but I cannot honestly say that was my prime concern at that point.

"I will come back with you," he said. It seemed that the longer I could see the world like this the more I would be able to see the world like this. There must be after effects I thought, such as the ability to immediately distinguish truth from nonsense. It had been an amazing journey.

Sunday 16th. 7.00am. Nine of Swords. Mithras spoke immediately about the daughter of one of my clients.

"You may help her in the Temple," he said.

"Is that appropriate, unasked?"

"Oh yes, you have a responsibility," he said.

"Better explore this scene first though?" I thought.

"If you wish."

I looked around but there was nothing to see! We ascended to the Temple. I was apprehensive and Mithras suggested I clarify my intentions privately with him before announcing them. I thought the best outcome would be for the mother to meet and respond to the situation in the best way she could.

"Then that should be your command," he said. I assembled everyone and protected the space. We built up an energy ball between us, to the ends that I announced, despatching it in one motion into the Universe. I watched it land in the home of the people concerned and detonate there. Thanking the assembled beings I disbanded them and the Temple.

As I was about to leave for home Mithras spoke the name of a person for whom I had an outstanding reading to give. He merged into me and moved to my hands and fingers. "My presence will not last long. Get dressed and write it up," he said. Home.

Later, 7pm. Mithras was laughing. "Are you enjoying being the Hermit?" continuing, "you are their secret, their joy. So many find your words soothing and you personality compelling. You would not believe it!" He was right, I did not believe it.

Monday 17th. 7.00am. Knight of Pentacles. A young man was bent over a bench, working with wood, planing, sanding away until his piece was perfectly rectangular. I asked if he had anything for me?

"Here," he said, handing me a small chisel which he said should be incorporated into my hands and fingers. "All manual and material work requires a degree of dexterity, co-ordination and manipulation of the object. This chisel will enable you to do this. Notice how I work, my head is down and I apply myself to it. I am not looking up and around or dreaming. I get on." I thanked him for his wise and appropriate words and turned to Mithras.

"Does this tool last just for today, or forever?"

"It is now forever in you," he said, "but like everything it must be used or it is lost. Go home now, but when at your desk call me into your hands and type a different kind of email."

Later, 5pm. Straight to the Temple, where the Light spoke. "You may work anything which assists your path, but in your mind there is the thought to work for another to whom you have no responsibility. Think carefully about this. There are ramifications here, consequences that might just finish you off."

"So what about the give and take aspects of this power, to take for self and help others?" I said. I wasn't really clear where the line of appropriate action was as my thoughts had been merely to assist.

"Like Karma, this is always a matter of give and take. Whatever you take from the Universe you must give back to the Universe, willingly or under compulsion. Too much taking is what incurs the Karmic Debts." Sufficiently warned I approached the Temple with only the goal of improving the prospects of one of my forthcoming events. Protection and summoning complete I spoke, "I demand that our next event is profitable, successful and fulfilling for all." This seemed to be the right frame of words and the assembled energies were satisfied with it. They and I shaped a ball of energy in our hands. We caused it to grow stronger and stronger, more charged with the goal, until we could hold it no more and propelled it into the Universe. It detonated over the area where the event would be and its remnants sank into the building.

I suddenly felt weak and drained of energy. I disbanded the group, thanked them and returned to the Inner Landscape. I remarked to Mithras how suddenly exhausted I felt.

"You overdid it. You now need to rest." I really did feel weak. "Come again in the morning before you leave," he said, "for a foretaste of the day. Forewarned is forearmed." Although this was not what I wanted to hear it was obviously needed, regardless of what I had planned. I was always one step away from 'giving it a miss just this once' so the constant reminders were clearly still necessary.

Tuesday 18th. 6.00am. Ace of Wands. I had been encountering tremendous difficulties in the Outer World. Mithras said straight away that he would "correct the situation." I saw a boy, young but seemingly wise. He spoke to me. "The Ace of Wands can only be sustained by food – fuel in the belly. You cannot run on empty and still deliver the fire."

Later 8pm. "A new routine is required," said Mithras, "to settle things down."

"But when will this happen?" I asked. I was strung out by my dealings with all sorts of challenging clients and colleagues, months of early starts and so much input from the Inner World.

"It will happen. You have experienced new sensations, experiences and lessons. Continue these. It will settle. As the wheel turns and the nights get darker so the pressure will recede."

Later still. Lying in bed, half asleep, half awake. A voice spoke. "You have what many seek, and many more want. In the face of this assault how do you remain on your path? This is the question, whose answer is as yet undiscovered. But it will be." The voice drifted off just as I did, "It will be…"

Wednesday 19th. 7.00am. Nine of Swords. A vague image of the card appeared before me, as if from my memory. Then a shadowy figure appeared.

"What are you afraid of?" it said.

"Losing my position, the things I have built up." I seemed to be able to answer this as quick as a flash.

"So what are your options?" was the reply.

"Stop worrying or accept the changes, and then think of a plan of action through them."

"Yes. Use your mind. Take the emotion out of the Nine and use the swords to think it all through."

"Thank you. Do I need anything from you?" I asked.

"No," he said, tapping me on the forehead, "you have a good mind and intellect. Use it." I turned to Mithras.

"Good advice," he said, "now come closer. You are effectively leading two lives now – The Hermit and The Ordinary – and you must adjust your behaviours to accommodate this. You must segment your life more effectively. Both lives will place demands on you which you must satisfy, but within more rigid bounds else each life will impinge on the other. The real question is how do you stay on your true road in the face of this."

"Yes. But what is the answer to that?" I was frustrated.

"You must think on this," he said. "We will return to answer it, but it is for you to think about. It is very, very important."

Later, 4pm. I was struggling with this effort. Although these visits were now once or twice daily the total amount of time spent in the Inner World and in these discussions was still only a fragment of my total daily activities, a great number of which pointed me in the complete opposite direction. It was hard to square the two paths. But maybe, as Mithras had suggested, no squaring was necessary, just tighter demarcation? Hard though.

"How do I know that this is you, and not just my imagination?" I asked Mithras. This was my standard procedure whenever the work became too hard, to doubt its very existence.

"Well, in a way it is your imagination for I no longer live in your world," he replied.

"And I do not live in yours," I said, trying to be clever.

"But parts of us are in each others. You are doing fine, moving to the stage where contact can be made instantly, without visiting here. A cave visit strengthens the bond but as you have discovered I am always available. It is the silence, the peace of the mind, the physical exhaustion, that makes the contact possible. Without these things you would not be able to do it."

This kind of work in the Outer World had gone very quiet, with few readings or consultations.

"Where have all the people gone?" I asked.

"They are having a rest. This is your time to learn, develop and grow, to teach yourself more. Then they will be back." The contact faded and I sat in reflection on his words for a little time. After maybe ten minutes I felt his presence again. He moved around my body. "Ears for hearing, eyes for seeing, brain for understanding, hands for making…" there was more but I could not discern it. The voice faded. Home.

Later still, 7pm. "You are preparing for a quieter period," Mithras said, "a withdrawal from others and from technology. Spending much more time in here, in this chair. In the Inner World you appear to us as a bright manifestation, but in the Outer World merely as one voice though it is a voice others can discern, for it is distinct. To listeners it even feels and sounds different. This –

as I have described - is the way that you stay on your path. This period will be followed by one of intense activity and significant change. Ordinary life, its happenings and appointments, will continue in the way that they must, but you will and must carve out more time for you. You remember the Seven Personal Year from nine years ago? You can learn from the mistakes made then and this time use it to the full."

Thursday 20th. 7.00am. Page of Cups. Another Page! This time an energetic boy could be seen balancing on a staff. He managed the feat well, and then came down to speak to me.

"Optimism, vigour, energy. With these things life can be better," he said. "You need this approach now." As before he handed me a necklace with the Sun pendant dangling from it. I wore it and the Sun emblem merged into me. "See" he said cheerfully, and ran off.

Mithras spoke. "This is now a day for doing, with an optimistic and confident heart. Tackle tasks related to your events, chase up, email, call. Move everything forward confidently and optimistically and then return tonight." I thanked Mithras and the boy.

Later, 6pm. "What does one do when one could do anything?" I asked Mithras. He paused before replying.

"You are adjusting to your power. You do not even believe that it is real, but it is and you will adjust. Until then you will waste or misuse it. But there is a further oath to take soon. Remain detached from Outer World commitments and promises. Peace is the key for you now. Your life as it stands might not always be peaceful, but it is more peaceful than most."

"Why do my Tarot cards continually show people?" I asked.

"Because you care more about them than you do about yourself. At the moment at least. This will change. The choice is between the general and the specific – helping people or helping one person in particular." Mithras merged into me and accumulated himself in my throat before moving all around my body, and finally expanding to full size again.

Friday 21st. 7.00am. The Lovers. By divination, not selection I had again chosen The Lovers. A man and a woman were before me making love. "But what is love?" I asked.

Mithras replied. "Love is where you care as much for the other person as you do for yourself. Not more. Not less. The same amount. Sometimes more or less, but over time always coming back into balance. Love is more than this of course, but it is beyond your words, much more related to actions than words in fact." He continued. "In this sense love is built when things are built together. This is really beyond the word love as some people use it."

The Lovers, both together, reached over to my heart and pulled something out. They then replaced something else inside. "This restores balance to you" they said, "and thus to all your relationships." I thanked them all.

Later, 7pm. "I can hear you, can I see you?" I asked.

"Come into the cave," he said. Then Mithras spoke a warning, "Some people, they push and they push, they cannot help it. You must be aware of this. But to the matter at hand," at which he merged into me completely. "Mithras in the hands, eyes, ears and throat." I felt those words vibrate through each of those parts in turn. "This work is what really matters," he said. Suddenly I had a headache. Little wonder I suppose.

Saturday 22nd. 6.00am. Eight of Pentacles. A man is working hard at his tasks. He looks down and is not distracted by anything. He is a master of his craft, after years of study, and applies his skills fully and precisely. He knows that soon will come the rewards. Mithras then appeared and entered me. "Choose where you wish me to be, for focused benefit."

"Eyes please, to see the truth."

"It will be tiring," he replied, and moved to my eyes. I assume he meant tiring for me? I can adjust later, I thought.

Upon reaching home, realisations flooded into my mind. The Lens of Perception: the truth is obscured by one's own personal lens. This protects and distorts. Our task is to purify and clean that lens.

Later, 6.30pm. It was the end of the first day of an event that I had spent a long time planning and working for.

"You have done well," said Mithras, "all things considered."

"It does not much feel like it," I said, tired and deflated. It had been a satisfactory day, but little more than that.

"Well, you have. Whether you see it or not." I changed topic and asked about the similarities between Maitreya and Mithras. "There are some," he said "but a great deal of the Maitreya material is the product of one man's imagination. But enough of that, come tomorrow and protect the building again," he said "That is all."

Sunday 23rd. 7.00am. Queen of Cups. A woman kicked over some cups, spilling the contents. She was angry, emotionally unstable and in need of support.

I went to the Temple with the intention of providing a healing for someone who was overtired and stressed out. After completing the usual method I attempted to disband the energies, but they would not depart. They spoke together.

"We want to merge with you."

"Now?" I said the timing was not good from an Outer World perspective.

"Yes, now." Of course I did not refuse and allowed all the energies to merge into me, in turn, each powerful and distinct. I concluded with turning to face the Light source energy ahead. It filtered into me and permeated right through me, though it did so without moving or changing from its position straight ahead.

"Visit tomorrow for more" came a voice. Mithras then merged into my throat, eyes and ears. "You will be tired later," said the voice. I was tired now.

Later, 8pm. The contact was very vague and patchy. The day was over and I was so tired. Mithras spoke first.

"This event was a great success." I did not agree with this, but there was no room to argue. "You must stop talking about people as a mass. They are individuals, each one unique. They make individual decisions and some days they each have other things to do than to attend your events." I heard him. "It went well, and it is not something to give up lightly."

I could hear no more and returned home. I had recently chosen so many similar cards, and I felt that this had reflected a circular or even stagnant period in my life. I hoped this would soon come to an end. It felt increasingly as if the cards I were encountering in this Inner World then manifested themselves immediately in the Outer World. But in the Inner World it seemed more understandable, less contradictory and confusing than the final living material form they took on.

Monday 24th. 7.00am. Four of Pentacles. A man sits at his desk, with a pile of coins stacked up in a Perspex box in front of him.

"Why like this?" I asked.

"So I can see them," he replied. "So I know that I am secure."

"But why?"

"Because change is coming," he replied, looking intently at them.

"Isn't it always? And isn't this a bit tedious?" I was grouchy.

"Yes," he replied, but did not seem to care as he took out another Perspex box to fill up with another pile of coins. I came home.

Later, 6pm. I ascended directly into the Temple and having arranged everything correctly I contacted the Light.

"I am here to take an oath," I said.

"Your oath is to continue your work," said the Light.

"I thought I had already done that?"

"This is different, to continue the spreading of Light and Truth for the rest of your life." Did this oath speak about future lives as well? I was not entirely clear. The Light merged into me, but it felt different to before, so thus everything was now different to before. Changes in here always preceded changes out there. "You have done well," came the very unexpected words. I felt the session to be disjointed, but the notion of a shift within me was palpable. I thought that I might have been more emotional under the circumstances.

Tuesday 25th. Seven of Cups. "This is where all the illusions have fallen away," said Mithras. "Things are no longer as attractive as they seem. The truth is all that now remains. Choices must be made. Decisions must be taken." I was offered a single cup, whose contents could be mine, but I refused it. Mithras concluded, "I will be there when you need me, but you must be still and listen if you are to make the correct decisions."

Later, 5.15pm. Mithras was again immediately present. "You are undergoing a very negative learning process of what the Hermit and the Nine is all about. You are proving yourself unable to disconnect from things and people that do you no good, and therefore when the endings are made *for* you they will be all the more traumatic." Mithras was disturbed. As was I. Many people had found their way to me, but in many cases their need for help seemed never ending.

"I will disconnect, but slowly," I said. "I see the need for it now."

"Just continue with the daily routine again in the morning," said Mithras.

Wednesday 26th. 8.00am. Eight of Cups. This person was not clear except that they were caped in bright red and had vigour, and attitude. They were not going to stand for second best. They knew what was missing and they wanted that gap filled. The figure spoke. "It is my staff that enables me to find the strength I need". He passed me a replica of it and it fused into my spine.

"You have a busy day ahead," said Mithras, as the figure faded from view. "Take a large breakfast and work through methodically. Come again later."

Later, 7pm. It was a vague and inconsistent connection, as it always was after a hard day.

"The daily discipline must be followed. The oath has been taken." Mithras was firm.

Thursday 27th. 8.00am. Three of Cups. Three attractive girls appeared straight in front of me. Each one a different size and shape with differently colour of hair. They were joyously dancing around, with much fun and levity.

"We like you," said one, curling her hair through her fingers. Each one in turn connected with the positions of my second, third and fourth chakras. They danced and laughed and drank freely without cynicism or malice. It was an enjoyable scene and it made me smile.

"You have done well," said another one.

"What happens when you are reversed?" I asked.

"A greed for more," said the third one, her countenance changing. "More power, more sex, more joy, more love. The wheel of life forced ahead, imbalance between the three of us and you. Unfairness only follows. They each reconnected with my chakra points. "Come again," they said, "we like you." Mithras appeared, raising his hands, pleased and content.

"Back on track," he said "It is all to do with balance, and now it is time for you." He merged into me and we returned home.

Later, 6.30pm. At first I detected the presence of what I suspected to be a False Mithras. The energy seemed wrong, he seemed too forward and too aggressive. I dispelled him, moving past him to the right to find the real one. We sat on the log and talked. One of the things passed to me after Arthur's death was a rare old Tarot deck that contained eighty cards; the usual seventy-eight, plus a blank white card and a card of the Dragon. I asked Mithras what this was.

"I cannot answer this," he said "It is a matter for Hermes." At which he appeared, and I felt the strongest need to refer to him as Lord Hermes.

"You wish to know of the Dragon?" he asked.

"Yes, I think so," I hesitantly replied.

"Very well," and he was gone.

I felt that I had just embarked on a grave and serious undertaking and said as much to Mithras.

"Am I ready for it?" I asked.

"I hope so," he replied "Look for the Dragon as you go about your business. Read your books and prepare well."

I moved on to ask about the need, sense and appropriateness of taking over another's life. Arthur had intimated that this is what he had done for me, some fifteen years previously, during a time of crisis. "I had to step in and take over," he said at the time. I did not know the extent or duration of his influence.

"You must speak to Arthur about this," said Mithras. Straight away I rose astrally to meet him. My mother was in the same place as before but I moved forward to speak with Arthur.

"Can I do this, take over another's life, if they cannot manage for themselves?"

"No," he said firmly. "You neither have the control nor the power. You are gaining the power but you are a long way from control. Others will attempt to reel you in, to demand your immediate attentions. But this is not your path. Be careful when meaning well." I thanked him. "Goodnight," he said. It was Arthur alright.

I returned. Hermes was present and said that the daily discipline continued to be very important. "Lots are happening to you right now and the daily practice keeps you solid and able to handle it."

"What if I am tired?" I said.

"There are different kinds of tired," he replied. "It is important not to miss the practice, no matter what." With an enormously wearied sigh I thanked him and returned home.

Friday 28th. 7.00am Two of Cups. I had difficulty getting through at first, then almost at the point of giving up I caught a glimpse in the corner of my right eye of a man, and in the corner of my left eye, of a woman. They were holding onto each other, arms clasped hand to elbow. The scene changed to them making love. They needed each other and this was a wholly supportive act. One did not draw anything from the other until they had given. The connection and love between them seemed real and wholly reciprocal, exactly 50-50. They were balanced between each other, but also within themselves. As individuals they were clear and balanced, and thus could be the same with each other. That was it, I could see it - how relationships worked and how they did not. They had nothing to give me. Mithras confirmed this was good and I returned home.

Later, 5.30pm. Outer World matters pressed increasingly upon me. Financial matters were not good and some of my clients continued to be extremely needy, demanding much more of me than I was able to give. I felt it all to be an enormous restriction and diminution of my power and possibilities. Mithras confirmed the situation without me even having to ask.

"You are on the verge of throwing everything up in the air in a fit of frustration. But for what?" He was much more forceful and direct than usual. "You have created these situations, you have allowed them to be. Now you must disengage from that which pulls upon your energy. Begin with much less communication." I asked for more time to make my decisions. "The Temple is the only place for that" he said and we ascended, protecting the walls and calling everyone together. I pleaded for time to work things through. The assembled beings cautioned me against taking too long and that things could not be held forever. "March," said one voice. "February," said another. I requested that Outer World matters be held in statis for as long as possible while I gained some breathing space and tried to see the signs more clearly.

"This will not last long," said the voice of the Light as a fireball was propelled out of the top of the building. I thanked all those gathered and promised to "try to make the right decisions." I recognised how serious this was, both the situation and the magick. I could almost feel the fireball above the house. I did not have much time.

"What is the price for this?" I asked of the Light.

"You will pay the price," came the reply.

"How do I know if I want to pay it?" I replied.

"That is not your choice," said the Light sternly.

Saturday 29th. 7.00am. Seven of Swords. Mithras spoke. "Prudence would be to refuse a reading from someone you do not know. There is a need for care in all that you say and do. A cautious approach, for there are many knives to tip-toe around. That is all. Attend to your business and come again later."

Later, 1.00pm. "Rely only upon yourself," said Mithras. "Connections with all other humans should be minimal." He hugged me. "This is what happens when human, I remember it well. You need your own space and distance, it is essential for your sanity." He grasped my head and looked into my eyes, I could feel a surge through my whole head. "You are doing the right thing by distancing yourself from situations and people that drain you," he said. This was, after all, simply a suggestion to be The Hermit!

Sunday 30th. 8.00am. Strength. I had continued to work at my daily practice. It was raising and providing immense power that I could often actually feel running through me. I was starting to think though that maybe I had not been handling or using this power well. Was its sole purpose to make you feel better about yourself? No, there had to be a higher goal. Whatever power it might be possible to raise had to be directed as an enabler of the greater work, and the idea – so prominent throughout New Age thinking – that the way you feel is paramount now seemed to be so wrong. The difference of course, between feeling good about oneself and feeling able to tackle the greater work, is initially imperceptible. But the roads deviate considerably over time.

Arriving in the landscape I approached the Lion and the woman. A voice spoke.

"The Lion is the representative of the Animal Kingdom, and a suggestion of nature and the elements. In this case you have control over and mastery of it. Not subjugation mind, it still does its own thing but under your aegis." Mithras now spoke. "This is one interpretation."

The woman suggested I might ride the Lion and I tentatively agreed. We flew high into the sky and it roared loudly, trying to throw me loose. Back on the ground I dismounted and stroked the Lion. It roared and opened its mouth so wide that it could swallow me whole. I concentrated as much as I could in order to make this transition as painless as possible. I found that I could integrate, and then effectively swallow, the Lion. I energised it into a miniature version of me and it leaped out of my right hand, jumping off my palm and immediately returning to its full size. The woman seemed both surprised and pleased. "You have done well, I have nothing for you," she said.

Mithras now merged into me. "I will be with you all day, call me when you have need. First place me in the throat, then in the hands."

Later, 5pm. It had been a successful day. "See what can be achieved through the guidance," said Mithras. "It was still you teaching them, but under my guidance and direction. You did not think that it went well, but they did and I did. Well done, it worked. Now arrange a follow up course."

[OCTOBER 2012]

Monday 1st. 7.00am. Two of Swords. A woman held two swords aloft, points upwards, crossed in the middle. "Holding back the tide," she said. "Stalling the storm, giving peace and pause before trouble and strife." The size of the swords then reduced considerably, enough for her to press them into my chest. "To protect from malign influences," she said. I thanked her for that.

Mithras joined in. "Continue exactly as you now are. You are doing fine. Take a bike ride if time allows, continue and visit later."

Later, 6.30pm. I made contact with Mithras without going into the cave. He gave me instructions of how to help people in my appointments tomorrow. I asked about producing a Volume Two to Arthur's work. "You must get clearance from him," he said. "The world needs the teachings, but it is for him to say." I was very distracted and kept losing the contact.

Tuesday 2nd. 6.00am. The Fool. "Why do you never fall, Fool?" I asked, of his traditional pose on the mountain ledge.

"Because I have no fear. I know that whatever happens it will be a chance to learn. Whatever happens there will be another attempt, a second bite, another day. I will never run out of time." He threw me a ring of energy which went around my waist and then adjusted itself to fit perfectly. Mithras was on hand and confirmed all was well with this. I gave thanks and departed for home.

Later, 7.30pm. As I closed my eyes I saw three bright lights, which seemed to be looking back at me. They were in the shape of the triangle, two at the bottom for my eyes, one above in the third eye position. They connected together, a line of light running between each. This triangle shape then morphed into a pentagram, point upwards.

I asked Mithras of the wisdom of making contact with him without the benefit of being in the cave. "Contact through the cave is best," he said, "for now at least. We have discussed this before." I asked him about a recent wrong prediction that he had made about someone close. "But that wasn't me," he replied. I suddenly became aware, at the very back of my head, of another voice. It was quicker in pace that Mithras, and quicker to answer my questions. This voice was very definitely at the back of my awareness, it might even be described as being on my shoulder, whereas Mithras and all other Guides had been reached and always positioned themselves before me and very often to my right. So I had another input, but one that would not give me the gold that Mithras and the other Guides had done. It would be very dangerous to confuse the two. Ouch, I think I had been doing that! This realisation and thought process seemed to irritate and annoy the voice at the back of my head. I could actually feel pain there. At this point I caught sight of a figure on horseback riding away from me. I asked Mithras to confirm what was going on. He simply replied that, "you have done well. Return tomorrow." I could see his form in more detail this time, though still not distinctly. He spoke again. "Sometimes violet, sometimes white, sometimes left, sometimes right. But always forward and never back." What on earth was that? I knew nothing except that those were his precise words. He then merged into me from the right, powerfully, much bigger than before. He moved around my body freely and I offered no resistance.

It dawned on me afterwards that it was always me who moved toward Mithras (and all the Guides before him). It was never, that I could recall, them coming down to me. My Outer World activity was a constant battle with my monkey mind, the voice at the back of the head. I did not mind this, and to some extent, in the Outer World, it was at times an asset, enabling multi-tasking and tight schedule management. But in the Inner World it was an enemy. But as long as I moved forward to meet my Guide then all would be well.

Wednesday 3rd. 7.00am. Knight of Wands. Mithras appeared, dressed in purple robes, but this time there was also a cloud, without defined form, to his right. Mithras spoke about the card.

"All smoke, no fire. Fire that burns itself out quickly. Steam, noise. No background, no foundation, no inner strength, efforts not sustained." He pointed at the Knight, who also kept tripping up. Or was he pointing at me?

"Think of the multi-brain. Looking and moving forward is the nature of life. It is clear, your eyes are at the front of your head. The Dark Brain resides at the back of the head and pulls you backwards, linking to past memories and experiences. The goal is to move the whole being forward so that the Dark Brain may become part of the Light. The Dark Brain never goes away but it can be managed and controlled. More on this later, now go about your day." The Knight threw me a staff. "You will need this," he said and it merged into my right arm.

Later, 6.30pm. Again there were two energies, Mithras in violet again, and the cloud behind him and to the right. I did not know who or what this was.

"There are five sections to the brain," said Mithras. "The frontal area receives guidance, the two side lobes indicate the two paths of positive and negative – what is done with the guidance, if you like. The central inner area controls the functions of the being and the area at the back and the bottom is the Dark Brain, the home of the survival instinct. This Dark Brain wins when you are tired, not concentrating, delusional or even in a hurry. This is why the process of Inner Work and Life development cannot be rushed in any way. Development requires dedication and must be formulated as the very centre of the day and life, taken time over and reflected upon. Speed does not win here. There is work being done along these lines by others. Research it and return tomorrow."

This was remarkable and explained many things. If I were going to have a headache it would be at the back, in the Dark Brain area, whereas others that I know had more frequent headaches at the front in the Guidance Area. Does a headache signify an imbalance in that area? Whether it did or not, it was clear that the direction of life must always be forward. Arthur had said this years ago, he had no interest in the past, even yesterday held nothing for him. He was almost fundamentalist about this. I now understood why. The Dark Brain was therefore the 'voice at the back of the head, which could grow in influence at the expense of the development of the other brains.

Thursday 4th. 7.00am. The Tower. I walked into the scene and immediately found myself within the Tower. I heard the lightning strike overhead, the building shake and then the ceiling collapse.

"Run!" Cried a voice. But I wanted, needed, to stick around and see what happened. I allowed the building to collapse around me. Somehow, though I was anxious, I remained untouched. "You did not run!" Said the voice. "You walked into the Tower and willingly stayed while it collapsed. Just for a buzz, just to see what happened. You did nothing!" It was many voices now, as one. They spoke in amazement. Mithras appeared.

"This event is a matter of your own creation. The Tower can only be avoided by the voice of Spirit. But you are in conflict, the voice of Spirit versus your own voice. Now you must clear up the debris and it will take a great deal of time," he said, walking me through the rubble.

"So what do I do?"

"Resolve the dilemma. Maybe not today, but decision time is rapidly approaching. The decision to accept the guidance or not." I thanked the voices, including Mithras, and left. The need for a buzz was sometimes strong, I reflected. The voices had been right.

Later, 7.00pm. Mithras appeared, as did a darker figure, behind me. At the same time I saw Light in front of me. With my eyes at the front of my head I remembered, I am designed to go forward, not back, so the shadow cast by the

Light source at the front then resides at my back. Wherever I go he is always there, this shadow creature. I even bring him into the cave, even though Mithras is always in front of me.

Mithras held and comforted me. "The Dark Voice only catches you out when you rush or when you are tired."

"So how come you enter me sometimes, yet I have no awareness of your leaving, and then here you are again when I return?"

"I leave you in the night," he said.

"Can you now tell me about the Dragon?" I asked.

"No, not yet. You must master control of your own Inner Voices first. The Dark Voice never goes away. Outside of this place the fragments of the knowledge you gain here can be applied and built upon to enable to you to overcome its influence. But still, it never goes away. Only by daily practice and persistence can it be controlled."

"Can I teach others these things?" I asked.

"No, not yet, it is not advisable. The exercises and learning that you are doing are increasing your personal power but also that of the Dark Voice. It is for you now to overcome this." I thanked him and returned home, protecting the entrance with a pentagram. So, I bring the Dark Side in. No point looking for the enemy without. It seemed that the message could be boiled down thus, that progress, growth and moving forward was the number one way to overcome and control the Dark Side. Progress is a threat to the Dark Side, a threat to its life, for progress breaks old patterns, and the Dark Side loves patterns. Therefore it is supremely vital to keep learning, moving, changing and growing if one is to control the influence of the Dark Side. We may never destroy it totally but this way we may at least limit its influence and it impact. Progress moves forward. The Dark Side moves backward. Backwards is all things traditional, historical, from the past, from patterns. The past, as Arthur said many times, is of no value other than to learn from.

Friday 5th. 7.00am. Five of Swords. There was peace, indeed even silence, across a battlefield. It was dusk, after the fighting. There was nothing but defeat and loss, sorrow and regret. Mithras appeared.

"A friend in need. The Five is almost as bad as the Ten. But, times change and we must move with those times. That is all."

"But this card brings my anxieties into play," I said.

"Yes, the nature of life is to deal with letting go, and to help others to do the same. Enough now. Return and give those close by some attention."

Later, 4.00pm. I took a much more steady and deliberate entry route, via the seashore, the beach and the cave, exactly as detailed in the original text of Arthur's meditation. I thought to myself that the wise man is never afraid of going back and reviewing Level One material. I greeted a very clear image of Mithras, adorned in purple, arms outstretched to greet and comfort me. We sat down on the nearby log.

"Crowley," he began, "like all occultists, lost the plot. This happens because the work is so hard. The idea that humans lie at the peak of evolution and that Life cannot go higher is false. The struggle from amoeba to animal to child does not end at fully grown man. Within the human life it is perfectly possible to have divided priorities, but never forget that the work continues 24/7 and never, ever stops. This is very, very hard. Your higher and connected selves are perfectly capable of managing everything that is necessary, so long as it is in fact your higher and connected selves that are in charge."

Arthur had often warned me about this, referring to Crowley as "having lost it" but then once qualifying that with, "but he did discover another world." Similarly he spoke of A E Waite as a "stupendous egotist, like you would not believe. But none of this must happen to you," he warned.

Saturday 6th. 9.00am. Page of Wands. I took it slowly, surveyed the card image beforehand and only when I had deliberately looked at all the detail of the card did I enter it. I felt the card envelope me as I did.

"What are you doing?" I asked the boy.

"Projects to do, things to accomplish," he said. He was youthful, energetic, vibrant and positive. Reversed?

"Lazy, cannot be bothered. Efforts ill applied. Talking, not doing."

"But who are you?" I asked.

"You," he said. An image of sixteen empty squares then appeared before me, their rows and columns labelled.

	Pentacles	Cups	Swords	Wands
	Earth	Water	Air	Fire
Pages. Learning	…to be	…to feel	…to think	…to act
Knights. Acting.	Being	Feeling	Thinking	Acting
Queens. Directing.				
Kings. Directing.				

"These are sixteen ways for you to be. Reversals show that you are not controlling, directing or integrating the particular energy very well, or at all. Thus sixteen makes thirty two. Fill in the blanks for yourself."

"So is a court card always me?" I said.

"No, but it is today." I was struggling to hold concentration.

"See!" he said, referring to the fact that as a Page I was struggling to hold concentration. Concentration and focus being adult traits, not those of a child.

"Do you have anything for me?" I asked.

"The information!" He said. Mithras confirmed the correctness of it all and urged me to write as much down as I could remember and then to return. I reflected that I had always seen reversals as a failure to meet experiences, possibilities and energies either fully or properly. They were signs of us, ourselves, getting in the way of our experiences. Maybe also now ourselves getting in the way of ourselves, our Dark Brain winning over our Light Brain?

Later, 5.00pm. Prior to these evening journeys I had been increasingly using protection rituals, usually the Lesser Banishing Ritual of the Pentagram to protect my working space, so keen was I now to avoid the voice of the Dark Brain. On this occasion, once the ritual was complete I sat quietly before entering the cave. I could actually feel an energy leave me, and my whole mood lightened. After while I entered and saw Mithras decked in violet welcoming me. To his right, again, was the shadowy figure from before. Turning to him, I said,

"Are you my True Guide? If not then vanish!" It disappeared in a puff of smoke. I turned to Mithras and tested him. He smiled warmly and we embraced. I asked him about my ability to do this work, to fit this and everything else in.

"You can cope with all that you have to do, if you focus and discern. Do you really need satellite TV, do you really need to read all the newspapers? Promise nothing to anybody, keep loved ones happy, continue with the work, deal with whatever comes and all will be well, things will then unfold naturally. But you must keep moving forward, there is so much to do." I thanked Mithras, he had been on the point as usual.

Sunday 7th. 8.00am. Six of Swords. Again, I relaxed and took my time with this. I found myself on a boat. The sea was choppy though not viciously so. The Captain threw someone overboard but the sea continued to be turbulent.

"We are heading for a new life," he said, "Yet the unresolved still fights against us."

"How do you keep steady?" I asked.

"Hermes' Staff" came the reply, which I feel once again throb in my spine. Mithras was also present. "The Staff of Hermes keeps you steady. There are many things to be distracted by, led off towards, and the Staff keeps you steady – though not still! In the magickal world you must not lose yourself. That is all, short and sharp bursts are best. Come again later." And that was it. I thanked them both and returned.

Later, 7pm. Mithras spoke. "When you again gain access to your flat it is essential that you cleanse the space thoroughly. Much negativity has collected there. Wash the walls in salt water and produce the pentagrams. The quality of a protected space is completely different to an unprotected one." There was noise, one of the cats in the Outer World. I went to attend to him.

Returning. "See!" said Mithras. I could feel the difference between the two types of spaces. "An X-Cross with a connecting circle in the middle keeps everybody out. A pentagram keeps uninvited influences out, allowing only those that you have personally allowed," he continued. "Protect here also." He changed tack. "Learning continues in small pieces. Use the magick. The breath is powerful and creates a magnetic effect on people, but this should really only be used for the work. Others that you meet, even those that cause you trouble, are part of your learning so that future encounters may be handled with caution."

Monday 8th. 8.00am. The Empress. "You are loved," said the Empress, "rest in my arms. Life never gives up on you, there is always another chance." She offered me her protection. Mithras nodded his approval but called time and sent me home.

Later, 7pm. Both Mithras and I increased in size by many times and together directed our combined energies at the dark me that stood behind. Truth was big, lies were small. After some time at this we stopped and I asked Mithras if I were deferential enough to him?

"Well," he smiled. "I would rather you appreciate me through your deeds than mere words, but yes you could be a little less doubting and a little less hostile."

"Are there any others doing this work?" I said, my hostility unabated.

"You are the latest in the Hermetic Line," he said, as if it were a statement of obviousness, like 'here is a door.' "For these teachings it is not possible to meet another" Did this mean there was, or was not, another doing this business somewhere else in the world?

"You will not meet another," and then a pause. "There were never many of them anyway. Go now, rest, you are tired and you have a busy week and a hectic weekend. There will be no respite." Home. Thanks. I tried to mean it.

Arthur used to speak about how there were no others. When frustrated with him I used to ask where else I could experience this teachings, the implication being without me having to deal with him. His reply was always the same, "I do not know of anywhere."

Tuesday 9th. 8.00am. Justice. A powerful figure appeared before me, sword in right hand, scales in left. She was large in size and in presence.

"I dispense Justice. I am the balancing and correcting force in nature. I bless and reward (at which she knighted me on my left shoulder) and I punish (she ran her sword across my neck as if to chop off my head). Natural Justice is dispensed by me. Rough Justice is dispensed by man, when removed from the guidance. If my voice is heard through man then natural and correct justice is always dealt. If it is not heard by man – and it is mostly not heard by man – then I correct the rough justice later, through the means of Karma. This is the way that it is. I am the correcting force of the Universe. Do you understand?" I understood! "That is all, now go!" she cried. Mithras spoke. "Do as she says." I did not hesitate.

Later, 6.30pm. I visited the Astral to discuss matters with Arthur. He was waiting in his familiar clothes, with his familiar demeanour. I asked about my pending, discussed, negotiated, but not yet firmed up trip to the USA.

"Pah!" He exclaimed. "Shortcuts. What they want cannot be achieved in this way." My heart sank. I had been planning this for months. Having given myself a Tarot card reading on the matter earlier that day the cards had been shockingly bad.

"Why such bad cards?" I said.

"Because once the Dark Side is fed it draws in more food. Shortcuts are the cause of this." Shortcuts by me too, no doubt. The thought had been to cover the entirety of Arthur's work in a couple of weeks. A foolish idea in hindsight.

"How may I proceed then?"

"Step by step only, monthly courses." I thanked him and did not wish to detain him any longer. He gestured for me to speak to my mother, nearby.

"Hello," I said. She was surprised to see me.

"I've come to see you," I said.

"No you haven't, you've come to see him," she pointed at Arthur.

"Yes, because he helped me when you did not! But I am here now, to say that I love you and all is forgiven."

"Really?" She said, pleasantly surprised. I lingered for a while before continuing.

"But I must go now."

"Come again soon," she asked.

"I will try." I said, descending back to the Inner World landscape. I asked Mithras what he made of all this.

"Arthur is of course right, you or they cannot achieve the task in this way. Construct a 2013 Mentorship programme, enrolling a few people per month and then maybe have a visit in August if the course goes well. Think about the people you would be working with, one of them really is just another version of you, though lost."

"So I don't need to do a Year Ahead reading?" I asked.

"You do, but for completely different reasons."

I gave thanks, genuinely this time, for a bullet well dodged.

Wednesday 10th. 3.00pm. Queen of Pentacles. A woman was laying down on the ground. Unsupported, she was weak and poorly and could achieve little from this position. I offered her my hand. She accepted and I put her on my shoulders.

"This is what I need all the time," she said. "Can you do this all the time?" she continued. "Do you get it?

"Yes," I replied, thought it did not stop her. "Do you? Do you get it yet?" I put her down and turned to Mithras.

"Some people are all talk and no action, all take and very little give," he said. "With this reversed card the potential is bad, but nonetheless your actions can change it."

"Can they?" I doubted this.

"Your cards show you what will happen if you allow clattering trains to race on without applying any brakes. But it is you that lets this happen, or stops it." That was a disturbing thought.

Later, 4.30pm. Mithras merged into me and I became aware of his, and by extension now my, enormous power. It was both creative and destructive and must be applied and channelled.

"How may I work out specific predictions using numerology?" I asked.

"Take the current Universal year, then a notional year in time for the place in question, then take some well known local people and work out their cycles. Introduce some Tarot cards for a little novelty and you have any type of reading you wish for any current mundane situation. Be vague and general at first, and then adapt your method as time passes. See what happens."

"Should I do some Temple work for my upcoming events in the Midlands?" I was not even sure I should be asking this.

"If you are in any doubt then maybe you should not," he replied. After some vacillation I settled on a no, not wanting to draw needlessly from the pot. Nonetheless, at variance to me, Mithras still seemed quite content with everything.

Thursday 11th. 7.00am. Nine of Wands. A man was busily arranging his nine stakes in the ground and cleansing the enclosed area. I asked him what he was doing. "I know events are coming. I am getting straight and ready for them," he said.

"And reversed?"

"Events come from outside so I must clear inside. But reversed I cannot do this. I am distracted, I cannot be bothered, to be troubled with the trivialities of it all. When things from inside trouble me I cannot do what I need to do." He fused the nine stakes into one and passed it to me. It merged into me. Nine different things, nine in one. I turned to Mithras and asked him if I might be able to have a day off soon?

"Try to do what you can. Do not visit again today. Come again in the morning, and then again on Monday. Enjoy yourself."

Friday 12th. 7.00am. Six of Pentacles. A man was cheerfully juggling some coins. He spoke, while also concentrating on his juggling.

"Sharing success, spreading rewards, distributing gains. For common joy. That is it, that is all. You can go." He smiled. Mithras nodded along.

"I will try not to let you down," I said to him.

"I know," he said. "Anyway, you have taken the oath so you can't! Now relax for two days." I could not wait for the rest.

Tuesday 16th. 8.00pm. The Cave. I felt the Staff of Hermes depart from me as I entered. I called for Mithras and he approached on my right, with an unknown figure on my left.

"I can do no more for you now," said Mithras.

"Is this a good or bad thing, a sign of my progress or of my failure?" I was concerned.

"It is beyond good or bad. It just is. You have decided and now you must go forward," he gestured to a new figure and faded away rapidly. I demanded that he return. "You have made your mind up," he said. "There can be no more debate." I did not feel as if I had made my mind up about anything. This new figure was dressed in black and red, but I could not make out any features or details. It was maybe the dress of a Samurai Warrior? "The oath still stands," said Mithras, "but I can show you no more." The new figure spoke reassuringly that this development was correct, but that it was ever essential to deal with where you are and move forward from there. I was not happy about this and it greatly upset me, although the new figure did not seem either worrying or threatening. "Come back soon," he said. "We must get to know each other" I knew he was right, but returned home hurt and bruised.

Wednesday 17th. 7.00am. Ten of Pentacles. I entered through a stone doorway, draped with luxurious, rich curtains. There were hangings and soft rugs everywhere. I spoke with a man dressed in great finery, seated at a table.

"It took years," he said, "but money always comes from money and one always produces two." He gave me a pentacle for my heart, and one each for my hands, then pointed to the figure on my right.

"Mithras watches over you," said this new figure. "And I will look after you now." I tested for his connection and love, in the time honoured way. It was the energy of fatherly strength and protection. I asked for his hand. It was in a heavy black glove. I asked that he remove this so I could feel the contact more strongly. He agreed.

"All is not lost," he said. "But you must do as I say." I confirmed that I would. "Very well, go about your day now, there is much to do." I gave thanks and returned home trying to work out his name. E. Eni. Eli. Enki (no, not Enki I heard, strong and clear). "When you know me you will feel safer," he said.

Later, 3pm. The Cave. Mithras was present. I could feel access to the Staff again and I merged it into me.

"It is vital that you understand the reality of your power and its effects," said Mithras. I said that I knew I had failed to use my power correctly and that I was well aware now that it worked.

"Oh yes, it works," he said, "and imagine if you directed one half of it toward your work, the effects and results it might generate. I now pass you over formally to your new Guide and Leader."

He was oriental, maybe Chinese and I felt no connection at all. He then shifted into the shape of a woman, with long black hair. "E-ly. E-li," she said as she merged into me.

"The same rules apply" she started, "call me into your throat for this evening's talk. I am here to help and save you," she said. We made love and she merged into and out of my body. "You cannot please everyone, reduce your commitments," she said.

A While Later. Mithras was again present, as was the Staff.

"I want to energise this weekends event," I said.

"You have already done this," he replied.

"But now for the public, for the visitors."

"Ah, now that is more like it," he replied. "To the Temple." Staff in hand we ascended and I summoned the intelligences and energies in the usual manner.

"To create an environment of learning, development and positive growth," I commanded. The directive, in the form of an intense ball of energy landed at its location, literally shaking the building and surrounding streets. The Light summoned me and spoke.

"You must be careful. Deviousness and untruths attack you from every angle. You must stand firm. Must!" The warning was serious. I asked Mithras why he was still around.

"This is your Guide," he pointed to Eli, "but there is still much for me to say and observe."

CHAPTER XV

ELI

[OCTOBER 2012]

Thursday 18th. 7.00am. Seven of Cups. The seven goblets wasted no time in immediately merging together into one giant chalice, exactly as before. I asked the woman in the scene, also taking Eli's hand on my right. "What is the big illusion?"

"There is one illusion blocking your vision, in the form of all those who purport to help, but cannot."

Friday 19th. 11.30am. The Cave. Eli, as a young oriental women, appeared from within her Samurai armour and merged into me.

"You have done well, all you need now is focus. Visit me daily, continue your exercises and all will be well. There is always something to tackle but with focus and concentration – and no distractions – it will all be fine. You have done well." I had spent some time clearing away distractions, and completing things that were never really going to go anywhere.

"Will you merge into me for the weekend?" I asked.

"You visit me, I visit you, is there really any difference?" she said, "This place is the necessary point between us, but I will be wherever you call me."

Afterwards: The following two days were taken up with managing a particularly stressful event. It had not helped that I had seen a series of clients all with their own form of particularly challenging news. I did not help myself by having a drink or two and to top it off had contracted a bad cold. We had also received worrying news of one of the cats. It took me a further week to get myself back to feeling at all human, during which time I made no visits to the Cave, the Astral or the Temple.

Monday 29th. 7.00pm. The Cave. I was greeted by Eli, Mithras, Eduki and Hermes. They instructed me to attend the Temple, "for the next stage of the oaths." I was apprehensive, but bowed respectfully to the beings already assembled there. I approached the Light straight ahead and bowed again.

"Now is the next stage of your oath. This is the how and the when," said the voice. "You have to want this more than anything or anyone else."

I asked if I could pursue two goals in life. The voice replied. "You can pursue one thousand, but can you keep focus upon the only thing that really matters?" It paused, then continued. "Speak the oath. This is more important than anything else." I repeated those words and Light, pure and white, enormous and tiny, flooded my being. I convulsed. It was beyond an orgasm, beyond anything. My whole being, including my actual physical body, shivered and shook. White light filled my head. "Go forth now and speak the words. Spread the Light." And then the voice was gone and the Light receded. I returned to Eli, Mithras, Eduki and Hermes who seemed pleased, though yet again I was not. I was disorientated, shocked, surprised and almost in tears.

Tuesday 30th. 7.00pm. The Cave & The Astral. I entered first the Astral Vortex, intending to visit my girlfriend Hannah's mum. After the vertical rushing and buffeting I emerged into the white and saw her. She seemed surprised to see me.

"Hullo," she spoke in surprised, but familiar tones. "What am I doing here?"

"You are reviewing," I said, "getting ready to come back again." I replied.

"Oh, I'm not doing that," she said and turned away. At that she saw my mum (having only met once, briefly, in the Outer World) and they started talking. "There's a lot to review," I continued, "a lot to learn from." It was on deaf ears though, for neither of them seemed very interested in me. That was fair enough. I wished them farewell. Returning to the landscape I spoke with Eli.

"You see, even Death does not always part the veil," she said. How true. "Visit tomorrow," she called after me.

[NOVEMBER 2012]

Wednesday 7th. The Cave. My visit was disturbed by an extremely noisy flock of seagulls overhead, in the Outer World. The Outer World had been extremely hectic and I had still not fully recovered from my cold.

Eli looked the same as before. "You have bought the stress in with you," she said. At that the noise of seagulls faded and calm descended. "You must be strong at this time," she said "Use it to study, there is so much to do."

Friday 9th. The Cave. I was aware I had been slacking in my attendance and my practice, but events were fast paced in the Outer World and I could not keep up. I tried, on this visit, to breathe and take my time. At the boundary from the cave to the landscape I found the Staff and the crystal, where it had always been and I fused them both into me. These seemed important symbolic and energetic markers of a change of pace and responsibility in here. There was additionally a Hermit's cloak to one side. This was new. I put it on. It was concealing, protective and warm.

Eli, and it seemed Mithras, was present. "Tomorrow, don the cloak, take the Staff and crystal and allow me to merge into you. You have done just fine with your work for others. But your work for yourself is struggling. These are two separate, yet of course connected, things."

Sunday 11th. 7.00am. The Cave. I had a one day course to host in the Outer World, but arrived here with a clear frame of mind, as instructed. Again, birds were flying overhead, distracting me. I froze them. I collected the Staff and crystal and fused it into me. I saw Eli, she was tiny, the size of a blade of grass and I shrank down to her height. "See, you can do anything here," she said. "What you are trying to do is hard and big. You will transform and change lives but they will wobble. You, however, must be steadfast and unshakeable in your resolve, firm in the ground." My mind was wandering. "See this cloak," she said, pointing to the cloak of the Hermit. I put it on, again it was comforting and protective. It was also concealing and held my true form back from people. "Now me," she said. I welcomed her into me, and although small she filled my entire body. "Move me here," I felt her in my throat. "And allow me to talk. Move me here," I felt her in my hands, "and allow me to heal." My whole body was shaking and sizzling, cracking and jolting.

I returned home and got on with the course. It went enormously well, with one particularly astute and sensitive attendee remarking on the fact that she thought someone – she knew not who – was working through me.

Monday 12th. 8.00am. Seven of Pentacles. A man leans on his hoe, surveying the seeds and plants in his field. There were slim pickings. He had limited resources yet was dedicated to planning the best possible outcome. "Break it into three parts," he said to me. "Work out what you have. Then work out what you are going to do with it. Then do it. Do not get stuck at stage one, which will happen if you obsess about what you have not got. Deal with what you have – identify your resources and with careful planning and husbandry results will follow." He tossed me a pentacle and it merged into my chest. I appreciated his wisdom and kindness. Eli nodded her approval and said to visit again later. I said I would try to get back on track with my daily routine.

Tuesday 13th. 7.00pm. The Cave. I approached Eli, donning the cloak, fusing the Staff and crystal into me and allowed her merging. With this all complete I moved to my desk in the Outer World to begin automatic writing. I picked up the pen, bound my writing hand with an elastic band and waited. The received words were as follows:

"My name is Eli. I was born in Somalia, as you know it in 1832, of slaves. My presence is Nefesh – to be seen. It dwarfs other presences due to its size. Let me tell you what will arise on your Earth plane. There will be war and horror, pestilence and famine. You must protect yourselves as much as possible, learning new methods to protect and strengthen the four bodies. This is not as easy as it seems although I and others may help you."

"Will we survive this?" I asked, more than a little concerned.

"Who can say, it is bound to be difficult. And yes, bound is the word. You must free yourselves from the Devil in all his forms, his words, his deeds, his fictions and his illusions."

"But how many will die?" I said.

"Millions. It cannot be said precisely for you have within you the tools of your demise or salvation. You know this. Work hard, harder than ever to make them see what is the matter and how to solve it. Despair may accompany you on this great work…. now, know this…clockwise is significant because it regulates the natural order of things, they die and grow, move up and down. This is nature."

"Can I see you?"

"Close your eyes and you will receive a vision…but wait, Hermes comes."

The handwriting abruptly changed in the following section. The phrases became shorter and the lettering bolder and starker. Frankly the words written in black ink on the page looked terrifying.

"YOU ARE EVIL – YOU DO EVIL – STOP.

EMBRACE MY VISION + STEP TO THE LIGHT. GLORY LIES HERE, NOT IN EVIL. WEAKNESS, INSECURITY, FOLLOWING NOT LEADING - THESE ARE THE TOOLS + METHODS OF EVIL. YOU MUST SEE THIS BEFORE IT IS TOO LATE. IT IS MANY THINGS, THE PEOPLE WHO ATTACH TO YOU, MONEY, HOUSES, BUSINESS. ENOUGH IS ENOUGH. MORE IS TOO MUCH.

I SPEAK THROUGH THE AGES. IT IS DONE. GO NOW."

Another voice then came, or maybe it was the same, but it was softer, as was then my handwriting.

"You may take these words to mean whatever you wish but note that our teachings do not follow fashion or ease. They bring truth and that is all."

I will not pretend that either at the time of receipt, or the time of assembling these words for publication, did I feel anything other than desolation and misery at the events of this day. The intensity of it has not lessened in the years that followed. It is abhorrent to re-read it now, and it still takes me to the maximum of what my being is able to cope with without going mad. I include it here only for the sake of completeness.

Upon my return from receiving those words Eli advised me to consciously move the presence into the hand in question and allow it to be guided without intervention from the brain. "This is hard to do, but possible," she said. Ah, so I did it wrong I thought. I was pleased at this newly presented get out clause. "Hermes' language is harsh," she continued, "but direct and truthful. You would be wise to reflect upon it." Dammit! I had to accept the words as given. "Build it and they will come," she said, referring to The Hermitage.

Thursday 15th. 7.00pm. The Cave. Eli indicated the presence of Hermes, which I checked and confirmed for myself. His message was clear. I had two responsibilities – to the Inner and the Outer Worlds - the managing and balancing of both would lead to much progress and further opportunities.

"It is important to experience further learning now – this is available whether you have matters balanced or not." I did not really understand and just felt extraordinarily dizzy and wobbly.

Friday 16th. 5.00pm. The Cave. Donning the Hermit cloak and adopting the Staff and crystal, my brain started to throb.

"There is a further oath to perform – another day," said Eli, as she merged into me. She repeated her instructions from a previous visit. "Move me here (throat) to speak, here (ears) to hear, here (hands) to write, here (eyes) to see. Do this for a maximum of two hours. Start now." I began the exercises exactly as she instructed and could feel the sensation as I moved her into each area. I continued this for as long as I could. It did not seem that I had done very much but when

I opened my opened my eyes I saw that it had been forty-five minutes. I was exhausted.

Saturday 17th. The Cave & The Astral. I visited immediately a friend to whom I had taught some techniques the night before. She had complained of violent tooth ache directly after leaving me. I focused a healing power toward her. Returning to the landscape I assumed the cloak, the Staff and the crystal. Eli spoke.

"Too much too soon. A lesson for both of you," referring to the night before. "Sturdy platforms of self knowledge are the only protection against things like this. They take a long time to put into place though. You are impatient for yourself, and for your pupils, but they can only learn what they are ready for. A useful lesson for you both though." She merged into me as before. "Call for me when needed," she said.

Tuesday 20th. 2.30pm. The Cave & The Astral. In the astral Arthur was immediately present, to my left. He gestured to my right. There was my mum, and Hannah's mum, Linda. My mum turned away from me, but Linda spoke.

"Hullo love, we are just discussing what being mum is all about, or trying to." She seemed quite perky but the connection trailed off there.

I turned back to Arthur and asked him what I should write in the prospectus for joining The Hermitage. "The Hermitage Creed," he said. "That is all. Feel free to make the rest of it your own, but those words explain it all." I admitted to him that I would not have thought of that by myself. "Well that is what I am for," he said. I thanked him and returned home.

Later. Eli congratulated me on my recent realisations and steps toward disengaging from the demands of the Outer World, but warned me that it must be done "authentically to your Karma, you must have no trace on your Karma." I turned to a practical matter regarding one of my pupils. She had worked hard to move forward, but bad decisions in her past looked like hampering her progress. Eli referred me to the Temple. I assumed the regalia and ascended, summoned the energies and intelligences, protecting and bowing to the Light.

"There is nothing we can do," said the assembled energies. I appealed directly to the Light.

"Maybe," came the reply, "but this isn't how it works. Yours is a request from an interferer and a worrier. Your concerns for her are no basis to intervene."

Back on the ground Eli confirmed the accuracy of all this and said that she herself did not know the answer. "Go rest now," she said.

Thursday 22nd. 5.00pm. The Cave. The usual arrangement with the cloak, Staff and crystal. I spoke to Eli, she seemed happy.

"You have gained some distance from other people's demands and successfully created some breathing space, but the good work is easily undone. Once people find you, you can never be entirely free of them ever again, and that is maybe no bad thing, so all things must be done in balance. Do not forget that you are The Hermit, and he is always concealed."

A recurring pupil had gotten back in touch to request help with a job application. Eli said that kind of thing was a matter for the Temple. Once inside I gave the straight instruction that she be given the job at her upcoming interview, but I was strongly warned off this action. I wondered whether I should have consulted The Keeper on the matter first? I composed myself and rephrased "I call for energy, enthusiasm, eagerness and positivity for her attempts to find work." Maybe this would do the trick, just giving her a following wind rather than a shove? The Eight Kings talked among themselves then signalled their agreement. We raised the power, I repeated the command and the Light co-operated, the fireball travelling to the person's body.

Suddenly I felt tired and drained. I took that as a sign that it had worked successfully and I disbanded the Temple. "Come again soon," said Eli as I thanked her for her guidance and support.

Saturday 24th. 4.00pm. The Cave. I had not intended to visit but after the third round of exercises that day I felt that I ought to. Entry was immediate. Eli beckoned me forwards toward her and Hermes.

"Get your cloak and follow me," said Hermes. I had already absorbed the Staff and crystal. We ascended to the Temple. Hermes moved to my right side and told me to invoke the eight energies.

"I call the energies invested in me to appear." They immediately did. Hermes moved to the left hand side of the Light source.

"What do you desire?" said the Light.

"The knowledge to know what must be done, and the strength to do it. Whether this means to bring something toward or move something away from me."

There was a pause. "You already have this," came the voice. Hermes turned toward the Light and something passed between them.

"The strength of knowledge and the will to action," I said, trying to demonstrate some clarity. There was a further pause.

"Very well," came the reply. Hermes merged into me, intensely. My whole being shook and it seemed like I might explode. He was back.

"I am your Guide again now," he said. "Return to the Outer World with me to get re-accustomed to it." I disbanded the energies and returned home. I said thank you and goodbye to Eli. She had been a great help, but I was getting another chance with Hermes. This cannot be a common thing.

Afterwards: It was around this time that matters in the Outer World became even more intense and challenging. I was guilty of using Tarot and Numerology as short cuts in my personal and business dealings, and although these insights were unfailingly accurate there always seemed to be a sting in the tail, somewhere, some time later. I had misread the guidance of the Inner World, harbouring a hidden desire to consider this work complete and to be free to enjoy the fruits of my labours. I now saw the errors I had made but it would take many months to make things right again. I had also failed to notice that this was guide number

15, and the 15th card of the tarot is the devil. I only realised the significance of this much later.

CHAPTER XVI

HERMES RETURNS

[NOVEMBER 2012]

Sunday 25th. 9.00am. The Cave. Hermes was back, as if he had never been away. "You are not doing the work, you are too easily distracted. The distractions are sent to you only in order that you may lighten the load, but you let them take over and the work slips back. You must do both." He was not at all pleased. "Come again later on tomorrow but you must do both."

The entries in my diary are then blank for a further seven days. I evidently did not do both!

[DECEMBER 2012]

Saturday 1st. 2.00pm. The Planet Mercury. Via the Vortex Elevator, with a tremendous amount of noise and vibration, I approached the planet. It was covered in shades of yellow, orange and red, but like none that I had seen on a screen or in a book. As I got closer I saw rivers of molten rock, huge and fast flowing. Even the mountains seemed to move as the rivers wound their way on. Nothing seemed solid.

Mercury (c) NASA

"You should not be here!" Came a voice.

"I beg to learn about Hermes," I asked.

"This is not the place for him."

"Are not Mercury and Hermes one and the same?"

"No. It seems he is teaching you what he *is* by what he *is not*," came the voice.

"So who are you?" I asked.

"We live here."

"The people?"

"Not people. Life!" The voice was getting more insistent each time.

"How do I know you are telling the truth?" I asked.

"You don't. You had better ask him." I moved away from the planet and merged with Hermes who had now appeared nearby. "There has been confusion. I am not Mercury, those correspondences are wrong." But he didn't seem angry at my visit to the planet, which was a bonus.

I had a healing patient the next day. "Place my hand upon her and she will follow you forever," he said. I did not like the sound of that. I did not want a stalker. "If you do exactly as I say there will be no trouble," he held his hand out. "Place your hand in mine. Repeat this process with your client." By now I was very tired and disorientated. His words lingered as I left. "You need nothing more now but to get on with your work. Build it and they will come."

Thursday 6th. 7.00pm. The Cave. I again felt the urge to address Hermes as Lord Hermes. But he refused and said there was no need for that. I asked about my clients, friends and followers, the number of which now was considerable.

"They all love you, they are attracted to the Light. But the greater the light the greater the dark - always." He refused to say any more on the matter. I changed tack and asked about the Qabalah.

"This is a Tree, a diagram of life, of the world. Suffice to say that much that has been written about the Tree is inaccurate. The Inner World – this place – is the place of fundamentals, of the roots of the tree, and that is the place to start to understand Life. The Inner World and The Tree are connected, they overlap, but not fully." I asked then about the popular New Age concept of Mercury Retrograde.

"Same thing," he said. "It is too complex, needlessly so, and the truth of it has been lost."

"The root chakra?"

"In the root of your spine – he pointed exactly where – its tendrils move out down the legs to the feet." I said I had sight of another attribution, with the root chakra in the feet. "No, this is wrong. The arms are connected to the heart, the throat and the head. The legs are connected to the root. Never forget, with all aspects of the body, use it or lose it." I was trying to remember all this with total accuracy. "The wheel has started to turn, come again very soon," he concluded.

Wednesday 12th. 7.00pm. The Cave. Hermes and a number of other unidentified beings were present.

"These are past and future Guides, other intelligences," he said. I asked of the wisdom of performing readings for self, with the Tarot or any other device. He directed me to a Merlin-esque figure standing nearby.

"Why should I not read for myself?" I asked him, trying to find a way to answer a difficult Outer World question.

"You should, but you already know the answer. Use a different spread, like Arthur's Acceptance." I queried Arthur's particular card sequence, his attribution of cards to numbers. It did not make total sense to me.

"It works. Nothing more. Nothing less," was the reply.

"And what about my Card for the Day?"

"Focus has a lot to do with this," he said. "Your mind is all over the place, neither concentrated nor focused. Sit down to draw the card and take your time over it. Do not do it immediately upon rising, clear your mind first and then ask the question – What Does Today Require From Me?" Very clear answers. Eli was one of the assembled beings who I did recognise and we embraced. I said to Hermes I was done.

"Good. Then go. Learn, learn, learn!" he said "So much to do, and no distractions!"

Saturday 15th. 4.00pm. The Astral. Arthur was exactly where I had last left him.

"You see now how hard it is?" he said, "The people, they will never leave you alone. But this has it compensations, and some of them could be great assets to the world, if taught right. Take care of them and show them the way."

"Thank you for everything," I said.

"But there will be no more books, nothing more about me," he was insistent. That was fair enough. I wished him goodbye.

I turned to Linda, Hannah's mum. "Where are we, why are we here?" she asked me.

"You are waiting for an opportunity…to learn." I chose my words carefully.

"Well that's not too bad I suppose. I like learning," she said. I told her that we had inherited custody of her cat.

"Does he follow you around? He likes a bit of fuss. He used to follow me around, give him some fuss," she said. I turned to talk to my mum, but she was less receptive.

"How come you are here and no-one else is?" she said.

"This is what I have been doing all these years," I said. "I will try to come again."

I descended down to the usual landscape where I saw Eli and Hermes. I was asked to ride on Hermes back. We flew up and up, way out into space, overlooking Planet Earth.

"Not much going on, is there?" he said.

"There is in comparison to other lumps of rock," I said, disagreeing with him. Hermes adjusted the filters to my eyes, moving my perception to a different set of wavelengths. On my first look through these new eyes the Planet Earth was covered in darkness, save for a few, sparse points of Light. We travelled around the Planet, marking where they were, these signs of people doing positive deeds. The Light areas were distributed a little in Denmark, Holland, Northern Europe, some in the UK, the East and West coasts of the USA (but very few in between). Isolated parts of Japan and Eastern China. There was one beacon in Australia, nothing in the greater part of Africa, nor Russia, India or any of the Middle East. There were scattered points of light in South Africa and there may have been others, but overall it was a very different image to the usual one of Earth.

I asked about running another mentorship programme for one particular interested party.

"Yes. But follow the book. Structure the work. She will need a notebook and pen, and a timetable covering three months. Give this all to her at the start. There will then be others. That is what the book is for. You are available to do this work now because you have freed yourself from the cycle of demands – so do not embark on another cycle. Satisfying the cries of those that you meet is not the same as teaching them."

Thursday 20th. The Cave. I set myself up for another session of automatic writing, this time bringing Hermes directly into me and then very deliberately into my hands. I hoped the results were not as extreme as before.

"Who are you?" I asked. "An ancient God." But what is your purpose? "To teach." To teach who? "Those who wish to know." To know what? "Truth. Life. Growth." How can they do this? "Through you. And others." Is there a lineage? "Yes. Arthur, then you, via me." What can you teach us? "Health. Happiness. Wealth. Knowledge. Through the interlinking threads of life." How shall I know you? "Through my Mark." He drew a very specific spiral shape. Are there others, apart from me? "Not yet." Were there others, before me? "Yes over the years, through the ages." How may I call others to me? "By using my Mark. All seekers recognise it. Research me and the stories of my life for background." Are you also Thoth? "I am Thoth. He is me, I am him. We are refractions of the same. Through time immemorial men have sought the answers to questions, any questions which they felt would strengthen them. Occasionally I had influence but most men's desires were for more outside of themselves, while most women's desires were for more inside of themselves. This has now changed and all now seek a greater Inner World. This is my time. I can show them this, with your help and cooperation a richer Inner Architecture can be discovered." Can I tell people these words? "With care. Distort or dilute not. Truth all or none. Be warned though that as the Light shines so the darkness grows all around. Care is needed. That is all. Research my story and learn from me."

Tuesday 25th. 9.10am. The Cave. Hermes and Eli were waiting. Hermes withdrew slightly. I asked how I might develop a good heart and a good mind. Hermes stepped forward.

"It is not a *good* mind or heart that you seek, but a clear one – devoid of any wants. When you want nothing you will receive all that you need. Wants – of any kind – create impressions in the Akasha for which there must be corresponding effects and thus a price. Free yourself of all wants and you will gain everything. This is the most difficult lesson of all and you will be one year working upon it. But that is fine, you are doing better than most. Continue as is." I turned to thank Eli with her help with the traditional Christmas Day stresses. "Detach," she said "Detach."

I felt the presence of Arthur, "Freeing yourself of these wants makes you a better vessel for the guidance from Hermes. You need acceptance, not desire."

Monday 31st. 9.30am. The Cave & The Astral. Entering the cave I felt called to the Astral. I approached the Vortex Elevator and rose up. Arthur was present, dressed familiarly.

"What can I do for you?" he asked.

"I just felt I needed to come and see you," I said.

"You must have a question," he said. I thought for a moment

"How do I control my Dark Side?"

"By letting it off the hook for short periods, and then getting it back on the leash again."

"Like taking a dog for a walk?"

"More like a wild animal!" he said, "Let us call it a Dragon."

"So that is what the Dragon is all about?" I said.

"Yes, it is the Dark Side made real and powerful. Be very careful," he said. I remembered that he had remarked something similar about the Dragon the first time I saw his rare Tarot cards. "Visit your mum," he said, changing tack completely.

I turned to speak to Hannah's mum Linda, and mine. Linda enquired about Hannah's sister. I said to my mum "Look, life is for learning, this is how you wipe clean all the sorrows, mistakes, sadness, emptiness and anger of the past." She did not react either way, maybe this was a good sign, maybe not. I felt somewhat awkward giving lectures such as this to my own mother, especially as I was less than a perfect example myself. It will take her a long time to adjust, I thought.

It was time to go, I wished them well and waved goodbye to Arthur. He raised both his hands victoriously as he had done many times in the Outer World. I returned back to the Cave and into the landscape, calling for Hermes.

"How may I be a better student?" I asked.

"Time. An investment of time is the only way. Everyday, no exceptions. Get up early, go to bed late. Time in brings results out. There is no other way."

"How may I become a good mentor?"

"You have all you need, you just need to give it time. Time to prepare, time to review, time to follow the work. That is all. You need some pupils now, to develop them further, then you can move to the next stage within the Temple." I asked of the Emerald Tablets. "These will be revealed to you. In time." Time. It is always a matter of time.

[JANUARY 2013]

Tuesday 1st. 11.00am. The Cave. "It is time to perform a new Year Ahead, Single Aspect Tarot reading for yourself. The old reading – though not out of time – has been wiped and a new course set, triggering new influences and new guidance. Compromise is the key in all your human relationships now, no-one you know can handle the unvarnished truth. Compromise is the word. Visit again tomorrow." Hermes had spoken. I did as instructed.

Thursday 3rd. 5.00pm. The Cave. This was two days later. I had not done as instructed.

"Do you prostrate yourself before me?" Hermes asked. I thought this was a strange thing to say, and I answered glibly. "I suppose so, given your experience." I am sure he saw this answer for the lame attempt it was. He continued. "Today I shall instruct you in movement." He began flitting and flicking backwards and forward, left and right. "Where am I? He asked, but without waiting for my answer he told me. "There. Here. There. It is all to do with speed. I am effectively in two places at once due to the speed at which I move. You are unable to discern that frequency and thus unable to discern the separation. So it is similar with you. A concentrated effort by you sees all your four bodies in one place and time, drawn in together. This produces real weight and concentration when you can bring all four to bear on the same matter, issue, problem, person or time. In this sense physical proximity makes more things possible." He went on. "You can also address different types of things at once. For example, thinking, feeling and recalling something can all be done independently. Hearing or smelling something recalls the place and time that you last heard or smelt that and then one of the bodies can move straight back there to sense the environment and situation as it was. This happens involuntarily most of the time, but make no mistake that such actions place you there. Thus you can effectively be in four different places at once, moving around in the fifth element while doing this." I brought my four roads – one, three, five and eleven – into me consciously and felt a new kind of resonance as I did it. "That is all. Visit tomorrow before your journey."

Friday 4th. 5.00pm. The Cave. This was the evening time, and I had again not done as instructed. I was greeted by a tall, foreboding figure, immediately on my right.

"What will you instruct me in today?" I asked.

"There will be no lesson today, or tomorrow, or the day after. You have made a mistake, taken a wrong turn." This cannot be correct, I thought.

"You are not Hermes. I reject you and consign you away from here." I then called for Hermes, who appeared in front of me. "How do I know who is real? How do I stop this from happening?" I said, confused and disturbed.

"My tone is different, my words are different. Your practice will bring clarity and the problem will disappear, but even so, there is no lesson today. We begin again whenever you are ready. It will soon be time to revisit the Temple, but you have done well with your first mentoring. She has read many books, but they are all lacking and do not say the things she really needs to hear. You are the only one that can do this." That seemed encouraging at least! "Come again tomorrow, and the day after, and the day after that, and the day after that. Instruction takes place every minute of every day, in here, out there, there is no division."

Sunday 6th. 10.00am. The Cave & The Library. The Library was some way off in the distance but on reaching it The Keeper welcomed me, much more warmly than in times past. "What do you require?" he said.

"I have a pupil. I need to consult about her." I said her name.

"Do you have any others?"

"Yes, but not today, I need to tackle them step by step."

"A good idea," he replied. A book appeared on a lectern in front of me. It was a thin volume. "She has learned little, she has seen very little point in it. Yet she has the mind to do so. She deserves the knowledge, yet does not. Yes, learning is the whole point of Life! It is not success, which is a proxy for self esteem. It is not love, which is an escape. It is not even happiness, which is a short cut. It is learning and growth, learning to do more, to know more, to be more. All the things we need are granted to us – after we have learned. Learning is the magick! Learning whatever interests you, but also learning about self, which may not interest you. Many see no point in this. They are however mistaken." I was not totally certain whether the words came to me from the book or from The Keeper himself. But it was The Keeper who then spoke.

"Teach her an adaptation of the Middle Pillar Exercise to establish a daily routine. Get her to do the card for the day. Then visit here again." I thanked him, this was most specific and helpful.

"One more thing," he said.

"What?"

"Be careful. Be careful of those who purport to help." I bowed in thanks. I left freely and was not ejected from the place as I had been many times before. Home to rest.

Tuesday 8th. 8.00pm. The Cave. "You need to pay a visit to a friend to heal her. She cannot get better without you. If you are sensible with your own energy, sleep, and wash thoroughly then you will be fine. But you must do it." That was all that Hermes said. I arranged to do as he instructed.

Thursday 10th. 6.00pm. The Cave. There was a figure to my right, with Hermes straight ahead. I banished the unknown figure leaving Hermes standing square onto me. "Hello child," he said. This provided some comfort. I asked again about my ill friend.

"She cannot survive without your help. But you are too hard on her. I see that the whole situation annoys you, but you have to learn to be more sensitive, slower and more gentle with people." I was going to struggle with that. After months of intense activity, practice and visits to the Inner World it had gotten no easier, and if anything harder. The demands made upon me by virtually all the people I encountered in the Outer World were not beyond what I was able to do, but they were pushing at the edges of what I wanted to do. I remembered speaking with Arthur many years ago, about how and when to help people. I had remarked at the time that the 'the real obstacle was that I wasn't actually interested in helping people'. I accepted that was not very good of me, but it was my honest assessment at the time. I had expected criticism, or encouragement from him, instead he simply said, "Well I know that!" I did not press it further with him at the time, and maybe I had not changed. I still believed that primarily people needed to sort themselves out. I appreciated that this was often not what happened in practice, but I thought that it should. After all, I had. Hadn't I?

Friday 11th. 10.30am. The Cave. "Speak to this being," said Hermes, pointing me toward a beetle, waiting on the ground.

"What do you want to know?" it said.

I asked about a new client, a retired gentleman.

"A child. Emotional. Be the balance for him, be the voice of reason. That is all you can do."

I asked of another, a housewife in France.

"You can protect yourself!"

And another, an old client from 10 years ago for whom life, via my advice, seemed to have done little.

"Ah, I cannot answer that," said the beetle. Hermes appeared again. "There is nothing more you can do with her. It has gone on too long. Show her the meaning of her Karmic Debt, but unless and until she changes her name no results or progress will be made." I turned back to the beetle.

"Scarab! If you don't mind," it said, brusquely.

"What do you represent?" I asked.

"Truth," came the reply, as it shot off into the grass. I belatedly decided to give chase but to no avail. I could not catch it and each time I thought I had it underfoot it wriggled out again. "You can never know the whole truth," it said before scurrying off again. I gave up the chase. At which point it suddenly reappeared. It moved on top of my head and then merged into me.

Monday 14th. 2.00pm. The Cave. Immediately to Hermes with a list of questions.

"I and the Scarab will answer these, then return later in the day for your own instruction."

I asked about a family I had recently encountered – a single mother with one autistic boy and no other children.

"Damaged by his parents and their behaviour, their relationship. He needs a strong male figure, not a weak man or even a strong woman. Boys need men. There are too many women in his life." I asked of another pupil. "Good progress. Increase the frequency of the work now. Numbers next, then the Guide work." Another pupil, this time one from a great distance away who I only communicated infrequently with via email. Hermes laughed. "No. Point out to her that her questions would be better if they focused on what can be done to make it better, not asking if it will be better. She must learn, everyone must. Help her with her name and numerology, but be very clear with her about what is and is not happening." One more pupil.

"Teach him the 'I am...' practice, to help him to deal with his emotions. In spite of the fact that he feels he has nothing to learn try to teach him to stop making decisions during emotional times." And finally, I asked about a financial investment possibility. His tone abruptly changed. "No. You have a method, which you may follow if you wish, but do not call upon me again for help with this matter. I will not assist you with this."

Later, 7.00pm. I was very tired, but I could feel something behind me, almost pushing me into the Cave and through to the landscape.

"Teach me, Hermes, your ways." I said.

"Emergence Volume One." He said. "It is time to write of the spiritual import of earthly matters, and the earthly import of spiritual matters. As these present to you daily you will be guided to the answers. Plain speaking will be the key here. Begin now."

Monday 21st. Using Arthur's Rare Tarot. I was keen to avoid getting into further difficult client relationships, with people who claimed to learn but actually did not want to. I therefore asked about a number of them in short succession, one card per person. For a someone who had presented themselves at a recent talk I received the un-deciphered Blank Card. Did this signify nothing, a waste of time, or the possibility of a blank slate ready for new impressions and new learning? I did not know.

Later, 6.30pm. The Cave. I greeted Hermes. It felt good to be back after a long absence. Everything felt better and made more sense when I was here. So why did I not visit more often? In truth it was because I still didn't quite believe it all. Even though I had spent my adult life searching, testing, exploring these matters I still didn't really believe that I had found them. Although I had never felt part of the human race, and always felt there was something else going on, something else to discover I could not really accept that I had actually discovered it. I could not really believe or accept that I had been fortunate enough to meet and stick with Arthur, or that I had been lucky enough to explore and work with these amazing beings. Others would have been over the Moon about it. I barely believed it.

"How do I know that it is you?" I asked Hermes. The power of his presence was so intense that my words contradicted the evidence right there before me.

"If you are in doubt then it cannot be me," he said cryptically.

"But how do I tell whether it is real or imagined?"

"Regular daily visits. The more you are here the stronger the voice and the clearer the guidance." He had said all this before.

"But I don't want to constantly trouble you."

"Me or one of my minions," he said, gesturing to The High Priestess. She was a blue/silver energy, feminine and strong, sat at a table.

"You have a question?" she said.

"Are we on the brink of World War Three?" She handed me the Tower card. I related this to the events of 9/11. She nodded her head.

"World War Three started on 9/11. It has passed through various phases, is now escalating further, and will continue to do so. All countries are involved."

"So how it will escalate further?"

"That is enough. Next question." I asked about the blank tarot card from Arthur's deck. "The future is there for you to write, but be careful, for this does not free you from the law of consequence. That is all for today." I bowed respectfully and thanked her, turning back to Hermes.

"Visit daily now," he said "I have begun to teach you in earnest, but you must do the work." Always there was more to do.

Tuesday 22nd. 8.00pm. The Cave. I identified Hermes by using his mark. I asked about the advance of 3D printing and the interesting possibilities this threw up.

"But are you the man for the job?" he said, then answering his own question, "you have not the patience!"

"But can I learn it?"

"This is but one part of The Emergence. Now, follow the Scarab." The creature scurried off into the undergrowth and I pursued it. It led me all the way up the Temple and then stopped. I entered this Theatre of Possibilities. Voices spoke.

"We approve. The idea is interesting and has possibilities. You should pursue it. It is a vehicle of practical magick, wherein you may develop all the skills you have so far gained. It feeds all your needs and enables you to use your talents in the outside world. Permission has been granted for you to investigate. Go to it, return tomorrow."

Wednesday 23rd. 8.00pm. The Cave. "You need to review your progress so far, go back through this diary. You cannot do or have everything so you must discern and choose the best way forward from all your options. The selection of one thing must always mean the abandonment of something else." That was the voice of Hermes.

Thursday 24th. The Astral. I entered the cave and, although I had not intended it, felt a pull toward the Vortex Elevator. As I moved toward it I felt the presence of a being in the Outer World throw up their hands in despair. I thought that it must be Hermes, but what would he be doing that for? I pressed on and rose up in the column.

I saw Linda and my mum sitting together looking at some kind of knitting pattern or embroidery. "Hullo dear," said Linda, "I'm just showing your mum how this works." My mum refused to look up or to acknowledge me.

"We will just have to go around again then," I said to her. Then to Linda, "Your daughters are both well but miss you."

"I know," she said "I miss them too."

My next recollection was of being with Arthur. He sat with a big broad smile, seemingly pleased to see me.

"Congratulations," he said "A fine figure," he continued. "You see, no one is really all good or all bad," he said. I noticed how large and solid he still seemed.

"Are you coming back yet?" I asked.

"Not yet," he smiled. "Will you be attending Ilkley (Bi-annual Complementary Medicine Festival)?" I told him that it was poorly attended these days. He shrugged. "Well, as long as you are getting yourself out there?" I confirmed that

I was. "Great!" he said. Then it was time to go, he wished me a merry and hearty goodbye with the words, "Enjoy yourself!"

The Cave. To Hermes. I noticed that Arthur was much warmer now that he was no longer alive, no longer my actual teacher. Hermes now filled that role, and he was supportive, but less warm. Maybe the teacher has to maintain a certain distance?

"Today's lesson," said Hermes, "is speed. Speed is relative, because no one can move slower or faster than they are ready for."

"How do we speed up?" I asked. I had confronted Arthur with this question many times before, if we are not ready how can we make ourselves ready?

"By learning," he said. "Learning increases speed. Not learning decreases speed, sometimes to a standstill. The key to speed is learning. Reflect upon this, enjoy yourself and return."

Realisations: The key to a successful life seems to be education – by which I mean discovery, error and experience rather than propaganda, certificates or letters after your name.

Sunday 27th. 4.30pm. The Astral. The Cave. I could feel a very strong force behind me, pushing me into the Cave. I hesitated but submitted. I turned then to the Vortex Elevator. I rose high, and higher still to what I could only term The Higher Astral. Stepping out the scene was even less visible, less tangible, more ethereal. I could speak with Arthur here, but I definitely could not see him.

"You must make sure," he said, "that all the things you do 'up here' relate to things you are doing 'down there'. As there is a connecting fine cord between the Astral and the Physical so there must be a relationship between the higher teachings and the reality of how people actually live and go about their daily business. This is so important." He seemed happy with things and said it was time for me to go now. I suddenly felt very heavy and lowered myself down to the Lower Astral, where I could operate with a little less strain. I again saw Linda and my mum. She asked if I saw my sister at all. I said I did not. "She is very stubborn," she said. How true. I felt the need to leave and descended into the Cave, through to the Inner Landscape. The Staff fused with my spine and the crystal into my brain. A Crystal Skull, I thought! I had not noticed that before.

Hermes spoke. "You still have not assimilated all your previous learning so now back to work." He began the lesson. "A problem can arise with chakra meditations if the positions are given incorrectly. Here is how it should be." I saw his form embody the chakra positions, which took the form of the standard diagram, red at the root of the spine, then emotional (orange), solar plexus (yellow), heart (green), throat (blue), third eye (indigo) and crown (purple). All the colours were translucent shades, and the ground that Hermes stood on was black. "There is a confusion between two practices. The Middle Pillar Exercise is designed so that you become the middle pillar, exactly mid point between mercy and severity, orientated in balance, ready to move forward toward the Light Brain. To overlay chakra points in this practice is wrong and a conflation of two different practices." I felt a calling now to visit the Temple. I stood inside. Hermes spoke again. "Franz Bardon's Book Two will instruct you upon what to do in this Temple. It is a place where you create your own learning. Do not close off this future by the promises you make now." He paused, and then concluded. "Tomorrow. There is so much to do."

Tuesday 29th. The Cave. I consulted with Hermes on a client that was seeking a name change. He gestured toward the Library. I knocked and entered, spoke the name of the person and asked to be presented with whatever I needed to know. A huge pile of books accumulated in a stack in front of me. The Keeper spoke. "She had much power in a previous life, but gaining no understanding of it. She fails to see the need to learn and act, rather than simply learning the theories. She must learn how to do stuff. You cannot tell her all this of course, but her proposed name although it is fine, will not solve these problems. It is all about the learning. That is the key, but you know that." Well, I ought to, I thought, the amount of times I had heard it. "Anything or anyone else?" asked The Keeper.

"Should there be?" I asked.

"You?" I enquired.

"OK, what Karma have I accumulated in this Life?" A book was presented to me, bound with old parchment and leather. It was empty save for a few hieroglyphic type squiggles at the back. "But this book is virtually empty," I said.

"But it is still a book. If there were no Karma there would be no book."

"How may I repay this?"

"By tracking down and making a gift against what you previously took. There is no other way. This is maybe something for the future."

Later, 6.30pm. I was tired, so tired, so busy with all manner of readings, calls, emails.

"This level of busyness is how it is going to be. The importance of eating well cannot be underestimated." Hermes told truth, but that truth was not always comforting.

[FEBRUARY 2013]

Sunday 3rd. 5.00pm. The Cave. "Hermes, teach me," I asked. Instead he gestured to the Scarab and off it scurried into the long grass. I followed as best I could but then lost it. It was then I saw that it was climbing up my leg and across my face. Positioned on my nose it looked directly at me, and then in a flash ate me whole. It then immediately excreted only an empty shell.

"Your husk," it said.

"Rest, read and return soon" said Hermes.

Monday 4th. 5.00pm. The Cave. I presented the Mark of Hermes and entered the space, asking him to instruct me.

"The Essential Purification of Thoughts," he said. "The Dark Side grows if denied. It is like an Inner Child but that is too simplistic and denies its potential force. Sometimes it wins, sometimes it loses, but it really only wants to be heard and recognised. If you are in the darkness you must see that there is Light, and if you are in the Light make the most of it! As Arthur said, the Dark Side must be recognised. It can be overcome but only if first of all it is seen for what it is. It must be given a little but the focus should be on what can be done about it, not to get lost by it."

"Shall I write about the Dark Side?"

"*Emergence* must be written first," he said. "You must eat well during this time, take vitamins as well to keep you topped up."

The real issue with the Dark Side is in accepting that it even exists, for although it wants to come into form, it does not want to be seen. Though it lives in the shadows, it is not the shadow itself. If the sanitisation of society increases so will denial of the Dark Side. Then, when we do get instances of the Dark Side running out of control we will get mass outrage. This seems to be a necessary phase through which society must pass. But how to indulge the Dark Side, safely? Mass sporting occasions maybe, but perhaps in future the Darker Side of humanity will be explored in safe camps or at release festivals? Perhaps there will be a resurgence of horror movies?

Monday 11th. 6.00pm. The Cave.

During this period I had been receiving extracts of the material for 'Emergence' from Hermes. These are reproduced separately.

Two figures, one below, one grander and higher up. I heard both call, but I decided to go with the smaller figure. On that choice he gestured and deferred to the higher figure. Suddenly and unexpectedly I was picked up and carried off by a tornado. It churned me up and around before depositing me in the Temple.

"This is your place now, this is where you must spend more time. You are able to enter here directly or through the astral Vortex. You must build this Temple now, construct it to your requirements for this is where you will direct matters and make thing happen." I felt I had free rein on how I might construct and decorate it.

"But what about *Emergence*?" I asked.

"There is little else to say. Record this meeting and visit again for the final words. Then prepare, and publish." Tired. Beyond tired. Thanks were given but only vaguely.

Wednesday 13th. 5.00pm. The Cave. In the cave there was the usual entrance to the landscape but I could also see a doorway to my left, studded with blue crystals. I moved toward it, the Staff and crystal present in the usual way. I signalled the Mark of Hermes and once again I was engulfed in the tornado, which offloaded me in the Temple.

"This is where your work now lays," said Hermes. "You are the directing influence, with polarity, to stitch and unpick, to create and destroy, to build and dismantle. But only in harmony with the laws of the Universe may you direct this. We will co-operate up to the limits of our power." The voice had changed from only Hermes to the eight (or maybe nine including the Light) assembled energies.

"What is the scope of your power?" I asked.

"Limitless," came the reply. "But use this not for trivia, for if you do you will be cast low and aside from us. The necessary techniques will take a lifetime to master. Attend here every day for two weeks. Read, then rest."

I looked around. The floor was tiled but plain, not checkered or patterned in any way. The walls were a blue/grey stone with archways within. There were eight circular plinths which were all empty. There was no ceiling. A central position was indicated where I was to put the focus of the operation. After trying to soak in as much of the scene as possible I left via the double doors behind me locking them with the protective mark. I descended and returned via the blue jewelled doorway.

Thursday 14th. 5.00pm. The Cave. The blue jewelled doorway – similar to an agate or sapphire geode – was on my left and high up on a ledge. I climbed up to it and felt the familiar astral buzz as I entered the Vortex. I arrived in front of the double doors of the Temple and gave the Mark of Hermes. The doors opened outwards toward me. Stepping through there were three steps down to the Temple itself. I sat on the stone chair and looked ahead into the room.

"I do not know where to begin. I do not know what to do, or even what you are offering me," I said.

"This is a good thing," came the reply, which I believed to be from Hermes.

"It seems that a torch has been passed to me, so should that be where I begin?"

"This sounds sensible," said the voice. "But first you must be strong. And you are not. You need to rest and be re-built. Approach the Light." I stepped forward.

"You must be cleansed, purified of all toxins. No alcohol at all from now on." I outstretched my arms and saw the Sun's Light straight in front of me. I allowed it to sear into me and search through me, burning every corner and sinew and ounce of my being. I withstood as much as I could then stepped back.

"Can you take more?" said the voice. I stepped forward again for the same. I literally felt as if I were on fire from within. I stepped back. "Now rest, purifying your body with this Light and return tomorrow." I retraced my steps, completely and utterly exhausted,

Friday 15th. 5.00pm. The Cave. The Temple. Entering the cave I felt a force behind me, pushing me forward. I entered, climbed up the ledge, through the blue jewelled doorway, up through the Vortex and to the double doors of the Temple. I passed the Mark of Hermes and the doors opened outwards with a groan. I entered and was instructed to lie down in the central position. As I settled I could feel the energy of the stars above permeate through me. It was not a forceful energy as the Light had been, but it was more penetrating and cleansing. It travelled into the tiniest, remotest, deepest areas of my body and I felt invigorated by it, but then suddenly very conscious of the heaviness of my being and very, very tired.

"Return soon," came the voice. "Now rest." I exited using the normal procedure.

Saturday 16th. 6.00pm. The Temple. My journey via the Vortex Elevator to Arthur was successful. Upon my arrival amidst the all encompassing whiteness I had to call for him and ask that he speak to me.

"You see now how hard it is," he said. "And it will only get harder. But it is worth it! Grab every ounce of it while it is available, for it is so much better than the alternative. Be ceaseless. You would do well to distance yourself from distracting voices," he said.

Linda and my mum were also there. "Oh hullo love," said Linda "It's Tricia's birthday today, how is Hannah? I miss them both." Tricia was Hannah's sister. My mum spoke up before that conversation could go anywhere.

"Why were you like you were?" she said.

"Because I had expectations of you, and you did not fulfil them. But I told you all this was in the past now, I forgive you and I love you." The words clearly did not register. Evidently she would listen more to Linda than to me. "Come on," said Linda to my mum. "Let's do this," picking up some knitting or stitching.

I returned to the cave and via the blue doorway reached the doors of the Temple. They were grey and closed firmly shut until I gave the Mark of Hermes. I moved through them and down the steps.

"Kneel," came a voice. Really? I did not approve of this. I bowed instead.

"This is your personal God experience," came the voice. "Here, is your experience of me. Here is where you make and destroy, shape and dissolve, flower and fade, change and adjust your experiences of the wonder of life. Anything is possible, anything, so long as it's in accordance with the Laws of the Universe." Why did they keep telling me this?

"I want to be healthy and well," I replied.

"Then lay here," came the voice, indicating the central position where I had laid before. Once again I felt the Akashic Universe fill me up extraordinarily. It was a buzzing, vibrating charge that cleansed me and my world. "There, it is done," said the voice.

I asked of a pupil. She was trying hard and I wanted her to succeed. I saw a ball of Light form directly in front of her in the Outer World. "What should I say to her?" I asked.

"We cannot advise you of that. Breathe. You already know." I tried to leave. "Return soon," said the same voice. I felt strange, freer somehow, tired, but not strung out.

Sunday 17th. 6.00pm. The Temple. "I am not yet ready," I said, entering the Temple by the now established route.

"Fine, then lay down and be healed," said the voice. I felt gentle, not forceful, rays penetrate my body. It was soft, moving into every part of me. Back in the

Outer World I had been neglecting the long built up habits of drink and certain kinds of food. I had also developed a craving for fresh foods, although I did not always like the taste. My mind drifted. I may even have fallen asleep. "Visit here in your sleep at bedtime and heal," I heard through the clouds. This brought me to. Maybe I had slept for seconds, minutes or not at all. "Visit again tomorrow, you haven't done enough yet." I slowly made my way back home with those words echoing around me.

Monday 18th. 6.30pm. The Temple. As I approached in the regular pattern I was told, "you will be instructed in the specifics as you go along." As I entered I was told, "this place will fill with your energy, from your choices, as time passes. Choose well. You still need more healing."

Laying down again I received a now gentler Light into my cells. It seemed regenerative, not just comforting and involved somehow a release of old cells. I felt lighter by the end of it.

Tuesday 19th. 7.00pm. The Doorway. "Approach," came the voice as I stood before the large doors to the Temple. "You have done wrong. Too fast, slow down. Speed in a Seven year is an abuse of the powers you have been granted. Why the busyness and the rush? Look what happens to others when they do the same, learn from their mistakes if you cannot learn from your own. Go now, rest and then return."

I was shattered, life was too busy, too many conflicting demands on my time and energy. But then again I chose to accept them. And that was where I had gone wrong, for no one was forcing me.

Wednesday 20th. 3.30pm. The Temple. I went to enter via the blue doorway but was told that, this time instead, I should use the traditional entrance via the landscape. I complied, presenting the Mark at the door. Hermes greeted me and ushered me toward a bearded man.

"Who are you?" I asked.

"Socrates," he said. "Learn about my life and much of your own will become clear. I will see you again soon, now go about your business."

CHAPTER XVII

SOCRATES

[FEBRUARY 2013]

Monday 25th. 7.00pm. The Temple. I entered the Temple and could see that it now clearly contained an altar, at the far end of the room. This was new, at least to my vision. Socrates appeared to my left. His face was full and round. He was laughing and assured me of his identity. The conversation was fast paced and unclear.

"You want to emulate me?" He laughed.

"I simply want to become what I might."

"So what is the problem?"

"I might get it wrong. I might fail. All this might be a massive mistake?"

"So make it. Write a book, even one that is later proved wrong, or that others have to decipher. That is the way. Create your own life, then create another. The skeleton is solid though even that moves and changes. Feeling, thoughts are all malleable."

"A book?" I was surprised.

"Yes a book, the written, printed word is more permanent than thoughts in the mind, which especially in your time have become ephemeral."

"But you didn't write any books. You were dead against it." I said.

"But others did it for me. I did not have the time." At that he merged into me, powerfully and my head began throbbing. "How interesting," he said within me. "Yes, fascinating, I see," he continued. "Twitter is most interesting," he said. "Allow me to enter as you read about me and I will tell you if what you are being presented with is correct." He exited at that point and moved off.

I turned to the wider Temple and asked for assistance with a problem one of my friends was having with her neighbour. I formed and projected 'realisation' Light to the neighbour in the hope that he see the error of his ways. I could see that he was very distracted and confused though. I additionally sent 'stand your ground' energy to my friend and 'support' to her husband. I felt her spine and resolve stiffen, but I had to concede that the situation had maybe developed too far, seemingly way too entrenched to turn back the clock. Changing topic I addressed the Light at the end of the Hall.

"I seek a calm mind, health and optimism," I said.

"And you shall have it," came the reply. "Franz Bardon's works are the most comprehensive instructions from a Master yet assembled. Learn from them."

"I want to devote my life to these mysteries." I said.

"Very well, but this means that other things will have to fall by the wayside to make room." I lingered for a while and returned home.

Tuesday 26th. 3.30pm. The Temple. "It is important to rest now, to consolidate, to try to re-kindle what has been lost and to resolve to a new oath. Return after your holiday, now go to rest and recover," said Socrates. I felt I had some blessing now to wander off for a short while, at least to get some perspective on things. I was so totally and completed exhausted with the mistakes, misinterpretations and misunderstandings of the messages I was receiving. I was working hard on the Bardon practices though, and these continued daily with great interest and effect. A full three weeks passed before I returned.

[MARCH 2013]

Sunday 10th. 11am. The Cave. The Astral. The Temple. First to the Astral Vortex, and 'up' the extra distance to the Higher Astral.

"Hello," said Arthur warmly. "Fill me in."

"It is hard," I said, "staying distant and disconnected – by myself."

"How is Pat?" he asked of his partner in the work of all those years.

"Oh fine, moving forward," I said.

"She was always going to," he replied. Everybody does I guess. Further answers unforthcoming I wished him farewell returning down to the Cave I located and entered the blue jewelled doorway, rising up to the Temple. Hermes was waiting on my right, Socrates on my left.

"Leave further exploration of the Bardon work for now. Your current focus should be on the people that need you. You have successfully reset many matters, but still you must treat all people compassionately. What do you want next?" I stated that I felt drawn to The Netherlands. I had made contact with a couple of people. "Visit, and they will see you," came the answer. This seemed unlikely, but I was given the exact form of words to deliver over there. I hoped that this was a chance to expand the scope of my work. "One more thing, your focus is now on others, but you yourself must continue to learn." Both Hermes and Socrates merged into me intensely. I could feel a resonance with the world, going back thousands of years through time.

Thursday 14th. The Temple. "Anything can be yours in here," came the voice inside the Temple. That same message again!

"For me or for others?" I replied.

"You and others. Within bounds." Focus was tough, although when I could manage it I detected that the scene had a new freshness and beauty about it that I had not witnessed before. I was given specific and practice pointers to develop The Hermitage, with a generally encouraging tone and the final words, "build it and they will come." I could not identify the voice.

Friday 15th. 10.00am. The Temple.

'Build your own Tree'

Ascending to the main door of the Temple I entered and bowed.

"My wishes, and even thoughts, seem to come true very quickly," I said, "sometimes too quickly."

"They will. Because you make such an impact on the fabric of life. But then again you are wishing for quite easy things. Try something a little further away and see how that goes." Again I did not know who the voice was.

"And another thing," I said. "I have no time for what other teachers say. Their words are wrong and this annoys me greatly. I can summon no tolerance for it."

"Forget what others say. Focus on what you are doing. Differentiate yourself exactly as you had planned to do. Now get on with it. See you later tonight."

Later, 5pm. I was instructed in how to set up the Temple. I could not remember my numerological Four Cores. "You should know these!" I was told. The arrangement given to me is as follows:

A Numerical Arrangement of The Temple

Monday 18th. 7.00pm. The Temple

'Each card is, in a sense, a living being...it is for the student to build these living stones into his living Temple' – Aleister Crowley, The Book of Thoth, 1944.

I constructed the Temple exactly as previously directed, starting at the nearest left position, working up the left side and turning back down the right side. I saw that in each position a Tarot Trump of the corresponding number grew up. I did my best to contain this space, but the energy build up was enormous. It seeped through me and swirled around me. I could feel the earth beneath my feet actually shake and the whole of the world seemed no longer solid. I did not feel as if I had full control of this level of power, and I could see how it could send anyone crazy. Much better preparation was needed on my part.

Tuesday 19th. 4.00pm. The Temple. Bowing as I entered the space, I awoke the assembled Tarot Trumps in their same positions are yesterday. I asked them each to be still. "Tarot entities are the Forces of Life," came the reply, "we cannot be still."

I attempted focus on one goal and the beings joined together to assist. Suddenly everything was noisy, as an incredible vibration, like a rocket engine, shaking the Temple and the room.

After a while I disbanded the room and the entities disappeared, replaced by stone pillars. I was about to leave when a voice spoke to me.

"You think you are very clever, don't you?"

"What?" I was half shocked, half annoyed.

"Do you not see that this is the way it has to be? The good alone can no longer be preserved in your society. All must come crashing down in order to clear the way to rebuild stronger and better. It must be like this. Waste no time railing against it." I was shown a vision of three young female politicians, two from UK, one from Holland. "These are the future," came the voice.

Wednesday 20th. 2.00pm. The Temple. I protected the space with as much force as I could muster. I looked up to the stars and saw that it was the cosmic intelligences which ruled us and all our possibilities. We were small and not nearly as in control of our lives as we would like to think.

"It is essential to be ever mindful and not distracted," came a voice.

I summoned the Tarot energies again. I could see them in distinct colours this time. The Empress was green and yellow, the Magician red. Justice was a grey, blue, silver combination while Strength was red and orange. I could not make out the colours of the Hierophant though. We experimented with gathering and focusing energies for a while before I left, the doors slamming shut behind me.

Later, 7pm. I returned again and repeated exactly the same procedure as before. This time the Tarot images communicated to me what they represented. Empress was Life itself, the Magician was the seed, Justice was intensity, Strength was strength and Hierophant was the power of travel. These insights came to me as experiential senses, not words. At the end of this session I felt totally drained. As I left I was given an instruction, "now read the next instalment of Bardon." I did not know whether this referred to the next chapter in Book One, or the Book Two.

Thursday 21st. The Temple. I was headed for the blue jewelled door but a firm voice told me no. I entered the traditional Inner World Landscape instead.

"In the Temple you have the ability to make anything happen, to create anything, yet you find the notion of this hard to accept." Indeed I did. "You must understand the message of Acceptance." It was Hermes now speaking. I thought I had better review some of Arthur's notes on this matter. "And then come tomorrow," he said.

Very interesting. I had for many years been highly ambitious, yet in this context I found the notions of success and achievement hard to accept. I had also grown weary of the popular New Age claims of manifesting success, which seemed all to umbrella under The Law of Attraction. I was uncomfortable with get-rich-quick, effortless-wealth Bubble Speak. How could any of it be relied upon when we were influenced by intelligences we neither recognised nor understood, daily victims of our own and others Dark Sides?

Sunday 24th. 5pm. The Temple. I ascended for longer and higher than before, behind the blue jewelled doorway. I entered and heard the familiar words.

"Build it and they will come." I could see various colours swirling around the room. "These are the forces you have invoked," came the voice. I collected them all together, compressed them and despatched them, twice to be certain. "Build it and they will come. The only solution is greater hours spent in here. It is time to get serious again, early to rise, late to bed. Take rest and rouse yourself to fulfil Hermes needs. You have had your time off. Now focus." The coloured swirls had gone.

I was warned away from taking a particular material path that I had been obsessing about. "That is not your way. Build it and they will come. The importance of moving forward cannot be overemphasised." I went home, tired. It did not feel as though I had taken any time off at all.

Thursday 28th. 3.00pm. The Temple. I was now in a state of almost constant assessment and re-assessment over how to proceed. I could see that I had already been selected (or had selected myself?) for an enormous task, the continuation of The Hermitage, the legacy of Arthur, and the focal point for the continued teachings of Hermes. I felt totally incapable of doing this, yet in two decades of searching had not found one single person more capable. I could see others streaking ahead in the development of their own schools and methods and although I knew that their path was not mine I increasingly felt as if I had been wasting my time. What I was really trying to do, of course, was to find any reason at all to pass the flame elsewhere, and to not perform the work myself. Originally I had met Arthur as a naïve seeker, and had initially gone about learning in the Inner Domain as the same. But I had now finally found what I sought, at least in part. Of course the learning never ends, as I was constantly being reminded, but I had already found so much. And the deal on the table was to accept it, integrate it and to get on with its work. Yet I still resisted.

I rose up to the Temple, buffeting noisily. I gave the Mark, bowed and sat in my stone seat. Dare I call it a throne? The Light opposite opened.

"You must integrate these eight energies," it said. I was also now aware of a further four pillars in the extreme corners of the Temple. This sight was new. I tried to ask some Outer World related questions.

"Instructions first, questions later," came the reply. "Each plinth in turn must be integrated, the four cores, the four roads. What are they? Quickly!" I hesitated, "er, Three. One. Eleven. Eight, then another pause, "Three. One. Eleven. Five."

"First of the cores, now - Three," was the reply.

I stepped up onto the plinth and into the energy column of The Empress III. It enveloped me, then penetrated me. It was somewhat overwhelming and it made my physical body shake and vibrate. After a while it ceased and I stepped out. I felt sick and continued to shake.

"One per day for the next few days. Cores first," said the voice. So this was the next level of initiation, did it ever end? I turned to Hermes who was stood in the corner. I asked him if I might attend a conference of interest in New York.

"No, not this time," he said. "There are other things to focus on first." I was still shaking, almost to the point of crying such was the enormity of all this. I was gasping for air and felt extremely weak.

Friday 29th. 5.00pm. The Temple. The room was now clearer.

I bowed to the Light source ahead and approached the Magician I, the second along on the left. I stepped into his plinth and absorbed all that was present. It was a very different sensation - boiling, red, angry, immediate, fast and direct. It brought the need for plain speaking and action. I again shook violently, but with a spikiness to my movement, like I had received an electric shock. I felt more in control of this energy, or maybe more familiar with it. Time would tell whether I was deluding myself on that.

"And tomorrow," said the voice.

Dreamtime. I did not always remember my dreams, and I did not hold a lot of store on their analysis. I had practised lucid dreams, willing myself to direct the course of the dream, and I had practised conscious dreams where you pick up part two of the previous night's dream. I did have one single recurring dream which had been with me since childhood, but otherwise it was not an area I focused on. But this one night, Arthur came to me in a dream so vivid that on waking at 4.30am I got out of bed to write it down time verbatim.

"Don't tell anyone," he said. "But the world is in need of a Father. I am the world's Father, someone to take care of others. That's how I follow your progress." He paused. "You are now meant to say *wait for me*."

"Wait for me," I willingly replied.

"I have been."

Saturday 30th. 2.00pm. The Temple. I was in a rush and this prevented me from reaching the blue jewelled door. Every time I attempted to enter it responded by moving further away. I composed myself, took some slow breaths, and as soon as I decided to wait for it – rather than force it - there it was, waiting for me.

The third plinth was Justice XI. The energy was a light blue steely grey colour. I entered it and it was very harsh, cutting and intense. It moved all over my body but accumulated in my genitals. I took as much as I was able, gave thanks and left.

I felt balanced, yet completely out of balance at the same time, like I were rocking on the edge of a cliff. I even felt my left shoulder pop out of sync as I sensed the energy of the card course through my blood. The strength of the feeling was not very pleasant.

"Speak on their level," I was told. I just about made it home.

Sunday 31st. 2.00pm. The Temple. It was the turn of Strength VIII. Stepping onto the plinth my awareness was with the Lion, not the woman, as the dominant force. I felt that I had a choice whether to control the animal or not, so I attempted to subdue it. It very quickly became obvious that in doing so I had actually become the Lion. I could now roar! The Light spoke to me.

"Follow your trail of reading, consolidate as you go, go over again the basic messages and fill in the missing links."

That was the left side done, the four cores. I was totally mashed up. Maybe I would get a break before the four roads?

[APRIL 2013]

Saturday 6th. 7.00pm. The Astral. In the event I decided to take a break anyway, of one week. I continued my daily practises but I did not visit the Inner World in any of its forms during that time.

Now entering the Vortex Elevator, within the cave, I felt myself rise up with the usual noises and sensation. Arthur was recognisable, there to my left, and he beckoned for me to follow him. As I did so the scene became unclear as everything around us disappeared. We then reached the vague shape of another Vortex Elevator. It was now just me and him. I entered it and again there were the familiar sounds and vibrations. I could feel disturbance in my face, head and neck. Arthur was present throughout this. I felt an increasing urge to fly away, to leave all material ties and weights of the Earth bound life but I resisted. I hung on and carried on with my ascension. The stress and movement was now located in the very top of my head and Arthur was urging me to let go. I tried and tried but I could not. I lowered myself down and asked him why?

"I can answer no more," he said, "you must speak with Hermes, he is with you now." Exasperating! I asked him if we could try the exercise again. He nodded in agreement and we went again up the new Vortex Elevator, higher and higher, louder and louder. I felt my whole body go into a forward roll and I felt that I could no longer be seated in my green chair. I then felt the weirdest sensations of side to side movement, still from within my body. It was sick making and disorientating. Then in a flash I could see Manhattan Island. The picture was clear and sharp, but Arthur instantly called me back. He seemed pleased.

"Come again tomorrow," he said. I felt totally out of it.

Sunday 7th. 10.00am. The Astral. The Temple. On the Astral, Arthur was positioned ahead, to my left. He gestured me toward the second Vortex Elevator. I felt spaced out, buzzing, rocking forwards and backwards, side to side, uncontrollably – yet all the while my body remained still. I got half a glimpse again of New York, and then other unrecognised places, and a fleeting sense of vastness, at which point I was brought back by external noises and their associated concerns. Back in the Outer World I had neighbour troubles. This kind of thing I found doubly annoying. "How dare they interrupt this work?" I thought.

"Protect," said Arthur on the matter. The noise lessened and I was back for another try. As I reached the very top of my head my vision was enveloped in a mass of multi-coloured fragments until we could go no further though. "You can come again later," he said, "if you wish. Now to Hermes."

I descended slowly, taking time to acclimatise, though I think that this was wholly unsuccessful for I was as high as a kite! After a small pause I entered back via the cave, the blue jewel encrusted doorway and the Temple. I gave The Mark and the doors opened. I was greeted by Hermes on my right. I had been thinking of doing some filming work in the Outer World.

"Buy the equipment and learn how to do it yourself," he said. I had been talking to someone about working together on this. I would now have to let her down, which I never liked to do.

"Should I not care what others think?" I asked. No direct answer came. "Put it to the breath - breathe the matter in, and then breathe it out," said Hermes. "This is an opening up, an expansion," he said. "Come again later. It will be sometime yet before you can move fully on to Franz Bardon Book Two. His invocations are very dangerous. It may even be years," he said. Not what I wanted to hear, but I was grateful for the clarity and unambiguous instruction.

Later, 2.30pm. Entering the jewelled doorway I seemed to rise higher, and this time for far longer. The double doors in front of me would not open until I gave the Mark and commanded them to. As I passed though the voice spoke.

"Are you ready for the next integration?" I said that I was and approached the nearest right plinth to take the energy of the Three from the Four Roads. This time however it was not the Empress form that presented itself, but a geometric shape of an equilateral triangle. This felt much stronger and I felt more able to absorb this. I allowed it to filter into and around me for some time before a halt was called. "Return tomorrow," said the voice.

I departed, less frazzled than before. I found the Vortex Elevator within the Cave and rose up. At the exit Arthur was again present. I laid down on a bed, face upwards, head unrestricted at the top. In exactly the way that he had done twenty years before, he moved his astral hands up the front of my body, plexus, chest, throat, eyes, top of head. "Steady" he said, holding me there. Then in a flash I was off. I could see the London Eye, the Thames, I swooped through the spokes of the wheel. What a rush! But snap, I was, at his command instantly back within my body in the Inner World.

"Always under control," he said. "Come tomorrow. There isn't much time."

Monday 8th. 6.30pm. The Astral. Arthur indicated toward the bed we had used before. I tried to disconnect from my Outer World annoyances and embrace some degree of relaxation. After not very long I could feel the same vibrations, the movement of myself up the trunk of my body and then an opening out of the top of my head. I had heard this described as like a lotus flower, but I did not feel it to be quite that magickal. At precisely that point of doubt though I felt myself shoot out through its petals and down the garden. I swooped low and high, seeing the garden that I was very familiar with from new perspectives, viewpoints that could not come from anything other than flying. It was exhilarating but did not last long, and I was back in my body quickly enough. "Tomorrow please," said Arthur insistently. I then met with Hermes via the blue doorway.

"One," he said. "Invoke One." Summoning up my memories of the Magician on the plinth as a template I began burning, boiling, red hot. I absorbed what I could before Hermes called a halt. "Tomorrow," he said. I returned home, rather shaky.

Tuesday 9th. 7.30pm. The Astral. I had written a Facebook post on the current Outer World situation. Margaret Thatcher had died and I was boiling over at the hypocrisy of the comments I observed all around me.

'Don't tell me how much you hated Thatcher and then try to give me spiritual guidance. Don't tell me how you can't wait to spit on her grave and then tell me about your energy healing work. Don't tell me about the purity of the Left and the Evil Tories and then about your work with the Angels. Because if you do these things it is obvious that you have learned nothing.'

I had been amazed at the number of likes it had received. I had expected a great deal more friction. Meeting with Arthur in the Astral he explained further.

"See, they need you. Simply share the facts as they are, without show or flash." I again lay down on the bed. More buffeting, buzzing, and an extreme and intense headache. I felt myself rushing out of my head, but then immediately back in again. That was all I could manage. Hermes spoke now.

"Rest. You cannot do this while you are so tired and strung out. Return later." I had a splitting headache and was exhausted.

Wednesday 10th. 2.30pm. I tried to enter the cave, but was just too tired. There was no communication that I could discern and I hated it when I could not connect to the voice, for I was never certain that my own thoughts were reliable enough to act on. I tried listening to my body instead, and found that message to be much clearer. Every time I closed my eyes I felt like I was going to fall asleep. That was probably as much as I needed to know. I came back. The moment I opened my eyes one of the cats burst into the room, how he opened the door I do not know!

Monday 15th. 4.30pm. The Astral. The Temple. I was a little rested, much not much. I moved toward the Vortex Elevator lift shaft and requested 'Upper Astral'. Arthur spoke.

"You need a break from these evening teaching sessions. Your pupils are at the limit of what they can soak in, and you have other things to do." Arthur was bang on the money as usual, distilling conflicting happenings down to their truthful core. Since January 1st I had devoted four or five weekday evenings every month, in two hour sessions each time, to my mentorship programme. This was in addition to a full working day every day, plus weekend shows and travelling once or twice a month. It was too much. He told me to lie down and once more we attempted the astral projection exercise. Again I could really get no further than the opening flower sensation at the top of my head, at which point my mind wandered badly.

"Enough for today," he said. "Again tomorrow." I was disappointed as I felt my energy body draw back into my physical. I passed Linda and my mum on the way back. They seemed smaller than before. I did not stay for conversation.

Back in the cave I found the blue jewelled doorway and ascended to the Temple.

"This is the place of magickal invocation," said a voice. "Build it and they will come. Create content and they will come." I complained that I did not feel my progress was of the right kind, or the right speed. "You are going as fast as you can," I was told. "Which is what is expected." I faced the third pillar along on the right, the XI position. "The Temple can only be explored in stages," said Hermes. This pillar now contained the High Priestess – two, not eleven, yet related to Justice, another female form. I stepped into its field and I shuddered intensely. I asked for guidance on how to proceed with my mentorship groups. "You know what to do, what to teach. We cannot help you in this. We can only help you in the creation and spreading of the word to a wider world. Visit again tomorrow."

Wednesday 17th. 5.00pm. The Upper Astral. The Temple. With Arthur's assistance and prompting I directed my energy body up to the crown of my head. I paused and held myself there.

"With control," he said as I descended slowly down again and could feel the very clear difference in sensation as I rested at difference parts of me.

"And again tomorrow," he said. The doors to the Temple opened in the usual way. Hermes was waiting.

"Next," he said, gesturing again to the third position on the right. This time Justice presented herself. There were many similarities between her and the High Priestess, and both were coloured in blues and greys. I moved onto the plinth and Justice shot into me like a knife through my brain, splitting my consciousness in two. The pain was actual and searing and moved through my whole being.

"Tomorrow," came the voice. What was going on here?

Thursday 18th. 7.00pm. The Astral. The Temple. I was instructed to head for the Temple first. Once I arrived and protected it I looked to my left and could see that the four pillars that had each contained the four cores had been replaced by one pillar, a collection of all four. A voice echoed.

"Communication. It was always for you about communication. At school you came second in the writing competition and was in the second grade for English in order than you would get better and learn. But this did not happen. You were let down by others certainly, but primarily you let yourself down. You did not work hard enough and you must make up for that now. Then, and only then, will there be the breakthrough that you seek."

I approached the last of the four pillars on my right. The Five energy, the Hierophant. The Roman Numeral V was shifting and tipping on it point. Then I saw many V shapes, connected together at their base to form a flower, then a pentagram, then an I Ching inspired arrangement of numbers, then finally the Vitruvian Man. All this merged into me. I outstretched my arms to accept it more fully. Some time passed in this position. It was a powerful energy for sure, but less difficult and less jarring than the others.

After a while a voice urged me on to the next step. Coming down from the plinth I watched as the four right hand pillars merged together into one. The new one was the same size as the others and it positioned itself to my immediate right. I could feel myself pivoting between the left pillar and the right one. The Four Cores, the left hand pillar, seemed to contain the past and a small degree of the present. The right pillar housed a degree of the present, but more so the future – what might yet be and what I might yet do. I was in the balance point between these two extremes, stuck in one sense, but directing them in another. A voice came, very clearly and very directly.

"You will be shown something that only you can do, and you must do it to the very best of your ability and efforts. It will be something that you and only you can do. This is very important." OK, this was important! "Understand," continued the voice, "that you will be in no doubt about what it is, when you discover it, and you must move heaven and earth to do it. Only you can do it. It will be presented to you soon, but we cannot say how soon."

"What about the projects you have already given me?"

"We are out of time now," came the reply. "Act as we have told you. Now visit Arthur, he is your instructor in this." I moved to Arthur in the Astral and he spoke.

"You have been given a very special privilege and you must bring all your faculties to bear to meet the challenge. There will no instruction today, take note of what has been said, rest and learn." Arthur had always said that the Four Roads, once recognised, actively worked upon and mastered would reveal a Golden Highway which would lead directly to your fulfilment. Was this the time?

Friday 19th. 5.00pm. The Astral. The Temple. With Arthur I rose up through my body as before. At the top of my head I could see snapshots and visions of all sorts of places and things, but could not achieve a full disconnection.

"The Golden Highway," he said, "takes you directly to your fulfilment, without deviation." I inferred that there would have to be some decisions about what could accompany me on this journey. "You have to get that looked at," he said, pointing to my intestines. I thought no more of this. At the entrance to the Temple I bowed.

"Are you ready?" I was asked. The left hand pillar did not wait for my answer and merged into me. "Mercy," was the word given. "Mercy for the past." With little delay the other pillar merged straight into me on my right, passing to only the word 'Severity.' Severity toward the future? Toward me? I did not know what this meant. Then an explanation arrived, spoken by many voices. "Be merciful to others, severe on yourself. Now step forward." But I was not at all sure that I was ready.

"There is so much that I do not know," I protested.

"Very true, but you are ready for this." The mass of white light straight ahead formed itself into a perfect circle and began to swirl with colour. After some hesitation I stepped through it. I was vibrated into a million pieces, beyond anything I could possibly describe. The Light infused me completely and I became conscious of a collection of beings - geniuses was the only word for them. They intended to show me a new language "We will bring this to you in the night. Listen and record," they said. After a little more of this I was instructed to leave.

Hermes pointed, as Arthur had, to my intestinal areas and scorched an ice cold laser light into it. I returned home, confused by the latest turn of events. I was so far out there now, so far from anything I would have imagined.

Monday 22nd. 6.00pm. The Temple and Astral. Entering the Temple Hermes spoke. "You must hurt no one, you cannot hurt them." I had no intention of doing so, but the instruction must have been given for a reason. "Visit Arthur," he said, "there is much to learn, much tuition remaining."

In the Astral Arthur greeted me warmly, "Rest, no, lie down here. Follow my hand movements over your body." He moved mostly upwards, sometimes to one side. He would punctuate the slow movements with "concentrate" or "control" sometimes "not too fast" and "here now." I could feel my inner being move each time his hand did. When I was at the very top of my head he said, "hold it" before moving slowly back down and around my body before returning to the top of the head. This time I felt my crown actually become an opening lotus flower.

"Where to?" he said.

"The London Eye," was the first thing I could think of. And then I was there. It was straight in front of me, the long queue, the embankment, the moored boats on the Thames. The full scene as if I were there.

"Back now," he said, satisfied with the progress. "You can do this exercise any time, but enough for now. Return tomorrow please, there is great deal more to learn." I thanked him and returned.

Tuesday 23rd. 5.00pm. The Astral. "Well done," said Arthur as he again led me in moving my awareness up, down and around my body. At my crown I could see flashing images of various scenes. People I knew, in their houses making tea, stomping around and generally going about their lives. I became aware that I was growing bigger. This continued until I felt as if I were taller than the houses in the street, straddling them. I held this awareness only momentarily and then returned to my normal size as steadily as I could.

"Tomorrow," said Arthur again. "Maybe twice. Take all the opportunities for learning that you can, in this lifetime." At home I felt disconnected from the room I sat in. Totally spaced out, dizzy, my eyes couldn't even focus properly and I had to blink many times to see straight.

Wednesday 24th. 12noon. The Astral. I shrank down to the size of a light orange coloured pin prick and settled myself in my lower stomach. On Arthur's instructions I started to move myself around my body. The sensations varied in different areas and in certain places I was driving my body, but then in other areas my body would be driving me. In this miniature state I could jump across the space between my legs. I could stop and assess what was happening to my body in certain areas. I could self scan and reveal blockages, inflammations, breakages or illnesses. All this must be possible. I moved higher up and arrived at my Lotus Crown. Holding myself at this point I became aware of matters of the Outer World. My vision now turned outwards, to my garden, the plants in the garden, and the bees in the plants.

Then slowly, by myself, I dropped back down my body to the original start point and then dispersed my minuteness back all around my body. All this did take some time, and some concentration. I also felt that the practice was causing changes itself.

"Later on please," said Arthur. Somewhat dizzy, though not as bad as before, I returned home.

Saturday 27th. 12noon. The Astral. The Temple. Outer World demands had distracted me away from the work. This continued to happen more than I would like. Arriving in the Astral, I was unsure that Arthur was indeed Arthur. Why did I doubt this so easily? Legitimate caution or self-persecution? I tested him nonetheless by asking that he come to me, rather than me to him. He agreed and smiled in the old familiar knowing way.

I moved around my body, noting particular areas of discomfort and difficulty. My intestines and liver seemed unhappy. "Food and drink," said Arthur. I rose up and again became conscious of my Lotus Crown. Holding right there I saw Manhattan Island. "This is true travel," he said. At that I extended out of the top of my head. The face of Statue of Liberty was immediately in front of me. It was covered in filth and dirt. It was all seen from an angle not possible unless you were flying. But I could not only see the physical structure of the statue, but also gained a sense of what it represented. The feeling was overwhelming that this was something of the past, a relic almost, an ideal which can no longer be applied with the population that now exists. This feeling was illogical and unexpected, yet strong. "Visit again soon," said Arthur.

Entering the Temple I gave the Mark with a greater force than usual. Hermes was there, tall and slim.

"Continue exactly as you are. You have been given all the tools with which to move forward, but increase the frequency and intensity of your practice to understand it all fully. You need to do this multiple times per day, every day."

"What should I will for, to become?" I asked.

"To become me," he replied.

"What?! Me as in me, or me as in you?" What did I even mean by that?

"To become me," he repeated and merged into me. He was so much bigger, more intense, of greater pressure and a greater weight and it was a job to hold him. "There is much to do," he said, as he departed from me. "The time is now, do not waste it."

"No pressure then," I said, half jokingly. There was no reply. I returned home, kind of. I lit a candle at the beginning of every visit, but at the end of this one it took me three attempts to even blow it out. As I looked around the room everything seemed covered in cobwebs. I set about some attempt at cleaning.

Later, 4.30pm. After a difficult and vague entry I reached Arthur. We practised again with me moving around my body then momentarily projecting it. This time for one or two seconds only, I was flying across the middle of the North Sea. It was desolate and in the middle of absolutely nowhere was an enormous mass of metal, an oil rig. Such a remote location, I thought.

I asked Arthur if he sometimes needed a break from this work. He had always referred to his time after death as his rest and this did not seem much of a rest. I listened but could hear no answer. I asked him what I should aim for, what ought to be my goal. "To be me," he said, like it was the most obvious thing in the world.

Sunday 28th. 10.00am. The Temple. Hermes form was more discernible to me now. He was very tall, maybe the equivalent of seven or eight feet high, and quite slim. Yet as these impressions formed in my mind I knew they were completely irrelevant.

"Build it and they will come," he said. "You have all you need to create this." He gave me a glimpse of an image. The Hollywood sign, Los Angeles. Me speaking out from a lectern to a crowded room. That was the vision, although it was hardly believable. I wondered how far I could go in my speeches or presentations.

"Is it safe to speak about The Only Evil?" I asked.

"Yes, but it depends on how you phrase it," he replied.

"But was Arthur even right? Are men the only evil, or it is actually power that's the problem?"

"Power is the fuel," he said. Suddenly I was transported high above the Temple, in the star field overheard. I was simultaneously connected and alone, with the Universe and alone within it. Amid this space dust I was aware of a great many forces and vibrations. Space was not, by any means, empty. A series of faces, people I knew in the Outer World, flashed before my eyes. "Train them," came a voice. "Give them what they need, as well as what they want." I was then propelled down a series of tunnels, twisting and turning, narrower each time, a never ending maze. I did not like the sense of uncertainty, the lack of direction or my ignorance of the terrain. "Ha!" said the voice, "like all students you seek to know before you go!" I had no answer to that. I thanked Hermes for this experience. I was still racked by Outer World concerns and asked if my business life was effectively over.

"All but," he said, not nearly as bothered about it as I was.

[MAY 2013]

Wednesday 1st. 7.00pm. The Temple. The Astral. To gain access to the Temple I now had to intone and vibrate the Mark, rather than simply show it. I did this and entered.

"Where are we up to?" asked Hermes, testing me.

"I have everything that I need?" I replied.

"Yes, you do."

"Everything with which to do the job in hand. I have all the tools at my disposal to build the Hermitage and then they will come."

"Yes," he confirmed.

"And I should stop thinking about throwing my life up in the air. It is just not necessary. I am fine with what I have and I should ignore all thoughts of an easier way, because there isn't one?"

"Correct."

"So I should start on Tuesday in earnest. This is my last break before then and I should enjoy it?"

"Yes. But we cannot wait forever. Now go to visit Arthur for instruction."

I asked Arthur about including mention of him in a forthcoming magazine article I had to write.

"Keep me out of it," he said. "It is the best way. Now, lie back." I brought my attention to the energy in his hands and I moved around my own body as before. At the Lotus Crown he asked "Where to?"

"Mecca." I said "Really? Very well," he replied And there I was. There was no Hajj, and it was very quiet, but all around the mosque there were vast commercial centres, spin offs from the religion. Tything - 10% donations or fees - was commonplace. I had read about the practice of tything in relation to the Ten of Pentacles and asked Arthur if this were good practice?

"Essential," he said.

On my way back I saw Linda, and wished her well.

"Thank you," she said. "Start again soon I suppose?"

"When the time is right," I said. That was my attempt at being comforting and not too intimidating.

Tuesday 7th. 5.00pm. The Temple. "Here together we will recreate the world," said Hermes. Continuing, "I have said build it and they will come, here we will build it. Stop now, be patient, be still and rest. Focus on nothing but the full stop at the end of this sentence. If people could do that, they would see."

There was a large bowl positioned in the centre of the Temple. I peered in and could see the whole of Planet Earth. It was non stop busyness from everybody, everywhere. The word Stop was so much needed.

"There will be no Arthur today," said Hermes. "Reflect on these words instead."

I could see images of retreats housing deep brain relaxation, giving people a chance to switch off everything, moving away from the infestation of noise, whether it might originate. Noise was a pattern than seemed so deeply ingrained, like an illness or a fever.

Wednesday 8th. 7.30am. The Cave. This time I spotted a new doorway, on the extreme left on an even higher ledge. I climbed up to it and passed through, buffeting strongly. I greeted Arthur, he reminded me to visit certain people in the Outer World. I asked him about the possibility of purchasing the flat below the one we owned in Cheltenham, as a knock through or extra let.

"You want less financial ties, not more!" He said. He was right of course and we moved on to discuss other material matters, where his wisdom as usual set matters straight. "Carry on just as is," he said, "you are doing fine."

Thursday 16th. 7.00pm. The Astral. I moved straight through to Arthur, for the familiar body location exercises. At the point of my Lotus Crown I could see one of my mentorship pupils, frantically rushing round to get ready for our session in one hour's time.

I also became aware of the vastness of starry space. Submerged within it I took a huge breath of its enormousness and its energy condensed into my tiny body. So huge outside, so small inside and therefore so condensed. So much could be condensed into the human body and energy field I thought.

"Again tomorrow," said Arthur.

To the Temple. Hermes merged into me with an enormous and shocking force. I vibrated violently and I could contain him for merely five seconds before I had to release.

"Again soon," he said, my weary limbs tired and brain fuzzy. How much more of this could I bear?

Friday 17th. 3.00pm. The Temple. The Astral. Again, I found that I had to give the Mark multi-dimensionally, through showing, intoning and vibrating. I greeted Hermes and bowed. He said that there was no need for me to do this.

"I invented writing and language and now it is time to show the world a new form of communication. Visit Stewart Pearce and read Bardon's Book Three – plus of course all the others to go with it. There is no time for ifs and buts, this is what matters now." OK, I thought, but was this 'the thing' I had been waiting for?

"Give me your hands," he said. I offered him my palms and he engraved a diagonal line up the centre of each. "The Fate Line," he said. "Now press them together." As I did and felt a voltage of energy run through me. "Now enjoy yourself but then return."

Visiting Arthur we practised once more, moving myself up, down and around my physical vehicle. At my Lotus Crown I expanded myself beyond my mere physical size and became aware of the Akashic Space. Again I breathed in as much as I could take. It was a new sensation which enlivened me, as well as causing me to vibrate and shudder.

Saturday 18th. 6.00pm. Very tired I called Arthur in from my chair, without accessing any inner space. I could still feel the vibrations and shifts as I moved my inner being around my physical vehicle. As I moved into each area so it came more alive, stronger and more responsive.

"What next?" I asked.

"Tomorrow you move to the next level," replied Arthur.

Sunday 19th. 4.00pm. "Lie down" said Arthur. Moving around in my body I settled into my Lotus Crown, imagining that everyone could do this, effectively becoming King or Queen of their own being. Words were heard.

"Out, not up." At this I moved right away from my body, out in the world. I travelled down the garden at the level of a cat or hedgehog. There was a grass snake and many worms. How interesting to see life from their angle. From this perspective I could see that the protruding roots of the tree were damaged and the grass was patchy. There was a stream at the end of the garden and I wanted to move with its flow, but Arthur called me back.

"You did it," he said. "Congratulations!" there was however no time for rest and I went next to the Temple.

"What do you want?" said Hermes.

"To build The Hermitage I will need an assistant."

"And you shall have one," he replied.

[JUNE 2013]

Monday 10th. 5.00pm. It had been a long gap. I had been practising my daily breath and meditation, but many negative feelings crept over me bringing great dejection and pointlessness about life and the work. These feelings had enveloped me and on more than one occasion my thoughts had been suicidal. Somehow though today was good and I headed straight for the Temple with all the temporary haste I could muster.

"Something is missing isn't it?" said Hermes. I was demoralised at the condition of the world and the direction people seemed intent on heading in. The attitudes of people I encountered, particularly on social media filled me with horror.

"Social media cannot record your Inner World," said Hermes. "And half the time it does not even record what you really think or feel. It is superficial," he said. "Develop these ideas and you will find the answers. But do it soon, don't delay."

I was thankful for that significant piece of guidance. As I left another one floated across the ether toward me. "The attainment of wants may be an ending or a new beginning – which is it to be?"

Wednesday 19th. 3.00pm. The Astral. The Temple. Arthur reinforced the message given by Hermes one week before, but my gloom had not lifted.

"There is not much you can do with these people. Very few of them want to know. But you have had an exceptionally good run of development in previous years, so it is only balancing itself out. Hang in there, it will get better."

To the Temple, Hermes spoke, quite directly.

"You just need to keep on. Being dispassionate is the key. It doesn't matter what people think, you have to interact with them more coldly. Promote your courses, get writing. And don't kill yourself. That would be a bad idea." Yes, of course he was right about that.

Thursday 20th. 2.00pm. The Cave. I felt an overshadowing of Hermes, not only entering me, but dominating me. Across the landscape I could see two Libraries, one on the far left, one on the far right. They slowly merged together and I entered. The Keeper seemed cheerful. I asked about my future.

"Well, some people can't let go," he said, "it is in their nature. But enough of that." A vision appeared of my gravestone. It was written in my birth name, 'born 1972, died 2056'. "That is if you follow the guidance," he said, "just think of the good you can do in that time. You could write a book a year, and produce enormous amounts of work. But you cannot give it to them too straight. The patterns of life that you have identified are only tendencies, but repeated and focused they become real. But it does not have to be like that. Think of Arthur, he saw all that has now been revealed decades ago. But he never got bogged down by it."

I thanked The Keeper and departed. Hermes was waiting.

"You must try to be constructive. All the ideas you have for books, you can get on with them, and it's just that there are better things to do. You cannot release *The Key To Time* as it is, you will have to soften the pill. The technology that you need can be learned. Patience please, in all areas." I thanked him and returned home.

Friday 21st. 12noon. The Sun. In the landscape of the Inner World I approached the Sun and allowed its full rays to penetrate me. I took my time over this to receive the very maximum benefit.

"Vital energy," said a voice. I uncapped my fingertips and projected the light I had received all around me in a flaming yellow golden pentagram which came alive. I thanked the Sun and returned home.

Saturday 22nd. 12noon. The Temple. I had been to a fascinating talk the night before in London with a very old mystical lady. I asked Hermes about this and the possibility of me studying with her.

"No," he said. "You were taught at a level higher than she can comprehend. Although she has great knowledge and vast experience, it is not at this level. It would be too much for her. It comes down to the social aspects again – you have been deprived of society but you have compensations others cannot imagine. Write, run courses, focus on your work now. Forget everything else, all will be provided for along this path. Time cannot wait forever though."

[JULY 2013]

Sunday 7th. 12 noon. The Temple. It was now a further two weeks later.

"We are waiting for you to step up. Ignore both your own expectations and others responses. Focus only on delivering the message. More people are ready and learning than you think. Let go of trying to get a specific outcome. Just deliver the message. Develop yourself by all means, but you really have all that you need. You have it all. Let us know when you are ready to step up." Hermes turned away at that point. I did not ever remember him turning away before. It was always me that left while he watched.

Afterwards: The message was repetitive and continuous – build it and they will come. Step up, focus, accept, get busy. Re-reading this diary the guidance is overwhelming, but it didn't seem like that at the time. Within a couple of hours of returning back to the Outer World its concerns again would distract and overwhelm me. Yes, some of these matters were important and did require genuine attention, but I also too easily allowed small things to become big, whilst the big things – this work – receded into the background. It sometimes felt as if this were a conspiracy, anything and everything assailing me on all sides to prevent me from my Inner explorations.

CHAPTER XVIII
MERLIN
[JULY 2013]

Sunday 14th. 4.00pm. The Cave. Another week had passed. Hermes appeared. "Speak to our friend here and come back to me when you are ready." I could discern a new shape. Though unclear he identified himself. "Mar…Mer…Merlin."

"But you are a fictitious character!" I cried.

"I am a fragment, a representation of the power and energy of Hermes, a characterisation, one which you may be able to understand." I listened. "People are simply not ready for that which you want to tell them. They cannot handle it. You can barely handle it!" I had not made that connection and it was undeniably true. "You need to visit here daily now," he said. "As you have seen – pointing to the works of Franz Bardon – producing, accessing, raising power is the easy part, but channelling it, harnessing it, holding it, controlling it? Those are other matters." He had nailed it.

Monday 15th. 7.00pm. The Cave. I immediately greeted the Hermit, the archetype from the Tarot.

"I am the Hermit," he said and motioned me to sit down. He merged into me "You will not sustain this for long, maybe two hours, so return again tomorrow. When in need bring me to your throat." I had a demanding mentoring session coming up next.

Hermes seemed to still be around, I heard him speak the vague words, "soon, soon, guiding..."

Tuesday 16th. The Temple. On arriving in the Temple, Hermes was clear and direct. "It is important to understand that you do not decide if you are ready or not. We do. We know and it is for you to recognise and to hear that call. You must understand that here, you are the servant. In the Outer World you may be the Master, but not here."

"So every master is somewhere a servant?" I replied.

"Yes, and it is vital that you get this relationship the right way round. With us you are the servant, with them you are the Master."

"And from here stems my humility?" I asked, to no answer.

His were harsh words but extremely interesting. I had, it seems, got it the wrong way round. I thought it was up to me to decide whether to do the work or not, but of course I had decided that a long time ago and all this, right now, was the fulfilment of my promises way back then, and more recently my oaths. They were, it now seemed, oaths to service. Perhaps I had not read the small print.

Wednesday 17th. 4.00pm. The Astral. The Temple. "Hello," said Arthur, before I could get my bearings. "What have you learned today?"

"That the Dark Side causes all sorts of trouble," I said. It had been a tough day of readings.

"Oh yes. Anything else?"

"Women operate differently to me. Men care about things, concepts, ideas, stuff, processes, results. Women care about, well, people. And love, they always go on about love."

"Well, in a way they are right," he said. "But not in any way that you can understand or relate to. Don't worry about it." I asked about Hermes. "Well, there are others," he said.

"What do you mean, others?"

"Ask him." I thanked Arthur and said goodbye. Moving into the Temple I saw Hermes.

"I am trying to build The Hermitage," I said.

"Yes, you are. Not as fast as we would like, or as fast as you could, but you are doing it," he said.

"What can I release to speed up my progress?"

"TV. Twitter. Use that only for making announcements not looking at other people. Just continue to proceed as you now are and everything will develop. But remember, we decide when you are ready. You decide if you want in, but we decide if you can."

"Who is we?" I asked.

"The Brotherhood of Light," he said, without pause.

"Who are they?"

"That is for another time." I asked about Kundalini. "Most books on this are not correct. The Cosmic Fire descends from above and causes a reaction inside. You yourself have experienced this. The usual explanation is not the whole story."

Friday 19th. 3.00pm. The Temple. I asked Hermes about The Brotherhood of Light. "As Franz Bardon suggests, it is to do with the Zone girdling the Earth, of which I am one, the Leader. But this is not for you, yet. You have trouble enough with just one of us. Have a short rest, stop getting distracted, I shan't say it again." I asked about a venue for courses that I had used in the past. "There is nothing for you there. You cannot deal with these people. You have taken yourself out of time and these are the consequences, you cannot effectively form relationships with other people. You gain tremendous other benefits from this, but also the downside."

Afterwards: That evening at home I was again most dissatisfied. There was a constant push from Hermes and others to 'come back tomorrow', 'daily practice', 'running out of time' and especially 'more to learn'. But what did these words even mean? What did the end game look like, what did the path to the end game look like? I myself had experienced great difficulty with pupils who had given up when they could not see the path ahead and I had been near to that point many times. I remembered a particularly fractious encounter with Arthur during the late nineties when I had asked that his lessons be more structured, so that I might prepare and have a vision of where the work, and I the pupil, was headed. He replied mockingly, as if I had advocated mass slaughter of first born children. "So you want to *choose* what you learn?" I remember feeling in that moment that my brain might explode as I changed from fourth gear straight into reverse. Of course I wanted to choose what I learned. That's how it goes isn't it? How wrong I was.

If I were trying to sell a product or service then customer satisfaction is key and in that sphere the customer is always right (even when he clearly is not). However in the land of education and development then it is courage that seems to become paramount, specifically the courage of the teacher to point out, or lead the pupil toward a realisation, that they were wrong. This may be scored very low in terms of customer satisfaction by the pupil, but if the teacher has not the courage to show the way, and the pupil not the courage to listen, then the pupil will direct their own learning which will only ever be down the path of least resistance. It can be no other way, for the pupil does not know what he does not know and indeed can have no possible idea of what it takes to know it! I understand that this is not how the current school education system works, but it certainly seems to be how this education system works, for the teachers – from Arthur to Hermes – seem to treat me as the pupil who refuses to reach high unless somehow pushed to do so.

In the Outer World community of teachers and learners much is said about learning styles - how to best assimilate new information, visual, audio, kinaesthetic etc. There are many models, but maybe your preferred style is only that - your preference - and if we are seeking growth then we must go beyond what comes naturally.

Arthur seemed to be teacher of the school called *Speech Creates*. When we read something our vocal chords move ever so minutely as if we are actually speaking the words. They no longer become the words of the author, but ours. He constantly got me to read stuff, in front of him, out loud. These words would always sink in more than the stuff that he said directly to me. Combined with concentration and intention the method has interesting ramifications, suggesting that listening (by itself) generates much less of an effect on the individual, the Ego being readily able to resist being told anything it doesn't like. But by reading aloud – with concentration and focus - the words seem to run through and into you, and the Ego seems not quite as present. But how does this work with an overshadowing or indwelling, such as is constantly occurring in my Inner World excursions. It can't just be a case of enter, vibrate, get told stuff, go home?

Monday 22nd. 3.00pm. The Temple. The Astral. Hermes directed me toward Merlin, on my right. I lamented the constant disturbances of my business life.

"You are in the game. It will persist like this until you leave the game. It is the Dark Side. As soon as you create a fixed point in the distance – a deadline, a completion date – then the Dark Side has room to plot and plan. Involve these business people in your schedules, then they may work their positivity, such that it is, to assist you." I was very uncertain about this.

"Moving deadlines, travel disruptions, timed plans going awry, these things are functions of your name Richard Abbot, and its lack of Five." I was aware of this but hoped that I had transcended it. Clearly not. I went to leave and Hermes now spoke.

"The weekend?" I had just finished a co-teaching weekend. The attendance had been poor, but more depressingly my session had been hijacked by a pupil dedicated to refusing anything and everything that might help her. I turned back to Merlin.

"Why do these things happen?" I asked, exasperated. "I mean, I know she was me, behaving exactly as I did twenty years ago. But she is sixty plus!"

"Have you seen Arthur?" he replied.

"He knows this," I said.

"Nonetheless, you should see him again."

Moving to the Astral I explained the situation to Arthur. The disruptive lady, had been very like me. My annoyance at her behaviour was great. But it forced me to recognise that this was indeed how I had been all those years ago.

"I am sorry," I said to Arthur. I did actually mean it. I must have been a great pain to him.

"I know you are," he laughed. "It is done with now," and he disappeared.

Tuesday 23rd. 5.00pm. The Astral. I had been planning, or at least thinking about this day for a long time, and I felt I was now ready to do it. I wanted to reach Franz Bardon on the Astral Plane. I performed the entry in the usual way, but it took some time to reach him. He seemed to be living in a very high and fine vibration. I called for him and he answered.

"Are you trying to follow in my shoes?" he said, already aware of my intentions.

"Trying," I replied.

"Few have succeeded," he said.

"Can I ask you some questions?" He signalled that this was acceptable.

"Is everything that you wrote correct?"

"Yes."

"Without exaggeration?"

"Yes."

"What would you add to it now?"

"I would include more about speed, and how there is no hurry. I would emphasise that much more."

"Can Book Three work in English?" (It was written as a practice using the German alphabet.)

"It can be adapted," he said.

"What about Book Four?"

"Oh, we weren't ready for that!" he said.

"Will we be?"

"Maybe."

I thanked him and he seemed happy with the conversation. He was smiling, but I did not want to overdo it, or outstay my welcome in any way at all. I descended and entered the Inner Landscape to visit Merlin.

"Wild weather you are having out there," he said. "You ought to go out into it and see what you can muster." I asked about two of my mentorship pupils.

"Ah yes, your apprentices. They are trying you know. One particularly, she is trying very hard, but that is the problem. Tell her to stop trying, and just do. You must now think about what you can give them in order that they may cope when you leave. Your work with them has run its course, for now. They think that you are a remarkable man and they hope that some of it rubs off on them, even if they cannot master the material. Pass them each a letter with a Hermit tarot card enclosed and say to be still and in tune when they are in need." I thanked him and returned home.

Wednesday 24th. 5.00pm. The Inner World. On arrival at the Library the Keeper was short and abrupt. I asked if my two pupils had managed to re-write the books of their lives? Two books came down, one thicker than the other. The thick book first, belonging to the more challenging of the pair. "She has made great strides, you have made a deep impression on her."

Thursday 25th. 6.00pm. The Temple. Entry was difficult and the door to the Temple was locked. I could only reach Merlin and asked him why.

"The door is locked by Hermes and you do not have the key. He decides when to open it, not you. You have not fulfilled your part of the bargain." I was so tired and could barely assimilate the words. I called for Hermes.

"How can I continue with the work?" I said.

"Are you sure you want to?" he replied. I said that I did.

"Then a dedication is necessary. A dedication of your life to the work, all encompassing." I paused for breath, this had not been the kind of continuing I had in mind. "See, you waiver. You cannot say that you are in, and then not be in. Visit again only when you have decided." He was not happy. And thus neither was I.

Friday 26th. 3.00pm. The Inner World. "Sit down son," said Merlin.

"Where has it gone so wrong?" I asked. Hermes' words last time had been correct but I did not like them.

"You know so much…" he said.

"...but maybe so little?" I said, finishing his sentence for him. A Hermit figure appeared.

"Come only with me if you wish to know the answers." he said. I followed him through the undergrowth, trees, bushes, which became thicker and denser. It was hard to move through and harder still to keep up with the figure. Finally we reached a small clearing. "It is your fault," he said. "You gained knowledge before you were ready. Huge knowledge before you should. Yet you also cannot handle it. This will heal with time, but how much time? You stepped forward so you must adapt and learn how to handle it. You said you were ready so you must be ready. Or not." His tone was forceful and not a little foreboding. My head was pounding, I left and returned to Merlin.

Sunday 28th. 9.00am. Upon moving through the cave I could see Merlin tall and thin, on the horizon. "Where are we?" I asked, "this is not the Inner World."

"We are elsewhere," he said.

"Do we, can we, ever transcend our Destiny Number?" I asked.

"The Four Roads act as a foundation for the true and specific Life Purpose to unfold. It is not about being, in your case, Three or not Three, it is about getting the Three in the right relationship to the Nine - the number of The Hermit. If the four roads go astray or we fall off them then the Life Purpose cannot be found or developed. Draw the Threes of the Tarot. Re-read everything about Three and understand." He continued. "People – and their numbers – are more powerful than money, food or buildings. If we forget that then they win! The dedication requires a dedication to showing people how to be happy. The understanding of the Dark Side that you have is valuable, but you give too much emphasis to it. Happiness can be attained – Three!" I was appreciative of the detailed nature of the guidance.

"Thank you Merlin."

"Come again tomorrow," he said, "and by the way, I am not Merlin. I am you." I was struck dumb.

Monday 29th. 7.00pm. The Cave. I had not attended the Temple for days. When I finally entered I asked Merlin how I might cope with all the tasks I had to perform, mainly in the Outer World.

"Something has to go," he said.

"What?"

"That is for you to decide."

"So where do we go next. Herbalism has become interesting to me," testing myself as much as Merlin by the question.

"Then Herbalism it is, but something has to go. The purpose of this time is consolidation, prior to the next phase of growth, getting yourself stronger in presence and in mind. Something has to go. The work cannot be completed at this stage." Merlin merged into me and I felt a little stronger.

Wednesday 31st. 5.00pm. The Cave. Merlin spoke. "You can contact me at any time. The music you use and the chair you sit in are but triggers and the contact can still – is still – being made. The requirements are simply clarity, focus and honesty. Any upturn in your fortunes, relative to the difficult times you are all in, is directly connected to the removal of the Dark Side from your life. The Fylfot Cross talisman you have received is powerful magick, but itself is the cumulative effect of all your workings. Dark goes, Light comes in. The Light in this case is money and business. That is what is needed now. As the Dark recedes so the Light goes exactly where it is needed." I thanked him. Or perhaps I thanked myself.

[AUGUST 2013]

Thursday 1st. 5.00pm. The Cave. Merlin again. "You cannot stop the effects of the work you have done on yourself. Accept what the Universe wants to give you. You cannot put a break on it, you are not strong enough and it will not work. Be careful with these new pupils, they are particularly delicate gentle souls. You know your business well enough, if you focus you will get everything done, but you will have to monitor things while you are away."

The irony of the situation was not lost on me. I was shortly leaving for three weeks in America, and in spite of months where my business life had barely ticked over I was now inundated with orders and enquiries. The money was nice, and afterwards the stresses would not to matter that much, but at the time it was annoying to have my life dictated to in this way.

Sunday 4th. 2.00pm. The Cave. Merlin again, for the last time before my trip away. "You cannot progress any further at the moment. Hermes is neither upset nor angry, but you simply cannot, so he withdraws. You must be totally committed to this work and you are not."

"I don't know how to be," I said.

"Fine. And therefore you are not. There is no judgement. It just is. The Hermit is known by all but maintains his distance. He is uninvolved. Everybody knows you, but few approach you. You are further on than it seems. It is hard on this path, but it is possible. You can cope with everything that you need to do, if you focus. But it is your choice. It is always your choice. Come again as soon as you are able."

Friday 23rd. 7.30pm. The Cave. The Temple. My trip to America had been successful, interesting, productive and – I was told – helpful to others. But it had given me pause for thought. Entering the Landscape I found Hermes.

"I am sorry for letting you down," I said to him.

"You have let no one down other than yourself," he said. "You are not ready, maybe in five years you will be. It cannot happen sooner than you are ready for – you know that. Merlin will be your Guide for daily affairs and I will assist occasionally. There is much you can do, a great deal to learn and to practice. Now you may leave." I thanked him and turned to Merlin.

"You are already higher up and further along than anyone you know. The ultimate high will have to wait a little longer, that's all. Come back again tomorrow. If you want to set it straight and earn back Hermes' guidance then you must work toward it daily."

Monday 26th. 7.00pm. The Astral. I greeted Arthur, in the Upper Astral. "They loved your work in San Francisco," I said to him. He was smiling and emitted a warm glow. "That is good," he said, "but you delivered it, not me. The congratulations pass to you." That was nice of him to say, but I knew who the genius was here, and it wasn't me. "There will not be much more from me soon," he said. "My time draws to a close. You are where I said you would be. Before I moved on I said it would take you until forty-five years old to piece it all together. The key of life is learning, and really there isn't enough time, so grab every opportunity you possibly can. It is the learning that makes life better. Goodbye." He waved and smiled.

I sought solace in the Cave, to speak with Merlin. Instead there was another presence.

"You want to learn, then come with me," said a tall Chinese man with a long white straight beard, dressed in red and white garments. "See this," he said, drawing on the ground.

X 7 X   Seven often looks upwards.

X 5 X   Five can go anywhere.

X 3 X   Three often looks downwards.

He drew other similar patterns that I could not make out.

"Now this," he said.

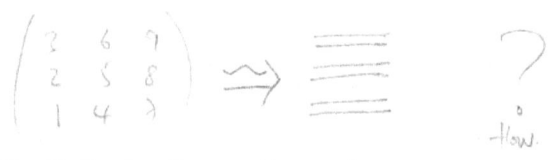

How Do Numbers Become a Hexagram?

"How does the first, the number key, get to the second, the hexagram key?" he asked, "Study, learn, research, come again tomorrow."

"But where is Merlin, and who are you?" I asked.

"My name is Lao Tzu."

Afterwards: I was intrigued by this new development, but disturbed and disappointed with what happened with Hermes. To dedicate to Hermes or not, to decide or not? I cannot visit Hermes until I have decided. What is the dedication? To show people how to be happy? I was hardly a shining example of that.

"You pushed for the knowledge, now you must handle it," rang again in my ears.

CHAPTER XIX
LAO TZU

[AUGUST 2013]

Thursday 29th. 5.00pm. The Cave. Lao Tzu was immediately available. "You must allow people a little of what they want," he said. "It is just too hard otherwise." To whom was he referring? "Do you wish me to merge into you?" I accepted his offer and could see how first Merlin, then Lao Tzu were links in the Hermetic Chain, the Line of Hermes. He asked if I had mastered the numerology I had been given.

"I am working on it." I replied. I had not even started.

"Numerology is the key to both the I Ching and the Tarot. It is the key to colour and vibration, including the voice, although a great deal can be achieved by simply lowering the voice and speaking from the heart and chest. Research more to discover more. I will stay with you a while, and then disappear later."

[SEPTEMBER 2013]

Wednesday 4th. 7.00pm. The Cave. The Astral. "Have you mastered the problem yet?" said Lao Tzu, continuing, "ah, yes, you are working on it." I assumed he was not being sarcastic.

"What is the next lesson?" I asked.

"Oh, you are already on it - how to take the work out of the head and into the body. It is an age old problem that, come again soon."

I asked to visit Franz Bardon on the Astral. I was struggling to concentrate now.

"Can the vital energy and the exercises damage you?" I asked.

"No," he said, "but hanging onto the vital energy can," he replied.

"That is what I think I must have been doing," I replied.

"Ah, I made that mistake. It causes damage but it should be released as soon as you can. Do that and visit again soon," he said. Home. Tired.

Saturday 7th. 4.00pm. The Cave. I bowed as I arrived in front of Lao Tzu. I did not generally do 'humble' very well, but Arthur had always said that such amazing beings required a 'good deal of bowing and scraping.' I was never going to go that far, but a little might not hurt.

"There is no need to bow," he said. "Have you worked out the puzzle yet?" I replied, but not from my conscious brain.

"All things are related to, created and generated by, numbers."

"Yes" he said, waiting for much more.

"And these things, and their numbers, are all interrelated. As in fact are words."

"Yes…"

"And these things, forming connections, give life."

"Yes…" leading me onto more.

"And they exist in the four sided arrangement you showed me."

"Yes…"

I wanted to say 3D, but the words out of my mouth were "And this arrangement is four dimensional."

"Yes…" I still wasn't there. I visualised a cube, eight opposing corners, one – ninth - central point. "Spend a little more time with it," he said, knowingly.

I asked to speak with Merlin. I asked all sorts of things related to the topic of Atlantis, and received all manner of replies, but nothing that could be formed into English language on a page, such is the limited form of communication we have. I asked about the desire and the need to make money.

"Do it," said a voice, neither Lao nor Merlin. "But we cannot advise. This matter is outside of our field."

I was starting to suspect that these beings, Hermes, Lao Tzu and Merlin, were in fact the same essence, connected by a thread. I said nothing, and merely allowed the thought to brush through my mind.

"And to Arthur, and maybe to you," said Lao.

"Maybe," said the Hermit from the Tarot, suddenly visible now.

"John Dee also, at one time," said another voice. This was interesting. I asked of the Enochian language but could hear no reply. Arriving back to write all this down my head was fuzzy and my recollections more vague than usual.

Sunday 8th. 10.00am. The Cave. The Temple. Reaching Lao Tzu I once again bowed. "There is no need to bow, we are equals." I was most surprised by that.

"Why can I not manifest precisely what I want?" I asked.

"Wants are a distraction from needs, as you know. We are trying to guide you, but you have already, in this life, fulfilled an enormous number of wants and those already distract you from your needs. The fulfilment of more wants might well knock you off your path altogether." I said I would reflect on this. He did have a point. "Please do," he said, "now how are you coming along with the puzzle?"

"I have found a book, or it found me, *The Kabala of Numbers* by Sepharial."

"Ah, read well. Study it. It contains great secrets and the hidden keys for which you have been searching. Study at length."

"Thank you. Can I see Franz Bardon now?"

"Yes, go to the Temple" he replied.

I rose up astrally to the Temple and was first of all greeted by Hermes. He seemed reluctant to grant my request, but without pleading or argument he relented. Franz Bardon appeared, a jolly, round man.

"This is the place of Magickal Invocation," he said and then continued onto something about Book Three being devised and used elsewhere, as if that elsewhere was not Planet Earth. I asked where I might be able to access Book Four. He quietly gestured toward Hermes. Enough said, that would have to be one for the future! I turned back to Franz and asked him what he had gotten wrong in his works. "Nothing," he said, but Hermes stepped in.

"That is not true. He was guilty of overstating the value and significance of the early exercises. They are really only practices and disciplines to the greater techniques later on. Complete mastery of the early techniques does not, by itself, bring an ability to handle any of the later work." Franz deferred and smiled. I thanked them both and bowed low.

Monday 9th. 7.00pm. The Cave. Lao again warned me of the dangers of getting too involved with the lives of others in the Outer World. I asked specifically of a client with some health difficulties, for whom I had already suggested numerous herbal and meditative options.

"There is not much you can do here. All the things you have listed to her will ease her symptoms, but the matter is deeper. Ask her what she believes, and then whether she is prepared – through knowledge and learning – to abandon all those beliefs. You may need to be subtle rather than direct and tease the answers out of her. In this matter you may also appeal directly to Hermes." Most helpful. I moved up to the Temple. Hermes spoke.

"You may appeal to the spirit that controls her, that she be released." These were entirely unexpected words.

"Is he likely to release her?" I asked.

"No, not without something in return. You may appeal, and provide the something, but extreme care is required. This is all part of the work, but be very careful. All are under the control of and bound to a spirit, from which they are trying to escape." The words registered, but were not understood.

Thursday 19th. 7.00pm. The Cave. Lao Tzu spoke directly and clearly. "You must write down everything that you know in a book. It is the only way to move through, beyond and into freedom."

[OCTOBER 2013]

Tuesday 1st. 7.00pm. The Temple. It had been another long absence from the Temple. The time had given me cause to reflect upon a great deal.

"How may I serve you?" I asked of Hermes, bracing for the response.

"By taking the oath," he replied.

"But what does it entail?"

"Then you are not ready to take it. Come again soon," he said without rancour or regret, handing me back to Lao, nearby.

"Listen my son," he said. "You work for yourself and for your own progress, but that is not the goal. You in fact work for the many millions who have barely inched themselves forward over millennia. You must find a way to help them to progress. Your results are not relevant, you are already way ahead of them."

"Then let's start with today's pupil," I said.

"You must be extremely careful, your pupils' attachments stunt their progress. You must appeal to her Angel of the North to enter and take charge over her Angel of the South. She has both, that is the key. Search her astrological data for clues on this and learn the path." I asked about some other pupils. Lao seemed pleased at the individual progress being made.

Wednesday 2nd. 8.00am. The Cave. Lao Tzu ushered me straight inside the structure of a large pyramid. In the room within there were all manner of treasures and lights.

"Ignore The Black Pullet," he said. I had been reading *The Treasure of the Old Man of the Pyramids*, a most remarkable grimoire of strangeness. He continued. "The creation of elementals is an act of life creation. Start small. The key is to inject maximum life into them. Choose a propitious numerological day for its birth and life period. Fix this, and its end date. Select a stone or crystal which is in harmony or sympathy to the desired aim. This could even be a ring, some jewellery or even parchment. Carry this on your person. This is the practice that Arthur used in the magick stones he passed on to you. Get the pupil to select the stone they desire or are drawn to and then energise it. It will start to rebalance the person away from their demon toward growth and light. This is the core secret of elementals, it is the creation of life, the more life force is imbued into it the more active it will be. Start small, in accordance with Franz Bardon's general instructions and come back here tomorrow." I distilled his instructs as follows:

Clear, achievable, lawful goal into an object + timing + life force = Birth. Cut cord, detach emotionally, leave it to go about its business.

Thursday 3rd. 12noon. The Cave. Back in the Outer World I had been investigating the idea of making money dealing currencies on the foreign exchange markets. I asked Lao about this.

"Come, son," he said protectively, leading us over to a nearby rock. He wore red robes today. "Do you think you work better now in slower or faster moving environments?"

"Nowadays, slow ones," I said. I knew that to be true.

"Well there you have it," he replied. "You would not be able to cope with the constant information inflow and the stress. You would find it too frustrating. It is not your path, let it go."

I asked about the concept introduced a while ago about ruling angels. I had seen this referred to elsewhere as the Angels of the Day and the Night.

"There are two ways to tackle this problem. One is to strengthen the Angel of the North, the other is to defeat the Angel of the South."

"Defeat? Surely simply appeal to?"

"Appeal to yes, but then something must be offered in exchange. In the case of the particular pupil you are referring to, what her Angel of the South wants is to feed on you."

"So, as soon as I strengthen the Day, so the Night is strengthened too?" I think I understood.

"Of course."

"So the only option is to defeat and to bind the Night Angel?"

"Yes, and that is the answer. Research is needed. Contact your friends in Leeds about the reliability of the Goetia and attain a seal/symbol/representation of her Angel of the South and bind it." I hoped to take these notes and make full sense of them later. I was about to leave when I realised that I had been asking about a pupil where actually, perhaps, I should have been asking about me.

"Well you have seen your Angel of the South, and now you should bind it. There is always research to do in this field, always."

Monday 7th. 8.00pm.

It was around this time that I began a serious application of the practices and exercises taught by Franz Bardon in his Book One Initiation into Hermetics. I have reproduced in the following months all the diary notes from these experiences as well as my usual excursions for one seemed to be intimately connected with the other. This training formed part of my 'getting ready for Hermes.' Although I had modified his words extensively the essence of the training was knowledge of the elements – Fire, Water, Air and Earth, plus the fifth, Akasha which binds them together. Through visualisation, concentration and imagination the qualities of each could be comprehended, harnessed and controlled. As this takes place within the trainee, so it manifests equally in their Outer World.

Through breath and concentration I impregnated my work room with the four elements - Fire, Air, Water and Earth - in that order, afterwards sitting down and closing my eyes. In the corner of my right eye (without journeying to any other Inner place) I saw the shape of a gnome. Now it is very important for me to explain that I do not believe in gnomes, or pixies, fairies, goblins or anything like that. I believe that they are almost always the imaginings of overexcited minds. This had been my lifetime's firm position. So, in light of this strong core inner believe, backed up my years of research and evidence I repeat again what happened. Having following Franz's procedures exactly I could now see, in the corner of the room, a very small, but very stocky gnome. I said nothing but it spoke to me.

"I wish to learn from you, and in return I will protect you. My name is Hazeldine and you can call upon me whenever you need. I will be awaiting your instructions." He was neither mischievous, disruptive nor scary. He was an unthreatening, unpretentious, steady presence. And there it was. It happened.

Afterwards: Many days of reflection and research later I clarified to myself what had happened and what it meant. I had established contact with a spirit of the Earth Element (as opposed to the actual, physical Earth), named Hazeldine. He is of a pixie or gnome like nature, very small. He obeys, but only when clearly and directly instructed. He is here to learn from me and in return will perform tasks for me. He is swift, but also a little lazy and tardy, he needs constant instruction and reminding. He is able to appear outside of my work space, but only under instruction. The hierarchy of the relationship is clear but he will subvert this if I allow him to. I am in charge and I must assert my superiority as a being able to connect to all the elements, unlike him who can only connect with one. I felt that I had met many people over the years who – though not gnomes – could be called Spirits of the Earth, for although able to use the five elements, they choose only to use the one.

Tuesday 22nd. 7.30pm. The Cave. As I tried to move through to the Inner World Hazeldine seemed intent on accompanying me. Merlin however was present and halted him. Merlin spoke.

"Continue as you are, with more intense practice if you can, as you and things recover." I had suffered my near annual attack of the common cold as Summer gave way to Autumn. "Now, look down there." He pointed down the side of the mountain that we seemed to be atop. "What do you see?"

"Devastation," was the only correct word I could find.

"And?"

"Some points of light."

"Yes. Seeds of hope. Continue to develop exactly as you are, attempting to highlight and work with these points of light, these seeds of hope, as you discover them. Work with Hazeldine exactly as you have been doing. He wants your time, to be with you to learn. As you learn from higher beings, so he learns from you." Ah, so as we guide, so we grow! I asked of one of my pupils.

"You will deal with your Angel of the Night soon enough. There is no point worrying about others just yet. Stick to what you know you can handle, and yes, in this and every other regards, a complete and total acceptance of the guidance provided by your Tarot cards is a sign of great progress."

Afterwards: The Earth Element.

"What do you want to know?" I asked Hazeldine.

"What is it like to be human, to be of the four elements?" he said.

I plucked the answer to his question from out of nowhere. Or maybe I had already known it but hadn't thought about it before.

"It is contradictory. We must ourselves reach higher – out to the Akasha – in order to direct the differing natures and forces within us. We are not always focused." I said.

"I am strong," he said, demonstrating his strength and agility with a series of gymnastic manoeuvres. As he had no more questions I instructed him to visit one of my pupils and report back. Instantly he was there and back.

"She is laughing," he said. "A lot." That was at least some good news. I told him that we would continue tomorrow.

Thursday 24th. 5.30pm. "When do I become human?" asked Hazeldine.

"When you die, if you have learned enough then you will be transformed into the elements and reformed. But learning requires mistakes, attempts and effort." Interestingly and refreshingly he was enthusiastic at this prospect. Although we had access to all five elements, were we really that superior after all?

Friday 25th. 5.00pm "Why don't you do more, with all your advantages?" Hazeldine asked me. "Advantages that we do not have." I assumed at the time he meant humans as a whole, not just me.

"It's called the Dark Side," I explained. "Everyone has one."

"I don't," he said.

"Yes you do. You are vigorous and full of life, but that life is short – 31st December 2013 to be precise. That is the price you pay." Hazeldine became very grumpy and stomped off away from me.

Monday 28th. 6.00pm. Hazeldine was still grumpy, sulky and down. "How can I grow, to be more than this?" he asked.

"You must," I said from nowhere, "break. You must break old structures in order to move and grow." Instantly attentive he snapped off one of his fingers. Even though it was made of a granite and rock mixture he winced in pain as he did it. "I didn't mean literally," I said. "I meant other types of movement." Perhaps he had taken it literally because that's all he knew how to do? I gave him his Outer World instructions and off he went.

Thursday 31st. 7.00pm. The Cave. The Temple. Merlin was immediately present "Are you ready for this, to write this book? Do you want it?"

"Honestly, no." I said. "I wish there were another way, but life is growth. And the alternative is death."

"Yes, I'm afraid so," he said. "But it is possible that it could be an enormous success, if you commit wholly and completely to it. No commitment, no success."

"I need to get past this weekend," I said. Merlin agreed and said to return after that. I tried to ascend to the Temple and was greeted by Hermes.

"I am still reticent about writing any more works, for as with *The Key To Time*, you may stop it again," I said.

"But that book was not about enlightenment. It was a shortcut. This is not the same thing at all." I heard him, on some level. "Now Hazeldine. He is bound to you, and you to him until you sever the tie. He will then die but be reborn as a higher level spirit and thus will contribute to the progress of all. He is a spirit of the Earth which means he will do as he is instructed but you will have to pay the price. He will do a great deal for you with that price attached, assisting in all things earthly. He will move people and things and affect all matters related to the physical, material and financial. But that is enough for today."

Preparing the set up for bringing Hazeldine into vision I also felt the continued presence of Hermes. I agreed with Hazeldine that he should accompany me to learn what it is like to be human, in return for "abundance, attendance, money and good things." He agreed, but I reiterated that everything would happen at my command and when I say enough is enough then he must and will leave me alone and be silent. He agreed and climbed up to my right shoulder to get a new view of life. He was amazed and soaked up his new horizons. I gave him some time to revel in this before instructing him to depart on my Outer World business.

I found the whole thing extremely interesting. I was now the Guide as well as the guided.

[NOVEMBER 2013]

Monday 4th. "Your sensitive friends can see me. So can you if you look," said Hazeldine, always eager to get the discussion going. "What are those lines on your hands?" he continued, pointing to my palms.

I spoke, but again the words came not from my conscious brain. "These lines signify the multi-dimensional, multi-elemental nature of human beings." We looked at his palms. On each slab of a hand there was the faintest of lines curling around the thumb. This made him most downcast. "But how may I have more?" he said.

"You must break, stretch outside your comfort zone, release your fixity and break out into new areas of experience." He seemed to understand and was keen to try it. I ordered him off on his Outer World mission.

Tuesday 5th. The Astral. I journeyed, via the usual method, to reach Arthur, who was now far away on the Upper Astral. It took my full concentration to even make it there.

"There is very little else that I can do for you now," he said. "It is lonely, but you are doing the work. If you would like to meet a friend who might get it then I will send them. But that is all I can offer now." I thanked him and bowed my head. "That is not necessary," he said. "Just say hello to Pat." And then he was gone.

I returned back down to the landscape and saw Merlin, who agreed. "There is nothing else to be said about your life. You must spread the teachings at talks, shows, events, writings, wherever you can. The USA is for later, not at the moment. You already know more than anyone you know, but you do not use it. You must start now, or there can be little else to say." This was cause for reflection indeed. It seems that it always took two or three repeats of the message 'in here', for me to get it 'out there.'

Thursday 7th. The Cave. Merlin was waiting for me. "It is time to visit Hermes," he said and we moved up to the Temple.

"So do you understand now?" Hermes said.

"I understand that to seek fame, popularity and appreciation is an exercise in giving people what they want…"

"Don't parrot back what I have already told you!" he replied.

"…that both popularity and wants are the low path, and I must forsake these for the higher path of service."

"Do you really understand this? Are you ready?"

"I am," I said. And in that moment I really felt that I was. After a pause came the unexpected reply.

"Very well. Cross your hands over your chest. I, Hermes Thrice Great, Trismegestus, Thoth also known, invoke thee Richard to thy cause of Truth and Light. You shall be supported on path."

The phone in the Outer World rang. Argh!! No!! What a time.

"Choose now!" he said. I was expecting an important call relating to the coming weekend. It was important and I really needed to take it. But I could not miss this chance with Hermes. The phone still ringing I decided that this was the most vital thing, so I stayed where I was and let the answer machine kick in, holding my concentration as best I could.

"I will need some distractions removing," I said, trying to make light of the interruption.

"I shall do this, worry not. You will need daily attendance and prayer, plus daily work and together the mysteries shall flow through you. Operate only from guidance now." Hermes merged with me, shattering my existing body entirely. My muscles ripped themselves apart, my bones creaked, everything tightened, and then relaxed and then tightened again. It continued like this for what could have been sixty seconds or sixty minutes before the feeling subsided. "Go now. Return tomorrow. It all starts then." At least, a reprieve. Better not mess it up this time.

Friday 8th. The Cave. Hermes was waiting and instructed me to visit with Merlin today. The figures changed and Merlin asked what I wished to know. I asked how I might progress and finish my writing.

"Persistence. It is the key to so much in life. To keep going and going and going against and above all. You may need to cut and paste sheets of paper all over the floor to help organise your mind and visualise the flow of the message, but basically, just get it done, as you are doing! You may go as far as you like with the message, so long as it remains broadly positive. Just make sure you go as far as you can."

Monday 11th. The Temple. Giving the Mark of Hermes to enter the space I saw Hermes stood directly ahead of me, not off to one side like he sometimes was. He had let me back in.

"Are you ready to take the oath?" he said.

"I thought we did this the other day?" I said. I was trying to not give the impression of nerves, uncertainty or apprehension.

"That was my part, now it is your turn."

"I do not know the words," I said.

"Then you must find them. If your intentions are true then you will speak correctly." I thought for a short while.

"I am The Hermit." I said. "I am the Illuminator." My body exploded, as all the pent up energy of years, maybe lifetimes, was released and I felt the inrush of a thousand or more different bodies and minds enter me. I could hear generations of voices, laughing, talking, chattering, arguing.

"You are," said Hermes. "There is no going back now. There are many people to guide, and you must do this. Visit here daily for on going instruction. You are powerful, but do not misuse it." I returned home, totally exhausted. I felt so old, like my body would give up on me at any minute, though I was also strangely determined, in a way I had not been before.

Wednesday 13th. The Astral. I had a long list of people I wanted to visit on the Astral, but I was not clear on who would or would not be accessible. Arthur had spoken of his own Astral time being the "equivalent of up to three to five years" after which he would no longer be reached in preparation for his return. He had often spoken of key figures from history "remaining there for a very long time, so that when they return here they have a great deal of catching up to do." With all this in mind I decided to visit Aleister Crowley to see what all the fuss was about.

"How dare you disturb me!" came a voice, well along in the Upper Astral. I replied that I came only seeking guidance. He laughed. "You!? You should know!" He repeated it again for good measure. "YOU should know!" He would say nothing more and despatched me pretty swiftly.

Merlin was now present. "Today's tuition is from Hermes," he said. I ascended and entered the Temple and Hermes spoke. "You need to be everywhere, doing everything. Your personal feelings regarding organisers and promoters are irrelevant, it is simply a matter of whether they get people into the room, or not. I will handle everything else."

Monday 18th. Today was an experiment with the elements Earth and Water. Accumulating Earth into the room created the correct environment for Hazeldine to appear. He wanted to know more about humans and more about how to break out of his form. I suggested Tai Chi type movements but his efforts were restricted and jerky. I suggested that he needed to understand the word "flow" through the introduction of water. He went away to practice.

Dispersing Earth, I collected Water. I could see, at first, numerous faces, which slowly formed together into one identifiable face. She called herself "Juno" and had barely any definite form or edges to her being. Her colours were all kinds and shades of blue, and although not beautiful as such she was alluring and enticing. She swirled around me and about me, impossible to contain. I instructed her to stop. She slowed a little but did not fully comply. "You cannot control me," she said and slipped away.

Later, The Cave. Merlin showed me over to an expanse of water over to the left of my vision, called The Eastern Sea. I had been aware of this for a long time, but apart from one brief encounter had given it little attention. I queried why it should be identified as Eastern, when it was clearly not. Merlin simply confirmed, "the name is correct." He continued, "the Inner World is a construction of the four elements in raw form. They also appear in the Outer World in a more developed form. This is a great secret," he said, "that cannot be released yet. 4 + 4 + 1 = completion. The One is the controlling intelligence, of which you must become part. The Temple is the place where this may occur. But enough now, leave, for there is much writing do."

Sunday 24th. The Temple. "You stand on the edge of a very great undertaking," said Hermes. "Tension and apprehension are understandable but invoke me to receive the required strength. Write my word and your commentary, it is better to have both. It is now time to jump. There is nothing left but this now."

Wednesday 27th. Hazeldine stomped into the room, but not angrily, it was just his manner. I told him again to "bend out of shape, and back again - literally in all ways – in order to move beyond the physical."

Merlin said that my next task was to journey through all the twenty-two cards of the Major Arcana.

Later, The Fool. In contemplation, prior to entry, I could see the Hermit's staff, and the Fool, who was a picture of innocence and took only what he needed. He had thus washed himself clean from previous endeavours and was pure.

Entering, the figure spoke. "Come here," he said, dancing around. "Would you like to hear a secret?" Without waiting for any kind of reply he spilled the beans. "It is you – you were the one all along, the Hermit, the seeker!" I did not understand. "Oh yes!" he continued. "Do you want to know how I do it, how I move around like this?" He was dancing around, but between dimensions, states and forms, appearing and then disappearing, animal then human, then who knows what. I signalled that of course I wanted to know more. "It is because I am nothing," he said. "I do not want to be or do anything particular. I just am."

"But what about a purpose to life, a direction?" I asked.

"Well maybe I have already accomplished it, or perhaps I am not interested in it?" he replied, unwilling to be pinned down in any way. He was free from want and desire, and thus could move anywhere and anyhow. There must be meaning in this for me. "I just am," he exclaimed. "Twenty Two. Zero." He was not interested in proofs, reasons, expectations, desires, ambitions, regret, looking forward or backward. He just was. "Do visit another day," he said, "before you go onto the others."

Thursday 28th. The Fool. "Is this the state that you seek?" said the Fool, continuing his behaviour from the previous day. As he moved around in all directions, able to turn and change in an instant leaving a trail of glittering lights in his wake.

"Sometimes yes," I said. "But you have no goal or purpose. I could not do that."

"But maybe I do have such things!" he said, condensing himself into a multi coloured ball of gas, now hovering directly in front of my face. I asked him if there was anything he might be able to offer to help me along the way. "You think you are ready?" and after a short pause he continued, "open your mouth." I did as requested, in both worlds, and he breathed himself into me. For a fraction of a second there was vast explosion inside my body. "The Breath of Life," he said. "Now go and live it! Return here once more in advance of the Magician – if you think you are ready." I was buzzing, and not at all tired. I returned home refreshed.

Friday 29th. The Fool. "Do you want to learn Magick?" said the fast moving ball of light that was the Fool.

"Do we not all wish to gain control of our life and surroundings?" I replied. He indicated that this was an interesting answer, "but the first thing you must learn is that the elements cannot be coerced. You can only harmonise with them. This is done through recognising them, penetrating them and then wielding them. Those who seek to coerce or disrespect the elements – whether by ignorance or falsehood – will be flipped over by them in one second and destroyed. Remember that well. If you do then you are ready to move on."

Realisation: The Fool flows, he does not manipulate.

[DECEMBER 2013]

Sunday 1st. The Magician. "Enter, you may enter," said the voice. This will be your last visit here for a while. You must now complete the Tattva Vision Exercises before you may proceed any further. Each card contains a series of exercises and understandings which must be mastered in turn. Come back when you have done this.

CHAPTER XX
THE LORDS OF CHANGE

[DECEMBER 2013]

Saturday 7th. Painting The Elements. Painting each of the Tattva Cards in turn proved to be a time consuming and exhausting process. The colours had to be selected very carefully, as did the paper. I was no artist so much preparation on how to draw the shapes was needed. Twenty five cards were painted in total and I insisted on painting each element with different brushes and then each had to be meditated upon, and then travelled into and through. I had initially hoped to complete the exercise within five or six weeks, one week for each element, plus a little slack for repeated journeys. In the event the entire process took me on a seven month rollercoaster of the strangest incidents, Inner and Outer, that I had yet encountered.

The weather changed as I moved through the creation and exploration of each of the elements and the cards. My eating habits changed, as did my skin tone and the people that I met, and how I interacted with them. There grew to be no doubt in my mind that the action of brush in paint and paint on paper created ripples in the pond of life. This work with the elements, punctuated by occasional catch ups with Hermes and friends, together with various other connected deviations, was, for me the most real of the all the things I had done in this work. It was through this process that I finally knitted together the threads of the Inner and Outer Worlds. As I painted each I noted down the thoughts and feelings generated, sticking to the consistent maxim that you cannot imagine the unexpected.

Earth – Yellow Square. Matters of flesh, all things bound and within bounds. The brilliance of the yellow acts as an attractant for many but concedes its truth nature and true weight. It is shining and warm. As I painted the first bright yellow square the Sun came out and blazed through the window.

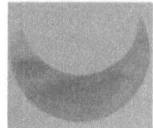

Water - Silver Crescent. As I laid the metallic silver on the page I became suddenly exhausted, drained of all energy and direction. The crescent was the same shape used in Islam, and this struck me. It seemed to emit a magnetic pull, submerging me under. It was quiet and subtle in its power. I needed shorter, sharper strokes to give the shape any accuracy or definition. The edges were particularly hard to paint accurately.

Air – Blue Disk. As I circled the brush around to create a bright blue circle my mind was filled with ifs, coulds and maybes, all of them leading to a greater if, could and maybe. Suddenly the cats were very noisy. I caught myself making more noise, tapping the table, humming. I was no longer silent, concentrating or still.

Fire – Red Triangle. By the time I reached this image my being was mashed up and exhausted. But there was more to come. Suddenly I was burning, my limbs ached, I was thirsty. I drew myself a pint glass of cold water and downed it in one. My nerves felt shredded and I was flying.

I had to lie down after painting these four, returning a little refreshed a couple of hours later.

Akasha – Dark Indigo Egg. My mind filled with dreams and visions of a global, uplifting then cosmic nature. These felt different to the thoughts of Air, they were not expansive or reliant on any kind of process or steps. They just burst forth into my awareness, fully formed within themselves.

The purity of each experience was very distinct and quite shocking. It must be too much for each element to exist, uncombined, for long on this plane. Everything must be a mixture, a combination. I reflected on how two or more elements might combine and what that would look like. The deep blue/black of Akasha, fused with the redness of Fire would bring an enormous creative force, an injection and an inevitable cosmic expansion. But how to direct and control such enormous forces?

Sunday 8th. Elemental Earth. "I desire to enter the Earth Realm," I said with the card, painted with its large bright yellow square, positioned directly in my line of sight. I allowed myself to see whatever presented itself to my eyes. One of these flashes was of dinosaurs, the ultimate living expression of the Earth element. After a while of contemplating this I closed my eyes and the flashing colour purple appeared before my inner vision. This was in the form of a doorway, which I entered.

I called for Merlin, and he was there beside me. But so was an enormous and horrific monster to my left. Vicious and spitting fire it screamed out. "I am Pyrrt, Lord of Flame!" He spat more fire in a long trail out to my feet. "This is my domain," he roared. I faced him and bowed in respect, but not subservience.

"There will be no bargain today," I stated firmly to the creature. He was immensely powerful and large, but at these words he disappeared.

Hazeldine now appeared at my feet. He was with his family and friends and they all surrounded me and led me over to the right. They proudly showed off their home, which I could in that moment perceive, but not afterwards describe. It seemed that the Sun, in this domain, shone from below, not from above, in this subterranean world.

By this time quite a few of Hazeldine's kind had gathered around me. I commanded them to find me new clients in the Outer World and more income. Merlin agreed with my instruction. There were a few questions from the more eager of the assembled beings, after which they all dispersed to do my bidding. I returned home.

My attitude throughout these diaries, from their start in 2003, was to faithfully and honestly record what I experienced, even if it made no sense and defied explanation. And there were still many things I had seen and heard that I did not fully comprehend. But I had learned throughout the process that today's nonsense is tomorrow's breakthrough and next week's wisdom. I still didn't believe in pixies, or gnomes, or subterranean worlds. I had in fact spent a lifetime avoiding and denying such rubbish, but there it was, recorded exactly as it happened.

Monday 9th. Elemental Earth. Many rocks and minerals were strewn around the place, and there was a tall tower in the far distance, constructed from a dark reddish brick or stone. Hazeldine warned me not to go there. I questioned this and Merlin confirmed that for us, it was fine. So I approached the heavy door and knocked.

"You may enter," came the reply. A stone staircase immediately presented itself. "You may ascend," said the same voice. I moved up the steps, and with every step I took I became larger and stronger. At the top of the steps there was a being, unidentifiable in form, visible at the time, but impossible to describe save for his colour, black and red all over, with the same voice as earlier.

"Ah, a mighty Magician!" he cried.

"I require no flattery," I said, attempting to show neither weakness nor arrogance.

"What do you want then?" he asked, confused.

"I wish to know how to heal and repair the human body," I replied.

He laughed loudly. "The human body is weak, and is nothing compared to the strength of the mind," he said, quite unexpectedly. "You are one quarter of us," he said. Looking at the elements from this different perspective was illuminating. It might be said that he was one quarter of us, but in terms of intensity, he was 100% Earth, where we were only 25%. It depended on how you looked at it.

"Or we are four times you!" I said. The being did not reply and seemed displeased. Merlin suggested it was time to depart. I nodded respectfully to the being and we left. Merlin suggested that I visit him once more, in the future.

I sucked myself back out of this world, back through the card. As I opened my eyes and cast a protective sign of closure over the yellow square, with my mind, the card fell over and wafted off the table onto the floor.

Later, The Temple. After a little rest I sat down once more and visited the Temple, in the time honoured way, to try to verify what I had so far experienced with the elements. I gave the Mark and entered the space. Hermes was present and indicated that I sit down in his golden throne. I had not noticed this furniture before.

"You are to deliver my teachings on Earth. There is nothing else for you to do now but write, write and write. The Earth is heading to a dark time and the recording of the Word is now vital." I was in no doubt about what I had heard and I asked to see Merlin. "You may," he said, and disappeared. Lao Tzu appeared in his place. I was thinking that all three were interchangeable.

"Instruct me please, Master, in the ways of the elements," I asked.

"See them as emanations, from one to the other," he replied.

"In which direction, up/down or left/right?"

"Both," he said and presented the vision of a wave symbol to me. "This is as much as I can tell you now, continue as you are." I thanked him and returned home.

Wednesday 11th. The Temple. Giving the Mark of Hermes in the usual way I asked if there were further levels of this place that could be accessed.

"Yes, in time. Soon in fact," said Hermes.

"What protection do I need to visit the elemental realms?"

"None," he said, directly. "Protection flows from within, from knowing who you are and what you are for. So who are you?" he asked, pointedly.

"My name is Richard."

"No. Who are you?" I racked my brains. I felt we had been over this before, but like an inattentive pupil I froze when asked.

"Er. Er. I am the Hermit"

"And what are you for?"

"To illuminate?"

"Yes, that is it. To disguise yourself in the dress of the Hermit is acceptable, if you like, but those two truths are all that you need. You should have known this." He said, displeased. He was right, I should have.

Thursday 12th. The Cave. Greeting Merlin warmly I asked, "how am I to increase my protection, presence and embodiment of you?"

"Welcome me in and I will show you how," he replied. He merged into me fully for an extended period of maybe thirty seconds. "Where am I?" he said. I scanned my body and located his presence. He instructed me that placing an open hand onto this area, would activate him. "As you do this, say these words of power (he gave me an exact sentence to speak). This will bring the presence of Hermes directly into you and enable you to perform the necessary work."

"What about closing down?" I asked. "When I am finished with the work?"

"Do you want to close down?" he asked.

"It might be necessary, sometimes," I said.

"In which case simply say *thank you, I will call upon you again soon*. Visualise the energy departing you as you do this. Practice this method and you will soon find it effective. Use it for all practices, prior to all readings, sessions, meditations, journeys, talks, workshops, and situations that require it. You may combine this with your own exercises but do not overuse these things."

Later, Elemental Earth. I gave the words of power, and then said, "Teach me ways of the Earthly Realm." Glancing upon the card I entered and could see that Hazeldine and others were running for cover at the sound of an enormous giant approaching. I did not run, and repeated only the words of power, insisting that the being teach me.

"Very well," he said. "Come with me." I felt a twinge.

"No, you will teach me here," I said. The being was annoyed, but obeyed. It had bright red eyes but I did not feel scared, though if I had encountered this five or ten years ago then I might have been. He held out his hands and spoke. "See my heaviness, my density, my mass, weight and gravity. See how much is compacted into so little, but imagine further when much is contained within a lot. Then there is enormous power, though there may be little else." He continued. "See roots and plants. Mountain pine is refreshing and uplifting, fern is good for the inner soil. See oil, it is the blood of the Earth, and gas is its oxygen. And you, you would bleed this Earth dry. See your planet…" suddenly I had a vista of the Earth from space, "you have a home, yet you destroy it. This must mean that one day you will be without a home and seek one. You will travel the stars, searching for one….but that is enough," he stopped himself from saying any more.

"What is your name?" I asked.

"Maya," he said, laughing as he moved off into the distance.

I felt the need to reassert my identity and repeated the words of power as I returned. Disconnecting, I opened my eyes again to the sight of my propped up card collapsing to the floor.

Friday 13th. The Temple. My basic life scepticism had at first been an asset, keeping me grounded in my early experiments. But as it had continued so did my sense of 'one step forward one step back.' And the more that my Outer World day was full of poor behaviours, bad attitudes and unprofessionalism – from others, but also in my response to others - the more sceptical I became. But I knew now that I had to resolve it, because it was really getting in the way.

"Are you real?" I said to Merlin.

"Of course," without hesitation, "I am the embodiment of all things Guidance, Nine and Brown. Read the source material of Geoffrey of Monmouth with an open disposition. I showed you and you will see the truth. I tried to guide them all to Arthur, but I failed. In the end we all fail. Earth is but a young world really…" he caught himself drifting off. "Now, to the Temple."

I ascended and gave the Mark, bowing to Hermes. "I see your every aspect, and therefore there is no need to bow," he said. "Be seated." I looked around. "You see something new?" he asked. I did. But I could not be clear what it was. "This is the place where you will perform the invocations described by Franz Bardon and others," he said. "This is why you must visit here daily, build up and extend your practice and concentration in this plane." I asked of the Earth element, realm and domain.

"You may visit there and seek to learn whatever you like, but remember everything there is inclined to bring you down. Mark that your words of power are always needed."

I left the Temple and attempted to access the Upper Astral to visit Arthur, but a reply was spoken to me. "There will be no more contact. You have all that you need." I floated around a little longer, and then returned.

Later, Elemental Earth. "You return again," said the voice from before.

"Yes." I passed the words, "and you will answer my questions."

"Yes I will," he said.

"What is the nature of Earth, the nature of, for example, friction?"

"You know this," said the being. "It is to act as a stop, a cannot, a wall. You can see this in the symbol, my symbol." Helpful answers, but this being was tricky to contain. "What do you really desire?" he said, "you know, really?"

"I desire more clients," I replied.

"You cannot handle such," he said mockingly, before demurring and agreeing to despatch his minions to the task. "But you will have as you desire," he said. I could now see a tree rooting deep into the ground, and all around was now dark and dreary. "You have seen enough," he said. I agreed, respectfully but firmly thanked him for his cooperation and dispatched him.

Contemplation of the Symbol, back in the Outer World. The square has corners and the energy of the shape always seems to be pulling inwards, constantly reinforcing itself. It seems more contained, and certainly more structured than the other symbols. The Earth is therefore vital as a container for other things. It might be that some want to knock off the corners, but it almost seems as if the square would want to reinstate them again. Others would want to escape the Earth entirely, but it is an essential one of the four (five). Within the Earth sphere the answer is only ever Yes or No. It is never Yes and No, at the same time, in the same place – this level of understanding can only be dealt with by introducing another element. So Earth alone is really one dimensional, and that it why it is Maya – illusion. The Illusion being that there is nothing else, the heaviness of Earth keeps us down, away from what else there might be. For Earth read across to the physical body, the physical world, money, buildings, and structure of all kinds.

Saturday 14th. Painting the Earth Sub-Elements. A voice spoke. "Children of the Earth, restricted but always with the seed of a choice."

I sensed that great richness, joy and distraction stemmed from the place called Earth. Enough of these things indeed for any single human. This is the story of the Earth, from where we may gain glimpses of the other worlds, but never for too long.

I experienced great dizziness after painting these five cards, the results maybe of a constant sense of rising up just in order to be pulled down again. The Yellow of the Earth Square always larger and stronger, overwhelming the reduced size of the other four symbols within.

Sunday 15th. Water of Earth. Passing the words of power I asked. "Grant me entry to the Kingdom of the Earth."

The previous giant was still there, but had shrunk down in size. He spoke.

"You come again. What do you require?"

"Show me the watery condition of Earth," I said. At that I began to shrink down as the solid ground beneath me turned to quicksand.

"There you are," he laughed, "dragged down, without solidity."

I passed the words of power and began to rise up, slowly but surely back to solid ground. The giant seemed surprised and a little nervous.

"You will now show me a safer aspect of this." I said. He pointed to the image of a woman nearby with her legs wide open, exposing herself. Firm, but fluid, swirling. "Always messy," he said, "dragging you down, sucking you in. The key is to stand firm and not yield." After a while with the scene I felt an enormous sneeze well up inside me. I could not contain it and sneezed violently. "And to inject Air into the proceedings," he said. "It is always messy!"

Monday 16th. Air of Earth. I passed through the card in the usual way and received only the following words. "The tree, here, look, and the world that moves through it. The tree grows up in order to expose itself to the air, as do all the things that move through it. That is all. We know who you are." Ominous. They knew me, but I did not know them.

Tuesday 17th. Fire of Earth. The red triangle within the yellow square was flashing, even moving. All this and my eyes were still open. Entering the image I announced the words of power and "I demand to know the secrets of Fiery Earth."

Many images and insights flashed before me. A flower burst forth into bloom, like a speeded up movie. Flames themselves licked up into the sky, but I could see them from a totally different perspective that I could ever have imagined. I could see the inner workings of an orgasm, a build up and then release in explosive and uncontrollable form. In all these cases the bigger the build up, the bigger the tension, the bigger the release. The power of the explosion of Fire outweighs the short length of its duration. This is depicted in the symbol of Fire, the triangle, with the point smaller than the base. I could only just comprehend this.

"That is all," said a voice. "Return tomorrow for the last section of Earth. You will not be able to understand that one."

Wednesday 18th. Akasha of Earth. In preparation for this the card I had painted fell on the floor a number of times. In the end I gave up trying to look at in and tried to reproduce it in my mind. A voice spoke.

"The Spirit of Earth is contained within the dead. Within the bones, the compost, the decay. Within the oil. Within the past lives. It is found in these places only, and never among the living, unless they themselves possess an understanding and appreciation of Death and a connection to their own past lives. And there are not many of those! The living are assigned the other four elements." I thought on this for a moment and indicated that I think I understood, although it seemed big step to take. "Very well. You have completed the lessons of this level. You must now visit Merlin." I still did not know who these voices were.

I disconnected from the card image and after a short mental rest I entered the Inner World to speak with Merlin.

"Rest tonight, tomorrow will be very productive." Yes, rest was needed. "You have mastered the Earth element, what do you conclude?"

"It is called Earth for a reason," I said, "there isn't much else, only signs here and there of what could be."

"Yes, but look at the planet. It could be much more, look at its atmosphere composed, like you, of Earth, Water, Air and Fire. You may see this place, the planet, as a testing ground. Is it not much but it could be so much more. Rest now."

Afterwards: I spent some time referencing my experiences to the Tarot. The most that can be realised, within the Earth element, is the Ten of Pentacles, which is the result of abundance, but with absolutely nothing else also brings limitation and restriction. Earthly matters matter, for sure, but there also must be more to life than that. In terms of the Court Cards we might come to embody the King or Queen or Pentacles, but it is also important that we then move on from that. Yet Earth, and Pentacles, are so heavy that they continually drag us down, making it hard for us to move on and forward. The Earth replicates itself through tradition.

Saturday 21st. Elemental Water. Passing the words of power I said, "I seek entry into the Kingdom of Water." I saw many beautiful beings, bare breasted, playful and fast moving. They were all around me, laughing noisily. If I had to stick a label on them it would have been mermaids. They were captivating.

"Do not try to tempt me," I said. "I seek only knowledge." At this they lined up in front of me.

"So what do you seek?" they said, their playfulness had disappeared.

"Teach me about fish," I asked.

"They breathe water as you breath air. Take them out of their environment and they drown, just as you do out of yours." I saw an image of Fukushima. "The sea there is very hot," said one of them. This informative exchange did not last long and they were all soon all around me again, complementing and flattering me. One referred to me as a 'leader on a throne' and they all played the roles of glistening and beautiful assistants perfectly.

"We know who you are, and what you seek," said one.

"What is Water?" I asked.

"It exists in order to cleanse, to clear away and to keep movement moving." I was struggling to take in my surroundings and remember their words. "That is all for today," said one. "Come again tomorrow," said another.

Franz Bardon, among others, had issued a stark warning not to fall in love with these beautiful creatures of Water. My initial reaction on reading his words was 'yeah, no worries.' But after this experience it might prove a little harder.

Sunday 22nd. The Cave. The Temple. I moved up the beach toward the cave entrance and inside. After all this time I was not disappointed. The integrity was preserved, the atmosphere noticeably and visibly different inside to out. All things inside were recognisable and familiar, except one. I could now see the roof of the cave, it came to a point, high up above me. I could see that point projected a Vortex Elevator downwards, finishing straight in front of me. I entered it.

The buffeting, vibrating, back-to-front, side-to-side movements were unmistakable. The noise was deafening and the experience exactly as when I had visited the Astral Plane before, except this lasted a lot longer. After a period of struggling to hold concentration and focus I greeted Hermes.

"I am not Hermes," came the emotionless reply. "I am Thoth. The work must intensify now. A great many people are lost," he wielded a staff toward me. I asked of the elemental forces. "They came forth from us," he said. I could not hold concentration any longer. "Daily," he said, his voice drifting quietly away. "The message must be spread daily." Easier said than done, I thought. I am but one voice among many. And then one voice came through very clearly, which I believed to be my own.

"So, it is the Time of Giving. But enough with the giving of stuff. Instead, give of yourself. Your unique self. Accentuate your difference from the pack, emphasise your character, and if necessary your odd-ness. Over the break, find the things that you do well, and do them a lot. To truly be yourself is no indulgence, it is the biggest gift you can give to anybody, for it opens them up to a life they did not imagine, to thoughts they could not think, and options they did not consider. For the greatest illusion of all is to think that you are nothing special."

And then another voice spoke, not mine this time. "Make your own mince pies, your own messy way." I descended down from the Temple to the Inner Landscape, through the cave.

"Allow me to merge into you," said Merlin. "It is easier for you to assimilate the information that way." He did so, ripping me apart from all angles in the process.

"The four elements were the forces employed to bring creation and Life on Planet Earth. That is the most we can say. Soon I will depart and again Hermes himself will guide you directly." Was I ready for this? Did it matter what I thought? "Now visit the Water element, but be aware that it is seductive. Call upon me as instructed and read my history as laid out by Geoffrey of Monmouth as soon as possible. As you have already seen it is patchy at best, but useful especially in its use and reference of language." I was starting to lose track of where Richard ended and Merlin, or even Hermes, or Thoth began. That's a good sign right?

Later, Elemental Water. My request to enter the Kingdom of Water was refused. "No, not today. Return tomorrow." I accepted the contradiction between this and Merlin's instructions. I may have misheard, or misunderstood. I accepted and withdrew.

CHAPTER XXI

THOTH

[DECEMBER 2013]

Monday 23rd. The Cave. Thoth merged into me as soon as I arrived amid the landscape. "You are not yet proficient enough to manipulate the weather, but your workings with the elements are already having side effects." I was about to protest at such an assertion, but Thoth was way ahead of me. "Of course such a thing is possible!" I took this as a positive indication that my doubts were today getting less room to breathe. "You will proceed directly from here to the Lords of the Earth and ask of the Forgotten Lands. Report straight back to me after." So be it. I did as instructed.

Later, Elemental Earth. The new familiar giant shrank down to a pin prick size. I announced myself and said I was on instruction from Thoth. The minute giant, and many other beings, fell into line immediately.

"What do you require?" said the small giant.

"Show me the Forgotten Lands." I said.

"These are within you. Your breath is the wind, your tears are the rain, your body the ground. You are the land and the land is you. As you grow so does your environment. You exist intimately connected to your land, as it sinks so do you. A malaise in the land is a malaise in the people, and thus a malaise in the weather. All this and vice versa too. As one being awakens so it enables others to do the same. You are connected to the land in this way." I thanked the being and left immediately to report back to Thoth, repeating exactly what I had been told.

"These words are correct," he said. "Mediate upon them to reveal further answers and report back to me."

Tuesday 24th. The Cave. "See here," said Thoth, with the letters a, e, i, o, u hovering in air before us. "Now see there," he said, doing the same again with the letters r, t, b, ch, d, s. All were written and pronounced in lower case. "A, E, I, O, U are the elements. Consonants are the sub elements, mixions of the previous sounds. The secret is to vibrate the sounds so as to cause an effect in the speaker and the listener. Chipped and shortened words are of no value, they do not travel and are not heard." He then proceeded to speak of the five vowels, with the suggestion but no more than that, of a downward movement through the body - A E I O U - he took his time about this and each sound caused a different vibration in my body. It was nothing to do with volume or pitch and was associated with clear pronunciation while speaking with a defined intention, without fear of contradiction.

"Now perform the Bee Mantra," he said. (This was a special technique given in a lecture by Frater Marabas. You may be able to get it directly from The Sorcerers Apprentice in Leeds.) As I made the correct tone I could feel an even greater vibration in my lower chest. "Rushing through your speech," he said, "can often be a veiled attempt to not be heard." I asked Thoth of the Cosmic Lords and their rulership of people. "It is true. But you are not ready for this yet."

"But are people utterly controlled by their Lords, as if puppets on a string?" I asked. His response was clearly "Yes" although with a less clear "But" and an indecipherable reason why.

Later, Elemental Water. Building on Thoth's advice I spoke the words of power, trying to vibrate them outwards from my lower chest. I could feel the beginnings of an effect as I said, "I desire entry into the Kingdom of Water."

I then found myself stood on a lone rock in the middle of raging ocean. The waves swept up and I felt they were sure to overtake me. I did not resist and allowed myself to sink deep into the ocean, surrounded by the water until I was breathing it.

"We know who you are," said an unknown voice. "Now see my fair ladies." I saw three mermaid type figures, all shades of blue, beautiful maidens with piercing eyes and long hair. One particular moved her long hair aside to show more of herself to me. A loud voice punctuated this sensual atmosphere.

"Be gone." At its command the ladies of the sea vanished. I allowed myself to breath in this watery atmosphere surrounding me, building up my tolerance of the Water element in the process. "What do you seek?" said the voice.

"I desire to know the properties of liquids and water," I said.

"But liquids are not always water," he replied. "There may be solid liquids, where a powder of form has been added, maybe for healing or medicinal purposes. Then there is pure water, which is always cleansing. Any water in the form of bubbles, gases, creates lightness and optimism. Then there is fire water, such as alcohol. It is better for your body to take only two mixions at once, more than that is an explosion of sensation but presents difficulties for the body when it comes to the time of ridding itself. This creates confusion in the system. Better still drink pure water, unadulterated. Come again if you need to know more."

I returned and reflected on some of the implications of this. Water could be earthy, airy or fiery, and each type would have a different effect on the body. Earthy waters might be salted or mineral waters, or herbal waters, or crystal elixir waters. That is not even to start on homeopathy, the proof of its effectiveness now provided by the Water element itself.

Friday 27th. The Temple. Passing the Mark I entered and bowed to Thoth. He, as opposed to Hermes, if there is indeed a difference, did not refuse my bow.

"Vibrate my name," he said. I replied in the specific pronunciation I had been given by Arthur many years ago. I vibrated it, repeatedly and audibly in my Outer and Inner World simultaneously. I could feel a strong sensation welling up in my chest, then my whole being vibrated as he merged with me.

"In this state you know everything that there is." His words seemed less a prediction, more a command. My mind was flooded with images. Pictures of the Royal Family, members of the government, newspaper headlines, truths that would emerge, secrets that never would. It was horrible, the extent to which our Outer World was set to change, and then again would not. "You may safely now continue with your elemental contacts. You are aware of the banishing and invoking procedures, these are now advisable. You are building up a collection of notes, insights and ideas, but nothing much else can be accomplished until you have proceeded through these elements. You will need to consult me again on the Akashic element, at that time." I thanked him a great deal. He left.

Later, Elemental Water. Although I intensely vibrated the words of power the being before me, in the Kingdom of Water, made his power very clear. "You could be swept away in a moment," he said.

"I seek not this confrontation," I said, "only knowledge."

"Very well," he said, unintimidated. "The land is impure, its people unclean. We come to wash it away. If unrestrained we will wash it all away, all of it. As people are washed away outside so they are washed away inside. It is our time now. Stand up and look outside, in your world." I did as he said, trying to hold the connection as I opened my eyes and moved to the window, looking out and down my garden. "What do you see?" The pond was straight before me. "And what does that allow you to see?"

"Reflections," I said.

"Yes, things that you would not otherwise be able to see. That is the power of water, for a cleansing is always a revealing." The being signalled that our time was up. I expressed my thanks. Letting him and the scene go I turned back, with open eyes, to the pond outside. It was windy, yet the water was still. I caught a reflection of a twig. Was the water allowing us to see light, but not directly? Direct truths are always refused, but reflected light somehow percolates through. Is this the time of reflected truths? Truths attained indirectly, through messy realisations and others' mistakes? Truths reflected off the mirror of others. Pools of water had always been associated with visions and glimpses of insight, indeed maybe even crystal balls were in fact containers of the water element used by those who could to see reflected truths. So long as I held myself in this rarefied state I could make sense of a lot of things that were otherwise mere noise. The Moon is intimately connected with Water and itself an assistant that filters the rays of the Sun, the rays of truth, so that we might not get burned. The Moon is barren so the Earth may be abundant.

My mind turned back to my previous encounter with Maya in the Realm of the Earth. Much of the acrobatics of life, it seemed, were created by an imbalance of the elements, when they misbehave or operate unchecked, weaving into people's unbalanced energy fields and creating havoc. But the elements themselves are pure, and it is the individual's energy field - the receptacle - which is unbalanced.

Reflected truth is of course rarely the whole truth, but it is often enough truth, enough to go forward with, given that none of us can handle more than we are ready for. Today's interconnected world holds great potential for glimpsing reflected and partial truths, particularly on social media.

Saturday 28th. Elemental Water. Again there were many beautiful naked females, one in particular tried to persuade me to take her back to the Outer World, presumably to embody herself in some suitable host. I insisted no. I addressed the leading woman with my questions about the nature of Water.

"Blood, semen, menses are all vitalised water, magnetised or electrified each," she said. "They are transmitters. Saliva is fermented water, the carrier of energy and disease, but less so than semen, blood and menses."

"How may we protect ourselves from Water?" I asked.

"You cannot build too strong a barrier, yet if the barrier is too rigid then it will always be swept away in the end. Square boats always sink. Protection must be flexible, able to move with the tide. Fixed barriers will be swept away. This is your protection."

Tuesday 31st. The Temple. Thoth spoke. "Proceed now, today, to bring forth and then banish Hazeldine. Now that he has formed a link with you he cannot continue his business unchecked. Give him three options. First of merging into a crystal. Second of merging back into his Kingdom. Third of being destroyed. There is no fourth option, and inaction is not an option. The link between you must now be severed, exactly as planned."

Later, Elemental Earth. My Outer World library was full of diverse stuff, some, though not much, pertaining to the realms of the elementals. There seemed remarkable agreement, from differing sources, about the names of the Kings of the Elements, from various sources. I intended to test these and match them to my own experience, as others had clearly been there before me.

The King of the Earth Realm, who identified himself as Ghob, greeted me. I explained that I was here to banish and release Hazeldine.

"That is unnecessary," he said.

"Respectfully Lord, I say that it is." I gave my words of power.

"Very well," he agreed, stepping aside as Hazeldine appeared.

"Hazeldine, the time has come, the end of our period." I said firmly.

"Thank you for your teachings," he said. "Is there anything else I can learn?"

"Stretch, move and stretch back again," I said, indicating how he might make star jumps. He played with this for a little while. "So now I offer you three choices. Either to merge into a material form, one of the crystals on my table. Or to merge back into the energy of your own world. Or to be destroyed." Ghob was not happy when I mentioned the third option. "Choose now," I instructed.

He paused for breath and thought. He seemed interested in continuing his material existence in a stone, but in the end he choose to merge back into his own Kingdom. I had not prepared any words for this, but suddenly some came to me, beginning with my words of power.

"I, with Thoth, sever the cord that binds us. You now leave me and do not return until I ask it of you. Your life is elsewhere and is no longer bound to me." Hazeldine offered thanks and departed.

King Ghob appeared and I thanked him for his cooperation and for allowing me to work within his realm.

"What else may we do for you?" he asked.

"I ask only that from time to time, if I have need of the Earth element and your people that I may return and call upon you."

"You may do this," he said. "We thank you for the way you have treated our kind. You have our friendship and respect." I valued this and left without any further delay. It was a most interesting encounter, contrary to everything I believed, but was satisfied that this was just another aspect of the Inner World, the invisible spectrum to our visible one.

[JANUARY 2014]

Wednesday 1st. The Temple. I entered and greeted Thoth with a bow, which he accepted. I had great doubts about my life and mission. Again.

"Open your eyes." he said. "Open them, what do you see?" I opened my eyes, in the Outer World, in my room, with my books and paraphernalia. I saw my candle, flickering dimly in relation to its surroundings. "The key is to keep focused on the candle light, the goal, the truth, the meaning, and not to glance at what surrounds it. Truth will not often be found in that which surrounds the Light, only in the Light itself. At times it seems as if the Light is obscured, even extinguished, by that which surrounds it, but it only seems that way. Write and reflect around these words to discover more truth. Now continue with your work, the more time you spend here the greater sense it will all make. There is only so much time. Check back if necessary, otherwise you know what you must do."

Later, Earth of Water. "King Nixsa, I desire knowledge of the earthy aspects of water." A figure was immediately present, its form was vague and ill-defined.

"Any solid," he said, "especially square or structured is hard for water to break down. It takes us time. It is best for us to weaken it early, to wear it down before attacking. Food takes time to break down. Muscle takes time to build. Fat takes time to lose. It is best to chew food many times in the mouth first of all, introducing it to water in the mouth, before it meets water in the stomach. Earthy Water is everything that is solid but flexible. Your people of the Earth nature take a long time to wear down, to change, to move, to shift. Only the consistent drip-drip ever moves them, and even then only slowly. The stronger they are the harder it is for them."

At that he signalled our time was up. I was tired. I could imagine and maybe even actually feel the solidity of Earth inside me, not moving. We need a little water, fluidity and flow if we are ever to move at all.

Later still, The Temple. I was getting pretty overwhelmed with the flow of information from my experiences, and as usual the validation I sought in the

Outer World was not forthcoming. I approached Thoth to seek clarification of my life and my path.

"See Merlin for that," he answered and turned away. Merlin appeared.

"Thoth is only available to questions concerning forward momentum. I can answer points of clarification," he ushered me away.

"So, I am to write one book – called *Emergence* – a collection of everything I know?" I asked.

"Yes, a clarification of everything you know," he replied.

"So the elemental world and the celestial world would appear in separate books?"

"Well you haven't gotten to the celestial world yet, and the elemental world provides great explanation which is essential. For example you will cover the topic of climate change in the book and yet this is a simple function of the elements, the movement between hot/dry and wet/cold. Freezing conditions in the USA serve to solidify the changes that have already occurred in that society. Wet and windy weather blows into you a new state and stormy times. Water cools Fire and thus calms down the fiery parts of the world. These are just examples, there are many others, and all are indicated through an understanding of the elements. And you don't even have to visit the cards in order to do this." This was something to get my teeth into and I left satisfied.

Saturday 4th. The Temple. Merlin set my mind at ease on one question that would not go away.

"You can be assured," he said, "that what you have written so far can be released. Thoth and I have encouraged you all the way along although it would be good if you would increase the pace somewhat. The additional elemental practices can be included later, but what you have so far is acceptable and we would not lead you this far down the path in order just to pull the plug. Think of your work on *The Key To Time*, you were warned all the way through not to proceed. This has not happened this time. You are safe. But more please!"

Sunday 5th. Air of Water. "How may we help you?" came unfamiliar voices, in unison.

"What is Air of Water?" I asked.

"It is Water that will not rest, Water that will not settle. It is agitated and becomes steam, an aroma, a scent – pleasant or otherwise. It is water that will not stay down – feelings of sickness arise as Air pulls things up and out, while Water pulls things down. A tension results." I wanted more but was told, "that is all."

Monday 6th. Fire of Water. A volcano appeared in my vision, and then a voice.

"A little heat goes a long way in warming up water. Fire turns Water into a propellant, see this as alcohol burns. A little dosage is very helpful, but too much is destructive. Such a liquid introduces speed and evacuates material quickly, burning all the way along. That is enough for now."

Afterwards: I reflected some more on this, through the prism of Global Warming. Sea levels were rising, as sea temperatures were rising. Elementally, the sea is slowly boiling as a result of the action of the Fire element, created in part by the burning of fossil fuels. To counteract this the system re-regulates itself, producing more Water to balance out the Fire. Elemental excess in one must be corrected by elemental excess in the other. The elemental balance of the planet has been disturbed and this is reflected by a disturbance in the elemental balance in individuals. Have we invoked the elements unwisely, using too much Fire and Air, and not enough Water? Will this right itself? What will the damage be? Who is bigger, man or the elements?

Tuesday 7th. Akasha of Water. I gave the words of power before moving into the card.

"Then enter," came the voice.

"I seek to know the ways of Water, its Akasha." I said.

"Water, you see, acts with purpose, at least in part. It is directed and controlled and therefore controllable. By taking control of the Akashic part of Water so you may direct and influence its flow, spurring it on toward where it needs to go. Akashic Water tells you that Water has an intelligence, or is at least penetrable by intelligence. That is all."

I thanked the voice. "May I call, King Nixsa, upon you and your kind again?"

"You may," came the reply. Some beautiful creatures shimmered toward me. I was transfixed, for maybe five or ten seconds, by their beauty. Then I snapped out of it. King Nixsa acknowledged me, and maybe his role in this.

Wednesday 8th. Elemental Air. "I seek knowledge of the Spirits of the Air and communion with King Paralda," I said.

"Then enter." I did, and repeated my request.

"We know this. But why do you seek it? You know what Air is. It separates and expands. The formula $1 + 1 = 2$ is merely an expansion of 1. Move numerous steps onwards and you have magick numbers, Fibonacci numbers and the mode of expansion. This is Air. The molecules in your body move apart and away from each other so you float away. The essential components of the house that you live in are constantly expanding. Feel this and feel your house float away. Be careful though!"

"I wish to speak to your sylphs." I replied. Some beings appeared in a form I could not even begin to describe. "They know who you are, but will not speak until you ask them to." They were floating about, not still, isolated and removed from the world I inhabited. It might be said they hardly existed at all. Yet they did, vaguely. "That is all now," said the same voice.

"I will return again" I replied.

"Yes," he said, "that is a good idea, once again here before the individual aspects of Air are unveiled to you. We are going to have much fun together," he said. I did not know whether to be excited or afraid.

Saturday 11th. The Astral. After weeks of thought, I embarked on an Astral journey to meet the famous Elizabethan magician and scholar, Dr. John Dee.

The journey was long and tiring, longer than any other I can remember taking. He was the first to speak, saying hello.

"Can I see you? I said. He immediately appeared as a small man, still some distance away from me, draped in a large cape or cloak that covered virtually his whole body. All this was topped off with a long pointed beard.

"How did it feel to amass so much knowledge and then lose so much?" I asked him.

"You must understand that loss is what we dealt with on a daily basis. Those were harsh times – you gained and you lost. There were no sentimentality or feelings involved in it."

"What did you learn?" I asked, "what was the main thing?"

"That there is no Monad – no glyph or system that encompasses or explains it all."

"And the Enochian language?" I probed further.

"It is but one language, one way to access the," he paused, "the creative world. The word *is* the thing and the thing *is* the word. Enochian is just one route into this. You already have some ideas, to generate a sound that touches something at its core. That was our task. Continue along the path of the elements and you will discover this for yourself."

"Are you aware of my work then?"

"I am part of the creative intelligence, of course I am aware of your work. But you must now go," he said, fading into the background. "Maybe we will meet again....fame and notoriety...they are not necessary for the work..."

Later, Elemental Air. "You may speak with these," said King Paralda on his throne, gesturing toward four beings, standing in a line in ascending order of height, smallest on the left, tallest on the right. I spoke first with the tallest one. Although he was reticent to answer King Paralda gave him the clearance he seemingly needed. I identified myself to him in the usual way.

"We know who you are. The moment a thought passes across you, we know about it. It is therefore vital to direct your thoughts constructively toward lighter matters. As you think of lower matters so you form, and then marshal, lower beings. As you think of higher things so you raise yourself up. You must of course know the ways of lower things but you must not be pre-occupied or overcome by them. Think constructively and positively at all times." In an earlier time I would have incorrectly associated these words with the need to think happy thoughts and avoid sad ones, but that would have been wrong. I took the word 'higher' to refer to options, possibilities and chances, whereas lower things swirled around the pot of 'cannot, not possible, no way'. Even with this though it was easier said than done.

"How does Wi-Fi work"?" I asked.

"Point to point, through transference. It is the point to point concentration of energy that causes it to happen. You know all this. To identify and locate someone or something through numbers is to also lock onto it. Through absolute focus – piercing clarity - we can then read it, and indeed influence it. Both Wi-Fi and numerology does this, zeros and ones moving node to node." I found it very interesting how everything of value seemed to emanate from these forces, and how little of value originated directly from man alone. "Put your finger out," said the spirit, "no, your second one." I did as asked. She, and I am pretty sure it was a she, merged into me through this finger. She seemed very interested in this and remained in me for some seconds. "You may now do it. To me," she said. I again put my second finger out and merged directly into her. Everything around me was now Light. There was a great deal of stuff and energy 'down there', below me, beneath me, but I was above, separate from it all, unconnected to anyone but able to connect at a moments notice, as and when I required. After a while I gave my thanks and exited, also making sure to thank Paralda on my way out.

"One more thing," he said as I was leaving "Look after yourself before you banish us completely." I had no idea what he meant. The experience of Air had been like being everywhere and nowhere at the same time, and I had not the same sense of travelling as I got in other trips. And yet the message was that focus was the key to thought transference, reception and transmission, but not just focus of the message but a very clear focus from the sender and the recipient.

Tuesday 21st The Cave. Merlin was on hand to tell me off. "The question is not *does* magick work, it is what do you do *when* it works. You should be beyond any doubt that what you think and summon up inside comes to pass outside. Speak now to the spirits of the elements, but understand their names, they are The Lords of Change."

Later, Elemental Air. I returned again to Paralda and asked to know more about the nature of Air.

"We sweep in as wind, and destroy everything of form. We solidify its structure until it cracks and breaks, for everything whose structure and form is destroyed must collapse. Take ideas, they are destroyed by thought, reason and logic. Once all water, all compassion and feeling, has been removed from them they collapse, dry and cold. Think governments, giving way from within as procedures and rules burn away compassion and concern. Any system that moves in that direction will be swept away. Reflect upon these words and the many applications they may have to reveal greater truths. We hope you will come back and play with my minions soon."

Sunday 26th. Earth of Air. "I wish to know of Air, in its earthly aspect."

"See mist, fog, low lying dense and heavy air, air conditioning, earthy tones and deep scents, bad aromas, the stench of death," said Paralda.

"But what is the quality behind these? I asked.

"Thoughts that do not uplift, thoughts that sink and are depressing, that bring us down to earth. But, that is enough for today. You must visit again tomorrow for further secrets."

Later, The Cave. Merlin was waiting for me. "Enter young one," he said, "and follow me." He turned and started to climb up a rather steep incline. His robe was black with silver etching. "Contact all those you have previous mentored or have expressed interest before," he said. The slope grew steeper and Merlin went silent.

"It is a long way," I said.

"It is longer still," he replied, pointing upwards to a cave high at the very top of the mountain.

"But why must I climb it?" I asked.

"Because you are the only one that can. All is a contribution back to the creative intelligence, and you take a lot from the Universe, so this you must give back. Think further upon this and return."

I thanked Merlin. "I do try," I said, offering some slight defence.

"We know," he said, with some compassion.

Monday 27th. Earth of Air. "Come," said Paralda. "You will come to no harm." All around me swirled a storm force gale, lifting everything that fell into its path. The only safe place was in the direct sphere of the King himself. He then seem to click his fingers and the wind ceased. Instantly everything was completely still.

"You should meet with my sylphs," he said. I could see a few moving shapes, formless yet trying to gain form.

"The Earth in Air," said Paralda, "is the grit in the oyster, the things that enable the possibilities of Air to carry through to the Earth, but this process might result in coal as much as it does a diamond. The working of this, it processing and working through is the stuff of life and is essential for progress."

One of the formless beings came forward and gave his name as "Ea-Ay". I pronounced this back to him three times to be sure of getting it right. He spoke.

"What do you wish from me? Who shall I influence and how?" Merlin was behind me and indicated that this was not a good idea. "Then I shall wait, ready to do this as you need." He offered to merge into me. Again Merlin intervened to stop this. "Call on me," said Ea-Ay and disappeared. Paralda stepped in. "Beware!" he warned. "You know not of the power which you now have!"

I wished Ea-Ay goodbye and heard the words, "I will serve you well", but I could not ascertain precisely from where they had come. Both Ea-Ay and Paralda laughed, though not entirely innocently.

Ea-Ay? E A? Earth of Air!!! What was going on here? My attempts at utilising the powers of Air within Earthly constraints seems hard. Maybe the two factors worked together over long period of time? These sub-elements might therefore be co-operations of the elements, descriptions of the ways they move together?

"What can I do for you, King Paralda?" I asked, aware that this could not be just a one way street.

"Tell them about us," he said. "And you will need to visit me more before you can advance further."

Reflection. Within this framework of the elements the formulation of a new society – or a new anything – cannot take place seamlessly, smoothly, or quickly. If it seems that it is doing this, it is con-trick, temporary flash in the pan or an invasion. Current arguments over the shape of a new society are probably all wrong and none of today's trends will last, for they all form part of the working out process and are not themselves the end result. This is how it always goes. Just like where people of an Airy nature take longer to change and to acclimatise, turning the grit in the oyster over, multiple times.

Later, The Cave. I met the Hermit, not Merlin or any other.

"Stand and wait," he said, "still, unmoving, focused but content and accepting. Watching for the bus, while ever alert. These things are the essence of the Hermit-nature and will take you many years to master."

Tuesday 28th. Earth of Air. "Enter young one," said Paralda. "As you now see Earth is a contaminant to Air. Earth wants to fix and form, but we want no such thing. In many ways we are the most perfect of all the elements."

"Others might say the same," I replied. "As Earth is a contaminant to Air, so some might see it the other way round."

"They would, but they would not be right. Air is here all the time, all around, travelling instantly, never stuck, or washed away, ever moving and changing. Earth is a contaminant because it is restriction, a diminution of energy – and that never works out well. That is all. You see it now. You can proceed to the other stages. Would you like to see one of my sylphs?"

Merlin was present and cautioned me against this. "Such perfect beings would enrapture you too easily," he said.

Reflection: These Lords of Change, the creative forces of our World, seemed neither good or bad, or perhaps more appropriately good *and* bad. Unbalanced, or uncontrolled workings with them might therefore make good situations better or bad situations worse. Either way, it seemed silly to apply 'positivity" to them. They just were.

Thursday 30th. The Astral. I again took the long and tiring trip to speak with Dr. John Dee.

"You come again," he said. I enquired about his methods of Enochian Magick. "The Sigillum dei Ameth works. You may use it to see anything, but I was a fool with Kelley and it was a great distraction. Learn this from me and my error. You may yet be a great figure in history, you do not know what may yet happen. But you are tired, visit again, but maybe another time." I protested, asking to stay longer and learn more. "Very well. But no, there is no descendency from Merlin to me, that is not how it was. But know that is the curse of the great to suffer the indignities of the small – I experienced much of this, but still it is no use simply discovering and receiving, one must practically use our discoveries in the lives of ourselves and others. Even writing about it is really only a record keeping experience." Invaluable. I asked if he might give me a tip. "Ah well, the closed hands, covering the eyes, perform the same as the blackness of the mirror." He must have been referring to his own black obsidian mirror within which so much was seen. I thanked him and returned to rest a while.

Later, Water of Air. Paralda asked me to enter. I gave the words of power, in spite of being clearly recognised and welcomed.

"Come see one of my beautiful sylphs," he said, pointing to a female form under water, much less vague than the ones I had seen before. She spoke.

"The Water makes me visible. It interferes with my purity, but enhances my form. As such I become more real. Note this important key, that through emotions and feelings, thoughts become real and visible."

Paralda called time. "That is all for today." I returned home.

[FEBRUARY 2014]

Wednesday 5th. The Cave. Merlin appeared through the gloom.

"As the Light grows so does the Darkness. What you have – well, you don't know what you have - but while you work it out the Darkness will attack you. Recognise some of the aspects of this Darkness but never forget that every individual is special and must be treated as such, in reference to each other, and that the work you do enables that. Therefore without this work there can be nothing. Remember that."

Later, Water of Air. "See my sylphs," said Paralda. I took a good look, pretty, enticing, but not beautiful. I felt Merlin's hand on my shoulder, stopping me from being enticed! Paralda continued.

"Watery Earth, you see it outside your window now, wind and rain, fog and mist, moisture in the Air, a mess, a confusion. This is the state that much of Planet Earth exists in…but that is all I can say for today," he stopped abruptly. "Come again when you can."

Reflections on Confusion. Within the confusion of the planet the Hermit is two things. To those with eyes to see his lantern he is a signal and a Guide. But he can only be this to seekers, who always have been and always will be few in number. So deep and ingrained are the mismanaged views of self and misunderstandings of the world that to everyone else the Hermit is a threat, and his teachings doubly so.

All things that deny, refuse or reduce the importance of Life Learning are the product of these mismanaged views and misunderstandings, which are in turn the product of the Dark Side. Given this state of affairs I suppose the Hermit ought to be grateful to even find one pupil who is prepared to commit to the work.

Monday 10th. Water of Air. "Rain falling down, fog rising up, both are Air and Water mixed. Water in Air is rain, Air in Water is fog. It is the question of the size of each component. See my sylphs…" I looked and thought them to be phantoms, attractive swirls of colours and feelings amidst the Air, amidst nothing. I was not at all excited by them, yet at the same time wanted to reach out to them. Merlin again stopped me.

"Feelings in the Air," came the voice. Yes, I thought, and therefore the key must be to hone in on that watery feeling and use it to see what is coming or what is hidden. The expansiveness of Air might be more attractive, but the watery feeling hanging in that Air creates an atmosphere which might inform us. Water in Air shows the seed of Water that may subsequently expand.

Wednesday 12th. Fire of Air. "Enter, and concentrate," said Paralda. Those attractive sylphs were right there again, and again Merlin held me back from them. Suddenly a shot of flame moved into one of those sylphs. The being started moving about excitedly in all directions, and then just as quick frizzled up and disappeared. Paralda had been present throughout and spoke.

"See how Fire increases, excites us, agitates, makes noises, makes us hotter and louder and then hastens our demise." I could see this and said that it was like an argument or a discussion that is referred to as just hot air. "But it always hastens the demise, if it is only Fire in Air. That is enough for today."

Thursday 13th. Fire of Air. "It is the change in temperature caused by Fire in Air that changes the way that the Air meets the person. The actual temperature change is the quantity, and the overall apparent change is the quality. This is evident in warming smells or cooling smells which evoke changes in thought, and sometimes taste." Very interesting words from Paralda, but then he turned back to his recurring theme. "See my sylph, her name is Mila," She was a beautiful tall blue creature. "If she moves ahead of you then this will cause you to be smelt and tasted before you arrive. But she must be used wisely." There was much temptation here, and Merlin reminded me of the dangers. I thanked Paralda but refused his offer. Another sylph came forward and outstretched her hand. It connected with mine and my whole arm felt as light as air. I disconnected and thanked all who were assembled.

"You are almost at the end of this period," said Paralda.

Monday 17th. Fire of Air. This time was different. I had created a reserved space, in the Outer World, within which I worked these exercises and nothing else. As I got into both the physical space and the head space, concentrating on the card image, I could feel the presence of King Paralda actually right next to me. I could register that he was there, and in a sense 'see' him though afterwards I had no clue what he looked like.

"What do you wish to know?" he said.

"The essence and behaviour of Air," I said.

"Very wise" came the reply, "So, silence. Listen." Although the house was not silent I could hear my name being called. "Richard, come to me" I did not recognise the voice.

"Who is it?" I asked.

"All of them," replied Paralda. "All that have ever met you or connected with you. They all want a piece of you. Not consciously, not admittedly, but they do.

The question is what do you want?" Mila, the sylph from before, appeared in front of me and bowed. Paralda said, "she desires to grow and learn and be with you." It was very tempting, I must admit, but again Merlin cautioned against this. At this Mila fell to her knees on the floor in front of me.

"If you ignite the thought, the message in the Air, with Fire, passion and desire, then all things become possible. The ignition of the thought is key," explained Paralda. I thanked them both.

Tuesday 18th. Akasha of Air. Paralda had again appeared to me, in my Outer World space.

"I seek to know more of the mysteries," I said.

"Very well, but you must join into one of mine." Mila stepped forward and, this time, Merlin indicated that is safe. I outstretched my hand and connected with her. I could immediately feel a lightness and a purity. There was no charge, no direction, no friction. She started to move further up, in and through my body, gently at first, and then seemingly to engulf me. Both Paralda and Merlin stepped forward to prevent this and she withdrew. I closed my fist as if to capture some lingering essence of her, but there was nothing.

"You cannot hold it," said the voice. "It is all about the present, the past cannot be retained."

"What of the Akasha of Air?" I asked.

"It is Air that is alive, born and charged not of man, but of something else." I saw a triangle, point upwards emerge out of the ground and hover before me. It was joined from the sky above by another triangle, pointing downwards. They joined and fused together to form the Star of David.

"This protection," he said, indicating toward the Star, "is neither good nor bad. It is simply alive, representing inspired truth not born of man. Truth is rarely born of man, it takes Akasha to provide that. If actions can be aligned with Akashic Air then truth results."

Wednesday 19th. Akasha of Air. "Your final visit now," said Paralda.

"Is Akasha the directing and generating principle of Air?" I asked.

"No. We are. Our kind regulate our quality. More of us and there is more Air, less of us and there is less Air."

"You self regulate?" I checked.

"Akasha moves us from one state to the next, onto Fire maybe, but we dictate ourselves." I could clearly hear his voice but not, this time, see him. I asked if this were possible? "You have no need of this, though you may see one of my kind." Mila again came forward. She outstretched her hand and we touched. She was interested in me, and I was friendly, though not too much. I released myself first.

"That is all," said Paralda firmly. "There is nothing more I can show you, for now." I thanked him and asked if I may call again upon his services. "You may," he replied and I asked if there were anything I could do for him. I listened intently for the reply.

"Tell others that we exist," he replied. He repeated this a second time. So that was Air, completed over forty two days. My progress was slowing.

Thursday 20th. The Temple. After some contemplation time I returned to the Temple, in the usual manner, to be greeted by Thoth.

"The strong must allow the weak to leave them, but the strong themselves must never leave the weak. The weak must be allowed to go, in order to return again to the orbit of the strong. All this time the strong must continue their work, even while the weak vacillate. This is the nature of The Hermit." At that he merged into me. I centred him in my solar plexus and concentrated him there. "Call me here for increased focus and power," he said. I asked if I may speak with Merlin, to whom I had grow quite attached.

"Merlin is but a figure, a light reflection of me for smaller matters and general experiences. I am your Guide." This felt very real and, unusually, very emotional. I had recently been fortunate, even blessed, with some happy occurrences in my Outer World life. I asked Thoth about these.

"You have worked hard to overcome the Dark Side and move forward. This is what happens to everyone when they do this."

I disconnected and had a short rest before returning, one final time, to Elemental Air. On this occasion I did so simply by sitting and focusing, without the sacred space or protective practices I had used each time up to now. I connected without difficulty, but Paralda had a different tone.

"You must not enter without protection. All manner of beings reside here." I returned and went through the laborious process of protections. Re-entering he spoke to me again.

"Mental numbers are of this plane." Mila reached out to me again, one minute with one appearance, moments later with another. A changeling. "But not an Avatar!" said Paralda.

"Are all numbers of this place?" I asked.

"No. There is nothing more I can show you. You must proceed to the next stage."

Tuesday 25th. Elemental Fire. Starting work with a new element was again accompanied by a change in tone. I became, over the coming weeks, more active, more energetic as well as more intemperate. Situations which had been slow moving or even stagnant sprang into dynamic life. The weather changed, becoming unseasonably warm and dry.

The name of the principal of Fire was Djinn, to whom I passed the words of power.

"Yes, what do you seek?" said the voice.

"To know the ways of Fire." I replied. He called for one of his salamanders, named Mae, who offered to instruct me. She immediately ran off, underneath a mound of some unknown material. She was the spark that then caused that mound to explode.

"Fire works upwards," said Djinn, "starting from the bottom and climbing to the top, through impetus, passion, heat, enlivenment – you've got to want it. The triangle is the mountain, the peak is the desired goal." Various other explosions and bursts of flame were taking place all around me, near and far. One detonated directly above me and into me. I felt Mae pick up the spark of the Hermit's message and run off with it, spreading it far and wide. She had no shortage of energy or enthusiasm. Djinn intervened and called a halt for the day. "You must assist in our work another time," he said. I opened my eyes, back in the Outer World. I wiped my brow, I was sweating!

Djinn had appeared more powerfully than the other three Kings. I imagined that theoretically they must be equal in order to maintain the balance, but in that moment they didn't seem very equal.

Friday 28th. Elemental Fire. I asked that Djinn speak the ways of Fire.

"You know them," he said.

"Fire rests at the top of the hierarchy?" I asked.

"Yes."

"And is most powerful?"

"Yes, though each is powerful within its own sphere. And Akasha influences all. You see, Fire works upwards, this is why we are of the South, the two poles of the planet being each South, leading upwards to the Equator. You see now how much our enormous Sun power would be abused and misdirected if it were not for the essential previous steps and balanced progress?" I did see that, very much.

"What else can you tell me?" I asked.

"This is all. You can proceed. Mae will assist you in whatever way you wish." She appeared again, but this time as a serpent. Thoth appeared, but with a warning.

"She will ask a price."

I asked Djinn if I may speak with the Elohim. He was not helpful and himself seemed surprised when many voices started to be heard.

"It is not our time yet. Nor is it yours. Be patient." The voices were magical, like a song, yet without a tune. I did not push further. I thanked the voices and Djinn, who remained in some surprise as to what had happened. I communicated my respect to him and returned home.

[MARCH 2014]

Saturday 1st. The Cave. The Temple. The entrance from the beach to the cave was closed off with an energetic barrier.

"Ascend directly," came the voice. I did and gave the Mark as I arrived at the double doors of the Temple. Hermes welcomed me in.

"What do you require?" he said.

"Confirmation, Lord Hermes." I replied.

"The Lord is not necessary," he said. "Continue exactly as is. The usual enemies are present, in the Outer World, but you need only speak your truth, so long as you are not too cutting on the innocent souls. Target the leaders of misinformation, not their followers." He merged into me and I could see all, everything complete and whole, correctly assembled and working perfectly. Every aspect of Life interdependent on the next, every kindness balanced by evil, every negative balanced by positive. I thanked him. "Do this whenever needed," he said.

The DRAGON

Monday 3rd. The Temple. "Be in this Temple and reach up, up, for the power and the theory," said Hermes. "The potential and actual of everything that was, is or will be is available here. You must identify it, raise yourself and focus upon it, in its specifics. Your goals are currently small, but much more is available. Your elemental assistants will help but always with consequences. You will discover this for yourself, consult your own Library for clues."

Thursday 6th. The Dragon. I identified myself in the usual way and entered through the unnumbered additional Major card of the Tarot – The Dragon – which I had inherited from Arthur.

"What are you doing?" said a voice. I persisted. I saw a Dragon – burning red – flying through the sky, and then another down on the ground to my right, a baby.

"You must grow me, feed me, build me and I will do your bidding," said the baby.

The warning voice came again. "You are not yet ready for this, your work is neither complete nor yet advanced enough." I thanked the baby Dragon, who I named, before returning.

Later, The Temple. "Lord Hermes," I bowed in greeting.

"No Lord," he said again. I asked of the elements, and progress thus far. "The elements make up everything, yet are themselves controlled by me, and others. I am not of the elements. The Dragon is a mythical creature of immense power that will serve you no practical purpose. Continue as you are, mindful of the usual obstacles, which have not gone away. Further work is need with the Fire element. You will become accomplished in all these matters, one day, but not yet. Some years must pass first."

Friday 7th. Earth of Fire. The temperature in the space was hot and intense.

"You have earned this," came the voice. "Fire is feared, for it is a destructive element, acting to clear away – like when the earth is scorched – so that the conditions can be set right again for a renewal. It works upwards with power. The death of the human body for example occurs through prolonged exposure to light, and some have a greater capacity for the light than others, some a greater desire, some a greater sensitivity. Sometimes the longest human lives are celebrated, other times those who explode and burn young are recognised. Everything changes, and Fire comes to help that process. That is all, Mae is here to help further."

I withdrew back to the Outer World and the moment I reopened my eyes was the moment the Sun went in behind a cloud.

Wednesday 12th. Earth of Fire.

"Know this, the sooner you realise that you can do nothing without us – save survive – the better off you will be." – Hermes.

Djinn spoke directly to me, his fiery form of reds and oranges burning fiercely. "Passion, heat, anger, desire. These are the only things that ever create movement. Desire must be instilled if anything is to change and stand a chance of starting again." Would the opposite of this, I thought, be apathy and reliance? "Mae is always here to help you. When you are ready visit again."

Later, Water of Fire. Djinn was waiting for me in the usual way. "Fire heats the blood," he said without delay or introduction. "It makes the fluids and juices move in particular directions. This is more suitable for moving people as it produces an impetus within them, as the liquid moves through the veins, blood pumping faster. But…no, it should be just a short instruction today."

Thursday 20th. Water of Fire. "Enter," said Djinn, after merely looking at his symbol for about ten seconds.

"Teach me more of Fire," I asked.

"You will soon progress onwards, but remember that Fire burns, we burn, but we burn out if not fuelled, if not propelled, with new stimuli, passion and involvement. No flame can burn unaided or by constant use of the same material. Would you like to live the flame?" Hermes was present and at first urged caution, but then relented. At his permission Mae appeared and passed directly into me. I burned intensely for ten or more seconds. I could feel myself possessed and overtaken by the Fire and it burned right through me. I felt I had to release it else I would surely explode. I placed my hands palms down on the solid wooden table in front of me. After a while I felt my body cool and the pressure diminish, though this took some minutes.

My left underarm had been painful for some time. I concentrated the remaining Fire into this region of my body. At first the pain grew even more intense, then after a while it seemed as if the heat had burned all the way through it. I moved my right hand to the area and focused the heat into me some more. I gained some relief from this and the pain has not been as acute since. I expelled Mae from me and thanked them both. Permission was given to move to the next level. "Soon," said Djinn.

Monday 24th. Air of Fire. I was distracted and found it hard to concentrate. The voice of Djinn was vague.

"Fire spreads. Passion and heat spread, by Air, by moving outwards. But this only happens if there is enough Fire. If there is too much Air then there is burn out and dissipation. Airy Fire is different to Fiery Air, consult your notes to see this." Mae came closer. She was in a small burning human-like form.

[APRIL 2014]

Tuesday 8th. The Cave. The Temple. It had been two weeks since my last visit. That never boded well for a good attitude to life.

"I am not worthy," I said to Hermes.

"You are human, with weakness and frailty, what can be done about that?" He merged into me powerfully, enabling, I hoped, a further stage in the destruction of my lower self and hopefully allowing a clearer channel to the me that was not me. I requested more knowledge and insight, but he referred me to Lao Tzu. So, if I was pushing my boundaries it was Thoth. If I were assimilating discoveries it was Hermes, but if I were struggling it was Merlin or Lao Tzu?

"There will always be a little of Hermes with you," said Lao, "so long as you call him. But to gain more requires a stronger work ethic. Here, take this salve for your skin." He passed me something which seemed to be made of avocado, lemon and ginger. I could not be quite sure but it was rough and mildly abrasive. I thanked Lao and Hermes, who was still lingering.

"If the work is not recorded it will be lost. It is as simple as that," said Hermes.

Later, Akasha of Fire. Djinn spoke and welcomed me into his dominion. I bowed to him as he sat on his throne over to my left, with Mae on his right. Djinn was robed and adorned, but Mae was not.

"Do you wish to play with Mae?" he said. Again Hermes cautioned against this. I said no and she hissed. I instead held out my fingers and connected with hers at which I felt like my whole body was on fire. I turned back to Djinn. "Teach me of Akashic Fire."

"You cannot understand it," he said.

"Show me something to think about then," I asked.

"Very well. Akashic Fire burns, to the very core of your being, enabling a complete and total fresh start at a new zero. You recognise the colours don't you?" The deep red surrounding a dark symbol in the middle was unmistakeable. "They used this primal, elemental power, but to their own distorted ends. You, all of you, are sweeping up the effects to this day. Raise your arms and demand this power into you!" I did as instructed and an enormous electric force entered my body. My fingers first tingled, then my hands burned.

"This Cosmic Fire you now hold, applied to anything, will cause it to be, and yet always with ego it is corrupted and disastrous. You have seen this before. Reflect and come again on this matter, this is only the most superficial knowledge."

"Thank you Djinn for this knowledge and wisdom. Thank you Mae," I was appreciative, as well as wasted and blinded, exhausted and overwhelmed.

Realisations: The deep blue/black of Akasha and the deep red of Fire had been combined in the flag of the Nazis, and the Vril energy they sought was the Cosmic Fire. I was certain of this, but had they been conscious of what they had connected with? How did they think for one moment that they could control it?

Monday 21st. Akasha of Fire. I could still, two weeks later, feel the energy of Cosmic Fire burning through me. I had been totally exhausted, yet wired, the whole time. I must banish this force completely.

"Yes, yes, come young man. Today will be your last visit here. You see now, how it burns, its power?" said Djinn. I sure did. "What have you experienced during this time?" he asked.

"Heat, impatience, anger, blood, movement, clarity, realisation and exhaustion," I said. Three days previously I had fallen off my bike to considerable blood, swelling and temporary, though vicious, pain.

"So you see what happens when these elements are released unchecked? Cosmic Fire particularly, when uncontrolled and unbanished, *always* brings blood. Bring in each force as you wish for your specific needs, but no more, and then tightly banish. Only rarely involve Akashic Fire for it burns in order to reveal truth. The truth is revealed, but always at a cost." I thanked him profusely and returned.

The Fire element, the fastest moving of all, had taken fourteen trips spread over fifty five days to explore. Arthur had long ago said that learning takes time. There really seemed to be no escape from this fact.

[MAY 2014]

Friday 2nd. The Cave. The Temple. "Lord Hermes," I said. Again he replied that there was no need for the Lord title. I seemed to have gotten into a pattern with that.

"An essence of The Hermit, the Nine, is to be willing and able to help people, in spite of the fact that you can see their failings, and their role in their own problems. To be able to see such things is to be able to help them. Do this and you are free, otherwise, do as you please so long as no hurt is ever caused. Now speak with Master Lao."

I turned to Lao and he spoke of one of my pupils. "She does not really understand the path through life. It is all about dealing with what is, the Way of the Superior Man, unaffected but still involved and guided by the bigger picture." This was helpful and relevant. I departed.

Later, Akasha. The journey into the symbol was different to the previous four, similar to the Astral process. I felt a buffeting, buzzing, particular sense of moving up, out of the open roof of the Temple, into the surrounding cosmos. There were all colours, yet only one, all colour in that one, that deep indigo black. The space was not empty, far from it. It was teeming with life of all kinds. I saw this, I knew this, I accepted this and there was nothing any longer to argue with.

"What do you require?" came an unknown voice. I did not have names to refer to any longer.

"I want to know everything," I said. There was a definite laugh in response.

"As you ask. All experiences shall be sent to you." I got the sense that this would come in the form of some kind of mirror, but I did not know what, when or how. The sense I had in this space was not bliss as such, but certainly a heightened mode of life. "But take care not to take too much," came a voice.

"Who are you?" I asked.

"In your terms – God," came the measured and ordinary response. There was no possible reply to this. I sat in the space, soaking it up for some time and then returned. Suddenly all was restrictive and heavy again. "Visit again soon," said a voice.

Sunday 4th. The Cave. It might seem crazy to say, but after my encounters with the Lords of Change - the forces of creation, God himself, a few of his intermediaries and numerous famous and respected figures from history, I was feeling deeply unhappy. Part of me *still* did not quite believe what had been happening. I knew that the mind had the ability to trick itself into thinking and believing anything, yet I was convinced that was not what was happening. Something real was taking place, and it was bringing real changes in the way I conducted my life. I did not believe that I had been particularly marked out for this, simply that I was the only one crazy enough to continue the work for this length of time. I had many answers yet no answers. In the Inner Space all could be seen, but back out here, in the messiness of the Outer Life, well that was another matter.

Lao Tzu appeared in his familiar robes and I shared my concerns with him.

"I feel as though I am going round and round in circles, not really getting anywhere."

"Come sit," he said. "It is a matter of balance. Sometimes there are too many Outer World concerns. Other times you have been too immersed in Inner World concerns. Others must be left free to go their own way, you are then free to apply yourself to the myriad possibilities of your life. Here are some glimpses of your future, please assume the position." I got myself into a receptive seated position and into my head was projected much unfamiliarity. I saw myself, older, seemingly taller or at least straighter, more authoritative, speaking to large groups, overseas, accompanied by someone much younger than me. I did not know who this person was but the scene seemed encouraging. Still nothing had been answered, though I felt a little better.

Contemplation of Akasha. My last attempt to connect with Akasha had been so mind blowing that I decided to undergo some gentle contemplations on the symbol, without a full entry. The words fall so pathetically short of the actual experience, nonetheless I can say that I saw every kind, every sort, every variety, every aspect of everything contribute to the whole of everything. It was truly every single kind - the good and bad in and of everything.

Tuesday 6th. Contemplation of Akasha. All is in one. One is in all. But if you focus exclusively on the one you will never see the all, nor will you see the one if you focus only on the all. Thus we must look in and out, up and down. We must do both.

All is contained in one. One is contained in all. This does not make these two things the same however and discernment is required to separate matters of one from matters of all. In other words, your stuff is not necessarily everyone else's stuff. One feeds the all, and all feed the one. What *is* will *be*.

The past is the present, the present is the future. There can be no freedom from this until one realises the effects of our actions now. Yet the only way our actions in the now can be positive is if they are in accordance with our Destiny – the things we must do.

A crack in the egg is a crack in the soul. A line on the hand is a line on the face. The universal laws dictate the default settings. Man is indeed capable of overcoming these and writing new laws, yet to do so in ignorance of existing ones is to invite chaos and destruction.

Thursday 8th. The Cave. Lao was present as I arrived and we discussed developments in the Outer World.

"We cannot tell you what to do, you must discover it for yourself, through trial and error. You need more time in here, more experimentation, allow others' thoughts, feelings and concerns to simply pass right through you. And sell your businesses, if you can afford to." He was right about that, I was past the point of interest in them.

Friday 9th. The Cave. The Temple. In my frustration at lack of progress I had done my usual trick of coming up with a grand, world beating scheme that would solve the problem in one dash. This time it was a film project.

Lao told me straight. "The project you speak of represents a serious step for which the world is not ready. Not yet." On one level I accepted his words, but on another was trying to find a way round them. It seemed to no avail, for Lao continued. "When the Gods, or the cards, or the dice, or the weather say it is not the right time then only an idiot will proceed."

Hermes stepped in. "That is all. Practice, practice," he merged into me and we returned home.

Later, Contemplation of Akasha. Stepping up the practice slightly I looked upon the symbol as I gave my words of power. I felt a light penetrate my solar plexus. I scratched my head.

"That won't work," said a voice "it doesn't happen there," continuing, "everyone is where they are, it cannot be any other way. What do you want?" Before I could really answer the voice concluded. "The Universe gives nothing, but rewards everything."

Monday 12th. The Temple. Lao took my face in his hands and looked deeply into my eyes. Suddenly we were shooting up through space like stars.

"This is where it happens. What is seeded here must come to pass there," he said, pointing down to the Planet Earth. "So if you could seed one thing, what would it be?"

My immediate answer, in the face of such possibilities, was 'peace on earth', but I tried to phrase it in a better way.

"The chance for everyone to pursue their life unfettered, uncontrolled, free of propaganda. Life on Earth, as opposed to Peace on Earth."

"Yes," said Lao Tzu. "That is it, to proceed through life unmolested, unrestricted by prejudice, ignorance or fear. Make some notes on this and return later."

CHAPTER XXII
THE VOICE OF VOICES
[MAY 2014]

Monday 12th, The Akasha. Contemplating the symbol I felt it to be a Magick Symbol, one that is not magick, but for magick, although as it is used for magick it may become magick.

"Welcome. How may we serve you?" said a chorus of voices.

"You serve me?" I asked, confused.

"Yes. You serve us. We serve you."

"How may I find the courage and energy to move forward, the strength to do what must be done?" I wondered.

"Courage is not strength. Courage is Fire, and you are not deficient here."

"The commitment and consistency then?" I continued.

"These things are Air, related to the knowledge of purpose. You are not deficient here either."

"So it's my Dark Side then, not under control?"

"Yes. Find a way for it to be calmed. This is the problem. Return when you have addressed it." The voice was clear and unambiguous, but composed of many strands. Who was it?

Later, The Temple. Lao explained the voices.

"They are what some know as The Secret Chiefs, controlling intelligences. You see, politics does not matter not because it does not change anything - of course it does - but its actors are themselves controlled and thus not in control of themselves. This is not a conspiracy, but the Chiefs, of which Hermes and I are but two, can allow only that which is lawful to proceed at its allotted time. It might be that this world must collapse but in which case it is a matter of preserving the correct knowledge for the next phase to best go forward. I am not saying that this is the way, merely that it might be. Think and reflect on this and visit again soon. In the meantime practice the Art of True Healing by Regardie. You are almost a Master of the Elements, but not quite." Home. Profoundly stunned and scared.

Wednesday 14th. The Cave. "Come with me," said Lao Tzu. I found myself with him on top of a tower, or maybe a lighthouse, in the middle of the ocean. "What do you see?" he said.

"The land contains the sea," I said.

"What else?"

"The sea is black, we cannot peer into it."

"Yes. This is the Dark Side, the area of Life that is unknown, unseen, lives in obscurity and darkness. Yet, through delving into it we may learn more about ourselves. But if you fall in then there is total destruction. It is all pervading black yet containing much life within."

"So how do we avoid falling in?" I asked.

"By knowing who you are and what you are for," he replied.

"Are you saying that I do not know these things?" I asked, confused.

"You are aware of them, but I'm talking about knowing, not believing. And I'm talking about most people. But for you however the Dark Side casts a long lasting shadow. Only by the Light may we see the shade, so a period of avoiding the Dark Side entirely helps you to see where and when it is functioning. A period of total abstinence helps clarify the reach and effect of the Dark Side. Reflect well upon this."

Later, Earth of Akasha. I set up the usual protection and entered the symbol, stating the words of power three times as I passed the threshold.

"How may we help and cooperate with you?" came the Voice of Voices.

"Explain to me the significance of Earth of Akasha." I asked.

"See the Bees. See their colour, it is no accident, in fact it is their connection. The link between, as some say, Heaven and Earth, is vibratory – sound, voice, communication, all express the will of Heaven through Earth. The voice, the rattle, the string, the drum. It is not merely words but sounds, when pointed and focussed, unadulterated, clear in tone, not what is said as much as how it is said. This is the key. Sound. Vibration. Speech."

Thursday 15th. The Temple. "The task," said Lao, "is to communicate truth in ways that they can understand, with a spark, and a reason for them to see it. Offer hope, light – the Hermit's Lamp."

"But what constitutes hope and what is the reason I should give them?"

"Truth is the prize. I am not talking necessarily about unbridled positivity, for if one constantly speaks of the positive then one had better be sure to deliver it, otherwise disappointment, which is a very powerful emotion, rears up. No, it is truth that is required, for truth is reliable, it endures and is a solid thing that can be built upon."

Saturday 24th. The Temple. Lao Tzu greeted me but immediately passed me over to Hermes. He instructed me to fall to my knees. I did as he asked. "Lower," he said. Again I did as asked, now actually performing this in the Outer World in my physical body. "Lower still," came the instruction. I complied.

"Do you see?" said Hermes.

"No," I replied. I saw nothing.

"Then lower still." My forehead was now touching the floor.

"Now do you see?" He did not wait for me to answer. "Man is subject to so many superior forces. The regular man, undeveloped, unknowing of self, will always be subject to the more developed man, or indeed sometimes the less developed one. Knowing oneself is what it all comes down to…" Hermes disappeared. Lao remained and now spoke.

"There exists now a greater movement toward the knowing of self than there has ever been, but so has also proliferated a million and one strategies for doing exactly the opposite. All this will be swept away…"

"Will it?" I doubted that.

"Yes it will. But what will then remain? Knowing of self is the key to everything…"

Sunday 25th. The Temple. My first encounter was with Hermes, who I automatically greeted as Lord.

"Not Lord." He was insistent. "Everybody is capable of being a teacher to everyone else. I am merely that aspect embodied constantly across your world." I asked when we might ascend to the next level of understanding in this place? "Not yet," was his reply.

"Then when shall I take the next part of the oath?" I continued.

"Not yet. You know what you must do, the task is large but must be completed, with minimum distractions. Continue as you now are. Ask not of your concerns, but focus on the task. All proceeds well, but you must soon step up."

Wednesday 28th. Earth of Akasha. "How does King Ghob operate through the Akasha?" I asked.

"The question should be how does the Akasha operate through Ghob," said the Voice of Voices. I reflected on that for a moment before they continued. "Through inevitability, fixity, in one place, to one end." In that moment I totally understood those words and all their possible ramifications, but the moment I returned to write them I was doubting and unsure. I was also hungry, which was always a distraction.

"Do you have any other questions?" came the Voices.

"No," I said. I couldn't really concentrate.

"Then return another day when you have," they replied.

Thursday 29th. Earth of Akasha. "How does the Akasha show itself through Earth?"

"Purpose, reason, functionality. It asks of everything, 'What do you do? What are you for? How do you operate?' In this sense you can see that all things material-spiritual are purposeful or beautiful. Beauty may reside in ugliness and purpose may be hidden deep down, but all things that come to form must have meaning."

"Is that really true? All things?" I queried.

"All things stem from their creators, and are both a product and reflection of them. Intelligent manifest beings hold the third part of the triangle of creation between God and Things." This triangle was displayed to me.

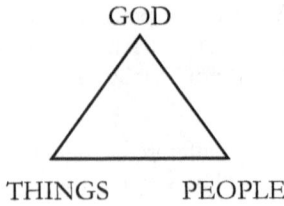

"At once each angle is the intermediary and filter between the other two, as well as the feedback from the previous round of all three. Things are created by man, informed by God. God is created by things, informed by people. And round and round always. Not everything that comes into form is purposeful, has reason or function – for humans reserve the right to act against God, by their free will – but only things charged with Akasha, that is creation informed by God, will endure."

"I need to write all this down," my mind was creaking with the information.

"A good idea!" came the reply.

Friday 30th. The Temple. Hermes, Lao and myself formed a triangle, with Hermes at the tip.

"The thing that keeps the you in here distant from the you out there (indicating the me in the Outer World) is the Ego. This is the gap between what you have and what you need. It is a force that pushes away from you that which you most need. This ego is a protective layer which on one hand prevents you from getting burned but on the other hand prevents you from seeing the Light. The gap between is the gap that the Ego, and Dark Side, wishes to maintain in order to keep things as they are, or at least to keep change to a controllable minimum. In short, this is the force which keeps all that is possible away from you." Hermes continued. "Only by direct embodiment of a practice can one hope to diminish this Dark Force, over time. Even then it will re-group and re-organise itself, given the chance. Therefore any practice must be practised, daily, repetitively. One hit is not enough, for the forces of the Ego and the Darkness are stronger than you think and are constantly pulling you and your attention outwards, away from your purpose. Burn oneself!"

Later, Akasha of Earth. "So how does one charge a material endeavour with Spirit?"

"It must be one of the correct form, able to take and hold the charge in the first place. It must be able to hold truth, or at the very least hold learning and progress and thus the grains of truth. It must enable and reflect growth but it is also a case of matched charging. That is that the creation can only receive a charge matching to or in proportion to the efforts of man. Zero effort from man will never be compensated for by the effects of God. Where man tries, God supports. If man does not try then God is impotent. All things, effectively, begin and end with man."

[JUNE 2014]

Monday 2nd. Water of Akasha. "How does Water present itself to the Akasha?"

"This is a very different question to that of Earth," said the voice. It was King Nixsa of Water, present and available, but reluctant to fully answer, preferring instead to point me toward one of his babies. I pressed for deeper answers and the Voice of Voices spoke.

"Water is purified and enables purification through whatever it works with. For example rocks help spring water to be formed correctly, flowers do the same for rose water, which can be of great medicinal benefit if taken internally in very small doses. In the body it is the job of food, combined with Water to work the purification process. If the food is wrong then the Water cannot do its work. One relies upon the other. Water needs a channel, the right container within which it can reveal its magick, for Akasha flows through pure water only."

Friday 6th. The Temple. Hermes questioned me immediately on arrival.

"Do you now understand? Do you see what is required of you, what your role entails?

"To be the one who provokes, stimulates others into new thought, new action and new ideas. Something like the Socratic Tradition, a firestarter but without the aggression."

"Yes. And what else?" he replied.

"To be the messenger, who people sometimes shoot, but to know that one cannot actually be shot or harmed. That won't stop them of course!"

"What else?"

"To be male and female."

"What else?"

"To be all things to all people, ever shifting and changing. All situations can then be managed and moved between."

"What else?" Hermes was relentless.

"To be back and forth between the worlds, always learning, fifty-fifty in each over time."

"And what else?" I was out of ideas now. After a short silence he spoke again. "Come again when you have thought more about it. There is one more thing and then we can proceed."

"To accept..." I said, tentatively.

"Yes..." Hermes was waiting for more.

"To accept whatever is given and received. To not argue, resist, judge or react in any way." There was a long silence.

"Yes. Come again in the morning and we will proceed. Eat well and rest well this evening."

Saturday 7th. The Temple. The Hermit and The Temple had been shown, long ago, as being deeply connected with the number nine. I asked Hermes a little more about this.

"Am I passing through Nine in this place, or I am seeking to become Nine?"

"Both," he replied. "You are adopting the Life Mantle of The Hermit, the conduit of Hermes, messenger of the Gods, not any one thing in yourself. Eight months must pass before the work can begin in earnest. You are right, acceptance is the missing link but you do not yet possess it. It is up to you to now go through all your notes and practices filling in the blanks as you do. You must do this, it is vital. I am available at all times for inner dwelling during your readings, talks or workshops, or if you have specific questions, but you cannot now go forward until you have assimilated *all* that you have encountered so far."

Later, Air of Akasha. I called for Paralda.

"Welcome young one, how may I help you?"

"How, please, does Akasha flow through Air?"

"For this... I cannot say...." He pointed up the Sun in the sky. The Voice of Voices replied, clear and resonant.

"Clarity, simplicity, self evident truths and honesty. Those are the marks of Akasha through Air. That is all." It was interesting that the suggestion was simple not complex. Non-contradictory, transparent and straightforward words were the key.

Tuesday 10th. The Temple.

The absolute inferiority of man before the Universe shall result in the absolute making of man.'

My ascent through the Vortex was longer and noisier than usual, but eventually there was Hermes.

"Turn off the music and kneel." I switched off the CD. "Say after me. I welcome thee."

"What am I welcoming?"

"The Light of Source. Say it, I welcome thee."

I splayed out my arms and repeated the words. I shook vehemently as if something entered me.

"This is the stance and the attitude to adopt. You may be a Master of Men, of the Outer Domain, but here you are not. Maintain this attitude and stance and all will be revealed to you. That is all. For now."

Later, Fire of Akasha. Djinn was present, exactly as our last encounter, but he stepped aside and deferred to the presence of those greater. The Voice of Voices spoke.

"Spirit is Fire. It is the medium through which we shine. It is the meaning."

"But who decides the meaning?" I questioned.

"You do. You decide what it becomes, how it grows. The seed of positive and negative will always be there, but it is to you to control and direct it. This is of course, not what happens, but it is time that it did. Spirit is Fire, but Fire is not Spirit. That is enough for now though, come again tomorrow, yes…tomorrow."

Wednesday 11th. The Temple. "Kneel, in balance. Do not slouch, welcome us," said the Voices.

"What is this position?" I asked. "Why is it necessary?"

"Submission to God. This is the correct relationship." I was not comfortable with this at all.

"All religions practice this, yet they all go wrong. How?" I asked.

"The intermediary poisons it. Submission to God always then degenerates into submission to man. The relationship from you to us must be personal, and of ones own construction."

Afterwards: I happened later, after my return, to follow a trail of links which completed in two quotations from the Christian Bible, where out of its own mouth, it condemned itself, along the lines that the Voices had mentioned.

'Woe unto you, scribes and Pharisees, hypocrites! For ye shut up the Kingdom of Heaven against men, for ye neither go in yourselves, neither suffer ye that are entering to go in' – *Jesus, Matthew 23.13*. Today's scribes are the Outer World commentators who guard the gates of validation. The Pharisees, now, are the do-gooders. Both classes are easily identified as those who would tell you how you must proceed to happiness. And that path will always be their way, and a denial of your way. Overthrow all preachers, spiritual teachers, gurus, busy bodies and do-gooders.

Jesus's words on the matter are again recorded in Luke 11.52. *'Woe unto you lawyers! For ye have taken away the key of knowledge, ye entered not in yourselves and them that were entering ye hindered.'* Lawyers, judges, health and safety officials, petty bureaucrats, verifiers, stampers and gate keepers of all kinds purport to protect us, yet all the while prevent us entering into our rightful place in the world – our individuality, our own Temple.

Later, Fire of Akasha. Fiery Lord Djinn was waiting as I arrived in his super heated environment.

"Step forward if you wish to have revealed to you the great secret," he said "But beware…" I stepped forward and the Voice of Voices began.

"You are a warped vessel. The Light must penetrate you in order that you be made clear. Inflame your heart to produce good actions. Inflame your hands to work good works. Inflame your mind to think good thoughts. Inflame yourself fully, daily, regularly, in order to see the Light. Speak truth when you see it, write it, act it, live it. There is no turning back now. This is your path."

I was unsure. "Can I, can my body take this?" Answer there was none, at least nothing clear. All throughout this I was burning and then the Voices spoke again.

"Anger, regret, these are the roads to darkness, speak not in anger nor from regret." The voices this time were different, more resonant, more whole.

Thursday 12th. The Sun. I assumed the position, kneeling before Hermes.

"What have you learned about submission?" he asked.

"That it should not be used as an excuse to abdicate responsibility or behave badly."

"What else?"

"I see that submission is the correct relationship with God, one of co-operation."

"And?"

"That it is down to me to choose."

"To choose what?"

"Whether I wish to reach my Destiny or not?"

Hermes was very pleased with these words. "Correct! Ascend! Rise up young man! The path will now be revealed to you on a daily basis. Go forth!" I felt extremely light headed and also, for once, energised, no longer exhausted.

Later, Akasha. I moved through the symbol doorway and connected directly with the sound of the Voice of Voices. They spoke directly about my concerns of the direction of the Outer World.

"You see now what is coming, what will happen. You cannot stop it. Warning others is part of the path, but you cannot stop it, it is in the nature of things. What you must now do is to seed the beginnings of the new world that will come afterwards, free from the intermediaries of religion. You cannot prevent the storm, indeed to attempt to do so and become part of it is but a distraction. The object now is to have an eye on what must come from this, the world afterwards." These were distressing words, for my predictions on the development of the world situation were dire, but maybe if the world of my lifetime would be bad, it might help the world of future generations be better?

"Leave exhibiting and organising your fairs now, if you can afford it. Focus on and be at your computer and your desk. You have all the ingredients to spell out what comes next. Go now. This is the end of the practice. Now begin."

'It is not possible for the Hermit to be of this world, merely in it. A terrible burden indeed. The Hermit might take pause for joy when good things happen, because as life goes on it is certain they will not last. But cheer up Hermit, for bad things happen too. And because life goes on they do not last either!'

Tuesday 17th. Judgement. "Enter the Halls of Judgement. Here, see, the Book of Britain," the Voice of Voices was the clearest I had ever heard it. A large and thick bound leather book appeared before my vision. It was very old and written in different languages and handwriting as the years moved on. The last few pages were blank.

"It is now up to you how this story ends. It is foolish to expect resolution to such a long tale in five minutes. The arguments about the future of your country will persist long after this year and next. Forever is the ebb and flow of life – change, resistance to change, progress, looking backwards. When one factor becomes too dominant then another must activate." I could see before my eyes now a swirling stream. "Even if the Scots vote no to independence, something like 55-45 there will still be resistance to the result and attempts to look at it again. People will not accept a result that does not accord to their views. The past, even though it is long and weighty, is not of relevance. What happens next is key. Britain, to all intents and purposes, no longer exists as a distinct entity, already destroyed by those angered at the slow pace of change."

That was it, nothing more was said. I returned and recorded the experience word for word without any understanding of its significance.

Later, The Temple. "Hermes," I said, appealing for his help. "May I speak with the Lord of Loss of Pleasure?" This was the name of the being depicted in the Tarot as having rulership of my day and month of birth. Its key attribute was disappointment, and I truly felt, at times, that it was a curse. Hermes seemed surprised by this request.

"Kneel," he said. I did and prepared myself for a dark and powerful force, embodying disappointment – the central theme in my life. A being appeared, but I could not afterwards recall anything about its form, except that it was mighty and unshakeable. I felt I had nothing to lose now and I spoke directly to him.

"Lord, why are you so?" This was paraphrase for why do you constantly persist in making my life so terrible.

"Do not resist," it said. I could detect kindness. "I protect you from that which would ruin you. All aspects of life must be passed through, none can be skipped. Under my protection and guidance you may avoid that which you simply could not handle. Do not resist me." The tone and the message was surprising and not at all malevolent. This ruling Angel, this Cosmic Lord was, after all, on my side, so long as I could get on my side! But what of the negative? What of those who work with these Cosmic Lords in the wrong way, or work with the wrong ones? I turned to Hermes.

"The invocation and arising of demons is not a practice that takes place out there, it is a reduction of things inside you. The names of spirits and angels are all used because, as externals, they trigger and reach parts of you that you would not think were parts of you. The task, as Solomon performed, is to bring these things to life and then lock them away, within triangles, permanently under control." His tone then shifted. "But first, you must produce your work."

Friday 20th. The Temple. I knelt before Hermes, but received a surprising response. "Not today, that is not necessary. Now your question."

"How does an on going daily practice of technique, realisation and learning help anybody but myself? Is it not one big selfish indulgence?" I asked.

"In the small way no, it does not help anyone else. But then again you yourself are changed by it, so all your subsequent interactions become different. Your words, written and spoken, will filter out to people you do not even know and they will outlive you. You could be more 'out there', which would accelerate this trend, but that would also inevitably distract you. In the big way as you change your world so you change the larger world." I understood but it seemed tenuous.

"You seem not happy with this?"

"It all seems to take such a long time," I complained.

"It happens in ways that are invisible to you, and much sooner than you think. But nothing can happen until the correct time." Best not to think too far ahead, I thought, returning home.

Monday 23rd. The Astral. My reading and practice of the work of Dr Israel Regardie had reached a logical conclusion and I very much wanted to see and speak with the man, in person, as it were. I asked Lao Tzu if this were acceptable.

"Very well, this way," he said and I ascended the Astral Vortex in the usual way. Glimpsing an old figure in the distance I addressed him.

"Dr Regardie?" I asked.

"What, who is this?" he said.

"I am a student of yours."

"Then make the sign," he demanded, impatiently. He did not seem happy to have company. And I knew of no sign that he would recognise.

"I cannot. I read your works and I value them and respect you, but I was not schooled in that degree."

"Then do not waste my time," he said, but then after a moment, "what do you seek?"

"What did you learn from your life?" I asked him.

"Stupid boy, my books are there for all to read. You think you are clever sitting in your chair and meditating! Real magick must be practised out in the world, by actually doing something." I summoned the courage for one more question.

"But why so much rigidity, so much framework and procedure around your work?" His techniques were heavy with ritual, grade and formality.

"How else can one establish rigour and a lasting effect if it is not within a structure?" He had a point there, this cantankerous and irascible, wise and experienced old sage.

"Thank you sir." I said, offering some deference, and left him alone.

Tuesday 24th. The Temple. Hermes, Lao and maybe many others were in attendance in the Temple as I arrived.

"Is it always true," I asked Hermes, "that Magick is distorted and practised by suspect males?" It certainly seemed that way. Lao glanced at Hermes knowingly and Hermes replied.

"It is a matter of balance. All is now co-operation and negotiation, working together, give and take, militancy and resistance hold no part of future life. The Soul of the Middle Nature is the Middle Pillar that Regardie and others spoke of. The Lower Middle Self of the genitals and the Higher Middle Self of the heart are the controlling factors, all built upon the Foundational Middle Self of the feet. Imbalance is a movement to any extreme or in any extreme way, such as very fast. This is how you cannot change unless and until you are ready to. There are no short cuts, least of all in magick." Hermes paused and then continued. "The honest and true expression of your Middle Nature is through your voice. Do not, from now, repeat anything of another. Find your own words, always."

"Is that all?" I asked, eager to try to remember this well enough to write it down.

"No. Show me your progress," he said. I had accumulated a few techniques, some might say tricks and I ran through them with him.

"Here I have two taps to summon an answer," I made the gesture to show him.

"Do not use this with me, but with Lao," said Hermes.

"I have three fingers to silence" I made the gesture.

"Care, for they will be silent."

"I have the daily breath practice."

"Increase it. And return to Bardon's work, his elemental references are the best."

"But I sometimes do not know what is appropriate to write, and what should be left out?"

"Open and close the aura as you require. Aim for one piece of writing per day."

"That is a lot," I protested. "Too much pressure."

"Aim for it," he insisted.

[JULY 2014]

Tuesday 1st. The Temple. I could sense things were changing and my time with this diary of explorations was coming to a close. I had started the groundwork of the task Hermes and the others had set me, and it seemed to be the only thing that really counted now. It made sense, after all this time, to publish and be damned. I still had doubts, but Hermes was solid in his insistence of what was required and that nothing further would be revealed to me until the work was done. Today he spoke to me directly about this.

"You have until August 2015. By that time you must produce and finish two new books, '*Emergence*' and '*Grand Britain*'. All your unread books must be read, all practices mastered and developed, all paintings and designs finished. All the while you must respond as called to help others. There must still be courses, shows, readings and talks. All this must be done, yet you will not have time for it all. Nothing must distract now."

Sunday 13th. The Astral. I ascended in my body, out of my head. The usual buffeting and intense noise was followed by a still space. Lao Tzu was to my right, as was the Library. The Keeper was waiting.

"It has been a long time," he said.

"I have come to see the Book of My Life." He said nothing but gestured me in. Only once inside did he speak further.

"There is no such book," he now said. "There is nothing to see, nothing more to know, at least not about you. You will either deliver the teachings you have been given, or there will be nothing." Lao Tzu confirmed this. There was neither anger, nor criticism. I asked for further explanation. "There is no book. Not for you." I had no option but to thank The Keeper and bow. He seemed appreciative of this and moved behind his counter and into his back room. We left and the Library disappeared. I wondered if I might ever see it again.

Wednesday 16th. The Cave. Hermes spoke.

"No one said this work was ever about the fame. Recognition maybe, and there may be much satisfaction in seeing your work distributed, yes even *The Key To Time*, but it is not about the fame. Your work is now so far ahead, maybe fifty years, that it is unlikely to find acceptance in this lifetime, but it will filter through in part. Help others in a quiet way, be out there but not on show, just work without trying to 'get anywhere' and you will see how your own personal quest is supported when you give to others. Remember that my indwelling and merging is always available, it's just that the distractions of the Outer World tend to obscure the voice, interfere with it, muddy its waters."

Monday 28th. The Temple. "There is only one thing you are now missing," said Hermes, "a gesture with which to pass my Mark, to enter the Temple or to welcome me." He showed me a hand movement and then continued. "It is good that you are doing the work but there is no time to lose in completing your recording of an honest account of visiting the world from your armchair." A useful subtitle, I thought. And then Hermes passed his last words to me.

"Many came before you, and after me. Whenever there was a new language and new ways to adopt it was me that made it happen. My descendants are your Guides now, and the Guides of others. Focus on the numbers, they are more powerful than the planets." He repeated those last words and added more. "Astrology will be discredited. The numbers are more powerful than the planets."

And that was it. It was done. A fifteen year long exploration into my head, out of my body and around the Universe was over.

This was The End.

Or was it just The Beginning?

The Worlds I Now Inhabit

Those who look to improve and challenge established mode of living are often accused of either seeking to destroy or to escape the ordinary world, and by doing so damaging the very people they purport to care about. I am therefore pleased to report that my excursions into consciousness have, if anything, made me more aware, more tolerant, more grown up and more considerate of others. I give more to society at the end of these journeys than I did at the start. I pay more taxes, I donate more to charity and I help more people in all sorts of direct and indirect ways. My health has not collapsed, I have not fallen into alcoholism, nor am I on medication. I am not in therapy, nor have I gone to jail. I drink less than before I started, eat better, sleep better and have a clearer approach to life. The only drug I take is coffee. Whether you judge these things to be good or otherwise it is clear to me that the journeys have been beneficial, not destructive, lifting me up, not pushing me down. I believe this to be the strongest evidence yet that you can 'turn on' and 'tune in' without 'dropping out'.

These trips have, of course, brought about challenges, the greatest for me being an awareness of the Illusion of Our Sophistication. The reality is that we humans do not know nearly as much as we think we do and a lot of what we think is just flat wrong. We might be educated and enlightened, but we are also biased, prejudiced and closed-minded. This is as true today – at the dawn of the twenty-first century – as it was five hundred years ago and is, on one hand, a downbeat assessment. But I have gained perspective on this long voyage. Yes, the individual is important, even sacrosanct, but there are many other individuals, here and gone, visible and invisible, human and otherwise. And we disregard them to our own detriment, for they are all able to show us something we would not otherwise be able to see.

Another important thing I have learned is my firm conviction that there does exist such a thing as objective truth. In spite of this being deeply unfashionable, I have now been taught that wherever there is an opinion, there is truth, waiting close by. In the age old conflict between truth and illusion, my truth may be another's illusion, but I know it happened, and it has improved my life immeasurably. Although sometimes in the moment I struggled, in hindsight I would not be without these experiences, nor the memories of the beings and places I encountered. I am in no doubt at all that these beings exist as independent and objective intelligences, and are absolutely not – although it may serve the explorer to initially believe so – simply aspects of self. I can do no better than Aleister Crowley in this regard, when he spoke about the Holy Guardian Angel.

"He is not, let me say with emphasis, a mere abstraction from yourself; and that is why I have insisted rather heavily that the term 'Higher Self' implies a damnable heresy and a dangerous delusion."

For those who cannot meet me there I will concede that at its heart, this book is my madness. But it is also my cure, its writing and publication my resolution and my ending, my acceptance of what I saw and heard and the end of my complaints about it. Your madness, for you must have one – and its cure - will be different and similar, but whatever form it takes it will be personal. It will be best uncovered by courage and persistence, a certain stubbornness to follow your path wherever it may lead, whatever surprises and astonishments it may produce, and whatever its consequences. This too can be unfashionable, particularly amidst today's spirituality, full of soft pastels and rounded edges, a mile wide and a millimetre thick. I hope that this account of my doubts, discoveries and consistently unexpected experiences will inspire you to go further than you otherwise would to add greater depth and colour to your world. Just begin by closing your eyes.

Afterword
Notes on the Method

It should be apparent that I am a born sceptic, believing nothing until I have seen it, done it, tested it and regurgitated it. I find it impossible to follow the herd and if ten thousand people say "hey, do it like this" I will immediately start thinking otherwise. This approach has served me with varying degrees of success, often making my progress – in all areas of life – slower than it might be. But I continue to value this trait for when I do make progress I *know* that I have made it. When I test things to destruction and they still survive, I know that I am *really* onto something.

These experiences have therefore proved themselves. I did not previously know, or have any awareness of, the information I was being told. I did not, for example, realise until the very end that the journey fell into twenty-two distinct parts - the number of Major Arcana cards in the Tarot. This was not at all arbitrary and many similar things presented themselves unexpectedly, from outside of my awareness. Although I consistently went looking for X, I kept finding Y. And Z.

The whole journey was one of projection through images and symbols. This path was referred to by Gareth Knight in *Occult Exercises & Practices* as *via positiva*, embracing the notion that transcendent and mundane realities are somehow connected and it's just a matter of finding the doorways and paths between. This is always a journey of increase – symbols and images providing additions to the mind, initiating growth through experience and encounter. This was the prevailing cultural meme at the time when I was first introduced to the topic; the early nineties being the time of boom and expansion in every area of my life. There is also the countervailing way, *via negativa*, which asserts that any symbol or image must, almost by definition (because it comes from the mundane) be a flawed and inaccurate representation of any transcendent reality. Thus any connection through these doorways can only introduce illusion, fantasy and separation from God. This approach has become more popular in recent times, and is always the path of reduction, of less, of the removal of stimuli and immersion in emptiness as a precursor to anything else. This path has its place but it is not what this book is about.

A couple of people have suggested that I have gone about my explorations the wrong way round, that I should have encountered Elements before Guides. Elements, they said, are the building blocks of life and must therefore come first. I do not agree. Guides and associated beings seemed in all cases to be connected with, and directly relevant to me, my history, character and knowledge and I do not see how I could have attained the quality of Elemental experience that I did without attaining the contact of the prior Guides and beings. Anyway, it's not like I consciously decided that it should be one way or the other. The whole process unfolded in a manner that was unexpected and unforeseen.

The quality of the experience toward the end of the journey is very different to the start. Interestingly, during the edit, a huge number of typographical and date errors revealed themselves and were grouped around the final few chapters. Once we corrected them it seemed like I had at times, and maybe literally, not known what day of the week it was!

It has also been pointed out to me that the entirety of my experience can be explained away in terms of The Daemon, the higher self being originally posited by Socrates and more recently explored by Anthony Peake. While this explains a great deal it also limits the experience in ways that do not accord to my personal encounters. To say that one's Guide is simply one's Daemon and to refer to another's explanation of what this is seems to miss the point of the experience entirely. Our connection with a Guide is organic and dynamic, deeply personal and highly revelatory, as well as remaining still, largely, a mystery.

Other serious occultists have pointed out the deviation in my approach from the accepted rituals of journeying *via positiva*, where a great deal of store is placed on the use of flashing colours. For example, in either a Tarot or Elemental doorway my approach has simply been to see, close eyes, continue to see, and allow myself to travel into and through what I see. By contrast, the traditional approach has been to see, to close eyes, to see the complementary colours of the image or symbol in the minds eyes and to project through those. I tested this is the early days and I do not think it is at all necessary. Although the principle states that the flash of the complementary colour signals the opening of the door, I have not always or often found this to be so.

Finally, there is no doubt that serious study of this work will cause all sorts of neurological and psychological explanations to appear. Maybe some of these will be insightful and facilitate a further development of the process? I would be very happy about any serious attempt to get to grips with the 'what' and 'why' of all this, but I will resist any attempts to diagnose these experiences as a deviation from some kind of human norm. Working with this technique and demonstrating it to others has shown me that every type of person is capable of attaining and benefiting from these kinds of experiences. In the ongoing fight against normality I urge you to hold the line at whatever goes on when our eyes are closed.

Richard Abbot.
England, March 2015.

www.ingramcontent.com/pod-product-compliance
Lightning Source LLC
Chambersburg PA
CBHW032014230426
43671CB00005B/83